A History of the Vietnamese

The history of Vietnam prior to the nineteenth century is rarely examined in any detail. In this groundbreaking work, K. W. Taylor takes up this challenge, addressing a wide array of topics from the earliest times to the present day – including language, literature, religion, and warfare – and themes – including Sino-Vietnamese relations, the interactions of the peoples of different regions within the country, and the various forms of government adopted by the Vietnamese throughout their history. *A History of the Vietnamese* is based on primary source materials, combining a comprehensive narrative with an analysis which endeavors to see the Vietnamese past through the eyes of those who lived it. Taylor questions long-standing stereotypes and clichés about Vietnam, drawing attention to sharp discontinuities in the Vietnamese past. Fluently written and accessible to all readers, this highly original contribution to the study of Southeast Asia is a landmark text for all students and scholars of Vietnam.

K. W. TAYLOR is a professor in the Department of Asian Studies at Cornell University. His career began in the US army, where he was deployed in the US–Vietnam War. He has now been researching Vietnam for nearly forty years, and his work has made a fundamental contribution to the development of the field.

A HISTORY OF THE VIETNAMESE

K. W. TAYLOR

CAMBRIDGE
UNIVERSITY PRESS

CAMBRIDGE
UNIVERSITY PRESS

University Printing House, Cambridge CB2 8BS, United Kingdom

Cambridge University Press is part of the University of Cambridge.

It furthers the University's mission by disseminating knowledge in the pursuit of
education, learning and research at the highest international levels of excellence.

www.cambridge.org
Information on this title: www.cambridge.org/9780521699150

© Cambridge University Press 2013

First published 2013
Reprinted 2013

A catalogue record for this publication is available from the British Library

Library of Congress Cataloguing in Publication data

Taylor, K. W., author.
  A history of the Vietnamese / K.W. Taylor.
    pages   cm
  ISBN 978-0-521-87586-8 (Hardback) – ISBN 978-0-521-69915-0 (Paperback)   1.   Vietnam–
History.   2.   Vietnam–Civilization.   I.   Title.
  DS556.5.T38 2013
  959.7–dc23   2012035197

ISBN 978-0-521-69915-0 Paperback

CONTENTS

FIGURES

TABLES

MAPS

ACKNOWLEDGEMENTS

I wish to acknowledge my gratitude to four people who have provided inspir-ation for this book. The late Paul G. Fried (1919–2006), whom I encountered at Hope College nearly half a century ago, gave me confidence in the importance of studying the past and in the possibility of becoming a historian; without his encouragement, I doubt if I would have subdued the disquiets of wartime experi-ence to commence a life of scholarship. John K. Whitmore, who initiated me into the study of Vietnamese history at the University of Michigan, demonstrated a commitment to academic study, an intellectual integrity, and an abiding curiosity about the past that have given me a deep appreciation for the craft of the historian. The late Oliver W. Wolters (1915–2000) taught me how to critique my ideas about historical study; his questing mind was a constant prompt to reread and to rethink texts with an awareness of the options exercised by those who wrote them. The late Alton L. (Pete) Becker (1932–2011), both during my training at the University of Michigan and during a summer seminary in 1992, taught me a love of words, of how language shapes and is shaped by thought, and of the pleasure of translation; his influence has gone deep into how I understand culture as a process of telling stories and of translating them. Olga Dror, my wife, has been my intellectual companion and most valued discussant for ideas about the Vietnamese past.

INTRODUCTION

Prologue

When people first began to live on Earth, terrain was very different from what it is today. For tens of thousands of years, what we know as the country of Vietnam was the mountainous western edge of a broad plain. Now covered by the Gulf of Tonkin and the South China Sea, this plain extended in places for hundreds of kilometers east of the modern coastline and included a massif that we now call Hainan Island. Today we can imagine that beneath the mud at the bottom of the sea lie the relics of the people who inhabited this plain. But our knowledge of their existence comes only from the remains of quarries and workshops where they crafted stone tools at the tops of mountains along the modern Vietnamese coast. During that time, people also inhabited the mountains in what is now northern Vietnam, and we know of them from what they left in the caves where they lived.

About twelve to eight thousand years ago, the coastline shifted westward as sea levels rose with the melting of the ice-age glaciers. The water reached to around 5.8 meters above the modern level of the sea and penetrated into the mountain valleys. Thereafter, the sea gradually receded to its present level, exposing a chain of coastal plains that became the lowlands of what is now Vietnam. The most important of these plains for early Vietnamese history is the most northern of them. This is the plain of the Red River. It was formed by grey oceanic sediment emerging from the receding sea that has been increasingly streaked by accumulations of the red silt that has given the Red River its name.

The Red River flows in nearly a straight line from the Yunnan plateau to the sea. It follows what geologists call the Red River Fault Zone. This is a major geological discontinuity where for millions of years the land south of the fault has been shearing a few millimeters each year southeastward under tectonic pressure from the Indian subcontinent against the Eurasian land mass. The plain of the

Red River, along with the smaller plains of the Ma and Ca Rivers immediately to the south, make up the scene in which Vietnamese history was lived until the fifteenth century.

Between four and five thousand years ago, people with stone tools began to live on these plains in agricultural communities with rice, domesticated animals, and pottery. It is fruitless to speculate about the origins of these people. They lived so long ago and left such meager evidence of their existence that they are impervious to our strategies for using archaeological, geological, geographical, or linguistic evidence to identify them as having arrived from a particular somewhere. They may have come from the continental land mass, they may have come from the lands submerged beneath the sea, or, most likely of all, they may have come from a mixture of peoples from both directions.

During the succeeding millennium, people with bronze weapons gained supremacy over these communities. At that time, advanced bronze cultures existed in several areas of the Asian continent. There is no surviving evidence that would allow us to specify from where the bronze-age people came to assert their rule over the Red River plain, or even to determine that they came from elsewhere and did not arise from the existing society as a result of bronze technology being introduced through peaceful exchange. Thereafter, contact with expanding political powers in the north, which we now associate with ancient China, increasingly exposed the people living here to northern influence and power and led to incorporation into the Chinese imperial realm.

The Dong Son Culture with its distinctive bronze drums decorated with boats, warriors, musicians, dancers, feathered garments, birds, animals, reptiles, and amphibians flourished during the four or five centuries preceding conquest by the Han Chinese in the mid first century CE, after which this culture disappeared. During the next nine centuries, the people here lived under a local form of imperial administration as the southernmost members of a succession of Chinese empires. During the past thousand years, local dynasties ruled as vassals of Chinese empires, save for the last century and a half during which a brief French hegemony gave shape to modern Vietnam.

Vantage

Vietnamese scholars have endeavored to project a sense of national identity back into the past as far as possible. In the modern period, it became common for Vietnamese to affirm a national history going back four thousand years to when archaeologists date artifacts that they have assembled and categorized under the name of Phung Nguyen Culture. Phung Nguyen is defined as a late stone and early bronze culture that represents a level of archaeological uniformity in the Red River Plain that did not previously exist. Many Vietnamese scholars are inclined to draw a line of continuity in cultural, and even ethno-linguistic, development from Phung Nguyen to modern Vietnam. This inclination, however, makes an exuberant use of evidence.

The search for origins in the distant past is a common intellectual endeavor among peoples in nearly all times and places. For example, historians at royal courts in northern Vietnam during the thirteenth and the fifteenth centuries were concerned to affirm their status in reference to rampant northern empires, the Yuan and the Ming. They did this not only by culling references from classical Chinese texts about what they imagined to have been their ancestors in antiquity but also by constructing a "southern" history for themselves that is largely parallel with and a response to "northern" imperial history. The urge for connections with the past is a means of self-affirmation, not a scholarly endeavor.

What we can know about the past with some degree of confidence is a meager residue of what remains from an ongoing process of accumulation and attrition, of gain and loss, of putting together and tossing away, a process in which all generations participate. Human efforts to remain oriented amidst change can take forms between the extremes of denying change and of seeking change. Historians are not immune to the implications of such efforts, and they do not agree on the appropriate pose to assume toward change in wielding the rhetoric of their craft. I believe that the task of historical scholarship is to look at what survives from the past as coming from people with their own existence, not as evidence of people who attain significance primarily as precursors of people today. The Vietnamese past does not display an internal logic of development leading to the present. Rather, it reveals a series of experiments designed by successive generations as solutions to perennial problems of social and political organization. These experiments have failed, have reached an impasse, or have been overcome by the possibilities or the violence of larger contexts. None has been a final solution.

Vietnamese history is a convenient name for what can be known about a certain aspect of the past. What makes it Vietnamese is that the events of which it is comprised took place in what we now call the country of Vietnam and that certain versions of it have been taught as a common memory to generations of people who speak the Vietnamese language, thereby inducing a sense of ownership. I find interest in the Vietnamese past not because it is Vietnamese but because it is about how human society has been organized and governed during many centuries on the edge of an empire.

Vietnamese history as we know it today could not exist without Chinese history. The manner in which Vietnamese history overlaps with and is distinguished from Chinese history presents a singular example of experience in organizing and governing human society within the orbit of Sinic civilization that can be compared with Korean history and Japanese history. Such a comparison is not the purpose of this book. The purpose of this book is to present a narrative of current scholarship on Vietnamese history that is accessible to students and general readers. But, this book is also written with an awareness of comparative possibilities within the academic jurisdiction of East Asia.

Vietnamese history can also be viewed in a Southeast Asian comparative context. The kingdom of Dai Viet that existed in Vietnam from the eleventh to the fourteenth centuries was contemporary with other major kingdoms in mainland Southeast Asia at Angkor (Cambodia, Laos, and Thailand) and at Pagan (Burma). Also, the southward expansion of the Burmese and Siamese peoples from the fourteenth to the nineteenth centuries is seemingly parallel with a similar movement of Vietnamese peoples at the same time. However, the disparity in surviving evidence, the great differences in culture and politics, and the exceptional imperatives of the Sino-Vietnamese relationship are obstacles to meaningful comparisons.

Language

A large proportion of the modern Vietnamese vocabulary derives from Chinese, but linguists categorize the Vietnamese language as a member of the Mon-Khmer family of languages. Although available comparative data for studying Vietnamese with other Mon-Khmer languages are limited, there is an abundance of materials documenting the historical relationship between Chinese and Vietnamese. Linguists continue to develop new methods for analyzing such data, and developments in Sino-Vietnamese historical linguistics enable new ways of theorizing how the Vietnamese language came to be. Building upon the work of scholarship in French and Chinese in the early twentieth century and of Japanese scholarship more recently, linguists are beginning to appreciate the great complexity of the relationship between speakers of the Chinese and the Vietnamese languages; both the speakers and the languages are products of great changes during the past two millennia from which documentation of this relationship exists.

Sino-Vietnamese historical linguistics has tended to focus attention upon words from the classrooms in which what we call Literary Chinese was taught for more than two millennia. This was the language of education, scholarship, literature, and government in both China and Vietnam until the turn of the twentieth century. While Literary Chinese in its written form has changed relatively little through the centuries, the phonologies of Literary Chinese have changed significantly in accordance with changes in spoken languages. Advances in phonological analysis enable greater understandings of the realms of spoken languages that have interacted with Literary Chinese. Literary Chinese, as the written form of the prestige language, was an aspect of a larger world of language contact between speakers of languages that we now identify as contributors to modern Chinese and Vietnamese. Modes of speaking Literary Chinese can be thought of as literary registers that became aspects of prestige versions of vernacular forms of language.

For over a millennium, up until the tenth century, speakers of Han-Tang Chinese accumulated in what is now northern Vietnam. Imperial government was based in the area of modern Hanoi where the most critical mass of Chinese speakers concentrated. During the thirty to forty generations of this time, the Chinese speakers developed their own regional version of Chinese, for which one modern linguist, John Duong Phan, has found evidence and that for convenience can be called Annamese Middle Chinese. It is possible that this was simply a dialect of a broader Southern or Southwestern Middle Chinese of that time.

The non-Chinese-speaking lowland population spoke a language that linguists call Proto-Viet-Muong, the most eastern member of the Mon-Khmer languages that at that time prevailed in the plains drained by the Mekong and the Menam. Proto-Viet-Muong can be imagined as having spread north at some earlier time from the passes linking the Mekong and Ca River valleys. During the ten centuries of imperial rule, many Chinese words were borrowed into spoken Proto-Viet-Muong and we can reasonably conjecture that there was a significantly high level of bilingualism among primary speakers of both languages.

Beginning in the tenth and eleventh centuries, when the governing connection with Chinese dynasties was broken, there were no longer regular infusions of Chinese speakers from the north and local kings appeared. The population of Annamese Middle Chinese speakers was increasingly concentrated in the Red River plain where political authority was based. As the diglossic situation collapsed, speakers of Annamese Middle Chinese gradually shifted into Proto-Viet-Muong, bringing with them a critical mass of vocabulary and grammatical particles, thus giving rise to the Vietnamese language as we categorize it today, the speakers of which at that time were called Kinh, meaning the people of the "capital" in the region of Hanoi. On the other hand, the speakers of various forms of Proto-Viet-Muong who did not participate in this "shift," namely those in the plains of the Ma and Ca Rivers, were eventually driven from the lowlands by the Kinh speakers, who referred to them as Trai, or "outpost" people; in the twentieth century, French ethnographers and colonial administrators identified the descendents of these people as Muong. The Kinh–Trai distinction is first mentioned in historical records from the mid thirteenth century, although it surely existed prior to that time; this is also the time when the writing of Vietnamese poetry is first documented and when the last generation of Vietnamese princes who spoke Chinese are known to have lived.

In the fifteenth century, two decades of Ming Chinese rule introduced new pronunciations for words already existing in Vietnamese from the Han-Tang/Annamese Middle Chinese experience. Some later Vietnamese scholars viewed the Ming pronunciations as less correct than the older forms. This is an example of a common phenomenon during the long history of Sino-Vietnamese interaction: Chinese words once absorbed by Vietnamese would be "re-borrowed" from a later version of the Chinese language with new pronunciations and sometimes modified semantic fields. The rejection of Ming pronunciations was part of a general reaction among educated Vietnamese to the memory of Ming rule. Nevertheless, from the fifteenth to the eighteenth centuries, during which Vietnamese began to flourish as a literary language, writers adopted or invented many classroom-inspired Chinese words to bejewel and elevate the vernacular in a process of "relexification."

A further complication is that, beginning in the sixteenth and seventeenth centuries, Vietnamese speakers in what is now central and southern Vietnam began to develop regional versions of the language as a result both of normal language change and of contact with non-Vietnamese speakers. In central Vietnam, many Cham speakers began to speak Vietnamese, and, in the late seventeenth century, a large wave of Ming Chinese refugees into the south also had a linguistic impact.

This new understanding of the Vietnamese language as arising from a long history of Sinic bilingualism gives formative significance to the centuries of Chinese rule that is more plausible than the well-established cliché of "a thousand years of Chinese domination" that imagines an already existing Vietnamese identity surviving many generations of participation in Sinic civilization while being fundamentally uninfluenced by it. It also requires a major shift in our view of Vietnamese history and culture away from the scheme of an ancient and enduring Vietnamese identity claimed by modern nationalists. Vietnamese culture and language came into existence as the result of a merging of what linguistic evidence reveals as speakers of Annamese Middle Chinese and Proto-Viet-Muong.

Apologia

In this book I combine a chronological political narrative, expositions of interpretive themes, and discussions of geography, education, ideology, language, literature, religion, society, government, economy, and warfare. Information surviving from pre-modern times is often very sparse, which is likely to disappoint the thirst of some readers for more knowledge than is available. I have sought to avoid excessive speculation or large generalizations that lack plausible evidence. At the same time I have endeavored to rise above a tedious account of random events by charting a narrative to stimulate the imagination, making thought about the past possible. I have excluded a mass of detail and have aspired toward coherence sufficient to satisfy both those who prefer to think diachronically across time and those who prefer to think synchronically with topics. An introductory survey, this book provides a point of entry into Vietnamese history and does not excavate the historiography from which my ideas have emerged. It aspires to provide a sketch of the Vietnamese past using political, administrative, economic, and cultural information.

I have given much attention to simply sorting out a basic sequence of events because this has never yet been done with the detail and method enabled by surviving evidence and recent scholarship. Although many detailed studies exist in Vietnamese, and to some extent in Chinese, Japanese, Russian, and French, English-language writings have for the most part referred to the pre-modern past with vast clichés and to modern times with relatively narrowly focused narratives that follow lines of argument about interpretive themes fundamentally unrelated to the Vietnamese. I have endeavored to provide as much opportunity as possible for readers to enter the past and to see events from the perspective of those who lived them or who recorded them. If we imagine the past with the dynamism of possibility with which it was lived, we can glimpse it looking back at us with the eyes of aspiration that each human life and each generation have aimed at the future.

The Vietnamese past is full of personalities and events both obscure and famous, and often the obscure have had greater effect upon the direction of culture, society, and politics than have the famous. I have tried to move beyond the propaganda of memory and memorializing to display a thicker layer of information that has accumulated about people and events. My purpose in doing so is to evoke a sense of the past as alive in its own time.

Because much of what survives from the past concerns the vicissitudes of political authority, some readers may view this as a "kings and battles" approach, which I believe would be a superficial impression, for I have endeavored to give serious attention to geographical contexts, language, literature, education, ideology, religion, ethnic and social formations, institutional developments, agrarian policies, trade, and commerce. Nevertheless, I have striven to sort out the political and military events because in the English language there has not yet been a sustained engagement with the history of Vietnamese efforts to structure authority and negotiate change.

Some readers will be disappointed by the lack of footnotes. The decision to avoid marking the text with notes was made out of consideration for the intended audience and from an expectation that readers looking for documentation can consult the bibliographic essays. I have done my best to stay close to the sources. There were times when I was tempted by an interesting thought toward an interpretation that in the end had to be discarded because the evidence was insufficient to bear its weight. I have indicated places where the evidence is too problematic to sustain any definite assertion. I am sure to have made errors and can do no more than to trust that other scholars will find them.

In this book, I have taken a pragmatic approach to the great morass of toponyms that have accumulated from past to present. The maps are provided as references for reading the book and do not indicate names and jurisdictions in their historical specificity. Places in the book have been known by various names during the two thousand years covered by historical records, and these names often covered different or overlapping territories at different times. Consequently, I have used a mix of historical and modern names, noting when I am using a modern name anachronistically for the sake of clarity. As much as possible, my aim has been to facilitate a narrative without digressions into the complexities and conundrums of historical geography, which require a separate study.

For example, the name Hanoi does not date before the nineteenth century. During the past millennium and a half, this place has been an administrative and dynastic center known by several names, the most prominent being Dai La, Thang Long, Dong Kinh, and Ke Cho. I have used these names in their historical contexts while at times also using Hanoi when doing so solved rhetorical problems, enhanced clarity, and seemed unobjectionable. In general, I have used modern names when historical names would introduce contextual inaccuracies and excessive explanatory asides.

The maps do not indicate jurisdictional boundaries for provinces and districts because that would introduce two unnecessary problems. First of all, the maps do not show every toponym but only those that come into the narrative; since we cannot begin to draw some boundaries without ending up by drawing all of them, we would need additional names that would clutter the maps with information of no use for the narrative. Also, since boundaries change and can be known but approximately, the project of sorting them out for each historical era, along with all the complexities and conundrums arising when doing that, is a task for a different, more specialized, kind of book.

I have endeavored to provide enough dates to maintain a sense of diachronic orientation but without cluttering the narrative with unnecessary information. The tables contain reign dates for rulers, but these are not unproblematic, particularly when times of transition occur near the end or the beginning of years as counted according to different calendars and historiographical rules. Vietnamese texts follow the lunar calendar in which the twelfth lunar month overlaps with the first solar month of the calendar currently in general usage. Furthermore, Vietnamese historians assigned whole years to rulers so that the remainder of a year in which a ruler died was counted in the reign of the deceased ruler and the successor's reign was considered to officially start only at the beginning of the next year. In some cases, sources provide different dates for the death of a ruler and the accession of the successor, or rulers were deposed so their death dates and the end of their reigns do not coincide, or the reigns of rival or coterminous rulers overlap, or there may be a gap between one ruler and another during times of dynastic turmoil or change. As a consequence of these considerations, readers will find a variety of dates in different books. Rather than drawing attention to these problems and analyzing them, I have followed a policy that privileges the solar calendar without the strictness and precision that a detailed study of dating problems deserves, seeking instead to provide dates that maximize the integrity and the readability of the narrative while remaining essentially faithful to a careful study of surviving sources.

Summary

The thirteen chapters of this book are organized on the basis of length and convenience and do not represent any scheme of periodization with which to conceptualize Vietnamese history. In terms of large themes, I am inclined to organize this material into four periods: first, the centuries during which what is now northern Vietnam was a province of Chinese empires (Chapter 1); second, the four centuries of the Ly and Tran dynasties during which Buddhist aristocracies in the Red River plain ruled (Chapters 2 and 3); third, the four centuries attributed to the Le dynasty during which kings came from Thanh Hoa Province, Confucianism was the ideology of rulers, the Vietnamese expanded into the south, and there were long eras of separate realms at war (Chapters 4, 5, 6, 7, and 8); finally, the two most recent centuries during which the modern country of Vietnam came into being (Chapters 9, 10, 11, 12, and 13).

During the millennium when what is now northern Vietnam was a frontier province of Chinese imperial dynasties, the people living there were acculturated to what we call East Asian civilization. In art, music, architecture, dress, cuisine, education, language, literature, religion, philosophy, social organization, and political behavior, nearly all the distinguishing features of Vietnamese culture were acquired at this time as a consequence of contact with the Han-Tang civilization of China.

A thousand years is a relatively long time in human history and it is hard to overemphasize the changes that occurred during this age of belonging to northern empires. The people who lived in the Red River plain before this time and those who lived there after this time would surely be unrecognizable and unintelligible to each other. Important changes can be attributed to any people during such a period of time, but the effect of being governed by a succession of imperial dynasties surely accelerated the pace of change in particular directions that reflected the course of imperial history. During these centuries, local culture, society, and political organization passed through many vicissitudes, some of them utterly transforming. Crafts, erudition, and political thought were mostly focused upon mastering the elements of imperial civilization. At the same time, from generation to generation and from dynasty to dynasty, a population of "northerners" accumulated and became a critical mass of people that were the governing class and its most reliable followers. Furthermore, there were a great variety of interactions, overlaps, and adaptions between local and imperial societies. It is not surprising that, intellectually, Vietnamese history later came to be written as a discussion, even an argument, with imperial Chinese history, for Vietnamese history can be understood only in reference to Chinese dynastic history. Accordingly, the earliest large event in Vietnamese history has to do with the arrival of northern imperial power near the end of the third century BCE and the eventual absorption of the region into the realm of northern dynasties. This situation was not altered until the tenth century after basic changes in imperial society and politics made it impossible for Chinese dynasties to continue to rule this region, thereby bringing the provincial relationship with northern powers to an end.

During the period from the late tenth to the early thirteenth centuries, political leadership shifted from the individual charisma of kings to leadership by men related to the mothers of kings. The Ly royal family came from the upper plains northeast of Hanoi.

Two brief wars with the Northern Song dynasty confirmed a relationship of formal vassalage with autonomy. The culture at royal courts combined popular spirit cults with the moral teachings of Buddhist monks, the occult skills of Daoist priests, and the erudition of Confucian scholars. The dynastic scheme of authority that was established at this time unraveled in synchrony with the decline of imperial power in the north. In the thirteenth and fourteenth centuries, the Tran dynasty, based on the coast downriver from Hanoi, endeavored to eliminate the power of maternal families by ensuring that queen mothers were always from the royal family itself. In place of individual charisma, a group charisma was nurtured among the many talented princes of the royal family, who gained fame by leading soldiers against Mongol invaders in the thirteenth century. In the fourteenth century, as the royal family lost interest in governing the country, kings nurtured a new class of educated commoners to provide talent for their courts. In the late fourteenth century, the dynasty failed to respond to new military, political, and ideological pressures from the rising Ming dynasty in the north and an echoing resurgence of Cham power in the south. The prevailing syncretistic attitude toward the "three religions" of Buddhism, Confucianism, and Daoism faded amidst dynastic collapse as the ascendant Ming dynasty trumpeted a new affirmation of Confucianism in China.

Beginning in the late fourteenth century, there were four successive experiments in government that responded to the rise of a new power base in Thanh Hoa Province, located immediately south of the Red River basin in the plains of the Ma and Chu Rivers. This opened a new age in Vietnamese history that would for the next four centuries be marked by regional conflict as Vietnamese migrated into the southern coastlands and began to challenge the ascendant position of the Red River plain. At the turn of the fifteenth century, a leader from Thanh Hoa assembled an entourage to pursue a series of experiments in educational, fiscal, agrarian, social, and political reform. Resistance to him in the Red River plain assisted the Ming conquest in the first decade of the fifteenth century. The Ming then experimented for two decades with efforts to turn the region into an imperial province. They built schools and propagated a curriculum that promoted Confucian forms of social and political organization. Although the Ming assembled a large local following drawn from erudite families in the Red River plain, resistance to them formed in Thanh Hoa. When the Ming eventually abandoned their policy in Vietnam, a coalition of Thanh Hoa clans proclaimed a new dynasty.

There was an era of relative peace, prosperity, and power in the late fifteenth century during the reign of a king who combined personal charisma with a court aspiring toward the forms of bureaucracy practiced in Ming China. During his rule, Confucian values were propagated as never before; new laws governing education, administration, land tenure, taxation, conscription, and public morality were promulgated; the writing of vernacular as well as classical poetry flourished; soldiers were sent to conquer lands along the southern coast and over the mountains as far as the Mekong River. However, in the early sixteenth century, royal authority collapsed and was superseded by a struggle for power between leaders from Thanh Hoa and a new dynasty in the Red River plain that survived for seven decades before being pushed aside by armies from the southern provinces.

In the seventeenth and eighteenth centuries, a new Vietnamese perspective emerged on the southern frontier. This perspective was produced by close contact with other peoples such as Chams, Khmers, Malays, Siamese, Japanese, Chinese, and Europeans and by a sense of options and possibilities that drew Vietnamese speakers away from the relative sense of discipline and confinement that prevailed in the provinces around Hanoi. Northerners and southerners tested each other on battlefields for fifty years in the seventeenth century; an uneasy truce then lasted for a hundred years before another era of warfare erupted in the late eighteenth century. By the mid eighteenth century, the southern kingdom had pushed its southwestern border to the extent of the current Khmer–Viet boundary. European merchants and missionaries arrived during this time and found two rival Vietnamese kingdoms that they called Tonkin and Cochinchina. The military and political deadlock was eventually broken at the beginning of the nineteenth century when a new dynasty established its capital at Hue, in central Vietnam, uniting for the first time all Vietnamese speakers in the territories that now make up the country of Vietnam.

In the nineteenth and twentieth centuries, the Vietnamese encountered the global forces that drove the emergence of what is commonly called the modern world, giving rise to various visions of social and political organization. In the early nineteenth century, the dynastic regime looked to China for culture and ideas about government. In the late nineteenth and early twentieth centuries, a French colonial regime subordinated Vietnamese life and thought to a European-based imperial system that for the first time cut the Vietnamese off from their historic relationship with China. When the French era came to an end in the mid twentieth century, northern and southern governments fought for twenty years over competing visions of a future Vietnam. The government in the north was allied with the communist world, being communal and disciplined. The government in the south was allied with the capitalist world, being relatively more individualistic and free. The northern regime conquered the south and then was at war with its neighbors and in relative international isolation for another fifteen years. At the end of the twentieth century, with the end of the Cold War confrontation, the Vietnamese state began a process of integration into the global system of economic and political relationships that presently exists. One of the most enduring features of Vietnamese history is that the rulers of China and Vietnam have maintained a common worldview amidst all the experiments undertaken through the centuries.

Pronunciation and spelling of Vietnamese names

This book does not include Vietnamese diacritical marks, which are an integral part of the Vietnamese alphabet. Some diacritics indicate tones and some indicate particular vowel or consonant sounds. Jesuit missionaries invented the

Vietnamese alphabet in the seventeenth century, largely in reference to Portuguese phonology. Consequently, readers who do not know Vietnamese but are familiar with European languages will not go far wrong in sounding out most pronunciations in Vietnamese. However, readers may be interested to know how to pronounce certain common names in Vietnamese history that have unexpected sounds. For example, Ly is pronounced "lee"; Le is pronounced "lay"; Tran rhymes with "bun"; Mac is pronounced "mock"; Hue is pronounced "way."

One consonant sound that may pose particular challenges to non-Vietnamese readers is the initial "ng" sound in Ngo and Nguyen, which is a nasalized "guh" made in the back of the throat, somewhat similar to the "ng" sound in "bingo" (which rhymes with Ngo). For Nguyen, this sound is combined with "we" and "in" to produce "ng-we-in," spoken as one syllable. When "ng" is combined with an "h" as in the name of the tenth-century ruler Duong Dinh Nghe, a "y" sound is added to the consonant cluster, producing a sound something like "Ngyay."

Without diacritics, the distinction between two consonants formed from the letter "d" is lost. The "hard d," indicated by a horizontal dash through the vertical line in either the upper (D) or lower (d) case letters, is pronounced as if in a European language. The "soft d" is indicated by the absence of that horizontal dash; northern Vietnamese pronounce it like a "z" and southern Vietnamese pronounce it like a "y." For example, Duong Dinh Nghe contains both a soft and a hard "D" and is pronounced "Zoong Dinh Ngyay" by northerners and "Yoong Dinh Ngyay" by southerners. Another example is the name of the president of the first Republic of Vietnam (Ngo Dinh Diem, 1955–1963), which also contains both kinds of "d," being pronounced "Ngo Dinh Ziem" by northerners and "Ngo Dinh Yiem" by southerners. On the other hand, the name of the tenth-century king Dinh Bo Linh is pronounced about the way it looks in English by both northerners and southerners.

One orthographic convention that I observe is that I spell Hanoi, Saigon, Cholon, Dalat, and Vietnam rather than Ha Noi, Sai Gon, Cho Lon, Da Lat, and Viet Nam, which is how these are rendered in the Vietnamese language. My reason for doing so, while leaving other Vietnamese place names in their Vietnamese forms, is that these names have been absorbed into common English usage without the space between syllables and without the capitalization of the second syllable.

1 THE PROVINCIAL ERA

The empire comes south

After conquering the Yangtze River basin and proclaiming the Qin Empire in 221 BCE, Qin Shi Huang, "The First Emperor of China," sent thousands of his soldiers over the mountains into the valleys and coastlands of what is now South China. He also sent convicts and women to establish a population of northerners there. After years of hard fighting against local people, Qin commanders built a city on the site of modern Guangzhou (Canton), the main seaport for trade into the southern seas. When the Qin Empire collapsed after Qin Shi Huang's death in the year 210 BCE, this coastal outpost became the center of a regional kingdom ruled by the senior commanding officer, Zhao To.

As armies fought for control of the empire in the north, Zhao To proclaimed himself King of Nan Yue (Southern Yue). Zhao To is among the first historical figures with a role in Vietnamese history. Sometime during the first quarter of the second century BCE, he extended his authority over the people living in the Red River plain of northern Vietnam. Yue had been the name of a state on the south-central coast of China (the modern province of Zhejiang) during the sixth to fourth centuries BCE. It was appropriated by Zhao To and eventually applied to the Red River plain by ancient Chinese dynasties; in Vietnamese, it is pronounced Viet.

Zhao To was not the first conqueror to arrive in the Red River plain from the north. Armed adventurers, apparently fleeing the Qin invasion of southern China, had previously arrived and defeated the local ruler. Their leader proclaimed himself King An Duong (Pacifier of the South; An Yang in Chinese). He occupied and rebuilt an existing fortress now called Co Loa. The earliest stories about this can be found in books compiled six or seven hundred years later. They tell about King An Duong and Zhao To struggling for control of the Red River plain. Several versions of this story have been recorded through the centuries; it is a tragic romance involving the transfer of political power.

The main line of the story is as follows. During a truce in the fighting between Zhao To and King An Duong, Zhao To's son, Shi Jiang, visited King An Duong's court. There, he and King An Duong's daughter, My Chau, fell in love and were married. The young bride and groom resided at An Duong's court until Shi Jiang managed to lay his hands upon the magic crossbow that was the source of King An Duong's power. He destroyed the crossbow and fled back to his father, who thereupon attacked and vanquished King An Duong. King An Duong escaped to the sea with My Chau in tow. She surreptitiously marked their way so as to be found by her husband. Perceiving this, King An Duong slew her for her treachery, and then disappeared into the sea. Finding his wife's body, Shi Jiang leaped into a well to join her in death.

This story exists today because it was interesting to compilers at Chinese dynastic courts in the third and fourth centuries CE, and maybe it was even created by them. At least three aspects of the story would have been popular at that time and place. One aspect is the theme of romantic love leading to tragic death, which was in literary fashion then. Another aspect is that it provides an explanation for how this remote part of the world was brought into the imperial political system; Zhao To's kingdom of Nan Yue (Vietnamese Nam Viet), which eventually expanded to include northern Vietnam, finally became part of the Han Empire, and all subsequent dynasties considered themselves to be heritors of Han.

Another reason why this story was interesting to people in the empire is the dissonance between a matrilocal society in which a man becomes a member of his wife's family, for which we have evidence from ancient Vietnam, and a patrilocal society in which a woman becomes a member of her husband's family, which for several centuries had already been the rule among educated people in China. Ngo Si Lien, a fifteenth-century Vietnamese historian, even commented upon how strange and "wrong" it was that in this story Shi Jiang lived with his wife's family and that My Chau did not go to live with her husband's family. It was hard for him to think that there had been a time when people in this country did not know the patriarchal Confucian family system.

In fact, the people whom King An Duong and Zhao To encountered in the Red River plain were very strange to educated northerners at that time. Two hundred years after the time of King An Duong, around the year zero, Han imperial administrators recorded their efforts to promote agriculture, to open schools, and to introduce the institution of marriage among the inhabitants of northern Vietnam. They wanted to expand agriculture to maximize the taxable surplus; schools were a way to win the minds of intelligent young locals; marriage practices governed the social system and consequently the form of political authority that could be exercised. Yet, according to the *San Guo Zhi* (Annals of the Three Kingdoms), an imperial administrator named Xue Zong, who two centuries later spent most of his career in northern Vietnam, wrote: "According to the records, civilizing activities have been going on for over four hundred years, but, according to what I myself have seen during many years of travel since my arrival here, the actual situation is something else ... In short, it can be said that these people are on the same level as bugs."

Until the middle of the first century CE, outside of a few imperial outposts, local rulers limited the influence of Han officials. These local rulers can be seen riding in boats that decorate the large bronze drums that announced their authority. In their graves of boat-shaped wooden coffins, they have left their weapons, tools, jewelry, and daily life items made of wood, pottery, bronze, and iron. From such things, and from brief written descriptions by imperial officials compiled in later books, we can vaguely see the society ruled by these people. Imperial officials called them Lac (Chinese Luo) and Au (Chinese Ou), which they understood as kinds of Viet (Chinese Yue), a name applied to southern non-Han people.

The Lac people were rice growers in the Red River plain. The Au had arrived with King An Duong, who combined his entourage with the existing class of rulers to produce what was recorded as the kingdom of Au-Lac. The Lac lords had previously served the ruler dethroned by King An Duong. In later centuries, historians used the name Hung for those who ruled before King An Duong at the place where the Red River emerges from the mountains, called Me Linh in old texts. It would have been easy for this place to be in contact with other bronze-age cultures up the Red River to the northwest in what are now the Chinese provinces of Yunnan and Sichuan. King An Duong's fortress of Co Loa was in the upper plain north of the Red River, located to dominate the plain while defending it from intruders coming from the north-east, either along the coast or through the upland passes leading to Zhao To's kingdom of Nan Yue in the modern Chinese provinces of Guangdong and Guangxi.

One detail in the earliest versions of the story of King An Duong and Zhao To can be related to the archaeology of Co Loa. Cao Thong (Chinese Kao Tong), a man described in such a way as to indicate that he was from China, was the chief advisor of King An Duong as well as the inventor of the magic crossbow. As long as King An Duong retained the loyalty of Cao Thong, Zhao To could not defeat him. However, King An Duong treated Cao Thong disrespectfully, and Cao Thong abandoned him. Thereafter, King An Duong lost the magic crossbow and was defeated. The archaeology of Co Loa reveals an adaptation of engineering practices from the Warring States of ancient China to the local terrain and a range of weapons similar to contemporary armies in China, which suggests that King An Duong's magic weapon may have been some kind of "new model army" trained and led by Cao Thong, which was no longer effective without his leadership.

After Zhao To had expelled King An Duong, he posted two legates to supervise the Au-Lac lords, one in the Red River plain, which was named Giao Chi, and one in the Ma and Ca River plains immediately to the south, which was named Cuu Chan. Some records suggest that he also invested a king at Co Loa who continued to preside over the Au-Lac lords. The legates established commercial outposts accessible by sea. Their presence was apparently unobjectionable to the Au-Lac lords, for there is no record of trouble between them. Access to stable markets with goods from the north was surely a benefit to the local rulers. For the next century and a half, no recorded information survives about this place. The local organization of society and politics apparently remained fundamentally unchanged in the transfer from Hung kings to King An Duong to the kingdom of Nan Yue. The next transfer of suzerain also did not bring any drastic change.

When the Han General Lu Bode conquered Nan Yue in III BCE, his army was met at the Giao Chi border by the two Nan Yue legates with cattle, wine, and tokens of submission. At that time, an Au-Lac lord received a titular reward from Han for overthrowing the king who had been invested by Nan Yue at Co Loa. Han subsequently established two new outposts as frontier garrisons, one facing northwest, up the Red River into the mountains at Me Linh where the Hung kings had supposedly ruled, and one facing the southern coast in Nhat Nam, on the plain between the Ngang and Hai Van Passes beyond Cuu Chan. The headquarters for Giao Chi and the entire region was at Luy Lau, a seaport amidst fields connected by river with the coast leading north.

Giao Chi, Cuu Chan, and Nhat Nam were given the status of prefectures in Han imperial administration. A total of twenty-two districts were organized, or at least theorized, in these prefectures, ten in Giao Chi, seven in Cuu Chan, and five in Nhat Nam. The districts were left in the hands of local lords who received imperial "seals and ribbons" as symbols of their status in return for what the lords viewed as tribute to a suzerain but which imperial officials over time began to view as taxes. Although this situation, so far as surviving evidence reveals, remained peaceful for the next century and a half, the accommodation achieved between a feudal aristocracy and the Han practice of prefecture and district administration was an expedient and would not be sustainable in the long run.

Han officials sought to maintain peaceful relations with the local population while pursuing the complex, sometimes contradictory, goals of imperial administration. These goals included patrolling the frontiers to ensure security, monitoring the local leaders to maintain domestic tranquility, nurturing trade and agriculture to produce a taxable surplus, encouraging northern immigration to consolidate a mass of people directly responsive to imperial authority, and seeking opportunities to change local ways toward northern norms with education and social reform. The perspective of the Han officials was largely limited to their prefectural headquarters and garrisons and the security of the river routes that connected these places. They met with the lords who governed districts to receive a portion of the local surplus and to confer tokens of imperial authority and benevolence.

For their part, the lords upon whom Han officials were dependent for governing the non-Han population inhabited a world very different from Han people. Theirs was the realm of the Lac, and of the Au who during this time were probably for the most part absorbed into the Lac. People today apply the archaeological name of Dong Son to their culture. Here were communities of agriculturalists settled along riverbanks beside rice fields. The rulers sent men by boat to collect rice and other goods, armed with crossbows, spears, swords, and their distinctive bronze pediform axes. They proclaimed their arrival by beating on bronze drums to summon the people to submit what was due. Many of these drums still exist and are decorated with scenes of the boats bearing warriors with weapons, large jars to carry rice, and the drums. There are also depictions of people wearing clothing decorated with feathers. Some are pounding rice in large mortars with long wooden pestles. There are musicians and dancers, men and women copulating, and warriors holding decapitated heads. The drums also bear images of birds, deer, crocodiles, and frogs. The rulers of this society met with Han officials to exchange gifts and to gain access to markets with goods from afar, and they were buried with their weapons, wooden combs, bracelets, ceramic pillows, and Han coins.

An imperial census was taken in the year 2 CE. It recorded 143,643 households and 981,755 people in the three prefectures of Giao Chi, Cuu Chan, and Nhat Nam. It is doubtful that these enumerations came from an actual registration of the population or even that they were a compilation of estimates. It was at this time that some prefects in remote jurisdictions endeavored to become famous for claiming to have promoted agriculture and patriarchal marriage rites, activities related to the taking of a census. They typically made impressive but unverifiable claims seeking to gain a reputation that would lead to more desirable assignments nearer the imperial heartland.

Despite many problems in evaluating the accuracy of this census, it is nevertheless plausible evidence for the existence of a settled population in the lowlands of what is now northern Vietnam that was significant and substantial in the context of imperial administration in ancient China. This is apparent in comparison with numbers in the same census recorded from the modern southern Chinese provinces of Guangxi and Guangdong, even allowing for the certainty of error and fiction: 71,805 households and 390,555 people, less than half the households and only around 40 percent of the people recorded for the prefectures in modern Vietnam.

Who were these people and what language did they speak? Han immigrants aside, we can plausibly conjecture that much of the lowland population spoke what linguists call Proto-Viet-Muong related to the Mon-Khmer language family that apparently expanded northward from the Ca River plain in modern Nghe An and Ha Tinh Provinces. The geographical connection with other Mon-Khmer languages appears to have been via the Mu Gia Pass from the middle Mekong plain to the Ca River plain. Another plausible conjecture is that the aristocracy that ruled these people, called Lac in Han texts, came from the mountains north and west of the Red River plain and spoke an ancient language related to modern Khmu, another Mon-Khmer language now spoken in the mountains of northern Vietnam and Laos. On the other hand, the Au conquerers who arrived from the northern mountains with King An Duong might be imagined to have spoken a language related to the Tai-Kadai language family that includes modern Lao and Thai. In any case, it is too early to speak of the Vietnamese language.

The Han conquest

During the years 9–23 CE, the empire was in turmoil as a so-called usurper named Wang Mang tried to supplant the Han dynasty. Uprisings spread disorder in northern China, and fighting continued until a Han prince restored the authority of his dynasty. During this time, officials in southern China remained loyal to Han. Many Han loyalists fled from the north seeking safety in what is now southern China and northern Vietnam. After the Han restoration, large numbers of the officials who had found refuge in the south returned north, but some remained and established families that would be prominent in local government for centuries after. This wave of refugees from the north strengthened Han officials in their dealings with local peoples during this short but tumultuous era and accelerated the ascendancy of imperial administration over the Lac aristocracy.

Han administrative activity in these years reflects an accumulation of immigration from the north as well as growing familiarity and experience with local conditions. Han officials began to extend the sphere of their direct authority over increasing numbers of inhabitants. Some of these were immigrants from the north settled near Han garrisons and administrative centers. Others were local people who either lived near these places or were attracted to migrate there for economic opportunities or for the security provided by direct imperial rule. Han centers surely attracted refugees from the politics of the Lac lords and the vicissitudes of local society. By this time, Han administrators had apparently established a presence at the district level where they were in a position to intervene in relations between Lac lords and local people. Han officials endeavored to draw the Lac lords into the hierarchy of Han government, to teach them to observe the norms of Han civilization and administration. This effort was probably successful in some cases, but in other cases produced non-cooperation and resistance.

Contradictions grew between Han government and Lac lords. Han officials were appointees in an imperial administrative system; Lac lords were hereditary aristocrats in something like a feudal system. Han officials organized and registered families in a structure that governed through the responsibility of patriarchs to control their subordinates and to pay taxes; the status of Lac lords passed through the family line of one's mother and tribute was obtained from communities of agriculturalists who practiced group responsibility. For Han people, land and inheritance rights were possessed by men; in Lac society, access to land was based on communal usage rather than individual ownership and women possessed inheritance rights.

Immigrants from the north included officials, soldiers, agriculturalists, and technical experts of various kinds who married local women and obtained land. The contradiction between the Han practice of land being inherited through the male line and the Lac practice of land rights being inherited through the female line came to a head with these people. In mixed marriages, the conflicting interests of male and female offspring were aligned with the discordant regimes of Han administrators and Lac lords. At stake was control of land and access to the taxable agricultural surplus.

While in Han society men inherited wealth through their fathers, in Lac society both men and women inherited wealth through their mothers. As late as the third century CE, an imperial administrator wrote disapprovingly that levirate was still practiced in areas where Lac traditions remained strongest. This meant that childless widows had a right to bear children with men from their deceased husbands' families in order to obtain heirs. This practice ostensibly provided an heir for the mother, although some patriarchal societies used it to provide an heir for the deceased father. A woman's prerogative to bear children for her family line may lie behind an observation from that time and place that local women were difficult to control and that aspiring patriarchs attached bells to the ears of their wives to prevent them from sneaking off at night to be with other men.

According to Han historical records, in the fourth decade of the first century CE, a Lac lord was "tied up with the law" by the Han prefect of Giao Chi. This provoked an uprising led by two women, daughters of another Lac lord, who were married to the "tied up" lord. These were the famous Trung Sisters who in later centuries became heroines of Vietnamese history. The details of what happened can only be conjectured. If the "law" referred to had to do with land ownership and inheritance rights, a plausible scenario is that Han officials endeavored to restrain a man who was championing the inheritance rights of women to whom he was related by marriage against efforts by the imperial regime to assert Han ideas about land ownership. But there may have been other issues at stake as well, for the Trung Sisters were from Me Linh, the locality where the Hung kings were said to have ruled before the time of King An Duong, so they may have been infused with a venerable tradition of authority.

Han descriptions of northern Vietnam compiled three to four centuries later say that the most distinguishing feature of Me Linh was the presence of big beautiful snakes that could be captured only by covering them with women's clothing. If this indication of female potency were imagined as a remnant of thought about there once being Hung queens rather than Hung kings in this place, it would offer an explanatory context to the fact that when Han settlements and garrisons were overrun in the spring of 40 CE the Trung Sisters then ruled as queens from Me Linh. These queens established their influence over the Han jurisdictions in northern Vietnam of Giao Chi, Cuu Chan, and Nhat Nam, and also a prefecture on the coast to the north that today is within the Chinese border.

The Trung Sisters reigned for two years until a Han expeditionary force was organized and put in motion. The only detail about their rule that remains from Han historical records is that they "adjusted taxes," which suggests that the most inflammatory issue leading to the uprising was control of land and agricultural surplus – an important target of Han taxation. It might also refer to control of the markets and taxation of local commodities that were sought by Han merchants. These were primarily luxury goods such as rhinoceros horns, elephant tusks, tropical bird feathers, pearls, aromatic woods, and slaves. Rulers in northern China had by then already been coveting these items for centuries. Two and a half centuries earlier, Qin Shi Huang's attention had been drawn to the south by the trade in these goods. Considerations of frontier security, revenue from a relatively large agricultural population, and access to tropical commodities all contributed to the Han determination to regain control of this region.

One climatic feature that has affected warfare in Vietnam for centuries is the monsoon rains. During the warm months when temperatures rise on the Eurasian land mass, winds from the sea bring rain, and sometimes typhoons, beginning in May and extending into October. The land becomes waterlogged and will not sustain the movement of large armies. As temperatures fall during the cooler months, from November to April, winds blow out to sea and the land dries out making it possible for large armies to move.

In the dry season of early 42 CE, General Ma Yuan led a Han army into the Red River plain, building a road along the coast as he came. Ma Yuan established his headquarters near King An Duong's fortress of Co Loa and camped there during the soggy months of the monsoon rain season, from May to October. Around the end of the year, as the land dried out and the fighting season opened, he captured and beheaded the Trung Sisters after a series of battles in which thousands of their followers were killed, were captured, or had surrendered. He spent the next year receiving the submission of local leaders, tracking down and killing those who refused to submit, deporting hundreds of prominent clans to the north, building fortified towns from which localities could be governed, establishing garrisons, and settling his soldiers on land from which they could supply their own provisions. He also issued regulations to eliminate the contradictions between Han law and local practice, and he took oaths of loyalty from those who submitted. Having established a foundation for direct imperial governance, he returned north in 44 CE.

The expedition of Ma Yuan ended the age that historians associate with Lac lords and that archaeologists associate with Dong Son Culture. It came two and a half centuries after Qin Shi Huang's imperial armies crossed the passes into southern China, initiating recorded history in this region with the frontier perceptions of Han administrators and the legendary struggle between King An Duong and Zhao To. Local society and the people who ruled it do not appear to have experienced any major disruption as Han officials garrisoned headquarters at a few strategic locations and began to attract immigrants from the north. As years went by, however, contradictions between imperial policy and local practice grew ever more apparent and eventually led to the violence of the 40s CE.

Stories about relations between imperial administrators and the local society during this long era of coexistence were compiled in a book annotated in its present form around five centuries later entitled *Shui Jing Zhu* (Commentary on the Waterways Classic). The stories are about boundaries between the realms of human beings and animals with the humans standing for imperial civilization and animals standing for uncivilized locals. Three stories are attributed to three regions of the Red River plain. One of these is the story, mentioned above, about the big beautiful snakes at Me Linh. This is where the Hung kings or queens are thought to have ruled and also where the Trung Sisters held court. The snakes are entirely in the animal realm, and the point of the story is how to capture and kill them.

Another story is located in the region of Co Loa, where King An Duong ruled. It is about chimpanzees able to transform themselves into creatures with handsome human heads that spoke using elegant language that moved the emotions of human listeners. Humans ate the delicious flesh of these creatures in time of famine. This story of an animal able to enter the human realm with its face and speech is a metaphor for local people who learned some aspects of civilization. But that they were eaten in an emergency indicates that for civilized people they nevertheless remained animals.

The third story comes from Luy Lau, the Han administrative center established at the seaport facing the northern coast. Here a Han administrator became famous for having transformed himself into a tiger and then later returned himself back into a man. This story is about a representative of imperial civilization penetrating the animal world and taking control of it in the form of the most ferocious of beasts, then returning to the human realm.

These stories reflect perceptions of three different regions, but they also reflect three phases in a process of contact between local people and Han officials. The big snake is utterly beyond human civilization and must be killed. The talking chimpanzees assumed some civilized characteristics and were interesting but could never become members of the civilized human world. The Han tiger-man learned to enter and master the realm of savagery yet remained a civilized man and an imperial official. These stories present metaphors for three policies: extermination of the uncivilized, allowing the uncivilized to acquire some aspects of civilization, and penetrating the uncivilized realm and dominating it with imperial versions of uncivilized potency.

In the same book where these stories are recorded, each of these three places is also associated with an emblematic military encounter. At Me Linh, Ma Yuan defeated and killed the Trung Sisters. Co Loa is the scene of the struggle for ascendancy between King An Duong and Zhao To, two aspiring monarchs on the imperial frontier. The battle recorded for Luy Lau is an event that took place in the year 411 when a rebel army fleeing from imperial forces in southern China entered northern Vietnam and attempted to seize control of it; the loyal imperial governor rallied the frontier province against the invading rebel and defeated him. These episodes show a shift of perspective on northern Vietnam from a place of disorder where uncivilized people were slain to a place where semi-civilized kingdoms competed for dominance on the edge of the civilized world to a loyal civilized province that overcame rebellious forces emanating from the imperial heartland.

For nine hundred years following the expedition of Ma Yuan, the southern-most province of successive dynastic empires was in northern Vietnam. During this time, every aspect of society and culture was transformed by education in the

Confucian and Daoist classics, by the arrival of Buddhism and its synthesis with local religious practices, by waves of immigrants, by imperial ideals of political organization and social behavior, and by a transformation of languages, both Annamese Middle Chinese that developed among the Chinese speakers and Proto-Viet-Muong spoken by the non-Chinese population, in a context of centuries of bilingualism. The series of acculturating episodes during this time progressively turned the lives and aspirations of people inhabiting this place toward the civilization in the north.

There was no further mention of the name Lac. Instead, the people here were recorded as Viet (Chinese Yue). As a name, Viet had a relatively prominent imperial pedigree. Although it was a designation for southern non-Han peoples, it nevertheless indicated a kind of uncivilized people that were redeemable. A kingdom named Yue/Viet was one of the "warring states" of ancient China in the sixth to fourth centuries BCE, on the southern coast of the civilized world near the mouth of the Yangtze River. Its most famous ruler, King Goujian (fifth century BCE), claimed descent from a sage-king in antiquity. His people, originally considered civilized, had assumed uncivilized aspects through long residence among uncivilized peoples. Consequently, the Yue/Viet were thought of as a kind of uncivilized people predisposed toward the civilizing process. This was a name for people on the threshold of civilization who had the options of going over the threshold, of turning away, or of looking both ways.

Shi Xie and the rise of the great families

For fifty years after Ma Yuan's expedition, Han power was at its peak. Very little information about the southern frontier during this time was recorded by imperial historians, which may be taken as an indication that, in the wake of Ma Yuan's frontier sojourn, the situation was relatively calm. When events began to be recorded, in the second century, they were about invasions, rebellions, and political turmoil. Ma Yuan left most of his army in Giao Chi, Cuu Chan, and Nhat Nam to form the core of what became a frontier garrison. Large numbers of Han soldiers, administrators, merchants, craftspeople, agriculturalists, and adventurers came and went. Many of these people remained to take advantage of opportunities on the new frontier.

Ma Yuan's expedition is the pivot for a dramatic shift in archaeological evidence. Han-style brick tombs replace Dong Son graves. These tombs are nearly identical with tombs found throughout the Han Empire, being underground chambers covered by mounds of earth and containing coins, jewelry, lamps, figurines, utensils, mirrors, ceramics, weapons, and other miscellaneous items, all typical of Han culture. Among the artifacts found in these tombs are clay models of agricultural compounds with wells, ovens, granaries, pens for animals, residential quarters, and walls with towers for defense. Such clay models are found in Han tombs everywhere and indicate the basic composition of Han society in the first and second centuries CE, a social structure that continued in various forms until the sixth century in southern China and northern Vietnam.

Historians of China refer to this as the age of "great family dominance," meaning that "great families," or agglomerations of people and property under the authority of kin groups, whether actual or fictive, constituted government at the local and provincial levels and dominated imperial administration outside of the capital region and of strategically located garrisons. These were similar to the latifundia in the Roman Empire and the hacienda of colonial Latin America, which emerged from contexts of imperial conquest and appropriation of land, manpower, and other resources. As economic units, they were typically based on control of large tracts of agricultural land worked by peasants and herders in various forms of servitude or dependency, but they could also include craftsmen with specialized skills, for example in ceramics, bronze and iron ware, woodworking, fishing and pearl diving, salt making, ivory carving, precious stones and metals, and the production of incense from aromatic wood. There would also have been scholars, scribes, teachers, medical doctors, priests, monks, soldiers, spies, assassins, alchemists, and magicians, all of whom were employed to serve the interests of the group of people composing the "great family," constituted by birth, adoption, marriage, or some other expedient.

The "great families" were economic and social units that brought together local people and immigrants or sojourners from the north. They were arenas with potential for upward social mobility for local people having skills, aptitudes, and attributes in demand by those in power. They were also places where northerners could find opportunities for employment and possible advancement. The people who presided at the very top of these "great families" were buried in the vaulted brick tombs. They were either northerners and their descendents or local people who had assimilated into the imperial governing class. The tombs indicate a fundamental regional stability of imperial society despite the vicissitudes of dynastic politics during the five hundred years following Ma Yuan's expedition.

During the first to sixth centuries, thousands of these tombs were built in the rice lands of Giao Chi, Cuu Chan, and Nhat Nam. They are today found as far south as the region of modern Quang Trach (Ba Don) in Quang Binh Province, on the Gianh River just south of Ngang pass. It is not coincidental that at this place the distribution of the brick tombs reached its southernmost extent. After the fall of Han, Ngang Pass became the southern border of the provincial jurisdictions inhabited by the ancestors of modern Vietnamese. The Han juris-diction of Nhat Nam had its northern border at Ngang Pass and it became a contested frontier zone between Sino-Vietnamese, later Vietnamese, and other peoples generally called Cham. Not until the fifteenth century did Vietnamese armies decisively conquer this area and open the southern coast to Vietnamese immigrants.

By the beginning of the seventeenth century, Vietnamese along this southern coast had established their own separate political system, and for two centuries the Gianh River was the border between northern and southern Vietnamese kingdoms. Decades of warfare ensued. Thirty kilometers south, at Dong Hoi, the southerners built a system of defensive walls from the mountains to the sea to block northern invasions. Seventy kilometers south of Dong Hoi is the Ben Hai River at the seventeenth parallel, the border between warring northern and southern Vietnamese states for twenty years in the mid twentieth century.

This region was the southern extremity of the Han Empire at its greatest extent, and thereafter it remained a border zone of one kind or another. There are at least four reasons for this: geography, climate, political history, and human activity in response to these factors. North of Ngang Pass, the plains of the Red, Ma, and Ca Rivers form a coherent geographical space of rice lands amidst large rivers and mountainous terrain with possibilities for defense against external threats. Major rivers all lead west-northwest into the highlands of southwest China and northern Laos. These plains are at the southern edge of the temperate climatic zone, having four seasons with cold, if brief, winters. Wresting an agricultural life from flooding rivers and the salty sea instilled a disciplined lifestyle. Internalizing the social organization and cultural ideals acquired from centuries of participation in an imperial world added new forms of discipline. Communal responsibility and deference to authority remain strong among northern Vietnamese.

The southern border of the Han jurisdiction of Nhat Nam was Hai Van Pass, located between the modern cities of Hue and Da Nang. South from Hai Van Pass, one enters the tropics and a coastal environment with greater exposure to the outside world of seafaring and maritime trade routes than is possible on the more northerly coasts facing Hainan Island. Here the Cham peoples, and later the southern Vietnamese, found scope for a more diversified economic, social, and cultural life than was possible further north. The mountainous hinterland communicates with the central Mekong and territories inhabited by ancient Khmer speakers and, more recently, by Tai speakers.

The coastal plain between Ngang Pass and Hai Van Pass is a transitional zone that includes both temperate and tropical climatic features. Han-era Nhat Nam was anchored in its north with a society in the plain of the Gianh River and its tributaries that produced the Han-style brick tombs. Here was sited the headquarters for commanders of garrisons and patrols that maintained watch as far south as Hai Van Pass. In the second century, as Han power began to decline, frontier disorders in Nhat Nam began to multiply, leading by the end of that century to abandonment of the entire jurisdiction. During that time, the people of Giao Chi and Cuu Chan repeatedly mobilized in response to these disorders and came to understand that with the ebbing of Han power their security increasingly depended upon their taking for themselves the responsibility of regional leadership. The story of how this happened is about the first inkling of local political initiative after the shock of Ma Yuan's conquest, which had been followed by several generations of immigration, intermarriage, and acculturation in the context of the "great family" estates.

At the center of this story is a family that traced its ancestry to refugees from Shandong Province in northeastern China that had fled into the south during the Wang Mang disorders at the beginning of the first century CE. This family settled at the headquarters commanding the frontier jurisdiction comprised of southern China and northern Vietnam, located at Cangwu (modern Wuzhou) on the present border of Guangdong and Guangxi Provinces in southern China. Here a main route over the mountains from the north met the West River, about 420 kilometers northeast of the modern Sino-Vietnamese border. During the years from the late 140s to the late 160s, the leader of this family, Shi Si, served as the chief administrative officer of Nhat Nam. These were critical years in the unraveling of the southern Han frontier, and Shi Si served there at a time when especially talented and trusted men were assigned to rule by force of personality in lieu of reliance upon military force only.

During the previous decade, in 137 and again in 144, Han outposts and settlements in Nhat Nam were overrun by uprisings originating in the southernmost part of the jurisdiction, provoking turmoil and the breakdown of Han authority in Cuu Chan as well. A disorder similar to these had been put down by force in the year 100, subsequent to which there were several episodes of local peoples immigrating into the areas of Han administration and submitting to Han authority. Since this was also the time when Han power began to decline, Han administration was apparently unequal to the task of carrying out its civilizing mandate among these new subjects or of keeping them at peace. When Nhat Nam erupted in 137 and 144, Han was no longer capable of sending large numbers of soldiers so far south. Consequently, a policy was implemented in which men were selected for their prior experience and success in dealing with non-Han peoples on the frontier and were sent to calm the situation through persuasion and charisma. Shi Si was such a person. In 160, when disorders once more broke out in Nhat Nam and Cuu Chan, Han officials again negotiated peace without resort to arms.

The progressive ebbing of Han power, however, continued to offer new opportunities for frontier adventurers. Nhat Nam was temporarily stabilized, but in the 160s uprisings began to break out further north in what is now southern China. The 170s were a time of contention among Han officials in southern China and northern Vietnam, where loyalty to the distant Han court was increasingly eroded by personal ambition. By the 180s, imperial appointments to prominent local men recognized an emerging arrangement of regional autonomy.

At that time, Shi Si's eldest son, Shi Xie, was appointed to govern Giao Chi. For the next forty years, Shi Xie kept Giao Chi and Cuu Chan in peace, while all around swirled the consequences of Han collapse. One of these consequences in the early 190s was the appearance of the kingdom of Lin Yi in southern Nhat Nam. The people of Lin Yi included groups from both the coast and the adjacent uplands along with Han renegades. Lin Yi must also have had some contact, if not connection, with Cham peoples led by kings in the region beyond Nhat Nam's border, south of Hai Van Pass. As portrayed in later Chinese records, the logic for the existence of this kingdom was to exploit opportunities for probing, plundering, and appropriating territories in imperial frontier jurisdictions. For much of the next four centuries, Lin Yi would be a chronic adversary for those who governed the Red River plain. It nevertheless appears that Shi Xie managed to maintain a modus vivendi with this nascent power.

In his youth, Shi Xie had been sent north to study with a famous scholar. He subsequently served as a secretary at the Han court, then returned south to mourn for his father, and thereafter served as an administrator in Sichuan in western China before being appointed to govern Giao Chi. This appointment was based upon both his personal qualities and his position as head of the Shi family, which had become prominent on the southern frontier. In the 190s, the lapse of imperial control in the south enabled Shi Xie to appoint three of his brothers to govern Cuu Chan and the coastal regions of modern Guangxi and Guangdong in southern China. Shi Xie governed from Luy Lau, about thirty kilometers east of modern Hanoi, where his tomb can be seen to this day.

Around a hundred scholars fleeing the collapse of Han found refuge with Shi Xie. Shi Xie was remembered among later generations of Vietnamese as the father of education in their land. He reportedly built schools and encouraged lively debates among the intellectuals who gathered around him, including Confucianists, Daoists, and Buddhists. Centuries later, he was credited with compiling a dictionary explaining classical terms in vernacular Vietnamese for use in schools. He surrounded himself with Buddhist monks, and the building of the earliest known Vietnamese Buddhist temples is attributed to him. The story about how Buddhism originated among the Vietnamese connects him to the first appearance of a Buddha in this land, a Mother Buddha who miraculously gave birth to a daughter who, via a tale entwined with the worship of trees and rocks, became embodied in images of four sister Buddhas with rain-making powers. One of these, the Dharma Cloud Buddha, was particularly worshipped by imperial governors and also by Vietnamese kings as late as the eighteenth century. Shi Xie's posthumous cult also credited him with Daoist powers of immortality. In short, Shi Xie is associated with the introduction of every major aspect of what came to define Vietnamese culture. This is why in his study of Shi Xie, Stephen O'Harrow called him "the first Vietnamese."

Giao Province

Shi Xie was termed a "king" in Vietnamese writings of later centuries, but during his lifetime he posed as a loyal official of the Han court until this was no longer plausible, at which point he shifted his allegiance to the rising Wu dynasty in southeastern China, one of the three kingdoms that partitioned the Han Empire in the early third century. After Shi Xie's death in 226, the Wu moved quickly to exterminate the Shi family and to gain control of northern Vietnam. Cut off from the Silk Road across Central Asia to northern China, the Wu wanted direct access to the maritime route to India and the Mediterranean Sea, for which northern Vietnam had become a terminus during the rule of Shi Xie. Wu exactions and resort to harsh expedients provoked resistance, and in 248 the leader of Lin Yi took advantage of this to seize northern Nhat Nam, inspiring local leaders in Cuu Chan and Giao Chi to rebel against the Wu regime. The Wu calmed the situation with conciliation, resorting to force only to suppress resistance in southern Cuu Chan led by a woman remembered in Vietnamese texts as Lady Trieu. Despite these successes, the Wu made no effort to re-enter Nhat Nam.

The Wu kingdom, locked in continual war with its rivals in northern and western China, treated Giao Chi and Cuu Chan primarily as sources of wealth, which was not a popular policy among the people who lived there. In the 260s, the Wei of northern China conquered the Shu Han dynasty of western China in Sichuan and thereafter became the Jin dynasty, thereby reducing the Three Kingdoms to two. Local leaders in Giao Chi sent envoys to Sichuan to offer their allegiance to the Jin, Wu's remaining enemy. In response, the Jin sent a governor with seven military commanders and their men to establish an anti-Wu regime in northern Vietnam. There followed three years of fighting between Wu forces attempting to regain control of the Red River plain and Jin forces endeavoring to prevent this. Local forces were initially allied with Jin. However, when Tao Huang, an astute Wu commander, sent treasure that he had seized from the Jin contingent to a prominent local leader, thousands of local troops shifted their allegiance to Wu. The Jin soldiers were soon besieged and forced to surrender.

Tao Huang thereafter governed northern Vietnam, now known as Giao Province, for around twenty-five years, until near the end of the third century; the exact year is unknown. Just as had been the case with Shi Xie, he governed during a time of dynastic change in the north. In 280, Jin conquered Wu. Based far away in northern China, Jin was content to confirm Tao Huang's appointment as governor of Giao, where he continued to serve until his death. Tao Huang was known as a patron of Buddhism. He also established an administrative structure for Giao Province that lasted through several dynastic regimes. A salient feature of this structure was the formation of three new frontier jurisdictions. Two of these were in Giao Chi facing the mountains to the north and to the west; one was in southern Cuu Chan facing the old Nhat Nam border. Tao Huang endeavored to re-establish some semblance of authority in Nhat Nam, proclaiming an economic embargo against markets in Nhat Nam and garrisoning soldiers on the frontier, but there is no evidence that he achieved more than a temporary stabilization of the border. On the contrary, his efforts appear to have done little more than elicit attacks by Lin Yi.

During the first two decades of the fourth century, warring princes tore the Jin dynasty apart and various groups of non-Han peoples conquered northern China, sending a great wave of refugees into southern China, where a Jin prince reassembled the dynasty from his base on the lower Yangtze. During this time, Giao Province was left to its own devices with a regime over which local leaders invited prominent members of old Wu families to preside as governors.

In the 320s, the newly constituted Jin court in southern China was strong enough to begin sending soldiers to Giao in efforts to gain control of the government there. As in the previous century when Wu attempted to gain ascendancy and local powers turned to the Jin in Sichuan, local powers in Giao now resisted Jin, inspired by the Cheng Han dynasty that had arisen in Sichuan in opposition to Jin. Meanwhile, Jin immigrants were seeking their fortunes in the south by pushing aside the old Wu families that had come to the fore in the late third century; Giao Province was the last place of refuge for these families.

The Jin dynasty finally established its authority in Giao in the 330s, after Jin troops had cut communications between Sichuan and northern Vietnam; within a decade, Jin gained control of Sichuan and removed that option entirely. Jin forces were concerned to get a grip on the southern frontier because the turmoil of the preceding years had attracted the unwelcome attention of Lin Yi. In the 340s, Lin Yi armies, commanded by a king of Han ancestry who had traveled extensively in China as a merchant and knew of conditions in China at first hand, began a series of raids into Giao, culminating in a full-scale invasion in 347. Jin mobilized soldiers from Giao and the province of Guang (modern Guangdong and Guangxi in southern China) for a major effort against Lin Yi. In 349, the Jin army advanced as far as the Gianh River, the former headquarters of Han-era Nhat Nam, where it was defeated and forced to withdraw. The Lin Yi king was mortally wounded in this battle, but his son continued the policy of attacking Giao until defeated by another Jin expedition in 359.

The mobilizations of men and resources for the expeditions of 349 and 359 bore heavily upon Giao and even provoked some dissention among provincial officials. But after Lin Yi had been quieted, Jin interest in Giao rapidly faded as the imperial court became preoccupied with other threats. In the late 370s, the governorship fell vacant and the prefect of Cuu Chan, the leader of a prominent local family named Li Xun, seized control of provincial affairs.

In 380, the Jin court sent Teng Dunzhi to be governor and Li Xun, perceiving that imperial power was weakening, opted to resist him. However, the head of another leading Giao family, Du Yuan, then serving as the prefect of Giao Chi, took the opportunity to further his ambitions by killing Li Xun and welcoming Teng Dunzhi. The Du family then stood at the head of provincial affairs for the next forty-seven years. Teng Dunzhi remained in Giao as governor for nineteen years, during which the Du family enjoyed preeminence in provincial administration.

Du Yuan's grandfather was originally from Chang'an (Xi'an) in northern China and had been assigned to a post in modern Guangxi near the Giao border early in the fourth century before the fall of northern China in 311. He subsequently settled in Giao during the time when Jin authority was being established there, apparently participating in that process. The family was prominent in Giao throughout the century of Jin rule.

Shortly after Teng Dunzhi's departure in 399, Giao was surprised by a Lin Yi invasion that succeeded in placing the provincial capital under siege. Du Yuan mobilized provincial forces and counterattacked, rapidly pushing the invaders back across the border. Shortly thereafter, the Jin court appointed him governor. When he died in 410, his son Du Huidu succeeded to the governorship. When Du Huidu died in 423, his son Du Hongwen succeeded to the governorship, which he occupied until 427 when he received an appointment at the imperial court.

The Du family left in Giao a reputation for good government, reportedly using benevolence and strictness as circumstances dictated. It was a time of dynastic change as the Jin court declined and was replaced in 420 by the Liu Song dynasty, which was content to confirm Du Huidu as governor of Giao. During these years, Giao faced a threat from its northern as well as from its southern border.

In 410, Lu Xun, the governor of Guang, the province in southern China adjacent to Giao, aimed to benefit from the feebleness of the Jin court by rebelling. When defeated by a Jin general in 411, Lu Xun led his army into Giao. There he lost his life when defeated in battle by Du Huidu, who thereby protected both his family's ascendancy in Giao and its reputation for loyalty to the imperial court.

The more constant threat to Giao was in the south, where fighting with Lin Yi became chronic, with serious episodes of warfare breaking out in 405–407, 413, 415, and 424. In each case, Lin Yi attacks were repulsed, but to eliminate the problem would take more resources than Giao Province by itself could provide. Although the ascendancy of the Liu Song dynasty in Giao was brief (for less than half a century), yet because of the need to respond to Lin Yi and because of major social, cultural, and economic developments during that time, important changes occurred in Giao. Unlike the expeditions organized in the fourth century by Jin against Lin Yi that relied heavily upon local resources, the Liu Song expedition came after several years of preparation that energized Giao with a prosperous imperial economy.

During the fourth century, Jin military leadership had been relatively diffuse, exercised by prominent émigrés who fled into the south after the loss of northern China in 311. These émigrés and their heirs continued to command the armies, keeping the emperors in a position of weakness. This changed when, in 420, the founder of the Liu Song dynasty concentrated control of the military in his own hands. The Liu Song era in the mid fifth century saw a major shift in the structure of politics and society with significant economic effects. Rather than martial prowess, the élite class of émigrés was encouraged to display literary accomplishments at court, where their status relations were carefully monitored. Those uninterested in this turned to trade and business, aiming their ambitions at the accumulation of wealth. The southernmost provinces, including Giao, attracted the attention of these people as a frontier of opportunity, a place to exercise their entrepreneurial and literary skills. This became an era of accelerating commercial activity and great prosperity.

As the élite émigré class shifted its attention away from military affairs to become a class of landed scholar gentry and urbanizing merchants, new wealth gained from agriculture and commerce opened possibilities for luxury, for taxation, for religion, and for investment. In Giao, this came after a century of stable government under the Jin and Liu Song dynasties and the administration of the Du family. In the 440s, borders with the dynasties in northern China were calm and did not distract merchants and adventurers from prospects in the far south, and a famously successful expedition against Lin Yi accelerated prosperity by destroying trading rivals on the southern coast and by infusing Giao with a great store of booty.

In 443, Tan Hezhi, the governor of Giao, was instructed to recruit soldiers and assemble supplies. He spent three years on this task, recruiting a formidable and well-trained military force, preparing a fleet to transport it, and gathering sufficient supplies for an extended campaign. He also enlisted the services of two commanders famous for their battlefield successes on the northern borders of the empire. In 446, the army advanced down the coast into the old territory of Nhat Nam. Defeating the Lin Yi king in several encounters, the expedition first sacked the seaport on the Gianh River where the headquarters of Nhat Nam had once been, then continued south to sack the citadel and palaces of the Lin Yi king near modern Hue, in what had been the southernmost part of old Nhat Nam. The expedition returned to Giao loaded with plunder. The Lin Yi that had contested the frontier during the preceding two and a half centuries had been thoroughly destroyed and the frontier was thereafter quiet for many years. What subsequently came to be called Lin Yi was from then based beyond the Hai Van Pass in the region of modern Da Nang, a major center of culture and kingship for Chams, who were ethno-linguistically related to the Malay peoples.

In Giao, the mid fifth century was a prosperous time. New lands were opened for agriculture south of the Red River in the region of modern Hanoi, resulting in the formation of a new prefecture there, an indication that the rural economy was expanding. Governors sent to Giao by the imperial court in the late fifth century had reputations for scholarly interests. They spent much time reading books; one was famed for his calligraphy and another discussed philosophical questions in a series of letters with two local Buddhist monks. Giao was a desirable assignment for some men at court because of opportunities there for making money. One man obtained appointment as governor in Giao after paying a large sum; he then sold prefecture appointments to others, a percentage of the profits from which he was obliged to pay to the court. These men believed that such investments would be easily recovered, with profit added, by taking posts in Giao. Giao was known as a place where private fortunes could be made.

The weak imperial court lost touch with distant provinces as government service gave way to opportunities for personal ambition. In 468, a local official prevented a newly appointed governor from entering the province and subsequently obtained for himself the appointment as governor. In the 470s, after this man died, his nephew successively turned away at the provincial border three men sent to be governor by the imperial court. Not until 485, after a new dynasty, the Qi, had restored some order to the empire, did an imperial army escort a new governor into the province, prompting the local strongman to go begging for mercy at the imperial court. But the potency of the Qi dynasty was brief and only five years later a local official took advantage of a bookish governor who neglected his duties to place him in confinement and report that he was mentally incompetent; the court simply appointed the reporting official as governor, acknowledging the existing situation. Provincial leaders in Giao had learned to govern their own affairs while posing as imperial officials. During the next century, as imperial power ebbed, Giao politics was primarily about contests for dominance among local strongmen.

Imperial weakness and local heroes

When the Liang dynasty replaced the Qi at the beginning of the sixth century, provincial leaders fell into factions that either resisted or favored the new dynasty. The pro-Liang group gained ascendancy and ruled the province for two decades, until a new system of imperial rule designed by Liang was extended to Giao in the 520s. During this time, unknown numbers of men from Giao traveled to the imperial court seeking advancement.

Since the Jin dynasty's loss of northern China in the early fourth century, the court was located at modern Nanjing, around 2,200 kilometers by land and 2,700 kilometers by sea from the Giao provincial capital. This distance is one reason why, during the preceding two centuries, leaders in Giao were sensitive to shifting dynastic fortunes at the imperial capital and developed habits of handling local affairs in their own way when it was necessary or possible to do so. Nevertheless, politically active people in Giao, despite their relative remoteness from the imperial center, were definitely educated and socialized to value their place in the empire, for ambitious men from Giao did not shrink from taking the long road to the imperial capital to advance their careers.

We know of two such men in the early sixth century, Ly Bi and Tinh Thieu, because they were prominent in a rebellion that in 541 drove Liang officials from Giao. Ly Bi's ancestors were reportedly among those who had fled into the south from northern China during the Wang Mang disorders of the early first century CE. For several generations, his lineage had been prominent in the military affairs of Giao Province, and what is known of his career places him among officers assigned to patrol the frontiers. He traveled to the Liang capital seeking a court appointment, but his ambitions were thwarted for unknown reasons, and he returned to Giao. He was joined in his frustration by Tinh Thieu, known as a scholar, who had also gone to the Liang capital in hopes of advancement. Tinh Thieu was chagrined to be disregarded because his family was unknown at court; his literary aspirations were disdained and he felt himself to be insulted by being assigned to oversee one of the gates in the city wall. Ly Bi and Tinh Thieu eventually returned to Giao together. No others are mentioned in the records, but there may very well have been a significant group of disappointed office seekers from Giao at the Liang capital who gathered around Ly Bi and Tinh Thieu. The subsequent rebellion led by them may have grown from the network of personal relationships established among members of such a group.

In 541, Ly Bi mobilized "heroes from several provinces" to attack Liang officials. These "heroes" are likely to have had unhappy imperial careers analogous to his and Tinh Thieu's. A time of relative imperial weakness encouraged an exuberance of ambition among those who were imaginative and daring. The "several provinces" is a reference to the Liang experiment in local administration implemented in the 520s, around the time that Ly Bi and Tinh Thieu returned to Giao. It was an effort to harness the ambitions of such "heroes" to imperial authority.

By this time, provincial government throughout the empire had, to a large extent, devolved into the hands of powerful local families, to the point that the imperial court aimed no further than to accept and regulate this state of affairs. The court appointed prominent local figures to be governors of newly organized small provinces while appointing members of the imperial family to be governors of larger, more strategic provinces. Military commands were established to oversee relations among the governors. Although Giao was divided into six provinces, the Red River plain remained intact; it was the dominant province in the region and was assigned to a nephew of the emperor. Ly Bi was appointed as military overseer of a province in the plain of the Ca River, on the southern frontier. From there, he mobilized an army that marched north. Reaching the Red River, he joined forces with a prominent local clan leader in the Red River plain named Trieu Tuc. In 541, the Liang governor paid a bribe to be allowed to escape north.

It took the Liang court four years, amidst several false starts, to organize an expedition against Ly Bi. During this time, while successfully resisting attacks both from Liang in the north and from Chams in the south, Ly Bi proclaimed himself an emperor and set about organizing an imperial court, directly challenging Liang's dynastic claim to the empire. It is no coincidence that the man who led an army against Ly Bi in 545, Chen Baxian, had imperial ambitions of his own and eventually supplanted the Liang by founding his own dynasty. Chen Baxian was among the best military commanders of his generation. Within a year he had driven Ly Bi into the mountains where he was killed by uplanders seeking to ingratiate themselves with the Liang army. Thereafter, Chen Baxian returned north where he was absorbed in the wars that eventually led to his proclaiming the Chen dynasty in 557.

Meanwhile, Liang forces remaining in Giao were sidelined by a struggle between the Ly clan, led by a kinsman of Ly Bi named Ly Phat Tu, who marshaled his forces in the southern provinces and along the upland frontier, and the Trieu clan, led by a son of Trieu Tuc named Trieu Quang Phuc, based in the lowlands of the Red River plain. In 557, when the Liang dynasty fell, the Ly and the Trieu, after many battles, made a truce, each recognizing the other's control in their respective territories. This truce was arranged with an eye on the new Chen dynasty, whose emperor had direct personal experience of Giao, having vanquished Ly Bi a decade earlier.

In 570, after stabilizing imperial control over the provinces just north of Giao, Chen Baxian sent an expedition to Giao, the main effect of which appears to have been the establishment of trading relations and the demise of Trieu Quang Phuc. This was the end of the brief moment of Chen power on the southern frontier and subsequently for three decades Ly Phat Tu governed Giao while watching the new imperial regime of Sui rise in northern China. By the 590s, Sui armies were operating in southern China near the Giao border and Ly Phat Tu found it expedient to formally acknowledge the authority of Sui officials head-quartered there.

In the sixth century, the Ly clan found scope for its ambition as imperial power ebbed from Giao. The Ly took on the trappings of an imperial court and, in the turmoil of the time, may have nurtured visions of glory beyond Giao's northern border. Less is known about the Trieu, but Trieu Quang Phuc's rise and fall were recorded in temples dedicated to his memory with a version of the story recorded in imperial texts about the rise and fall of King An Duong in antiquity, described earlier in this chapter. This sixth-century version explains how Ly Phat Tu defeated Trieu Quang Phuc. It associates these men with Sinic lore about frontier heroes that celebrated loyalty to one's father over romantic attachment to a spouse. It is a clichéd tale that had been recycled through the writings of imperial literati, and it shaped how these sixth-century heroes were remembered through the writing brushes of aspiring local scholars such as Tinh Thieu.

The rule of Ly Phat Tu, literally "The Son of Buddha with the Ly Surname," was congenial to the prosperity of Buddhism. The first Sui emperor reportedly asked about Buddhism in Giao and was informed by a prominent monk that in the provincial capital of Giao there were twenty Buddhist temples and five hundred ordained monks. Sutras had been translated there and prominent monks were teaching. The first Thien (Chinese Chan; Japanese Zen; Korean Seon) master was considered to have arrived in Giao at this time, initiating a lineage of patriarchs in the School of Dhyana (meditation), which was beginning to flourish at that time.

As Sui inaugurated a new imperial era in the north, a residue of resisters and adventurers from the old order of the Southern Dynasties crowded into Giao, and Ly Phat Tu presided over the last outpost of a passing age. After years of equivocating with Sui officials, he was unprepared to resist when, in 602, a Sui army, under the able leadership of an energetic commander named Liu Fang, unexpectedly emerged from the northern mountains. Ly Phat Tu surrendered and was taken prisoner to the Sui capital in northern China. Liu Fang took the submission of local clans while tracking down and executing the few recalcitrants. To punctuate Sui dominance on the frontier, he then led his army down the coast to a Cham royal center at Tra Kieu, near modern Da Nang, which he put to the torch. Loaded with plunder, Liu Fang and his army encountered an epidemic en route back north and reportedly perished to the last man.

Despite this disaster, Sui officials easily established their rule in Giao. They brought a new way of organizing society, economy, and government as well as cultural and educational fashions that superseded the imperial ebbs and flows that had characterized the preceding four centuries of belonging to the Southern Dynasties. The Sui inaugurated an imperial age that brought fundamental change to Giao.

The Protectorate of An Nam

Less than two decades after having extended its southern frontier to Giao, the Sui dynasty collapsed in 618 and was superseded by the Tang. This transition was peaceful in Giao as Sui officials transferred their allegiance to the new dynasty. The Sui and Tang dynasties established a regime based on the success of prior Northern Dynasties in centralizing their authority against the great families that had dominated the empire since Han times. The basis of this regime was the so-called "equal field" system of land distribution that limited the amount of land any one person could own and instituted a periodic redistribution of farmland to individual taxpayers organized into military units. This ensured a stable source of tax revenue and of soldiers for the imperial armies. It was most effective in areas that were newly opened up for agriculture and that did not already have powerful local families. Accordingly, in the seventh century, for the first time, the imperial headquarters for Giao was shifted south of the Red River, to the site of modern Hanoi. This was adjacent to lands in the southern and western parts of the plain that were prone to flooding from the Red River and where, beginning in the fifth century, the building of dikes had been making large-scale agriculture increasingly feasible. The appearance in the seventh century of an administrative center at what is now Hanoi was related to the organization of peasant-soldier communities south of the Red River as the foundation of Tang power in the region.

This was a time of peace and prosperity. Giao was a major stop on the land and sea routes between the Tang Empire and lands beyond. The sea route to India was well traveled by merchants and by Buddhist monks on pilgrimage. Fortunes were made from trade in tropical luxury goods. Imperial administrators garrisoned the upland frontiers and kept an eye on the peoples and markets there, under orders to enforce an embargo on trade in weapons. Information from Giao during the first three-quarters of the seventh century includes much detail about changes in administrative jurisdictions, culminating in 679 with the formation of the Protectorate of An Nam ("pacified south"), a kind of Tang jurisdiction that combined civil and military authority in the hands of a protector general that was considered appropriate for an exposed border region.

Tang records reveal concern about building walls and ramparts in the Hanoi area. During the three centuries of Tang rule these walls were repeatedly repaired, rebuilt, and expanded, and the place was known by several different names, most of them referring to particular kinds of wall. When the city was rebuilt near the end of the eighth century after a destructive war, it became known as Dai La, "big wall," the name that will be used in this chapter for the sake of convenience. This was where administrators organized a peasant militia based on the "equal field" system.

There is only one report of political violence in the seventh century, and it reveals the presence of a large peasant militia in the Dai La area. In 687, a new and inexperienced protector general endeavored to double the rate of the harvest tax, provoking an uprising that besieged him within the walls of Dai La. Before Tang forces could be effectively mobilized from the north, the walls were breached and the protector general was killed. This episode shows that the peasants affected by harvest taxes also held the balance of military force and were capable of successfully besieging the seat of government. It would be a mistake to imagine that these rebels represented some kind of non-Chinese resistance to Tang authority. The rank and file included many local people, but the hierarchy of command and the specialized skills necessary to organize a siege of the protectorate headquarters required officers, engineers, and other experts that included men from the Tang heartland. The issue was not resistance to imperial government but rather to an inept governor general. The 687 uprising was focused on the administrative center and limited to the region south of the Red River that the Tang peasant militia had brought under cultivation during the preceding decades. This is the only recorded domestic unrest during the first two centuries of Tang rule, and it came from within the Tang system of government itself, not from supposedly indigenous anti-Tang forces seeking to expel the imperial regime altogether. For the most part, people in the lowlands accepted Tang government.

North of the Red River, in the region where the great families of the Han and the Southern Dynasties had been based, a different socio-economic situation developed as powerful local families transformed their private estates into temple estates. Some of their sons entered officialdom and others entered the monastic communities that presided over the temples. The Buddhist temples across the river north and east from Dai La flourished during Tang times. The earliest people to be cited in later works as prominent Buddhist patriarchs date from this time. In addition to the prominence of Buddhist relics and miracles, which date from the time of Shi Xie at the turn of the third century, there are indications of a new emphasis on erudition and the study of sutra texts among Buddhist monks in An Nam. Also, popular religious cults developed in Tang times to worship local spirits that protected imperial government.

Some historical events appear with such little context that it is impossible to evaluate what exactly happened or what significance they might be imagined to have had. One such event is the great spasm of violence that broke into the southern Tang frontier in 722 under the leadership of a man remembered in Tang records as the Black Emperor, presumably because he was black. He came from a coastal village at the extreme southern frontier of the Tang Empire, in modern Ha Tinh Province, near Ngang Pass at the Hoanh Son massif. This was not only on the border of Tang with peoples on the southern coast; it was also near the terminus of the main route from the middle part of the Mekong over the mountains through Mu Gia Pass to the coast. According to Tang records, the Black Emperor assembled a host of four hundred thousand, comprised of a multitude of peoples from the mountains, the coasts, and the seas beyond the Tang frontier. What led to this breakdown of Tang frontier vigilance is as mysterious as what may have elicited and enabled the Black Emperor's leadership. The Black Emperor and his followers marched north and, surprising the fleeing Tang authorities, soon had the entire Protectorate of An Nam under their plundering regime. Tang forces in the north immediately mobilized, marched back into the Protectorate, and slaughtered the Black Emperor and his horde.

Forty-five years later, in 767, a somewhat similar episode occurred when people identified in Tang records with terms generally applied to the islands of what is now Indonesia invaded from the sea and briefly overran the Protectorate of An Nam until armies mobilized in the north arrived to expel them. As in the case of the Black Emperor, our knowledge of events in Southeast Asia during that time is insufficient to allow any sense of clarity about what may have provoked or elicited this event. What bears consideration, however, is that the Protectorate of An Nam was organized to prevent such threats from materializing or to respond to them when they did. The fact that during the course of two centuries there occurred only two such episodes of frontier security being breached, and that in each case a successful Tang response was organized with alacrity, shows the stability of Tang authority during that time.

During the last half of the eighth century, the Tang Empire was greatly weakened by a series of rebellions led by commanders of the peasant-soldier armies that had been the basis for the rise of the dynasty. These rebellions came on the heels of serious defeats in the early 750s suffered by Tang armies in Yunnan, in Central Asia, and in Manchuria. In the late 750s and 760s, military units were withdrawn from An Nam to fight against the rebellious generals in northern China. News of this may have encouraged the 767 seaborne invasion mentioned above.

By the 770s and 780s, Tang government in An Nam gave way to military commanders vying for ascendancy. Some of these men were of local origin. Tang records identified one of them, named Phung Hung, as a "frontier garrison indigenous leader." He came from the region of old Me Linh, associated with the Trung Sisters and pre-Han traditions. According to local lore, he was from a prominent family and claimed an indigenous rather than an imperial title.

Phung Hung gained control of An Nam sometime in the mid 780s as Tang authority faded from the southern frontier amidst the fighting among contenders in northern China. It is recorded that he peacefully entered Dai La after the death of a protector general. When Phung Hung died in 789 there was a struggle in the Phung family between partisans of his brother and of his son. Those in favor of his son prevailed. Phung Hung's son reportedly honored him with a posthumous title that contains the earliest known use of what became the Vietnamese word for king (*vua*), which is generally considered to be related to another Vietnamese word for father (*bo*), and which some have also conjectured to be related to a word in the Tai languages of Southeast Asia that means chieftain.

By this time, the rebellions in the north had been put down and the Tang Empire was regaining a measure of stability. In 791 a newly appointed protector general appeared and the Phung family submitted peacefully. The brief ascendancy of the Phung family was a local response to a temporary withering away of imperial government in An Nam, an effort by local powers to maintain a semblance of political order in a time of dynastic emergency in the north. Tang government in An Nam was fundamentally stable. This is evident considering that it held together for thirty years after the outbreak of rebellions in the north, and when it was reconstituted in the 790s the local people readily acknowledged it without resistance.

The Nan Zhao War

The reconstituted Tang Empire that emerged in the late eighth century was based on a social and economic foundation that once again facilitated the rise of great families. The "equal field" system was abandoned and restrictions on land ownership were abolished. Taxation was shifted from a per capita enumeration to calculations based on cultivated land. Wealthy local families came to occupy prominent administrative positions. Over the course of several decades, this led to increasing dissention within An Nam between leaders from Giao in the Red River plain who supported Tang authority and leaders from peripheral upland areas and in the southern provinces who were driven by other ambitions. What gave momentum to this developing confrontation was not only the rise of contending local powers but also the progressive weakening of Tang central government during the course of the ninth century. This was accompanied by the rise of new threats from beyond the frontiers. The peoples in the mountains were being stirred by the rise of the Nan Zhao kingdom in Yunnan, and on the southern coast the Chams were resurgent.

After the Phung Hung episode, Tang government in An Nam benefited from a series of astute protector generals who cultivated popular support for rebuilding government in the protectorate. The first of these, Zhao Chang, wrote a book about An Nam and earned a good reputation among the people in the Red River plain. He was in An Nam from 791 to 802 and was sent back a second time from 804 to 806. His protégé, Zhang Zhou, succeeded him from 806 to 810 and during that time organized an army to beat back the Chams who, during the time Zhao Chang had been absent from the protectorate, had seized the southern coastal provinces in alliance with local leaders there.

However, the situation turned grim in 820 when a military commander, whose ancestors had been administrators on the Cham frontier since the early eighth century, managed to seize Dai La and to kill the protector general along with a thousand members of his entourage. For the next sixteen years, the protectorate was rent with disorders; imperial officials struggled with local strongmen and frontier threats. The situation eased somewhat in the late 830s with the leadership of some capable protector generals, only to worsen again in the late 840s and early 850s as protectorate politics were superseded by the ascendance of Nan Zhao and its mobilization of peoples in the mountains for a policy of raiding and plundering the lowlands of An Nam.

Despite the chronic raiding, trade in horses and salt continued between people in the uplands and lowlands. In 854, a seemingly inept protector general's effort to gain control of this trade led to its breakdown and an escalation of hostilities. Do Ton Thanh, the governor of the Ma River plain, whose family had been prominent in the region since the fifth century, allied with Nan Zhao, whether in resistance to the protector general or in response to spreading disorder is unclear; he was seized and executed by the protector general, which stiffened resistance to Tang authority in the southern parts of the protectorate. Then, the protector general neglected, whether by bungling, by the manipulations of local officials, or by lack of resources is unclear, to reinforce the garrison at the head of the Red

River plain during the dry season when raiders habitually burst from the mountains. The commander of the garrison, caught in a hopeless situation, shifted his allegiance to Nan Zhao.

Such are the main events cited in historical records for the outbreak of a war that devastated An Nam during the next decade. Imperial historiography assigned blame for this war to the hapless protector general at that time, a shadowy figure named Li Zhuo, of whom virtually no information has survived. While a more capable man may have been able to master the situation, this war was about much more than one man's mistakes. It had been brewing for decades. Not simply a problem of frontier security, it had to do with local politics in the protectorate and how to respond to the decline in Tang power.

The people of An Nam experienced imperial rule differently, depending upon terrain and upon proximity to centers of government. Agriculturalists in the Red River plain were most directly affected by Sinic civilization. They understood themselves as members of the civilized world that relied upon the Tang shield for protection against the barbaric forces of disorder that threatened them. The inhabitants of provinces in the southern plains of the Ma and Ca Rivers were vulnerable to and less hostile toward neighboring peoples in the mountains and on the southern coast who lived beyond the imperial order; they could relate to these peoples as potential allies in times when northern dynastic power was too weak to maintain order in their lands.

The rising prestige of Nan Zhao, combined with the ebbing of Tang strength on the southern frontier, posed a problem for leaders in the southern provinces. They considered that it was time to take affairs into their own hands. Nan Zhao was breaking Tang's grip on the region, but they aspired to be the ones who would benefit by eventually extending their power over the population of the Red River plain. Nan Zhao, with its center far away through the mountains in Yunnan, could plunder the lowlands and destabilize the imperial regime, but it was not capable of governing the agriculturalists of An Nam, which was the ambition of leaders in the southern provinces. Thus, we see in this war a theme that would reappear more than once during the course of later Vietnamese history: competition for dominance between the provinces in the Red River plain and the provinces in the plains of the Ma and Ca Rivers.

After the collapse of the Red River border garrison in 854, Tang armies were mobilized into An Nam, but turmoil in neighboring jurisdictions to the north distracted Tang attention. By 858, a local military commander, of whom nothing is known, had pushed aside the protector general. But shortly after, a competent general from the north arrived with Tang reinforcements, and, for two years, until his departure, he built new fortifications to protect Dai La, prevented Nan Zhao forces from entering the lowlands, and restored stable administration among the agriculturalists in the Red River plain. However, in 861, within a year of his departure, the family of Do Ton Thanh, the southern governor whom Li Zhuo had executed in 854 for negotiating with Nan Zhao, mobilized an army in league with Nan Zhao and captured Dai La while Tang forces were tied down in the mountains further north. Tang reinforcements soon arrived and restored a semblance of order as imperial officials endeavored to calm the protectorate by placating the Do family with apologies for Do Ton Thanh's death.

This policy of conciliation failed, however, as the Tang weakness it was meant to conceal was unmasked by a full-scale Nan Zhao invasion in early 862. Tang armies fought until early 863, when Dai La fell and large numbers of Tang soldiers drowned trying to escape across the Red River. Tang forces in An Nam were utterly defeated. Nan Zhao plundered the Red River plain without hindrance as a multitude of refugees fled north and tens of thousands of perished soldiers were mourned in the towns and villages of central China where they had been recruited, provoking one Mencian scholar at the Tang court to write a song blaming the disaster on bad government and criticizing the empire's waste of human life, thereby knowingly ruining his own career in officialdom.

It took two years for Tang to organize a military response to the defeat of 863. The population of An Nam was scattered by marauding bands from the mountains, and a large refugee population accumulated just over the northern border where Tang armies assembled. Men from the southern provinces of the protectorate occupied the administrative center at Dai Lai and allied with Nan Zhao, preparing to resist the expected Tang reaction. The Tang court considered the situation sufficiently dire as to require the skills of Gao Pian, one of the most famous generals in the empire, who had made his reputation fighting Turks on the northern frontier. In 865, after months of training and preparing his troops, he advanced into the protectorate, chased Nan Zhao contingents into the mountains, and besieged recalcitrant forces at Dai La, which he took by the end of the year, reportedly executing some thirty thousand men captured there.

The Tang Empire's remarkable effort to recover An Nam at a time when imperial authority was moving rapidly toward a general collapse is an indication not only of the primacy of frontier security but also of how An Nam was considered an integral part of the dynastic inheritance. Young men from An Nam took the official examinations and served in officialdom all over the empire. One of them rose to be prime minister in the late eighth century and two of his essays have been preserved. Another wrote a poem that was collected by Tang anthologists. One governor general of An Nam, despite being forced to flee the protectorate by a mutiny in the 840s, felt so at home there that he later retired to a village east of Hanoi, thereby establishing a family that in later centuries produced many famous scholars at Vietnamese royal courts.

Gao Pian was himself quite taken with An Nam. He spent three years there before being called north to deal with more urgent problems. During that time, he supervised emergency shipments of food for the population. He rebuilt Dai La, restored and extended dikes and canals, and constructed roads, bridges, and public inns. He also removed rocks that impeded coastal shipping, researched geomantic features of the terrain, investigated existing popular spirit cults, patronized shrines and temples, and instigated the worship of new deities to buttress An Nam's connection to the imperial supernatural realm. Furthermore, he wrote poems about An Nam propounding Confucian and Daoist ideas. Later Vietnamese scholars credited him with authoring the first book on local geography and several maps and geographical texts were subsequently attributed to him. Popular tales of his deeds entered Vietnamese lore and Vietnamese literati sang his praises into the nineteenth century. He was the hero of the people in the Red River plain, for he had restored to them their membership of the civilized world. In the early eleventh century, a ruler from the Red River plain explicitly cited his legacy for inspirational authority after wresting power from a regime based in the southern provinces.

When Gao Pian departed An Nam in 868, he left in charge one of his grandsons, Kao Xun, of whom nothing is known. In the 870s, Zeng Gun replaced Kao Xun. Zeng Gun had been Gao Pian's most trusted assistant during the Nan Zhao War and remained in An Nam for fifteen years. He wrote a book about the Red River plain that no longer exists but was cited by Vietnamese scholars in later centuries. In 880, he left when the last Tang garrisons were withdrawn amidst spreading anarchy in the north. Thereafter, the people of the Red River plain were left to their own devices as a host of warlords began to carve up the empire. For the next half-century, a relatively stable and peaceful regime was led by the Khuc family. As for the southern provinces, Gao Pian had halted their separate political trajectory and subordinated them to the structure of power based in the Red River plain.

A lesser empire

The Khuc were a prominent family from the old heartland of Giao Province, east of Hanoi. When the Tang dynasty was officially replaced by the Later Liang dynasty in 907, the leader of this family was Khuc Thua My. He transferred his allegiance from Tang to Later Liang and claimed legitimacy as a loyal imperial official. The Later Liang exerted little influence beyond northern China, but, as late as 918, Khuc Thua My continued to send envoys with tribute to Later Liang to maintain the benefit of whatever moral support could be obtained from imperial appointments. In central and southern China, adventurers were striving to expand their authority with dreams of founding their own dynasties. In 917, one such aspirant proclaimed the Southern Han dynasty in Guangdong and Guangxi, on the northern border of Giao. When Later Liang fell in 923, the powers contending for northern China gave no more thought to affairs in the south, and Southern Han began to nurture designs on An Nam.

The Khuc did not follow the model of other regional powers in China by founding a dynasty. They continued to pose as officials of an empire that no longer existed, ostensibly waiting for a new imperial house to re-establish order in the north. Unlike other parts of the empire that since the late ninth century had been ravaged by the uprisings and turmoil of Tang's long decline, An Nam rested quietly with the legacy of fifteen years of stable government led by Gao Pian, by his grandson, and by Zeng Gun. The men who inherited this legacy shrank from the anarchic violence they observed in the north. Claiming to be more than imperial servants would simply attract unwanted attention and stoke the ambitions of their Southern Han neighbor. For several years, they had an alliance with the Min kingdom of Fujian, located on the northeastern border of Southern Han, which discouraged Southern Han from launching an attack on either of them. However, when Min fell apart into civil war in 930, Southern Han immediately took the opportunity to attack An Nam.

There is no record of any resistance being offered by Khuc Thua My. It appears that he and his advisors considered it best to submit. After all, their sense of identity was with the empire, and the Southern Han were claimants to the imperial throne. Khuc Thua My was taken into custody and removed to the north where he spent the rest of his life. The Southern Han army could not resist the temptation to march down the coast to sack the Cham capital at Tra Kieu. After that, Southern Han was content to appoint a governor of Giao Province with responsibility for the Red River plain.

The southern provinces, in the Ma and Ca River plains, were left in the hands of a subordinate of Khuc Thua My, a man native to that region named Duong Dinh Nghe. While the people in the Red River plain may have been relatively phlegmatic about Southern Han rule, Duong Dinh Nghe and the people who assembled around him had their own ambitions. In 931, Duong Dinh Nghe marched his soldiers north to Dai La, expelled the Southern Han officials with their garrison, and attacked the Southern Han army that was sent as reinforcement, killing its general in battle. He then proclaimed himself to be the governor, and Southern Han, stinging from defeat and unprepared for further fighting, recognized him as such.

Duong Dinh Nghe's mobilization of the southern provinces was the first indication after the Nan Zhao War that these territories were prepared to re-enter the competition for control of the Red River plain. There were two main political centers in the plain, Giao in the agricultural heartland with Da Lai at its center and Phong, formerly Me Linh, at the head of the plain where the Red River emerges from the mountains. For centuries, the headquarters for patrolling the upland hinterland had been located in Phong. Duong Dinh Nghe endeavored to rule from Da Lai, but, in 937, Kieu Cong Tien, a leader of Phong, killed him and called on Southern Han for assistance against the southern provinces. In response, Southern Han mobilized a fleet of warships, commanded by the crown prince, to bring an army to the aid of its would-be ally in Phong.

Meanwhile, Duong Dinh Nghe's son-in-law, Ngo Quyen, also from Phong but in command of the southern provinces, marched north and killed Kieu Cong Tien. He then stationed his men at the estuary of the Bach Dang River where the sea routes entered the plain and where he prepared to receive the Southern Han fleet with iron-tipped poles planted in the bed of the river. When the Southern Han fleet arrived in late 938, it was trapped on the poles as the tide fell and was annihilated; the heir to the Southern Han throne perished, and that was the end of Southern Han ambitions in An Nam.

What was left of the empire was now divided up among several regional kingdoms and it was no longer plausible to maintain the fiction of posing as an administrator-in-waiting for some new dynasty to restore the imperial peace. Ngo Quyen accordingly rode the momentum of his battlefield victory at the Bach Dang estuary and took the step of entering the realm of jostling post-Tang states by claiming royal status and proposing to found a dynasty of his own. He organized a court with titles, ritual etiquette, and dress code modeled on imitations of imperial practice then current at the various regional capitals in the north. Furthermore, he set his capital north of the Red River at the ancient site of Co Loa, the fortress supposedly built by King An Duong over a millennium before, located in the heartland of old pre-Tang Giao where the Chinese-speaking population was concentrated.

Ngo Quyen's adoption of the forms of imperial authority at a site north of the Red River shows that, although he had avenged his father-in-law by killing the leader of Phong, he had also come to terms with the people of Giao. Preparing for the Battle of Bach Dang had required the active assistance of these people, for the Bach Dang estuary was in eastern Giao. Despite his career in Duong Dinh Nghe's entourage and his command of the southern provinces, he was as noted earlier originally from Phong, the same district that had produced Phung Hung in the eighth century, whose posthumous cult he patronized. He achieved an alliance between the southern provinces and the Red River plain. The court at Co Loa was designed to elicit the loyalty of prominent people who believed in maintaining membership in the northern political realm, whatever form that might take.

When Ngo Quyen died in 944, Duong Tam Kha, his brother-in-law and a son of Duong Dinh Nghe, proclaimed himself king. The eldest of Ngo Quyen's sons, not yet an adult, fled and was protected by a powerful family in eastern Giao. Duong Tam Kha brought people from the southern provinces into the court and pushed aside the men of Giao. In 950, leaders in Giao rallied behind Ngo Quyen's second son, who had remained under Duong Tam Kha's tutelage, and deposed Duong Tam Kha, banishing him south of the Red River. At this point, men from the southern provinces were pushed out of the royal court and the powerful families of Giao stood behind Ngo Quyen's two eldest sons, who presided over a weak two-headed monarchy. When the eldest brother died in 954, the younger brother announced himself as a vassal of Southern Han, but this was of no help to him. Enmity between the Kieu and Ngo families produced chronic fighting between Phong and Giao, and in 963 the Ngo king was killed in an ambush while campaigning on the Giao–Phong border. His successor, very likely a younger brother, was unable to resist a new leader emerging from the southern provinces named Dinh Bo Linh, who forced him and the Ngo family into his entourage with multiple marriage alliances.

Dinh Bo Linh's father had been in command on the Cham border in the far south under Duong Dinh Nghe and Ngo Quyen. Dinh Bo Linh was based at Hoa Lu, a natural redoubt among the rocky outcroppings of the southeastern edge of the Red River plain in modern Ninh Binh province. Hoa Lu commanded the main land route from the plain to the southern provinces. It was also an outpost of the southern provinces looking out upon the Red River plain. From there, Dinh Bo Linh built up his forces, allied with neighboring strongmen along the lower Red River, and attacked those in the upper plain who resisted him, the most valiant of whom were three brothers, sons of a Chinese merchant and a local woman. He subdued all his opponents by 965 when he sent envoys to the Southern Han court. At this time the empire was being reconstituted by the Song dynasty, which conquered Southern Han in 971. In 973 and again in 975, Dinh Bo Linh sent envoys to establish and then to expand relations with the Song court in northern China, which, being occupied with urgent problems elsewhere, provisionally acknowledged the Dinh family's authority in An Nam.

In terms of geographical extent and military power, the Song dynasty did not compare with the Han and the Tang. The reason for this was that the warrior aristocracy that for centuries had founded dynasties and ruled the empire had, beginning in the last half of Tang, been superseded by a class of scholars and administrators who advanced their careers through a system of academic examinations and were distrustful of military men. Armies were organized with multiple chains of command to prevent any single person from gaining control of soldiers. Military campaigns were bureaucratized with pre-set itineraries and the need for cooperation among men chosen for their personal animosity toward each other. Consequently, the Song dynasty did not expand to the north, the northwest, and the northeast to the extent that previous major dynasties had, but instead was blocked by other powers along these borders. As for the southern frontier, the Song court waited for an opportunity to reclaim the legacy of Han and Tang. This opportunity came in 980 with news that Dinh Bo Linh had been assassinated and that his followers were fighting among themselves. This came at a time of relative quiet on the northern frontiers and an expedition was quickly organized to reclaim the far south.

A courtier who reportedly had visions of grandeur stabbed Dinh Bo Linh and his eldest son to death in their sleep. A brief struggle for power was quickly resolved in favor of Le Hoan, a native of the province south of Hoa Lu, now called Thanh Hoa, who was commander of an army that had been recruited by Dinh Bo Linh in the Red River plain. Le Hoan prepared to resist the Song expedition, which was en route both by land and by sea. The leaders of the Song forces were unimaginative and confounded by strict instructions from the imperial court. The land force arrived on the northern edge of the Red River plain and spent over two months in camp waiting for the arrival of the fleet, which was held up by fighting with Le Hoan's forces at the Bach Dang estuary. When the fleet arrived, the Song officers argued about what to do next, dismayed by the loss of time and the approach of the monsoon rain season when warfare was impracticable. One senior official, believing that Le Hoan was about to submit, embarked part of the army and advanced by river toward Hoa Lu, but he was ambushed and killed. News of this led the other senior officers to abandon the campaign and return north, where they were executed for incompetence.

This war exemplified how the situation had changed from that in previous centuries. In the past, new dynasties had no problem establishing their control over the plains of the Red, Ma, and Ca Rivers. The generals who led imperial armies adapted to circumstances and improvised their strategies, taking calculated risks, being confident of victory. In 980, the Song army came with a committee of arguing officers constrained by their instructions and fearful of defeat. This was a new kind of empire led by a different kind of people. It lacked the martial prowess and strategic vision of the old Han-Tang aristocracy. Rather, it was focused on civil administration, bureaucratic procedure, the management of wealth, and literary excellence.

In the wake of the Song expedition's withdrawal in 981, Le Hoan moved quickly to establish relations with the northern empire. Hoa Lu diplomacy had initiated a precedent during the previous ten years. After the Song conquest of southern China in 971, Dinh Lien, Dinh Bo Linh's son, had traveled to the Song court and obtained an imperial appointment as governor; during the 970s, envoys from Hoa Lu bearing rich tribute repeatedly went to the Song court and Song envoys arrived at Hoa Lu to confer additional honorary titles on both Dinh Lien and Dinh Bo Linh. After the uproar of 980–981, Le Hoan initially conducted diplomacy with Song in the name of the last Dinh king, an infant son of Dinh Bo Linh whom he had deposed and adopted when taking the throne. When it became clear that Song was uninterested in further warfare and, moreover, was open to conciliation, Le Hoan stepped from the shadows and informed Song that he had supplanted the Dinh. The Song court responded in 986 by recognizing him as the local ruler and conferring on him titles of vassalage. Throughout Le Hoan's reign, envoys from Hoa Lu regularly carried tribute to the Song court and Song envoys arrived to bestow further titles on Le Hoan. One Song envoy, Li Jiao, became famous for exchanging poetry with the Buddhist monks assigned to greet and entertain him. In modern times, the verse produced in these exchanges has been anthologized as the first poems in what is imagined to be the history of Vietnamese literature.

In the mid 990s, when Le Hoan was beginning to enforce his ascendancy in areas adjacent to the Song border, the emperor accused him of plundering Song settlements both by land and by sea. Le Hoan replied that the depredations were the work of rebels and bandits whom he was endeavoring to suppress. The Song court, determined on a pacifist policy, accepted his explanation and amicable relations were soon restored. Many men at the Song court began to understand that the imperial inheritance on the southern frontier, as on the northern frontier, was beyond their capacity to reclaim. Le Hoan understood that the Song would leave him alone so long as he observed the protocol of vassalage and displayed a respectful attitude.

The millennium of belonging to the empire ended because of fundamental changes in the outlook of the rulers of the empire and in how imperial government was organized. What for centuries had been Giao Province or the Protectorate of An Nam was now beyond the reach of imperial armies because, in comparison with earlier times, military commanders were kept on a short bureaucratic leash. But this was also more than just an administrative matter. Song rulers were less cosmopolitan than those of Han and Tang; their relative weakness in relation to neighboring powers produced a more embattled perception of the civilized world, narrower and less confident of being able to accommodate cultural diversity. While earlier dynasties had no problem accepting the people of Giao/An Nam as more or less legitimate members of the empire, Song rulers viewed them as beyond the edge of civilization. This was revealed in the imperial edict published in 980 announcing the reasons for the expedition against Hoa Lu. The rhetoric of disdain for and outrage at the uncivilized behavior of Le Hoan and the people he ruled was unprecedented in the long history of official imperial relations with this part of the world. Beyond giving lip service to the historical task of reclaiming a part of the imperial inheritance, this edict dilated upon the task of eradicating savagery, indicating a more constricted mental world than that of previous generations of imperial officials who had lived, worked, and permanently settled in Giao/An Nam.

The Song attitude effectively redefined this place as outside the realm of civilization. Le Hoan was able to go his separate way not only because Song was not strong enough to subdue him but also because Song no longer considered him and the people he ruled sufficiently civilized to be deemed proper subjects of the empire. Song's diminished martial prowess was closely related to this more demanding, less inclusive, view of the civilized world because men in government were now products of literary education and civil administration more than of military training and battlefield experience. One effect of this fundamental change in Chinese government was that the people in the Red River plain began a new trajectory of cultural and political autonomy.

Every aspect of Vietnamese culture is deeply imprinted by contact with China. To assume that these aspects have been either imposed by imperial oppressors or freely borrowed by indigenous people requires a clear demarcation between what is called Chinese and what is called Vietnamese. Such a demarcation did not exist during the time we have discussed in this chapter. In the tenth century, the people of what is now northern Vietnam were an amalgam of settlers from the north and indigenous peoples; for centuries they had lived together, intermarried, developed bilingual habits of speech, and formed a regional perspective on imperial civilization.

By the end of the tenth century, as described in the Introduction, the version of the Chinese language spoken in northern Vietnam, which we can call Annamese Middle Chinese, was cut off from regular contact with the north and from fresh infusions of Chinese speakers. It nevertheless remained the prestige language even as it became more isolated in the region surrounding Hanoi and began a process of merging with and shifting into the prestige version of Proto-Viet-Muong, a process that produced what we can recognize as the Vietnamese language.

2 THE LY DYNASTY

Hoa Lu

During the forty years that Dinh Bo Linh and Le Hoan ruled from Hoa Lu (965–1005), possibilities for rustic leaders from the southern provinces to govern the more populous Red River plain with its temples, schools, and heritage of imperial culture were fully explored and ultimately reached their limit. However, before this line of events had run its course, Le Hoan's reliance upon a new class of leaders from Giao opened the way for an exit from this impasse. Le Hoan's quarter-century reign reveals both his astuteness in solving immediate problems and his failure to establish a basis for long-term political stability.

Events of the tenth century were narrated in the previous chapter in the context of a progressive disengagement from the imperial world. When viewed from the perspective of local politics, these events become a story about relations between the population of the Red River plain and the population of the southern provinces. These provinces have been differently organized and named through the centuries. They comprise the modern provinces of Thanh Hoa, Nghe An, and Ha Tinh. Ha Tinh was separated from Nghe An only in recent times. For centuries, the basin of the Ma and Chu Rivers was Thanh Hoa and the basin of the Ca River was Nghe An. The uplands of Thanh Hoa communicate with the region of Sam Neua in the modern Laotian province of Houaphan. The uplands of Nghe An communicate with the modern Laotian province of Xieng Khouang, a region known in Western languages as the Plain of Jars and which the Vietnamese call the Tran Ninh plateau. These uplands were a borderland between Tai and Vietic peoples.

In the tenth century, the Red River plain was composed of three major politically defined areas. The heart of the plain was Giao, centered on a region bounded by the modern cities of Hanoi, Bac Ninh, Hai Duong, and Hung Yen. In the northwest was Phong, old Me Linh, where the Red River emerged from the mountains in the modern provinces of Son Tay and Vinh Phu. In the southwest was Truong, the region of Hoa Lu in modern Ninh Binh province, on the border of Thanh Hoa. Leaders in Phong drew upon the resources of the upland valleys inhabited by Tai-speaking peoples. In Truong, Hoa Lu drew upon the resources of the southern provinces. Giao contained the greatest residue from the imperial experience and leaders there vacillated between pursuing local experiments and looking north for alliances and political ideas.

The men who stood at the head of politics in the tenth century lived amidst shifting contexts, which, in the absence of an imperial regime, tested the unity of An Nam while at the same time opened the way for new kinds of leadership. Khuc Thua My was from eastern Giao, a man loyal to the empire who preferred to submit to a northern regional power than to resort to war. He perceived no vital benefit in fighting for local autonomy. However, Duong Dinh Nghe, from Thanh Hoa, was prepared to fight for local autonomy but did not aspire to more than that, resting content with being acknowledged by the neighboring northern power as the local governor. But this also meant subordination of the Red River plain to men from the southern provinces. Men of the Red River plain resisted this, and, after only six years, the leader of Phong killed Duong Dinh Nghe and made a bid to restore a closer political connection with the north. Ngo Quyen mobilized an alliance among warriors both from the southern provinces and from Giao to bring this scheme to naught at the Bach Dang estuary in 938. He then established a royal court in the mode of the so-called "ten kingdoms" that then ruled various regions in what had been the Tang Empire.

Ngo Quyen died at the age of 46, before he had time to stabilize his accomplishment. His entourage splintered under the pressure of regional tensions, with men from Giao supporting his young sons against his brother-in-law, Duong Tam Kha, the son and heir of Duong Dinh Nghe, who stood at the head of men from the southern provinces. Proliferating ambitions inhibited unity even within the Red River plain with warfare breaking out between the deltaic plains of Giao, led by Ngo Quyen's heirs, and the region of Phong where the Red River issues from the mountains. Then, within fifteen years of Duong Tam Kha being pushed aside by leaders in Giao, the southern provinces were resurgent under the leadership of Dinh Bo Linh.

One feature of politics at that time is the extent to which it was related to personal and family relations. Duong Dinh Nghe was a retainer of Khuc Thua My, and Ngo Quyen was a son-in-law of Duong Dinh Nghe. Dinh Bo Linh reportedly began his political career by fighting battles with his paternal uncle over the leadership of the southern provinces, where his father had governed in the time of Duong Dinh Nghe and Ngo Quyen. This brings to mind the struggle between Phung Hung's brother and son in the late eighth century, a contest between lateral succession among brothers and patrilineal, or father to son, succession; such rivalry between uncle and nephew, also apparent in the case of Duong Tam Kha and the sons of Ngo Quyen, was not characteristic behavior in Giao, where a large Chinese-speaking population, isolated from regular contact with the north, began to shift from bilingualism to developing a high-register version of the local vernacular. This population tended toward the practice of strict patrilineal succession; on the other hand, brother-to-brother succession was apparently more plausible among the inhabitants of the southern provinces at that time.

After he had forced the submission of the Ngo clan in the 960s, Dinh Bo Linh endeavored to bind the Ngo to his family through marriage. He married one of his daughters to the last Ngo king; he married a younger sister of that king to his eldest son; and he took the Ngo queen mother as one of his wives. His practice of marrying prominent women from other powerful families established a tradition of multiple queens that was followed by his successors for a century. However, marriage politics were not always effective. The last Ngo king repudiated his Dinh wife and fled south to the Chams. When he heard of Dinh Bo Linh's death, he persuaded the Cham ruler to launch a seaborne attack on Hoa Lu, though the fleet was destroyed by a typhoon.

Hoa Lu was rustic, but some quasi-Buddhist ideas related to exorcising demons and to karmic retribution were apparently current at Dinh Bo Linh's court. Dinh Bo Linh's eldest son and designated heir, Dinh Lien, erected one hundred stone columns inscribed with the Ratnaketu Dharani, a Buddhist text that is thought to expel demonic powers. In early 979, Dinh Bo Linh demoted Dinh Lien and replaced him as heir with an infant son. According to the annals, he did this out of extreme love for the infant's mother. Unwilling to accept this, Dinh Lien slew the small boy, then erected several stone columns inscribed with the Usnisa Vijaya Dharani Sutra, believed to provide deliverance from the consequences of one's evil deeds, ostensibly seeking to spare his dead brother's soul from the torments of hell. The columns bear an inscription explaining that it was necessary for Dinh Lien to "bring doom to the life" of his brother because his brother had "strayed from the path of loyalty and filial piety toward his father and elder brother." Here was the creative use of a Buddhist sutra to shift the karmic force of fratricide from the murderer to the victim.

Within a few months of this, Dinh Bo Linh and Dinh Lien were slain by a courtier as they slept off their drunkenness in a palace courtyard. The assassin, reportedly mesmerized by portents indicating his own elevation to the throne, was quickly seized, killed, and, in an unusual case of cannibalism, eaten. Not much is known about Dinh family politics, but behind these events probably lay a struggle among the maternal clans of Dinh Bo Linh's sons, and possibly even Le Hoan's design, for the mother of the only surviving son of Dinh Bo Linh was

Duong Van Nga, who was believed to have been intimate with Le Hoan even before Dinh Bo Linh's death.

The fighting that immediately broke out between Le Hoan and a group of rivals after the deaths of the Dinh father and son was reportedly provoked by an expectation that Le Hoan would take advantage of the king's youth and of his relationship with the queen mother to seize the throne for himself. The queen mother reportedly encouraged Le Hoan to attack his enemies. It was this fighting that stimulated Song expectations of a successful intervention.

The role of men from Giao in the accession of Le Hoan is apparent from an event recorded for early autumn 980. News had arrived of the Song expedition's approach. A prominent commander of soldiers from Giao, Pham Cu Lang, together with his subordinate officers crowded into the palace and confronted the queen mother. Pham Cu Lang argued that his men would not fight for a child unable to discern their battlefield merit and incompetent to bestow appropriate rewards for their fighting prowess. He demanded that Le Hoan be made king, for only then would the army march. Duong Van Nga responded by sending the royal regalia to Le Hoan.

The Dinh family murders in 979 and the emergence as queen mother and regent of a woman believed to be the lover of Le Hoan can easily be imagined as the result of plans by men from Giao to replace the volatile leadership of Dinh Bo Linh and Dinh Lien with the more trusted hand of Le Hoan. An unexpected consequence was the Song attack, but even this served to bind the fortunes of Giao and Le Hoan more firmly together. Nevertheless, the situation was not as simple as this might suggest.

One of the men who had joined the unsuccessful alliance against Le Hoan was an elder brother of Pham Cu Lang. The brothers were from a powerful family in eastern Giao; their grandfather and father had served the Ngo family, and they both served the Dinh at Hoa Lu. When resistance to Le Hoan broke out during the 979–980 dry season, one brother went with each faction, apparently to ensure that the family would be on the winning side no matter the outcome. Pham Cu Lang's brother was one of three leaders in the anti-Le Hoan coalition; while the other two leaders, both closely associated with the Dinh family, were killed, it is recorded of Pham Cu Lang's brother only that he was captured.

Duong Van Nga was remembered in later generations for her prominent role in passing the throne from her son to Le Hoan. Her son, who at the age of 6 had been king for eight months in 979–980, was adopted by Le Hoan and served him loyally; in 1001, he died at Le Hoan's side when caught in an ambush while fighting rebels in Thanh Hoa. Because of her role in effecting royal succession from the Dinh to the Le and because of her being the queen of the two major Hoa Lu kings, Duong Van Nga was regarded as a woman of extraordinary power, which apparently explains why a shrine was eventually built at Hoa Lu to worship her. In this shrine, her statue was placed between statues of Dinh Bo Linh and Le Hoan. This was a scandal to later Confucianists, who considered such a reputation to be immoral. According to later writings, in the fifteenth century, after the royal court began to adhere to a relatively strict Confucianist code, an official was sent to Hoa Lu to destroy this shrine and to punish Duong Van Nga for adultery. The official tied the statue of Duong Van Nga to a rope and pulled it behind his boat all the way back to the capital at Hanoi, ritually drowning her for her sin. A popular tale claims that this official died suddenly in great pain after reaching the capital, thereby paying the price exacted by Duong Van Nga's spirit for his disrespect toward her.

The rebels at whose hands Duong Van Nga's son perished were people against whom Le Hoan arduously and continuously fought in the later years of his reign. They were from the southern provinces and neighboring upland areas. This may seem to be odd considering that Le Hoan was himself a native of Thanh Hoa. As a boy he had shown sufficient intelligence to be adopted into a prominent family, which gave him an opportunity to earn the notice of Dinh Bo Linh's eldest son, chief assistant, and designated heir Dinh Lien, who brought him into the Dinh entourage. In the 970s, when he was in his 30s, he was assigned by Dinh Bo Linh to command soldiers recruited in Giao as well as to command the palace guard at Hoa Lu. This shows that Dinh Bo Linh felt safer under the protection of disciplined soldiers from Giao than with men from the southern provinces, who were difficult to control. It also shows that Dinh Bo Linh was careful to place a southerner in command of the Giao military units. After both Dinh Bo Linh and Dinh Lien were assassinated in 979, Le Hoan defeated his rivals with the Giao army, and it was Giao that supported his taking the throne and that supplied the wealth and manpower that enabled him to resist the invasion from Song China in 980–981.

In the Song War, and in later diplomatic relations with Song, Le Hoan relied heavily upon the advice of an erudite Chinese named Hong Xian. When Hong Xian died in 988, Le Hoan began to assign fiefs in Giao to his sons, suggesting that until then Hong Xian may have held administrative responsibility for Giao. Le Hoan built his primary base of support in Giao, and he championed the interests of Giao against the southern provinces. This is very understandable considering that Giao was the center of agricultural resources, of manpower, of educated talent, and of expertise in dealing with the northern empire.

After decades of turmoil, from the Southern Han expedition of 930 to Dinh Bo Linh's conquest in the 960s, political leadership in Giao came to rest in the Buddhist temples among the monks who administered the extensive lands that had been donated to or acquired by these temples. A new generation of young men were educated in the temple schools of Giao, both in the Confucian classics and in the Buddhist sutras. The monks were indispensable to the Hoa Lu kings for administering Giao and for dealing with the Song Empire, and these monks found ways to introduce the most promising of their student protégés into the Hoa Lu court. Within four years of Le Hoan's death, one of these young men, Ly Cong Uan, became the king and shifted the royal court from Hoa Lu to Dai La in the center of Giao.

About eighty-five kilometers almost directly north of Hoa Lu (one hundred kilometers by boat) lay Dai La, surrounded by rice fields and at the center of the riverine communication network uniting the Red River plain. By contrast, Hoa Lu is a natural fortress of limestone outcroppings at the southern extremity of the plain; it commands the main land route to the southern provinces. Hoa Lu lies at the entrance of what resembles an antechamber to the Red River plain, about twenty square kilometers bounded on three sides by uplands and open to the plain on the east; this is modern Ninh Binh province. Hoa Lu is about forty kilometers northwest of the seacoast. It is comprised of two connected natural antechambers located in a small but impressive massif. Enclosed on three sides by towering cliffs, brick walls were built across their open sides. In one of the enclosures the kings kept their personal wealth and family retainers; in the other, they stationed the soldiers of their principal followers and held court. Dinh Bo Linh was known for rough justice, boiling malefactors in large cauldrons and feeding them to caged tigers. However, such resort to cruelty for enforcing obedience was not attributed to Le Hoan. During the course of his reign, Hoa Lu became the base for Giao to dominate the southern provinces rather than the other way around as it initially was under Dinh Bo Linh.

The Cham king, ruling at Tra Kieu near the modern city of Da Nang, was emboldened by Dinh Bo Linh's death and by the Song invasion to pursue an aggressive policy toward Hoa Lu. Enemies of Dinh Bo Linh had assembled at the Cham court and news of his death entangled the Cham king in their hopes for revenge. As noted previously, a Cham fleet was lost in a storm when about to attack Hoa Lu in late 979. In 982, after the Cham king detained his envoys, Le Hoan led an expedition that plundered and destroyed the Cham capital, killing the king and capturing hundreds of soldiers along with scores of palace women and even a Buddhist monk from India. A Vietnamese adventurer ruled from the devastated Cham capital until his death in 989, meanwhile fending off soldiers sent by Le Hoan to capture him. Shortly after his death, a man sent to collect taxes in the southern provinces instead led them in revolt and petitioned the Cham king, then ruling at Vijaya near the modern city of Qui Nhon, to accept his submission and to join him against Hoa Lu. The Cham king refused to embroil himself in this scheme and Le Hoan led his soldiers south, killing the renegade tax collector as well as "immeasurable" numbers of this man's followers in the southern provinces. In the 990s, the Cham king relocated back north at Tra Kieu, and there was chronic fighting between his soldiers and those of Le Hoan.

Much of Le Hoan's reign was spent in recruiting armies in Giao and sending them into the southern provinces to build roads, dig canals, and kill rebels. The Cham frontier beyond the southern provinces, in the old Han jurisdiction of Nhat Nam, became a lair for renegades and adventurers from both north and south; it was patrolled by both Le Hoan and the Cham king but controlled by neither. Nevertheless, the balance of power was tilting against the Chams. After the death of the Cham king in 999, his successors ruled from Vijaya further south and never again attempted to rule from Tra Kieu.

Le Hoan's policy of using soldiers from Giao to discipline the southern provinces and to establish in them an infrastructure for transport and communication was the initial step in a long process of bringing people from the Red River plain into this region and of pushing rebels into the uplands. Many of those who resisted this process went further south beyond Ngang Pass into the Cham frontier where they found larger scope for their ambitions and where eventually they and their descendants would be caught up in the patrols and expeditions of Le Hoan's successors during the eleventh century.

Le Hoan acknowledged eleven sons and one adopted son with the rank of prince. The three eldest, all of similar age, were given titles in 989 when they were 6 or 7 years old. While these three remained at the Hoa Lu court, the younger sons were entitled and assigned fiefs during the years 991–995. Being children at the time, the small princes were served by trusted adults. Eight of the nine princely fiefs were in Giao and one was in Thanh Hoa. The fiefs of the fourth, fifth, and sixth sons were the most strategic locations for defending the Giao heartland: Phong, modern Viet Tri, on the northwest, where the Red River and its confluents flow out of the mountains; Phu Lan, modern Pha Lai, on the northeast, where a large fortress guarded the land route to China and access to four rivers; and Dang, modern Hung Yen, on the south, where watch was kept over points of coastal access to the Red River. Ambitious men gathered in the entourages of these three princes. None of the other fiefs offered comparable prospects as a potential base for promotion in what, as the years went by, was expected to be a fraternal competition for the throne. Le Dinh, the fifth son, based at Dang, nearest to Hoa Lu, was best situated to be in the middle of events.

The eldest son and designated crown prince died in 1000. Le Dinh, then 15 years old but already a strong personality, pressed his father to make him the crown prince. Le Hoan was disposed to agree to this but was dissuaded by advisors who argued that Le Dinh's full brother, the third son, Le Viet, outranked him in age. In 1004, Le Hoan accordingly designated Le Viet to be his heir while at the same time he promoted Le Dinh, Le Viet, and the second son, Le Tich, all three, to the same rank equivalent to crown prince. Le Hoan's death in the following year, at the age of 64, was immediately followed by eight months of fighting in which Le Tich, Le Viet, Le Dinh, and the ninth son, Le Kinh, were all involved in ways that surviving information does not reveal, but it is clear that the primary conflict was between partisans of Le Tich and Le Viet. Le Tich was eventually defeated. He fled south seeking protection with the Cham king but was killed near the southern border.

Shortly thereafter, Le Viet was proclaimed king at Hoa Lu. Three days after that, Le Dinh killed Le Viet. After proclaiming himself king, conferring high rank upon his mother, and naming four women as his queens, Le Dinh proceeded to besiege Phu Lan, where Le Kinh had taken refuge with the sixth brother, Le Can. At the point of starvation, Le Can gave up Le Kinh to be beheaded by Le Dinh in exchange for being allowed to submit. Le Dinh then moved his army to confront the fourth brother in Phong, who quickly surrendered. He then completed his wars of accession by marching into the southern provinces to suppress the people with whom his father had been fighting for years and who had taken the opportunity to once again rebel. Le Dinh was 19 years old when he became king. He died four years later, reportedly of hemorrhoids brought on by his debaucheries. He was the last king to rule from Hoa Lu.

Le Dinh's short reign was portrayed by later historians according to the Confucian idea of "the last bad king" of a dynasty whose depravity justifies the rise of a new dynasty. He is said to have delighted in cruelty. Much of his energy was spent campaigning in the southern provinces and attacking the uplands, in the course of which he assembled large numbers of prisoners, whom he roasted alive, drowned in cages, felled from trees, or fed to poisonous snakes. He was known for a nasty sense of humor. He entertained himself by having a Chinese actor spend several days dissecting a man to death with "a small dull knife" while making jokes in response to the man's screams. He thought it was funny when he used a seated monk's head to support a stick of sugar cane he was whittling and seriously wounded the man when his hand slipped. He cooked and fed cats and lizards to his court officials and laughed when they vomited. He surrounded himself with actors and jesters who kept up a constant chatter, making light of all that was said and twisted the words of officials to make them ludicrous. He slid into a state of drunkenness and unrestrained self-indulgence. His final days were spent in a prone position because of his hemorrhoids, which is why later historians gave him the posthumous title Ngoa Trieu Hoang De, "Emperor who Held Court Lying Down." The speed with which he dissipated his youthful vigor may indicate that the stereotype of a dynasty's last bad king may in this case not be entirely amiss. Those eager for him to pass from the scene possibly even encouraged his excessive behavior. These were the monks from temples in the region just north of the Red River from Dai La, in modern Bac Ninh province.

Ly Cong Uan

The Le succession wars were the context of Ly Cong Uan's rise to the throne. Educated by monks in the heartland of Giao, Ly Cong Uan had a reputation for both erudition and martial prowess. Born in 974, he apparently began his career at the Hoa Lu court in the 990s when entourages formed behind Le Hoan's sons, for his eldest son was born at Hoa Lu in 1000. When Le Dinh struck down Le Viet in 1005, Ly Cong Uan was 31 years old and in Le Viet's entourage. Everyone present fled the scene except for Ly Cong Uan, who, unafraid, was said to have cradled Le Viet's corpse in his arms and wept. Le Dinh reportedly praised his loyalty and made him commander of the palace guard.

Ly Cong Uan's seemingly smooth transition from the entourage of Le Viet to that of Le Dinh may be a tribute to his personal qualities, but it is likely also to be an indication of the influence exercised by his patrons at court, the monks of Giao. The advisors who persuaded Le Hoan to give Le Viet precedence over Le Dinh were unconcerned with the seniority of Le Hoan's second son, Le Tich. They were definitely partisans of Le Viet, among whom Ly Cong Uan stood. Ly Cong Uan was the star protégé of the monks. His reputation for "virtue, mercy, and magnanimity" resonates with the reputation for "upright humaneness" of Le Viet, the prince he served, and echoes the lessons of temple teachings. During Le Hoan's reign, the influence of the monks grew as the Hoa Lu monarchy increasingly relied upon the wealth and manpower that they could provide. By the time of Le Hoan's death, the position of Ly Cong Uan, and of the monks who stood behind him, was secure. They were indispensable even to Le Dinh, known for his "ruthless cruelty," the most determined and unsavory of Le Hoan's brawling, fratricidal teenage sons.

Although families of the mothers of potential kings were often important factors in royal politics in early times, this was probably not the case with the mother of Le Viet and Le Dinh, who was from the class of palace servants and not from a politically prominent family. The phrase in historical texts that identifies her has been variously recorded and interpreted to mean "beautiful woman," "secondary wife," or, according to some Vietnamese scholars, even "uncivilized slave woman," which has led to a conjecture that she was one of the Cham palace women seized by Le Hoan in 982. It may have been precisely because of her low status that the monks supported her sons, to avoid complications arising from the ambitions of already powerful families.

Ly Cong Uan's family background is no less mysterious than that of the mother of Le Viet and Le Dinh. According to the court chronicle, he was conceived when his mother had intercourse with a "divine being" at a temple in the heartland of Giao and at the age of 3 was given for adoption to a man named Ly Khanh Van, of whom no information has survived. A fourteenth-century historian wrote that some thought he was from Fujian Province in China but that this was incorrect. He was educated by Van Hanh, the most eminent Buddhist patriarch of the time, in the village of Dich Bang, a short distance across the Red River from Hanoi to the northeast. According to some accounts, Van Hanh was not only the teacher and patron of Ly Cong Uan but also his father. In the mid 990s, as Le Hoan's sons were being entitled and their entourages were being assembled, Ly Cong Uan began to serve at the Hoa Lu court, eventually rising to a high position of trust at the side of the designated heir to the throne. It is not clear whether the Ly family was a prominent clan in its own right or a clan of convenience for the monks into which were adopted the most promising students from the temples. Van Hanh, just prior to Ly Cong Uan taking the throne, reportedly asserted that, considering all the families in the realm, the Ly family was "exceedingly large," and the expression recorded could even be read as meaning "the largest."

Incapacitated by declining health, Le Dinh watched helplessly as the monks of Giao launched a propaganda campaign that nurtured belief in the inevitability of Ly Cong Uan becoming king. Poems, riddles, portents, and prophecies pointed to the demise of the Le family and to Ly Cong Uan taking the throne. Van Hanh's intemperate talk in this vein at Hoa Lu made Ly Cong Uan sufficiently nervous that he ordered a kinsman to escort Van Hanh back to Dich Bang and keep him quiet there. Le Dinh reportedly sought to have Ly Cong Uan killed, but nothing was done. Ly Cong Uan commanded the palace guard and enjoyed the support of the monks, who controlled what at that time passed for public opinion.

Two days after Le Dinh died in late 1009, Ly Cong Uan became king, reportedly by general acclamation. Within a year, Hoa Lu was abandoned. The royal court relocated to the site of Dai La. Dai La was known as the city that the Tang general Gao Pian had built in the 860s after the ravages of the Nan Zhao War. In 1010, Ly Cong Uan published an edict explaining why he was moving his capital to this place. Citing kings who moved their capitals during the Shang and Zhou dynasties in classical antiquity, the edict compared Hoa Lu unfavorably to "King Gao's old capital at Dai La," which was centrally located amidst the abundance of a broad plain and which displayed the marks of geomantic potency. Dai La was only ten kilometers from Dich Bang, where Ly Cong Uan had been raised and educated by Van Hanh. When Ly Cong Uan's boat docked at the new capital, a dragon, symbol of sovereign authority, reportedly soared above his head; he accordingly renamed the place Thang Long, "ascending dragon."

The successive reigns of Ly Cong Uan (1009–1028), of his son Ly Phat Ma (1028–1054), and of his grandson Ly Nhat Ton (1054–1072) appear in historical records as an era of soaring power for the kingdom over which the house of Ly presided. All three kings were learned and capable. They all came to the throne as adults and ruled during their years of vigor. They were all men of action who traveled incessantly to personally survey the affairs of their realm. They were all interested in the problems of government. They presided over six decades of internal peace and prosperity and of an expansion of royal power outward from Thang Long that met no effective barrier.

Relations with Song were given high priority. One of Ly Cong Uan's first acts was to send envoys to the Song court to report that the Dinh family had lost the capacity to rule and to ask for recognition. During the disorders following Le Hoan's death, Song border officials had argued in favor of military intervention, but the emperor refused to act and admonished officials to avoid becoming embroiled in the violent affairs of distant uncivilized people. In 1010, Song recognized Ly Cong Uan without delay, conferring upon him the usual titles of vassalage. Thereafter, Song maintained a pacifist policy, doing the minimum necessary to preserve border security, even willing to suffer minor violations. The aim of Song policy was to preclude any provocation that might arouse a major crisis requiring mobilization of armies into the south that were more urgently needed on the northern frontier. This policy, begun in the 980s in the wake of the failed expedition of 980–981, has been termed "appeasement control" by some historians. It prevailed into the 1050s when, as we will see, dramatic events emboldened Song border officials to shift toward a more aggressive posture in response to the rising power of Thang Long in the border regions.

Ly Cong Uan's activities as king went through three phases. His early years were occupied with gaining a firm grip on the material resources of his kingdom, building his capital, and leading soldiers into vital borderlands. Beginning in 1016, he focused on establishing his authority in the spiritual realm, placing local cults under the eye of court patronage. His final years were a time of personal withdrawal in preparation for death and of releasing worldly affairs into the hands of the next generation.

One of Ly Cong Uan's first acts was to summon fugitives and vagabonds to return to their native places and to command all villages and hamlets to repair shrines and temples that had fallen into ruin. These measures reveal Ly Cong Uan's priorities: population control and the encouragement of religion. Very little can now be known about Ly Cong Uan's method of administering his kingdom, but there is no evidence of any kind of bureaucratic organization.

His authority was based on personal charisma and the loyalty of his aristocratic and monastic entourages.

The Ly family controlled the agricultural heartland of the Red River plain where both the Ly home estates and Thang Long were located. This was where the power of the Buddhist temples was strongest, and there was a close relation between the monarchy and the temples. Ly Cong Uan supervised the ordination of monks and appointed officials to oversee both the monks and the lands belonging to temples. Because of this, the Ly family effectively controlled temple estates as well as lands held directly by family members. Ly Cong Uan began his reign with vast expenditures, bestowing robes on monks, distributing cash and silk to elderly people in his home district, building over a dozen palaces in the royal compound at Thang Long, and erecting at least fifteen new temples in Thang Long and adjacent areas. Ly Cong Uan's wealth was enough to cover these expenditures, for, at the same time, he announced an amnesty for all tax delinquents, declared a tax holiday for three years, and abolished all taxes for orphans, widows, and the elderly.

Three years later, in 1013, Ly Cong Uan published a scheme for taxation on ponds (fish and pearls), fields (rice), and mulberry trees (silk); on goods traded in upland markets, such as salt, lumber, aromatic wood for making incense, fruits, and flowers; and on precious luxury items such as rhinoceros horns and elephant tusks. He also specified that members of the Ly family could collect taxes according to their rank. In 1009, he had assigned ranks to his father, his mother, six queens, an uncle, and a host of brothers, nephews, sons, and daughters, an indication that his family background may not have been as muddled as various accounts have suggested.

The outer regions of the Red River plain, beyond the Ly heartland, were in the hands of families allied with the Ly by marriage. Ly Cong Uan abandoned a scheme of dividing the plain into "ten circuits" that had been devised by Dinh Bo Linh and replaced it with "twenty-four routes"; these were not administrative jurisdictions but rather itineraries designating various localities. He organized the southern provinces into "military outposts," indicating a policy of garrisons and patrols.

In 1011, Ly Cong Uan raised a large army and attacked "rebels" in the southern provinces, in what is now Thanh Hoa and Nghe An. He campaigned there for two years, burning villages and capturing local leaders. While returning by sea in late 1012, a great storm threatened to sink his boat, which he understood as a divine judgment upon him for the violence he had brought upon so many people. A speech was recorded that he reportedly made amidst the storm, addressed to the heavenly power, in which he acknowledged that the innocent might have been harmed in error but that he nevertheless could not refrain from attacking these people because of their wickedness, cruelty, and savage resistance to "civilizing instructions"; he begged forgiveness for his soldiers and expressed his personal acceptance of any required punishment. In response to his appeal, according to the story, the storm abated and the sea became calm.

This speech in the storm shows the religious sensibility of Ly Cong Uan, which later Confucian historians criticized as "superstitious." Ly Cong Uan represented his people before the divine powers, and his was a civilizing task. He understood the moral dilemma as well as the necessity of using violence on behalf of a worthy cause. His sensitivity to the supernatural realm became increasingly evident as the years passed.

For three years, 1013–1015, Ly Cong Uan sent soldiers into the northern mountains, primarily the upland valleys of modern Ha Tuyen Province, to chastise people there who were falling under the influence of the Nan Zhao kingdom in Yunnan. Soldiers commanded by a brother reportedly killed or captured thousands of people and obtained many horses. Song border officials felt the reverberations of these events, which they interpreted as threatening to their security, but the Song emperor commanded them to remain uninvolved.

In 1016, at the age of 42, Ly Cong Uan appears to have achieved a sense of success and contentment sufficient to enable a new focus for his attention. In that year, there was an exceptionally good harvest, and Ly Cong Uan accordingly declared a three-year holiday from having to pay land rents. He also took the opportunity to obtain three more queens, ordain over a thousand monks, build two Buddhist temples, dedicate four new images of the "heavenly emperor," and embark on a series of peregrinations to enjoy the famous sights of the Red River plain.

During the course of his travels he initiated a kind of royal experience that would be repeated by his son and grandson and that would accumulate a pantheon of spirit guardians for the Ly realm. The pattern was for the king to be visited in a dream by the most prominent spirit in the place of his sojourn, having been aroused by the presence of the king's virtue to announce itself as a protector of the kingdom; in response to this, the king then worshiped the spirit and built a temple for it in the capital. In this way, during the first half of the eleventh century, a pantheon of spirit protectors was assembled from all parts of the kingdom. All of the first three Ly kings were students of the Confucian classics and devout Buddhists. They were also patrons of Daoist priests and honored the supernatural realm of earth spirits, mountain spirits, water spirits, and spirits of departed human beings, over which the "heavenly emperor" was believed to rule. This eclectic attitude became characteristic of Vietnamese religious practice, which today remains attached to popular spirit cults that are often incorporated into Buddhist and Daoist pantheons.

In 1024, a temple was built for Ly Cong Uan to use for reading and reciting the Buddhist scriptures, a copy of which he had requested and received from the Song court a few years earlier. Thereafter he began to withdraw from public affairs. In 1025, Van Hanh died. He had been Ly Cong Uan's teacher, mentor, and, to some extent, father figure. He had previously been an advisor to Le Hoan and was a central figure in effecting the transition from the Le family at Hoa Lu to the Ly family at Thang Long. It seems that Ly Cong Uan's royal personality was in some degree animated as an extension of Van Hanh's expectations of him, for from this time little of note is recorded about Ly Cong Uan until his death in the spring of 1028.

Ly Cong Uan's achievement in shifting the throne from Hoa Lu to Thang Long without bloodshed owed much to the power of the Buddhist temples in Giao that mobilized manpower and resources on his behalf. But his personal qualities, so far as they can be understood as a combination of martial valor, classical erudition, and religious devotion, were also important in setting a standard of leadership for his son and grandson.

Ly Phat Ma

Ly Phat Ma, Ly Cong Uan's eldest son, was the most vigorous and charismatic of all the Ly kings. He was born in 1000 at Hoa Lu when his father was rising to prominence at the Le court. In 1012, he was assigned to reside in the "eastern palace" built outside the walls of Thang Long, because his father wanted him "to understand all about the people." He thus escaped, to some extent, the stifling fate of a palace-bound prince. Like his father, he received a broad education in the Confucian classics, in the Buddhist sutras, and in military affairs. In 1020, at the age of 20, he and an experienced general were sent against a Cham army that was threatening the southern border. The two armies met in what is now northern Quang Binh Province and the Chams were decisively defeated. In subsequent years, he led soldiers to repress rebels in the modern provinces of Nghe An, Vinh Phu, and Lang Son, giving him familiarity with the kingdom's borderlands.

An uncle and two younger brothers of Ly Phat Ma also led armies to patrol the frontiers and to attack rebels during these years. On the day of Ly Cong Uan's death, these three men, for reasons that have not been recorded, led their soldiers into Thang Long and besieged the royal compound to dispute Ly Phat Ma's accession. The palace guard opened the gates and burst out, killing one of Ly Phat Ma's brothers and most of the rebel soldiers. The uncle and surviving brother escaped, but the next day, when Ly Phat Ma formally took the throne, they returned to beg forgiveness, and the new king pardoned them. The commander of the palace guard, who had killed the rebellious prince, was later honored with a posthumous cult and made a protector spirit of the kingdom.

Another of Ly Phat Ma's brothers had for fifteen years been assigned to oversee Hoa Lu, which during that time had become a bandit lair. When news of the battle at the palace gates reached Hoa Lu, this prince raised his standard in revolt. Ly Phat Ma mobilized his soldiers and, before marching against Hoa Lu, paused to have his officers drink a blood oath of personal loyalty to him at the shrine of the spirit of a mountain in Thanh Hoa that he had encountered in 1020 during his expedition into the southern frontier. He believed that this spirit had helped him to obtain victory against the Chams at that time and also that this spirit had appeared to him in a dream to warn him of the treachery of his brothers. As Ly Phat Ma's soldiers approached Hoa Lu, the rebellious prince submitted and was forgiven.

In dialogues between Ly Phat Ma and court officials that have been recorded from the days following his father's death, Ly Phat Ma expressed a strong sense of family feeling for his disloyal brothers. Hoping that his kinsmen would submit of their own accord, he sought to delay a resort to violence, saying: "I want to hide my brothers' crimes and allow them to yield willingly, for, of all things, my own flesh and blood is most precious." There is no way to know whether these words reveal Ly Phat Ma's attitude toward family solidarity or are the handiwork of later historians seeking to give a didactic gloss to a sad episode of fraternal strife. In either case, Ly Phat Ma was a strong personality whose quarter-century reign has been recorded with a relative abundance of words attributed to him.

Two months after his father's death, after settling affairs with his brothers, Ly Phat Ma designated his 5-year-old eldest son, Ly Nhat Ton, as crown prince and sent him to live in the "eastern palace" outside the city gates, away from the ritualized life of the royal compound. At the same time he appointed seven women as queens, appointed men to serve in his immediate entourage, and established a new hierarchy for the monkhood. His next act was to organize a grand festival to feast, entertain, and distribute gifts to his followers. The occasion was ostensibly his birthday celebration and it followed a precedent dating back to 985 when Le Hoan began the practice of royal birthday festivals, which was continued by both Le Dinh and Ly Cong Uan. A distinctive feature of these festivals was the construction of a bamboo mountain that over the years came to be decorated with images of birds and animals, the calls of which royal guests competed to imitate. Ly Phat Ma began a new style of "five-peaked bamboo mountain" with elaborate decorations beyond precedent. It was only after having thus attended to the joy and expectations of his followers that Ly Phat

Ma finally buried his father, seven months after Ly Cong Uan's death, a delay that later Confucian historians severely criticized.

Ly Phat Ma appears from the records as one of the most intelligent, vigorous, and interesting kings in Vietnamese history: intelligent because the comparatively large amount of information preserved from his reign shows a mind constantly in motion, growing in its understanding of how to exercise royal authority and in a dynamic and creative relation with a shifting circle of advisors and the rush of events; vigorous because he was typically at the forefront of events and the prime mover of them; interesting because, despite the intervening centuries, a living personality shines through the words attributed to him. Vietnamese kings followed the practice of Chinese emperors of designating the years of their rule by reign titles, phrases that expressed the aspirations of the time. Ly Cong Uan had used but one reign title at Thang Long: Thuan Thien, meaning "in Agreement with Heaven," expressing the Ly view that the Hoa Lu kings had not been in harmony with the natural order of things. In comparison, Ly Phat Ma successively proclaimed six different reign titles, and each one represented an evolving phase of his focus and activity.

His first reign title was Thien Thanh, "Heavenly Completion," as if to signal that he aspired no further than to complete what his father had begun. During the six years of this period (1028–1034), he was compliant with the advice of men who had been close to his father, filling in the blanks of what his father had initiated and maintaining the peace that had been achieved under his father's leadership. Nevertheless, there were already indications of his energy. He went to hunt elephants and personally captured one, a sport he would enjoy throughout his reign. He regularly attended plowing and harvesting ceremonies at royal estates. He built new palaces at Thang Long and 150 temples and shrines throughout the kingdom. He compiled a register of Daoist priests. He attacked rebels in the southern provinces and in the northern mountains. And he married a daughter to a local chieftain on the Song border in the modern province of Lang Son, showing a keen and fateful interest in expanding his power into the northern borderlands.

In 1034, Ly Phat Ma proclaimed a new reign title: Thong Thuy, meaning "Utterly Auspicious." This was the beginning of an era (1034–1039) in which he often argued with or surprised his advisors. The event considered "auspicious" that occasioned the change of reign title was the self-immolation by fire of two monks who thereby produced potent relics in the form of their ashes and bones, which Ly Phat Ma installed for veneration in a temple. The two monks had been lifelong friends who through years of study and meditation had attained a high level of erudition and spiritual enlightenment. Self-immolation was not unknown among Buddhist monks in China at that time, but this is the first recorded example of it in Vietnam. Shortly after this event, a box of Buddhist relics was unearthed in the home district of the royal family, giving emphasis to the idea of welcoming change. Ly Phat Ma marked the new reign title by demanding that his officials use a more grandiloquent form of address with him.

From this time, Ly Phat Ma stepped beyond the perspective of his father's generation and took more direct personal control of the royal agenda. Aside from irritating his court by promoting a favorite concubine to the status of queen, thereby provoking conspiracies that he seems to have openly elicited and then ruthlessly put down, he began to build ocean-going ships and to build storehouses in frontier areas, suggesting an initiative to develop trade with foreign lands. During the annual ceremonies to open fields for agricultural work, he shocked his entourage by insisting on actually taking the plow. When his officials objected, saying "This is farmer's work," he replied, "If I do not plow, what rice can I use for my sacrifices to the spirits and what kind of leadership will there be in the realm?" Previously, at these ceremonies he had simply received a symbolic stalk of rice from a farmer. Now, not content with ritual, he wanted to lead by example and believed that true sacrifice required his direct participation in producing the rice to be offered up.

When the royal prison became overcrowded with people whose cases were not being decided and he suspected that the judges were corrupt, his solution was to lay the matter before the "heavenly emperor," who replied by informing him in a dream that the spirit of Pham Cu Lang, the general who had served Le Hoan during the Song War of 980–981, was being appointed to take care of the matter. He accordingly built a shrine for Pham Cu Lang and made him the patron deity of the court and prison, the practical effect of which presumes widespread respect for Pham Cu Lang's supernatural powers.

In 1039, Ly Phat Ma marched an army north to the upland valley of Cao Bang, on the Song border, to attack Nung Ton Phuc, leader of the Tai-speaking population there. For several years previously, Nung Ton Phuc had been a Ly vassal, sending annual tribute to Thang Long, but in 1038 he had renounced his allegiance to the Ly and proclaimed himself a sovereign. Ly Phat Ma captured him and four other prominent male members of the Nung family and brought them to Thang Long where he publicly put them to death. In the wake of this campaign, veins of gold and silver were discovered in the mountains of Cao Bang. At about the same time, by coincidence, five Cham princes arrived at Thang Long seeking refuge from political troubles in their kingdom and offering their submission.

Court officials argued that the pacification of the Nung, the discovery of gold and silver, and the arrival of submissive foreign princes were indications of good government that required literary acknowledgment with a new reign title meaning "Having the Way that Tallies with Heaven" (Can Phu Huu Dao) and the addition of a phrase to the royal honorific meaning "Gold Flows, Silver Appears, the Nung are Controlled, the [Cham] Frontier Yields" (Kim Dung Ngan Sinh Nung Binh Phien Phuc). They cited the golden age of Yao and Shun, the sage-kings of classical antiquity, whose virtue was so great that simply donning their robes and folding their arms was enough to bring peace and order to the human and natural worlds. The royal advisors sought to establish the idea of ruling in accordance with principles, and to do that they needed to capture the attention of a king who had his own intellectual momentum. At that time in China, Fan Zhongyan (989–1052) was advocating a stronger role for scholars in government. Vietnamese envoys regularly visited the Song court and knowledge of trends there was promptly communicated to Thang Long.

Ly Phat Ma did not like what his advisors were saying. He is the first king whose words have been recorded in relative abundance revealing a strong personality. According to the court annals, eventually compiled as *Dai Viet Su Ky Toan Thu* (Complete Book of the History of Great Viet), he replied to his entourage that as for the golden age of Yao and Shun, when everything was perfect "simply from the ruler putting on robes and folding his arms," he did not understand it, because, being "a mere man assigned to stand above the officials and the people," he had to work hard at being king, "rising early and retiring late, as if passing through a deep abyss, not knowing the way to understand Heaven and Earth or the virtue that rises to the level of Yao and Shun." Referring to the events of pacifying the Nung, receiving the submission of Cham princes, and finding gold and silver, he rhetorically asked: "How did ideas cause these things? Or what was there to give prior notification of them? I am very worried about this. What is a sufficiently noble and beautiful reign title? You must stop this discussion." Ly Phat Ma believed that good results came from hard work, not from consulting books. He apparently considered that his advisors' proposal was intended to diminish his own role, which he was endeavoring to expand. He thought that he was in contention with them for control of the royal agenda. Nevertheless, when they "obstinately" insisted, he finally gave in.

What happened during the three years of the ensuing reign period (1039–1042) is an indication that the argument was about how to take up the slack between Ly Phat Ma's vigorous personality and the disorganized manner in which he was ruling. Rather than smothering Ly Phat Ma's initiative with erudition, those who won the argument sought to strengthen his leadership by codifying laws and procedures. The result was a book of law "suitable for the current age." The book no longer exists, but edicts recorded from these years indicate detailed attention to military discipline, corrupt tax collectors, the storage of rice against times of shortage, and cattle thieves. Issues related to a new class of wealthy households, apparently from the rising Ly aristocracy and allied families, were also addressed. These households were prohibited from buying able-bodied male peasants as slaves, who were thereby removed from the tax and conscription registers. On the other hand, householders were allowed to kill nocturnal intruders who sought to molest their women. The court was protecting both its source of revenue and the morale of its supporters.

The administration of royal justice, which Ly Phat Ma had attempted to reform by establishing the cult of Pham Cu Lang a few years before, was now reorganized and placed under the direction of a living person, the 17-year-old crown prince, Ly Nhat Ton, who subsequently became an expert in the law. Queens and concubines, often used to advance the interests of their families, were a perennial source of intrigue, so it is not surprising that at this time the hierarchy of palace women was reorganized. The monks and people attached to temples were another focus of royal attention, and an Arhat Assembly was instituted to legislate monastic and temple affairs. When the book of laws was published in 1042, the Minh Dao, "Clear Way," reign period was initiated, indicating that codifying the laws had made clear the way to govern.

The short Mind Dao reign period (1042–44) was occupied with preparations for and the actualization of a seaborne expedition more than a thousand kilometers down the coast to sack the Cham capital. This was the climax of Ly Phat Ma's reign. In consulting with his entourage, he asked why he had never received any envoy from the Cham king and wondered if it was due to some fault of his own or if it was simply a matter of the Cham king trusting in the protection afforded by distance and terrain. His advisors replied that the Cham king would not acknowledge him without being attacked and thereby being forced to do so. Moreover, they said that vassals at home would also become arrogant and disrespectful unless he attacked the Cham king. Ly Phat Ma's advisors were ready to follow him on a difficult mission to a remote place in order to ensure obedience and submission near at hand, an indication of the high degree to which Ly kingship depended upon the momentum of charismatic leadership. In 1043, coins were minted, soldiers were recruited and trained, supplies and weapons were assembled, and several hundred warships, of eight different classes, were built.

Amidst these preparations for war were auspicious episodes of material objects being mysteriously moved by Ly Phat Ma's will. For example, while visiting the ruins of an abandoned Buddhist temple, Ly Phat Ma saw a tilting stone pillar on the verge of falling. He was about to order his men to set it up straight, but before the words were out of his mouth the pillar suddenly straightened up by itself. Literati at court, identified by a term indicating Confucianists (*nho*; Chinese *ru*), the first appearance of this term in the Vietnamese annals, were directed to compose a rhyming narrative "to make known this extraordinary supernatural event." Royal advisors interpreted other signs and wonders before and during the expedition as Heaven's blessing on the king's plans.

At the beginning of 1044, Ly Phat Ma left Thang Long in the hands of Crown Prince Ly Nhat Ton and embarked. He encountered the Cham king, Jaya Sinhavarman II, in the vicinity of the modern city of Da Nang. Ly Phat Ma immediately landed his soldiers and attacked. The Cham king was killed and his soldiers fled. Many thousands were slain and five thousand were captured along with thirty war elephants. Re-embarking, Ly Phat Ma arrived in early autumn at the Cham capital of Vijaya, near the modern city of Qui Nhon in Binh Dinh Province, where he took possession of the royal treasury and the palace women, including a group of girls skilled in singing and dancing to "Indian tunes." At the end of the year, back in Thang Long, he celebrated victory by proclaiming a 50 percent reduction in taxes and a new reign title, Thien Cam Thanh Vu, "Heaven Inspires Saintly Martial Prowess."

There followed an era of prosperous contentment as plunder from the southern coast was digested and many fortunes were made. Edicts were published against corrupt storehouse officers and prison guards. Ly Phat Ma used captured elephants from Champa to pull him around in a lavishly ornamented wagon and as decoys for his elephant hunts. He built a new palace for the exclusive use of the women taken from Vijaya. Markets and post houses were built. An army was sent to the Xieng Khouang plateau in modern Laos and returned with large herds of cattle and many human captives. All this seemed to be a fulfillment of Ly Phat Ma's punning prophesy on the eve of his Cham expedition when an unusually large gallstone the size and shape of a citron was found in a sacrificial goat. Since the word for "citron" is a homonym of the word for "pleasure," Ly Phat Ma suggested that the big gallstone in the sacrificial goat was an indication that "with a bit of hard work we will gain great pleasure and happiness."

Among Ly Phat Ma's vassals who traveled to Thang Long to congratulate him on the success of the Cham adventure was Nung Tri Cao, son of Nung Ton Phuc, the chieftain of the northern border valley of Cao Bang whom Ly Phat Ma had captured and executed for treason in 1039. At that time, Nung Tri Cao had escaped capture, but in 1041 he was seized and brought to Thang Long after attempting to follow his father's rebellious path. Having already put to death his father and other male kinsmen, Ly Phat Ma "took pity" on Nung Tri Cao, pardoned him, and sent him back to govern Cao Bang. For the next seven years, Nung Tri Cao was a loyal vassal of Ly Phat Ma. But in 1048, perhaps judging that Thang Long had grown soft with Cham plunder and could be challenged, he raised his banner in revolt. After three years of heavy fighting, Ly armies drove Nung Tri Cao out of Cao Bang and into Song territory where he wreaked havoc across the length and breadth of southern China, the modern provinces of Guangxi and Guangdong, all the way to modern Guangzhou, before Song forces ran him down and killed him in early 1053.

Ly Phat Ma may have been disturbed in his declining years by the Nung Tri Cao affair and by chronic fighting against rebels in Thanh Hoa, but these worries did not disturb his preparation for death. In 1049, he dreamed of Avalokitesvara, the bodhisattva of mercy, seated on a "lotus throne" growing out of a pond; the bodhisattva reached down and lifted Ly Phat Ma up to sit on the throne. When he recounted this dream to his circle of advisors, they interpreted it as a portent of Ly Phat Ma's death, his departure to a higher realm of consciousness. A Buddhist monk recommended that a temple be built on a stone pillar in the middle of a pond with an image of Avalokitesvara seated on a lotus throne as in the dream. This was done and monks continually circumambulated the pond chanting a liturgy asking long life for their king. This temple, repeatedly rebuilt through the centuries, exists in Hanoi today, known as the "One Pillar Pagoda" (Chua Mot Cot). The beautiful and fragrant lotus blossom, with its stem rooted in the filthy mud of a pond, called a "lotus throne," was a popular symbol for the enlightened mind rising above the turmoil of worldly affairs.

The reign title was changed in 1049 to Sung Hung Dai Bao, "Reverencing and Raising the Great Jewel," referring to the "great jewel" of the kingdom, Ly Phat Ma, being lifted up to the lotus throne and into the company of the bodhisattva. Elaborate gardens and fishponds were built in these years to create a restful environment for Ly Phat Ma during his last years on earth. At the same time, the palace guard was reorganized, elderly advisors of merit were promoted, worthy officials were feasted and given gifts, princes and princesses received new ranks and titles, and a bell was hung in the palace courtyard to be rung by anyone appealing to Ly Phat Ma for justice, indicating withdrawal of the king from the accessibility of his accustomed routine.

In 1053, after a series of earthquakes, a dragon was reportedly sighted at a pavilion in the inner courtyard of the palace. While some considered this to be a good omen, one Buddhist monk said: "Dragons are supposed to fly in the sky. This one has appeared on the ground. It is not a good omen." In mid 1054, Ly Phat Ma formally handed governing authority to his 31-year-old heir, Ly Nhat Ton. He died a few weeks later.

The reign of Ly Phat Ma stands out as a remarkable time of unfolding the potential of Thang Long as a regional power. Ly Phat Ma had a vigorous personality and he responded to events decisively, but he also assembled an entourage of astute men with whom he was in a continuous and evolving conversation about what to do next. In his early years as king, he followed his father's style of taking the advice of men he respected. Then, there was a period in which he argued with his advisors, disputing with them about how to govern. The major achievements of his reign in codifying laws, ravaging Champa, and pushing into the Sino-Vietnamese borderlands came when a mutual appreciation was established between him and his entourage and they had learned to work together. His son, Ly Nhat Ton, had a less dynamic personality yet at the same time a more grandiose vision of himself.

Ly Nhat Ton

Ly Nhat Ton was the first king of the post-Tang era to enjoy an uneventful accession. Unlike his father and grandfather, he had not lived in the disturbed atmosphere of Hoa Lu. He came of age witnessing and participating in the exuberance of Ly Phat Ma's reign. His father had readily delegated important tasks to him. He led soldiers against rebels, he judged offenders, he presided over the court in his father's absence, and he always knew that he would be king. Later Vietnamese historians remembered him as a good military strategist, a promoter of education, an aesthete who enjoyed music and dance, a man who was both compassionate toward his people and harsh toward his enemies, and also a man who wasted wealth and manpower on the construction of palaces and temples; historians cited as particularly extravagant a pleasure palace on the shore of West Lake, adjacent to the royal compound in Thang Long, and a spectacular multi-storied stupa, located beside a temple on the site now occupied by the Hanoi cathedral.

According to Chinese historians, Ly Nhat Ton violated propriety by arrogantly proclaiming himself an emperor, and he violated the border by sending his soldiers to attack Song outposts. He was the first king at Thang Long to capture the close attention of Chinese historians, and this was because, in the wake of Nung Tri Cao's rebellion, the buffer zone between Ly and Song had been removed and soldiers from the two sides began to encounter one another on a regular and increasingly hostile basis. Chinese historians argued that Ly Nhat Ton bore much responsibility for provoking the Sino-Vietnamese war that broke out in the 1070s. Ly Nhat Ton's fearless attitude toward the Song borderlands can be included among factors contributing to that war, but there were many other factors as well. As for claiming imperial status, Ly Nhat Ton was generally careful to maintain a correct posture as vassal in all dealings with Song, but he also "reformed letters" and "nurtured propriety" in ways that gave a rhetorical and ritual appearance of following the forms of an imperial dynasty.

In the 960s, Dinh Bo Linh had named his kingdom Dai Co Viet, a linguistically hybrid term that included both Literary Chinese and vernacular Vietnamese. In Literary Chinese, *dai* (Chinese *da*) means "great"; the vernacular Vietnamese word *co* also means "great." The pairing of these words in this name expresses a phase in the linguistic shift from bilingualism to the emergence of the Vietnamese language. By the time of Ly Nhat Ton, the formal acknowledgment of bilingualism was no longer necessary. When he became king, Ly Nhat Ton dropped the word *co* from the name of the kingdom, henceforth known as Dai Viet, a reformation of letters conforming to imperial usage by removing a non-classical word. Ly Nhat Ton also honored his father and grandfather with posthumous titles that followed the usage of imperial dynasties in the north. Furthermore, he ordered the members of his court to wear ceremonial hats and boots according to the fashion at the Song court. Perhaps most provocative of all, given the context of growing border conflict with Song, he had three characters tattooed on the foreheads of his soldiers meaning "The Son of Heaven's Army"; "son of Heaven" was a term that could mean only "the emperor."

Despite aspiring toward usages prevailing in the Song Empire, Ly Nhat Ton also followed the practices that had grown out of the Hoa Lu and Thang Long experience of kingship. He named eight queens, celebrated his birthday festival, plowed fields at agricultural ceremonies, convened Arhat Assemblies, and personally led soldiers against rebels. The number of dragons recorded as having been sighted during his reign is considerably more than for any other Vietnamese king. A great lover of Cham music, he had Cham songs translated and performed with singing and dancing to the accompaniment of drums.

For routine government affairs, he apparently relied upon Ly Dao Thanh, a royal kinsman, whom he appointed to serve as chancellor at the beginning of his reign. Ly Dao Thanh remained chancellor for the duration of Ly Nhat Ton's reign and was a prominent leader at court in the early years of the next reign. Chancellors, functioning as royal advisors, are recorded from the time of Le Hoan, but Ly Dao Thanh was the first to eventually emerge as more than an advisor. This was because Ly Nhat Ton never had an adult heir with whom to share the duties of government.

Ly Nhat Ton's chief preoccupation during the first twelve years of his reign was to father a son. This led him to visit shrines and temples throughout the kingdom to pray for an heir. In 1063, 40 years old and still without a son, he traveled to the temple of the Dharma Cloud Buddha, about thirty kilometers east of Thang Long at the ancient site of Luy Lau, where Shi Xie had governed at the turn of the third century. This was among the first Buddhist temples to be built in the Red River plain. It was dedicated to a female Buddha famous for her ability to send or stop rain. As the royal procession made its way through the fields across the countryside, all the local people crowded around to catch a glimpse of the king except for one young girl who ignored the hubbub and continued her task of picking mulberry leaves for feeding silkworms. Her nonchalance attracted the attention of Ly Nhat Ton and he brought her back to Thang Long. Three years later, she gave birth to Ly Nhat Ton's heir, Ly Can Duc. She was known as Lady Y Lan and, during the reign of her son, she would exert a dominating influence at the royal court. The Dharma Cloud Buddha consequently became a prominent object of royal patronage, and its temple is today called Chua Dau, "mulberry temple."

Although Ly Nhat Ton found the mother of his heir in the mulberry fields near Chua Dau, the prayer believed to have actually produced the happy event was made at a temple in a western suburb of Thang Long. Ly Nhat Ton had sent a servant to make prayers there on his behalf. Despite the success of his mission, the servant was later beheaded at the door of the temple when it became known that he was studying magical arts with the resident monk. Prowess in the use of magic is a strong theme in the record of the Ly dynasty.

Ly Can Duc was born in early spring of 1066. This event was the watershed of Ly Nhat Ton's reign. More sons were born later, but Ly Can Duc was immediately named the crown prince, and the remaining six years of Ly Nhat Ton's life were an echo of his father's vigorous style. The centerpiece of these years was the re-enactment of Ly Phat Ma's 1044 expedition to Champa. In 1068, Ly Nhat Ton ordered the war boats to be repaired. In making plans for the campaign he relied on Ly Thuong Kiet, the ranking military man at court.

Ly Thuong Kiet, born in 1019 in Thang Long, had begun his career in royal service as a eunuch during the reign of Ly Phat Ma. He advanced quickly in rank, being a skillful military leader. He was not a member of the Ly family but had been given the royal surname to honor his service. He lived long and became a major figure in the late eleventh century.

Ly Nhat Ton embarked on his expedition in spring 1069 and six weeks later landed near modern Qui Nhon. The Cham capital of Vijaya lay some fifteen kilometers inland from there. It is worth noting that the only battle fought by the Vietnamese during the long voyage down the coast was at the modern site of Dong Hoi, in Quang Binh Province, where a Cham army was positioned to intercept them at the border. This is the very same place where, for fifty years in battle after battle, southern Vietnamese stopped northern invasions during the seventeenth century. The explanation for this lies in the coastal terrain. It is the most defensible natural choke between mountains and sea for any force marching by land on the entire Vietnamese coast, and it was very difficult for a pre-modern naval force to advance south of this point without first taking control of it, for there are seventy kilometers of barren sandy beach without fresh water before the next river mouth.

When the Cham army was defeated at Vijaya, the Cham king, Rudravarman III, fled to seek refuge with the Khmers. Ly Thuong Kiet pursued and captured him before he could make good his escape. Ly Nhat Ton lingered for some time to enjoy the Cham palaces, to feast his officers, and to personally perform "the shield dance" and play a game of shuttlecock in the Cham throne room to symbolize his conquest. After conducting a census of Vijaya, which totaled 2,560 households, he burned it to the ground and departed. He returned to Thang Long after an absence of five months, entering the city parading several thousand prisoners, among whom Rudravarman III was prominently displayed.

Rudravarman III was allowed to return to his kingdom after promising to cede what is now the province of Quang Binh, giving the Vietnamese control of the Dong Hoi choke point. Despite this, the Viets and the Chams continued to fight for control of this region until the fifteenth century. Many Cham prisoners were settled on the royal estates of the Ly family in modern Bac Ninh Province, across the river from Thang Long, where they would exert a discernible cultural and political influence into the thirteenth century.

In contrast to happy adventures along distant southern coasts, relations with Song on the northern frontier went from bad to worse during Ly Nhat Ton's reign. Ly Phat Ma had used a policy of punitive expeditions and marriage alliances to gradually extend his influence over chieftains in territories beyond the effective control of Song outposts, most importantly in the modern provinces of Lang Son and Cao Bang. Nung Tri Cao's uprising had been to some extent a reaction against this policy. While engaged in fighting with Ly armies in Cao Bang, Nung Tri Cao requested to be accepted as a vassal of Song, hoping to elicit Song assistance, but the Song emperor rejected the advice of officials eager to use him against Thang Long and refused the request, observing that "he belongs to the Viets." When the Vietnamese forced Nung Tri Cao out of Cao Bang and into Song territory, he was treated by Song as, and played the part of, a plundering invader, and Song soldiers eventually put an end to him. The buffer of local chieftains between Ly and Song had thus been eliminated, but without a clear demarcation of the border.

Ly Nhat Ton became king with an ongoing and volatile border situation in the wake of the Nung Tri Cao episode. There were opportunities for misunderstandings and resentments as each side endeavored to secure the most favorable terrain. The distant Song court took a passive attitude toward the potential for trouble, at that time being more concerned with its northern frontier. However, from the mid 1050s, local Song officials, led by a man named Xiao Zhu, agitated for military action against Thang Long to settle the border question. They secretly trained military units and sheltered refugees from the Vietnamese side, including army deserters. The contradiction between the pacific pronouncements of the Song court and the devious, provocative policy of local Song officials angered Ly Nhat Ton. He believed that Song officials were conspiring to provoke war, shielding their activities behind the professions of amity issuing from the imperial court. In 1059, "hating Song's back and forth," he ordered a raid upon the Song coast at modern Qinzhou, about eighty kilometers northeast of the modern Sino-Vietnamese border, "to dazzle [Song] with soldiers and return." There followed a series of attacks and counterattacks in which local Song forces fared poorly, resulting in a parley between Song and Ly envoys that temporarily calmed things down. Seeking to avoid being drawn into a larger conflict, the Song court accepted Thang Long's explanation of the trouble and dismissed Xiao Zhu and the other activist officials.

In the mid 1060s, Han Qi, a prominent official at the Song court, explained the rationale of the appeasement control policy that had been observed for eighty years, apparently in response to arguments against it. He wrote that the lesson of the 980–981 war was that negotiation and conciliation were more effective than punitive expeditions in eliciting Viet affirmations of obedience; that the Viet territory was remote, its climate unhealthy, and even if conquered could not be controlled; that no conceivable benefit could be obtained from sending soldiers against Thang Long. Nevertheless, new incidents occurred, and, although the official Song policy forbad direct provocation, local Song officials went so far as to conspire with the Cham king to put pressure on Thang Long. During the 1060s, Song border officials were divided in their opinions with some conspiring to engineer military action against Thang Long and others denouncing these efforts as foolish and contrary to instructions. Meanwhile, Ly Nhat Ton, emboldened by the passivity of the Song court and unaware that Song policy was about to change, allowed his border officers to maintain an aggressive stance. By the time of his death, in 1072, the Song court was implementing plans to attack Thang Long.

The Cham adventure exhausted Ly Nhat Ton's vitality; two and a half years later, he died at the age of 49. His final years were full of worry: declining health, border problems with Song, successive years of drought that depleted royal granaries, but especially the lack of an adult heir. The prospect of a child king lay behind the building of a shrine in 1070 dedicated to the Duke of Zhou, Confucius, and Confucius' disciples. The Duke of Zhou was famous for ably governing on behalf of a child king and then relinquishing power when the king came of age. Confucius, the great teacher of good government, considered the Duke of Zhou to be a model of righteousness and loyalty for officials serving a child king. For centuries, historians had credited the Duke of Zhou with a decisive role in establishing the house of Zhou, one of the greatest and longest-lasting dynasties of Chinese antiquity.

The Thang Long shrine built in 1070 contained statues of the Duke of Zhou, of Confucius, and of Confucius' four best disciples, as well as painted images of seventy-two of Confucius' other disciples. Seasonal sacrifices were instituted at the shrine to worship the spirits of these men, and 4-year-old Crown Prince Ly Can Duc was sent there to study. This combination of spirit cult and study hall focused attention upon the small crown prince as the true and correct object of loyalty. Famous men in the past were invoked as dynastic spirit protectors, models of loyal service, correct teaching, and sincere learning. This shrine combined appropriate worship with lessons in loyalty for officials and lessons in kingship for the crown prince.

In the fifteenth century, when Confucian thought first dominated the Vietnamese court, historians seeking to extend the genealogy of Confucian practice as far as possible into the past recorded the 1070 shrine as a Temple of Literature (Van Mieu), which indeed it became in the fifteenth century, a type of temple that in Ming China was dedicated to Confucius. However, the first Van Mieu in China was built in 1410, so an eleventh-century Van Mieu in Vietnam is implausible. After years of dereliction during the twentieth-century wars, the Van Mieu in Hanoi has been rebuilt and is now a major tourist site, claimed as the first university in Vietnam.

Ly Dao Thanh, the leading figure at court in the 1070s, was definitely familiar with the Confucian classics, as were all educated people at that time. But he was also a devout Buddhist. He valued the teachings of Confucius because they exhorted officials to serve their sovereign loyally and instructed rulers how to govern wisely. Yet, in time of need, he turned to Buddhism.

The death of Ly Nhat Ton in early 1072 opened a perilous era. Song was preparing to attack. The king, Ly Can Duc, was a child born of an ambitious peasant mother, Lady Y Lan, who was intolerant of her low status in the hierarchy of aristocratic palace women. Presiding at court was an old man, Ly Dao Thanh, who was quickly surrounded by intrigues beyond his ability to fathom. The commander of military forces, Ly Thuong Kiet, was experienced and decisive, but also foolhardy and difficult to control.

The first three Ly kings made Thang Long a rising regional force, eventually attracting the concerned attention of the Song court. The ensuing Sino-Vietnamese war in the 1070s coincided with the beginning of an age of successive royal minorities when mothers of kings and the men they favored exercised authority.

Outbreak of the Ly–Song War

The war of the 1070s was closely related to the Song reform policies of Wang Anshi (1021–1086), who became powerful in 1069 with the patronage of Emperor Shenzong (r. 1067–1085). At this time, Song government was rent with conflict between reformers led by Wang Anshi and those who opposed reform, generally called traditionalists. Wang Anshi initiated a broad range of fiscal, military, and administrative reforms intended to increase state revenue, administrative efficiency, and military preparedness while improving the economic position of peasants and curbing the power of wealthy families. The emperor's support enabled him to attempt to implement his reforms, but many powerful traditionalists, supported by the empress dowager, mother of the emperor, opposed him. The result was an era of fierce bureaucratic factionalism.

As for the traditional appeasement control policy toward Thang Long, Wang Anshi considered it cravenly unprincipled and encouraged activist officials to take a more "positive" attitude toward the border situation. He and his bureaucratic allies had developed a pattern of successfully dealing with irritating frontier situations on the Tibetan border in modern Gansu Province and against upland chieftains in Hunan and Sichuan Provinces. In each case, local military forces were used to build up pressure on the frontier until the enemy forces began to break up into groups that could be individually worn down and suppressed. When, in 1070, the emperor received a complaint lodged against an official on the Viet border for engaging in provocative activities, Wang Anshi denounced the complaint and decided to apply his experience of "nibbling operations" against tribal leaders to the far south, imagining that Thang Long could be subdued in the same way.

Xiao Zhu, the aggressive official who had been dismissed several years before, was reinstated and tasked with implementing the activist policy on the southern border. However, he had meanwhile shifted his view and had no heart for the enterprise. He reported that the Ly army was very strong, and he was accused of going so far as to destroy documents on military plans. In 1073, he was dismissed and a man named Shen Qi was sent to replace him. Shen Qi was enthusiastic. He reported that Thang Long was "small and ugly" and could be "squashed like a bug." But Wang Anshi lost confidence in him because his excessive confidence led to carelessness, so he was replaced in 1074 with yet another official, Liu Yi, who rapidly reorganized preparations for war on a sound basis.

Part of the problem with local leadership in these years was that policy on the Viet border had become enmeshed in the factional conflict between Wang Anshi and his bureaucratic enemies. The emperor continued to receive complaints about the aggressive activities of officials on the Viet border even as Wang Anshi was endeavoring to initiate such activities. Opposition to Wang Anshi reached a crescendo of intensity in 1074 as his enemies, with the support of the empress dowager, mobilized against two of his reforms, the so-called Agricultural Loans Act and the Public Service Act. He was forced to retire from office for several months until, with the emperor's support, he returned to power in early 1075, at which time the situation on the southern frontier was sliding toward open war.

Despite the ostensible incompetence of Song border officials, much had changed in the early 1070s. Song officers aggressively expanded their system of supervision over upland chieftains, competing with the Ly for their loyalty with considerable success. Local troops and tribal levies were recruited and trained. Weapons were distributed. Supplies were stockpiled. War boats were built. Élite land and naval units were assembled. The trigger for initiating hostilities was an effort to cut the trade routes between Nan Zhao in Yunnan and Thang Long. This occurred in spring of 1075. Meanwhile, at Thang Long, the adjustment to a child king had not been without drama.

For one year following the accession of 6-year-old Ly Can Duc in early 1072, government was in the hands of Ly Dao Thanh, a member of the royal family who had presided over Ly Nhat Ton's court, and the senior queen, subsequently known as the Duong queen mother, who served as the regent and official adoptive mother of the king, for Ly Can Duc's birth mother, Lady Y Lan, was a commoner and ineligible to hold the rank of queen. During that time, the court busily attended to routine matters as if making a studied effort to project an appearance of normalcy: the king made sacrifices at shrines, visited various palaces, celebrated his birthday festival, attended a "Buddha-bathing festival," granted an amnesty to prisoners, presided over an examination of monks to test their literary skills for appointment as scribes at court, chose two queens, and conferred promotions upon Commander-in-Chief Ly Thuong Kiet and his senior officers.

When the monsoon rains continued well into autumn, the Dharma Cloud Buddha was paraded to the capital from its temple in the native district of Lady Y Lan. It was taken to a temple in the royal compound where the king prayed for the rain to stop, and the rain immediately stopped. This demonstration of supernatural power by a deity from Lady Y Lan's natal village came shortly before a palace coup in which Lady Y Lan seized control of the court and was named queen mother and regent. The Duong queen mother and seventy-two other palace women were interred in Ly Nhat Ton's tomb, whether dead or alive is unclear, and Ly Dao Thanh was exiled to the southern border in modern Nghe An Province.

According to the court chronicle, Lady Y Lan was unhappy at "not being able to participate in government" and complained to her son that the Duong queen mother was "working hard to accumulate power, riches, and honor"; the king, "although a child," knew who his real mother was and accordingly ordered the retirement of the Duong queen mother and the elevation of Lady Y Lan. Historians have tended to assume that this coup was accomplished with the assistance of Ly Thuong Kiet, the general who had captured the Cham king in 1069 and was commander of all military forces, which is plausible because he was presumably the only person in a position to accomplish it, although evidence of this has not been preserved. Assuming that this, nevertheless, was the case, it is not hard to imagine, in the light of later events, that Ly Thuong Kiet championed Lady Y Lan's resentment as a way of bringing into the court new leaders who understood the urgency of the situation developing on the northern border. During Ly Can Duc's first year as king, activities recorded at court show no indication of addressing what an alert military commander would have understood as a serious threat.

In Nghe An, beside the provincial shrine for local deities, Ly Dao Thanh built a garden for the bodhisattva Ksitagarbha and erected in it a Buddha statue and an ancestral tablet for Ly Nhat Ton where he worshipped "at dawn and at dusk." Ksitagarbha is the bodhisattva believed to be responsible for instructing the unfortunate souls who live in the age of darkness, from the historical Buddha's death until the arrival of Maitreya, "the Buddha of the future." Ly Dao Thanh viewed himself as living in the benighted age from Ly Nhat Ton's death to Ly Can Duc's maturity. He wanted to instruct his contemporaries about how to survive this dangerous time and took comfort from the bodhisattva for his task. He may have been too preoccupied with Ly Can Duc's minority accession to take adequate note of events on the northern border. On the other hand, Ly Thuong Kiet may have been too preoccupied with military affairs on the border to appreciate Ly Dao Thanh's leadership at court. But the urgency of events required that these two men work together.

In 1074, Ly Dao Thanh was called back to resume his duties at court. He lost no time in seeking new talent to serve at court. Although the wisdom of the old generation was acknowledged, with officials over 80 years of age being issued staffs and chairs for leaning and sitting at court, provision was also made for raising a new generation of young men to positions of importance. Early in 1075, three levels of examinations were held to select men educated in Confucian studies; what exactly this meant in that time and place is not known, but presumably it included the "five books" of the traditional Confucian education in history, poetry, ritual, prognostication, and annals. This is the first recorded instance of the Vietnamese royal court holding an exam to identify talent among commoners educated specifically in Confucianism. The highest honors were conferred upon Le Van Thinh, who was immediately assigned to be Ly Can Duc's teacher. Later that year, in time of drought, the Dharma Cloud Buddha was again paraded to Thang Long, this time to hear the king's prayer for rain, a prayer that was reportedly efficacious. This is the last felicitous event recorded before Thang Long passed into the shadows of war.

In late spring and early summer of 1075, fighting erupted in Cao Bang between Viet soldiers and a chieftain who had submitted to Song and cut the route by which Thang Long had been receiving horses in trade with the Nan Zhao kingdom of Yunnan. Warfare continued through the year and spread as Liu Yi's military preparations along the border became impossible for Thang Long to ignore. Ly Thuong Kiet decided to take the initiative with a pre-emptive strike to ravage Song border jurisdictions and destroy accumulated supplies. Late in 1075, as terrain was drying out from the monsoon rains and large-scale military campaigns became practicable, Song border officers reported indications of a major attack, and within a week a combined land and sea force of between eighty and one hundred thousand Viets crossed the border.

Ly Thuong Kiet led naval forces and within three days easily captured the main Song ports facing the Viet coast, at modern Qinzhou and Hepu. He disembarked his soldiers and, joined by an army marching down the Zuo River from Cao Bang and Lang Son, lay siege to Nanning, the Song headquarters facing the Vietnamese border. Caught by surprise and fearing a naval attack on Guangzhou, Song officials in the region were ordered to avoid battle and wait for reinforcements. After a siege of forty-two days, Nanning fell, much to the astonishment of Wang Anshi who had confidently predicted that the city was too strong to be taken. After destroying Nanning and killing tens of thousands of people, the Viets withdrew back across the border, taking with them much plunder and many captives. In a campaign of less than three months, Ly Thuong Kiet set back Song war preparations and stung Wang Anshi into an angry haste.

Wherever Ly Thuong Kiet's soldiers had gone on Song territory they set up signs at crossroads proclaiming three reasons for the attack. The first two reasons were closely related to the actual situation along the border. First, Ly Thuong Kiet accused Song of harboring rebels against Thang Long and refusing to surrender them. This referred to the immediate cause of the fighting when Nung chieftains who had been Ly vassals shifted their allegiance to Song. Just prior to the outbreak of fighting in early 1075, Thang Long had requested the return of an upland chieftain who had gone over to Song with seven hundred of his followers; Song refused, saying that these people had submitted to Song and consequently belonged to Song. This was different from prior policy during the decades of Song pacifism when Song strictly refused to meddle with Thang Long's vassals and even returned those who sought refuge with Song. Second, Ly Thuong Kiet accused Song of training and organizing soldiers on the border for the purpose of attacking Thang Long. This, of course, was true, and later Chinese historians considered the war preparations of Liu Yi and his predecessor as provocative.

The third reason is remarkable for the knowledge it reveals of Song politics. It is seemingly a riposte to a Song edict, reportedly composed personally by Wang Anshi and published early in the campaign, which denounced the invasion and declared Song's intention of attacking the Viet kingdom, among other reasons, to rescue the people from Thang Long's harsh exactions. Ly Thuong Kiet, for his part, claimed that he had come to rescue the people suffering from Wang Anshi's Agricultural Loan and Public Service Acts, the controversial reforms that had provoked such resistance in the Song government as to force Wang Anshi into temporary retirement in 1074–1075. Ly Thuong Kiet was inserting his campaign into Song bureaucratic factionalism by claiming to be an ally of Wang Anshi's political enemies. This was said to have especially nettled Wang Anshi and to have hardened his eagerness to strike back.

One of the successes of Ly Thuong Kiet's pre-emptive strike was to provoke a Song response so motivated by a desire for revenge that it was poorly prepared. Ly Thuong Kiet had also taken many captives that would be used as leverage in future negotiations. Furthermore, many upland chieftains who had gone over to Song now returned their allegiance to Thang Long. But his most important achievement was the destruction of the Song navy that had been assembled at Qinzhou and Hepu. This had decisive repercussions for future battles. The surprise of Ly Thuong Kiet's attack, as perceived by Song, was achieved by his sailing directly from the Cham frontier to attack the Song coastal ports. Ly Thuong Kiet spent several months prior to his Song attack in the far south skirmishing with Cham border forces, mapping terrain, and settling military colonists. Song diplomacy was exciting Cham kings with visions of revenge for Thang Long having twice plundered Vijaya during the previous thirty years. Cham–Viet hostilities were nearly constant during this time.

Wang Anshi's enemies at the Song court made sure that the decision to launch a full-scale invasion of the Viet kingdom was not made without extensive discussion and spirited dissent. Fu Bi, a traditionalist who opposed Wang Anshi's reforms, argued that the Viet lands were remote and difficult to conquer. Zhang Fangbing, another traditionalist, submitted a nine-point argument against the projected expedition, saying that Viet military strength was greater than in the past, having successfully attacked and inflicted great damage upon Song border jurisdictions; that cavalry was of no use in the Viet lowlands, which were screened by rugged mountains and wide rivers; that if success could not be obtained in one winter's campaign the army would have to be withdrawn when the summer rains began; and that the Viet kingdom had been an important frontier jurisdiction of the old Tang Empire but had now become a major regional power that could not be knocked out in one blow. A naval expert, Su Ziyuan, cautioned that the Viets had a powerful navy and were "skilled in water battle"; he pointed out that it would be impossible to take Thang Long without naval control of the Red River, which would be no easy task.

Wu Chong, another enemy of Wang Anshi, although unsuccessful in arguing against the expedition, obtained the emperor's approval of his recommendation to appoint Guo Kuei as senior commander of the army. Wang Anshi's candidate, Zhao Xie, was named second-in-command. As can be expected, Guo Kuei and Zhao Xie did not get along. While Guo Kuei was slow and methodical, Zhao Xie was alert to tactical opportunities. Furthermore, despite being recommended by Wang Anshi, Zhao Xie did not want this assignment and repeatedly requested to be excused, unconvinced that the expedition was well advised.

The Ly–Song War

The Viets spent 1076 preparing defenses. It is recorded that, in late spring of this year, the 10-year-old king was taken to inspect a "water barrier," which, considering the course of later battles, was likely an underwater obstacle sealing the Bach Dang estuary. The naval war began three months before major land battles and continued for two months after withdrawal of the Song army. No details of the naval fighting survive except that there were "many sea battles," that the Song navy never penetrated the Red River plain, and that Thang Long's navy continued attacking long after the withdrawal of Song land forces. Viet supremacy at sea, demonstrated against Champa in 1044 and 1069, was guaranteed by the crippling blow dealt to Song naval forces by Ly Thuong Kiet in 1075, from which Song had not taken time to recover before launching its attack.

Guo Kuei advanced his headquarters to Nanning in late autumn and within a month had advanced to the border opposite Lang Son. There he waited for over two months while one of his generals took a side trip to secure Cao Bang. Zhao Xie was critical of the Cao Bang campaign, believing that too much time was lost bringing the soldiers sent there back to join the main body of the expedition before advancing. He argued that these soldiers should be sent directly through the mountains toward Thang Long from Cao Bang, allowing the main force to press on, but his opinion was ignored. Furthermore, stubborn Viet resistance in Cao Bang prolonged the delay. Finally, near the end of the lunar year, the Song expedition, numbering around 50,000 troops and more than double that number of porters, crossed into Viet territory, pushed aside border guard units, marched down to the lowlands, and arrived at the Cau River where the Viets had prepared their defenses.

On the road from the border to Thang Long, the Cau River is the only natural obstacle between the mountains and the Red River. Around forty-five kilometers northeast of Thang Long, it is anchored upstream in the valleys leading to Cao Bang and downstream it joins its waters with other rivers at Pha Lai, beyond which lie soggy plains unsuitable for the movement of large land armies. It shielded the heartland of old Giao that was filled with Buddhist temples and the royal estates of the Ly in modern Bac Ninh Province. The Viets waited for the Song army on the southern bank of the river, where they had built multiple layers of bamboo fences and anchored over four hundred war boats. The Song army arrived on the northern bank of the river and there it stalled for lack of naval support.

Zhao Xie sent soldiers to cut down trees for building catapults and floating bridges. The Song prepared an attack at a place where a hill on the northern side of the river enabled soldiers to assemble out of sight of Viet observers perched in watchtowers on the southern bank. Song catapults are said to have sent stones falling like rain upon the Viet war boats to open a way for the attack. Several hundred Song soldiers crossed the river on floating bridges before the bridges were destroyed. They set many bamboo defense walls aflame but the walls were in so many layers that they could not break through. Song reinforcements arrived by raft and advanced a maximum of eight kilometers toward Thang Long, but Viet troops eventually succeeded in killing or capturing all the Song soldiers who had crossed the river. This turned out to be the furthest advance of the Song expedition.

After more than a month of repulsing further Song efforts to cross the river, Ly Thuong Kiet was emboldened to essay a frontal assault to disperse the Song army. Under cover of night, he led thousands of soldiers across the river. The Song front line began to collapse until all the reserve forces, including cavalry units and Guo Kuei's bodyguard, moved up and forced the Viets back into the river, capturing a Viet general and resulting in the drowning of two Ly princes.

With each side having demonstrated the best that it could do in battle but without dislodging the other, the stalemate began to work against the Song forces. Provisions were nearly depleted. Over half the army was dead from battle, heat exhaustion, or tropical fevers, and most survivors were weak from illness. Furthermore, the monsoon rains were about to begin. The Song generals wanted to withdraw but they dared not do so without some token of success. The Viets understood this, and a message from Ly Can Duc to the Song emperor was delivered to the Song encampment apologizing for having violated Song territory in the past, promising not to do so again, requesting permission to send tribute and re-establish normal relations, and offering a proposal for marking a mutually acceptable border.

Guo Kuei and Zhao Xie decided to regard this as a formal submission and hastened to withdraw as their rearguard held off Viet attacks. Song forces endeavored to retain control of Lang Son and Cao Bang, but within a few months, attacking Viet forces regained Lang Son and began to put pressure on Cao Bang. Song officials used criminals to work the gold and silver mines of Cao Bang until late 1079, when the Ly and Song courts reached a settlement. The Song abandoned its claims in Lang Son and Cao Bang. The Ly returned a couple hundred remaining captives seized during Ly Thuong Kiet's pre-emptive attack and resumed their pose as loyal imperial vassals. After further negotiations over districts at the upland extremity of the frontier in northeastern Cao Bang, a border agreement was finalized in 1088. The border drawn at that time, with minor changes through the centuries, was basically the same as the Sino-Vietnamese border today.

The war we have described was a war of mutual aggravation. The factors contributing to its outbreak emerged from the context of internal imperial politics. Although the Viets had to some extent drifted away from the imperial world after the fall of Tang, they were still connected to it, as Ly Thuong Kiet's use of Wang Anshi's reform legislation in his war propaganda revealed, not to mention the sharing of a single civilization. The Nung Tri Cao uprising, Ly border exuberance, and Wang Anshi's activist inclinations shook Song policy from decades of passivity on its southern frontier. The question of drawing a border to separate regions that for centuries had belonged to the same imperial world was delayed for so long because of the rugged mountains and the screen of tribal vassals. The rise of Thang Long under the first three Ly kings, however, accelerated the dangers of an unmarked border and the resolution of border irritations became a priority for both sides.

The consciousness of a fixed border between northern and southern domains of the same imperial world is expressed in a poem that later historians attributed to Ly Thuong Kiet. It was supposedly sung in temples along the southern bank of the Cau River during the weeks of fighting to motivate the Viet soldiers: "The mountains and rivers of the south are the dwelling place of the southern emperor; the border has been fixed in the book of Heaven; how dare these uncouth rebels come in for plunder; you will all go out to see their defeat and ruin."

If this story is true, it is unlikely that the poem was sung as it exists today, for it is written in Literary Chinese following Tang-style prosodic rules, which would probably not have been wholly intelligible to Viet soldiers. Furthermore, it is unlikely to have been written by Ly Thuong Kiet, who was neither a literary man nor known to have produced any other literary works. The story of singing in temples to give heart to soldiers on the eve of battle is very plausible, but whether it was exactly this poem that was sung and whether this poem was written in the eleventh century or at a later time are questions without irrefutable answers. Nevertheless, it is plausible to imagine that the border consciousness expressed in the poem arose in the context of drawing the Sino-Vietnamese border in the eleventh century. This poem also expresses what became a tenet of Vietnamese historiography in the thirteenth century when China was conquered by the Mongols and Thang Long posed as the last remaining outpost of civilization: a southern imperial tradition with its own mandate of Heaven. Whatever else it did, by emphasizing a border separating two imperial mandates, the poem simultaneously emphasized the connectedness, if not unity, of the two mandates as northern and southern parts of a whole.

When Ly Thuong Kiet returned from his foray across the Song border in 1076, his deeds were announced before the tombs of the three first Ly kings and Ly Can Duc's reign title was changed to trumpet a "heroic, martial, glorious victory." However, mobilizing to meet the impending Song invasion had been a sobering experience. While Ly Thuong Kiet trained soldiers and prepared defenses along the Cau River, Ly Dao Thanh selected a cadre of educated men to supervise the military camps, to stockpile supplies, and to staff a communications network. An edict was also published "to request straight talk." This appeal for plain speaking, without fear of reprisal, was an unusual, if not desperate, call for any and all ideas. In late 1076, as Song forces were entering the kingdom, Le Van Thinh, the man selected the previous year to serve as tutor to the king, was made minister in charge of all military affairs. A few months later, as Song forces were withdrawing in early 1077, an exam was organized to select men with knowledge of "letters and laws." Looking beyond the military emergency, Ly Dao Thanh was endeavoring to build a system of government capable of operating without the firm and constant hand of a vigorous adult king.

The monks were also active. In spring 1077, at the peak of fighting along the Cau River, an assembly was convened at Thang Long to recite the Nhan Vuong (Chinese Renwang) Sutra, "Sutra on the Benevolent Kings," which was commonly recited to avert disasters. According to a popular explanation for the outcome of the war, the Song generals believed that their inability to obtain victory was due to the power of the Dharma Cloud Buddha, whose temple was not far from the battlefield. Song soldiers were sent to raid the temple and take away the statue of the Buddha, which was later abandoned in a forest as Song soldiers fled from a Viet ambush on their way out of the country. The Buddha was thought to be lost until a forest fire during the next dry season consumed all the trees in the region except for one spot of dense and luxuriant foliage in which the Buddha was found. This miracle was reported to the king, who returned the Buddha to its temple with great honors.

The Ly–Song War of the 1070s emerged from the specific problem of defining a border where none had existed before. There was aggression on both sides. The negotiations that followed the hostilities and that led to a resolution of outstanding issues are more typical of Sino-Vietnamese relations than are the few episodes of war during the past millennium.

Ly Can Duc

Ly Dao Thanh died in 1081. In 1085, 19-year-old Ly Can Duc announced his majority by proclaiming a new reign title and appointing Le Van Thinh as chancellor. Le Van Thinh had risen rapidly as a protégé of Ly Dao Thanh. In

1084, he successfully negotiated border questions with Song officials. From 1085 to 1096 he was the dominant figure at court.

According to historical records, in the late 1080s there were a series of initiatives that appear to have been concerned with establishing positions and hierarchies. In 1086, a literary exam was held to select a man to be a Han Lam Hoc Si (Chinese Hanlin Xueshi), the first reference in Vietnamese history to a Han Lam Scholar. In Tang and Song government, such men were assigned to what was called the Hanlin Academy where erudite men were called on for various tasks requiring academic knowledge or literary skill. A privy council (Bi Thu Cac; Chinese Mishu Ge) was instituted in 1087, a kind of secretariat where the most secret matters were handled. In 1088 a Buddhist monk was appointed Quoc Su (Chinese Guoshi), "Teacher of the Kingdom," a title that had been given to a pre-eminent monk since the time of Le Hoan. At the same time, ten clerks were given appointments, seemingly to assist in administering the Buddhist temples, for, also at that time, all the Buddhist temples in the kingdom were categorized into three classes depending upon their wealth in fields, slaves, and treasure; high-ranking officials were appointed to oversee temple affairs. In 1089, a classification of positions was determined for "civil and military officials including those who personally attended the king and those with miscellaneous duties." All of these initiatives apparently came from Le Van Thinh.

Le Van Thinh's appointment as chancellor in 1085 came as Lady Y Lan ended her regency on behalf of her son the king. From this time Lady Y Lan began to occupy herself with traveling and with building temples and stupas. She became famous as a lavish patron of the Buddhist monks. Her pursuit of interests away from the court opened an opportunity for Le Van Thinh to make changes that brought increasing authority into his hands. As the king's former teacher and chief advisor, Le Van Thinh enjoyed much power, particularly since surviving information portrays Ly Can Duc as unassertive.

Le Van Thinh's ascendance diminished members of the Ly royal family. The king had a younger brother and many uncles. It is recorded that, in 1095, the king called all the nobles of the royal family to come to court. No further information is recorded about this, but shortly thereafter the king ended a drought by proclaiming an amnesty for prisoners and by canceling or reducing the collection of taxes. Whether or not these measures were intended to reduce Le Van Thinh's control of affairs can be no more than a matter of conjecture, but within a few months, in early 1096, a curious episode brought an end to Le Van Thinh's career.

Ly Can Duc was in a small boat on West Lake, adjacent to the royal compound at Thang Long, on an excursion to watch fishermen. Suddenly the lake was covered with a thick mist. The splashing of another boat's oars was heard approaching and the king threw a spear into the mist toward the sound. A moment later the mist lifted to reveal a tiger in the royal boat. A fisherman in a nearby boat threw his net over the threatening form, which turned out to be Le Van Thinh. Le Van Thinh was found guilty of plotting to murder the king and sentenced to die. In consideration of his earlier "merit," however, Ly Can Duc remitted the death penalty and instead banished him to a frontier outpost in the mountains; no further information survives about him.

Court historians glossed this event by explaining that Le Van Thinh had acquired a slave from Yunnan who could do "strange tricks," and this slave taught him how to masquerade as a tiger. No further information survives about Le Van Thinh, but modern archaeologists have discovered an elaborate burial place prepared for him, though never used, located in his home district in modern Bac Ninh Province. Without further information the most plausible conjecture is that senior members of the royal family acted to secure their interests against a commoner upstart. The brave fisherman was later honored as a guardian deity of the kingdom.

Shortly before Le Van Thinh was undone in the boat, whether by coincidence or as part of some larger set of events, Lady Y Lan gave a feast for monks at Thang Long and asked the Quoc Su, a senior monk and "Teacher of the Kingdom," several questions about the Buddha, the source of enlightenment, and the "patriarchs" who transmitted enlightenment. The monk explained how the Buddha had transmitted enlightenment to the lineage of patriarchs in the Thien (Chinese Chan; Japanese Zen) School where it was passed from generation to generation outside of scriptural teachings. He explained how this lineage had entered the Viet lands and identified the patriarchs who possessed the "mind seal" of the Buddha's teaching at that time. Lady Y Lan was very pleased with this explanation and gave the Quoc Su gifts and a new name, Thong Bien, "Understanding and Discrimination." Lady Y Lan's interest in the authoritative lineage of correct teaching suggests the possibility of a similar concern at that time with the royal bloodline, a concern that grew from year to year as Ly Can Duc was childless.

After the Song War of the 1070s, there is no record of Ly Thuong Kiet playing any part in court affairs, although it is recorded that he patronized many famous monks. He appears to have spent most of his time away from Thang Long, in particular in the southern provinces and on the Cham frontier, where the few bits of information recorded from his later years took place. He has been credited with building Buddhist temples in Thanh Hoa Province and with being particularly active in stamping out the worship of "evil spirits." He seems to have been a man of action with small tolerance for the palace life of Thang Long, or perhaps the Ly royal family enforced upon him a quasi-banishment to work in the southern provinces to preclude his involvement in court politics. His final campaigns, in 1103–1104, when he was already in his eighties, show him as Thang Long's lord of the southern marchlands.

In 1103, a rebellion broke out in the southernmost province, modern Nghe An and Ha Tinh Provinces, led by a magician named Ly Giac, who was thought to be able to conjure soldiers out of trees and bushes. Ly Thuong Kiet attacked Ly Giac and sent him fleeing to the Cham king (Jaya Indravarman II). With Ly Giac whispering in his ear, Jaya Indravarman II seized border districts and raided deeper into Viet territory. Ly Thuong Kiet led his men south, defeated the Chams, and re-established frontier defenses. One year later, he died and was accorded great honors.

Many stories have been recorded about Buddhist monks during the Ly dynasty. The poems of an official at court in the 1080s and 1090s, Doan Van Kham, give written portraits of two contrasting kinds of monks, those who withdrew from human society to meditate as hermits and those who served society as teachers and royal advisors. In the late 1080s, as Le Van Thinh expanded the size of officialdom, Doan Van Kham described himself as "roped and fettered" among the "flock" of officials at court, frustrated in his desire to visit the monk Quang Tri, who dwelt in seclusion on a mountain. When news of Quang Tri's death arrived with his desire still unfulfilled, Doan Van Kham comforted himself by writing that despite leaving behind no tomb where he could be venerated, Quang Tri had left his pure essence, which could be encountered everywhere. Doan Van Kham wrote another poem on the death of the monk Chan Khong in 1100. He describes Chan Khong as a pillar of society, surrounded by disciples, and in death continuing to serve others with his tomb as a place of pilgrimage and meditation. Behind these two classical stereotypes, however, were monks famous for magic and sorcery, the most famous of whom was Tu Dao Hanh.

According to Tu Dao Hanh's biography, his father, a temple administrator in Thang Long, had an altercation with a Ly nobleman who hired a magician named Dai Dien to kill him. Tu Dao Hanh, after spending years acquiring supernatural powers, killed Dai Dien to avenge his father. He then wandered from temple to temple in search of enlightenment and eventually achieved his goal. He thereafter became famous for taming snakes and wild beasts, producing rain, and curing sickness. In those days, the king was advancing in years and remained childless.

In 1112, a small boy about 3 years old appeared on the seashore in Thanh Hoa. He spoke like an adult, knew all about Ly Can Duc, and called himself "Giac Hoang," "emperor of enlightenment," a term for the Buddha. He was taken to Thang Long and lodged at a temple in the royal compound. Ly Can Duc was so taken with him that he wanted to make him the crown prince, but the entire royal court opposed this. Some advised that if the boy was truly what he seemed to be then he should be able to reincarnate himself into the royal family, and if he could do that then there could be no objection to making him crown prince. Ly Can Duc accordingly organized a reincarnation ceremony for the child.

When he learned of this, Tu Dao Hanh realized that Giac Hoang was a reincarnation of his enemy, the magician Dai Dien, so he used his own magical powers to disrupt the ceremony. When Ly Can Duc investigated the matter, Tu Dao Hanh confessed to what he had done and was arrested. Tu Dao Hanh implored the Sung Hien Marquis, a brother of Ly Can Duc and also childless, to help him, in which case he promised to assist the marquis to become the father of the next king. The Sung Hien Marquis told Ly Can Duc that Tu Dao Hanh's power was demonstrably greater than that of Giac Hoang and that accordingly it would be better to rely upon Tu Dao Hanh to supply an heir to the throne. Ly Can Duc agreed with this. According to one account, Giac Hoang died shortly after and was buried at a prestigious temple.

During a later visit to the Sung Hien Marquis, Tu Dao Hanh supposedly used his magical powers to cause the nobleman's wife to become pregnant, and he told the marquis to inform him when the baby was about to be born. In 1116, when a messenger from the marquis arrived at the temple where Tu Dao Hanh resided to say that birth was imminent, Tu Dao Hanh prepared to die and passed away. He was reincarnated as the son of the Sung Hien Marquis and was named Ly Duong Hoan. Two years later, Ly Can Duc, 52 years old and still childless, selected Ly Duong Hoan to be the crown prince. In this way, Tu Dao Hanh was reincarnated to become the fifth Ly king.

This odd tale, a mixture of fact and fancy, was forced out of the human imagination by the same desperation to have an heir that had oppressed Ly Nhat Ton until the birth of Ly Can Duc. Ly Can Duc never had any children, and by the 1110s, as he approached and entered his sixth decade of life, the future of the dynasty became an urgent question. The story that explained how the matter was resolved features a Buddhist monk, a feud between magicians, and the bloodline of the Ly family, three prominent elements in the minds of educated people at that time.

Another aspect of this is that Ly Can Duc designated a crown prince in late 1117 only two months after the death of his mother, Lady Y Lan. Lady Y Lan exercised strong influence over Ly Can Duc to the end of her life. Five months before her death, she complained to her son about the depredations of water buffalo thieves and he responded by prescribing a series of punishments for such people. After her death, three other palace women were buried with her remains, punctuating what in effect was a revolution in the palace, making way for the mother of the next king. Lady Y Lan had inhibited a resolution of the succession question.

The deaths of two other high-ranking people in 1117, shortly before the death of Lady Y Lan, may also have had implications for the naming of a crown prince. They were both Ly noblemen with the rank of marquis, among the brothers and uncles of Ly Can Duc, although the exact relationships are unknown. In 1104, during a royal audience, one of them had publicly struck the other with the ivory tablet held by noblemen during royal audiences at court; these symbols of rank were about a meter long and just wide enough to be held in the palm of one's hand. No additional information was recorded about the incident, so it remains a mystery, but the attacker was the same man who had hired Dai Dien to kill Tu Dao Hanh's father in the story about Tu Dao Hanh, suggesting that he may have been a rival of the Sung Hien Marquis, with whom Tu Dao Hanh was allied. That he was easily angered and quick to act suggests a man of definite views who was likely to have had a stake in the naming of the crown prince. Perhaps the deaths of the two antagonists of 1104 removed options with which Lady Y Lan had involved herself but that were opposed by other members of the Ly family, in particular the Sung Hien Marquis and others who were willing that his son, Ly Duong Hoan, be made crown prince.

One option that was ostensibly taken seriously was Giac Hoang, the strange boy who came from outside the royal family. Lady Y Lan, who came to the court as an outsider and who resorted to mass murder to push her way into the Ly aristocracy, may have favored Giac Hoang or others like him. Her well-known devotion to Buddhism may have led her to consider spiritual achievement superior to a royal bloodline in selecting the next king.

A dominant theme during the remaining history of the Ly dynasty, which lasted for another century, was a struggle to draw a boundary around the royal family to distinguish those eligible to be king from those who were not. Except for the childless Ly Can Duc, the practice of multiple queens, along with hosts of royal concubines, produced several potential kings in every generation. The political logic of the Ly experiment in government was based on marriage alliances with other powerful families who provided queens, the potential mothers of kings. Ly Nhat Ton had resorted to designating the son of a peasant girl as his heir. This was accepted because there was no other plausible alternative, but Ly Dao Thanh's effort to maintain the fiction of Ly Can Duc's adoption into the clan of the senior queen succumbed to Lady Y Lan's homicidal ambition.

Four decades later, Ly Can Duc, apparently under the influence of Lady Y Lan, wished to make Giac Hoang the crown prince. Giac Hoang came as if having sprung from the sea, without a mother or any family at all. He did not threaten Lady Y Lan's dominant position among the palace women. Senior Ly noblemen foiled this scheme, and five of them offered their sons for consideration instead. Ly Duong Hoan was chosen from among these five Ly offspring just three months after Lady Y Lan's death. His mother, Do Thanh Anh, would be a strong influence in the palace until her death in 1147. Her kinsman, Do Anh Vu, would dominate the court from the late 1130s until his death in 1159.

Do Anh Vu and To Hien Thanh

Just as his father had sought to re-enact his grandfather's expedition to Champa after designating him as crown prince in the 1060s, Ly Can Duc, after his mother's death and the settling of the succession question, showed an uncharacteristic exuberance by personally leading an army in the field for the first time in his life. In 1119, after great preparation and accompanied by signs and wonders, Ly Can Duc led his soldiers to attack people in the mountains surrounded on three sides by the great curve in the Da River, a major affluent of the Red River, in the modern province of Hoa Binh. In his proclamation announcing the expedition, Ly Can Duc charged the leader of these people with raiding, plundering, and ignoring royal authority. The object of the expedition was around seventy kilometers west of Thang Long, twice that distance by boat upriver. The campaign was a great success.

One man who may have taken the opportunity of this expedition to demonstrate his abilities to the king and thereby advance his status at court was Le Ba Ngoc. He first appears in records as a palace eunuch in 1114. He had risen to a mid-level position by 1118, at which time he was demoted to a clerical post under unrecorded circumstances. Beginning in 1121, he received a series of promotions and advanced rapidly in rank. In 1125, he led an army against Nung rebels in Cao Bang and thereafter became the ranking military commander. At the time of Ly Can Duc's death in 1127, he was entrusted with guarding the palace and ensuring Ly Duong Hoan's accession. He was the dominant figure at court until his death in 1135.

Le Ba Ngoc's success came from insinuating himself into the family of the crown prince's mother, Do Thanh Anh, by adopting as his son one of her kinsmen named Do Anh Vu. According to written records, Do Anh Vu was a brother of Do Thanh Anh, but inscriptional evidence suggests that he was more likely her cousin. In 1124, at the age of 10, Do Anh Vu was brought to live at the court and became a companion of the crown prince Ly Duong Hoan, who was two years younger than he. Do Anh Vu was reportedly a handsome and lively lad skilled in singing, dancing, and playing games.

The court did not linger in mourning after Ly Can Duc's death. After only twenty-two days, the new 11-year-old king began to hold court on the same day that he witnessed the palace women being burned on Ly Can Duc's funeral pyre.

This sweeping away of women in the palace put a definite end to the regime of Lady Y Lan, who had initiated her control of the palace by doing away with women of aristocratic status. Royal women and highborn women of families at court now regained control of the inner palace.

One of Ly Duong Hoan's first acts was to elevate his mother to the rank of queen mother and to eliminate tax obligations for one hundred members of her family. Within two months, two royal consorts were designated. One was from the royal family and was named queen. The other was a daughter of Le Ba Ngoc's nephew and was given a lower rank. The hierarchy of palace women was the dynasty's spine. In 1131, even their distinctive hairstyle was forbidden to other women in the kingdom.

One of the men sent to announce Ly Can Duc's death to the parents of the new king was Do Thien. The only other surviving information about this man is that he wrote a book of history. The book has not survived, but it was cited in a fourteenth-century compilation for several stories that celebrate historical figures famous for loyal service to their sovereigns, a theme that Le Ba Ngoc and Do Anh Vu cultivated to justify their exercise of power in Do Thien's time.

Ly Duong Hoan's relatively short reign (1127–1138) was a time of major change in the strategic environment of the region. In the 1120s, the Song dynasty was driven from northern China by the Jin dynasty, which originated in Manchuria and was led by people called Jurchen, ancestors of the Manchus who conquered China in the seventeenth century. Thereafter, the Southern Song dynasty was ruled from Hangzhou in south-central China. Constantly threatened by its northern neighbor, Southern Song was a relatively weak dynasty that posed little potential threat to Thang Long. This significant reduction in pressure on the northern border is an underlying reason why Ly dynastic politics became increasingly diffuse and troubled during the twelfth century. The fate of the Ly dynasty was closely connected to the fortunes of Southern Song, for the necessity to maintain strong leadership at the Ly court faded away along with the sense of danger from the north.

On the other hand, this was in the time of the greatest conqueror to rule the Khmer kingdom of Angkor, Suryavarman II, whose reign began in 1113 and lasted into the 1150s. During much of this time, Suryavarman II dominated the Chams, and allied Khmer and Cham armies attacked across Thang Long's southern border in 1128, in 1133, in 1135, and in 1137. Each time, Viet armies mobilized and successfully repelled the invaders. The border nevertheless remained unstable for many years with chronic raids, Cham princes seeking asylum, and Cham slave merchants seizing local people to sell at Angkor.

In 1138, Ly Duong Hoan lay on his deathbed at the age of 22. It is recorded simply that he was "unwell." Two years earlier he had suffered a severe illness that resisted all cures until he was miraculously made well by a monk named Minh Khong who had been the favorite disciple of Tu Dao Hanh. According to the story, Tu Dao Hanh had forewarned his disciple that after he was reincarnated as the next king he would be ill, and he asked that Minh Khong cure him when that came to pass. According to an inscription, Ly Duong Hoan's fatal illness began in 1137. Apparently, the king had a weak constitution and was not expected to live long.

Ly Duong Hoan had three sons, aged 6, 2, and 1. He intended that his eldest son should succeed him, and the implications of this for the family and allies of that son's mother are likely to have been an increasingly important factor in court politics. However, on his deathbed he was visited by three of his wives who pled with him to designate his second son instead because the mother of his eldest son was of a lower status than the mother of his second son, being only a concubine, and she would become jealous and bring harm to them if her son were made king. Here we see the shadow of Lady Y Lan's murderous rampage in 1073. The dying king acknowledged the justice of their appeal and accordingly named his second son, Ly Thien To, as his heir. One of the three wives, Le Cam Thanh, was Ly Thien To's mother. She was from a high-ranking family claiming paternal descent from Le Hoan and maternal descent from the Ly royal family.

When Ly Duong Hoan died, Do Anh Vu immediately stood up to exercise actual power in the name of the child king, Ly Thien To. Do Anh Vu became the lover of Le Cam Thanh, Ly Duong Hoan's widow and Ly Thien To's mother, and he stood at the head of the court for the next two decades. Do Anh Vu had accompanied an army sent in 1135 to expel Cham and Khmer invaders on the southern border, and his career shows close attention to military affairs. A major challenge to his ascendance at Thang Long materialized within a year of Ly Duong Hoan's death. In 1139, a man named Than Loi, identified in Vietnamese records as a sorcerer, appeared in the northern mountains. He posed as an abandoned son of Ly Can Duc and laid claim to the throne, proclaiming himself king. Chinese records tell of a man at this time claiming to be the son of a concubine rejected by Ly Can Duc. He asked the Southern Song for assistance but the emperor refused to be involved. Than Loi gained a reputation for supernatural powers and gathered a large following from the lowlands as well as from the border regions and the mountains. He concentrated his forces in the foothills of modern Thai Nguyen Province about seventy kilometers north of Thang Long, and defeated all armies sent against him.

When Than Loi marched against Thang Long, Do Anh Vu personally led an army out to attack him. Than Loi suffered a crushing defeat and escaped back north to the mountains to assemble new forces. After displaying the heads of dead rebels for many kilometers along the roads north of Thang Long, Do Anh

Vu marched out to attack Than Loi along the upstream of the Cau River, in modern Thai Nguyen Province. He captured two thousand of Than Loi's followers, but Than Loi fled toward the Song border. One of Do Anh Vu's lieutenants, To Hien Thanh, pursued Than Loi and captured him in modern Lang Son Province. Than Loi and his most prominent followers were beheaded in Thang Long. Other captives received various punishments depending upon the measure of guilt assigned to them. They all received pardons a year later.

The Than Loi episode suggests rather serious disaffection with the Thang Long court. What it has in common with previous and later moves against the dynastic regime is that it originated from outside the circle of royal blood and of those who posed as guardians of that circle. The rupture of that circle when Lady Y Lan swept out the highborn women of the palace in 1073 was a haunting memory for later generations of nobles. The Ly dynasty was based on alliances of aristocratic families, among which the Ly were preeminent. But over time, in the absence of strong adult kings, competition among these families for precedence at the Ly court played out among the palace women following the vicissitudes of giving birth to an heir, and this gradually began to pull the dynastic system apart.

Meanwhile, men like Do Anh Vu guarded access to the palace and supervised the government. The campaign against Than Loi is the first mention of To Hien Thanh in the records. To Hien Thanh, probably a kinsman of Do Anh Vu's wife, who was from the To family, was Do Anh Vu's protégé and most trusted assistant. After Do Anh Vu's death in 1159, To Hien Thanh stepped into the role of guarding the dynasty for another twenty years, until his death in 1179.

Four laws proclaimed in 1141 give a glimpse into the rural economy. They show that the royal court was concerned with disputes over the ownership of fields, orchards, and ponds. The laws specified the difference between a mortgage and a bill of sale; a mortgage could be redeemed or litigated under certain conditions but a bill of sale was final. They also protected the ownership rights of people bringing abandoned fields or orchards under cultivation for one year without anyone disputing their claim. Anyone disputing ownership of fields or ponds with weapons and killing or injuring another person lost any claim to the disputed property. Violation of these laws earned eighty strokes of the rod.

These laws do not have any discernible applicability to the relatively stable regime of large ecclesiastical and aristocratic estates that were typical of the Ly dynasty and that dominated the rural economy of the Red River plain from the tenth century into the early thirteenth century. However, we know that in the twelfth century lands along the coast where the Red River meets the sea were being desalinized and brought under cultivation. This is the modern province of Thai Binh where in the early thirteenth century the Tran family rose up to penetrate the system of Ly politics and found a new dynasty. Do Anh Vu's family estates were located on the Thai Binh frontier downriver from Thang Long, and he was surely interested in promoting the extension of agriculture into the tidelands.

The 1141 laws were concerned with buying and selling lands and with litigating disputes over land ownership, problems typical of an emerging rural economy on an expanding agricultural frontier, which is what Thai Binh was at that time. In 1144, another law was published specifying that anyone relying upon family power and influence in a dispute over fields, ponds, and property was subject to eighty strokes. Judicial concern then shifted from disputants to corruption, for in the following year yet another edict prescribed sixty strokes for judges who unlawfully used coercion in settling litigation.

Economic expansion along the coast at this time attracted foreign trade. In 1149, merchant ships from Java and what is modern Thailand arrived asking to trade. A seaport was established at Van Don, on what today is called Quan Lan Island off the coast north of the Red River plain, where local products were exchanged for goods from overseas. Merchants from Southern Song were prominent at Van Don, which became part of a thriving trade route from China down the coast to what is now Thailand, Sumatra, and Java, with connections to islands further east and to India in the west. Van Don was thereafter an important entrepôt for more than three centuries.

Do Anh Vu was particularly concerned with military authority and the loyalty of the palace guard, for this was his main defense against enemies both in the countryside and at court. In 1143 he instituted a new regime of training and discipline for the army. As the Than Loi affair demonstrated, without a strong adult king, the Ly court was vulnerable to pretenders.

In 1144, a man from Song crossed into the border province of Cao Bang and proclaimed that he had received an imperial mandate to govern An Nam. He attracted a large following from the peoples in the mountains and along the border. Song border officials asked Thang Long to capture and extradite him. A Viet army attacked the rebels and captured many followers of the imposter, who escaped back into Song territory where he and his entourage were captured by Song border guards. Recognizing five of those captured as rebel chieftains owing allegiance to the Ly, Song officials returned them to Thang Long for justice. The Sino-Vietnamese border had become a relatively well-policed frontier with the Song and Ly courts cooperating to maintain order.

A more immediate danger to Do Anh Vu was disaffection in the palace guard, for as the young king, Ly Thien To, grew from childhood to adolescence he became a focus of loyalty for those who were alienated from Do Anh Vu. In 1145, an edict specified that in selecting men to fill vacancies in the palace guard, local officers were to select men from large, powerful families and were not to select orphans. The reason for this was that someone without a family would be more susceptible to a conspiracy than someone with a prominent family to guarantee his loyalty. Furthermore, the families indicated here were aristocratic allies of Do Anh Vu.

Nevertheless, many at court detested Do Anh Vu's adultery with the queen mother. The *Complete Book of the History of Great Viet* records his reputation for cruelty and his arrogance in "sitting as emperor in the hall of audience while belligerently daring anyone to oppose him." It also records that "servants, officials, and officers . . ." gestured with their chins and exchanged glances; they all looked askance at what was happening but dared say nothing." Perhaps barriers to Do Anh Vu's enemies were removed by the deaths, in the mid 1140s, of Do Anh Vu's kinswoman, the queen dowager, and of Mau Du Do, an influential official at court who had supported both Le Ba Ngoc and Do Anh Vu since the death of Ly Can Duc nearly twenty years before.

In 1149, a conspiracy broke out in the palace guard, which imprisoned Do Anh Vu and appealed to the young king. Do Anh Vu's enemies temporarily gained control of the court and he was exiled to a village outside of Thang Long. Within a short time, however, the queen mother, Le Cam Thanh, had mobilized her allies to secure his return to court. Do Anh Vu organized and trained a personal guard of five hundred men and used it to seize his enemies and have them killed. After these events, the young king reportedly fell ill and regained his health only after Do Anh Vu re-enacted a famous episode from the life of the Duke of Zhou, celebrated in Confucian texts as the model for those ruling on behalf of young kings, in which he prayed that the king's illness be placed upon himself. What lay behind the performance of this historical cliché is unknown, but Ly Thien To remained docile for the rest of his life.

In 1150, the daughter of a paternal cousin of Do Anh Vu named Do Thuy Chau became a queen of Ly Thien To and during the next several years gave birth to several sons, thus ensuring the continued ascendance of Do Anh Vu and his family at court. Opponents of Do Anh Vu nevertheless tried once more to bring him down.

In early 1159, an envoy returned from the Song court and reported the practice of a box being placed in the palace courtyard to receive anonymous messages addressed to the Song emperor. He requested that this practice be instituted at Thang Long, and the king agreed. After a month, the box was opened and a message was found that accused Do Anh Vu of plotting to seize the throne. Do Anh Vu said that this was surely the work of the person who had suggested to emplace the box, and so the king exiled that person to an outpost in the mountains where he was compelled to drink poison. Perhaps this last effort of Do Anh Vu's enemies was emboldened by intimations of his mortality, for within a few months of this episode, Do Anh Vu died. He was buried with great honors.

To Hien Thanh, his trusted assistant and wife's kinsman, immediately picked up the reins of government.

Later historians condemned Do Anh Vu for his adultery with the queen mother, but they evaluated To Hien Thanh highly, praising his principled leadership and incorruptibility. To Hien Thanh maintained the level of leadership established by Do Anh Vu in campaigning successfully against Champa and suppressing rebels to protect the borders and maintain the peace. In his time there were literary exams to select civil and military officials, and he discouraged the proliferation of palace eunuchs by forbidding self-castration; these measures were litmus-test issues for Confucian historians in later centuries. Furthermore, in 1174, Thang Long achieved a major diplomatic success when Viet envoys persuaded the Song emperor, against the arguments of some of his advisors, to promote the status of the Ly king in the imperial hierarchy of vassalage from King of Giao Chi Prefecture, the title first given to Dinh Bo Linh, to King of An Nam Kingdom.

What earned To Hien Thanh his greatest appreciation from later historians was his resistance to the schemes of the queen mother, Le Cam Thanh, during the royal succession of 1175. As the ranking woman at court, she commanded considerable authority. When, in 1149, the palace guard had imprisoned her lover, Do Anh Vu, she bribed his jailors and returned him to power. In the early 1170s, the crown prince, Ly Long Xuong, was around 20 years old. Information about his mother has not survived, but the queen mother had fixed her hopes on him, and she exercised a strong influence over him. According to what has been recorded, her love of intrigue blighted Ly Long Xuong's prospects because she underestimated To Hien Thanh's loyalty to the king, Ly Thien To, her son.

The king grew to hate the crown prince because the youth made a point of having affairs with all of his favorite women. The queen mother, for reasons not recorded, took exception to a particular favorite of the king named Lady Tu and wanted to alienate the king from her. To this end, she secretly introduced Ly Long Xuong into Lady Tu's chamber and endeavored to have the lady fall in love with the prince, thinking that this would cause the king to abandon her. When Lady Tu told the king about this, the king angrily demoted Ly Long Xuong and replaced him as crown prince with Ly Long Trat, who was less than 2 years old. This occurred in 1174.

The queen mother was not reconciled to this turn of events, and, when the king died a year later, she repeatedly tried to put Ly Long Xuong on the throne, first by bribing To Hien Thanh, then by banqueting court officials, and finally by trying to bring Ly Long Xuong into the palace with an entourage of his followers. To Hien Thanh stood fast to the dead king's decision and refused all bribes. The court officials all remained loyal to him and ignored the queen mother's appeal. When Ly Long Xuong attempted to enter the royal compound, court officials barred the way and advised him that, if he did not desist, the palace guard would be called. The queen mother did not cease her conspiracies on Ly Long Xuong's behalf until 1182, after he had become a leader of bandits. She lived to a fine old age, dying in 1200.

To Hien Thanh's presumed loyalty to the wishes of Ly Thien To in protecting the accession of Ly Long Trat was probably not as important as his loyalty to the network of friends and associates that he inherited from Do Anh Vu. The mother of the child who was put on the throne by To Hien Thanh in 1175, the new queen mother, was Do Thuy Chau, a kinswoman of Do Anh Vu. Her brother Do Anh Di became second-in-command to To Hien Thanh.

When To Hien Thanh died in 1179, Do Anh Di succeeded him as the dominant person at court. He did not have the moral stature of To Hien Thanh, who apparently persuaded others with appeals to what was thought to be correct. Instead, he instilled in others a fear of him personally, which led to a breakdown in government functions and became the object of public jokes made onstage at the Thang Long opera. Grim humor during his ascendancy may have been exacerbated by a famine in 1181 that reportedly carried away more than half the population.

Perhaps because of the lowering of respect for authority after the death of To Hien Thanh, there was a particular emphasis on education and the next generation of leaders, starting with the small king. Within weeks of To Hien Thanh's death, the king, Ly Long Trat, and his mother observed children of temple officials competing to read a Buddhist sutra and a competition of lads in poetry and mathematics. They also attended an examination in which children of Buddhists, Confucians, and Daoists competed in writing poetry and rhyming prose and were tested on their knowledge of classical books, moral principles, and practical sciences such as making calculations and organizing transportation. A course of instruction was instituted for the king and a program of public education was begun to teach the people about filial piety and loyalty to rulers. In 1185, an exam of those 15 and older with knowledge of poetry and history resulted in selecting thirty for further study. These exams were presumably held to identify talent for assignments at court, but there is no information about people coming through these exams occupying positions of significance. Despite these educational activities, later historians viewed Ly Long Trat as a hopeless playboy with no interest in government, and they dated the beginning of the collapse of the Ly dynasty from this time.

Collapse of the Ly dynasty

After Do Anh Di's death in 1188, his assistant Ngo Ly Tin attempted to direct affairs but became the object of public humor instead. Ngo Ly Tin was a soldier who rose to prominence in the early 1180s, first by suppressing the banditry that had reached the level of rebellion under the leadership of the disgraced crown prince Ly Long Xuong, and then by leading an expedition into the mountains of modern Laos. In 1189, the court was in some disarray due to the influence of Mac Hien Tich, who was the lover of the queen mother, Do Thuy Chau. Court officials obtained an order from the 16-year-old king for Ngo Ly Tin and another official to investigate Mac Hien Tich, but these two were afraid of him and nothing was done. A song was sung in the streets of Thang Long comparing the two ineffectual men to a pair of famous idiots in the city at that time.

The situation changed rapidly in 1190, beginning with the death of the queen mother. Bereft of her protection, Mac Hien Tich was exiled to a distant outpost in the mountains. Within a few months Ngo Ly Tin died and was succeeded by Dam Di Mong. Dam Di Mong was a kinsman of a general whose daughter had entered the palace in 1186 and who in 1194 gave birth to Ly Sam, the last Ly king. Dam Di Mong was the leading figure at court for the next quarter-century. Later historians described him as uneducated, without guile, lacking backbone, and indecisive.

This characterization of Dam Di Mong might encourage an identification with the palace guard officer of the same name who in the coup of 1150 had prevented his fellows from killing Do Anh Vu immediately upon arresting him, arguing that they should follow proper procedure. If indeed this was the same person then he must have lived to a very old age. Dam Di Mong never exercised the dominant position held by Le Ba Ngoc, Do Anh Vu, To Hien Thanh, or even Do Anh Di. This was not simply due to his lack of personal quality. It was also due to the breakdown of the Ly political system, based initially on the personal charisma of kings and then increasingly on the swords of the families of aristocratic women brought into the palace.

Lady Y Lan's challenge to this system was mitigated by the emergency of the Song War, but her dominant influence in the palace and Ly Can Duc's lack of an heir froze any practical consideration of the future of the dynasty for over forty years. By the time of her death, Ly nobles had mobilized a consensus about how to proceed. However, without strong adult kings, able and ruthless men with high connections in the hierarchy of palace women became the leaders of the dynasty. Any powerful family could aspire to have their women enter the palace and give birth to a king, and the competition for this opportunity gradually superseded attention to the actual business of governing. Dam Di Mong was the first strongman to attain pre-eminence on the expectation of his kinswoman giving birth to a prince rather than on the actual birth of such a prince. The prejudice in favor of child kings, easily controlled by their adult mentors, had made this increasingly likely as time passed. During Dam Di Mong's era, the Ly court disintegrated into open warfare among powerful families based in various regions of the Red River plain.

In the 1190s, Dam Di Mong appeared to demonstrate a certain level of energy putting down rebellions in the southern provinces and in the region just north-west of Thang Long. He also inspected the performance of officials to decide whether they should be promoted or demoted, and exams were held on the "three religions" of the Buddhists, the Confucians, and the Daoists and to select scholars to teach the king. Nevertheless, he perceived that the authority of the court was fading, and he decided that the Buddhist temple population had become too large and unresponsive to the monarchy. In 1198, Dam Di Mong blamed the Buddhist monks for subverting public morality. He told the king that monks were as numerous as the working population, flocking together in groups to indulge in drunken orgies, sleeping during the day and carousing all night. He accordingly gathered the monks and defrocked most of them, tattooing their hands to permanently mark them.

Dam Di Mong's purge of the monks did not stop the spread of disorder. That same year, 1198, rebellion again broke out in Nghe An led by someone claiming to be a descendent of Dinh Bo Linh. This rebellion was suppressed, but the following year floods and famine spread over the land, and in 1200 the court was distributing food to the starving. In 1202 an official in charge of the monks addressed the king in response to the popularity of Cham music at court, which was sad and mournful, making listeners weep with emotion. He quoted from a classical text, "Preface to the Odes," about how the sounds of a disordered kingdom are plaintive, lamenting, angry, and resentful. He then described the present time: "The people rebel, the kingdom is in distress, the ruler pursues pleasure without limit, government is in a state of anarchy, the hearts of the people are perverted." His conclusion was that the current fashion in court music was "an omen of ruin."

The following year, the 30-year-old king, Ly Long Trat, unimpressed by the "omen of ruin," embarked on a vast project to build a complex of more than ten palaces, some with upper stories and towers, surrounded by ponds and gardens. For the next three years he entertained himself there, playing games and carousing with his eunuchs, women, and favorites. To pay for these pleasures, he opened his hand to bribes, which led to royal decisions being made by the highest bidder. Gangs of robbers sprang up and spread through the countryside, opening the way for the ambitions of rebel leaders. Construction of the palaces caused much distress among the people. A bird built a nest in an uncompleted tower and was viewed by some as an evil omen, but a eunuch persuaded the king that it was a good omen. Dam Di Mong's efforts to maintain some modicum of order in the kingdom were to no avail. At one point, Dam Di Mong whipped another official in an altercation over the construction schedule and was publicly denounced to the king. This led to a brief period of symbolic demotion for Dam Di Mong to appease his enemies.

An episode on the Cham frontier is an indication of how things had changed from previous eras when Ly armies kept a close border watch. A Cham prince appeared with several hundred armed men in some two hundred boats on the coast of modern Ha Tinh Province, just north of the border. He claimed to be fleeing from enemies in his own kingdom and had come to ask for help. Dam Di Mong went south to investigate. Fearing that "an anthill can break a dike," he advised local officers to beware the strangers and to maintain guard against them. The local officers scoffed at his caution and asked how there could be anything to fear from people fleeing trouble. Angered by their attitude, Dam Di Mong left them to their own devices and returned to Thang Long. Belatedly, the local officers began to fear treachery and planned to attack the Chams. Hearing of this, the Cham prince struck first, ambushing and defeating local forces, killing the local leaders, and plundering the region before returning south.

A rebellion broke out at Hoa Lu and armies sent against it were repeatedly defeated. Dam Di Mong built a defensive wall to contain the rebels and mobilized expert archers from the northern uplands to lead an attack, all to no avail. By 1207, two other major rebellions had also broken out, one based at modern Son Tay, west of Thang Long, and one at modern Hai Duong, east of Thang Long. Ly Long Trat was sufficiently sobered by the situation that he allowed an edict to be published apologizing for his misrule, promising to "make a new beginning with the people," and saying that all the land and merchandise that had been confiscated by officials would be returned.

In a more prosaic vein, Dam Di Mong and Pham Binh Di, the eunuch who had erased concern about the bird's nest in 1203, marched against the most threatening rebellion, led by Doan Thuong, the leader of Hong Province in the region of modern Hai Duong, fifty kilometers east of Thang Long. As the king's men approached, Doan Thuong requested that he be allowed to surrender to Pham Du, a prominent man in Khoai Province, a neighboring locality to the southwest. Money was passed from Doan Thuong via Pham Du to Ly Long Trat, who consequently ordered Dam Di Mong and Pham Binh Di to withdraw their troops. As a result of this, Pham Binh Di acquired an intense hatred of Pham Du for outwitting him in the game of royal sycophancy.

Pham Binh Di was the leader of Dang Province, fifty kilometers down the Red River from Thang Long at modern Hung Yen, southwest of Khoai, which was the bailiwick of Pham Du. The feud between these two men was about access to the king, which had to do with streams of money. Pham Binh Di had gained access to the palace through castration. Despite efforts to ban the practice, during the Ly dynasty, men submitted to self-castration as a way to get into the palace. Ly Thuong Kiet is only the most famous of such cases. Sometimes, as with Pham Binh Di, these men had wives and children and were prominent leaders in their localities. Pham Du was apparently not a eunuch, but he was very successful in gaining the king's ear because of the wealth he channeled to the king. It was the manner in which he gained his wealth that offered Pham Binh Di an opportunity to openly oppose him. The competition of these two men for the king's favor was the catalyst for an outbreak of violence that pulled the Ly court apart and brought Ly Long Trat's reign to an end.

The court was endeavoring to recruit soldiers to fight the increasing numbers of rebels and bandits. When the king appointed Pham Du to be in charge of the southern border region in modern Nghe An and Ha Tinh, Pham Du requested and received the king's permission to recruit an army of personal soldiers. Pham Du quickly became a notorious robber baron and his soldiers became expert bandits. This encouraged an outbreak of banditry and rebellion that paralyzed communications and transportation in the kingdom. Pham Du organized a network of marauders allied with Doan Thuong in Hong.

In 1208, amidst floods and famine, Pham Binh Di received a royal commission to attack Pham Du's allies south and east of Thang Long. Pham Du returned from the southern border and joined with Doan Thuong against Pham Binh Di. After months of fighting and repeated setbacks, Pham Binh Di finally defeated Pham Du in 1209 and proceeded to inventory and confiscate or destroy all of Pham Du's considerable property. However, when he went to report to the king, Pham Binh Di was detained under arrest in a palace, for Pham Du had arrived before him and brought the king to his side. Hearing of this, Pham Binh Di's general Quach Boc broke down a gate into the palace intending to rescue his leader. But before he could do so, Pham Du slew Pham Binh Di. Pham Du and the king fled as Quach Boc went on a rampage, retrieving Pham Binh Di's corpse and taking the 15-year-old crown prince Ly Sam, along with his younger brother, his mother, and his two sisters, before hastening downriver for refuge with allies of Pham Binh Di.

The most powerful of Pham Binh Di's allies was Tran Ly, grandson of a man named Tran Kinh, who had come from Fujian Province in China. Tran Kinh had arrived when the opening of new lands and a quickening of trade with Southern Song and Southeast Asia had stimulated an expanding economy, attracting people with an eye for opportunity to the Red River's coastal region. Tran Kinh reportedly started out as a fisherman, but by the time of Tran Ly the family owned vast estates, commanded soldiers, and dominated the coastal region of the Red River. Tran Ly had married into the To family, and his wife's brother, To Trung Tu, was a powerful ally; whether these people were related to To Hien Thanh is not known, but such would be a plausible conjecture. Tran Ly had three talented adult sons, Tran Thua, Tran Tu Khanh, and Tran Thu Do, all of whom would be prominent in coming events. Another of his assets was daughters, potential mothers of kings.

The arrival of Quach Boc with the crown prince suddenly expanded the horizon of Tran Ly and To Trung Tu. Dam Di Mong, along with other members of the court appeared on the scene, following the winds blowing his kinswoman, the mother of Crown Prince Ly Sam. In a series of events orchestrated by To Trung Tu, Ly Sam and a daughter of Tran Ly, later known as Thuan Trinh, were married, and Ly Sam was proclaimed king.

Meanwhile, Ly Long Trat had rallied his followers and regained Thang Long. He sent Pham Du to join with Doan Thuong to attack Tran Ly and To Trung Tu. Pham Du, distracted by a princess, missed his pre-arranged rendezvous with Doan Thuong and was captured by men who sent him to Tran Ly, who killed him. Tran Tu Khanh, Tran Ly's second son, then mobilized Tran and allied forces and attempted to seize control of the capital, but a sudden storm scattered his boats and he lost over three hundred men to Thang Long's defenders.

After this, those who had gathered with Tran Ly and To Trung Tu to make Ly Sam king were dismayed, and many crept back to Thang Long, including Dam Di Mong, who endured a public rebuke, but nothing more than that, for his lack of loyalty to the king. In 1210, Ly Sam returned to Thang Long as the crown prince, leaving his Tran wife behind. Soon after, bandits killed Tran Ly, and, shortly after that, the king fell sick and died. When a clique of warlords opposed the accession of Ly Sam, To Trung Tu attacked and defeated them and was accordingly given a high rank at court by the new king. Of course, Dam Di Mong was given the leading position at court, now that his kinswoman was indeed the queen mother.

There followed six years of intrigue and fighting. Beneath the surface of seemingly random violence was a consideration that had become the basic principle of Ly dynastic politics and that motivated the combatants. It was a struggle to the death for the possibility of one's kinswoman becoming the mother of a king. The Tran had struck first with the marriage of Ly Sam and Thuan Trinh, but the queen mother was determined not to allow the Tran clan to gain a foothold in the palace. Her efforts to do away with Thuan Trinh would not reach the level of homicidal fury until 1216 when a pregnancy signaled the potential imminence of a crown prince's birth and moved Ly Sam to the most decisive act of his life. Until then, the hopes and fears of many men led them from battlefield to battlefield. Without a strong decisive king or a dominant court master, there was nothing for the men of the kingdom but to fight the matter out among themselves.

It was not until To Trung Tu had gained a strong position at court in the spring of 1211 that the Tran sent Ly Sam's wife to Thang Long. However, within a few weeks, To Trung Tu was dead, struck down by the husband of a princess with whom he was having an affair. The queen mother then shifted the influence of the court behind the most formidable enemy of the Tran, Doan Thuong in Hong, who had been charting his own course since 1207.

Tran Tu Khanh, Queen Thuan Trinh's brother, accordingly attacked Hong. The fighting was long and bitter. At one point Tran Tu Khanh broke the dikes and flooded large parts of Hong. At another point, Doan Thuong was invited to Thang Long where he was feted and granted high titles. After a significant victory, Tran Tu Khanh arrived at the capital hoping that his battlefield deeds would translate into access to the court, but the queen mother refused him entry. To emphasize her point, she had Thuan Trinh demoted in the hierarchy of palace women. Tran Tu Khanh saw nowhere to go but back to the battlefield. The fighting continued through 1212. Ly Sam was so discouraged that he had to be talked out of retiring to a monastery. In early 1213, royal armies were sent to attack Tran Tu Khanh. The queen mother plotted to seize Tran Tu Khanh's mother, matriarch of the To family, who had entered the palace when her brother To Trung Tu had been ascendant. Tran spies heard of it and Lady To escaped downriver.

Dam Di Mong raised armies and joined Doan Thuong against Tran Tu Khanh. Tran Tu Khanh fended them off and even captured Nguyen Non, the Ly general in charge of a region centered on the modern city of Bac Ninh, thirty-five kilometers northeast of Thang Long. Nguyen Non's bold demeanor and lack of fear were so impressive that Tran Tu Khanh made him a son-in-law and gave him a command. However, within a year, Nguyen Non became the most implacable enemy of the Tran family, greatly complicating its ambitions.

The year 1214 began with an all-out attack on Thang Long orchestrated by Tran Tu Khanh. Defeated everywhere, Ly Sam and his mother fled to Lang Son on the northern border, and the last information recorded about Dam Di Mong is his departure to seek help from Doan Thuong. Doan Thuong could do nothing, for Tran Thu Do, the third Tran brother, had just ravaged his home province of Hong. Tran Tu Khanh sent messengers to Lang Son inviting the king back to Thang Long. The queen mother said no. She and the king, abandoned by all their followers except for around thirty guardsmen, wandered through the mountains waiting for a turn in events.

Tran Tu Khanh, giving up on Ly Sam and his intransigent mother, tried to raise another prince to the throne in Thang Long, but this merely provoked Nguyen Non at Bac Ninh and others to turn against him. In exasperation he plundered and burned the palaces. The king and queen mother then emerged to place themselves under the protection of Nguyen Non. By the time Nguyen Non fought his way into Thang Long, the entire city had been looted and burned to ashes by Tran Tu Khanh. Thang Long having become a battlefield, the king and his mother took residence in a thatched house built beside a shrine outside the city.

Fighting between Tran Tu Khanh and Nguyen Non went back and forth through 1215 with Tran Tu Khanh facing upstream, Nguyen Non facing downstream, and Thang Long the center of attention. With the king and queen mother was the residue of the Ly court, noblemen susceptible to the spies and bribes of both sides. At one point, Ly Sam shaved his head to be a monk, but the press of events and the appeals of his entourage did not allow him that luxury. A thatched palace was built on the western edge of Thang Long and by early 1216 Ly Sam and the queen mother were holding court. The queen mother had become a partisan of Nguyen Non while Ly Sam was pulled toward reconciliation with the Tran under the influence of his wife. Tran Tu Khanh endeavored to show a friendly face by returning some of the royal loot he had taken. In spring 1216, Ly Sam asked Tran Tu Khanh's help against an obstreperous nobleman who was resisting his authority, and Tran Tu Khanh obligingly attacked the man, who fled to Nguyen Non.

The most fateful event at this time was that Thuan Trinh, Ly Sam's Tran wife, was pregnant, and the queen mother wanted to do away with her. The queen mother commanded Thuan Trinh to commit suicide, but Ly Sam intervened. She sent poisoned food to Thuan Trinh, but Ly Sam kept his wife with him constantly and had her eat only from his own bowl. The queen mother's homicidal schemes finally alienated Ly Sam from her. What began as a turning point in the mind of Ly Sam became a turning point in the morass of violence that had engulfed the Ly dynasty. When the queen mother sent a draught of poison with servants instructed to force Thuan Trinh to drink it, Ly Sam stopped them, and that night he took his wife and sought refuge with the soldiers of Tran Tu Khanh stationed near the palace. The 22-year-old king and his wife were quickly passed along up the chain of command to be welcomed with great joy by Tran Tu Khanh at his headquarters downriver from Thang Long. The queen mother found refuge with Nguyen Non.

Ly Sam's flight from Thang Long in the summer of 1216 violated the principle that kings obeyed and belonged with their mothers, which had governed the Ly court since the time of Lady Y Lan. This principle had become increasingly disconnected from actual events, despite its hold on the minds of the politically alert. Without his mother and her men, Ly Sam would either have to be a leader in the mould of the first three Ly kings or he would have to disappear. He was not a leader. His one decisive act had come out of desperation, at best, not conviction. He was now in the hands of the men who led his wife's family.

If one is inclined to favor the stereotypes of Ly Sam as irresolute and of Tran Tu Khanh as implacable, it might be tempting to imagine that the story of Ly Sam seeking refuge with the Tran to protect his wife was conjured by Tran historians to sanitize some less romantic event. In that case, one might conjecture that Tran agents forcibly took Ly Sam captive while rescuing one of their women, possibly pregnant with a future king, from homicidal schemes. Such might be thought to be more in keeping with the general atmosphere of the times as recorded in surviving annals. However, without further information, such would also be to choose the fatalism of violence over the possibility of the human spirit breaking out in unexpected ways. Whatever was going through the mind of Ly Sam as he and Thuan Trinh hastened through the night, be it a naïve sense of escape or a despairing sense of entrapment, the remaining ten years of his life were an agony of powerlessness as he watched the men of his wife's family fashion a new regime.

3 THE TRAN DYNASTY

Tran Thu Do

The Ly family was based in the upper plains of the Red River where they enjoyed direct control of what was then the agricultural core of the country. The Tran family viewed matters from the perspective of the coast, which by the mid twelfth century had become part of a lively network of foreign trade stimulated by the economy of Southern Song. The port of Van Don was a gathering place for merchants and travelers from the coasts of southern China and elsewhere. Here, local products found a market and foreign goods were available. Wealth accumulated in the hands of producers, traders, officials, and those who were politically and militarily ascendant, namely the Tran. The founding of the Tran dynasty brought a new perspective to Thang Long, linking it more directly to the economy and culture of Southern Song than was possible by any overland connection. It was the result, however, of a long and violent struggle during the second and third decades of the thirteenth century. Nguyen Non and Doan Thuong partitioned the Ly dynastic heartland and resisted the upriver advance of the Tran.

Possession of the king gave the Tran an advantage that they were quick to exploit. Within days of finding protection with her brother Tran Tu Khanh, Thuan Trinh gave birth to the princess Thuan Thien. A thatched palace was quickly built on the southern edge of Thang Long for Ly Sam, the king. Thuan Trinh was elevated to the status of queen. Tran Tu Khanh, his eldest brother Tran Thua, and Tran Thua's eldest son Tran Lieu, then 5 years old, all received prestigious court appointments. Reinforced by men who followed the king, Tran Tu Khanh resumed his attacks on the two local strongmen who were his chief enemies, Nguyen Non at Bac Ninh and Doan Thuong at Hai Duong, pushing both men back and putting them on the defensive. An effort to present a façade of royal normalcy was undertaken in 1217 with the king's birthday festival, replete with a five-peak bamboo mountain and outings for the king to watch fishermen.

In 1218, a second daughter, the princess Chieu Thanh, was born to the queen. The king reportedly began to suffer from epileptic fits and to act irrationally. Whether this was an actual illness, an expression of sadness, or a flourish of Tran historians to indicate incompetence is hard to say. In the events leading to his death, during 1225 and 1226, there is nothing to suggest that he was not in good health at that time.

Fighting with Nguyen Non and Doan Thuong continued. Tran forces gained the upper hand in battle but could not eliminate these old foes. In 1218, Tran Thua broke dikes to devastate Nguyen Non's territories with floodwater, but Nguyen Non remained undefeated. Meanwhile, Tran Tu Khanh sent men to secure the southern provinces and the Cham border. He also sent patrols into the northern mountains to bring over to his side the chieftains there. Nguyen Non and Doan Thuong were too weak to threaten the Tran outside of their home districts but strong enough that the Tran preferred to avoid forcing the issue. They were neighbors, and the Tran found ways of keeping them at odds with each other. With possession of Thang Long and of the monarchy, the Tran had more urgent matters to address.

In 1223, Tran Tu Khanh died. His younger brother, Tran Thu Do, immediately stepped forward. For the next quarter-century he was the actual ruler of the country and the architect of a new dynasty. The elder brother, Tran Thua, was given formal precedence and did take an active part in government. But Tran Thu Do always had the last word. In 1224, Tran Thua was on the southern border pacifying rebels in Nghe An while Tran Thu Do was in the palace attending to court affairs.

Tran Thu Do was determined to ease Ly Sam off the throne and did so with the expedient of having him abdicate in favor of his second daughter, Chieu Thanh, then 7 years old. Ly Sam's eldest daughter, Thuan Thien, then 9 years old, was passed over because she had already been married to Tran Thua's eldest son, 14-year-old Tran Lieu. Tran Lieu had been introduced into the court in late 1216 at age 5 to be the playmate and eventual husband of Thuan Thien, born six months before. However, Tran Thu Do did not view Tran Lieu as a plausible king and instead favored Tran Thua's second son Tran Canh. Chieu Thanh and Tran Canh were the same age. At the end of 1225, Tran Thu Do brought Tran Canh into the palace and arranged for the two children to be married, making Tran Canh king and his father, Tran Thua, the "senior king." Ly Sam and his mother were sent to a temple in Thang Long. Within a year, worried that latent loyalties to the Ly dynasty might focus on the retired king, Tran Thu Do induced Ly Sam's suicide. Tran Thu Do then took Ly Sam's queen, his half-sister Thuan Trinh, as his own wife, for he dared not entrust a woman of her status to any other person. The death of a queen dowager was recorded in 1230, which can only have been Ly Sam's mother. All the remaining women of the defunct Ly court were married to upland chieftains.

Nguyen Non continued to be a thorn in the side of Tran Thu Do. In 1228, Nguyen Non killed Doan Thuong and took possession of all his lands, people, and treasure. In combining the resources of the two remaining anti-Tran regions, Nguyen Non was in a position to launch a serious challenge to the new dynasty. Tran Thu Do reinforced his defenses and sent a letter to Nguyen Non appointing him to a high rank along with a Tran princess to be his wife, hoping that she and her entourage would be able to maintain close watch on him. However, Nguyen Non isolated her from his household and took for himself an even grander rank. But only three months later he fell ill. When Tran Thu Do sent members of his entourage to visit him, Nguyen Non made a great effort to appear strong and healthy, eating and riding his horse, but he died shortly after.

Nguyen Non's second-in-command was a Cham slave who had previously been a merchant in Laos and was famed for his mastery of weapons and of battlefield strategy. Much of Nguyen Non's success was attributed to him. Some Vietnamese historians have pointed out that Nguyen Non's home region included the estates of the Ly royal family where large numbers of Cham prisoners were settled after the expeditions of 1044 and 1069 and that this gave a distinctive cultural and linguistic character to Nguyen Non's ambitions. It is commonly thought that Nguyen Non's long and successful resistance to the Tran was in some measure a result of his use of cavalry, which the relatively elevated and hilly terrain of his region made practical. After Nguyen Non's death, his Cham lieutenant galloped off on horseback to no one knew where, and the Tran, after nearly twenty-five years of war, finally stood unchallenged in the Red River plain.

In 1226, the new king, Tran Canh, celebrated his birthday festival, following a tradition that had been initiated by Le Hoan two and a half centuries before. In 1227, the Tran revived the annual oath of loyalty to be taken with a draught of blood by their men at the shrine of the mountain spirit where Ly Phat Ma had begun this practice after his accession in 1028. In these ways, the Tran continued some ritual practices of kingship from the previous dynasty. However, the Tran had participated in the long and painful disintegration of the Ly dynasty and were determined to learn from that experience. The lesson they took from the Ly failure was the importance of maintaining the integrity of the Tran family by ensuring that the mothers of future kings be Tran women. The only exceptions to this were Ly Sam's daughters, who had been absorbed by marriage into the Tran family at an early age and thereby separated from the Ly.

In 1232, determined to have done with any nostalgic intrigues among the Ly aristocracy, Tran Thu Do arranged that a ceremony for Ly noblemen to honor their ancestors be held in a hall prepared over a deep pit. In the midst of the ceremony, when all were drunk with banqueting, he collapsed the floor and buried them alive. After this, the Ly family, for the most part, ceased to exist. Some members of the Ly royal family fled across the sea and found refuge with the Koryo dynasty of Korea, where their descendents maintained a memory of their royal past into modern times.

Once he had finally erased the likelihood of any resurgence of loyalty to the Ly, Tran Thu Do began to worry about who would be king in the next generation. The next king's legitimacy would be difficult to challenge if his mother was Chieu Thanh, former child queen and the king's consort. In the mid 1230s, however, Chieu Thanh remained childless. On the other hand, her elder sister, Thuan Thien, had already given two sons and a daughter to the king's elder brother, Tran Lieu. In 1234, the death of Tran Thua, father of both Tran Lieu and the king Tran Canh, left Tran Thu Do free to solve the problem in his characteristically callous style. In 1237, Tran Thu Do and the mother of the two young women, now his wife, decreed that Tran Canh abandon his wife and take the wife of his brother, who happened to be three months pregnant.

One year earlier, Tran Lieu had suffered a reduction in his rank for having been intimate with a former concubine of the Ly court. Now, suffering the humiliation of being deprived of his wife, he went into rebellion. Tran Canh, dismayed by the turn of events, rebelled in his own way by running away to a temple on Mount Yen Tu, some 120 kilometers east of Thang Long, begging to be allowed to abdicate and become a monk. Unable to persuade the 19-year-old king to return to the capital, Tran Thu Do began building a palace complex around the temple where the king had taken refuge, saying that wherever the king happened to be was where the capital would be. This was too much for the Buddhist patriarch at the temple, a former teacher of Tran Canh, who told the young king to go back to the capital before the precious solitude of the temple was ruined.

A couple weeks after Tran Canh had returned to Thang Long, Tran Lieu, despairing of his prospects as a rebel, eluded Tran Thu Do's men by pretending to be a fisherman and approached the king's boat to ask for mercy. The two brothers embraced and wept. Tran Thu Do, in a nearby boat, came rushing over and ordered his men to "Kill that rebel Lieu!" Tran Canh clung to his brother and refused any harm to him. Tran Thu Do was angry and reportedly said, "I am nothing but your dog! How can I know what's going on between you two brothers?" Tran Canh spoke to calm down Tran Thu Do and asked him to withdraw his soldiers. Tran Thu Do grudgingly complied but made sure that everyone who had followed Tran Lieu in his rebellious adventure was tracked down and killed. Tran Canh assigned his brother a fief where he lived quietly until his death in 1251. Five years later, one of the sons that Thuan Thien had borne Tran Lieu, harboring resentment at the treatment of his father, took his family and dependents and attempted to escape to Song China. He was captured and returned by an upland chieftain who was loyal to Thang Long.

Tran Thu Do's policies opened fears of a feud within the Tran family. Some thought that Tran Lieu, as the eldest son of Tran Thua, should have been king. These people looked for a champion in another son that Thuan Thien had borne Tran Lieu, the man later to be famous as commander-in-chief of all military forces during the Mongol invasions of the 1280s, Tran Quoc Tuan (later known as the Hung Dao Prince, or Tran Hung Dao). Tran Quoc Tuan was able and bold. Because of this, and because of the wrong done to his father, relations between him and the king, his uncle, were strained.

Tran Quoc Tuan famously tried the king's patience in 1251 when, at the age of 19, he broke into the house of a Tran prince whose son had been promised the hand of the king's daughter in marriage. The princess had been sent to reside in the household of her future father-in-law. Tran Quoc Tuan, enamored of the princess, his half-sister, surreptitiously entered her bedchamber at night and carried her away. He was spared punishment and allowed to keep the girl, who was at most in her early teens, only through the intervention of his aunt, the king's full sister, who had raised him as her son after his father's rebellion fourteen years before.

In 1240, Thuan Thien bore the king a son, Tran Hoang, who became the crown prince. In order to knit the two sides of the family together, a daughter that Thuan Thien bore Tran Lieu, Princess Thien Cam, became the queen of Tran Hoang, her half-brother. She subsequently became the mother of the next king, Tran Kham. Tran Kham's queen was his cousin, a daughter of Tran Quoc Tuan, who became the mother of the next king, Tran Thuyen. Tran Thuyen took as queen a granddaughter of Tran Quoc Tuan, but her failure to bear an heir would, among other things, lead to a breakdown in the Tran marriage policy in the fourteenth century. What the Tran had learned from the failure of the Ly dynasty is that mothers of kings must come from within the royal family. This rule was the initial basis for the Tran dynastic experiment. So long as it functioned, the Tran dynasty remained strong.

The Tran policy to exclude other families from the palace was consonant with centralizing policies in other areas as well. In 1228, village leaders in Thanh Hoa, notoriously difficult to govern, were instructed to conduct annual censuses to update population registers that distinguished people of different ages, abilities, states of health, and family status as a basis for military conscription and recruitment of officials. This was the first recorded effort by rulers in Thang Long to connect their authority directly with villages in a southern province. Three years later, perhaps building on this, a canal was dug to connect Thanh Hoa with the Ca River plain further south. In 1234, Tran Thu Do took direct personal responsibility for Thanh Hoa, an indication that after settling matters in Thang Long he directed his attention to the southern provinces. In 1238, he approved the population registers of Thanh Hoa after four years of work.

In 1242, a new scheme of jurisdictions was established for the entire kingdom. Groups of officials responsible for each jurisdiction were sent to categorize villages according to their sizes and to establish population registers indicating how much land, if any, was owned by each family and the amount of taxes to be paid accordingly. This is the earliest surviving evidence of a centralized land tax regime being proclaimed by a royal court at Thang Long. Nevertheless, the differences between the Red River plain and the southern provinces were great and in 1256 the kingdom was divided for certain purposes into two categories. The Red River plain and the people there were called Kinh, meaning "capital." The southern provinces of Thanh Hoa and Nghe An, which at that time also included the modern province of Ha Tinh, and the people there were called Trai, meaning "garrison" or "outpost." The Tran instituted an unprecedented centralization of authority in both areas, but relied primarily on the Kinh people for soldiers and taxation, since they were most numerous, most accessible to the capital, and most socialized to respond to authority. The distinction between Kinh and Trai people gave rise to the usage, still current today, of referring to the Vietnamese as Kinh in contrast to other ethnic groups in the country. The Trai people can plausibly be associated with ancestors of the various groups of people categorized as Muong in modern times.

Within the Red River plain, the dynastic regime built by Tran Thu Do expressed the rising power of the coast based on trade and land claimed from the sea. The Tran homeland was in the region of the modern city of Nam Dinh. The most stubborn enemies of the Tran were based in the upper plains in the Bac Ninh and Hai Duong areas, which had been the heartland of old Giao Province. While the Ly had looked from Thang Long across the river to their home estates in that old heartland, the Tran made the river a pulsing artery connecting Thang Long with their second royal palace complex near Nam Dinh, which was connected in the other direction with the international commerce centered at the seaport of Van Don. This is an example of change and vitality breaking into old centers from frontier areas, a theme prominent in Vietnamese history as it also is in the histories of many other countries.

Early Tran literati

The Tran did not simply replace the Ly but fought for many years to destroy the local powers that had been an aspect of the Ly system of government. While the Ly presided over a coalition of powerful local families, the Tran made sure that members of the royal family were in dominant positions everywhere. This was practicable only with a cadre of educated commoners to serve the Tran nobles. The need for administrative personnel led the Tran to develop a system for recruitment based on the model of civil service examinations in Song China.

The Ly dynasty had held occasional examinations to select people with skills in demand at court, most commonly with little more than knowledge of letters for reading and writing. In addition to this, a small cadre of scholars was needed to serve as palace teachers and as envoys to the Song dynasty. Most of the educated people in the Ly dynasty were Buddhist monks or classical scholars who were also Buddhists. This began to change in the thirteenth century under the influence of educational ideas about curriculum and examinations for government service that had developed in Song China and were brought to Thang Long by the Tran. This curriculum began to produce men with a more secular sense of moral cultivation based on relatively rational ethical principles and hierarchical human relationships. Devotion to deities or the cultivation of spiritual knowledge and of supernatural powers did not cease among educated people but rather declined and came under more critical scrutiny.

The first recorded mention of the new curriculum comes from 1253 when Confucian scholars were summoned to teach "the Four Books and the Five Classics" at a newly built palace academy. In 1272, a search was made for scholars to teach the king about "the Four Books and the Five Classics." The Five Classics (*Changes, Odes, Rites, History*, and the *Spring and Autumn Annals*) were standard texts that had been studied for centuries by ancestors of both the Song Chinese and the Vietnamese. However, the Four Books (*Great Learning, Doctrine of the Mean, Analects* of Confucius, and *Mencius*) came into prominence only from the time of the Song philosopher Zhu Xi (1130–1200), the architect of what is sometimes called Neo-Confucianism.

In 1232 and in 1239, examinations were held at the capital with a total of nine people being selected in those years. These exams were for "advanced students," but they did not follow the system of awarding academic degrees that was later viewed as standard. One of those selected in 1232 was Tran Chu Pho, who is known to have written a book of history that no longer exists but was used by later historians. His other claim to fame was to be an object of public laughter during a royal banquet in 1242 when everyone was drunk and taking turns to sing songs; he stood up to sing but could only murmur over and over: "What I will now sing is . . . What I will now sing is . . ." The few people selected in these exams were most probably used as teachers and as consultants in relations with Song China.

In 1246, a new system for examinations was established that began a standard format for awarding degrees to successful candidates. In 1247, the first examination under this new academic regime was held and forty-eight men were graduated. Similar exams were held in 1256, 1266, and 1275, producing forty-three, forty-seven, and twenty-seven graduates, respectively. Thus, in thirty years, 165 men were produced by these exams. Most of these graduates were from the Red River plain. The only examination to record the number of Kinh and Trai graduates is that of 1256. In that year, only one of the forty-three graduates came from the southern provinces.

The men who participated in these examinations presumably had the advantage of coming from families able to educate their sons and of being recommended by members of royalty. Many of these men were descendents of immigrants from the north who maintained family traditions of learning. The examination system provided an avenue for such people to gain public attention and opportunities for advancement in service to royalty. These men did not receive appointments in a bureaucratic structure of government, for such did not exist. If not assigned to pedagogical, scholarly, or consulting tasks in palace offices, they were assigned to the entourages of noblemen to assist with the miscellaneous tasks of administering various localities. Two men of that time who are remembered as historians represent these contrasting experiences.

One of the graduates of 1247 was Le Van Huu (1230–1322), who in 1272 presented to the throne a book of history from early times to the end of the Ly dynasty. Although this book no longer exists as Le Van Huu wrote it, it was used in compiling the official court chronicle in the fifteenth century, which preserves Le Van Huu's comments on various historical events. Beginning with Zhao To in antiquity and continuing through the period of the Ly dynasty, his comments critique what he regarded as laudable, disorganized, improper, or immoral conduct by historical figures and reveal a strong Confucian bias. He spent his long life in Thang Long as a palace erudite.

Le Trac was a man of learning in the entourage of Tran Kien. Tran Kien's father, Tran Quoc Khang, was a son of Tran Lieu, but born after Tran Thu Do sent Tran Lieu's wife to Tran Canh. Tran Quoc Khang was adopted as a son by Tran Canh and remained loyal to the throne throughout his life, but his son Tran Kien nurtured the resentment of his grandfather, and in 1285, while on campaign in Nghe An, he surrendered the army he was leading, along with his family, dependents, and entourage, to the Mongols. Le Trac surrendered with him.

When Mongols escorted this group north to China, local chiefs prepared an ambush at Chi Lang, a strategic pass on the watershed over the highlands into Lang Son Province. With those lying in wait was a slave of Tran Quoc Tuan, Tran Kien's uncle and commander of the Tran armies. The slave, a marksman with the bow and arrow, recognized Tran Kien and shot him dead. Le Trac retrieved the body of his patron and escaped on horseback. He spent the rest of his life in China where, in the early fourteenth century, he compiled a history of "An Nam" that still exists today.

After 1275, no examinations are recorded until 1304, apparently because of the disruptions of the Mongol Wars. The 165 men selected during the examinations of the mid thirteenth century were but the peak of a mass of literate officials serving at all levels of dynastic affairs. In 1228 all officials were tested to compile a register for ranking them. A royal audience for students passing an exam was recorded in 1236, and on that occasion rules and regulations for lower-level exams were established. Also in that year a school was established for the sons and younger brothers of "literate" officials and of officials who "follow," two categories of people apparently meant to include all those in the entourages of Tran noblemen, both the literate and the illiterate. In 1261, an examination was held in writing and mathematics for applicants seeking appointments in officialdom. In 1267, an examination in writing was held for people to be given official appointments. In 1274, people specifically identified as Confucian scholars were selected to teach the crown prince. There were also examinations in the "three religions" of Buddhism, Daoism, and Confucianism recorded in 1227 and in 1253. These examinations continued an educational tradition from earlier times and apparently selected people to supervise Buddhist and Daoist temples.

In 1253, a shrine was built at Thang Long with statues of the Duke of Zhou, of Confucius, and of Mencius, along with pictures of seventy-two of Confucius' disciples. This is reminiscent of the shrine built in 1070 with statues of the Duke of Zhou, of Confucius, and of Confucius' seventy-two disciples. In 1156, Do Anh Vu had built a shrine for Confucius, an indication that the 1070 shrine no longer existed in his time. The 1156 shrine apparently perished when Thang Long was looted and burned in the last years of the Ly dynasty. In 1253, the addition of Mencius reveals the influence of Song Neo-Confucian thought, which put particular emphasis upon the Mencian idea that everyone had the potential for goodness if properly educated. This shrine was part of the palace academy, already mentioned, which was established to teach the "Four Books and Five Classics," the new curriculum from Song China.

Despite formal attention to a curriculum of study and a system of academic examinations, men resorted to other means to gain promotion as well. One scholar secretly used incantations to advance his career, which, when revealed, provoked the king to veto his appointment to the royal academy. Full of resentment, he joined the Mongols during their invasion of 1287–1288 and was subsequently beheaded as a traitor when captured by the Tran.

Solidarity among the princes

The Tran kings and princes were exceptionally well educated, and not only in the Confucian classics. They were also trained in Buddhism, and they were great builders of temples and stupas. Tran Canh read widely in the Buddhist sutras and the writings of Chan (Japanese Zen, Korean Soen, Vietnamese Thien) masters of the Tang dynasty, particularly Huineng (638–713). Tran Canh was an original thinker, abreast with Buddhist thought in Song China, and he developed an inclusive view of various currents in Buddhism. He wrote many sermons and essays during his lifetime that were subsequently compiled as *Khoa Hu Luc* (Instructions on Emptiness). His grandson, Tran Kham, followed his deep engagement with Buddhist thought and practice and became the founder of a royal sect of Buddhism, the Truc Lam (Bamboo Grove) School.

Tran Canh's writings moved beyond the miscellany of devotional, thaumaturgical, and meditational practices that had characterized the Buddhism of the Ly dynasty and earlier. Similar to the way Confucian studies were reoriented by trends in Song thought, Tran Canh's writings express a distinctive response to issues in Song Chan Buddhism. In the late eleventh century, the monk and patriarch Thong Bien (d. 1134) had propounded a distinction between the "scriptural school" and the "mind school," a divide that was typical of Song Buddhist thought. At issue was whether one achieved enlightenment gradually through the study of books or suddenly by meditative intuition.

Tran Canh moved beyond such dichotomous conundrums toward a sense of the unity of all things and all beings. The Tang Chan patriarch Huineng, who taught that all sentient beings were endowed with the Buddha nature, was an important influence on his thought. Tran Canh believed that all perceivable phenomena were parts of a single underlying unity in the mind of Buddha and that the highest wisdom transcended all distinctions. This idea, "not-two" (*bat nhi*; Chinese *bu'er*; Sanskrit *advaita*), meaning "non-separation," is generally translated into English as "non-duality." An emphasis on non-duality is prominent in the poems of the monk Tue Trung (1230–1291), who was Tran Kham's teacher, and is characteristic of Tran thought generally. Among members of royalty, the idea of non-duality tended to be conflated with a sense of family solidarity and of unlimited power over the country.

Tran princes had a strong sense of ownership over every aspect of the kingdom and were unwilling to distinguish between themselves and the people and property over which they ruled. They resisted any tendency to affirm separation, division, or alienation from the realm in which they were masters. We see this in successive generations of adherence to a marriage policy designed to heal the wound between the brothers Tran Lieu and Tran Canh. Tran Canh's protection of Tran Lieu against Tran Thu Do's wrath was an act against the duality, or irreconcilable separation, expressed in this feud. On the other hand, Tran Kien's choice to avenge his grandfather's humiliation with the separatism of a traitor earned him an arrow of death, for what was not in harmony with the group could not be allowed to exist.

The relatively strong sense of solidarity among the Tran princes was expressed by Tran Hoang when, as king, he addressed a gathering of his royal kin in spring 1268. His words were recorded as follows:

> All that is in the world is nothing but the realm of our ancestors, and it is only right that the elder and younger brothers of our royal house together enjoy the riches and honors that are the inheritance of our ancestors. Although outwardly there be but one person on the throne to receive the world's respect, yet inwardly you and I are the bone and flesh of the same womb. If there is something to worry about, we worry together; if there is something to be happy about, we are happy together. You must all pass these words on to your sons and grandsons so they will never forget them, for only then will our royal house have good fortune for ages to come.

Tran Hoang's emphasis on solidarity was surely aimed at ameliorating the volatile relations among his royal kin and uniting them under his authority.

In typical Tran fashion, the matter was not left at the level of words. The king followed up his remarks with a decree that whenever there was a royal audience, his kinsmen were to remain after everyone else was dismissed and go with him into the inner palace to eat and drink together and afterwards to bring out a long pillow and a large blanket for them all to sleep together, "in order to have true feelings of brotherly affection." At the same time, a strict hierarchy was to be observed among the royal kin at public occasions. The result of these policies, according to later court chroniclers, was that at that time all the royal kinsmen were united in mutual harmony and respect and none was arrogant or disdainful toward another.

In reality, as already noted, there were many tensions among these men, and the emphasis upon solidarity was surely intended to lessen the dangers of this. Aside from the accumulation of resentments produced by escapades such as Tran Quoc Tuan's stealing away the bride of a kinsman, there remained the founding feud of the royal house between the "senior line" of Tran Lieu and the "junior line" of Tran Canh. Marriage policy and habits of friendship could not entirely push this feud out of sight. A remarkable indication of this is an episode recorded from the Mongol invasion of 1285 as the royal entourage fled from the enemy. Tran Quoc Tuan carried a wooden staff with a sharp iron point. Since dissatisfied members of the "senior line" considered that the throne rightfully belonged to him, the king's men kept a sharp watch upon him, afraid that he might stab the king. When he realized this, he discarded the iron point from his staff.

A famous exception to Tran solidarity was Tran Ich Tac, a son of Tran Canh who, when growing up, was extraordinarily bright and competitive, good at everything and particularly known as an expert chess player. It was said that he had sent a letter to the Mongols via merchants at Van Don requesting that they come to make him king. When they came, he went over to their side with his entourage and dependents; three other men with their dependents went with him, one of whom had been an envoy to the Mongols in 1263. Tran Ich Tac subsequently spent the rest of his life at the Mongol court as the "King of An Nam." Annalists recorded a story to explain his treason. At the time of Tran Ich Tac's birth, he had announced himself to Tran Canh in a dream, saying that he was a northern prince being punished by his sovereign for misbehavior; he would be reborn as Tran Canh's son and later would return north. Reincarnation was a common explanation for otherwise unaccountable behavior.

Considering the magnitude of the Mongol challenge that would test the Tran house, and considering the number of people who eventually failed the test of loyalty, the degree of solidarity among Tran leaders was nevertheless remarkable. This was not by chance but grew from the spirit of inclusion and reconciliation that was the hallmark of Tran Canh's personality, religious sensibility, philosophy, and policy. His son and grandson, Tran Hoang and Tran Kham, who stood at the head of the Tran family during the Mongol invasions of the 1280s, imbibed his attitude and understood that the fortunes of their dynasty depended upon the unity of the royal house, preferably mobilized willingly with a spirit of group solidarity but enforced by coercion if necessary.

Poetry and language

Tran kings and princes were trained to appreciate and write poetry in the form of "regulated verse" that had developed during the Tang dynasty (*jintishi* in Chinese, "new style prosody"). Very few poets during the Ly dynasty mastered this form, but in the Tran dynasty it became the dominant mode. Ly dynasty poetry was mostly written by Buddhist monks and tended to focus upon abstract religious thought. However, Tran dynasty poetry celebrates the beauty of the natural world, the joys and sorrows of human life, and the remembrance of events. The poems were written in Literary Chinese following complicated and difficult tonal and rhyme schemes. The skill of being able to express a scene or an emotion in poetry was a way of processing individual experience into a form of knowledge accessible to others in writing. The discipline required to do this was understood as a mark of being civilized. The many Tran princes who wrote and enjoyed poetry shared a realm of aesthetic appreciation.

The writing of vernacular poetry began at this time. The court chronicle says that an official at court in the 1280s named Nguyen Thuyen was the first to write poetry in the vernacular. None of his poems has survived, and no vernacular poetry at all has survived from before the era of Ming dynasty rule in the early fifteenth century when vernacular writing was collected for destruction. Vernacular writing, called Nom (written with a character that means "gibberish" but is usually glossed as "southern speech"), used Chinese characters in various ways to represent Vietnamese words. One common way of Nom usage was to use a character for its sound. Another common way was to invent a Nom character by combining elements of two Chinese characters, one to mark sound and one to mark meaning. The use of Nom was facilitated by prior knowledge of Literary Chinese characters and of their pronunciations in the vernacular language. Consequently, it was a writing system designed to maintain the élite's monopoly on literacy or, according to a once well-known aphorism, for the amusement of retired scholars.

The preface for a dictionary compiled no later than the seventeenth century claimed that Nom had existed in various forms since the time of Shi Xie in the early third century as a pedagogical aid for students studying literary texts. But its use to write poetry in the thirteenth century was an aspect of the emerging class of educated commoners, the most prominent of whom won recognition in the mid-century examinations. That these people began to use Nom for writing poetry shows that vernacular sensibilities were being brought into the realm of literacy to an unprecedented degree. It also suggests that, prior to this time, there was a high degree of bilingualism among educated people, who were for the most part from the aristocracy.

Some, if not all, Tran family members were bilingual in the thirteenth century. In 1282, Tran Quoc Tuan was able to pose as a Chinese monk in an interview with a Yuan dynasty envoy. Tran Ly, Tran Canh's grandfather who had led the Tran family into court politics, was the grandson of an emigrant from Fujian. The Tran were based on the coast near the entrepôt of Van Don where Chinese language, cuisine, and style of dress were the currency of social and business relations. Whether the family had ever maintained contact with kin in Fujian is unknown but nevertheless plausible, for the Tran dominated the coast where trading connections with China produced wealth.

Many of the educated commoners coming into the entourages of Tran noblemen in the mid thirteenth century were bilingual, though some may at best have mastered the high-register language of Literary Chinese and not necessarily spoken Chinese. For them, writing vernacular Vietnamese poetry opened a literary community based on the idioms of their experience as students struggling upward into the governing class. Spoken Chinese gradually died out among upper-class people during the Ly and Tran dynasties as an aspect of the process of linguistic shift in which bilingualism gave way to a monolingual vernacular pattern of speech, thereby bringing into being the Vietnamese language through infusions of Chinese vocabulary and grammatical particles.

Mobilizing resources: eunuchs, slaves, dikes, and war

An important class of people at court was eunuchs. As had been the case during the Ly dynasty, Tran eunuchs were typically the products of self-castration. Some young men took this route to gain access to the palaces and to the powerful people in them. An example of someone becoming a eunuch was recorded in 1254 when Tran Canh, on an excursion into the city, saw a student who looked exactly like a person that a divine being had pointed out to him in a dream as deserving a senior appointment in his entourage, which was reserved for eunuchs. Tran Canh paid the boy a large sum of cash to be castrated and to enter his service as a eunuch. Eventually, this eunuch proved his worth and was promoted to reach the high position indicated in the king's dream.

Eunuchs served in many capacities. In 1231, a eunuch was sent to supervise the digging of a canal to link the provinces of Thanh Hoa and Nghe An. In 1280, when Tran Canh was hailed in the street by someone seeking justice against the brother of a powerful official of whom judicial officers were afraid, he had a eunuch investigate the matter and thereafter placed eunuchs in charge of handling such cases. Confucian scholars generally disdained eunuchs, considering them a pestilence of intrigue and corruption, and some tension between the two groups also existed at Thang Long, as demonstrated in an episode from 1288, which nevertheless was recorded with a happy ending in keeping with the Tran court's emphasis on harmony.

A feud had erupted between the scholar in charge of the office that prepared proclamations and the eunuch whose task it was to read out the proclamations in public. The proclamations were written in Literary Chinese, but the eunuch's knowledge of Literary Chinese was rudimentary, so in order for him to read out the proclamation before an audience at court he needed sufficient time to study it beforehand. The feud between the two men reached a point that on one occasion the scholar decided to keep back a proclamation until just before the court session at which it was to be read. The result was a public scandal with the eunuch being unable to read the proclamation. Afterwards, the king took the eunuch aside and said: "This man is a scholar. You are a eunuch. You both watch over the royal capital and are mere worms to me. Send him some oranges as a present and the two of you will give gifts back and forth. What is the problem?" Thereafter, the two antagonists reportedly became good friends.

As the king's blunt words made clear, both scholars and eunuchs were members of the royal entourage and neither had any base of power or support outside of royal favor. There was no choice for them but to get along. But it was significant that it was the eunuch whom the king pulled aside for a reprimand. Eunuchs belonged to the king in a way that scholars did not. Scholars had their own families and friends beyond the palace, but it was difficult for a eunuch to exist outside of the king's entourage.

Another class of people was slaves. These could be peasants who sold themselves into slavery to improve their lives, or prisoners of war, or people from other lands brought by merchants. They served many functions from manual laborers to skilled craftspeople. As time went by, Tran princes accumulated increasing numbers of slaves. During the Mongol Wars, many military units were composed entirely of slaves. In the thirteenth century, slavery was not a particularly bad fate. Slaves were generally well cared for and, in wartime, served their masters loyally. The condition of slaves, and also of peasants, would change dramatically for the worse in the fourteenth century when, lacking the kind of leadership provided by the first three kings, Tran government faltered.

The infrastructure of transport, communication, and water control was centralized to an unprecedented degree in the thirteenth century. The canal built in 1231 connecting the southern provinces of Thanh Hoa and Nghe An has already been mentioned. In that same year, Tran Thua ordered that statues of Buddha be built in all the rest houses so travelers could worship while on the road. In 1244 the kingdom was divided into jurisdictions and officials were sent to establish a base in each of them for transporting goods. Transportation and communication, as in the past, were mostly by boat. In 1248, a system of dikes was designed for defense against floods in the Red River plain. A cadre of officials was tasked with maintaining these dikes. Owners of land lost to dike construction were compensated in cash by the court. In 1255, an official was sent to oversee dike construction throughout Thanh Hoa Province. Previous dike construction was done locally or regionally. Royal interest in building and keeping watch over dikes throughout the kingdom began from this time.

By 1250, the Tran court had mobilized the human and material resources of the Red, Ma, and Ca River plains to a degree of central direction never before achieved. Tran Canh was then 32 years old. He had been king since the age of 7. He had a 10-year-old crown prince, Tran Hoang. His uncle, Tran Thu Do, architect of the dynasty, was 57 years old and still strong. Following the example of Ly Phat Ma and Ly Nhat Ton, Tran Canh expressed the exuberance of his well being by an expedition to the Cham capital of Vijaya.

In the late twelfth and early thirteenth centuries, Cham rulers were in large measure subservient to Jayavarman VII, one of the great kings of Angkor, under whose direction Khmer and Cham armies had pushed north against the faltering leadership of the Ly dynasty. By the 1220s, this era of Khmer ascendancy had passed and Cham kings regularly sent tribute to Thang Long. The Tran court was nevertheless irritated by demands for its recognition of Cham authority in disputed border territories in modern Quang Binh Province that each side claimed but neither controlled. Even more irritating were periodic raids along the southern coast by people whom the Tran believed to belong to the Cham king. Consequently, to display Tran power on the southern coast, in 1252 Tran Canh personally led an expedition to sack Vijaya. Departing Thang Long at the beginning of the year, he returned at the end of the year with much plunder and many captives, including the wives and concubines of the Cham king. The two kingdoms were thereafter at peace for many years, and they even became allies during the Mongol Wars of the 1280s.

The First Mongol War

The situation on the northern border became volatile as Southern Song power faded under the blows of Mongol invaders. Conditions on the Song border deteriorated to the point that tribute goods could not be sent to the Song court because of bandits. Then, in late 1240, officials on the border in Lang Son Province reported that "northern people" had raided and plundered the province. A year later, Tran Canh sent soldiers by land to attack Song border jurisdictions. He himself led a naval force in small boats to attack up the rivers in the same Song coastal jurisdictions that Ly Thuong Kiet had attacked in 1075, at modern Qinzhou and Hepu. The aim of these attacks was to clear away bandit lairs on the Song side of the border and to advise Song border officials that incapacity to control disorderly conduct from their side would not be matched by Tran passivity. In 1242, after further campaigning along the border by a Tran general, secure communications were restored between the Tran and Song courts.

In the 1250s, Kubilai, a grandson of Genghis Khan, was campaigning against Southern Song. He took Chengdu in Sichuan Province in 1252. In 1256, his general Uriyangqadai moved further south to overrun the Nan Zhao kingdom in Yunnan. In summer and autumn of 1257, Uriyangqadai advanced downriver through the mountains toward Thang Long. He had sent envoys to the Tran but waited in vain for them to return. He led a force of around 25,000 men, 5,000 Mongols, and 20,000 local levies from Yunnan. His aim was to contribute to Mongol attacks on Southern Song from the north and west by passing through Tran territories to attack from the south. It was an unprecedented crisis for the Tran, who threw the Mongol envoys into a prison and had no intention of allowing Uriyangqadai to pass.

The Tran manufactured weapons and trained soldiers as the Mongols moved steadily through the mountainous terrain between the Yunnan plateau and the Red River plain in two columns, one along the left bank of the Red River and one along the right bank of the Chay River. Then, in the last month of the year, when the dry season had started and it was feasible for cavalry to enter the lowlands, Uriyangqadai emerged from the mountains northwest of Thang Long. His two columns converged at modern Viet Tri, where the Red and Chay Rivers meet, and proceeded eastward, north of the Red River.

Tran Canh personally led his men to block the invaders near the modern district of Binh Xuyen, around thirty-five kilometers northwest of Thang Long. Meanwhile, Tran Thu Do's wife, Thuan Trinh, the former queen of Ly Sam and the mother of Tran Canh's queen, being the ranking woman in the palace, had organized the evacuation of Tran women and children, including the crown prince, from Thang Long. She made sure that the boats also carried as many weapons as possible for soldiers gathering downriver.

Tran Canh could not hold back Uriyangqadai. His general Le Phu Tran skillfully delayed the Mongols as Tran Canh hastened to his boats to make his escape. The Mongol captain tasked with capturing him chased after the royal boats with his men on horseback along the riverbank, but could not keep up. His failure earned him a cup of poison. Tran Canh withdrew downriver past Thang Long, leaving the rearguard in the hands of General Le Phu Tran. Uriyangqadai occupied Thang Long, where he found his envoys trussed up in a dungeon, one of them dead. The city was empty of people and provisions. Forays out of the city to collect food met with stiff resistance and returned with little of value.

The initial defeat and the flight downriver broke the morale of some Tran commanders. As the crown prince's boat moved upriver in search of the king's boat, the boat of one officer fleeing rapidly downriver sought to avoid him by passing on the far side of the river. The men with the crown prince shouted to ask him where were the Mongols. He replied: "I don't know. Ask the guys who ate the mangos." He was referring to an occasion before the campaign when the king had gathered his men and distributed mangos to them. This man had distinguished himself by being so overcome with fright that he could not eat his mango.

Later, in a small boat with the 17-year-old crown prince at his side, the king encountered the boat of one of his brothers, Tran Nhat Hieu, and asked him what he advised. Tran Nhat Hieu remained silent but using water wrote with his finger two characters on his oar meaning to flee to Song. The king then went to Tran Thu Do's boat. The 65-year-old dynastic rock reportedly said: "My head has not yet fallen to the ground, so there is nothing for you to worry about." Relying upon the counsel and battlefield prowess of Le Phu Tran and others, Tran Canh rallied his men and returned to the offensive, attacking and pushing back the Mongol force at Thang Long. From when battle was joined until the Mongols retreated upriver was only twelve days.

The Mongols were a new kind of enemy. This brief encounter, later numbered as the first of three Mongol invasions, would be remembered as relatively insignificant in comparison with the other Mongol wars in the 1280s. But it was a scare, and some Tran nobles fled, not bothering to assemble their soldiers for battle. Le Phu Tran, a man who in 1250 had risen to the rank of general on the basis of his martial merit, was celebrated as a hero. Tran Canh honored him with marriage to his former wife, the Ly Princess Chieu Thanh, who had been separated from him in 1237 by Tran Thu Do. Although Chieu Thanh had been unable to bear children for Tran Canh, she bore a son and a daughter for Le Phu Tran and died with honor twenty years later. In 1274, Le Phu Tran was assigned to teach military strategy to crown prince Tran Kham, Tran Canh's grandson, who would be king during the second and third Mongol invasions.

Living with danger

Alerted to the danger posed by their new Mongol neighbor, the Tran family moved quickly to further strengthen royal leadership. Within two months of expelling Uriyangqadai from the lowlands, in early 1258, Crown Prince Tran Hoang was made king and Tran Canh became the senior king. The practice of having two kings, one senior and one junior, became a stabilizing feature of the dynasty.

The older generation was passing away. In early 1259 came the death of Thuan Trinh, the heroine of the evacuation of Thang Long. She was the queen of the last Ly king, the mother of Tran Canh's queen, the grandmother of many talented princes and princesses, and for many years the wife of her half-brother,

Tran Thu Do. She had borne the title "Mother of the Kingdom" with the rank and privileges of a queen dowager.

Tran Thu Do died five years later at the age of 71. He remained lucid and active to the end. Only six months before his death he was leading patrols on horseback to inspect border terrain in Lang Son Province. He had not received a literary education, but in political acumen and foresight he had no peer, and for forty years his had been the final word on all matters of consequence. Tran Canh instinctively deferred to him, and he exercised the personal authority of a king.

Tran Thu Do was strict but also fair in his own way. According to one anecdote, a certain person from "the flock of officials" once had the temerity to approach Tran Canh during a public audience and with tears complain that Tran Thu Do acted like a king and took advantage of the king's youth. Tran Canh immediately adjourned the audience and, taking with him the entire "flock of officials," went to Tran Thu Do's residence and reported to him what the man had said. Tran Thu Do replied, "Yes, it's exactly as he says," and gave the man a reward for his honesty.

This story tells of utter transparency between Tran Canh and Tran Thu Do and also of Tran Thu Do's knowledge of human character, being able to see the loyalty and concern for royal authority that had motivated the complainer. After the death in 1234 of Tran Canh's father, Tran Thua, Tran Thu Do was effectively the "senior king" to Tran Canh. The quality of this relationship between uncle and nephew was a model for the close and trusting relationships that existed between senior and junior kings in later generations.

In 1262 a royal complex with a palace for the senior king was built near the home of the Tran family at the site of what is today Pho Minh Temple, about five kilometers north of the modern city of Nam Dinh, some seventy kilometers downriver from Thang Long. A second palace was built next to the senior king's residence for the junior king to use when coming to visit and consult. Tran kings, especially senior kings, established a particular relationship with Buddhist temples on Mount Yen Tu, where Tran Canh had sought refuge during the family crisis of 1237, as a place for study, meditation, and rest.

The regime of registering the population and recording land ownership to mobilize manpower and to collect taxes that was begun in the 1230s and 1240s produced a wandering population of landless, homeless people without any means of livelihood. These were people who failed to find a place in the new rural economy. Some may have resisted the registration procedure, preferring to remain anonymous in the eyes of officialdom, perhaps because of misdeeds in the past, perhaps because of family associations with the Ly dynasty, perhaps because of criminal or socially marginal ways of life. Others may not have been successful in registering their ownership of land, being victims of people quicker than they were to ingratiate themselves with a new regime. Still others may have found pleasure and opportunities in the wandering life. In 1254, an edict allowed people to buy communal land and turn it into private property. People who depended upon communal land would have thereby lost their means of livelihood and many likely joined the vagabond life.

The Tran responded to this by having the royal family take direct responsibility for these people. In 1266 Tran nobles were allowed to "recruit" these people as slaves and put them to work opening up uncultivated land for agriculture that then became their personal estates. This was the beginning of royal estates farmed by slaves that became a characteristic feature of the Tran rural regime and which in the fourteenth century would contribute to an era of peasant rebellions. For several decades, it proved to be a successful way to stabilize the rural population.

In 1267, in order to limit the number of people who could participate in the privileges of royalty, an edict cited the rule of venerating one's ancestors to the fifth generation to allow people to claim kinship with the royal family only within five generations of the throne, meaning all who were the great-great-grandchildren, or closer, of a king. Only a king's children and grandchildren were qualified for the ranks of nobility that gave ready access to the palace. The king could nevertheless assign a title of nobility to anyone he wished, and he could promote and demote his kin from one rank to another as he considered appropriate. Being within five generations did not automatically confer nobility but merely qualified one for receiving appropriate titles from the king. Commoners of exceptional quality could be adopted into the royal family or given a status commensurate with royal kin, but they could not pass this benefit on to their children. These regulations, combined with the rule of kings being the children of Tran women, removed any threat of a non-royal family gaining a foothold in the palace.

A famous example of a prince losing and then regaining royal status is Tran Khanh Du. His actual relationship with the kings is unknown, but he was adopted by Tran Hoang as a son and given all the privileges of that rank because of his battlefield prowess during the Mongol invasion of 1257. However, when he forced intimacy upon a princess who happened to be the wife of Tran Quoc Tuan's son, the king sent men to beat him nearly to death, confiscated all his property, and expelled him from the royal family. He became a coal merchant. Years later, in 1282, when the kingdom was in a flurry of military preparation, the king, while traveling to a conference of royal princes, noticed Tran Khanh Du rowing a boat loaded with coal. He restored him to the royal family and gave him a high military command. Tran Khanh Du won a major naval battle against the Mongols in 1287. Because of his battlefield merit, he was never again expelled from the royal family, despite his many misdeeds and his reputation for greed, lust, and arrogance.

Kings kept a close watch over their family members. In 1270, one of Tran Hoang's cousins was building an elaborate palace with extravagant architectural features in Nghe An. He sent someone to take a look, which so embarrassed the man that he installed a Buddha statue and turned the edifice into a temple. On the other hand, kings were sometimes thwarted by the opinions of their kin. For example, in 1264 Tran Hoang wanted to promote his uncle Tran Nhat Hieu to a higher position, but Tran Nhat Hieu's faintheartedness in wanting to run away to Song during the Mongol invasion had so embarrassed him among the other nobles that he dared not accept.

From Uriyangqadai's retreat upriver to Yunnan in the winter of 1257–1258 until Mongol armies under the command of Togan began to penetrate the borders in the winter of 1284–1285, envoys shuttled regularly between the Tran and Mongol leaders. The Tran were prepared to acknowledge Mongol suzerainty to the same degree that they acknowledged Song suzerainty, with triennial tribute missions. The Mongols demanded more than this, but until the mid 1260s were too occupied with internal struggles and events in China to pay very much attention to the matter. In 1261, Kubilai agreed to the traditional tributary relationship, but also insisted that a Mongol military overseer, called a Daruhaci, be stationed in Thang Long.

From 1262 to 1268 the Daruhaci spent little time at Thang Long and there were reports that the Tran had corrupted him. In 1267, Kubilai sent his son Hugaci to take charge of Yunnan, at the same time sending a list of six demands to Thang Long: that the Tran king come to the Mongol court, that the king's children be kept as hostages at the Mongol court, that census registers be sent, that taxes be sent, that a Mongol garrison be stationed at Thang Long, and that all affairs be under the supervision of the Daruhaci. A new Daruhaci was sent in 1268. During the next ten years, there was a stalemate with envoys carrying back and forth Mongol demands and Tran demurrals.

Until 1271, Kubilai was occupied with internal disputes among the Mongol princes and with organizing his control over northern China. In that year he proclaimed the Yuan dynasty and summoned the Tran king to appear at his court in Dadu (modern Beijing). Tran Hoang excused himself, saying that he was ill. It was probably no coincidence that at this time Le Van Huu submitted his book of history to the Tran court. One of Le Van Huu's arguments in this book was that the kings of Thang Long were heirs of a southern imperial tradition established in the second century BCE by Zhao To, King of "Southern Viet," who had proclaimed himself emperor during a period of confrontation with the Han dynasty.

Le Van Huu claimed that, in the tenth century, Dinh Bo Linh had carried forward Zhao To's imperial claim, which was then inherited by the Le, the Ly, and the Tran kings. The poem attributed to Ly Thuong Kiet during the Ly–Song War of the 1070s expresses the idea of northern and southern imperial realms with a clear border defined by separate heavenly mandates. Whether or not this poem pre-dated Le Van Huu is a matter for conjecture. If it did, it was but an ideological elaboration of Ly Nhat Ton's application of imperial titles and ranks to his own royal house and court in the mid eleventh century, a rhetoric followed by all later kings in the realm of ink on paper.

Le Van Huu's writing of this perspective into history was a response to the Yuan dynasty's claim of universal empire at a time when Thang Long's suzerain of nearly three centuries, the Song, still existed in southern China. Kubilai may have been an emperor in the north, but there remained a Song emperor in the south, not to mention Tran pretensions to imperial status, which were kept private among the Tran and never acknowledged to the Song or the Yuan. An interest in borrowing history to argue about the present was not confined to the Tran, for in 1272 a Mongol envoy demanded to know the exact location of the bronze pillars reportedly erected by Ma Yuan in the first century CE to mark the southern limit of the empire. After an investigation, the Tran reported that no trace of Ma Yuan's pillars could be found.

Meanwhile, relations with Southern Song went slack as Song became completely absorbed in its struggle for survival. In 1263, a border chieftain who had been a vassal of Song submitted to the Tran, indicating the shrinkage of Song authority away from the border. The Song Empire was fading fast. In 1274, a fleet of thirty ships loaded with Song refugees and their families arrived and, being mostly merchants, were allowed to settle in Thang Long where they established a new commercial district. This was the beginning of a major emigration of Song refugees.

As Song fortunes sank, the Tran became more determined and watchful as the Mongol attitude toward them became more imperious. In 1275, the Tran court requested dismissal of the Daruhaci. Kubilai responded by naming a new Daruhaci and renewing the six demands of 1267. In 1276, as Kubilai was engaged in heavy fighting with Song, a Mongol envoy arrived demanding that the Tran assist by also attacking the Song. The Tran refused. In that year a Tran spy masquerading as a buyer of medicines was in the north gathering information about the Mongols.

Amidst this threatening situation, the Tran mechanism of leadership functioned perfectly. Tran Canh died in 1277 at the age of 59. In 1278, the 38-year-old king, Tran Hoang, became senior king and the 20-year-old crown prince, Tran Kham, became king. Tran Kham's eldest son, Tran Thuyen, 2 years old, became crown prince. During the Mongol invasions of the 1280s there would be two kings, one in his forties and one in his twenties, as well as a crown prince in early adolescence. They would stick together in complete harmony throughout the ordeal.

In 1278, led by a man named Chai Zhuang, Mongol envoys for the first time came to the border through Guangxi rather than Yunnan. The Tran sought to redirect them through Yunnan, explaining that the route was not secure, but Chai Zhuang brushed aside objections and arrived at Thang Long with a letter from Kubilai full of accusations and demands. Chai Zhuang was turned away without any satisfaction.

In 1279, the Mongols finally extinguished the Song dynasty and ruled unchallenged in the north. In that year, Chai Zhuang arrived again to reiterate Mongol demands, and again he was sent away empty-handed. Mongol power was growing on the northern horizon. An episode in 1281 alerted the Tran to this changing situation. An uncle of the king had been made the leader of a group of envoys sent to the Yuan court. Kubilai appointed him "King of An Nam" and sent him back with a mounted escort of one thousand men under the command of Chai Zhuang, ostensibly to place him on the throne at Thang Long.

This expedition was met at the border by Tran soldiers who let Chai Zhuang pass but went after the royal renegade and seized him. Chai Zhuang was angry about what had happened at the border. He arrived in Thang Long at the head of his armed column and, without dismounting, unceremoniously rode through the palace gate. When a guard officer attempted to stop him he wounded the man in the head with his whip and rode on. When he came to the pavilion for foreign envoys, he dismounted, went in, and sprawled out. Tran Quang Khai, a brother of the senior king, who had given hospitality to Chai Zhuang on his previous visits, came with a poem full of polite and diplomatic sentiments to greet him, but Chai Zhuang refused to acknowledge him.

Tran Quoc Tuan, half-brother of the senior king, then decided to approach the disgruntled envoy. He shaved his head, donned monk's robes, and went into the pavilion where Chai Zhuang and his officers were. He spoke and acted exactly as a Chinese monk, and Chai Zhuang in astonishment stood up to receive him. As they drank tea together, Chai Zhuang became aware of Tran Quoc Tuan's true identity. He had one of his attendants poke Tran Quoc Tuan's head with an arrow, causing blood to flow. Tran Quoc Tuan acted as if nothing had happened and, according to Thang Long annalists, thereby tamed Chai Zhuang with politeness. After Chai Zhuang departed Thang Long, again without anything to show for his long journey, the royal uncle who had been used by the Mongols to humiliate his kin was demoted and assigned to a minor military post.

During the twenty-five years following the First Mongol War, the Tran kings concentrated on enforcing unity and discipline among the princes, strengthening their grip on the human and material resources of the kingdom, and maintaining a vigilant eye on the north. There was a growing conviction among the kings and senior princes that the prospect of living in peace with the Mongols was remote.

The Mongols return

Military preparations preoccupied the Tran kings during 1282 and 1283. Weapons were forged and soldiers were trained. Men recruited to protect the kings were not allowed to study literature for fear it would diminish their fighting spirit. In autumn of 1282, the two kings called a conference of all their military leaders at a location near modern Pha Lai, around fifty kilometers east of Thang Long. Pha Lai was a strategic point that had been fortified for centuries. It was at the western terminus of the range of mountains along the northern edge of the Red River plain where four major rivers flowing from the north and west joined their waters before separating into several channels leading to the sea. Any invader from the north would have to pass by this point. Nearby were the personal estates of Tran Quoc Tuan at Van Kiep, which became a major object of battle in the coming wars. The conference was held in this place not only for the importance it was expected to have in future battles but also to be away from Mongol spies stationed in Thang Long.

It was at this conference that Tran Khanh Du, retrieved from the coal business, was rehabilitated and assigned to command the seaport of Van Don, where, back to his old tricks, he soon made a small fortune by buying up thousands of distinctive hats made in a particular village and then ordering all the local people to buy and wear them in order to distinguish loyal people from strangers and spies. Tran Quoc Toan, a grandson of Tran Quoc Tuan, was chagrined that he was considered too young to participate in the conference. He went home to recruit and train over one thousand soldiers from among his slaves and retainers. His men became famous as a crack unit that the enemy learned to fear, and he would himself die in battle. In contrast to this, Tran Kien, a disgruntled nephew of Tran Quoc Tuan, refused to attend the conference, excusing himself to stay home and "study Daoism." Later, when in the press of battle he was ordered to lead his men into the field, he immediately surrendered and assisted the enemy as a guide. One Tran prince was excluded from the conference for a different reason, having been demoted to be a common soldier for writing a letter that "disparaged the kingdom."

Following this conference, the Tran nobles and their followers returned to their home estates to recruit and train their soldiers. The text of a speech commonly regarded as having been made at this time by Tran Quoc Tuan to his officers has been preserved in Literary Chinese. The text is full of erudite allusions to Chinese history that were added by later writers. Nevertheless, the basic argument is that his officers owe him their obedience because he had given them everything they have and without him they would be nothing. Furthermore, if they do not fight for him they will lose everything they have to the enemy, but if they fight with him he will reward them with even more in the future. In terms of what they have and of what they will additionally receive, he refers to wives, children, slaves, land, and treasure. Here we see the strong proprietary mentality of the Tran family, with its sense of possessing the kingdom and everything in it, being extended as the motivating appeal to its constellation of entourages.

A different kind of appeal was made to the thousands of Song soldiers who had fled from the Mongols and found refuge with the Tran. Tran Nhat Duat, a brother of the senior king, gathered and organized these men into an army that would win a major battle against the Mongols. Tran solidarity with Song against the Mongols during the previous thirty years came from a sense of shared membership in a common civilization under siege by an uncivilized enemy. With the demise of Song, pride of membership in this civilization and confidence in the superiority of being civilized was concentrated in the exercise of Tran dynastic leadership to resist the Mongol foe. Song soldiers were welcomed, placed under their own officers, and allowed to wear Song uniforms. The Tran were careful to alert their soldiers who campaigned with this army not to mistake them for the enemy.

Soldiers were tattooed with characters reading "death to Mongols," and signs were distributed reading: "When the invaders come, everyone must fight them. If you are not strong enough to resist them, you are permitted to flee, but you must not surrender to them." In autumn 1284, as Tran spies reported that Mongol armies were marching toward the borders, soldiers were sent to their assigned stations in the mountain passes. Tran Quoc Tuan commanded the armies facing the modern Chinese province of Guangxi, and Tran Nhat Duat led Song and Tran troops to watch the border with Yunnan.

When all was in readiness in late 1284, the senior king, Tran Hoang, summoned the "elders" in the kingdom to Thang Long. He discussed with them the situation and asked for their response. They reportedly shouted in unison: "To war!" Held just days before the first battles, the purpose of this meeting was to alert these village leaders to what would be expected of the people under their supervision and to rally them to follow wartime instructions.

One of the Mongol demands was that the Tran give provisions and passage to their armies en route to Champa. Kubilai was attacking in all directions at that time, through Korea into Japan, into northern Burma, and also into Champa, which he viewed as a stepping-stone for further seaborne conquests in Southeast Asia and India. The Cham coast was the safest route to avoid the dangerous reefs in the South China Sea. Emboldened by the stiff Tran attitude toward the Mongols, the Cham king, Indravarman V, refused to cooperate with Mongol ambitions, even daring to detain Mongol envoys on their way to Siam and India. In the winter of 1282–1283, a large army led by the Mongol general Sogetu arrived by sea at the Cham capital of Vijaya near the modern city of Qui Nhon. Sogetu defeated the Chams and entered Vijaya, but Indravarman V refused to submit and instead held fast in the nearby mountains, mobilizing more soldiers from distant places. Sogetu abandoned Vijaya and fortified a camp on the coast where he spent a year waiting vainly for reinforcements.

In spring 1284, Sogetu embarked his army and sailed up the coast to the northernmost Cham districts in the modern provinces of Thua Thien, Quang Tri, and Quang Binh, where he won some battles, gathered provisions, and waited for reinforcements. Instead of reinforcements, however, in late 1284 he received orders to march north to Thang Long in support of other Mongol armies marching against the Tran from Guangxi and Yunnan.

The Mongol army, under the command of Kubilai's son Togan, included a core of Mongol units, many trusted units recruited in northern China, and some less reliable units recruited from the old Song territory in southern China. It emerged from Guangxi, crossed the border into Lang Son Province, and fought its way through the passes to a rendezvous at Pha Lai/Van Kiep with the Mongol fleet coming upriver under the command of a Mongol general named Omar. With an army mobilized from nearby localities and over one thousand war boats, Tran Quoc Tuan attempted to prevent this rendezvous. Togan and Omar brushed aside the Tran forces and advanced to Thang Long along the Duong River. Tran forces could not hold them back, and, less than one month after crossing the border, Togan entered Thang Long. The Mongol army in Yunnan commanded by Nasirrudin had meanwhile advanced downriver, pushing away all resistance to their progress, and also arrived at Thang Long.

Withdrawing Tran armies concentrated in the region of the modern city of Nam Dinh, near the Tran home estates. Togan and Omar advanced down the Red River against them, defeating a series of counterattacks meant to delay them. One of these counterattacks became famous because of the person who was captured while leading it. Tran Binh Trong was a descendent of Le Hoan who, because of his valor, had been adopted into the royal family and given a widowed sister of the senior king as wife. When his Mongol captors offered him riches and honor if he would turn to serve them, he is reported to have replied: "It is better to be a ghost in the southern kingdom than a prince in the north." He was beheaded.

Sogetu had penetrated the southern border and was advancing northward through Nghe An Province where Tran Quoc Khang, a full brother of Tran Quoc Tuan, was in command. All available Tran armies were sent south to stop Sogetu and prevent him from linking up with Togan. Tran Nhat Duat, Tran Quang Khai, and Tran Ich Tac, brothers of the senior king, were ordered to lead their armies south, and even Tran Kien was stirred from his Daoist reverie and sent to lead his men to join his father, Tran Quoc Khang. However, unable to overcome the store of resentment he had been nursing for years, Tran Kien immediately went over to the Mongols and guided them against other Tran units hastening south. Tran Ich Tac, with a different store of resentment, also joined the enemy, bringing several other generals with him. Sogetu advanced through Thanh Hoa.

The Tran leaders attempted to slow down Togan by sending envoys to negotiate peace, even sending him the senior king's full sister as an ostensible token of sincerity. At the same time, Tran Quoc Tuan and his son-in-law Pham Ngu Lao led a force in several hundred war boats through the rivers back to Van Kiep, the headquarters for Togan's supply line from the border to Thang Long. Unable to retake Van Kiep, they nevertheless organized Tran forces along the Mongol supply routes to keep them under constant attack. This gained the attention of Togan and prompted him to worry about his rear. He paused and requested reinforcements from Kubilai, but when the Tran kings refused his demand that they appear before him in person, he continued his advance to link up with Sogetu, who pressed forward from Thanh Hoa into the Red River plain.

The two kings were faced with the prospect of being crushed between the two Mongol armies. Tran Quang Khai from the south and Tran Quoc Tuan from the north had rejoined them and together they made plans to lure Togan's attention back north while preparing to reconcentrate in Sogetu's rear, in Thanh Hoa. As Togan's and Sogetu's armies linked up, the kings and generals fled by boat out to sea and up the coast to the Ba Che River in Quang Ninh Province, near the Chinese border. Omar's war boats chased after them down the Red River but they disappeared into the sea and Omar returned with no idea of where they had gone. Disembarking at Ba Che, the Tran leaders sent the royal boats further up the coast to the border to attract the attention of the enemy and then walked on foot over the mountains to the Bach Dang River. With news that the Tran leaders were in the north, Togan went back to Thang Long, concerned that some new threat would materialize in his rear. Meanwhile, the Tran leaders embarked from the Bach Dang River and went directly by sea to Thanh Hoa, where they rallied their scattered armies.

After the Tran leaders had disappeared into the sea, many followed the example of Tran Ich Tac, Tran Kien, and others. Large numbers of Tran officials and soldiers surrendered, convinced that the war was finished. Togan was in Thang Long while Sogetu was at Ninh Binh with some units posted along the Red River between the two points. Hearing that Tran forces were reforming in Thanh Hoa, Togan ordered Sogetu to take some of his men back south to confront them and sent Omar with sixty war boats to assist with water transport. The summer rains were beginning. Suddenly, Tran armies arrived from Thanh Hoa by boat, moving rapidly up the Red River.

Tran Quoc Tuan defeated Mongol forces stationed at modern Hung Yen, and the Tran armies proceeded upriver. Around twenty-five kilometers south of Thang Long, Togan attempted to stop them. In a series of running battles the Mongols were pushed back. Tran Quoc Tuan's grandson Tran Quoc Toan led the attack at Tay Ket, Tran Nhat Duat's Song soldiers led the attack at Ham Tu, and Tran Quang Khai led the attack at Chuong Duong, on the edge of Thang Long. As Tran forces broke into Thang Long, Togan withdrew to Gia Lam on the north side of the Red River.

Sogetu and Omar looked in vain for the Tran armies in Thanh Hoa, for the two Tran kings had led their remaining forces north to attack the Mongols left behind by Sogetu at Ninh Binh. These Mongols fled and just had time to join Togan at Gia Lam before he began his retreat toward Van Kiep. The Tran armies that had taken Thang Long followed in close pursuit, inflicting many casualties with attacks and ambushes. Togan fought his way through the mountains to the Lang Son border and safety. At the same time, Nasirrudin had a similar experience of many ambushes as he withdrew back to Yunnan.

Sogetu and Omar, lacking good information, returned from their Thanh Hoa sojourn and, hoping to rejoin Togan, came up the Red River toward Thang Long. The two Tran kings defeated them in battle at Tay Ket. Sogetu was captured and killed as Omar fled downriver and out to sea. The Tran kings returned to Thang Long six months after the Mongols first crossed the borders.

After proclaiming punishments for those who had gone over to the enemy during the fighting, one of the first post-war tasks taken up by the kings was to order that a census be taken, which occasioned the first recorded argument between a Tran king and his scholar-officials. The officials reasoned that the turmoil and distress occasioned by the war made a census unpropitious. The king replied that it made a census all the more necessary in order to assess damages and losses and to know the condition of the kingdom.

In early 1286, enemy prisoners were released to return north, but a few months later came news that Kubilai had issued orders for a new invasion, and the Tran kings again looked to their soldiers. Stung by Togan's defeat, Kubilai took a vengeful view of the Tran. He cancelled plans underway for a third invasion of Japan and concentrated military preparations in the south. But uprisings in southern China and the time needed to recruit and train new armies forced him to postpone his attack for one year.

In the winter dry season of 1287–1288, Togan again crossed the border into Lang Son Province and moved through the mountains into the lowlands for a rendezvous with the Mongol fleet at Van Kiep. Tran Khanh Du, at Van Don, could not prevent the Mongol war fleet, commanded by Omar, from passing down the coast and upriver to Van Kiep. However, several days later the Mongol supply fleet came along, and he completely ruined it, capturing or sinking every ship, save a small boat in which the Mongol commander fled to Hainan Island. The loss of their supply fleet doomed this Mongol campaign.

At Van Kiep, Togan and Omar waited in vain for the supply fleet before proceeding to Thang Long where they were joined by the column from Yunnan. Together they pushed Tran forces down the Red River and out to sea. Running out of provisions, Togan returned to Thang Long and sent out foraging parties. Omar paused at the Tran home estates to despoil Tran Canh's tomb, then went in search of the supply fleet, of which he found no trace.

After a month of sitting at Thang Long, Togan withdrew to Van Kiep, where Omar joined him after fighting and foraging his way back up the Bach Dang River. Tran armies gathered and hemmed in Togan and Omar at Van Kiep. After a month had passed, the Mongols were running out of food and had no choice but to break out and return to China. Omar went downriver where he was captured and his entire fleet was lost when Tran Quoc Tuan ambushed him at the Bach Dang estuary. Meanwhile, Togan fought his way through the mountains to the Lang Son border, and the Yunnan contingent returned the way it had come.

Kubilai was not reconciled to this defeat. He continued to issue plans for another invasion until his death in 1294. But Mongol expeditions were engaged in Burma and in Java during these years, and Kubilai's followers were growing weary of conquest. In 1289, the Tran released most of their prisoners of war, but Omar, whose return Kubilai particularly demanded, was intentionally drowned when the boat transporting him was contrived to sink.

It is recorded that during the Mongol invasions "many noblemen and officials went to the invader's camps and surrendered." After the wars, those who returned to allegiance were examined and suffered punishments appropriate to their cases, whether death, banishment, confiscation of property, or changing of surname as a mark of treason. After this procedure was completed, a trunk captured from the Mongols that was filled with lists of the names of those who had surrendered to them was burned to symbolically put an end to the matter and "to soothe rebellious inclinations."

After punishing traitors, the Tran kings presided over another round of rewarding the meritorious. When some expressed dissatisfaction with what they had received, the senior king is reported to have won them over by saying: "If any of you can guarantee that the enemy will not return, I will promote you to the highest rank possible and not be sorry to do it. But supposing it turns out that you are wrong, and I have already given you a generous reward; if you earn more merit when the enemy returns, what more can I give to reward you then?" The appeal was to material rewards. And the prospect of another Mongol attack remained alive.

In the winter of 1289–1290, the king, Tran Kham, led an attack into what is now Laos. He brushed aside the objections of scholar-officials who argued that the land was still suffering from the effects of war by saying that it was necessary to do this precisely for that reason, so the people in the mountains who were inclined to raid the lowlands would not get the idea that war had exhausted Tran defenses. Another reason may have been to offer opportunities for his men to earn more merit and plunder.

Farewell to tattoos

In late 1288, tax exemptions were published proportional to wartime damages. But there were also long-term economic and social effects of the war. By autumn of 1290, a famine began that lasted for two years, causing taxes to be cancelled entirely. The Tran court distributed food to the poor for a time until overwhelmed by the starving. There is no record of what caused these crop failures. Perhaps a decade of preoccupation with war had led to neglect and breakdown of the water control system. Perhaps the mobilization of men out of the rice fields into the battlefields had disrupted the planting and harvesting calendar. Perhaps there were floods, drought, and pestilence that have not been recorded.

Whatever the case, the result was a socio-economic shift with a drastic reduction in population from death by starvation, the abandonment of villages, and large numbers of people selling their land, and also selling their children and themselves into slavery, in order to survive. In 1292, as the famine eased, a law was published that people who had sold themselves into slavery during the famine could be redeemed, but land and property could not be redeemed. The people in a position to acquire the land, property, and slaves made available at bargain prices during this long famine were the Tran noblemen and their entourages with their riches and honors earned in wartime. The trend toward large aristocratic estates worked by slave labor or the labor of peasants in a serf-like condition accelerated from this time.

It was amidst this dire famine that the royal family passed through another generational transition. Tran Hoang, the senior king, died in 1290 at the age of 50. He had been the center around which the clashing egos of Tran princes had revolved during the dramatic events of the 1280s. He was a master of discipline, of consensus, and of delegating authority. His father, Tran Canh, had taught him the importance of family solidarity. His son, Tran Kham, and his grandson, Tran Thuyen, learned to exercise similar attitudes toward maintaining dynastic leadership.

In 1292, the 16-year-old crown prince, Tran Thuyen, was married to a granddaughter of Tran Quoc Tuan, and the following year he was proclaimed king. Tran Kham, still in his mid 30s, became senior king. He remained very much in command until his death in 1308. He encouraged his younger brothers, Tran Duc Viep and Tran Quoc Chan, to play more active roles at court. Tran Duc Viep died in 1306, but Tran Quoc Chan was a prominent member of the court for the next thirty years. He became a trusted advisor of Tran Thuyen, and the circumstances of his death in 1328 came to symbolize for later historians a major turn in dynastic fortunes.

Shortly after Tran Thuyen's accession, his mother, a daughter of Tran Quoc Tuan, died. She was much respected for her bravery. Stories were told of how she once protected her husband, Tran Kham, from a tiger that had escaped from its cage, and how she had confronted a runaway elephant that had broken into her palace. She was typical of many Tran women who were praised for their courage and loyalty during the era of the Mongol Wars.

In the late 1290s, tension erupted between the senior and junior kings. In his early twenties, Tran Thuyen developed a habit of going out into the city at night with a group of companions and carousing until dawn. His fondness for alcohol led to many days when the palace dozed away the daylight hours while he slept off his hangover. Tran Kham spent most of his time at the downriver palace. However, when he discovered what was going on in Thang Long, he became exceedingly angry and severely rebuked the young king, threatening to dethrone him and replace him with a brother. Tran Thuyen eventually took his father's reprimands to heart and for the rest of his life forswore drinking alcohol. He came to be regarded as a strong and competent king, strict but fair, loyal to friends but also a good judge of character. Yet, his youthful rebellion left a lasting mark on the dynasty with a loosening of pride in the Tran martial ethos.

In 1299, Tran Kham summoned Tran Thuyen to a palace where, before an audience of Tran princes, arrangements had been made for him to be tattooed in the manner of Tran men. Tran Kham's explanation to his son was recorded as follows: "Our family comes from the river mouth and our ancestors were blessed with good fortune. For generations we have respected martial valor and our profession has been war. We all have dragons tattooed on our thighs to show that we have not forgotten our origin." The Tran sense of family solidarity was based on a warrior ethos that was expressed by the tattoos on their thighs. According to an explanation recorded at that time, the dragons on Tran thighs were associated with the crocodiles found at the mouth of the Red River. The dragon was also an old and enduring symbol of royal authority shared with other Asian thrones. Perhaps the Tran journey upriver to Thang Long was celebrated with a visual reminder of how a crocodile became a dragon.

Tran Thuyen, however, did not want to be tattooed. He watched and waited for a moment when his father's attention was taken in conversation with others, and then he quickly slipped away from the palace. He was the first Tran king not to be tattooed. A generation later, in 1323, men selected as officers for the palace guard could no longer wear tattoos, which by then were considered old fashioned and ugly. The abandonment of this mark of family identity came amidst a gradual but fundamental shift in the composition of dynastic leadership.

Farewell to the princes

For a few decades, the heroes of the Mongol Wars continued to lead soldiers, govern assigned territories, and offer advice at court. But they passed steadily from the scene. Tran Quang Khai, Tran Quoc Tuan's closest friend and the hero of the Battle of Chuong Duong, died in 1294. Tran Quoc Tuan, commander-in-chief and the hero of the Battles of Tay Ket and Bach Dang, died in 1300, as also did his full brother Tran Quoc Khang, who had spent his career in Nghe An and had fought running battles with Sogetu's army as it came north from Champa. Tran Quoc Tuan's son-in-law Pham Ngu Lao, who gained fame for laying ambushes for Togan in the northern mountains, actively led soldiers on the frontiers until just before his death in 1320. The longest surviving members of that generation were Tran Nhat Duat, Tran Khanh Du, and Tran Khac Chung, and they each represented particular tendencies in the royal family.

Tran Nhat Duat was born in 1255. A son of Tran Canh and the hero of the Battle of Ham Tu, he was active as a loyal member of the royal entourage throughout his life. Whether suppressing rebellion in the mountains or leading armies against Mongols, he was always reliable. He spent much time with non-Viet people and never needed an interpreter, whether talking with Chams, with upland peoples, or with Chinese. His personal estates were in Thanh Hoa and all of his wives were from that province, but he remained attentive to affairs in Thang Long for many years and was deeply concerned about the future leadership of the dynasty.

Tran Thuyen's senior wife, a granddaughter of Tran Quoc Tuan known as the Bao Tu queen, had no children, and sons born to lesser wives had not survived infancy. Then, in 1300, Tran Thuyen finally obtained a son and heir when Tran Manh was born to the Chieu Tu queen, a daughter of Princess Thuy Bao and Tran Binh Trong, who had been captured and killed during the Mongol Wars. Although not from the senior line of the Tran family, the Chieu Tu queen was nevertheless a high-ranking Tran woman, so there were particularly strong hopes that her son would survive to inherit the throne. Fearing that the palace was not propitious for the health of infants, Chieu Tu's mother, the Princess Thuy Bao, was asked to take responsibility for rearing the baby. She excused herself from the task and asked her brother, Tran Nhat Duat, to do this in her place.

Tran Nhat Duat reared Tran Manh as if he were one of his own sons, training him in martial skills, seeing to his education with books, and teaching him to have concern for public affairs while at the same time living simply and viewing himself as but one member of a dynastic team. Tran Manh would be king during a time of unprecedented challenges to dynastic authority. That he would be able to maintain a measure of integrity and competence amidst a general shift in social and political values away from Tran leadership is a tribute to the quality of Tran Nhat Duat as an adoptive father and mentor. When Tran Thuyen spent six months away on an expedition to Champa in 1312, Tran Nhat Duat was left in charge at Thang Long with the young crown prince. By the time Tran Manh had come of age and became sole king in 1320, Tran Nhat Duat was advancing in age and became less active at court. He died at age 75 in 1330.

Tran Khanh Du, with his checkered yet illustrious career, represents the tendency of some Tran princes to withdraw from public affairs and pursue private gain, ignoring Thang Long and settling down to a life of leisure on their estates. He had a reputation for corruption and making trouble, but his seizure of the Mongol supply fleet in 1288 made him a hero and virtually untouchable for the rest of his long life.

Tran Kham disliked him and considered him to be a bad influence in the royal family. In 1296, Tran Kham summoned him to answer charges that his coarse and greedy behaviour was causing distress to the people in his jurisdiction. He replied, "We are hawks and the people are ducks. The purpose of ducks is to feed the hawks. What's so strange about that?" Tran Kham was so incensed with this arrogant reply that Tran Khanh Du hastened from Thang Long before judicial proceedings could be initiated against him. He kept away from court affairs until after Tran Kham's death. When Tran Thuyen attacked Champa in 1312, he was placed in charge of the seaborne units, but his lust for plunder and disregard of instructions angered Tran Thuyen. His last recorded public act was in 1316 when he was sent to conduct a census and to collect taxes in Nghe An. The king made sure to send along with him an official known for integrity, but that did not prevent accusations of fraud from being made. Thereafter, Tran Khanh Du is not mentioned in the records until his death in 1339, at which time he must have been around 100 years old.

The trend among Tran princes in the fourteenth century was for there to be fewer and fewer in the mold of Tran Nhat Duat and increasing numbers who withdrew from public life to their own private lives in the mode of Tran Khanh Du. Tran Khac Chung represented a different and more portentous trend of people entering the royal family from outside and compromising it for their own ambitions. This man was originally named Do Khac Chung, but he was given the royal surname and adopted into the royal family as a result of his high-risk but successful performance in a side drama of the Mongol invasion of 1284–1285. When Togan and Omar were camped across the river from Thang Long shortly before occupying it, the senior king, Tran Hoang, called for a volunteer to go into the Mongol camp and pretend to negotiate for peace while in fact spying out the situation there. Do Khac Chung, a famous gambler, was excellent at presenting a bold front and engaging in clever talk; he immediately asked to be given the assignment. In the course of his successful visit to the Mongol camp he had an interview with Omar in which, as recorded among the Tran, he audaciously bantered with the Mongol general. He then got safely away despite efforts by Omar to have him detained. He was subsequently admitted to high councils and given the royal surname with the rank of a Tran nobleman.

In 1298, Tran Khac Chung was appointed to administer the royal capital of Thang Long. In 1303, he was elevated to a coveted rank with close access to the king, normally reserved for eunuchs. During a visit to Champa in 1301, Tran Kham had promised a marriage alliance with the Cham king. In 1305, when Cham envoys arrived with gifts, asking for fulfillment of this promise, all of the court officials argued against it except for Tran Khac Chung and one other prince. Tran Kham sent a princess to marry the Cham king. Two years later, the Cham king died and the Tran worried that the princess was in danger of being burned on his funeral pyre. Tran Khac Chung was sent to rescue her from that prospect. He arrived back in Thang Long many months later after dawdling at sea to prolong an affair with the princess. This earned him the hatred of some Tran princes, in particular a son of Tran Quoc Tuan who, referring to the meaning of the characters in Tran Khac Chung's name, said: "This guy is unlucky for our house. Does not his name mean that we are finished?" (Tran Khac Chung literally means: "the Tran can die.")

Thereafter, Tran Khac Chung kept a low profile for a few years, but after Tran Kham's death he insinuated himself back into the center of things, obtaining promotions in 1313 and 1315. He was so prominent at court in 1315 that some officials blamed him for a drought in that year, saying that it was a sign of his wickedness. He once suffered a demotion for publicly making a joke and causing laughter in the palace when the Tran royal tombs were struck by lightning, but it was a temporary setback. With a glib tongue he talked himself into the confidence of the young and unsuspecting king.

In 1319, Tran Manh's first son, Tran Vuong, was born to a non-royal woman from Tran Khac Chung's home village in the eastern part of the Red River plain. She had apparently been introduced into the palace through Tran Khac Chung's influence. Tran Khac Chung posed as a "teacher" of Tran Vuong and began to nurture hopes of the boy inheriting the throne.

Despite Tran Khac Chung's aspirations for Tran Vuong, there remained a strong belief among senior members of the dynasty that the mothers of kings must be from the royal family. The leader of this group was Tran Quoc Chan, a brother of Tran Kham. In the 1310s he twice led armies against Champa and became the most trusted advisor of the senior king, Tran Thuyen. Before he died in 1320, Tran Thuyen established Tran Quoc Chan as the mentor of his heir, the young king Tran Manh. In 1323, Tran Quoc Chan's daughter, Hien Tu, was appointed Tran Manh's senior queen. Her age is not known but she was still too young to bear children. Tran Khac Chung and others argued for making Tran Vuong the crown prince. Tran Quoc Chan argued forcefully against this, asking to wait until his daughter, a Tran woman, could produce an heir.

Frustrated by Tran Quoc Chan's influence, those who wished to see Tran Vuong made king conceived a plot. Tran Phau, a member of Tran Quoc Chan's entourage, was bribed with a large amount of gold to falsely accuse Tran Quoc Chan of treason. In 1328, Tran Quoc Chan was imprisoned in a temple. The young king was uncertain what to do. Tran Khac Chung advised that "it is easier to capture a tiger than to let one go," and Tran Quoc Chan was left to die of starvation. In the following year, Tran Vuong was made king, with Tran Manh becoming senior king.

Tran Khac Chung did not live long to enjoy the fruits of his schemes. He died in 1330. One of Tran Quoc Chan's sons sent a slave to dig up his corpse and to chop it into bits. It was not until 1344 that Tran Quoc Chan was posthumously rehabilitated when a dispute among the wives in Tran Phau's household brought the conspiracy into the open. Tran Phau was condemned to die by slicing, and Tran Quoc Chan's son ate his flesh as it was cut away. Tran Vuong, the young prince who became king as a result of the conspiracy, died in 1341 at age 22. Meanwhile, Queen Hien Tu had begun to have children, and one of these, 5-year-old Tran Hao, was immediately raised to the throne.

In his later years, Tran Manh was haunted by his "error" in not preventing the death of Tran Quoc Chan. The death of Tran Quoc Chan ended the mutual trust and family discipline that had been the strength of previous generations of Tran leaders. Tran Manh was thereafter a lonely king. The counsel of senior princes and the loyal service of junior princes became more attenuated than it had ever been for a Tran king.

Already in 1300, the right to contribute to discussions at court was restricted to those who had participated in the wars. Anyone speaking up who did not have a veteran's identification card was demoted. However, some cards were issued during a time in 1258 when the royal seal had been lost and temporarily replaced with a hastily carved wooden seal, and there were questions about these having been counterfeited. So an inquest was initiated to examine such cards for authentication. The same issue came up again in 1316, and Tran Thuyen, who experienced the wars of the 1280s as an adolescent, commented: "People at court who are not familiar with references to the past will make big mistakes in their work."

Even as the older generation resisted the loosening of its grip on public affairs, new fashions took hold, stimulated by the cosmopolitan energy of the Mongol Yuan dynasty. Sorcery and fasting to obtain supernatural knowledge and power had been practiced for centuries, but a Daoist master from Fujian stimulated an unprecedented popularization of these practices in the early fourteenth century. A royal servant famous for training horses, playing chess, and mixing medicine studied with Daoist experts to perform exorcisms. A Buddhist yoga master from China claiming to be 100 years old amazed people with his curious skills and even obtained the admission of his daughter into the palace. Performers from China introduced tightrope walking and rope dancing as well as Yuan dynasty classical opera (called *tuong* in its Vietnamese adaptation).

The strangest case of all was connected with Tran Hao, who in 1341 became king at the age of 5. When he was 3 years old, he had fallen into a lake while watching fish and was apparently drowned. A doctor named Trau Canh revived the boy with acupuncture. Trau Canh's father had been a doctor with the Mongols during the 1280s, was captured by the Tran, and then chose to remain in Thang Long. He treated members of the royal family and became rich with land and slaves. Trau Canh followed his father's profession and was known as a skillful physician. In 1351, he prescribed a cure for the 15-year-old king's impotence that involved human sacrifice and sexual intercourse with his sister. The cure was declared successful, although Tran Hao never did have any children, and Trau Canh thereafter became a popular physician among the palace women. With free access to the palace he began to carry on affairs with the women there. Informed of this, Tran Manh, the senior king, wanted to have him killed, but he was spared because he had saved Tran Hao's life.

Tran Manh hated Trau Canh so much that when Trau Canh came to his deathbed in 1357 and repeatedly informed him that his pulse was "melancholy,"

Tran Manh roused himself to write a satirical poem before he died: "When examining the pulse do not speak of too much melancholy; Mr. Trau's medicine should blend the ingredients; If one unceasingly speaks of melancholy, I fear that melancholy will only be aroused to increase." The reluctant mercy shown to the doctor was emblematic of Tran Manh's intelligent yet inclusive spirit, the last echo of his great-great-grandfather Tran Canh's teachings about non-duality. Although in 1347 he ordered a kinsman to be killed for stealing one of his robes and then having the cheek to wear it at court, Tran Manh sometimes substituted poetry for justice. Within a decade of his death, Tran Hao's palace became a playground for clever commoners. It was also at this time that an unprecedented challenge began to materialize on the Cham frontier.

Tran Kham's visit to the Cham king in 1301 had built upon the anti-Mongol alliance to achieve a marriage agreement. In return for a Tran woman as wife, the Cham king relinquished his claim to modern Quang Tri and Thua Thien Provinces. The death of the Cham king in 1307 dissolved the marriage and gave rise to Cham demands for the return of those territories. Tran Thuyen's expedition of 1311–1312 was in part a response to those demands and resulted in deposing the Cham king and replacing him with a brother who agreed to be a Tran vassal. In 1313, a Tran army was sent to repulse a Siamese army from Sukhothai, a kingdom in central Thailand, which had emerged from the mountains to attack the Chams. In 1318, a Tran expedition expelled the Cham vassal, who had rebelled, and replaced him with another Cham leader. In 1326, that vassal also rebelled, defeated a Tran expedition, and thereafter sought to regain the lost territories. The Tran took no initiatives toward Champa for over two decades, being occupied for several years in the 1330s with fighting against encroaching Laotians along the upper Ca River in Nghe An. In 1353, an attempt to intervene in a Cham succession dispute failed when Cham war boats prevented supply ships from reaching the Tran army, which had advanced as far as modern Quang Ngai Province before turning back. Thereafter, the Tran were on the defensive in the south. In the 1360s, a Cham king appeared, called Che Bong Nga, who in the 1370s and 1380s would strike deadly blows upon the Tran dynasty.

Tran Manh and the late Tran literati

In the 1320s, as the older generation of Tran nobles died and the younger generation showed little interest in government, Tran Manh came to rely increasingly upon a new generation of educated commoners, scholars of the Confucian classics who entered government by taking written examinations. There had been no exams since before the Mongol Wars when, in 1299, a call was issued for students to prepare for an examination. The exam was held in 1304 and graduated 44 men with 330 others selected to pursue further study. The curriculum for exams was clearly announced and included taking dictation, writing essays on the Confucian classics, writing poetry, and demonstrating knowledge of mourning regulations and of how to write royal proclamations and petitions to the king. Until the 1370s, when the political situation changed drastically, the court annals record further examinations in 1314 and 1344; another source indicates an examination in 1364, and there may have been others for which information has not survived. Other kinds of exams were also held during this time, for example in 1304 officials in the judiciary were examined on their knowledge of the law, and in 1321 monks were examined on their knowledge of the Diamond Sutra.

Apparently stimulated by the exam of 1304, a new type of poetry became fashionable. The exam included a type of prose poem that had been developed in the Han dynasty, called *phu* (Chinese *fu*). Subsequently, *phu* began to be written in the vernacular using Nom characters. Nguyen Si Co, a scholar and official with a reputation for being good at making jokes, is associated with this new poetic form. Younger scholars fondly remembered his collegial, friendly, and entertaining manner.

Quite different in personality were Truong Han Sieu and Nguyen Trung Ngan, both of whom had long and illustrious careers at court in the mid fourteenth century. After the death of Tran Thuyen in 1320, and with the thinning out of Tran princes interested in public affairs, Tran Manh brought many talented scholars into service at court. The court annal notes in 1323 that scholars had become more numerous at court and from that time were taking a larger role in court discussions. The names of thirteen scholars were listed in that year as the most prominent, and two of these were Truong Han Sieu and Nguyen Trung Ngan.

Truong Han Sieu (?–1354) had come to notice in the entourage of Tran Quoc Tuan, who introduced him to service at court before his death in 1300. Because of his erudition, the kings called him "teacher" rather than referring to him by his name. In the 1320s he had risen to the highest position at court for someone not a member of the royal family, a position that gave him personal access to the king. He had a reputation for being distant and arrogant toward other scholars. He socialized with eunuchs and married his daughters to men of wealth rather than of learning. In 1326 he accused two scholars working in the judiciary of taking bribes. When Tran Manh ordered an investigation, Truong Han Sieu remarked to someone that an investigation should not be necessary because he was himself someone of high position and his word should be good enough. When Tran Manh heard of this remark, he rebuked Truong Han Sieu, saying that no matter what their rank or position all officials served him and he would not take the word of one against another. The investigation revealed that Truong Han Sieu had no grounds for his accusation and so he was fined heavily. One of the men whom he had accused was found to be "honest and meticulous" and was accordingly promoted.

From the late 1330s into the 1350s, Truong Han Sieu again received important assignments at court. In 1339 he wrote an inscription on the occasion of renovating a Buddhist temple, and in 1343 he wrote another inscription on the occasion of renovating a stupa. In these inscriptions he expressed a complicated attitude that combined his Confucian education with both appreciation for Buddhism as a moral force and criticism of superstitious and corrupt practices that he believed were undermining this moral force. Later Confucian historians took his critical comments out of context to argue that he opposed Buddhism. Buddhists, in turn, have pointed to a poem of his that refers to his having made an "error" to suggest that he was expressing repentance for having opposed Buddhism; in fact, the poem says that the "error" was in being defensive about his reputation and plausibly refers to the 1326 episode. Truong Han Sieu died in 1354 on his way back from supervising soldiers sent to reinforce the southern border against Cham attacks after the unsuccessful expedition of the previous year.

Nguyen Trung Ngan (1289–1370) was a child prodigy who passed the examination of 1304 and irritated colleagues with his boundless pride. He was famous for writing a poem that read as follows: "I am a talented scholar at court; from childhood my spirit could swallow a water buffalo; at twelve I was an advanced student; at sixteen I passed the examinations; at twenty I was a government official; at twenty-six I was sent as envoy to Beijing." In addition to excessive pride, he was also known to be careless with details, which led to a setback in 1326 when he incorrectly recorded the rank of a Tran nobleman. Tran Manh appreciated his ability so did not punish him for this but rather reassigned him away from court in Thanh Hoa. Six years later he was back at court and received a series of promotions until in 1342 he was placed in charge of the Privy Council. In that year, the Privy Council was given responsibility for selecting the palace guardsmen, and he personally supervised the guard units in Thang Long. In consideration of this, from 1351 he was allowed to wear a military uniform.

Another man found on the 1323 list of scholars was Doan Nhu Hai, who had begun to serve at court in the 1290s. He gained favor when he assisted the reconciliation between Tran Kham and Tran Thuyen during their feud over Tran Thuyen's drunkenness. He later distinguished himself as an envoy to Champa and with administration on the Cham frontier. In 1335, he led an army up the Ca River in Nghe An against encroaching Lao. After initial success he led his army into a trap. More than half of his men were lost, and he was drowned trying to escape. Tran Manh eulogized him by warning his officials to beware of excessive ambition and of trying to achieve too much. In fact, this class of scholars was socialized to compete for the attention of the king, and the desire for acclaim was for them conflated with public service. They were not members of a bureaucracy in which promotions and demotions followed a prescribed procedure. As Tran Manh made clear in 1326, they were members of the royal entourage and stood equally in relation to him for assignment as he saw fit; he did not recognize any appeal to hierarchy among them.

An episode demonstrating Tran Manh's attitude toward court officials occurred in 1342 when he appeared early one morning at the Censorate office after it had been renovated. The two ranking Censorate officials had not yet arrived, so a subordinate greeted the king and facilitated the visit. When the two officials arrived later and discovered what had happened they petitioned the king to punish the subordinate for allowing anyone to visit the Censorate when they were not present. Tran Manh replied that he could go wherever and whenever he wanted and instructed them to drop the matter. They nevertheless persisted and became very heated. Although Tran Manh repeatedly told them to stop, they stubbornly continued the argument until they were finally dismissed. Commoner officials were beginning to be excessively attached to what they considered to be the privileges of court appointments.

The increase of educated commoners at court reached a point where many unauthorized people gained admittance to the royal compound and loitered about. In 1337, an edict specified that all people coming to court must present their credentials, and that those found without proper identification, "doing nothing," were to be expelled. In 1342, an edict specified that all officials were to be reviewed for retention or dismissal, making it clear that they served only at the pleasure of the king.

From the 1340s, Pham Su Manh and Le Quat, two scholars on the 1323 list, became increasingly prominent in royal service. They were both students of Chu An, the son of an immigrant Chinese and a Vietnamese woman from the outskirts of Thang Long. Chu An was a highly respected scholar who instead of entering government service remained a teacher and a critic of public affairs. Eventually, Tran Manh persuaded him to be the teacher of the young king, Tran Hao. After Tran Manh's death, Chu An criticized Tran Hao's favorites in high position as disreputable characters and advised that seven of them be beheaded. When Tran Hao ignored him, he withdrew from the capital and went to live in retirement at Chi Linh, sixty kilometers east of Thang Long.

Pham Su Manh and Le Quat, like their teacher, were known for their integrity. They were also competent royal officials who were given important assignments.

However, when they petitioned Tran Manh to "change the system of government" to be in accord with their understanding of Confucian principles, Tran
Manh understood them to mean a bureaucratic system such as existed in China
since Song times and reportedly said: "Each country perfects its own pattern;
South and North are different from each other. If I listen to pale-faced scholars
seeking to market their plans, there will be rebellion."

Despite increasing reliance upon men whose education encouraged a Confucian bias, Tran Manh considered their arguments as excessively drawing
distinctions and establishing unnecessary hierarchies. His bias was toward
the non-duality and sense of inclusiveness that traced back to the thought of
Tran Canh and that had been a core value of Tran leadership for over a
century. In his time, however, there were no external conditions in the form
of a cohesive band of princes to give material expression to this thought.
Instead, he had to work with bickering intellectuals who were full of self-
importance, erudite theories, and their own competing ambitions. The echo
of Tran Canh's thought that reached him after four generations was
expressed in naïve, sometimes self-effacing, even simplistic, assertions that
there was nothing to worry about. He instinctively looked beyond the
posturing of his officials to a firm belief that everyone and everything was
in some fundamental way related and that there were no insurmountable
incompatibilities in his kingdom.

For example, a son was born to the Bao Tu queen after Tran Manh had
become king. Since the Bao Tu queen was from the senior line of the Tran
family while Tran Manh's mother was from the junior line, it could be
claimed that her son ranked ahead of the king. When some sought to give
his half-brother the rank and privileges of a crown prince, he quickly agreed,
despite many officials advising him to think more carefully about it. His reply
to objections was that there was nothing to worry about since he believed that
his half-brother did have a stronger claim than himself and so he was merely
occupying the throne temporarily until the other came of age. The potential
problem foreseen by his advisors never came to pass because the half-brother
died young.

When officials reported to him that there were great numbers of unemployed
people wandering around who did not have families, did not pay taxes, and did
not obey royal edicts, he replied, "If this were not the case, how would I be able
to follow my calling to pacify the realm? You want me to punish these people,
but to achieve what purpose?" He understood that attempting to punish people
in distress would push them into rebellion. He also understood government to be
a process and not a plan to solve everything to perfection. Later historians
considered him to be wise, intelligent, humane, and deeply conservative in

resisting any change to what he had inherited from his forbears. He was also motivated by a Buddhist, even Daoist, sensibility that was reluctant to take any unnecessary action for fear of an inevitable and unwanted reaction. He did send soldiers to attack rebel leaders, but he wanted nothing to do with activist schemes for disciplining mere unfortunates. He made a point of instructing his sons to be kind and gentle to their subordinates.

He imagined that the political stability achieved by his fathers would last forever. He did not know that his world was on the brink of disaster and that later historians would see his reign as the last sunny era of his dynasty. His was a time when, despite accumulating worries, the momentum of Tran power remained a plausible source of confidence and comfort for educated people. Consequently, books were compiled that mapped the past from a Tran vantage and took the Tran achievement for granted.

The *Thien Uyen Tap Anh* (Compiled Extracts about Zen Worthies) was first arranged some time in the fourteenth century, almost certainly during the reign of Tran Manh and probably in the 1330s. It consists of biographies of monks and nuns who lived from the sixth to thirteenth centuries in Giao Province/An Nam/Dai Viet. The intent of the compiler was to document lineages through which the "mind seal" of enlightenment was passed to the Tran dynasty. It was modeled upon "transmission of the lamp" texts written during the Tang dynasty and aimed to show that the Tran had received true Zen doctrine. The last people mentioned died in the time of Tran Canh who had developed a particular line of Buddhist thought that became characteristic of Tran royalty. Tran Canh, as well as his son and grandson, Tran Hoang and Tran Kham, were regarded as Zen masters by some temple dwellers. Tran Kham spent his last years, died, and was cremated on Mount Yen Tu, where he propounded the Bamboo Grove (Truc Lam) School, a short-lived royal sect that later writers associated in various ways with worthies in the *Thien Uyen Tap Anh*.

In the 1320s, Ly Te Xuyen, the royal librarian of Buddhist texts and sutras, compiled two books. The *Co Chau Phap Van Phat Bon Hanh Ngu Luc* (Record of What has been Said about the Origin and Deeds of the Cloud Dharma Buddha at Co Chau) is a history of the cult of the first Buddha in the land, dating from its origin in the time of Shi Xie at the turn of the third century. It is an accumulation of materials over a period of a thousand years. The text as it presently exists contains several "endings" where compilers at particular times finished their work. The last ending before the eighteenth century contains a description, dated in 1322, of Tran royal officials giving thanks to the Buddha for answering prayers for rain, and it also gives a description, written by Ly Te Xuyen, of the new year festival of this Buddha as it was celebrated both at its temple and in Thang Long.

In 1329, Ly Te Xuyen compiled the *Viet Dien U Linh Tap* (Departed Spirits in the Vietnamese Realm). This book contains biographies of twenty-seven deities beginning with Shi Xie and ending with cults established during the Ly dynasty. These deities were considered to have responded to the prayers of Tran kings to grant success to their armies during the Mongol Wars and the 1312 expedition to Champa. Information is cited from earlier texts and from oral tradition about the spirits worshipped by Tran kings as guardian deities of the kingdom. Titles conferred on the deities by Tran kings in gratitude for their protection of the realm are recorded.

These works view the Tran dynasty as sustained by the divine forces that govern human affairs and by the wisdom of correct teaching about the Buddha. The rising class of scholars included those inclined to look askance at what they perceived as superstition, corruption, or wastefulness among the adherents of Buddhism. However, at least until the death of Tran Manh in 1357, they knew that they served a king who venerated the Buddha. Tran Manh was inclined to dismiss their ideas about how to organize society and government but appreciated their loyalty and competence. He shrank from interfering in the existing scheme of things to bring change but dutifully intervened, when necessary, to restore order.

Agrarian unrest, Tran Hao, and Nhat Le

While royalty and literati maintained the forms of dynastic rule, an undercurrent of agrarian distress gathered momentum. The post-war famine of 1290–1292 had initiated a pattern of land being absorbed into the estates of royal family members and of peasants shifting into the status of royal slaves. Land once transferred to royal estates was never returned, but people who had sold themselves into slavery were given a term in which to redeem themselves. This term came to an end in 1299, after which redemptions were no longer allowed. Rural poverty was endemic. In 1303, Tran Kham summoned an assembly of wealthy people to contribute money to the poor. At the same assembly he initiated a program to distribute copies of a sutra to the common people for their edification, indicating that he and others viewed poverty as both a material and a moral issue.

The rise of slavery apparently led to disputes on royal estates, for in 1315 an edict forbad mutual denunciations among fathers and children, husbands and wives, and family slaves. Without more information, it is impossible to understand the situation being addressed, but in 1320 an edict forbad false claims of ownership over fields, indicating continued litigation over control of land. There is no indication of whether such litigation was between disputing aristocratic family members or between aristocrats and their slaves or peasants. Whatever the case, it is clear that the agrarian regime was not stable.

There was drought in 1315, and in 1317 it was recorded that banditry was a growing problem. In 1326 there was no rain. In 1333, there was flood and famine. In 1337, granaries were organized to feed the hungry. The following year, floods washed away crops and a big windstorm blew down trees and houses. These troubles were not out of the ordinary; a certain level of rural misery was normal. But the expansion of aristocratic estates and of slavery on those estates significantly reduced the capacity of rural society to respond flexibly to economic distress. In the 1340s the agrarian regime fell into a prolonged crisis that produced rebel armies.

A drought in 1343 initiated a famine that lasted for three years. There was no harvest that year, and the court reduced taxes by half. Many people turned to banditry, especially slaves on royal estates. When the famine continued in 1344, people continued to join bandit gangs, and many who did not want to do that became monks and entered the temples. A rebel leader named Ngo Be assembled an army in the eastern plain near modern Dong Trieu and Mao Khe. Tran officials organized local military units to fight bandits and sent soldiers against Ngo Be. In 1345, Ngo Be's army was defeated, but he continued his career as a rebel leader, and the famine also continued. An edict reduced the punishments for many crimes to encourage the surrender of bandits and rebels. In 1348 there was more drought and flooding. Rebels accumulated in the provinces of Thai Nguyen and Lang Son in the northern mountains and were not pacified until 1351. Then, in 1352, the dike on the Red River below Thang Long broke and flooded a vast region southeast of the capital.

In 1354, another famine brought misery to the rural population. Insects destroyed the harvest, and another 50 percent tax reduction was proclaimed. A fresh outbreak of banditry contributed to the formation of another rebel army, this time led by one claiming to be a descendent of Tran Quoc Tuan. This man rallied large numbers of royal slaves and occupied extensive territories from his base at Van Kiep. In that year, news arrived from the northern border that a son of the traitor Tran Ich Tac intended to attack with an army he was raising in China, which at that time was rent by war as the Mongol regime was in collapse. Nothing came of this, but it added to the sense of unease in Thang Long, as did reports of the foreboding appearance of a wild black tiger in the palace complex. In 1355, there was drought and also floods.

In 1356, amidst these unsettling events, Tran Manh, perhaps seeking some mercy for himself and his tormented kingdom, visited the tomb of Tran Quoc Chan, the father of his senior queen whom he had unjustly condemned to death three decades earlier. While returning to Thang Long by boat he was stung by a bee on his left cheek and fell ill. Despite the efforts of doctors and the prayers of his entourage he died six months later, in early 1357.

Rural unrest continued as Tran Hao, a young man of 21, and not very interested in government, became the only king. In 1358, there was drought, crops were infested with insects, and fish died of pestilence. The court's response was an appeal to wealthy people to give rice to the hungry. Ngo Be reappeared at the head of a rebel army. From his base at Chi Linh, he controlled the north-eastern part of the plain and adjacent uplands. The court ordered the mobiliza-tion of soldiers to fight the rebels. In 1359, floods washed away entire villages along with crops. In 1360, Ngo Be was finally captured and killed along with thirty of his lieutenants. In that year an edict required slaves belonging to royal family members to be tattooed on their foreheads. Anyone found without this tattoo would be treated as a rebel, which implies that the options available to many were now either slavery or rebellion. In 1362, drought again led to crop failure, a 50 percent reduction in taxes, and appeals for rich people to feed the hungry. To set an example, even the king distributed food. Banditry and rebel-lion continued. In 1366, robbers attacked the king himself as he traveled in the countryside at night, and took his royal seal and sword.

Meanwhile the situation on the southern frontier was grim. In 1356, shortly before his fatal bee sting, Tran Manh took Tran Hao on a two-month inspection tour of the southern provinces. Cham relations were deteriorating at this time and efforts to maintain communications with the frontier were urgent; within a year orders went out to dredge and upgrade the canals and waterways in the southern provinces. In 1361 Cham sea raiders were fought off in modern Quang Binh. In 1361, Cham raiders plundered the Hue area and seized many captives. Cham raiders were repulsed in 1366, and the following year more soldiers were sent south to engage the Chams. In 1368, Cham envoys demanded the return of territories that the Tran had acquired with the ill-fated royal marriage alliance of 1305. The Tran response to this demand was to send an army to attack into modern Quang Nam, where it was repulsed.

Soldiers were also mobilized to watch the northern border. The founder of the Ming dynasty was expanding his power in southern China, and the Mongol Yuan dynasty was no longer able to police the border, which inspired disorders. In 1359, Ming envoys appeared in Thang Long for the first time. The Tran sent officials north to investigate what was happening. In 1361, Thang Long politely refused a Ming request to send soldiers to help fight the Mongols. In 1368, Ming envoys arrived to announce their new dynasty and Tran envoys were sent to establish normal relations.

Tran Hao paid little attention to the internal disorders and external threats of the 1360s. Before he died, Tran Manh had made Tran Hao's mother, Queen

Hien Tu, promise to remain in the palace and not withdraw to a nunnery. He must have foreseen that Tran Hao was not competent to be king and hoped that she would exert a positive influence on him. Tran Hao was mainly interested in money, amusements, and drinking. In a thinly veiled scheme to gain cash, he summoned rich people to come to the palace to gamble with him. On another occasion, he found a pretext to confiscate the property of a wealthy pearl merchant.

Many people were gaining access to the palace by virtue of their wealth or entertainment value. One man was given a rank at court simply for performing a trick in which he appeared to drink huge amounts of wine. Tran Hao ordered all members of the royal family to send their opera troupes to his palace; he spent much time watching the Yuan-style opera (*tuong*) that had become fashionable after the Mongol Wars. He also restored Trau Canh to the rank and privileges of which Tran Manh had deprived him. This clever doctor, hated by Tran Manh to his dying breath, had been closely associated with Tran Hao from the time he had revived the prince at the age of 3 from a near drowning accident. Trau Canh's return to the palace was typical of a time when sycophants and adventurers gained ascendancy at Tran Hao's court. In a collection of tales compiled a century later entitled *Linh Nam Chich Quai* (Strange Tales Collected South of the Mountains) can be found a story of a young man, supposedly the son of a divine father and a human mother, who became a favorite of Tran Hao and made a career as a sexual predator until he was killed by a Tran nobleman.

In 1364, Tran Hao went for a drunken swim in the river at night and fell sick. Trau Canh mixed medicines for him and he was cured after two months. But he did not abate his heedless way of life. His nocturnal encounter with robbers in 1366, however, reportedly gave him an intimation that he did not have long to live, in response to which he indulged all his favorite dissipations until his death in 1369 at the age of 33. He had no children. It fell to his mother, Queen Hien Tu, to mobilize the court behind a successor.

Hien Tu was a niece of Tran Kham and the ranking woman at court. After the death of her father, Tran Quoc Chan, she had borne Tran Manh three children, two sons and a daughter. Tran Hao had been the second son. For unrecorded reasons, the eldest son, Tran Duc, had not been considered a good choice to be king. He apparently loved the theatre as much as his brother did, for he married an actress who was known as Vuong Mau, meaning "Royal Mother," because she was famous for performing that role in the opera. It did not matter to Tran Duc that she was already married to an actor named Duong Khuong, nor did it matter to him that she happened to be pregnant with a child of Duong Khuong at the time he married her. She gave birth to a son named Nhat Le. Tran Duc, who had no children of his own, adopted Nhat Le as his own son. By the time Tran

Duc died in 1364, Vuong Mau and Nhat Le were established in the palace as members of royalty.

When Tran Hao died, Nhat Le was the ostensible male heir of Tran Manh by Hien Tu, his only Tran wife. Nhat Le's age is not known, but he could not have been out of his teens. There were three sons of Tran Manh who had established reputations as competent members of the royal family: Tran Nguyen Trac, 50 years old; Tran Phu, 48 years old; and Tran Kinh, 33 years old. However, none of their mothers was a Tran woman. Hien Tu officially recognized Nhat Le as her grandson and the legitimate successor to the throne. Despite Nhat Le's questionable pedigree, she followed the Tran dynastic rule of succession, for which her father had paid with his life. She is recorded as saying: "Duc was the eldest son of the legal wife. He was not able to be king and died young. Is not Nhat Le his son?"

Hien Tu had a reputation for being strictly fair in her relations with the women and children of the palace and for seeking to avoid conflict. Once, when Tran Manh was still alive, evidence surfaced that one of the palace women was using magic to bring harm to Hien Tu's children. When Tran Manh wanted to bring the matter into the open and apply punishments, she persuaded him to let it pass because the woman in question was the daughter of a prominent Tran prince, and she valued harmony in the royal family above all else. She had accepted Nhat Le as the legitimate heir of her son Tran Duc, and she was not prepared to shirk from the implications of this when Tran Hao died.

Nhat Le was raised to the throne. Tran Nguyen Trac was given a high appointment at court, and a daughter of Tran Phu was made queen. Six months later, Nhat Le killed Hien Tu when she expressed regret for his having become king. Nhat Le was reportedly a lascivious drunkard who spent his time in idleness watching opera. In this he may not have been very different from Tran Hao. What was most demoralizing to the Tran nobles and court officials, and what probably turned Hien Tu against him, was that he began to talk about changing the dynastic name to Duong, the surname of his real father. This was a repudiation of his adoption by Tran Duc and an unacceptable threat to the existence of the Tran royal family. Resistance to him gathered around the senior Tran princes.

Tran Phu

Nine months after the death of Hien Tu, a group of Tran nobles led by Tran Nguyen Trac advanced into the palace to depose Nhat Le. Nhat Le escaped over a wall and hid under a bridge. His pursuers could not find him and dispersed.

Nhat Le then gathered his followers and sent them to track down and kill his enemies, eighteen men in all, including not only Tran Nguyen Trac and his son, but also two sons of Hien Tu's daughter Ngoc Pha. This signaled open war between Nhat Le and the Tran royal family.

Tran Phu retrieved his daughter from the palace and fled to the safety of his mother's family in Thanh Hoa. Tran Kinh also fled thither, for his mother and Tran Phu's mother were sisters. A nephew of these sisters, Le Quy Ly, was the leader of the family. They were joined by Tran Nguyen Dan, a great-grandson of Tran Quang Khai, and by Hien Tu's daughter Ngoc Pha. All the soldiers that Nhat Le sent from Thang Long against these people joined them instead of attacking them.

Tran Phu was the senior member of the group. Everyone looked to him for leadership, but he was diffident. Ngoc Pha and others urged him forward. After several days of hesitation he set out for Thang Long with Ngoc Pha and Tran Kinh at his side, leading a growing army of Tran followers. When they arrived at Vu Ban, about fifteen kilometers southwest of Nam Dinh, Tran Phu was proclaimed king and an edict was published dethroning Nhat Le.

On the occasion of proclaiming his accession at Vu Ban, Tran Phu is reported to have said:

> Formerly, our court established the country with its own governing system and did not follow the regulations of Song, for in the north and in the south each ruler has his own kingdom and they did not imitate each other. In the Dai Tri era [1358–1369], pale-faced scholars were used in public service who did not understand the exact purpose of drawing up laws, and all the old laws of our ancestors were changed to go toward northern customs; whether it be things like clothing or like music, they are too many to count. Consequently, we will now begin to govern according to the regulations in the Khai Thai era [1324–1328].

This remarkable statement rallied members of the Tran aristocracy who flocked to join Tran Phu in his triumphal march on Thang Long. It analyzed the troubles in the country as the result of excessive northern influence instigated by educated commoners.

Tran Phu singled out the time of Tran Hao as the time when northern influence threatened the Tran dynastic legacy. He believed that the scholars, with their arguments based on northern books, did not understand how the southern country really worked. Only the Tran princes understood this because, after all, their house had established the country, and the country belonged to them. They had more at stake in governing the country than did the scholars, whose ideas about government were detached from loyalty to any particular dynasty. Whether in the ephemera of opera, medicine, sorcery, dress, music, or in the stiffer legal framework that disciplined a society, Tran Phu and the people around him were convinced that change had destroyed the basis of their country's strength and prosperity. The unrest and rebellion that had broken out since the 1340s, the inability to maintain ascendancy over the Chams, and the fact that a traitor had been nurtured in the bosom of the dynasty were all indications that something had gone wrong.

Tran Phu proposed to go back to the time before the death of Tran Quoc Chan in 1328. That event had resulted in a king whose mother was not a Tran woman. The premature death of this king, Tran Vuong, unexplained in the records, may well have been the work of people who sought to rectify that event after a grandson of Tran Quoc Chan, Tran Hao, was available for the throne. With the failure of Hien Tu's experiment to legitimize Nhat Le by adoption, there were no surviving male heirs of Tran Manh with Tran mothers. Nothing could be done about that. In fact, Tran Phu was able to restore a semblance of the Tran heritage because he could call upon the resources of his mother's family in Thanh Hoa. As it turned out, this was the most important aspect of the events in 1370, for Le Quy Ly, the leader of his mother's family, spent the next thirty years gradually gaining control of the country until he was in a position to completely destroy the Tran dynasty.

Tran Phu with his entourage and army entered Thang Long in triumph. Nhat Le offered no resistance to his demotion, but then he strangled a Tran nobleman who had remained with him as a secret agent of Tran Phu, and because of this he was killed. For the next four months, in late 1370 and early 1371, Tran Phu and his followers were busy celebrating and thinking about how to set things right. Chu An came out of his retirement to congratulate Tran Phu, then died soon after. Tran Nguyen Dan, the next most senior Tran prince, was a literary man and had deep respect for Chu An. Despite the repeatedly expressed scorn of Tran noblemen for "pale-faced scholars" with their schemes for reforming governance, many of these men were nevertheless valued for their loyalty and learning. Furthermore, many scholars were dismayed by the leadership of Tran Hao and of Nhat Le and were ready allies of Tran Phu.

Le Quat, one of Chu An's disciples, wrote an inscription at this time that expresses his respect for how Buddhism had penetrated people of all social classes, for how eagerly people contributed their money and possessions to the temples and monasteries, and for how temples were to be found everywhere and were constantly being repaired or renovated. In comparison with this, he expresses his embarrassment that, although he had spent his youth studying the sages of antiquity and how to instruct the people in proper behavior, there was not yet even one hamlet that followed these teachings and nowhere in the land could he find a school or shrine that was dedicated to classical learning. This reveals that scholars were intellectually alienated from the mainstream of Tran society and culture, which remained focused on Buddhist temples. They earned a place in dynastic affairs with their literary skills, their competence, and their loyalty. Despite Le Quat's gloomy inscription, which apparently described conditions in the countryside, Truong Han Sieu, who had died in 1354, was honored at a shrine to Confucius in Thang Long in 1372. When dynastic affairs fell into disarray in the late fourteenth century, the scholars were in a position to increase their role in government and society.

Tran Phu had time to celebrate his birthday festival and to abolish two laws from Tran Hao's time before an unexpected disaster struck. One law had regulated the reclamation of land from the sea by Tran nobles and one had provided that when a man died his property would be inventoried for royal inspection and potential confiscation. Abolishing these laws removed ways for a greedy king to bite into the aristocracy's freedom to amass land and wealth. But the agenda of re-establishing the prerogatives of the Tran nobles was suddenly superseded by calamity.

Nhat Le's mother had fled to the Cham king Che Bong Nga and, seeking revenge against the Tran lords, suggested to him that following the recent turmoil the situation at Thang Long was an opportunity. In spring of 1371, Che Bong Nga led his seaborne forces up the Red River to plunder Thang Long. He burned down the city along with the palaces before withdrawing unscathed. The Tran were caught completely off guard and no defense was offered against this attack.

Tran Phu had no heart for dealing with this crisis. Within days, he elevated his half-brother, 34-year-old Tran Kinh, to be crown prince. A year and a half later, Tran Kinh was made king and Tran Phu became senior king. The next few years were spent in mobilizing the resources of the kingdom to send armies into the south. Tran Kinh was the leading spirit in this endeavor and made it clear, despite protests from officials at court, that he would lead the soldiers in person.

Le Quy Ly

Tran Kinh's rising profile as leader of the royal family was accompanied by the appearance of Le Quy Ly, his maternal cousin, at a high level of government. Within two months of the Cham invasion, Le Quy Ly was put in charge of the Privy Council and given as wife a Tran princess who had been widowed by Nhat Le. Tran Kinh, in turn, took a woman of the Le family as his queen. In autumn 1371, Le Quy Ly was given a title of nobility and sent to inspect the southern border regions. From his family base in Thanh Hoa, he became the master of the southern provinces and the frontier jurisdictions.

Thang Long palaces were rebuilt in a rustic manner with labor from royal slaves so as not to trouble the rest of the population, which was being mobilized for military purposes. Bandits and drought interfered with and delayed military preparations, but gradually transportation routes into the south were put in order, weapons were manufactured, soldiers were trained, rice was requisitioned, and officers were selected. Tran Kinh was single-mindedly focused upon obtaining revenge for Che Bong Nga's sack of Thang Long.

By early 1376, Tran Kinh was poised to lead his armies south. Le Quy Ly was in charge of gathering supplies from the southern provinces and transporting them down the coast for the campaign. Do Tu Binh, a high official who in 1372 was given overall responsibility for military affairs, was sent to the southernmost Tran jurisdiction, in modern Thua Thien Province, to repulse Cham patrols and report on the situation at the border. It was later rumored that Che Bong Nga sent a large amount of gold to Tran Kinh and expressed a willingness to settle matters peacefully, but Do Tu Binh pocketed the gold and reported to Tran Kinh that Che Bong Nga's colossal insolence required punishment. This was what Tran Kinh wanted to hear, for he had nurtured a consuming anger toward Che Bong Nga.

Tran Kinh embarked his army at Thang Long and went by sea to the Giang River in what is now northern Quang Binh Province. From there he led his army on horseback, pausing for a month at modern Dong Hoi to train and reorganize his troops and to gather prisoners from the Cham population fleeing south. After a month of marching, he arrived before the Cham capital of Vijaya, near the modern city of Qui Nhon. Che Bong Nga enticed him into attacking what he thought was a deserted encampment. After an argument with one of his generals who suspected a trap, he excitedly led his soldiers forward. In a rush of exuberance, his men melted into an undisciplined mob, which the Chams ambushed and utterly defeated. Tran Kinh and three of his generals were killed. Do Tu Binh, in command of the rearguard, abandoned the field and fled north for his life. When the news reached Le Quy Ly, he hastened back to Thang Long.

The death of Tran Kinh in early 1377 reopened the issue of dynastic leadership. Tran Phu had two adult sons. Tran Ngac had been assigned to patrol modern Thai Nguyen Province, in the foothills north of Thang Long, a notorious gathering place for bandits and rebels. His brother Tran Huc had accompanied Tran Kinh's expedition and had not returned. Exercising his accustomed diffidence, and perhaps also revealing what subsequently became his habit of deferring to the suggestions of Le Quy Ly, Tran Phu passed over Tran Ngac and instead raised to the throne his 16-year-old nephew, a son of Tran Kinh named Tran Hien, whom later historians evaluated as muddleheaded. A daughter of Tran Phu, Thuc My, was married to Tran Hien and made his queen. In the midst of sorting out these dynastic arrangements, Che Bong Nga arrived by sea and found a way past coastal defenses to suddenly ascend the Red River. He once again plundered Thang Long before disappearing back into the sea.

In early 1378, Tran Hien celebrated his birthday festival amidst urgent efforts to manufacture more weapons and war boats. Tran Huc appeared in Nghe An married to a Cham princess and claiming to be king. Allied with Che Bong Nga he rallied many people in the southern provinces to his side. Che Bong Nga arrived in the lower Red River plain with an army. Do Tu Binh was sent to stop him but could not. The Chams plundered Thang Long for the third time.

During the next six years, with neither of the kings capable of providing leadership, Le Quy Ly and a group of men associated with him struggled to keep the Chams out of Thang Long. The treasury was empty but money was needed to train, equip, and supply soldiers. To increase revenue and military manpower, the basis of taxation was shifted from land to households. Following the equal field system of the Tang dynasty, able-bodied men were organized into military units, assigned land, and taxed on a per capita basis. The old system in which taxes were levied only on land was not functioning because so much land had disappeared into the estates of royal family members who did not pay taxes. The new system was also designed to stem the flow of impoverished peasants into the ranks of slaves on royal estates. This was the first step in what would be a long-term policy of Le Quy Ly to build a socio-economic base beyond Tran aristocratic control.

In 1379, despite drought, famine, fears of Cham attacks, and a major rebellion in the northeast of the Red River plain, enough taxes were collected that soldiers were assigned to transport money to the mountains for safekeeping. In 1380, the Chams, who then firmly controlled the frontier region of modern Quang Binh, Quang Tri, and Thua Thien Provinces, tightened their grip on Nghe An and attacked into Thanh Hoa. Le Quy Ly led armies south and, gaining victories, pushed the Chams back into the borderlands. In 1381, a local leader in Nghe An was executed for having served the Chams, as was Tran Huc, Tran Phu's son who had rallied support in the southern provinces behind his alliance with Che Bong Nga.

Despite some victories in the field, Tran resources were near exhaustion and the Cham threat remained unabated. In 1381, Buddhist leaders were sent to mobilize all able-bodied monks both from temple monasteries and from mountain retreats to temporarily serve as soldiers against the Chams. Statuary and other treasures from temples and shrines in the lower Red River plain were taken and stored for safekeeping in the mountains. In 1382, the Chams again attacked into Thanh Hoa but were repulsed after desperate fighting by Nguyen Da Phuong, a protégé of Le Quy Ly.

In 1383, Le Quy Ly sent a fleet of large new ships down the coast. They did not advance far, being damaged in a storm, but nevertheless did prevent Cham attacks by sea. Instead, Che Bong Nga led his army through the mountains of Thanh Hoa to emerge into the Red River plain west of Thang Long. A general sent by Tran Phu against him was captured and Che Bong Nga closed in on Thang Long as Nguyen Da Phuong hastily built and garrisoned a defensive "fence" to protect the city. Amidst heavy fighting, Tran Phu fled across the river and took refuge at Bao Hoa Palace, which was located beside Phat Tich Temple, around twelve kilometers northeast of Thang Long near modern Tien Son. There he spent his time compiling a book of instructions for the young king.

Nguyen Da Phuong's defense of Thang Long was successful and the Chams withdrew. Thereafter, Che Bong Nga did not threaten the Tran capital for six years, although fighting continued along the southern coast. At Thang Long, Le Quy Ly and his growing entourage made decisions as the young king and people near him gnawed powerlessly on their resentment. Tran Phu remained at Bao Hoa Palace. Among other things, he supervised an examination held at Phat Tich Temple that graduated thirty men in 1384.

The other senior Tran prince, Tran Nguyen Dan, went into retreat at Mount Con near Chi Linh on the northeastern edge of the plain. He clearly perceived that the Tran dynasty was nearing its end but saw no way to prevent this. He was in his sixties and had made his peace with Le Quy Ly, marrying his son to Le Quy Ly's stepdaughter, who in giving birth to two grandsons thereby ensured that his posterity would survive beyond the age of Tran. The strongest words that he had about the fate of his dynasty were in two lines of poetry: "From past to present, prosperity and decline can truly be seen; Gentlemen, how can it be endured that remonstrations are so few?" Tran noblemen were paralyzed by the daunting disorders of the time, their lack of strong leaders, and the ambition of Le Quy Ly that put him far ahead of any rival. Tran Ngac, who in 1377 had been passed over for the throne, commiserated with Tran Nguyen Dan with a poem that said: "I was tossed aside years ago; You are not a great talent in our house; It happens that we are alike in being old and weak; Fields and gardens will soon revert back to nature."

Tran Nguyen Dan, although without political ability, was nevertheless a talented poet and, until his death in 1390, kept about him a circle of like-minded literary men. One of his later marks of note was that in 1380 he became the grandfather of Nguyen Trai, the most prominent scholar, poet, and statesman of the early fifteenth century. Nguyen Trai's father, Nguyen Phi Khanh, as an aspiring young scholar, was employed as the tutor of one of Tran Nguyen Dan's daughters. When she became pregnant, her father allowed Nguyen Phi Khanh to marry her. However, Tran Phu, the senior king, was offended by this marriage of a Tran noblewoman with a commoner and barred Nguyen Phi Khanh from any appointment at court. Nguyen Phi Khanh later followed Le Quy Ly.

In 1387, Tran Phu returned to Thang Long from his sojourn of nearly four years at the Bao Hoa Palace. His presence in the capital emboldened the 27-year-old king, Tran Hien, to plot against Le Quy Ly. Learning of this, in 1388 Le Quy Ly manipulated Tran Phu into deposing Tran Hien and replacing him with his youngest son, 10-year-old Tran Ngung, once again passing over Tran Ngac. A daughter of Le Quy Ly was made the queen. Tran Hien and all his co-conspirators were killed.

In 1389, more secure after being rid of Tran Hien, Le Quy Ly appointed to high positions at court a group of eleven scholars of whose loyalty he was sure. By mid year, however, rebellions in Thanh Hoa opened the way for a new Cham invasion. Le Quy Ly led an army into Thanh Hoa but was defeated, after which Tran Phu lost confidence in his battlefield skills. When Le Quy Ly returned to Thang Long to obtain reinforcements, Tran Phu relieved him of further military duty and instead appointed Tran Khat Chan, a descendent of Tran Binh Trong, the famous martyr of the Mongol Wars, to lead soldiers against the Chams. Le Quy Ly's prestige had suffered sufficiently that Nguyen Da Phuong, his former associate who had kept the Chams out of Thang Long in 1383, dared to publicly oppose him until forced to commit suicide. Then, a monk suddenly appeared at the head of a rebel army from northwest of Thang Long. The two kings fled north of the Red River as the rebel army flooded into Thang Long. Tran Phu called on a general who had been campaigning against Chams and their allies in the mountains west of Thang Long to suppress this uprising. For a few critical months, Tran Phu demonstrated a hint of the leadership for which his ancestors were famous.

Tran Khat Chan, although repulsed in Thanh Hoa, retreated in good order to the southern Red River plain. There, in early 1390, benefiting from information given by a Cham turncoat, Che Bong Nga's boat was identified and ambushed with firearms, the first recorded use of firearms in Vietnam. Che Bong Nga was killed and his followers fled south. The Cham wars ended after twenty years. During that time, the people in the territories of modern Quang Binh, Quang Tri, and Thua Tien had mostly followed the Chams. The people in Nghe An and Ha Tinh had been divided with about half following the Chams. Officials and soldiers were sent from Thang Long into these areas to re-establish Tran authority and to administer a round of rewards and punishments.

With the lifting of the Cham cloud, Le Quy Ly regained his momentum. In 1391, he personally led soldiers down to the vicinity of modern Hue on the border. He sent an army to penetrate into Cham territory, but it was decisively defeated and he returned to Thang Long. This reminder of past defeats and of Le Quy Ly's skill in turning disaster for the country into personal success encouraged criticism from many quarters, despite the fact that Le Quy Ly's spies and agents seemed to be everywhere.

When an official drew attention to a song sung by children in the streets of Thang Long that suggested Le Quy Ly was coveting the throne, the official was forced to go into hiding. Two officials in a province far from Thang Long had a conversation in which they expressed dismay at how Le Quy Ly was acting as the king; the conversation was reported to Le Quy Ly and the two men were killed. A Tran nobleman was killed for plotting to kill Le Quy Ly. Tran Ngac, Tran Phu's son, had been on the edge of several conspiracies against Le Quy Ly. He thought that he should be the king and was a focus for Tran resentment against Le Quy Ly. Fearing for his life, he fled from the capital, was caught in the countryside, and was killed.

In 1392, having disposed of all immediate enemies, Le Quy Ly published a book that propounded his version of the Confucian canon. The Duke of Zhou, who loyally served a young king in antiquity, was "the first sage." Second in importance was Confucius, "the first teacher," whose *Analects* Le Quy Ly criticized passages for where Confucius appears to show lack of attention to ethical and practical matters (visiting a lewd woman, talking with rebels, failing to bring along enough food while traveling). The Tang philosopher Han Yu (768–824) is praised, apparently because of his practical attention to the importance of a strong central government and his criticism of Buddhism as a waste of manpower and resources. On the other hand, the line of Song philosophers from Zhou Dunyi (1017–1073), Cheng Yi (1033–1107), Yang Shi (1053–1135), La Congyan (1072–1135), Li Tong (1093–1163), and Zhu Xi (1130–1200) is described as erudite but with little ability, not sufficiently attached to actual facts, skilled only in collecting bits and pieces from ancient texts. Le Quy Ly proposed that action is more important than thought and that his model for action was the Duke of Zhou who accepted the responsibilities of kingship during a time when the king was too young to do so. He did not share the disdain of Tran royalty for "pale-faced scholars," but he wanted an intellectual agenda that was under his control.

Given the curriculum followed in previous generations, which accepted the teachings of the Song philosophers, this was a change in ideology that was sure to provoke unease among some scholars. A teacher in the royal academy had the temerity to publicly disagree with Le Quy Ly's book and was consequently demoted. Le Quy Ly immediately moved to reorient education toward his ideas.

An examination in 1393 produced thirty new graduates and was followed by another examination for officials who already had appointments, apparently to reinforce the perspective of the new book.

An even larger difficulty in Le Quy Ly's new emphasis would seem to be that, with a senior king at hand, there ought to be no need for a "Duke of Zhou" to assist the young king, Tran Ngung, then in his early teens. In 1394, however, Tran Phu, 73 years old, set this worry to rest by presenting a painting to Le Quy Ly that demonstrated his approval of Le Quy Ly's new conceit. The painting was entitled "Four Helpers" and depicted four ministers of state in times past who were famous for helping young kings: the Duke of Zhou himself, who helped Zhou Cheng in the eleventh century BCE; Hua Guang, who helped Han Zhao in the first century BCE; Zhuge Liang, who helped Liu Shan in the third century CE; and To Hien Thanh, who helped Ly Long Trat in the twelfth century.

A month after this painting was shown in public, Tran Phu reportedly had a dream in which he saw his half-brother Tran Kinh, the former king, leading his army and reciting a poem: "In the center is no one but the marquis with a red snout; He is about to climb up into the tower of the white chicken; The decision of whether the kingdom will prosper or perish has already been made; It is not in front of you but behind you." Reference to the "red snout" and to the "white chicken" indicated Le Quy Ly and Tran Phu, respectively, based on horoscopes and puns. The "tower" was the throne. The last two lines affirmed that it was already determined that the Tran were about to perish. It is recorded that Tran Phu brooded over this dream and was troubled by it, but that he saw no way out.

Another month passed and, after the annual blood oath was administered, Le Quy Ly met with Tran Phu, who is reported to have said: "You and I are of the same family. Together we are in charge of the country's affairs. Now the country's strength is declining, and I am an old man. After I depart this life, if the king can be helped, then help him; but if he shows no merit, then take the throne for yourself." He understood what was happening and, despite his personal dismay, publicly blessed it. Four months later, he died.

Tran Phu had passed from the family of his father to the "same family" that he shared with Le Quy Ly, the family of his mother. Whereas Ly Sam had marked the end his dynasty by turning away from his mother's family, the end of Tran Phu's was marked by turning toward his mother's family. The Ly dynasty developed an experiment in governance by maternal families. The Tran dynasty was an experiment in excluding non-royal maternal families from access to the throne. Both experiments worked for a few generations and both ultimately failed.

There is no way to know whether the tremble of doubt that passed briefly through the mind of Tran Phu after dreaming of his brother was the last quiver of courage radiating from the deeds of his ancestors, or a shudder of loathing at how he had betrayed his own bright hopes on that day in Vu Ban nearly twenty-five years before when he was proclaimed king, or simply the anxiety provoked by the approach of death. His brother's ghost came to comfort him. The outcome of the Tran story had been determined, and he could die in peace.

4 THE LE DYNASTY

Destruction of the Tran aristocracy

The fortunes of the Ly and Tran dynasties waxed and waned in step with the Song and Yuan dynasties. There was a vital connection between regimes in the Red River plain and the successors to the northern dynasties that had governed there during earlier centuries. Both sides carefully observed the tributary relationship. Books, medicine, theater, music, weapons, and government policies in the north were easily perceived, understood, and adopted in the south. Disorders and political troubles in the south were monitored and any potential for requiring or enabling intervention was evaluated in the north.

In both the Song–Ly cycle and the Yuan–Tran cycle, the rise of the northern dynasty was accompanied by the rise of the southern dynasty, and the decline of the northern dynasty was accompanied by the decline of the southern dynasty. The relative sizes of the two sides ensured that initiative in the relationship came from the north. The role of the south was to answer northern initiative. Moments of warfare climaxed both cycles, the outcomes of which confirmed the general basis of the relationship between vassal and suzerain. The ebbs and flows of power and prosperity in the north and in the south reveal that, in the eleventh and thirteenth centuries, northern challenges evoked southern responses. Similarly, in the twelfth and fourteenth centuries, northern weakness gave slack to the relationship and led to weakness in the south.

In the late fourteenth century, the rise of the Ming dynasty fundamentally altered the strategic and cultural environment in eastern Asia. The Ming rulers redefined civilization and the sphere of government while at the same time they sought to restore the borders and to equal the glories of the Han and Tang Empires. Early Ming policies are commonly considered to be conservative and expansionist in aiming to erase the humiliation of Mongol rule by reanimating the Han–Tang imperial legacy. The result was a centralizing mobilization of human and material resources that led to extending Ming rule over neighboring regions.

At the same time, and not by coincidence, there was a fundamental change in the structure of politics among Vietnamese speakers with a strong effort to centralize control of resources. However, this was insufficient to prevent the Ming from asserting regional dominance and restoring imperial government in the lands of old Giao Chi and An Nam. Although the Ming would eventually abandon this ambitious policy and return to a reformulation of the tributary relationship, the Vietnamese regime that emerged from these tumultuous events was shaped not only by the challenge from the north, but also by an internal shift of power away from the Red River plain and into the southern provinces, with dramatic consequences for the structure of dynastic government. Le Quy Ly was the first Vietnamese leader to respond to the Ming challenge and to envision a new future for Vietnamese government.

Le Quy Ly traced his ancestry to an immigrant of the Ho surname who in the late 940s came from Zhejiang Province on China's east coast and received an appointment as governor of the province in the Ca River basin, presumably from Duong Tam Kha, who was endeavoring to rule at that time. Leaders in subsequent generations of the Ho family served as commanders of an outpost in that province and on one occasion were honored with marriage to a Ly princess. In the thirteenth century, a branch of the family moved to the region of modern Vinh Loc district, beside the Ma River in the foothills of Thanh Hoa Province. It was adopted into the clan of a local strongman with the Le surname. Le Quy Ly, born in 1336, was in the fourth generation with this surname. Although information is lacking, the family probably earned merit with the Tran kings during the Mongol Wars, for two of Le Quy Ly's aunts had entered the palace in the early fourteenth century as consorts of Tran Manh.

Le Quy Ly was well educated, a writer of both prose and poetry. He promoted writing and reading in the vernacular. He learned how to organize and lead armies, with some successes yet many failures on battlefields. But he was first of all an astute politician who spent most of his adult life preoccupied with the question of dynastic change. He was ruthless yet rational. He imposed radical solutions upon a society that in the 1370s could no longer protect itself. He did not care if he was hated so long as he was obeyed. With great energy and willpower he laid the foundations of a new dynasty at a new location and with a new base of power.

Unlike the founders of the Tran dynasty, who had time in which to establish their rule before being tested by the Mongols, Le Quy Ly had to deal with Ming expansionism before he had gained the loyalty of the people in his kingdom, many of whom remained attached to remnants of the Tran dynasty. By the late fourteenth century, the Tran aristocracy had become an accumulation of autonomous private estates that had to be destroyed before an effective central government could be rebuilt. Le Quy Ly did not shrink from the task. He understood the Ming threat and hastened to prepare for it.

After the death of Tran Phu in 1394, Le Quy Ly tightened his grip on the Tran court. He wrote a book of instructions for the 16-year-old king, Tran Ngung, who showed no aptitude for government and was easily isolated from court affairs. Le Quy Ly moved into a palace beside the central court where his close associates were given the highest positions. Officials were prohibited from wearing robes at court with large sleeves in which objects, such as weapons, could be concealed, and anyone heard conversing about people previously killed for conspiring against Le Quy Ly were put to death.

Before directly challenging the Tran royal family, Le Quy Ly moved to gain control of the four other major groups with influence in the kingdom: monks, merchants, scholars, and soldiers. In 1396, he attended to all of these groups. Monks younger than 50 years old were defrocked and returned to secular life, and an examination for knowledge of Buddhist sutras was given as the basis for appointing people to govern temples, shrines, and monasteries.

As for those who accumulated wealth by commerce, Le Quy Ly attempted to cut down their power by prohibiting the use or possession of coins, which until then were the only form of money. All coins had to be exchanged for paper money. This measure was intended to force the wealth of merchants out into the open, to make it difficult for them to avoid paying market taxes, and to make their assets vulnerable to government inspection.

Scholars were given a new curriculum for the civil service examinations. Le Quy Ly issued an edition of the classical texts in vernacular Nom characters. This edition no longer exists, but, according to annalists, he wrote an introduction that presented "his own ideas" rather than following the orthodoxy of Zhu Xi. Aware of the importance of palace women, he sent female teachers to instruct them with this edition. The exam for scholars was prescribed to have four parts: an essay of at least 500 words on the classical texts that followed a prescribed format for developing a philosophical theme; a poem following Tang prosodic rules and an essay of at least 500 words in rhyming prose (phu, which had become popular in the fourteenth century and was often written in the vernacular); examples of proclamations, remonstrations, and petitions in prescribed styles; and a 1,000-word essay based on the classics, histories, and current affairs. The first exam under this new regime was held in 1400. Until then, education officials and aspiring scholars were fully absorbed in preparing for it.

To keep soldiers busy, military leaders were aimed at Champa. An expedition into Champa in 1396 resulted in the capture of a Cham general, who was given a military command and who faithfully served Le Quy Ly thereafter. In the following year, another Cham general along with his family and entourage submitted. He was assigned to guard the southern border. These men owed their allegiance to Le Quy Ly and not to the Tran dynasty.

With the ranks of monks limited to the elderly and erudite, the monetary assets of merchants inventoried and shifted from metal to paper, the scholars busy studying for exams, and generals occupied with the Cham borderlands, Le Quy Ly was ready to confront the Tran nobles. Thang Long was a Tran city. Le Quy Ly decided to move the capital to his home district of Vinh Loc in Thanh Hoa Province, thereby removing the seat of government from the Red River plain where loyalty to the Tran was strong. The new capital was 115 kilometers south of Thang Long over mountainous terrain; it was 170 kilometers by boat downriver from Thang Long to the seacoast then up the Ma River.

In 1397, within a few months, a wall of about 850 meters square was built nestled among the foothills on the north bank of the Ma River. Palaces were hastily constructed within. Near the end of the year, the 19-year-old king was taken to the new capital; officials who attempted to warn him that shifting to the new capital was part of Le Quy Ly's plan to seize the throne were killed. Thang Long palaces were dismantled for transport to the new capital, which became known as Tay Do (western capital). Thang Long was known by different names over the next few years but in the second quarter of the fifteenth century became known as Dong Kinh (eastern capital), from which derives the modern term Tonkin.

In 1398, Tran Ngung, the king, was persuaded to yield the throne to his 2-year-old son, Tran An, a grandson of Le Quy Ly. A year later, Tran Ngung was sent to a Daoist temple near modern Dong Trieu in Quang Ninh Province, where he was killed on Le Quy Ly's orders. A conspiracy among Tran nobles against Le Quy Ly was uncovered at the annual blood oath ceremony, held at Tay Do in 1399. Le Quy Ly took the opportunity to kill over 370 people and to imprison hundreds more. This dealt the Tran royal clan a mortal blow. Le Quy Ly imposed tight security measures throughout the kingdom; travel permits were required to be outside of one's home district and villagers were afraid to give hospitality to strangers. A rope was stretched across the Ma River downriver from Tay Do, forcing boats to stop for inspection. Prisoners were set to work digging canals in the southern provinces or were scattered among colonies in the mountains.

Resistance nevertheless emerged under leadership from an unexpected source. Someone identified as a counterfeiter gathered an army of rebels, reportedly ten thousand strong, in the northwest of the Red River plain. Le Quy Ly managed to suppress this uprising after six months of fighting.

As he shifted his government to Tay Do, eliminated the potentially obstreperous young king, and subdued the royal family by killing and imprisoning hundreds of nobles and their followers, Le Quy Ly also enforced limits on land ownership that were aimed at the Tran aristocracy, families allied with the Tran, and ambitious commoners, all of whose power rested upon large private estates worked by peasants in a slave or serf-like status. Except for the very highest princes and princesses, land ownership was to be limited to ten hectares. Le Quy Ly particularly targeted land that in recent generations had been reclaimed from the sea in modern Thai Binh and Nam Dinh Provinces, which is where many of the largest private estates existed. All landowners had to declare the size of their holdings, with excess land passing to the state. Strict rules were laid down for establishing claims of ownership, and those convicted of crimes had their land confiscated.

At the same time as these measures were being put into effect, a new system of provincial government was instituted with differently organized jurisdictions and new names. Provincial officials were required to make annual reports about men available for military conscription, tax revenues in rice and in money, and judicial proceedings. Public land was set aside to support schools, and teachers were to annually send their best students to the capital for further study or for appointments in the government.

In 1400, Le Quy Ly took the throne and restored to his family the surname Ho. He named his kingdom Dai Ngu, "Great Ngu" (Chinese Yu), thereby claiming kinship with the ancient sage-king Shun, also called Yu Shun (Vietnamese Ngu Thuan), a descendent of whom had later received from the founder of the Zhou dynasty (around 1000 BCE) a ducal appointment with which he acquired the surname Hu (Vietnamese Ho), from whom Ho Quy Ly now claimed descent. This did not signify an effort to be associated with the imperial history of northern empires, for Vietnamese considered their inheritance of classical antiquity to be as authentic as that of the northerners. The invocation of Shun as Ho Quy Ly's ancestor evoked the principle of succession based not on blood but on merit, for Shun was related neither to his predecessor, who chose him, nor to his successor, whom he chose. Ho Quy Ly aimed to portray the change of dynasty from Tran to Ho as following a pattern for which the sage-kings of antiquity were praised.

Ho Quy Ly demoted his small grandson Tran An from the throne, then raised his second son, Ho Han Thuong, to be king, himself becoming senior king. He passed over his eldest son Ho Nguyen Truong because his mother was not a Tran woman. Ho Han Thuong's mother was a daughter of Tran Manh, so, when Ming envoys began to invoke the legitimacy of the Tran dynasty, Ho Han Thuong could be presented as Tran Manh's grandson. Ho Han Thuong seems not to have had any particular ability. On the other hand, Ho Nguyen Trung ably served his father in making plans and leading soldiers.

Ho Quy Ly

During the few years of his rule, Ho Quy Ly presided over a blizzard of activity aimed at monitoring and suppressing dissent, mobilizing available resources to push back the Chams, and preparing for an impending Ming attack. His efforts to control officialdom, private property, the marketplace, manpower, and education were steadily expanded. He sent out trusted officers to check on provincial and local officials. Based on their reports, officials were promoted or demoted. An important criterion in these investigations was an individual's sense of loyalty to the new dynastic regime. At the same time, new regulations for administering law and conducting local government were published.

A census in 1401 was more thorough than previous enumerations had been and discovered a great increase in the number of men available for conscription as soldiers. The ownership of slaves was restricted, with excess slaves being appropriated by the state; this provision was applied even to remaining Tran nobles, whose landholdings were also restricted at this time. Taxes on land were dramatically increased and were to be paid in paper money. Market inspectors were sent to enforce uniform weights and measures and to ensure the use of paper money, which was resisted by merchants. New taxes were levied on boats that carried merchandise. Ho Quy Ly was gathering manpower, land, and metal coins from people who could potentially oppose him.

The degree of disaffection toward Ho Quy Ly was so significant that in these years there was a large turnover in officials, as many resigned or retired or were dismissed. The prevailing system of examinations to select men for officialdom was inadequate to meet the need for new officials. In 1400, an examination was held under the existing scheme and twenty men were graduated. In 1404 a new plan to mobilize more students into the examinations was published, but it was not implemented because of the urgent preparations for war with Ming that began to absorb Ho Quy Ly's attention. Consequently, in 1405 an ad hoc examination was held that selected 170 people for government appointments. At the same time an even more informal examination produced appointments for an unrecorded number of officials.

The rapid turnover of officials in these years prevented implementation of a plan to establish a system of granaries to provide food in times of want. Instead, when a famine broke out in 1405, inspectors were sent to inventory the rice supplies of wealthy families and to force them to sell rice to the hungry. At that time, the brewing of rice wine was prohibited to save rice for eating.

One ritual change indicated a shift from loyalty enforced by religious belief to loyalty enforced by a police system. The annual blood oath, which appealed to one's fear of spirits and deities and had been practiced since 1028, was abandoned. In its place was a cadre of spies and special police who monitored any detectable sign of disloyalty. Ho Quy Ly, rather than supernatural powers, now commanded fear and respect. In place of the oath ceremony, Ho Quy Ly instituted an annual sacrifice to Heaven on behalf of the kingdom to pray for good harvests and prosperity. This sacrifice was called *giao* (Chinese *jiao*), indicating a tradition of Daoist sacrifices that developed in China during preceding centuries to supersede what were considered to be old-fashioned sacrifices to unorthodox and demonic spirits.

Another ritual change was abandonment of the birthday festival that had been held upon the accession of kings since the time of Le Hoan during the Hoa Lu monarchy. Instead, in 1405, Ho Quy Ly celebrated his seventieth birthday by holding a grand reception at Tay Do and by distributing gifts to people in the kingdom who were the same age as he or older. He reformed the traditional royal birthday festival from a legitimizing formality to an act of venerating longevity, bringing to mind the sage-kings of ancient times.

Many people in the Red River plain viewed Ho Quy Ly with sullen disenchantment, being aggravated by his hard policies and nursing nostalgia for what they imagined to have been a better time under the Tran kings. Facing south, however, Ho Quy Ly found people who were ready to respond to his leadership, and there he achieved a brief but significant expansion of his regime. Considering that for the first twenty years of his public career he was almost exclusively occupied with desperate efforts to fight off Cham attacks, it is no surprise that after taking the throne his first order of business was to settle accounts with the Chams. An initial expedition against the Chams in 1401 was unsuccessful, but in the following year, after building a road with post houses from Tay Do to the border near modern Hue, Ho Quy Ly forced the Cham king to cede to him what are now the provinces of Quang Nam and Quang Ngai. Some of the people there followed the Cham king in his withdrawal from those territories, but many Chams remained and were organized into militia units with Vietnamese officers. There are families in Quang Nam Province today whose genealogical records indicate that they were originally Cham and that they took Vietnamese surnames in the time of Ho Quy Ly. Officials were appointed to govern these new border provinces. Landless people were settled there and water buffaloes were sent to assist in developing agriculture. In 1404, in a time of food scarcity, rice was sent to these provinces.

In 1403, Ho Quy Ly, determined to utterly destroy the Cham threat, sent another expedition into Champa and besieged the Cham capital at Vijaya in modern Binh Dinh Province. However, he was forced to lift the siege and withdraw when supplies ran out. Thereafter, his attention was turned to the north where a much more serious threat was materializing.

During the reign of the founder of the Ming dynasty, Zhu Yuanzhang (r. 1368–1398), a disturbing pattern of peremptory demands had developed. In 1384, Ming demanded provisions for its soldiers fighting in Yunnan. In 1385, Ming demanded elephants and transportation facilities for moving soldiers south to fight Champa. In the same year there was a demand for tropical fruits and for Buddhist monks. In 1395 came demands for monks, masseuses, and eunuchs. In each case, the demands were at least partially met or plausible excuses were made. One of the eunuchs sent in 1395 arrived at Tay Do with a Ming envoy in 1403. Accused of serving as a Ming spy, Ho Quy Ly ordered him seized and killed.

By this time, Emperor Zhu Di (r. 1402–1424) was on the Ming throne and pursued an expansionary policy. Zhu Yuanzhang, his father, appears to have viewed Thang Long as a vassal that had acquired bad habits during the Mongol–Yuan dynasty and needed to relearn proper imperial discipline. He took a dim view of the fighting between the Vietnamese and the Chams and tended to put most of the blame on the Vietnamese because they should know better than to behave like disorderly uncivilized people. On the other hand, Zhu Di viewed Ho Quy Ly both as an obstacle to the "great peace" of his imperial order and as an opportunity, because Tran dynasty partisans persuaded him that Ho Quy Ly did not have the support of the people and could be easily removed. Zhu Di was uncharacteristically outward looking among the Ming emperors. He allocated resources to build and outfit the fleets of Admiral Zheng He, which during his reign made several voyages through Southeast Asia to South Asia, the Middle East, and East Africa. Filled with the exuberance of reasserting imperial power on the scale of the Han and Tang dynasties, Zhu Di was tempted to bring Giao Chi/An Nam back under direct rule.

By 1403, Ming envoys were, in the words of annalists, coming and going between Zhu Di's capital at Nanjing and Tay Do "like the shuttle of a loom," and tension between the two newly established regimes increased rapidly. Diplomatic exchanges became difficult and unpleasant. In 1404, a Ming envoy appeared suddenly, delivered an accusatory message, and headed back to the northern border as unexpectedly as he had come. Ho Quy Ly sent men to kill him, but he escaped across the border before they could catch up with him. In 1405, Zhu Di demanded cession of certain border territories. Ho Quy Ly, seeking to buy time, agreed to deliver some land, but relations did not improve, and later that year Zhu Di imprisoned one of Ho Quy Ly's envoys sent to negotiate an accommodation. It was becoming obvious that Zhu Di was intent upon striking at Ho Quy Ly.

From 1404, Ho Quy Ly prepared for war with Ming. Landless, unemployed, and indigent men were organized into special army units. Boats were constantly on patrol at the border to intercept spies and watch for signs of an imminent attack. Wooden stakes were planted at strategic points in the rivers to obstruct invading boats, both from the sea and from Yunnan down the Red River. People with skills to make weapons were gathered at newly established arsenals. The army was reorganized and Ho Quy Ly traveled through the kingdom to inspect the terrain and make plans for defense. He ignored the advice of one general to engage invaders in the mountainous terrain on the borders and instead prepared a riverbank defense in the heart of the Red River plain. The key to his plan was the Da Bang fortress built on the southern bank of the Red River northwest of Dong Kinh, at the point where Ming armies from Yunnan and from Guangxi would most likely attempt to join forces.

An anecdote about the construction of Da Bang fortress is emblematic of Ho Quy Ly's subsequent reputation. When, in the course of construction, the shrine of a local spirit was destroyed, the spirit reportedly appeared in a dream to the official in charge and requested that the shrine be rebuilt. In reply the official wrote a poem with the words: "It is too bad, but there comes a time when old trees must suffer axes." Later historians commented that when "knowledgeable people" heard about this poem they knew that Ho Quy Ly would come to a bad end. This idea that Ho Quy Ly and his followers were the victims of their arrogant disregard for tradition was useful to later historians as an explanation for Ho Quy Ly's failure, but in fact he did not have the luxury of time to plant his regime in the minds of a new generation before having to face a powerful foe that was determined to dominate the region. When he met with his generals and advisors in 1405 to discuss the situation, his eldest son Ho Nguyen Trung prophetically said: "I am not afraid to fight. I fear only that the people will abandon us." The people whose loyalties were most in doubt were the inhabitants of the Red River plain. Ho Quy Ly could not rely upon the Red River plain as the source of his military strength as the Ly and Tran courts had been able to do when resisting invaders in previous centuries. Instead, the Red River plain became a forward line of defense for his base of power in the southern provinces and his seat at Tay Do.

A small Ming army came across the northern border in late spring of 1406 escorting a man who claimed to be a member of the Tran royal family. The Ming proposed to place him on the throne and to demote Ho Quy Ly to a provincial post in the far south. Ho generals engaged the Ming as they emerged from the mountains into the northeastern foothills of the Red River plain. After a day of bitter fighting, Ho Quy Ly's men captured the Tran pretender along with many Ming officers and soldiers. The Ming commander barely escaped back to the border. This triggered Ming plans to invade that already had been in preparation for two years.

In the few months before the end of the monsoon rain season, when the land would be sufficiently dry to enable the movement of large armies, Ho Quy Ly made his final arrangements for war. Stakes were planted at the river mouths, the population in the northeastern part of the Red River plain was evacuated to the south and west, and retired officers were called to duty. But no serious resistance was given to the Ming armies as they came through the mountains and entered the Red River plain.

Modern historians have estimated that an army of 135,000 men set out from Guangxi and an army of 80,000 advanced from Yunnan. By the end of 1407, the two armies had joined forces in the northwestern part of the plain, had overrun Da Bang fortress, and had occupied Dong Kinh. Ming officers spread the news that they had come to restore the Tran dynasty. More than half of Ho Quy Ly's soldiers deserted. Prominent families in the Red River plain led by Mac Thuy and his brothers, descendents of a famous scholar-official in the early fourteenth century named Mac Dinh Chi (1272–1346), offered their allegiance to the Ming.

In early 1407, as most of the people in the Red River plain and many members of the Ho government defected to the Ming, Ho Quy Ly and his eldest son Ho Nguyen Trung rallied their soldiers and led a final desperate attack up the Red River to dislodge the Ming from Dong Kinh. They were decisively defeated and retreated to Tay Do. Pursuing Ming forces quickly expelled them from Thanh Hoa and chased them down the coast. Ho Quy Ly, his sons, and other family members along with their followers were captured in what is now southern Ha Tinh Province and taken to the Ming capital at Nanjing. Ho Quy Ly and Ho Han Thuong were imprisoned and disappear from recorded history. Ho Nguyen Trung found a new career as a manufacturer of weapons near the northern Ming capital at Beijing and died after authoring a book about his native country that was published in 1438.

Pre-modern Vietnamese historians, following historiographical rules established by the Song scholar Sima Guang (1019–1086), viewed Ho Quy Ly as an illegitimate usurper, and he was scorned for having failed to defend the country. In modern times, scholars have variously viewed him as a feared, even hated, reformer; as a savior of the Vietnamese state amidst the disintegration of the Tran dynasty; and as a ruthless yet astute man who deserves some recognition for what he accomplished under difficult circumstances. He lived in hard times, but rebuilt a crumbling dynastic regime with imagination and will. He was stymied by Zhu Di's expansionist policy, which was beyond his control.

A historic watershed

By mid 1407 the Ming announced that the Tran family was extinct and, reportedly in response to petitions from local leaders and elders, proceeded to organize the imperial province of Giao Chi. Huang Fu, the senior civil official, immediately began to establish a structure of government staffed by both local men and men from other imperial provinces. He spent the next decade in Giao Chi as the senior administrator. According to the official Vietnamese history (*Complete Book of the History of Great Viet*) compiled later in the century, he "was intelligent, was able to cope with changing circumstances, had talent for government, and was respected by the people." His stated aim was "to make a fresh start" after the turmoil of the preceding thirty-five years. He used the expression *canh tan* (Chinese *gengxin*), "change to the new," the literary equivalent of the vernacular term *doi moi*, generally translated as "renovation," which has become famous as the designation of government policy in Vietnam beginning in the late 1980s.

This expression has a venerable pedigree in pre-modern Vietnamese political thought and shows a perception of discontinuity that is at least as characteristic of historical experience as the more common assertion of continuity. Since the tenth century, no experiment in establishing a structure of political leadership has lasted more than a few generations, whether it was personal charisma, maternal kinship, group solidarity, merit, or despotism. Now there would be an experiment in going back to the empire. None of these experiments led logically from one to the next. They each exhausted the possibilities for developing a particular solution to the problem of leadership in the context of a specific time and place. Each experiment turned in a new direction that did not necessarily develop from what had gone before. These experiments were enabled, shaped, or thwarted by the vicissitudes of powerful empires rising and declining just beyond the northern border.

Vietnamese historians have unanimously viewed the experiment in Ming rule as a tale of woe with no redeeming features and sure to fall beneath the weight of its own corruption and the righteous wrath of Vietnamese patriots. However, this was not a story with a pre-ordained narrative. It was initiated and abandoned as a result of decisions made at the Ming court. Like the interventions of Wang Anshi, Kubilai Khan, and Che Bong Nga, this was not a struggle with an outcome determined by a law or theme of history but rather by the ambition and limitation of a particular man, in this case Zhu Di. Furthermore, Ming rule had a transforming effect on the development of Vietnamese culture and politics. For one thing, it completed the destruction of the Tran aristocracy begun by Ho Quy Ly. For another, it inculcated a generation of students with the Confucianism of Zhu Xi, which thereafter replaced Buddhism as the primary ideological vantage of rulers. And it also aroused a new style of monarchy that built upon the brief experiment of Ho Quy Ly in Thanh Hoa.

The senior Ming military commander in Giao Chi, Zhang Fu, was among the most competent military figures of the early Ming period. After preparing and leading the Ming invasion, he spent most of the next two decades in Giao Chi attending to security matters. His main post-invasion task was the suppression of resistance led by surviving members of the Tran royal family. In autumn of 1407, a son of Tran Phu named Tran Ngoi rallied soldiers to the Tran banner and proclaimed himself king at Yen Mo district in Ninh Binh Province, near Hoa Lu. Within two days Ming soldiers attacked him, and he fled south to Nghe An Province. There, he and his men killed two Tran nobles along with five hundred of their followers because they refused to abandon their allegiance to the Ming. Within weeks, Zhang Fu attacked Tran Ngoi and forced him further south. By mid 1408, Zhang Fu had returned to Dong Kinh and Tran Ngoi had returned to Nghe An, where he was joined by a general named Dang Tat leading soldiers from the far southern frontier.

With Ho Quy Ly's defeat, the Cham king had reoccupied Quang Ngai and Quang Nam. Dang Tat and other officials from those jurisdictions began to fight among themselves as they withdrew northward. Dang Tat prevailed over his erstwhile colleagues and then sealed his ascendant status on the border by pledging allegiance to Ming. He now abandoned this pledge and joined his forces with Tran Ngoi. He rallied a large army and led it north through Thanh Hoa and into the Red River plain. Near the end of 1408 in Y Yen district, Nam Dinh Province, on the road to Dong Kinh, he defeated a Ming force that had been sent to stop him. This was the last hurrah of the Tran dynasty, but it was achieved under the leadership of a headstrong and careless man. Dang Tat brushed aside Tran Ngoi's desire to follow up the victory with an immediate attack on Dong Kinh and instead led his soldiers from place to place in the lower plain to disperse Ming garrisons and rally more people to his banner. In early 1409, when rumors spread that Dang Tat was thinking of pushing Tran Ngoi aside to proclaim himself king, Tran Ngoi had him killed.

This turn of events caused dismay among Tran partisans, and a son of Dang Tat went south to rally support for Tran Quy Khoang, a son of Tran Phu's son Tran Ngac, a nephew of Tran Ngoi. Tran Quy Khoang was proclaimed king in Nghe An. His partisans captured Tran Ngoi and brought him to Nghe An. By autumn 1409, the two kings had worked out an arrangement with Tran Ngoi as senior king and Tran Quy Khoang as junior king. The two kings led their forces north but were defeated in Thanh Hoa by Zhang Fu in an engagement resulting in Tran Ngoi's capture by the Ming. Thanh Hoa was thereafter pacified and incorporated into Giao Chi. Tran Quy Khoang attempted to invade Thanh Hoa in 1410 but was repelled. He was thereafter inactive and survived for two years until Zhang Fu expelled him from Nghe An, pursued him to the southern border and captured him there in 1413. The Ming had completed the pacification of the Red River plain and Thanh Hoa by 1409; Nghe An, which included modern Ha Tinh, by 1412; and the southernmost territories down to the region of Hue by 1413. Quang Nam and Quang Ngai were left to the Chams. Irreconcilable opponents of the Ming fled to Champa and Laos.

Later Vietnamese court annalists criticized Tran Ngoi and Tran Quy Khoang for being weak leaders and for being addicted to wine and women. Their most ardent followers and boldest generals came from the Cham frontier. They relied upon residual loyalty to the Tran dynasty, but their failures and internal rivalries accumulated, giving them no prospect for overcoming such a strong and relentless foe as Zhang Fu.

As long as Emperor Zhu Di remained alive, until 1424, the project of making Giao Chi a Ming province was firmly supported by the imperial court and, despite problems, was plausibly a success or at least on the way to success. Huang Fu was governor throughout this time, giving a continuity of leadership that generated administrative momentum. The later propaganda of the Le dynasty that developed in resistance to Ming rule portrayed Ming Giao Chi as a cruel, oppressive, exploitative regime. In fact, like nearly every regime that has tried to govern anywhere, Huang Fu's administration was a mixture of positive and negative characteristics. Overall, the positive was no less important than the negative, depending upon the perceptions of particular localities.

People in the Red River plain tended to support Ming government. People in the lowlands of the southern provinces of Thanh Hoa and Nghe An were generally responsive to Ming government as well. But in the foothills and uplands of these southern provinces was an endemic resistance to Ming rule. In other words, following a distinction first reported during Tran times, many Kinh people perceived value in being part of the northern empire, but the Trai people did not. Thus, in the 1420s, after the death of Zhu Di, it was among the Trai population of the southern provinces that active resistance to Ming developed most rapidly, particularly in the lower valleys of the foothills south of the Red River and west of the coastal plains. The Tran terms Kinh and Trai represented different tendencies on a spectrum of cultural and linguistic practice that in modern times have been perceived as a difference between Vietnamese and various peoples collectively called Muong. This difference began to assume a significant political aspect in the fifteenth century with the building of Tay Do and with Thanh Hoa becoming the home of kings. Ming rule exacerbated latent tensions between the Red River plain and the southern provinces that became a prominent feature of Vietnamese politics for the next four centuries.

Ming Giao Chi

The year of conquest, 1407, brought a social and economic disaster. With disruptions caused by military operations, there was no harvest. Famine combined with an epidemic, and corpses piled up faster than they could be buried.

Huang Fu rapidly established an administration that was integrated with government elsewhere in the empire and conditions gradually improved. Thousands of local men received appointments at all levels of administration. Thousands more went to the Ming capital to be trained and evaluated for appointments both in Giao Chi and elsewhere in the empire. At the same time, men arrived from the north to receive appointments. They came from all parts of the north, but most of them were from neighboring provinces and many of them were students who failed in their examinations or were officials suffering demotion or exile. The quality of administrative personnel was mixed and not significantly different from comparable imperial jurisdictions on relatively remote frontiers. By 1416 it was possible for Huang Fu to integrate administrative personnel into the system for government appointments that prevailed elsewhere in the empire. In that same year, the procedure for setting up local police and defense forces was finalized.

Ming educational policies left a strong legacy among the Vietnamese. The emphasis on a Confucian education that opened the way to civil service examinations was but part of a much larger educational effort that included schools for the study of Buddhism, Daoism, medicine, physiognomy, and astrology. People with knowledge in these areas were recruited to teach, and some of them were sent to contribute their knowledge at the imperial court in Nanjing. Many shrines to Confucius (Van Mieu) and to the God of Agriculture (Xa Tac) were built throughout Giao Chi, but popular religion was also encouraged with the building or repair of hundreds of shrines to local deities and nature spirits. Confucian scholars, Buddhist monks, and Daoist priests were all regulated and supervised. In 1419, Ming sent a new edition of the classical Confucian texts to Giao Chi, as well as erudite Buddhists to instruct the monks in Giao Chi.

Ming officials organized an up-to-date communication and transportation system with roads, bridges, waterways, and post houses. This contributed not only to administrative efficiency but also to trade and commerce. Ming tax policy in Giao Chi was intentionally light to assist post-war reconstruction and to foster good will toward the regime. In 1411, rewards were distributed to local people who had earned merit in suppressing the Tran resistance, indicating that by then Zhang Fu considered the resistance to be under control. At the same time, a three-year tax holiday was declared for major commodities such as gold, silver, iron, ivory, plumage from tropical birds, aromatic wood for incense, pearls, lacquer ware, tea, fans, fish, and salt. These were items traded to cities in the north. Even rice was exported to the north in 1413.

In 1407, immediately after the conquest, several thousand skilled craftsmen were sent to Nanjing. In 1413, shipbuilders along with their families were relocated to the north, apparently to assist in preparations for Zheng He's fourth voyage, which began that year. In contrast to those with useful skills were those uprooted by the conquest and its attendant disorders, homeless and wandering from place to place. This floating population was gathered and assigned to productive work or to military service.

In 1414, at the end of the tax holiday, a schedule for taxes on rice fields and mulberry orchards for silk production and for levies on marketable commodities was instituted. According to the *Complete Book of the History of Great Viet*, compiled by Le Dynasty historians, in 1415, "Taxes were heavy, levies were substantial, and so the people had nothing from which to make a living." This evaluation is excessively colored by the need to see no virtue in the regime supplanted by the Le dynasty. But it does indicate the beginning of Giao Chi's integration into the imperial system of revenue collection. Corruption, a normal and ineradicable feature of government, was particularly common in the collection of lucrative commodities. Enterprising officials found ways to make personal fortunes at the expense of those who were defenseless against their demands. There were examples of corruption in nearly all the commodity markets, but salt was a special case. A government monopoly on salt production became enmeshed in the assignment of contracts to salt merchants to supply Ming garrisons in Giao Chi, which offered unusual opportunities for unlawful enrichment.

The most negative features of Ming Giao Chi came from the arrogance and prejudice of Ming people toward the local population. Routine corruption easily became malignant in a situation where northerners viewed local people as less civilized than themselves. The underworld of corruption can be more biting and brutal in a colonial context than it otherwise would be. Ming soldiers garrisoned in Giao Chi dismayed some local people who felt their presence as an intrusion, an imposition, or even as a subversion of good social relations. The conceit of a civilizing mission animated positive features of Ming policy in Giao Chi, but it also contributed to the negative effects of the Ming adventure among the Vietnamese.

This was particularly obvious in the policy that sought to collect all "heterodox" writings. These were writings in the vernacular, but also historical and literary writings in the classical language that expressed the perspective of a separate kingdom in the south or that were in any way critical of northern dynasties. Many of these writings were destroyed on the spot and many others were transported north. What is certain is that nearly all of them disappeared. Consequently, writings by Vietnamese from before the fifteenth century are very rare. Several works of history disappeared along with collections of poetry and other writings. The only book among those taken to the north that is known to have survived, an annal of the Ly dynasty, surfaced in a Qing anthology three centuries later. Other than that single item, of the books collected by Ming officials, nothing remains, although today it is possible to encounter myths about a hidden cache of books waiting to be discovered somewhere in China that will restore to the Vietnamese their pre-fifteenth-century literary heritage. Some historical and literary works did escape this effort to eradicate the corpus of "southern" writings and became the basis of later knowledge about the previous five centuries.

In addition to changing the ideas in people's minds and the books that were available for educated people to read, Ming civilizers also endeavored to change more material aspects of life. According to the *Complete Book of the History of Great Viet*, they "forbade unmarried boys and girls to cut their hair and forbade women to wear short skirts, in order to change customs in conformity with the north." Presumably, the lengthening of skirts promoted a female modesty valued by proponents of Ming's dominant Confucian ideology. Similarly, the forbidding of children to cut their hair follows a rule of filial piety associated with Confucianism that hair, being a gift from one's parents, should not be cut. These rules predictably targeted women and children, the most vulnerable people in any society.

Huang Fu and the best of Ming administrators in Giao Chi espoused an idealistic desire to provide good government and to foster prosperity and happiness among the people. On the other hand, the underworld of corruption and the arrogance of northerners who considered themselves superior were more immediate to many local people than were those good intentions. Nevertheless, there is no evidence from which to judge Ming Giao Chi as significantly more corrupt than the indigenous regimes that ruled the Vietnamese both before and after the Ming episode. Resistance to the Ming regime would presumably have faded away with the passing of generations, but this would have required a longer Ming commitment than the lifetime of a single emperor.

The abandonment of Ming Giao Chi

After 1424, Zhu Di's successors abandoned the Giao Chi project because they deemed its cost to be greater than its benefit. Despite the accumulation of private fortunes by some Ming officials in Giao Chi, government there was a net loss for the state treasury. This problem may have abated if Zhu Di's successors had been as committed as he was to completing the task of governing the Vietnamese. As soon as he was gone, however, Ming Giao Chi rapidly collapsed.

One result of Ming rule is that for two decades Chinese was again the prestige language and most educated people learned to speak Chinese. This resulted in certain words and pronunciations of words that were particular to Ming entering the Vietnamese lexicon. For example, a seventeenth-century dictionary indicates that some words had both pre-Ming and Ming pronunciations. The dictionary registered a preference for the pre-Ming pronunciations over the Ming pronunciations, which were not considered as authoritative as more venerable usages. Another feature of the linguistic dimension of Ming rule was to hasten, if not provoke, a phonological trend to abandon sesquisyllabic words, which had an initial "half syllable," in favor of true monosyllabic forms.

In 1416, Zhang Fu yielded military matters to Li Bin, a competent commander who had participated in the initial conquest in 1407. The security situation was basically stable, but the potential for rebellion, particularly among people in Thanh Hoa and Nghe An, lay beneath a surface calm and it required constant vigilance. When uprisings broke into the open, Li Bin was able to suppress or to contain them with relative ease. Nevertheless, there were large numbers of people living in the shadow of the law, particularly in the foothills, who readily rallied behind plausible rebel leaders, and there were local men serving in Ming government who could not always be trusted.

In 1419, a local officer in Nghe An, angry about the extortions of a Ming official, rebelled and besieged the provincial citadel. Li Bin led reinforcements that quickly raised the siege and dispersed the rebels across the Laotian frontier. Meanwhile, a group of six men in localities surrounding Dong Kinh, noting that the best soldiers had left with Li Bin for Nghe An and that only a small force remained in the city, united their followers to attack the capital. Li Bin returned and easily defeated them.

One of Li Bin's officers, a man named Lo Van Luat from Thach That district just west of Dong Kinh, had disappeared into the mountains during the Nghe An campaign. He reappeared in 1420 leading a rebel army in Thach That. Li Bin quickly defeated him. He fled to Laos as Li Bin destroyed the villages of his followers and pursued them into the nearby mountains where they took refuge in caves. Li Bin built fires at the mouths of the caves and filled them with smoke, killing the people inside.

The most famous event of 1420 was the uprising of Le Nga, a former slave who was reportedly handsome and charismatic and who, seeing how aspiring rebel leaders were fighting among themselves in the mountains northeast of the Red River plain, rallied large numbers of their followers by saying: "If you want to be rich, follow me!" He proclaimed himself king in the mountains of Lang Son Province and marched down to seize Xuong Giang (modern Bac Giang). His former master recognized him and attacked him but was defeated. Li Bin then arrived and sent Le Nga and his followers fleeing into the mountains. News of Le Nga having captured a major town, however, had reached the imperial court and

Zhu Di angrily demanded that he be captured and transported to the Ming capital. Unable to lay his hands on Le Nga, Li Bin seized an innocent man and sent him instead, claiming that he was Le Nga. This caused a stir among local people against this injustice, which required Huang Fu's intervention.

During these years, a local strongman in the foothills of Thanh Hoa named Le Loi was a minor nuisance. He was from the region of Mount Lam, around twenty kilometers southwest of Tay Do, where Kinh and Trai peoples mingled. Born in 1385, he became the head of a prominent family that gained control of a parcel of land during the years of Tran dynastic decline. After the Ming conquest, he became a follower of Tran Quy Khoang. In 1413, after Tran Quy Khoang's defeat, he swore allegiance to Ming. He then became involved in a feud with a neighboring strongman who denounced him as a rebel to the Ming. Attacked by the Ming, he fled into the mountains.

Early in 1418 he mobilized an army and openly challenged Ming authority. He successfully ambushed a Ming column on the upper Chu River but was then betrayed by a turncoat who showed Ming units a way to attack him by surprise from the rear. His followers scattered and he briefly went into hiding before collecting enough men to ambush a Ming patrol and force it to withdraw. In 1419, he seized an outpost near Mount Lam held by another local strongman, apparently the man with whom he was in feud, and he reportedly beheaded 300 men captured there. He then spent more than a year marching around in the uplands recruiting more men. In late 1420 he ambushed a Ming patrol. Li Bin responded by mobilizing Ming and local military forces against him, but Le Loi achieved a victory over them in the region of Quan Hoa district on the upper Ma River.

In late 1421, a large Ming army ascended the Ma River valley to attack Le Loi. A Laotian army approached down the valley from the opposite direction. Le Loi was under the illusion that the Laotians were his allies. However, Lo Van Luat, who had fled to Laos after being defeated by Li Bin the previous year, viewed Le Loi as a rival, and he persuaded the Laotians to join the Ming in attacking Le Loi. After a year of fighting, the Ming and Laotians gained the upper hand. By the end of 1422, Le Loi was utterly defeated and sued for peace. In 1423, he returned to Mount Lam, paid an indemnity with unspecified amounts of gold and silver, and promised the Ming that he would live in peace. In return, the Ming provided him with fish, salt, rice, and farm implements. This was the situation when news arrived in 1424 of the emperor's death.

Within a month of taking the throne, Zhu Gaozhi (r. 1424–1425), Zhu Di's son and successor, issued a proclamation indicating a dramatic change of policy in Giao Chi; calling for "reform," he abolished the collection of commodities. In other initiatives, he moved to end Zheng He's voyages, and he downgraded the role of the military. He wanted to consolidate the core of what had been achieved by his father and grandfather but had no taste for costly adventures. He recalled Huang Fu from Giao Chi and lowered the priority of holding that distant place. After only one year as emperor, Zhu Gaozhi died suddenly of a heart attack, but his son and successor, Zhu Zhanji (r. 1425–1435), continued his policies. Zhu Zhanji considered affairs in Giao Chi an unnecessary distraction from more serious threats on the northern frontier. In 1425, he expressed the opinion that it would be better to restore the Tran dynasty and return to the old tributary relationship. When in 1426 Zhang Fu requested permission to reassume command of Giao Chi to deal with the worsening situation there, the emperor refused.

In 1426, Zhu Zhanji proclaimed a general amnesty and abolished all taxes in Giao Chi except for land taxes to be paid in rice, needed to supply Ming garrisons. The abandonment of commodity collections and taxes was the beginning of an administrative withdrawal from Giao Chi that represented a more realistic appraisal of the long-term interests of the Ming dynasty. Zhu Di's exuberant expansionism exceeded what the Ming empire was capable of sustaining given its governing structure. The relatively high degree of bureaucratization and the pacifist tendencies of Confucian scholar-officials made the Ming more like the lesser empire of Song than the greater empires of Han and Tang.

Considering the degree to which Ming government had been established in Giao Chi, the promises made to local people, the commitments made by local leaders, the interests that had become attached to the imperial project, and especially the fact that tens of thousands of Ming soldiers and officials were still stationed there, Zhu Di's successors could not terminate imperial policy in Giao Chi simply with the strokes of a writing brush. The emperor had severely diminished the priority of holding Giao Chi, but he had no plan for implementing the logical conclusion of having done so. Instead, the shift in Ming policy offered an opportunity for Ming enemies in Giao Chi, and it was they who drove events to a final conclusion. Ming officers went on the defensive amidst a lack of imperial interest in their plight and minimal pro forma responses by officials in neighboring jurisdictions.

Le Loi

In late 1424, news of the new emperor's proclamation and of Huang Fu's recall prompted Le Loi to set out on a new trajectory. His earlier five-year career as a rebel leader in the Thanh Hoa uplands had ended with him back at where he had begun. During that time he had simply endeavored to survive in the mountains of Thanh Hoa, laying ambushes and avoiding encirclement. Now he went on the offensive, striking south through the mountains into Nghe An. After ambushing a Ming force in Quy Chau district, he advanced to Con Cuong district on the upper Ca River. From there he moved downriver, defeating Ming and local pro-Ming armies until by the end of the year he had forced his enemies to take refuge at modern Vinh, which at that time was the provincial headquarters for Nghe An. He rallied thousands of new recruits into his armies from the upland population of the Ca River basin.

In 1425, as the Ming court was preoccupied with the death of one emperor and the accession of another, Le Loi sent armies both to the south and to the north. In the south, his men defeated a Ming army in modern Quang Binh and then marched through modern Quang Tri and Thua Thien to gain control of the southern border. In the north, Le Loi's men captured a Ming supply fleet in northern Nghe An, then pursued Ming forces through Thanh Hoa to besiege them at Tay Do. Gaining momentum from these spectacular successes, in 1426 Le Loi sent his armies through the mountains north of Tay Do to emerge at the head of the Red River plain, threatening Dong Kinh and cutting it off from the road to Yunnan. When Ming soldiers were recalled from Vinh to reinforce Dong Kinh, Le Loi, leaving some troops to besiege Vinh, followed the Ming forces as they moved north, rallying thousands of men from Thanh Hoa as he went. Pushing into the Red River plain he proclaimed as king a certain Tran Cao, supposedly a Tran prince. Men from the Red River plain began to join his ranks as he called for those who had favored the Ming to come to his side and arrested those who did not. Wang Tong, at Dong Kinh as Huang Fu's replacement, was prepared to surrender, but local men who were loyal to Ming persuaded him to resist. They frightened him with the story of Omar whom the Tran had drowned in 1289 while pretending to let him return north. Consequently, there followed a year of waiting for Ming reinforcements.

Le Loi was later recorded as saying that at first he had no intention of overthrowing the Ming regime or of becoming king: he had simply been trying to stay alive and one event had led to another. This seeming diffidence may have been true in the years 1418–1423 when personal enemies aroused Ming and Laotian armies against him in the Thanh Hoa uplands. However, upon news of the death of Zhu Di, he embarked on a three-year campaign that showed forethought and a bold, aggressive spirit. Attacking Ming and allied forces at their most isolated and vulnerable points, he quickly gained control of the southern provinces and recruited into his armies large numbers of men from both the uplands and the lowlands. Without pause he had rushed his men into the Red River plain and swiftly placed his enemies under siege.

By the beginning of 1427, five major strongholds were under siege. These were Dong Kinh and Tay Do; Co Long, a fortress built to guard the southern entrance to the Red River plain in Y Yen district, near Vu Ban in Nam Dinh Province, on the road between Dong Kinh and Tay Do; a fortress at Chi Linh, near Pha Lai, that guarded the eastern part of the Red River plain; and Xuong Giang, a fortress at the modern city of Bac Giang that guarded the route out of the Red River plain to the northern border. All the Ming garrisons south of Tay Do had surrendered. Le Loi established his headquarters at Bo De, in Gia Lam district, directly across the Red River from Dong Kinh.

Le Loi understood that Ming Giao Chi was at its end. The Ming were unlikely to make any serious effort to reassert their control in Giao Chi. By making Tran Cao king, Le Loi satisfied the aim of restoring the Tran that had ostensibly led to the initial Ming intervention and that Zhu Zhanji now considered to be the basis for terminating intervention. Nevertheless, with imperial forces under siege, Ming could not be idle. Maintaining the appearance of empire required efforts to reinforce or to rescue the besieged remnants of Giao Chi. At a more prosaic level, the routine habits of Ming military officials produced soldiers in response to Wang Tong's call from Dong Kinh for help, although they would be relatively few and without the quality of leadership that had been demonstrated in the past by Zhang Fu. While waiting for this final crack of Ming's whip, Le Loi pressed the siege of remaining Ming fortresses, prepared to defend the borders, and began to act like a king.

Le Loi appointed Nguyen Trai to have responsibility for organizing civil administration and for writing letters to solicit the submission of Ming officials and of local people serving the Ming. Nguyen Trai was a grandson of Tran Nguyen Dan, one of the last prominent Tran princes. Nguyen Trai's father, Nguyen Phi Khanh, was a scholar who had served Ho Quy Ly and had been taken as a prisoner to the north after the Ming conquest. Nguyen Phi Khanh has left many poems expressing his aspirations for public service. Nguyen Trai had received an excellent classical education and was a graduate of the examination held in 1400 under Ho Quy Ly. After the Ming conquest, he remained in Giao Chi and apparently lived for several years in hiding to avoid serving the Ming. Eventually, he joined Le Loi and served him as an advisor.

Nguyen Trai's surviving works include several letters to Ming officials and to local men serving the Ming explaining why they should surrender, a famous proclamation of victory over the Ming, a history of Le Loi's career, a geography, and many poems both in Literary Chinese and in vernacular Vietnamese. Consequently, he has become a towering figure in Vietnamese literary history, particularly since very little has survived from before his lifetime and because he is the first poet to leave a significant corpus of verse in the vernacular language. Consequently, although largely based on conjecture, it has been widely assumed that he was a great statesman and military strategist who devised the plans that resulted in Le Loi's success.

There is no firm record of when Nguyen Trai joined Le Loi, although there is a well-known tale about him traveling to Thanh Hoa to meet Le Loi at Mount Lam and then deciding to join him. It is very unlikely that this occurred before Le Loi began to resist the Ming in 1418, because at that time Le Loi had no particular reputation that could possibly have drawn Nguyen Trai's attention. It is most likely to have been after the five years of fighting in the mountains of Thanh Hoa that ended in Le Loi's defeat and submission to Ming. Le Loi's reputation as a fighter and a survivor was established by then, and during the truce of 1423–1424 it would have been possible for visitors to find Le Loi at home.

Part of the significance of Nguyen Trai's role in the events of that time comes from the fact that he was a man of the Kinh people in the Red River plain while Le Loi and large numbers of his followers came from the Trai peoples of the southern provinces. A century later, the differences between these two populations and regions would lead to prolonged civil war. The image of Le Loi and Nguyen Trai as a team of brawn and brain representing the two parts of the country was a useful and comforting symbol of unity, particularly since so many Kinh people in the Red River plain had supported the Ming. In fact, there is no firm evidence that Nguyen Trai's contribution to Le Loi's regime was more than as an erudite writer of letters and proclamations, a knowledgeable administrator, an expert on court music and ritual, and a voice of moderation amidst Le Loi's bloodthirsty lieutenants, all of which, while a bit short of the myth, was still a substantial role in the tumult of that time.

The most plausible way to conjecture an even larger role for Nguyen Trai is to associate him with the shift in aim, strategy, and tactics that we have noted between Le Loi's activities before and after the death of Zhu Di. From a defensive mentality and merely staying alive in the mountains of Thanh Hoa, Le Loi suddenly acted to mobilize the upland population of the southern provinces, to strike at the most vulnerable points of the Ming defense, to build on the momentum of his successes without delay, and to methodically lay the foundation for a new dynastic regime. This dramatic change may have come from Le Loi's own meditations or from consultations with his trusted battle leaders, but it may also owe something to Nguyen Trai, who possessed a large knowledge of history, had closely observed Ming administration while evading it, and held strong opinions about good government. Nguyen Trai is likely to have been more alert than others to understanding the implications of Zhu Di's death and of Zhu Gaozhi's proclamation of a new policy in Giao Chi. It may even have been these events that prompted him to join Le Loi and to urge Le Loi to take advantage of the changing circumstances.

A new dynastic structure

In early 1427, aside from collecting rice to feed soldiers, the chief aims of Le Loi's civil administration in the Red River plain were focused upon accumulating know-ledge of the population, finding qualified officials, and establishing rules for their behavior. Family registers were compiled. Displaced people were sent back to their villages to grow rice or to engage in trade. In a proclamation, Le Loi called upon educated "men of ability" to come forward to serve. In one of his first acts after establishing his headquarters at Bo De, Le Loi authorized a literary examination that selected over thirty scholars who became the core of a civil court.

Officials who had served Ming but readily turned to serve Le Loi were assigned to posts in the southern provinces. Checkpoints were established to authenticate the travel documents of officials, who were admonished to strictly follow their itinerary and instructions, to report everything that they saw and did, and to observe "the three proscriptions": do not be without human feeling; do not be oppressive and rude; do not be crafty and avaricious.

As more local people who had served the Ming began to come over, proced-ures for evaluating degrees of guilt by association were devised and levels of punishment were prescribed. A schedule of ransoms by which guilty men could redeem their wives, children, and slaves was published. Chieftains in the moun-tains also began to submit, and trade in salt and fish was forbidden with those who did not. Envoys from Champa and Laos arrived to make peace with Le Loi, showing that the shifting tide of power was felt beyond the frontiers.

During the first half of 1427, Le Loi was preoccupied with turning a rabble into an army. Thousands of men were hastily recruited during his march through the southern provinces. Thousands more were recruited in the Red River plain. After a spate of fighting around Dong Kinh early in the year, Le Loi not only rewarded some officers but he also had others executed for failure to follow instructions. He issued a proclamation to his soldiers urging discipline and obedience. He informed them that if they obeyed his commands he would take care of them and their families but disobedience would be punished with death. He also announced that when the war ended two-thirds of them would be allowed to return to their homes and fields.

Le Loi announced ten prohibitions that give an indication of what he meant by indiscipline in the ranks: boisterous behavior; talk of omens that caused loss of fighting spirit; pretending not to see the flags or hear the drums ordering an attack; not stopping when the signal to stand fast is given; not retreating when the gong for retreat is sounded; sleeping or abandoning one's post when on guard duty; getting involved with women; hiding unreported wealth or taking bribes from deserters; venting anger and hatred that obscures the merit or the crimes of others; being dishonest, thievish, cruel, or at odds with others. Violations of these prohibitions were to be punished by beheading. Shortly after, another punishment was announced: all members of units that flee battle and leave some of their members behind were to be executed.

Meanwhile, catapults and siege engines were being constructed and iron forges were built to produce and repair weapons. Dikes and walls were piled up to tighten the siege of Dong Kinh. The northern border was put under the command of Le Sat, one of Le Loi's most able commanders. In late summer, a small Ming army attempted to cross the border but was repulsed. Thereafter the families of soldiers on the northern border were relocated out of danger and the siege of Xuong Giang (Bac Giang) was pressed to eliminate this stepping-stone for any Ming army on its way to relieve Dong Kinh or for any retreat of Ming forces from Dong Kinh to the border.

The Ming commanders at Xuong Giang understood the importance of their post and resisted to the death. Le Loi sent troops to throw up earthworks from which to gain access to the fortress. Élite units with long swords, crossbows, flaming arrows, and firearms joined the battle, and Xuong Giang fell ten days before the arrival of the main Ming relief army. Le Loi instructed his generals to prepare what might be called a "deep dead end" for the Ming army on the road from the border to Xuong Giang with Xuong Giang as the end of the road and with units closing in around the Ming force as it advanced. The commander of the Ming relief force did not know that Xuong Giang had fallen so plunged ahead until he was well caught in the trap. The Ming army was utterly annihilated.

Banners, standards, and prisoners from this campaign were conveyed to the Ming army marching downriver from Yunnan, which persuaded its commander to turn back, and to Wang Tong at Dong Kinh, which persuaded him to surrender. Le Loi's generals wanted to attack and kill remaining Ming forces, but Nguyen Trai argued that nothing was to be gained by this and that they should be allowed to return north without further injury. Le Loi took Nguyen Trai's advice and arranged for the Ming and their supporters to leave the country in peace.

Le Loi promulgated six rules to be observed by his military officers to curb their enthusiasm in victory, prohibiting cruelty, bullying, and criminal behavior. Most local people who had supported the Ming decided to remain and face the consequences of that. The rest were allowed to depart north with what remained of the imperial garrison. Within weeks, the Ming court recognized Tran Cao as king and abolished Giao Chi. Only a few weeks after that, Tran Cao was dead, probably poisoned, though many stories have been told of his demise.

In 1428, Le Loi presided over an extended session of conferring rewards and meting out punishments before entering Dong Kinh and taking the throne.

During the five years of his reign, he and his followers attended to all aspects of a royal court: law, administration, personnel, public morality, finance, defense, diplomacy, ritual, and succession. The role of Nguyen Trai and other civil officials was mainly concerned with ritual, diplomacy, and the details of law and administration. The most influential voices at court belonged to a group of generals from Thanh Hoa who had served Le Loi from the beginning of his military campaigns, of whom Le Sat was the most prominent.

Le Loi endeavored to maintain some sense of continuity with the Tran past by rebuilding the tombs and shrines of the Tran royal family that had been destroyed by the Ming. He conducted sacrifices to all former kings and to all prominent deities that had received royal recognition in times past. He also reinstituted the blood oath and the royal birthday festival, which had been abolished by Ho Quy Ly. These were occasions to encourage loyalty and to distribute gifts among large crowds of new followers.

The business of rewards and punishments continued for quite some time. Assemblies were organized to distribute rewards to various military units. In 1429, after a year and a half of investigation, a "register of merit" honoring ninety-three men who had particularly distinguished themselves in wartime service to Le Loi was published. An official was assigned to investigate anyone claiming to have been unjustly left out.

Measures for dealing with those who had served Ming reveal that this included a significant number of people. Stubborn Ming partisans who tried to avoid Le Loi's justice were tracked down and beheaded. On the other hand, those who surrendered to Le Loi could regain their confiscated property. The investigation to itemize the land and possessions of various classes of people who had served Ming took ten months, and for several months after the completion of this procedure officials were still sorting out the disposition of those who had served not only the Ming but also the Ho, along with their families, dependents, land, and property. The official dynastic doctrine was that the Le succeeded the Tran dynasty, and that Ho Quy Ly was an unlawful usurper.

Administrative jurisdictions were reformed and regulations for conducting censuses, collecting taxes, conscripting soldiers, and authenticating paperwork were published. Government at village, district, and provincial levels was organized, and officials were assigned their posts. Literary exams to fill positions were held in 1429, 1431, and 1433. Officials were called upon to recommend others for appointment, but they were punished if anyone they recommended proved to be incapable. Officials were investigated and categorized into four groups: first, those with energy, acumen, and both literary and military skill; second, those with energy, acumen, and knowledge of letters; third, those who could write and do arithmetic; and the fourth category was for "others." The emphasis on "energy and acumen" expresses an appreciation for enthusiasm and intelligence, and for being able not simply to follow orders but also to take initiative.

At the same time, several edicts were published against corruption, and officials were repeatedly admonished to refrain from evil and oppressive behavior. Some such problems were a normal part of any administration, particularly at the start of a new regime. However, there were likely to have been contradictions between the Le dynasts, whose base of power was in Thanh Hoa, and the people in the Red River plain, who for twenty years had been governed as a Ming province. Ho Quy Ly, the first king from Thanh Hoa, never won the allegiance of people in the Red River plain. Later events would show that Le Loi and his successors mitigated this regional antagonism for a time but did not erase it.

In 1429, after a grand military review, four-fifths of the soldiers were demobilized and sent to work in the fields. An especial concern of Le Loi was to put land back into production. Abandoned and confiscated land was assigned to demobilized soldiers and to other worthy people. Magistrates were instructed that no land was to be left uncultivated. A new agrarian regime emerged out of Le Loi's legislation on land ownership and village government. There came an end to large estates farmed by slaves or peasants in a serf-like status. Instead, villages were organized on the basis of free peasants with enough land to support their families and pay taxes.

This agenda built upon the work of Ho and Ming administrators. The Ho, the Ming, and the Le all targeted the estates not only of aristocrats but also of temples. Le Loi ensured that Buddhist temples were restricted not only in their ownership of land but also in their manpower. He held an examination of all monks to determine whether or not they would be allowed to continue as monks or would be returned to lay life. The effort to put people into productive work was reinforced by Confucian ideas about public morality. One of the first edicts in 1429 was against gambling, playing chess, and sitting around drinking wine.

During the Le dynasty, the standing army was primarily recruited from the southern provinces. Le Loi collected weapons from the population in the Red River plain. At the same time, arsenals and shipyards were established to manufacture new weapons and war boats. Several campaigns were launched into the mountains against upland people deemed uncooperative in the modern province of Lai Chau. Despite tribute missions from Champa and Laos, the Le court nurtured a long-term desire for revenge against these kingdoms. Champa had taken the opportunity of Ming rule to recover the territories that Ho Quy Ly had conquered in 1402, the modern provinces of Quang Nam and Quang Ngai. Laos had assisted Ming in its pacification of Le Loi in 1421–1422. The Le court would take its time to prepare replies to these grievances. Meanwhile, more urgent matters preoccupied Le Loi.

One of these was finance. Annalists observed that Ho Quy Ly had destroyed nearly all coinage. As early as 1428, Le Loi began to cast his own coins, but demand was initially greater than what could be produced. In 1429 the court debated the issuing of paper money, but this was not done. After a few years, the monetary situation was stabilized as the production of new coins gradually filled demand.

An important matter was to regularize the tributary relationship with Ming. For four years, Ming demanded the return of all Ming people and of weapons left behind in Giao Chi. In fact, a significant population of Ming people chose to stay, and Le Loi had no intention of forcing them to leave. Ming repeatedly demanded that Le Loi find a Tran descendent to restore that dynasty, and Le Loi repeatedly replied that none could be found. Finally, in 1431, the Ming court recognized Le Loi as king. Thereafter, relations with Ming were amicable and uneventful.

Le Loi's eldest son, Le Tu Te, was an adult and had held high positions in his father's entourage. However, he had a reputation for being rustic, rash, and foolish, and Le Loi did not regard him as capable of being king. In 1429 he designated his second son, Le Nguyen Long, born in 1423, to be crown prince. Shortly before he died in 1433, Le Loi demoted Le Tu Te and confirmed Le Nguyen Long as his choice to succeed him. After Le Loi's death, Le Tu Te was ostracized from the royal family and eventually demoted to commoner status.

Le Loi led a rough and vigorous life, full of danger, daring, and drama. His energy was spent enforcing order, discipline, and hierarchy, first among the people in the uplands of the southern provinces and then among the Kinh in the lowlands as Ming rule faded away. Rising as a frontier chieftain on the margins where Trai and Kinh people intermingled, he mobilized the Trai to make himself king of the Kinh. Although he established his regime at Dong Kinh, the "eastern capital," he also maintained a dynastic "home base" at Ho Quy Ly's old "western capital" of Tay Do, which lay near his native estate at Mount Lam and near which he and his descendents would be buried.

According to a popular story, Le Loi's achievement was made possible by a magical sword that he received from Heaven as a symbol of his destiny. After founding his dynasty, Heaven took the form of a great turtle that surfaced in a Dong Kinh lake and reclaimed the sword as Le Loi passed by in a boat. Today, a lake in downtown Hanoi is called the Lake of the Returned Sword (Ho Hoan Kiem) to commemorate this mythical event.

Later Vietnamese historians have understandably chosen to see Le Loi's war with Ming as a war of resistance against foreign aggression, but it was also a civil war between the Kinh and the Trai, between the Red River plain and the southern provinces, between those for whom the northern empire was the source of civilization and those for whom the uplands and southern frontiers were places of freedom from the restraints of civil discipline. Le Loi built his dynasty as an alliance between these two groups, but it was a fragile alliance, relying upon unity among men from the south whose personal ambitions were a centrifugal force seeking new horizons of fulfillment. The alliance lasted for a century before lapsing into a new civil war that continued in various forms for three centuries. For three decades following Le Loi's death, his generals became great lords and enforced a peace in which educated men of the Red River plain accumulated at the royal court.

Great lords and Le Nguyen Long

During ten years of warfare, Le Loi gathered a large entourage of battle leaders. Ninety-three such men were listed on the 1429 roll of honor. They were not united by a common ancestor, as were the Tran princes two centuries before. They came from many families and many places, and most of them held the Le surname as an honorific, given to them by Le Loi in recognition of their service to him. They were nearly all from the southern provinces and were illiterate. Later court annalists quoted an unknown writer of a non-extant history to describe them as "avaricious, boastful, licentious … everywhere putting their relatives and favorites in positions of authority … openly corrupt … utterly stupid … like a noisy swarm of bees … like dogs and rats baring their teeth … so thickheaded that they could not tell the difference between a pig and a goat … so ignorant that they did not know the four seasons of the year … full of envy and murder." This is seemingly an excessively jaundiced view, but these men probably tended toward rusticity and arrogance. Le Loi kept them under control with his strong will and severe discipline. After his death, the great lords who emerged at the forefront of these men passed in succession across the stage of power, each being pushed aside by the next. This came about because there was no adult king until the 1460s.

Le Nguyen Long was 10 years old when he became king in autumn of 1433. He was precocious, strong-willed, and high-spirited. There are stories that his mother had been particularly close to Le Loi, but she had died in the boy's infancy. According to one tale, in 1425 she had volunteered to be sacrificed to a local Nghe An spirit in exchange for Le Loi gaining victory and her son becoming his heir. This unlikely story provided a popular explanation for her untimely death and her son's elevation to the throne at the expense of his elder half-brother. Le Nguyen Long had made his way through childhood without maternal vigilance. As a small boy, he had witnessed the final stages of the war with

Ming and the events of his father's reign. He ostensibly ruled without a regent from the time of Le Loi's death. The adults who surrounded him were outwardly deferential while busy with their own affairs.

Le Sat was the most powerful person at court. Although the young king was consulted on matters of consequence, he was often at odds with Le Sat and with other officials, showing that the court was in a certain state of contention, with some people finding access to the boy king as a way of furthering their influence. In recorded differences of opinion, the king always had the last word, which indicates either the force of his personality or, more likely, the power of those seeking to harness him to their ambitions. For his part, Le Sat carried the daily burden of government, but he did not know how to deal with the boy king.

Already in the first year of his reign, 1434, Le Nguyen Long found himself in the middle of a long argument between two groups of officials, one aligned with Le Sat and one seeking to push Le Sat aside in favor of those with royal blood, including the king's elder half-brother, Le Tu Te. After many arguments that thoroughly frustrated Le Sat, the king was finally made to understand that bringing his brother into the court would be a mistake, and the leader of Le Sat's enemies was exiled to a distant post.

Also in this year, two of Le Loi's prominent generals who were not on good terms with Le Sat suffered demotion or censure. Le Kha, who was Le Sat's particular enemy for unrecorded reasons, was demoted to Lang Son Province on the northern border. Another man, Le Thu, was accused of using soldiers and dynastic revenue to build an elaborate mansion, something many others of his class were also doing. After lengthy judicial procedures, he eventually escaped punishment in consideration of his former service. These two men, among others, were eager to unseat Le Sat.

Le Sat had a habit of killing people. Shortly after Le Nguyen Long's accession, a conspiracy was uncovered and the leaders were beheaded. Not long after that, perhaps still in a grim mood, Le Sat insisted on beheading a workman at a Buddhist temple he was building who, reportedly suffering from fatigue, cited a Confucian cliché to jokingly suggest that the drought then being experienced was an indication that royal virtue was lacking. Then, when two officials were found to be making a business of selling royal slaves to other officials, Le Sat beheaded them. He routinely beheaded officials found guilty of corrupt practices. This was about the same time that he became angry with Nguyen Trai over an argument that Nguyen Trai was having with two other officials who wanted to change some words in a document that he had written. Le Sat was easily angered and expected everyone to obey him as his soldiers had done. He could not understand why people had to get into arguments and behaved in what he considered to be a disobedient manner.

Meanwhile the small headstrong king attracted much concern. In 1435, one official had the temerity to confront the king with six accusations: the king refused to study with the teacher assigned to him; he disdained, scolded, and ignored the governess who had been chosen by his father to look after him; he shut his door against the palace "aunties" who attempted to correct his behavior; he abandoned his studies to shoot birds with his bow and arrow, and when his attendants tried to stop him he shot arrows at them; he shunned the children of high officials sent to study with him and instead played with his servants; he spent too much time with eunuchs and gave them gifts. Le Nguyen Long was so angry at this series of rebukes that he sent eunuchs to harass the temerarious official at home and elsewhere. However, the official persisted and explained that he was arguing for the king's best interests, and eventually the king relented. Despite his adolescent exuberance, Le Nguyen Long seems to have had a rational mind that could be engaged in argument and discussion.

A few weeks after this fuss, a case came up of seven criminals who were not yet adults. According to the law, they deserved death, but Le Sat hesitated because he realized that already there had been "too much beheading." Nguyen Trai argued for mercy, so Le Sat assigned him to take responsibility for rehabilitating the young offenders. Within a very short time, Nguyen Trai reported that they were incorrigible. Two were accordingly beheaded and the rest banished to remote places. This demoralizing lesson in efforts to educate wayward youth resonated with the problem of educating the king.

The king still refused to study. Nguyen Trai and other prominent scholars were assigned to take his education in hand, but he would not cooperate, which so infuriated Le Sat that for a time he refused to attend court and demanded the death of a eunuch whom he considered to be corrupting the king. Finally, an official reasoned with the king and explained the serious consequences of his behavior for the whole kingdom and the episode passed.

Shortly after, the king was learning to ride an elephant, and when a wild deer was presented to the palace he decided to set the elephant and deer to fighting for sport. When the deer gored the elephant, the elephant in fear backed up, fell into a well, and died. Le Sat and other officials put a stop to this kind of amusement. The king held his peace, but he did not forget his accumulation of resentments.

Le Sat had made many enemies with his old-soldier no-nonsense mentality. He had once gotten into a losing argument with a scholar over whether or not widows and widowers should have a reduction in taxes. His argument was that military people worked hard to protect the country and had to pay their taxes, so it was not fair that people who contributed nothing to the country be given special consideration simply because they had lost their spouses. He was very protective of the martial legacy of Le Loi as he understood it, but he could not grasp the arguments of scholars that were based on books and ancient history. Meanwhile, the cadre of scholars at court grew.

The biennial literary examinations to select officials that were begun under Le Loi continued until 1435. In 1434, a plan for instituting regular literary examinations in a five-year cycle was published. A preliminary examination that year selected over one thousand to be given the right to continue their studies, the best of them being allowed to go to the palace academy.

At the beginning of 1437, an ad hoc examination in writing and arithmetic selected 690 people to be assigned administrative posts throughout the country. Education officers were dismayed by how the examination process was subverted by the great lords who owed their positions to wartime merit. Such people, in the words of the Confucian annalist, "were not fond of the Confucianists and used them only for keeping records, preparing documents, and inscribing litigation; positions of responsibility were given to sycophants." Great lords filled vacant administrative posts with their followers and dependents, regardless of ability. The annalists reported that half of those chosen in the 1437 examination had not studied but simply feigned knowledge in order to obtain an appointment.

Le Sat was unaware that the king had nurtured a great hatred of him because of how he exercised authority at court. He consequently found himself at a loss in 1437 when the 14-year-old king insisted on appointing his enemy, Le Kha, as commander of the palace guard. When Le Sat opposed this, saying that this would cause him to fear for his life, the king summoned accusations of insubordination against Le Sat and obtained his death. There followed a round of promotions for Le Sat's enemies and demotions for his friends. Among those who benefited most were Le Kha and Le Thu.

The opinion of the workman executed early in Le Nguyen Long's reign for suggesting that bad government caused drought eventually became the official view of the court. Year after year the country experienced both drought and insect infestations that ruined harvests. The Dharma Cloud Buddha was brought to the capital to pray for rain. Sacrifices were made to popular spirits and deities in the country, also to the god of agriculture and to Confucius. Punishments for criminal acts were reduced to show mercy as a way of eliciting rain. In 1438, a royal edict observed that the successive years of drought and insects might be due to the king's failure to appoint good officials, and consequently the king promised to try harder. Two years later, a similar edict was published. In these years, Le Nguyen Long was coming out of his adolescent fog and becoming aware of public affairs.

In 1437, the year in which he ostensibly came of age and obtained Le Sat's death, Le Nguyen Long presided over a reform of court music and ritual, the details of which were entrusted to Nguyen Trai and a eunuch named Luong Dang, who was a favorite of the king. The work on court music went smoothly enough because the eunuch was uninterested and Nguyen Trai made arrangements to his own satisfaction. Nguyen Trai supervised the manufacture of musical instruments and sent stonecutters to make chimes. He also unveiled a painting of stone chimes and explained the importance of music to influence people toward study and good behavior. Luong Dang did not dispute Nguyen Trai's work on music, which was based on Ming precedents, and this part of the task was completed easily enough.

In the midst of his work on music, Nguyen Trai also prepared a compilation of Ho Quy Ly's vernacular poetry in response to a request from the king. This was a curious task considering that Le historians considered Ho Quy Ly to have been a usurper and consequently a "bad" model for royal behavior. These poems are not known to have survived, but there was apparently something about them that attracted the interest of this teenage king. Perhaps it was a certain intellectual adventurousness and spontaneity that resisted the orthodox verities of Song–Ming Confucianism. At the least, this would explain the fuss that arose between Nguyen Trai and Luong Dang when they turned to matters other than music.

The two men could not agree on clothing regulations at court. Luong Dang was not a scholar and was uninterested in bookish precedents. He had his own ideas about what would look good. The king chose his plan over Nguyen Trai's recommendation, which was based on erudition. Offended, Nguyen Trai asked to be excused from any responsibility for this topic. More serious was the difference of opinion between Nguyen Trai and Luong Dang over court ritual. Again, the king was inclined to agree with Luong Dang. Nguyen Trai held his tongue, but another official exploded, excitedly affirming that ritual forms manifested eternal truths and that Luong Dang's haphazard schemes would "destroy the country." This dire prediction infuriated members of Le Nguyen Long's entourage, and the intemperate official was banished, barely escaping with his life.

Beginning in 1439, Le Nguyen Long led annual punitive expeditions into the mountains against rebellious vassals. Around the same time he ordered that the Ming people who had settled in the country must cut their hair and wear clothes according to the custom of the Kinh people. He was getting out of the palace and starting to pay attention to what he saw in the city streets and in the countryside. Whether he had the makings of an energetic and intelligent king or would have never overcome the feckless frustrations of his youth is a matter for conjecture. The manner in which he dealt with the question of succession before his untimely death suggests that he was easily manipulated.

In 1439, his first son, Le Nghi Dan, was born, and in the following year Le Nghi Dan was made crown prince. In 1441, a revolution among the palace women deprived Le Nghi Dan of this position. Le Nghi Dan's mother was demoted for being "proud and obstreperous" and Le Nguyen Long then announced that the question of crown prince was not yet decided. Shortly after this, "wayward and insolent" palace women were imprisoned. Finally, an elder half-sister of the king who had been captured and adopted by a Ming general, then raised to adulthood in China before being repatriated during Le Loi's reign, was forced to commit suicide, being accused of endless conspiracies. Meanwhile, two more sons were born, and the third son, Le Bang Co, born during the course of the upheaval among the palace women, was designated crown prince. Le Nghi Dan was demoted and assigned as prince of the northern border province of Lang Son. The second son, Le Khac Xuong, was assigned as prince of the southern border province of Thuan Hoa (modern Quang Binh, Quang Tri, and Thua Thien).

The guiding hand behind these events in the women's quarters was Nguyen Thi Lo, Nguyen Trai's young and beautiful wife, who had been assigned as teacher of the palace women and who exercised strong influence over the young king. Behind each woman in the palace was a family aspiring to greatness through being related to a king. There were plots to induce abortions in rivals, and, in this case, to rescind a decision already made about the crown prince. Nguyen Thi Lo, an intelligent, well-educated, good-looking, and spirited woman with the benefit of the king's eye, was in the middle of these affairs. The king was infatuated with her and kept her at his side "day and night."

In early 1442, the pregnancy of a particular woman in the palace, Ngo Thi Ngoc Dao, caused great concern. She was a daughter of Pham Tu, who had been a follower of Le Loi and who was also a close friend of Nguyen Trai. There are stories about the discovery of an image of the infant crown prince Le Bang Co that was designed to summon demons to harm him. Nguyen Thi Anh, Le Bang Co's mother, was persuaded that Ngo Thi Ngoc Dao was behind this act of sorcery. Consequently, there was a plot to harm Ngo Thi Ngoc Dao. Nguyen Trai and Nguyen Thi Lo intervened to protect her, reportedly with hopes that she might bear a son who would be king. There are stories of spiriting her out of the palace to safety.

In early autumn of 1442, Ngo Thi Ngoc Dao gave birth to a fourth prince, Le Tu Thanh. Seven days later, the king paid a visit to Nguyen Trai's home at Chi Linh, around fifty kilometers east of Dong Kinh down the Duong River. On the journey back, he was found dead one morning after spending the night with Nguyen Thi Lo. She was accused of poisoning him. Twelve days later, Nguyen Thi Lo, Nguyen Trai, and all members of their families were executed. Two eunuchs who protested their innocence were also executed. The mother of an unborn son of Nguyen Trai fled to the mountains of Nghe An. Twenty-two years later, the boy received a provincial appointment when his father was exonerated and given posthumous honors.

Insufficient information has survived to explain the death of Le Nguyen Long and the alacrity of Nguyen Thi Lo's and Nguyen Trai's condemnation. Their involvement in palace intrigues had surely earned them powerful enemies. Given the eunuchs' suicidal protest, as well as Nguyen Trai's later exoneration and his venerable status in later historical and literary writings, everyone who has written about him has assumed that he was innocent of the king's death. After all, he was credited with saving Le Tu Thanh, considered by many later historians as the greatest of all Vietnamese kings, from infanticide. Official historians also assumed that Nguyen Thi Lo was innocent and attribute the king's death to "a sudden grave illness" or to "a malarial fever." If the king's death was from natural causes, the fact that it was taken as an occasion to eliminate Nguyen Trai and Nguyen Thi Lo suggests that powerful people perceived them as a threat to their ambitions. If this was a regicide and Nguyen Trai was innocent, then casting the onus of guilt upon him would have deflected blame from the conspirators. Nguyen Trai was the most prominent of Le Loi's wartime associates who was not a warrior and was not from Thanh Hoa. Consequently, he was vulnerable and defenseless.

For nine years, the Le court had experienced the vicissitudes of a rebellious, adolescent, orphaned king who was susceptible to the influence of others and finally mesmerized by Nguyen Thi Lo. It may appear as if he learned how to use eunuchs and officials to have his way when he obtained the death of Le Sat. But it is more plausible that Le Sat's enemies, chief of whom was Le Kha, learned how to use the young king to eliminate Le Sat. As Le Nguyen Long entered adulthood, great lords and aspiring hegemons, taking a lesson from Le Sat's fate, found cause for dismay in the potential for the king becoming more unpredictable and dangerous. Le Kha and Le Thu benefited from the deaths of both Le Sat and Le Nguyen Long, but whether regicide was one of their means of advancement can only be conjectured.

Great lords and Le Bang Co

Six days after Le Nguyen Long's body was carried back to Dong Kinh, Le Bang Co was made king. Nguyen Thi Anh, the queen mother, became the pivot of authority at court. She was designated as regent to rule "from behind the curtain." She was from a Thanh Hoa family and established a working relationship with Le Kha and Le Thu. She took care to educate and discipline her son to the task of kingship with seemingly acceptable results. Later court historians praised her wholehearted concern for public affairs, the respect she showed toward the great lords, the care she took to follow established rules, and her willingness to retire when her son reached the age of 12. This rather cheery interpretation does not take into account that she was also pliant to the intrigues of others, was apparently forced into retirement with the fall of Le Kha and Le Thu, and was ridiculed by a later writer with the cliché of a hen crowing at dawn, commonly used by Confucian historians when referring to women in positions of authority.

While the queen mother presided over the court, Le Loi's old battlefield associates attended to affairs beyond the capital. There were five such men who in 1442 stood forth to ensure an untroubled accession for Le Bang Co. All five were prominent on the roll of merit published in 1429. Le Kha, Le Sat's old enemy, was one of the five, as was Le Thu, who, although initially allied with Le Sat, had been harassed by court officials for his extravagance and did not rise to prominence until after Le Sat's death. Le Kha and Le Thu formed a partnership with the queen mother and their power grew during the 1440s.

Two others of the five, Le Boi and Le Liet, had been early allies of Le Sat, but they had mainly occupied themselves with leading soldiers on the frontiers in the mid 1430s and had escaped the palace dissentions of that time. They now appeared at court and stood with those raising Le Bang Co to the throne. Le Boi apparently did not care for court life. He was soon leading soldiers on the Cham frontier, but then succumbed to a lingering illness. He felt well enough in 1449 to pay a visit at court and receive a sum of money in recognition of his service, but played no further leadership role.

Le Liet had been rising to prominence in the last years of Le Nguyen Long's reign. In 1441, amidst the palace intrigues of that year, he was assigned to announce that Le Bang Co was crown prince. However, he was not part of the partnership between Le Kha and Le Thu, and in 1444 he was slandered to the queen mother who imprisoned him and his family. His case could not be resolved for lack of evidence, and he was finally released in 1448 after the intervention of several great lords and a princess. His wife and children were not released to him until 1450. He thereafter stayed out of the way until returning to the center of court affairs in 1459 with Le Xi, the remaining man of 1442.

Le Xi had received a promotion after the death of Le Sat in 1437, but nothing further is thereafter recorded of him until 1442. Like Le Boi and Le Liet, he seems to have gravitated toward service on the frontiers. Shortly after leading an army against Champa in 1445, he was dismissed. By 1448 he had been reinstated with responsibility for administering the army, but thereafter he played no recorded role until 1459. In that year, he emerged to finish his career with an important act of leadership and great honor.

Three of these five men are recorded with different surnames in some records because they were given the royal Le surname as a mark of merit: Trinh Kha, Dinh Liet, and Nguyen Xi. The careers of Le Loi's generals in the mid fifteenth century reveal a great diversity of characters with many vicissitudes and intrigues, but few of these men became leading figures at court, and those who did achieve prominence enjoyed but a brief time in the limelight.

In the 1440s, Le Kha and Le Thu managed to push aside Le Liet and Le Xi and, with Le Boi in failing health, to gradually gain ascendance at court. They exerted increasing influence over the queen mother and brought into their circle of power a third great lord named Le Khac Phuc (his original surname was Trinh). In 1434, Le Khac Phuc's younger full brother had been killed by Le Sat, and he was demoted to a minor post. He had not immediately benefited from Le Sat's death because at that time he was under investigation for protecting an official accused of corruption and with making unlawful appointments. He was apparently slow to master the skills of maneuver at court, but by 1445 he was a major figure, and in that year his eldest son received a princess in marriage.

Le Kha, Le Thu, and Le Khac Phuc tightened their collective grip on the court during three years of war with Champa. In 1444, Cham attacks in Thuan Hoa prompted Le Boi to lead an army to the border, after which he became ill and played no further role at court. In mid 1445, Le Xi was sent to attack Champa. He was dismissed a few months later for an unrecorded offense. During the winter dry season of 1445–1446, Le Kha, Le Thu, and Le Khac Phuc all joined an army as it assembled in Nghe An and advanced down the coast to modern Binh Dinh Province. There, the Cham capital of Vijaya was taken and the Cham king was captured. They appointed a new Cham king and surrounded him with Chams who had resided in Dong Kinh during previous years. Three years later, in 1449, the man designated as the Cham king was killed and replaced by an elder brother. Thereafter, relations between the two kingdoms began to deteriorate again.

The Dong Kinh court was quick to report to Ming the details of the expedition to Champa and to explain it as a response to unprovoked attacks. The Le court was particularly sensitive to the Ming in these years because of a territorial dispute that had arisen on the coastal border. The two sides held discussions about the problem in 1447 and 1448, and at one point a false rumor that a Ming army was about to attack prompted an emergency mobilization of soldiers and the collection of large amounts of beef and wine with which to beguile the expected invaders.

Meanwhile, scholars continued to accumulate at court. The first examination under the new academic system announced in 1434 was held in early 1442, shortly before Le Nguyen Long's death. This and subsequent examinations held in 1448, 1453, and 1458 produced a total of eighty-nine graduates, although only four of these were from 1458. This was a new generation of educated men who came of age in a time when, according to a comment in the *Complete Book of the History of Great Viet*, "culture and education were in eclipse, those with ability crouched under injustice, and old scholars were tossed into retirement." Many of these graduates would play prominent roles at court later in the century, some of them still haunted by the fragility of civilized behavior. The examinations were seldom without scandal. The top graduate in 1448 was publicly satirized with graffiti and street songs as "professor pig" when it became common knowledge that he slept with his mother-in-law.

The great lords did appreciate and protect scholars who attended competently to their assigned tasks. For example, Nguyen Thien Tich went to China three times as an envoy to the Ming court and wrote an inscription for Le Nguyen Long's tomb. He was known for being strictly impartial when grading examinations, which was so unusual as to be a point of particular praise. When, in 1448, another official who had falsely slandered him was caught embezzling tax revenues, Le Kha had the man killed, even though the offense did not require such a severe punishment, simply because he was so incensed that anyone would dare to disparage a man of such integrity as Nguyen Thien Tich.

Le Kha's presumption of authority at this time seemed to extend to the smallest details. The whole court would periodically go to Tay Do for a holiday. On such an occasion in 1448 the local boys and girls in Thanh Hoa Province presented a performance of dancing and singing, which Le Kha stopped because he considered it too lewd for the young king to see. Later that year in Dong Kinh he ordered that a hunting net hanging in a palace courtyard be discarded so as not to encourage the king to become addicted to hunting. He personally went to convey the Dharma Cloud Buddha to the capital to pray for rain, and he also made a trip to Tay Do specifically to build a shrine.

He supervised court appointments and judicial proceedings, advising the queen mother about how cases should be decided. The employment of mercy and severity appears random without more information but surely had to do with Le Kha's circle of friends and clients, and his list of enemies. In one case, the son of a great lord who murdered someone in the marketplace escaped punishment in consideration of his father's merit. On the other hand, the son of another great lord was executed for being a thief and a gambler and his father was demoted for having failed to control him. An example of Le Kha's idea of justice being disconnected from the opinions of others comes from 1449 when he insisted on beheading an official accused of corruption despite nearly everyone else at court arguing for mercy.

For his part, Le Thu seemed more interested in reaping personal benefit from his position at court than in exercising authority. In 1448 his son was to marry the 10-year-old elder sister of the king, who happened to be mute. His preparations for the wedding were attended by such extravagance and corruption that a scandal erupted, which nevertheless was quickly smoothed away. Le Khac Phuc, who was in charge of the wedding arrangements, had married one of his sons to a princess three years before and was in the middle of many unsavory activities. He dispensed royal largess by presiding over banquets at which gifts were distributed to selected officials. He instituted the practice of examination officials taking a blood oath as a caution against corruption, yet he admitted an unqualified student to the palace academy in a transparent case of bribery.

The greatest failing of these men was their inattention to agriculture, to keep the dikes in repair, to guard against the loss of harvests to insects, and to provide for times of famine. Rural distress is a major theme of the era of great lord ascendancy. In 1445, a flood destroyed one-third of the rice stored in the palace compound; an edict was published noting that there had been several years of excessive rain, floods, broken dikes, villages being washed away, insects ruining harvests, ponds drying up, and vegetables rotting on the plant. The edict, following Confucian logic, suggested that these troubles resulted from bad government, so, in an effort to make a new beginning, criminal punishments and taxes were reduced.

In 1448, there was more famine and prayers for rain. Once again an edict lamented several years of successive floods, drought, and plagues of insects. A year later, in 1449, another edict noted drought, failed harvests, famine, and misery. This edict expressed royal self-criticism and the same day there was rain. Thereafter, altars were erected to worship all kinds of spirits, including the gods of wind, clouds, thunder, and rain. Schools were repaired as an act of good government to solicit rain. Le Kha and Le Thu sent a public message to the queen mother suggesting that she consult more extensively with them in order to bring order to the court and thereby elicit rain. When she issued a statement agreeing with their suggestion, it rained again. But the overall situation did not improve.

In 1451, another royal edict was published about the chronic disasters in the countryside. Questions were posed. Why is this happening? What can be done about it? Many people were asking these questions, and the most plausible answer was that something was wrong with how the country was being governed. The standard Confucian explanation was that blame rested upon the ruler and his ministers. The king was 10 years old and represented by a regent. With the country in such distress, the men who exercised authority in collaboration with the queen mother could not hide from what were widely believed to be the consequences of dereliction. Accordingly, in the space of two years, a shift of leadership brought a new regime to court.

The 1451 edict was issued at a time when Le Kha's harsh, increasingly homicidal rule had infected the court with fear to the point that his enemies gathered their courage against him. The queen mother was persuaded that Le Kha was plotting against the throne, so she ordered him to be killed. Le Khac Phuc was also killed since there seemed to be no way to retain one without the other. Less than a year later, Le Thu was imprisoned for not preventing his son from using sorcery to harm others. In 1453, the queen mother was persuaded to withdraw from court affairs, thus ending the regency. The 12-year-old king, Le Bang Co, began to personally hold court.

Very little is recorded from the six remaining years of Le Bang Co's reign. Coins were minted. A census was taken. Edicts on military discipline and public morality were published. Le Thu was released from prison in 1456. In that year the king enjoyed a music and dance performance during a visit to Tay Do that featured two favorite items entitled "Defeat of the Ming" and "The Great Lords Come to Court," indicating a congratulatory imagination fixed on past glories.

The most memorable event from this time for later historians was the completion in 1455 of the official court history of the Tran dynasty, including the reign of Ho Quy Ly and the era of Ming rule. Phan Phu Tien, a graduate of the 1429 examination, supervised this work. It became the most important source of information available to later generations about the Tran and about Ho Quy Ly. Phan Phu Tien emphasized that the last Tran rulers were incapable and had lost the heavenly mandate to govern and that Ho Quy Ly was an illegitimate usurper. Thus, he presented the historical basis for proclaiming the Le dynasty.

Many obituaries of great lords are recorded as the generation of Le Loi's followers dropped away. But there remained a constellation of aging men who carried the responsibilities of government. They had been previously elbowed aside by the more ambitious men of their cohort such as Le Sat and Le Kha, who had each attained great heights of power before being cut down. The survivors tended to be men who had kept to the edges of the great factional conflicts of their time by busying themselves in the provinces, leading soldiers on frontiers, preferring the open life in the countryside to the headaches of palace intrigue. Consequently, they were diffident about taking a prominent and open role at court, even when the king's youth would appear to require it. The fates of Le Sat and Le Kha were lessons against seeking the limelight.

The most prominent of the surviving great lords were Le Xi and Le Liet, both of whom had briefly come forward in 1442 during the emergency of Le Nguyen Long's death, after which they faded into the background as others pushed ahead. They were relatively sober men whose sense of public service was at least equal to their desire for personal acclaim. They continued to stand outside the circle of power, ready to step forward if necessary.

Many court affairs fell into the hands of the sons of great lords, but there was no one of stature among them able to exercise leadership. Le Bang Co wandered into adulthood amidst a royal entourage composed of elderly men filled with self-importance and fond of recalling the deeds of their youth and the sons of these men who had grown up learning how to leverage their fathers' reputations for personal gain. According to the comment in the *Complete Book of the History of Great Viet* mentioned above, there was "injustice without appeal" and "all public matters were upside down"; prominent civil officials were "almost 80 years old" and leading great lords "could not read one word"; "the young men, without memory or forethought, acted with savage cruelty, and the old men, not dying, became agents of ruination."

The manner in which the reign and life of Le Bang Co came to an end shows that proper attention was not being given even to the basics of palace security. Court historians considered that Le Bang Co was a well-educated and well-behaved young man who gave indications of becoming a good king, but he lacked the benefit of experienced advisors able to ensure that routine precautions were observed. One night late in 1459, his elder half-brother Le Nghi Dan, who as an infant had been demoted from being crown prince during the palace turmoil of 1441, benefiting from the complicity of a palace guard officer and accompanied by around three hundred followers, climbed over the walls of the palace compound with ladders and killed both Le Bang Co and the queen mother. Four days later, Le Nghi Dan proclaimed himself king.

Le Nghi Dan's feat of suddenly penetrating into the center of power, along with his claim to the throne as a former crown prince, gave him an opportunity to be king. However, it soon became evident that the homicidal manner in which he had advanced his claim would be typical of his rule. Le Thu, who had survived imprisonment during 1452–1456, became one of Le Nghi Dan's victims. Furthermore, Le Nghi Dan was perceived as the tool of other men about whom nothing has been recorded except their names and that they came from a region in the Red River plain east of Dong Kinh. For reasons now lost, except for conceivable conjectures based on class or regional animosities, these men and the great lords regarded each other as mortal enemies. Resistance to Le Nghi Dan among the great lords was ostensibly based upon their revulsion against regicide, but eight months passed before Le Xi and Le Liet brought their men into the palace to kill the regicide and his followers in an apparent act of striking first to avoid calamity for themselves.

Le Bang Co's other elder half-brother, Le Khac Xuong, played an ambiguous role in these events, for which he was later killed. Le Xi and Le Liet passed him by in favor of the younger half-brother, 18-year-old Le Tu Thanh, whose birth had been safeguarded by the intervention of Nguyen Trai. Two days after Le Nghi Dan's death, Le Tu Thanh was proclaimed king, thereby opening the most celebrated reign in all of Vietnamese history. Bringing Le Tu Thanh to the throne earned Le Xi and Le Liet great merit among later historians. It was also the last event of any consequence that can be attributed to the great lords.

The nearly three decades separating the death of Le Loi and the accession of his grandson Le Tu Thanh contrast sharply with comparable times in Ly and Tran dynastic history. Whereas the Ly dynasty began with the successive reigns of three strong kings and the founders of the Tran dynasty quickly organized a collective leadership of talented kings and princes, in the early years of the Le dynasty the royal family was eclipsed by a parade of great lords whose energies were in large measure absorbed in mutual competition. This was an aspect of Thanh Hoa political culture that became a fundamental feature of Le dynastic history with the exception of the reigns of Le Tu Thanh and his son, Le Tranh.

Le Tu Thanh as teacher

In 1442, only fourteen days before the death of his father Le Nguyen Long, Le Tu Thanh was born in the countryside where his mother had found refuge from homicidal intrigues in the palace. After three years, he was brought to the palace to be educated with his three elder brothers, all being about the same age: Le Nghi Dan, Le Khac Xuong, and the king Le Bang Co. According to the annalists, he was in good relations with all his brothers and in particular earned the affection of both Le Bang Co and Le Bang Co's mother who was then serving as regent queen mother. Annalists described him as unusually handsome, digni-fied, intelligent, courageous, resourceful, humane, and decisive. He was drawn to good and gentle people. Most importantly, he was diligent and untiring in his studies. As time went on, he withdrew from contact with others and spent all his time with books. The luxury of spending the energy of his youth in study made him the most erudite man of his generation.

Tran Phong, an examination graduate of 1431, was the head of the palace teachers. Some historians recorded that he quickly perceived that Le Tu Thanh showed indications of greatness. But others wrote that he favored Le Nghi Dan and scorned Le Tu Thanh. When Le Nghi Dan seized the throne, like many other officials, he had no qualms about serving this fratricidal king. Then, a few months later, when Le Tu Thanh became king, Tran Phong turned to serve him. For twenty-five years, Le Tu Thanh endeavored to give Tran Phong the consideration due to a former teacher while at the same time repeatedly rebuking him for his reprehensible behavior and urging him to mend his ways. Tran Phong held positions in the judiciary and the Censorate. He became famous for following the crowd while shamelessly fawning on people of high rank.

In 1465, Le Tu Thanh rebuked Tran Phong for joining others in lodging an accusation against his own younger brother, thereby abandoning correct brotherly feelings. In 1467, the king turned the tables on his former teacher to ask: "Why do you not read the books that illuminate the way to correct yourself?" At that time, Tran Phong had joined a group of officials seeking to denounce Nguyen Duc Trung, a man who had joined Le Xi against Le Nghi Dan in 1460 and who had subsequently become the maternal grandfather of Le Tranh, the crown prince. Immediately after doing this, Tran Phong hastened by night to the house of Nguyen Duc Trung to apologize. Then, seeking to ingratiate himself further with the maternal family of the future king, he asked to marry the daughter of Nguyen Duc Trung's brother, Nguyen Yen. He finally achieved this after spending an entire day lying prostrate in Nguyen Yen's courtyard. Le Tu Thanh observed that, in his unprincipled search for greatness, Tran Phong "licked Nguyen Duc Trung's hemorrhoids and sucked Nguyen Yen's boils." In 1474, the king rebuked Tran Phong for his corrupt schemes and asked: "Why do you not stop your despicable behavior so that you can have a good name when you retire?"

Finally, in 1485, Tran Phong was put to death, accused of obstinate disloyalty. On that occasion, the official who prepared the accusation against him noted the king's repeated warnings and wrote that, among other things, Tran Phong treasonously resisted Le Tu Thanh's organization of the royal government, denouncing it as imitating the Ming instead of following dynastic tradition. Tran Phong's dismal career introduces three large aspects of Le Tu Thanh's reign: the importance of education, an intense relationship between the king and his officials, and an unprecedented renovation in the structure of government.

Education was the cornerstone of the half-century "golden age" initiated by Le Tu Thanh's accession in 1460. Of the 2,896 men listed as having graduated at the level of countrywide, or capital, examinations from the eleventh to the twentieth centuries, 502 graduated in the twelve triennial exams, from 1463 to 1496, that were held during the reign of Le Tu Thanh, which is more than 17 percent of the total. If we add the six additional exams, through 1514, held during the reigns of his successors before the Le dynasty began to collapse, the total is 714 graduates, which is nearly 25 percent of all graduates in the history of the country. In 1484, steles were erected inscribed with the names of all capital examination graduates beginning with the exam of 1442. Thereafter, the names of graduates were routinely inscribed on steles, which can still be seen today in Hanoi at the Temple of Literature (Van Mieu).

Behind these few who achieved the honor of participating in the palace exam, which was held to rank the graduates of the capital exam, there were thousands who graduated from the regional exams, thereby earning the right to compete in the capital exams. In 1463, nearly 4,400 men participated in the capital exam. In 1514 there were 5,700. An average of about 4,000 men graduated from the regional exams to participate in the capital exams every three years, and only about 1 percent of these graduated to take the palace exam.

The proportion of candidates to graduates in the regional exams was surely greater than it was in the capital exams. The rules for entering the regional exams involved an investigation into one's family history, an evaluation of one's moral character, and a preliminary dictation test to eliminate non-competitive candidates. Being away from direct scrutiny by the court until 1492, when the court took direct responsibility for the regional exams, the supervision of regional exams was not as severe as it was for the capital exams. Consequently, the percentage of regional candidates who graduated to take the capital exam was certainly greater than the 1 percent success rate for candidates at the more rigorous capital exam. How much greater can be no more than conjecture, but a hypothetical calculation based on a plausible yet conservative 10 percent success rate will yield an average of 40,000 candidates at regional exams in any given year.

The 1490 census reported approximately 8,000 village-level jurisdictions throughout the country including the thirty-six urban wards that lay between the royal compound and the Red River at Dong Kinh, the only "city" in the country. There were at least seven different categories of rural village-level jurisdiction. One of these, the *xa*, was the most typical form of lowland rice-growing village and made up the great majority of village-level jurisdictions. During the fifteenth century, the trend of Le dynasty administration of the *xa* was toward fewer and larger *xa* as rural administration became more entrenched, the agrarian regime became more systematic, and the population grew. Surviving records do not enable any calculation of an average size of *xa* in number either of households or of population, but, according to one text, by 1490 the number of households in a *xa* could range from fewer than sixty to more than 600, which is not a particularly precise or useful piece of information.

Taking the reasonable but arbitrary hypothesis mentioned above that in each of the triennial exam years there was an average of 40,000 regional candidates, there would have been an average of five of these candidates for every village-level jurisdiction in the country as counted in the 1490 census. This is not implausible and strongly suggests, even if it does not indicate with certainty, that education had spread widely into the villages. Of all those who studied, relatively few were likely to have gained admittance to the regional examinations, which suggests that many others nevertheless attained a certain level of literacy.

Behind these thousands of examination candidates were thousands of students preparing for examinations as well as thousands who failed and took relatively minor government appointments or became teachers or went into the military or turned to agriculture or business. They all had some modicum of literacy and to some extent had passed through the discipline of a pedagogical process, learning the rudiments of Literary Chinese and the prestige vocabulary. During these years, the ambitions of young men for fame and fortune were to a large extent focused upon the mastery of a curriculum based on philosophy, literature, history, and government.

The examination curriculum during the reigns of the first three Le kings followed educational policies established during the period of Ming rule. It was based on the Four Books, which had been emphasized in Song Neo-Confucian thought and had become the basis of orthodoxy for the Ming dynasty. These Four Books were the *Great Way*, *Doctrine of the Mean*, *Analects* of Confucius, and *Mencius*. These were philosophical texts that emphasized the importance of education in the development of human morality. The curriculum published for use in the regional examinations of 1463 included the Four Books but not the Five Classics, which had been part of the curriculum during the Tran dynasty. In 1467, the Five Classics (*Changes*, *Odes*, *Rites*, *History*, and the *Spring and Autumn Annals*) were published and teachers were assigned to teach them in the palace academy. An edict noted that prior to this time only the *Classics of Odes* and *Classic of History* had been studied, not the others, but that from then all of them were to be studied. The 1472 exam included both the Four Books and the Five Classics, giving particular emphasis to the *Spring and Autumn Annals*. In 1473, there was an exam for teachers on the Four Books and the Five Classics. Subsequently, the 1475 exam contained a more elaborate scheme of questions about the Four Books and the Five Classics than there had been in 1472.

The restoration of the Five Classics to the curriculum reflects an intellectual eclecticism that eschewed a dogmatism based on authoritative texts oriented toward ideological certainty in favor of more general fields of knowledge with practical utility. The *Spring and Autumn Annals*, along with its various commentaries, is a storehouse of historical situations with lessons for how to govern. The *Classics of Rites* and *Classic of Changes* contain blueprints for ceremonial behavior, for analyzing the present, and for thinking about the future. Paying attention to the Five Classics indicates a wider horizon of thought than is generally associated with the Neo-Confucian school of Zhu Xi. The 1473 teacher's exam also covered the Tang poet Li Bo's style of *phu* (Chinese *fu*), a Han dynasty prosodic form that had been introduced in the 1304 exam of the Tran dynasty and adapted into the vernacular during the early fourteenth century. This is another example of turning to pre-Song pedagogical authority, which cautions against a widely accepted view of this as a time when the Le court adopted Neo-Confucianism. In terms of pedagogy, the Neo-Confucian legacy of Ming Giao Chi was contextualized in a larger realm of erudition.

The credibility of the educational system rested upon a perception that the examinations were administered fairly. Consequently, officials who supervised the examinations were closely monitored, were quickly promoted or demoted depending upon their performance, and were the recipients of frequent royal edicts exhorting them toward excellence. In 1492, presumably in an effort to upgrade standards, the responsibility for supervising regional examinations was given to court-based officials rather than being left to provincial officials. The regional, capital, and palace examinations that dispensed academic degrees were only the most prestigious in a broad system of exams, but they set the criteria for objectivity that gave credibility to the many other exams that became part of dynastic educational policy, including exams in medicine and astrology.

Those who taught the élite students who were accepted into the palace academy were kept alert to maximize the learning process. Edicts warned them against taking books to their homes, thereby rendering them inaccessible to the students. They were also instructed to arrange programs of study so that students would not all be assigned to read the same texts at the same time, which would inevitably cause an excessive demand for some texts while others were not being read at all. This level of classroom detail as the subject of royal attention is typical of Le Tu Thanh. He ruled as if his reign were one long study session for the entire country.

Exams in letters and math were regularly organized for the children of officials, and sometimes for others as well, including soldiers and peasants, which could lead to appointments in officialdom or admission to schools in the capital. The lives of students at the capital were carefully regulated in terms of study periods, levels of achievement, tax exemptions, and exemptions from labor and military service. Poor performance led to assignments in the army. A particular educational stream was created for the sons of nobles and high officials that led to examinations for appointments in officialdom. If they failed they were sent to study the military arts. If they failed the examination in military arts, which could lead to military appointments, they were sent to serve as menials in administrative centers outside of the capital. In 1478, an examination was held for military officers to certify their skill in archery. The 1471 expedition to Champa, which was personally led by Le Tu Thanh, became an extended training session for soldiers. The king published a book of instructions for military drill and discipline for use during the campaign that was translated into the vernacular and used "to teach everyone" as the army marched and drilled its way south.

Le Tu Thanh sought to create an atmosphere of study and of literary prowess in his palace. When the crown prince, Le Tranh, was 4 years old, the king surrounded him with teachers. In 1467 he selected thirty officials to take an examination in writing *tu* (Chinese *ci*) poetry, six of whom he chose for the luxury assignment of being allowed to do nothing but read books in the palace library. In 1471, Ngo Si Lien, a graduate of 1442 who had not particularly endeared himself to Le Tu Thanh with his equivocal behavior during the Le Nghi Dan episode of 1459–1460, was sent to work in the Office of History. Eight years later he produced a work that reorganized the history of the Ly dynasty written by Le Van Huu in the thirteenth century and the history of the Tran dynasty completed by Phan Phu Tien in 1445 and adorned them with his commentaries. Later historians extended this work, entitled the *Complete Book of the History of Great Viet*, to the end of the seventeenth century, making it the official court history up until that time.

Ngo Si Lien's innovation in historical consciousness was to extend the history of the kingdom back to the time of the Confucian sages of antiquity. He did this by drawing upon a collection of tales that were circulating among educated people at this time, known today as *Strange Tales Collected South of the Mountains* (*Linh Nam Chich Quai*). These tales were ostensibly written down during the Tran dynasty based on oral lore then current among common people. They had been subjected to a process of revision and rewriting to discard what was considered lewd and demonic and to infuse them with Confucian didacticism. Ngo Si Lien used them to give content to an ancient dynasty named Hung that he purported to have ruled beginning in the third millennium BCE, preceding the first dynasty in Chinese history. This dramatic and unprecedented excursion into the past might conceivably be attributed to the episode of Ming rule. In asserting a hoary imperial prerogative, the Ming could be imagined to have provoked a counterargument negating that claim by making an even more extravagant assertion of local sovereignty. The *Linh Nam Chich Quai* and Ngo Si Lien differently recorded the details of how the line of Hung kings originated, but the basic idea is that the first king was acknowledged as the most worthy of one hundred brothers. Half of the brothers followed their father to the sea and half followed their mother to the mountains. Versions of this story have also been recorded in modern times from oral lore among the peoples called Muong and can be understood as affirming the common ancestry of upland Trai/Muong and lowland Kinh. This tale became popular at the royal court in the late fifteenth century because of the Le dynasty's origins in the Thanh Hoa foothills.

In 1470, Le Tu Thanh published a book entitled *Dao Am Thien Tu* (One Thousand Words from a Wayside Cottage). According to the summary of it that has survived, it described the analogous relationships between, on the one hand, the unyielding authority of divine Heaven, of a sovereign ruler, and of a husband, and, on the other hand, the responding pliancy of the Earth, of a loyal subject, and of a wife, each of which willingly and harmoniously follows its leading partner without compulsion. He was interested in how to exercise authority without coercion. His literary interests seem always to have contained an element of didacticism. In his later years, Le Tu Thanh gathered selected officials to write poetry with him on assigned themes related to ethics and good government and then published them in anthologies. He loved poetry and enjoyed the excitement of competing to display literary skill.

As became the custom of the Le kings, early each year Le Tu Thanh made a visit to Tay Do and to his ancestral tombs in Thanh Hoa. On one such occasion he wrote about the scenery and terrain as he observed it while going up the Ma River by boat. He used the imagery of a dragon and identified various features of the landscape as the dragon's nose, its mouth, its jaws, etc. His seeing "the dragon" of sovereignty in Thanh Hoa symbolizes the historic reorientation of political geography that had been underway since the time of Ho Quy Ly. Dong Kinh had been the place of the "rising dragon" (Thang Long) for four centuries and, according to some texts, before that it had on occasion been referred to as the "dragon's belly" (Long Do), the heaviest and most immovable part of the dragon. Now, with the Le dynasty, the dragon of sovereignty had shifted south, and for a time it would reside in Thanh Hoa. The "great lords" of Thanh Hoa who had been mobilized by Le Loi became a force that would drive Vietnamese politics for several centuries. One of Le Tu Thanh's achievements was to wrap his authority around these men and to subordinate them to his will. He did this in two ways. He absorbed some in study and civil administration; for others he offered war.

Le Tu Thanh as ruler

Most of all, Le Tu Thanh's intelligence and erudition enabled him to stay ahead of his entourage, to truly be "the leader" of the royal court. This was already clear during the first six months of his reign when, according to court annalists, virtually every aspect of government was in some way addressed. For three decades the Le court had been an arena of competition among jostling great lords, child kings, eunuchs, and palace women. Agriculture, the main source of wealth for the kingdom, was neglected. Men of ability were elbowed aside by clambering sycophants. The royal compound was not even kept secure for the safety of the king. According to the *Complete Book of the History of Great Viet*, "It was as if no one was there." Suddenly, with Le Tu Thanh's accession, a higher level of brainpower was at work with royal attention being given to every detail of public life.

The educational system produced unprecedented numbers of educated men. Most of Le Tu Thanh's energy was spent in mobilizing, organizing, supervising, disciplining, admonishing, counseling, and enjoying the company of these people. He created an entirely new kind of extended royal entourage with a structure and a body of rules and regulations that enabled the royal will to be effective beyond the palace walls to a degree never before achieved. The structure was inspired by Ming imperial government but cannot in any practical way be considered as comparable to it. The criticism attributed to Le Tu Thanh's evil teacher, Tran Phong, that the government had abandoned dynastic tradition to follow Ming practice, was superficial at best; at worst, it showed nostalgia for the corruption and disorder of earlier reigns.

In 1471, detailed administrative regulations were published. The basic structure was built upon the Six Ministries (Luc Bo) that had been the core of imperial government in China for centuries and which, in various partially adapted forms, had also existed in Vietnam since the Ly dynasty. In 1466, Le Tu Thanh reorganized existing offices into the Six Ministries. The Ministry of Personnel (Lai Bo) handled administrative appointments, promotions, and demotions. The Ministry of Finance (Ho Bo) handled revenue collection and monetary disbursements, including the census and other tax-related records. The Ministry of Rites (Le Bo) was responsible for education and examinations, ceremonies and festivals, diplomacy, astrology, medicine, religion, theater, and music. The Ministry of Justice (Hinh Bo) administered the courts of law. The Ministry of Public Works (Cong Bo) was responsible for all construction projects, fortifications, dikes, canals, steles, and transport/communication posts. The Ministry of War (Binh Bo) supervised military affairs, including the palace guards. Before the time of Le Tu Thanh, the specialized functions of these ministries were for the most part handled by relatively low-ranking officials. Le Tu Thanh gave the ministers a high status at court, just below the inner circle of his military commanders and personal advisors. He also reinforced the leadership in the ministries with each having two high-ranking deputy ministers.

The most significant innovation of Le Tu Thanh, a departure from Ming practice, was the formation in 1471 of the Six Departments (Luc Khoa). A department was assigned to watch the work of each ministry to ensure that all was done according to rules and regulations. Departments functioned as inspectorates with power to report directly to the king. This was in addition to the less specialized Censorate, which had existed for centuries to report irregularities and corruption among officials. The emphasis on vigilance to monitor performance and to evaluate results was a key factor in the remarkable success of Le Tu Thanh's reign. He understood the distance that separated the formation of policy from its implementation and accordingly built into the structure of his government a system for self-scrutiny.

Another innovation, dating from 1466, was to reorganize several areas of responsibility into the Six Courts (Luc Tu) that performed specific tasks directly related to the palace. The Supreme Court of Justice (Dai Ly Tu) was attached to the Ministry of Justice. Four courts were attached to the Ministry of Rites: the Court of Seals (Thuong Bao Tu) was responsible for safeguarding royal seals; the Court of Ceremonies and Proclamations (Hong Lo Tu) organized public events that displayed royal majesty; the Court of Sacrifices (Thai Thuong Tu) conducted all sacrificial rituals on behalf of the king at temples and shrines; and the Court of Banquets (Quang Loc Tu) organized official culinary occasions. The Court of Equipage (Thai Boc Tu) was responsible for royal transportation and procurement; its relationship with any particular ministry is not apparent from information available today, but, at least, it must have had to coordinate with the Ministries of Finance, Rites, and War. The Palace Academy (Quoc Tu Giam), the most prestigious center of education in the country, collaborated with the Ministry of Rites in administering examinations and with the Ministry of Personnel in recommending students for official appointments.

The Office of Academicians (Han Lam Vien) and the Secretariat (Dong Cac) reported directly to the king. Many scholars simultaneously held positions in both of these offices. They were experts in education, in writing edicts and proclamations, and in diplomatic correspondence with Ming. Le Tu Thanh tended to stock the Academy and Secretariat with scholars whose opinions he particularly trusted. Other scholars, if they were not considered suitable for administrative responsibilities, such as Ngo Si Lien, were sent to the Office of History, which ranked rather low in the hierarchy of the court.

Provincial governments were organized as triumvirates of military commanders, civil administrators, and judicial officers. Censors were also stationed at the provincial level. After 1471 there were twelve provinces: four surrounding the capital in the Red River plain, four in the northern mountains facing the Ming border, and four in the south strung out along the coast. According to a map of the kingdom prepared in 1471, these provinces were comprised of 54 prefectures, under which were organized 178 lowland districts and 50 upland districts.

The dynastic hierarchy was based on a schedule of overlapping aristocratic ranks and administrative grades. After the king (*hoang de*), the crown prince (*hoang tu*), and lesser princes (*vuong*) came more junior members of the royal family bearing the ranks of duke (*cong*), marquis (*hau*), and count (*ba*). The ranks of viscount (*tu*) and baron (*nam*), which could be assigned to people who were not members of the royal family, overlapped with the highest two grades in officialdom. These were typically men with military assignments or who personally advised the king and crown prince. Below these people were sixteen grades. Examples of appointments in this scheme, in descending order, are: commander of the palace guard; the Six Ministers; the head of the Censorate and the commanders of provincial garrisons; the twelve deputy ministers, and the provincial civil governors; the head of the Office of Academicians; the heads of the Secretariat and of the Palace Academy; the heads of the Six Courts; the head of communications and information; the heads of provincial judiciaries; prefects; the heads of the Six Departments and the provincial censors; district magistrates; the head of the Office of History; the head of land reclamation; the head of stockbreeding; the head of water control for agriculture.

Members of the royal family received annual cash salaries in addition to allotments of servants, salt makers, rice fields, ponds for raising fish, and mulberry fields for raising silkworms. Officials in the top eight grades received annual cash salaries and allotments of land. Lower-ranking officials received cash salaries only. In 1477, Le Tu Thanh ordered an examination of the workload of all officials and a corresponding adjustment of their salaries up or down. In 1481, when available cash was insufficient to pay all the salaries, the king ordered to reduce the number of officials by weeding out the incompetent, corrupt, or unproductive.

The expansion of government had been significant enough that in 1467 the royal compound was enlarged because it was "too small and cramped." According to a census of officialdom in 1471, there were around 2,700 officials with appointments at court; 70 percent of them were military. A similar number of officials were in the countryside; of these, only 30 percent were military. The army and the navy were both headquartered at Dong Kinh, which is why military officers were so numerous there. The army was organized under five major commands, all stationed near the capital, in addition to which were the palace guard units. Provincial garrisons, border guards, and local militia kept watch in the countryside and on the frontiers. Le Tu Thanh met daily with his top military commanders, and after every public session of court he met privately with the commanders of the five armies along with the Six Ministers.

Le Tu Thanh was a keen judge of character and kept a sharp eye on the thousands of men in his government. Early in his reign he established a strong sense of connection between himself and his officials, praising and admonishing them individually, revealing detailed knowledge of their lives, careers, and litigations. On one occasion he sent fruit jam to all his officials as a token of his appreciation and as encouragement to work hard. Another early edict advised officials against castrating themselves in a "foolish" effort to gain admittance into the inner palaces, identifying a temptation that some ambitious officials may have entertained. Time and again he issued warnings, rebukes, exhortations, and words of appreciation to officials. He dismissed one military official because the man's son had galloped a horse through the streets of the capital and had let his slaves beat people passing by; the official was held accountable for not teaching his son how to behave. He once had an official beaten and banished because he had failed to report corruption existing among those he was supposed to supervise. He dismissed a provincial official because "in his jurisdiction there were many insects eating the crops yet he did not report it but simply sat and watched calamity come upon the people."

Le Tu Thanh paid particular attention to officials being recommended for promotion. He would refuse to promote those he considered unworthy. He once imprisoned an official for recommending someone he viewed as bad. He insisted that a man must be in a position long enough to be evaluated before being promoted to another assignment. Evaluations of officials were to be conducted every three years, and supervising officers were punished if their evaluations were not completed on time. Officials in remote upland areas could be reassigned to lowland appointments after six years if their work had been good. If not, they would have to spend at least six more years in the mountains. On the other hand, officials in sensitive border areas were reassigned after relatively short periods to prevent their "going native" and losing a spirit of vigilance.

Le Tu Thanh's reign displays a constant stream of edicts instructing and warning officials about bribery, corruption, dishonesty, greed, laxity, self-indulgence, wild and undisciplined living, wine, women, marriage procedures, marrying a woman from the jurisdiction where one was assigned, mourning regulations, competition for burial plots, excessive feasting, laziness in collecting taxes, not completing work on time, gathering with others for gossip and not keeping office hours, hanging around the guard posts as if having nothing to do, tossing betel quids in the palace yard before entering the court, correct dress and ways of holding one's hands at court, how to address one another, not taking paperwork out of the office to one's home, returning all papers when leaving a position, not to speak of court affairs with family members or people outside of the court, reporting at the palace first before going to one's home when returning from assignments outside of the capital, the preparation and submission of paperwork, apportioning the workload between officials and their subordinates, and the importance of filling vacancies promptly. The annalists record that, when the extent to which the king kept a close watch over his officials became well known, everyone became very careful about their behavior.

At the same time, Le Tu Thanh made it clear that evaluations, promotions, and demotions were not to be a matter of public discussion or factional struggle; he announced that if an official was at fault it was a matter between him and the official and not a case for public accusations at court. He was famous for giving those who had been disciplined, demoted, or dismissed a second chance so that they might redeem themselves. He once revealed a sense of humor when he satirized two officials who pretended to be ill in order to avoid participating in a poetry competition; he suggested that their jobs were too demanding for them, causing them to lose their health. He displayed a very rare mixture of strictness, fairness, and mercy.

Le Tu Thanh valued the opinions of his officials. Administrative innovations were often the result of suggestions made by his officials. He wanted his officials to be perfectly open and honest with him, and he once issued an edict against speaking equivocally. He eventually divided his court into three groups with which he met separately: the heads of the Six Departments and the Censorate to discuss the conduct of officials; the heads of the Six Ministries and of the Six Courts to discuss plans and policies; the nobles and the military commanders to discuss security matters. He made a point of insisting that everyone speak when called on and that they address topics of discussion thoroughly, clearly, and decisively; they were not to follow a faction or be evasive. One man was appointed to be the "invigilator" for each court session; he was not to participate in the discussion but was to bring charges against anyone violating the rules of discussion. These arrangements reveal an effort to maximize the application of group intelligence to any given problem.

In an edict of 1485, Le Tu Thanh expressed his purpose in building an administration of officials trained to be moral and efficient. He proclaimed that government had two main goals: to maintain the happiness of the people and to nurture agriculture to provide enough food and clothing. He explained that happiness comes from a moral life and that his officials must do more to teach ethics to the people and to keep a close watch over the state of agriculture and the moral behavior of the people, implying a connection between these two aspects of rural life. Officials in the countryside were expected to react quickly to drought, flooding, and other rural calamities. The king often inquired about the condition of agriculture and the well being of the people. He made provision to send out doctors with medicines to areas affected by epidemics. Local officials were expected to instruct people in the laws affecting them, particularly laws about land ownership. They were to take care in appointing village heads and were not to allow more than one person from a family to serve as a village head in order to avoid factions and feuds among villages.

Le Tu Thanh was aware of and engaged with how village people lived, both in meeting their material needs through agriculture and as a society of human relationships. As king, he believed it was his responsibility to ensure that government be the best it could possibly be. He had no expectation of attaining perfection. But, during more than thirty years, extending his voice beyond the circle of his officials with the studied repetition of a born teacher, he endeavored to raise the ethical consciousness of increasing numbers of people with exhortations to moral excellence. His education had taught him that social morality was fundamentally defined by Confucian ethics. He gave public honor to people known for their chastity and filial piety. Abortion was prohibited. He issued an edict forbidding singers and actors from ridiculing parents or officials.

Stories were later written about his view of Buddhism as a vain superstition that wasted the productive energy of the people. But he was not an agnostic about supernatural powers and advised his officials to pray to all available spirits and deities in times of drought, flood, or pestilence. Village ritual life began to change in the fifteenth century with the development of the village community hall, called *dinh*, as a place for the conduct of local administration and for the worship of village protector spirits called *thanh hoang*.

There are references to *dinh* in Tran times as places to shelter travelers and where Buddhist statues were sometimes placed. The distinctive architectural features of *dinh* with raised floors bring to mind stilted longhouses still found in upland regions and suggest that there was a tradition of such structures for community events. In China, *thanh hoang* were protector deities of cities, towns, and walled administrative centers. Beginning in Tang times and extending through Tran times, three different *thanh hoang* were recorded for Dai La/Thang Long. During the era of Ming Giao Chi, imperial officials followed the system current in Ming China of establishing shrines to *thanh hoang* at centers of administration down to the district level. During the reigns of the Le kings in the fifteenth century, *thanh hoang* cults came to be placed in the *dinh* where they were regulated as an aspect of local administration. Ritual observances associated with *thanh hoang* were conducted by men, in contrast with the prominent role of women and nuns at many Buddhist temples.

There is little information about Buddhism from Le Tu Thanh's reign. In 1467, he decreed that Buddhist and Daoist temples that did not have "old thresholds" could not be rebuilt without permission, implying some effort to place limits on these religions. A 1470 edict against people shaving their heads unless they were legitimate Buddhist monks or temple wardens suggests a suspicion of people seeking to impersonate temple dwellers to avoid field work. Despite this seeming inclination to curb the activities of monks and priests, in 1467, amidst an invasion of crop-destroying insects, the king sent Daoist priests to exercise their occult powers against the calamity; he also ordered that sacrifices be made to "all the deities" to stop the infestation.

There were several recorded times of drought and hunger during Le Tu Thanh's reign and each time he responded vigorously. In 1467, in addition to sending Daoist priests against the insects and ordering prayers for rain, he also lowered taxes due to the poor harvest. This same year a typhoon devastated coastal provinces, breaking dikes, flooding fields with seawater, and causing the deaths of many people. The king halted all construction projects in the capital and sent the workers to help in the countryside. Soldiers were excused from drill and training exercises to assist with repairing the damage from the storm, including rebuilding the coastal dikes. The price of rice in Dong Kinh was excessively high, so rice was transported from Nghe An where it was more plentiful and cheaper.

The drought continued in 1468 and prayers for rain also continued. When rural distress led to disorders and banditry in the coastal province adjacent to the Ming border, the king closely monitored the situation and sent new officials with reinforcements to restore calm. Shortly after this, in 1469, weapons were collected from private homes. In 1473 and in 1476, droughts were combated with prayers that were followed by rains. A drought that began in 1489 led to harvest failures in some provinces in 1490. When people began to die of hunger, the court distributed rice and declared a suspension of taxes. In 1492, a famine was met with people being instructed to plant and eat yams instead of rice. Le Tu Thanh's government paid closer attention to village life than any previous regime. This resulted from the increase in the number of royal officials assigned to rural localities, from the way that officials were organized to implement policies and monitor performance, and from Le Tu Thanh's repeated exhortations.

Expanding the borders

Le Tu Thanh's agrarian policy was based on Le Loi's effort to keep all land in production by nurturing a peasantry of small landowners able to support themselves and pay taxes. One of his first edicts was against idleness, exhorting rural people to grow as much rice as possible. Tax rates for rice fields were fixed and family registers, along with records of land ownership, were updated and scheduled for revision at six-year intervals. Land could be sold only under certain conditions to prevent small landholders from selling land to pay their debts and to prevent large landholders from accumulating more land than they could cultivate. Mortgages dating from before the founding of the dynasty in 1428 were declared void and could not be redeemed. Land disputes were to be settled promptly by judicial officers. Severe punishments were announced for those who took over the fields of others by force, pulled up or changed boundary markers, or cut down trees and bamboo hedges belonging to others. Officials were repeatedly reminded to check that all available land was in production. If fields became waterlogged or dried out, officials were responsible for adjusting the water control system to make them productive again. Coastal lands were being brought under cultivation as early as the twelfth century, and, while this process accelerated under the Tran dynasty, evidence of a major rise in the population of the coastal regions comes from the fifteenth century.

This agrarian policy was designed for the Red River plain. In the southern provinces, land ownership remained vulnerable to the greed of predatory great lords. In 1467, Le Tu Thanh lamented in an edict that although the region around Tay Do in Thanh Hoa was the "homeland of the royal family," "prominent local families" had unlawfully appropriated all the land there so that members of the royal family could not find any available land to call their own. There is no further information recorded about the rural regime in Thanh Hoa, but Le Tu Thanh presumably shamed the great lords into making land available for at least some prominent members of the royal family. This is very different from the Ly and Tran royal families that, in times past, directly controlled much of the most productive land in the country. Le Tu Thanh endeavored to shift the basis of the dynasty from the pool of martial manpower in the Thanh Hoa uplands to the peasantry of the Red River plain. As long as he lived, this experiment was alive, but however much he brought rational government to the Red River plain, the feuds and ambitions of Thanh Hoa men, which had propelled the dynasty to power, remained in the background. Le Tu Thanh sought to address this potential source of ruin by keeping these men busy with military adventures.

Early in his reign, Le Tu Thanh ruled that military officials were to have no authority over civil affairs. He also forbad military officials from engaging in trade. He wanted to focus the concentration of his military officers on assignments along and beyond the borders. In 1467, after consultations with military commanders, new instructions were issued to units stationed on the borders. Incidents on the Ming border that year were followed by warnings to border officers to be especially vigilant. An army was sent to attack Laos and returned in victory. Military exercises were held at which regulations for issuing rewards and punishments were announced. In 1469, soldiers were once more sent into the mountains to attack people along the Lao border.

Relations with Ming received careful attention. Envoys regularly departed to and arrived from the Ming court. Close attention to border incidents was part of Le Tu Thanh's method of maintaining peace. This required demonstrations of alertness and preparedness. In 1472, indications of potential border trouble in modern Quang Ninh Province triggered plans to mobilize soldiers from neighboring jurisdictions. In 1480, incidents along the border in Cao Bang and Lang Son were promptly investigated. Le Tu Thanh decreed that all correspondence with Ming about these problems be discussed and vetted by three separate groups of officials to preclude any errors. At this time, perhaps provoked by rumors about border troubles or some other unknown cause, the officials in charge of governing the capital began to force all the resident Ming people to return back north to their own country. Le Tu Thanh immediately stopped this, rebuking the officials for overstepping their authority, for harming commerce, and for destroying an important source of tax revenue.

Patrolling the northern border was not a task sufficient to absorb the ambitions of military commanders. It was on the southern border that Le Tu Thanh found opportunities to entertain the attention of his soldiers. After the expedition to Champa of 1446, Vietnamese efforts to hold the Cham king as a vassal quickly failed and relations between the two kingdoms deteriorated. The border was at Hai Van Pass between the modern cities of Hue and Da Nang. In 1469, a Cham raid across the border was recorded. In 1470, a Cham army arrived and besieged the Vietnamese garrison at Hue. The local commander sent appeals to Dong Kinh for help. The alacrity and scale of Le Tu Thanh's response shows that this situation was anticipated. Within weeks, soldiers were mobilized, rice was collected and transported south, and envoys hastened to inform Ming of what was planned. Only three months later, at the start of the winter dry season, after publishing detailed campaign orders to his generals and proclaiming in a long edict the reasons for the expedition, Le Tu Thanh set out to attack Champa.

As he went south, Le Tu Thanh paused along the way to make sacrifices at temples and shrines. When he rendezvoused with his soldiers in Nghe An he was dismayed to find not an army but crowds of undisciplined men. He called in his generals and warned them that their soldiers were acting "like children playing games" and that he expected them to bring the army to attention. In the early weeks of 1471 as he moved down to the border and into Cham territory, he put the army and navy under strict discipline and kept them busy drilling and conducting exercises. He wrote a book of instructions for the expedition and had it translated into the vernacular and taught to the men. He observed terrain, corrected maps, and monitored the transport of rice to ensure that the expedition would not run out of food. He also scrutinized the behavior of his officers and occupied himself with promoting and demoting them based on his evaluation of their ability. In short, he brought with him on campaign the clarity of thought and the habits of critical supervision that he had been practicing for ten years within the halls of the royal court. He was 29 years old.

As he moved through modern Quang Nam and ascertained the disposition of the Cham army, he devised a plan that was spectacularly successful. Marching with his main force down the coast, he sent his right wing through the mountains to lay an ambush and advanced his left wing by sea to land behind the enemy. He soon had the Cham army surrounded, causing it to melt and scatter. He pursued the Cham king and captured him at his capital in modern Binh Dinh Province. A Cham general fled and established himself as ruler at modern Phan Rang, more than 250 kilometers further south. He and two others, a ruler in the Central Highlands (the region of Kon Tum and Play Ku) and a ruler on the coast immediately to the south of Binh Dinh, in the modern provinces of Phu Yen and Khanh Hoa, submitted to Le Tu Thanh as vassals. The modern provinces of Quang Nam, Quang Ngai, and Binh Dinh were annexed to become Quang Nam Province. Le Tu Thanh assigned garrisons and appointed officials to be responsible for this new jurisdiction. The Cham king was embarked with his multitude of wives, requiring an additional boat, to be brought to Dong Kinh; he reportedly died of illness en route.

Certain classes of marginal or undesirable people were subsequently settled in Quang Nam. In late 1471, descendents of people who had served the Ming, unreliable upland chieftains, unsatisfactory royal slaves, criminals, resident Chams, resident Laotians, and people of mixed Ming and local ancestry were identified and selected to be pioneers of Le authority in the new lands. Officials who were convicted of corruption or other offenses were sent to establish administration there. Officials along the coast of the Red River plain that had been devastated by the typhoon of 1467 were particularly warned that unless they worked harder to restore the dikes and return inundated fields to production they would be reassigned to Quang Nam. Quang Nam was categorized along with the northern border provinces as an unhealthy assignment. Many Cham people remained in Quang Nam and Vietnamized their names. In 1472, an edict specified that these names could be only three characters in length. At the same time an edict warned against Vietnamese officials and people concealing their possession of Chams, presumably meaning Chams unlawfully enslaved. In 1474 a schedule of banishment for criminals to Quang Nam was established with those guilty of more serious crimes being sent further south.

Le Tu Thanh did not accompany the other major expedition during his reign. In the 1479–1480 dry season, a large army advancing in five columns set out into the western mountains. It sacked Luang Prabang, the capital of the Laotian kingdom of Lan Xang, and, according to Vietnamese annalists, continued west as far as the Irrawaddy River in Burma before turning back. The return of this army is not recorded, but the presence in Dong Kinh of the generals who led it is noted by mid year 1480 when Ming envoys inquired about reports from Ming administrators in Yunnan that a Vietnamese army had attacked people on the Yunnan–Burma border. A result of this expedition was that from this time Vietnamese rulers considered it important to have a foothold on the Xieng

Khouang plateau of Laos (called the Tran Ninh plateau in Vietnamese and known in Western writing as "The Plain of Jars") to secure their western frontier.

The opportunities for adventure in Quang Nam and in the western mountains momentarily occupied the lords of Thanh Hoa. In his later years, Le Tu Thanh distributed gifts to those who accompanied him on his annual pilgrimages to Thanh Hoa and made a point of publicly honoring the descendents of men who had fought with Le Loi. He had seemingly pacified his turbulent dynastic homeland. Yet, he harbored resentment at having had to endure the bluster of old heroes. On his deathbed he reportedly said that he had erred in two regards. First, he violated what was right in his desire for fame, seemingly referring to his military conquests in the south and west. Second, he disturbed the government by keeping in high positions incompetent men with merit from the past; he named three men in particular, one of them being Le Liet, who, with Le Xi, had raised him to the throne in 1460.

A historian who was at court during that time lamented that Le Tu Thanh "excessively visited women and consequently his body was afflicted with chronic illness." As a result of this, his senior queen, the mother of Crown Prince Le Tranh, later known as the Truong Lac queen mother, had retired to a separate palace and had no contact with the king as his illness increased in seriousness. His symptoms were described as tumors, swellings, and open sores. Although annalists did not name the disease, their descriptions of it and their observation that it came from excessive sexual contact point to syphilis. When Le Tu Thanh took to bed for the final time in late 1496, the queen was allowed to wait on him. She was apparently angry toward him, for historians recorded that she hid poison in her sleeve and secretly applied it to his sores to increase the intensity of his illness.

After proclaiming Crown Prince Le Tranh king and writing a final poem, Le Tu Thanh died in early 1497 at age 55. He was the father of fourteen sons and twenty daughters. Commonly called the Hong Duc King because the last twenty-six years of his reign were counted as the Hong Duc ("immense virtue") reign period, he has been celebrated as the greatest king in Vietnamese history. Confucian scholars in later generations viewed his reign as a golden age of good government. His most significant achievement was to unite the human and material resources of the Red River plain and the southern provinces and to organize these resources to maximize prosperity and to push back the southern and western frontiers. He did this by promoting education and by mobilizing a generation of officials trained to respond to moral appeals. The military achievements would not have been possible without the unprecedented level of efficiency in civil administration that he achieved, which produced the necessary supplies of recruits and of rice.

The relatively short reign (1497–1504) of Le Tranh was a mild echo of his father's more famous reign. Educated by the best teachers available and by a father with definite ideas about the responsibilities of kingship, at age 36 he stepped into the pattern of royal leadership created by Le Tu Thanh without discernibly disturbing the established habits of government. For seven years he gave the same kind of attention to education, examinations, appointments, promotions, demotions, moral exhortations, relations with Ming, agricultural production, local administration, and writing poetry that had been typical of his father. And, finally, he died in the same way as his father, suffering, in the words of the annalist, "chronic illness" from "excessively visiting women." In providing a worthy successor, however, he did not follow his father's model.

In the fifteenth century, Le dynasty rulers effected a fundamental reorientation of government and culture that established norms of public life that would be honored into modern times, at least in word if not always in action. However, this was a fragile achievement of one man's unusual personality. Regional tensions remained unresolved. When leadership faltered, these tensions erupted into a series of wars between rival regimes that continued for three centuries and that coincided with the expansion of Vietnamese speakers down the coast and into the Mekong River plain.

5 THE BEGINNING OF INTER-REGIONAL WARFARE

Return of adolescent kings and great lords

Le Tranh had six sons. The eldest, although reported to have been intelligent and well educated, was so obstinate that while still small he poisoned his mother because she opposed his will. But what most disqualified him to be king was that he liked to wear women's clothing. The second and third sons were born only seventy-five days apart in 1488. In 1499, Le Tranh had designated the third son, Le Thuan, as crown prince. He reportedly passed over the second son, Le Tuan, because he was "immature, without moral goodness, incompetent, and unworthy." While the younger three sons and members of their entourages appear to have played roles in later intrigues, no further specific information about them has been recorded. Le Thuan's mother, a royal concubine, had died when he was small. His paternal grandmother, the Truong Lac queen mother, was his adoptive mother.

Objections to Le Tuan being named crown prince were about more than his personal qualities. His mother had begun as a poor peasant across the river from Dong Kinh. Destitute, she had sold herself into slavery. When her owner was arrested for some unrecorded offense, she was confiscated and became the property of an official who brought her into royal service where she became a servant of Le Tranh's mother. Le Tranh took her as a concubine. She died shortly after giving birth to Le Tuan. Another royal concubine named Nguyen Kinh raised the motherless boy and attached her aspirations to the prospect of him becoming king. Nguyen Kinh and members of Le Tuan's mother's family were disappointed when he was not named crown prince. However, this did not put an end to their hopes.

When Le Tranh died, despite his having designated Le Thuan as his successor, there was a struggle for the throne among "all the princes." Le Tuan appears to have been the most determined of the claimants, but the actions of two officials thwarted him. Dam Van Le, an examination graduate of 1469, was Minister of

Rites and had possession of the royal seal. Nguyen Quang Bat, an examination graduate of 1484, was the head of the Censorate. They considered it their duty to ensure the accession of the designated crown prince. Dam Van Le hid the royal seal in his home and the two officials, with the support of the queen mother, called on the nobles and high officials of the court to proclaim Le Thuan king, which they did.

Le Thuan died after less than seven months as king. No cause of death has been recorded. Le Tuan and his supporters moved with alacrity to take the throne. The main obstacle to Le Tuan's elevation was opposition from the Truong Lac queen mother, his paternal grandmother. She was the daughter of Nguyen Duc Trung, a prominent Thanh Hoa lord who had helped Le Xi raise Le Tu Thanh to the throne in 1460. She did not want her former servant, a peasant waif and confiscated slave, to be the mother of a king, even posthumously, because it would open the palace gates to her low-class relatives, a rabble of peasants and slaves. Furthermore, she was endeavoring to bring another prince to the throne. Historians have been unable to ascertain the identity of this prince, but it appears that he was not one of Le Tranh's sons. Her plans were in vain, however, for a eunuch in Nguyen Kinh's clique named Nguyen Nhu Vi moved quickly upon Le Thuan's death to seal off the palace and isolate the Truong Lac queen mother from potential allies. It is recorded that large sums of gold passed from Le Tuan's surrogate mother Nguyen Kinh into the hands of certain great lords.

Three months after becoming king, Le Tuan had the Truong Lac queen mother killed. Several weeks after that, he obtained the deaths of Dam Van Le and Nguyen Quang Bat, the two officials who had prevented his accession after the death of his father. These two men, who stood in the first rank of officialdom, had such a reputation for rectitude that their murders provoked a widespread outcry of dismay. Le Tuan was consequently moved to cast all the blame for their deaths upon Nguyen Nhu Vi and to have him killed. The murder of a queen mother by a new king was not unprecedented, but the appearance of Dam Van Le and Nguyen Quang Bat in the middle of a succession dispute is an indication that Le Tu Thanh's new structure of government offered the possibility of scholar-officials participating in royal politics to an unprecedented degree. However prophetic for the future it may be thought to have been, their case was nevertheless an episode enabled by the residue of Le Tu Thanh's reign and not part of a trend for the future.

In 1505, Le Tuan was 17 years old. Gathered around him were relatives of his deceased mother, men of low origins with little respect for the royal family. In 1506 he brought into the palace the family of two sisters with whom he became infatuated, making the eldest his queen. The family of these sisters claimed descent from the mother of a Tran king and came from a village near the capital named Nhan Muc, by which name the family came to be known. There was also the family of the king's adoptive mother, Nguyen Kinh, which came from Thuy Nguyen district in the east of the Red River plain, just north of the modern city of Hai Phong. The influence of her family members and of those allied with them spread through the eastern plain and brought people from that region into the capital. One such person was Mac Dang Dung, who was appointed an officer in the palace guard in 1508. Twenty years later he would be the king.

During Le Tuan's short reign, his deceased mother's family dominated the region north of the capital and the Nhan Muc family dominated the region west of the capital. Roving bands of armed men scoured the countryside for plunder and for pretty girls to bring back to the palace. Villagers fled at their approach and hid until they had passed.

Although the examination system continued to function and produced large groups of new officials in 1505 and 1508, the atmosphere of officialdom had become stormy. Officials were dismissed or imprisoned for speaking against the will of the king. Those who in previous years had been cashiered for various offenses were reappointed. Those who had not supported Le Tuan's accession were killed. In one famous case, a relative of the king's mother seemingly beat a scholar-official to death and the corpse was tossed over the palace wall, but the man revived as his family prepared to bury him, and he thereafter lived in hiding until after Le Tuan's death.

Le Tuan organized new groups at court, mainly using eunuchs and the relatives of his birth mother, of his queen, and of his adoptive mother. He established a new military unit to guard his palace and also units of men armed with staves who staged mock battles for his amusement. He instigated a pogrom against the Cham population at the capital that came from captives brought north in 1471. He reportedly developed a nightly habit of drinking himself into a stupor while cavorting with women whom he afterwards murdered. The relatives of his deceased mother who seized the powers of government presided over a homicidal regime that produced shock and fear in the population.

Terrorizing common people was one thing. But Le Tuan's crowd of followers came to understand that the royal family was their mortal enemy and that with it there would be a fight to the death. In 1509, Le Tuan ordered surveillance on twenty-six princes, his brothers, his uncles, and his cousins. One fled and was not heard of again. The others were imprisoned. Only one of these managed to escape after passing bribes to his jailors. He was Le Dinh, the second son of Le Tu Thanh's fifth son. Meanwhile, lesser members of the royal family and refugees from officialdom gathered at Tay Do under the leadership of Nguyen Van Lang, a brother of the murdered Truong Lac queen mother. Nguyen Van

Lang was leading an army out of Thanh Hoa when he encountered the fleeing Le Dinh. Together they returned to Tay Do, issued a call to rally people behind them, administered a blood oath, and marched against Le Tuan. There followed days of bitter fighting at Dong Kinh, during which Le Tuan killed his prisoners, including Le Dinh's mother and three of his brothers (his father had died in 1502). These murders so infuriated Le Dinh that after Le Tuan was captured and forced to drink poison the royal corpse was shot from a huge cannon with but a few grains of ash retrieved for Le Tuan's tomb. Le Dinh was proclaimed king without delay. He was 15 years old.

Despite the king's youth, many officials entertained optimism about the future, believing that after the reign of Le Tuan things could only get better. Luong Dac Bang (b. 1472), a graduate of the 1499 examination, was a Deputy Minister of Personnel when he was forced into retirement in the time of Le Tuan. Now he was recalled for reappointment. He refused, being pessimistic about prospects for improvement. His refusal was denied, and so he wrote a long appeal in which he detailed how officialdom had been corrupted and listed fourteen points that he considered necessary to correct the government. His fourteen points restated all the essential lessons that Le Tu Thanh had endeavored to drill into the minds of his officials during his long reign, revealing the shortness of the court's institutional memory. It was recorded that the king agreed with what Luong Dac Bang wrote.

The educational system continued to function normally. The examinations of 1511 and 1514 were held on schedule and yielded numbers of graduates comparable to previous years. In 1512 an exam in reading and math was held for children of officials to select students for higher study in the Confucian classics. There was a strong interest in historical writing at this time. In 1511, a book produced by the court developed the points that had been made by Luong Dac Bang. It presented a record of all the iniquities of Le Tuan and argued that now there would be a return to the ideals and practices of Le Tu Thanh, which were elaborately itemized. Also in 1511, Vu Quynh (1452–1516), an examination graduate of 1478, presented a revised version of the history of the country that had been compiled by Ngo Si Lien in 1479. In 1514, Le Tung, an examination graduate of 1484, presented an interpretive summary of the works by Ngo Si Lien and Vu Quynh. Around this time, Dang Minh Khiem, an examination graduate of 1487, also wrote a book of history and a collection of poems in praise of exemplary people in the past. The perspective on public morality and good government shared by these men had been formed during the reign of Le Tu Thanh. They sought comfort for the present in connections with the past.

Regardless of whatever degree of administrative competence that may have been retrieved from Le Tuan's witless reign, something had gone seriously awry in the kingdom. It was easier to tear down a structure of government than it was to build it back up. The disorders of Le Tuan's reign had weakened, where it had not removed, a regime of authority that had given decades of peace to the Red River plain. The serpents of chaos had been awakened and were testing the currents of change. Literally, in 1513 and 1514, plagues of snakes emerged from the Red River at high water during the summer rains. In 1514 the infestation lasted for four months. There was a constant shooting of guns and a beating of drums in Dong Kinh to frighten the reptiles off. The dragon of sovereignty had become a mass of writhing serpents.

In early 1510, shortly after Le Dinh took the throne, an attempted coup by supporters of another prince led to a battle in the palace. Less than a year after this, an official who had graduated in the exam of 1508 and who had served Le Tuan organized a rebellion northeast of the capital, the home region of Le Tuan's mother. This rebellion was quickly put down, but later, in 1511, Tran Tuan, a grandson of an official who had served Le Tu Thanh, led a rebellion in the region northwest of the capital that was much more serious. As the rebel army marched on Dong Kinh, the city's inhabitants fled across the river for safety, leaving the streets deserted. The king was so angry at what he viewed as cowardice that he sent an official to investigate which families had sent their wives and children away. When he discovered that this very official had also sent his family back to his home village he had the man publicly executed. Armies sent against the rebels were defeated and Tran Tuan's men were breaking through the defenses of Dong Kinh.

At this point, a general named Trinh Duy San, in desperation, strode boldly into the rebel camp and slew Tran Tuan with his sword before anyone could react. The rebels fled. Trinh Duy San was from Tho Xuan district in Thanh Hoa, near Mount Lam, the hearth of the Le dynasty. He and his elder full brother Trinh Duy Dai had followed Nguyen Van Lang and Le Dinh during the march from Thanh Hoa against Le Tuan. The brothers were subsequently honored for their service in raising Le Dinh to the throne. They had the same surname and were from the same village as the woman who became Le Dinh's queen, which makes it likely that they were related to her.

In 1512, groups of Tran Tuan's followers were still being tracked down through the mountains when a rebellion broke out in Nghe An. The army sent to suppress it was defeated and the rebels advanced into Thanh Hoa, causing panic in Dong Kinh. Trinh Duy San once again proved to be the royal protector as he led his men south and put down the uprising.

In 1515, Trinh Duy San successfully attacked rebels on Mount Tam Dao, about forty kilometers north of Dong Kinh. A rebellion in Thanh Hoa later that year was also suppressed. In early 1516, the king, now 21 years old, personally directed soldiers that repulsed rebel armies gathered north of the capital. Two months later, the most spectacular rebellion of this era emerged from the eastern plains led by a man named Tran Cao. This provoked a series of events that brought a sudden end to Le Dinh's reign.

The great rash of uprisings in these years, emerging from virtually every part of the kingdom, show that the administration emplaced by Le Tu Thanh had ceased to govern. For more than a decade the kings were teenagers without the education, the moral judgment, the experience, or the sense of duty needed to supervise a structure of administration that could not be maintained without a strong, competent royal hand. Moreover, it was not simply a matter of neglect. Like Le Tuan, Le Dinh became a force of negativity at the center of the government. In 1513, a Ming envoy reportedly remarked to a colleague that "his face is handsome but his body is tilted; he is fond of debauchery and is nothing but a hog king; rebellion will soon put an end to him!"

His appetite for women was seemingly insatiable. Large numbers of women were brought into the palace. Annalists disapprovingly noted that he also spent time with the women of his predecessor. He relished staging battles between elephants and tigers. But it was his neglect of government and administration that opened the countryside to rebels. His attention was absorbed with building projects at the capital.

In 1512, amidst a drought and famine, he consulted with an engineer named Vu Nhu To who had plans for a palace with more than one hundred rooms. In 1513, he announced a major construction project, which was the beginning of an unending frenzy of remodeling and construction that involved expanding the walls of the royal city, raising extravagant palaces, and digging canals between palaces and West Lake. Over the next three years these schemes consumed the energy of thousands of soldiers, laborers, and craftsmen. Presiding over it all was Vu Nhu To, whose grandiose and constantly expanding visions gave pleasure to the young king.

Agricultural work and military training suffered as peasants were dragooned to the construction sites and soldiers were exhausted with digging and carrying. The sucking of human and material resources out of the countryside and into the capital, including the transport of logs from the mountains and of food to feed the workers, disrupted normal military, agricultural, and administrative activity, leading to chaotic conditions that encouraged rebellion. The king was apparently unconcerned about this. He was not an astute ruler. He could not discern between what was important and what was not. For example, he was constantly sending people into the countryside to collect cotton blossoms; when a court official objected to this wasteful practice he had the man demoted to a post in Thanh Hoa.

However much misery he brought to his people, Le Dinh brought disaster upon himself personally by turning against the royal family and the great lords who were its protectors. In 1514, excited by false accusations against prominent Le princes, he had fifteen of them killed. Trinh Duy San, a stalwart of the dynasty who had repeatedly risked his life fighting against rebels, had begun to irritate the king with his arguments against the way he was ruling. The king had him publicly flogged. It was a fatal error.

In late spring of 1516, riding widespread rumors that a sovereign would arrive from the east, a man named Tran Cao, from Thuy Nguyen district, just north of modern Hai Phong, proclaimed himself king. He claimed descent from the Tran royal family on his father's side and from Le Tu Thanh's mother's family on his mother's side. He also claimed to be an incarnation of Indra. He gathered a group of talented followers, including a Cham named Phan At, who became his chief military strategist. In less than a month, Tran Cao's army was camped at Bo De, just across the river from Dong Kinh. Armies sent to dislodge him were defeated and three royal generals were killed.

A new army was advancing to attack Tran Cao led by Nguyen Hoang Du. He was the son of Nguyen Van Lang, brother of the murdered Truong Lac queen mother, who had rallied against Le Tuan and raised Le Dinh to the throne. Nguyen Hoang Du had ridden with his father on that occasion and had accordingly been given honors upon Le Dinh's accession. Nguyen Van Lang had died in 1513 and Nguyen Hoang Du was now the leader of the family, which came from Ha Trung district in Thanh Hoa, about twenty-five kilometers east of Tay Do, on the main route leading north from Thanh Hoa to the Red River plain. This family would be prominent in Vietnamese politics into the twentieth century, by which time it was the royal family. In the troubles of 1516, Nguyen Hoang Du was a potent but unpredictable figure. Just as he was about to attack Tran Cao, news reached him that the king had been slain.

Burning with anger at being publicly humiliated by Le Dinh, Trinh Duy San took advantage of the confusion in the palace provoked by Tran Cao's approach to track down the king and kill him. The princes and great lords who gathered around the king's corpse shed no tears, but they were in disarray about what to do next. Two nephews of Le Dinh, both of their fathers having been killed by Le Tuan, were considered candidates for the throne. Trinh Duy San favored Le Quang Tri, 8-year-old son of a younger brother of Le Dinh. Others proposed Le Y, 16-year-old son of Le Dinh's elder brother. The leader of those who supported Le Y was murdered, and Le Quang Tri was proclaimed king.

Nguyen Hoang Du's reaction to the news of Le Dinh's death was not exactly rational. Apparently dismayed that anyone would kill the king, he led his army into Dong Kinh intent on seeking revenge against the regicides. Then, apparently excited by the chaos that had seized the city and frustrated by what had become of the kingdom, he went on a rampage of looting and destruction that found an object of rage when he captured the evil architect Vu Nhu To, to whom he gave a lingering public death that delighted the mob. Trinh Duy San, seeking to placate Nguyen Hoang Du, sent Le Quang Tri to Tay Do and proclaimed Le Y king instead; then, fearing what Nguyen Hoang Du might do next and perceiving the need for more soldiers, he hastened to Tay Do with Le Y in tow. Nguyen Hoang Du withdrew from the city as Tran Cao crossed the river and took possession of the capital.

At this point, some people of reputation decided that Tran Cao held the best prospect for restoring order to the kingdom. The most prominent of these was a senior prince of the royal family named Le Quang Do, who had supported the accessions of both Le Tuan and Le Dinh. He and others joined Tran Cao. Within days, however, fighting erupted in and around the city as Tran Chan, an adopted son of Trinh Duy San whose home base was in the region west and north of the capital, fought a series of battles with Tran Cao's general Phan At. Nguyen Hoang Du soon joined him, as did Trinh Duy San, arriving with reinforcements from Thanh Hoa. Only twelve days after entering Dong Kinh, Tran Cao was forced to flee. Two days later, Le Y was paraded into the city as king. Back at Tay Do, Le Quang Tri was killed to erase any future repercussions from his brief abortive reign.

Fighting continued through 1516 as Tran Cao was gradually pushed north-eastward away from the capital. During the course of this fighting, both Phan At and Trinh Duy San were captured and killed by their enemies. By the end of the year, Tran Chan had driven Tran Cao beyond the Cau River. Tran Cao stepped aside in favor of his son Tran Cung, shaved his head, and disappeared into the monkhood. For the next five years, the Cau River was the border between the competing dynastic courts of Le Y and Tran Cung.

In 1417, Nguyen Hoang Du and Trinh Tuy, a younger brother of Trinh Duy San, joined their forces to campaign against Tran Cung, but without success. The two Thanh Hoa armies returned to Dong Kinh, where junior members of the two families publicly disparaged one another. Angry words provoked a feud resulting in battles being fought between the two sides in the streets of the capital. When the matter was discussed at court, the Nguyen spokesman accused the Trinh of plotting to overthrow the king. In the uproar that ensued, a royal command was obtained for the deaths of leading Trinh family leaders, including Trinh Duy Dai, the eldest of the Trinh brothers and the nominal head of the family. Nguyen Hoang Du took advantage of this to launch a sudden attack on the Trinh warriors and to drive them out of the city. Trinh Tuy withdrew to Thanh Hoa. Tran Chan, the Trinh ally based near Dong Kinh, then led his soldiers into the city and attacked Nguyen Hoang Du, who was defeated and also took the road back to Thanh Hoa.

Rise of the east

The fighting of 1516 and 1517 had devastated much of the Red River plain. Armed men brought destruction. Fire ravaged markets and villages. Famine spread through the countryside. Officials watched helplessly or ran for their lives. The dead lay unburied in heaps. The eastern part of the Red River plain, in the region of the modern cities of Hai Duong and Hai Phong, neither of which yet existed at that time, was least affected by the fighting but had become dynamic and volatile. It lay off the beaten tracks between Dong Kinh and Thanh Hoa and between Dong Kinh and the Lang Son border with Ming. It was nevertheless open to the outside world by sea. Merchants from China and from countries in Southeast Asia gathered at Van Don, the nearby island seaport. When government faltered during the reigns of Le Tuan and Le Dinh, this region quickly felt the slack and began to exude a spirit of energy and anticipation.

Le Tuan's adoptive mother came from this region and the conduit she provided for local men to enter the palace was the first indication of this spirit. Already in 1511 rumors that a king would come from the east prompted the Le court to send a group of officials to Do Son, the easternmost projection of land into the sea, and today a major resort town, to perform an exorcism to dispel any royal aura that may have been accumulating there. Tran Cao was from this area and his followers were initially from this region, though after 1516 they were displaced by the vicissitudes of war and terrain to the northeastern corner of the plain. There, just beyond Chi Linh and the Cau River, the royal pretension of Tran Cao's heir, Tran Cung, offered an alternative focus of loyalty apart from the Le court at Dong Kinh, which was preoccupied with Thanh Hoa and its seemingly inexhaustible store of great lords and their soldiers. In the dire conditions of 1517, two men in the east successively gained large followings as healers and performers of miracles. They were both taken into custody and killed by officials of the Le court.

By 1517, the east had begun to develop a political personality of its own. The man who came to embody this personality was Mac Dang Dung. He was a descendent of a famous scholar of the early fourteenth century named Mac Dinh Chi, a man of very short stature but of high reputation for his astute and erudite diplomatic work at the Yuan imperial court. A grandson of Mac Dinh Chi, Mac Thuy, had been in the forefront of those who welcomed and served the Ming in the early fifteenth century. With the rise of Le Loi, the Mac family sought obscurity, moving from place to place. A grandson of Mac Thuy named Mac Binh eventually settled in the coastal fishing village of Co Trai, several kilometers west of Do Son at the entrance of the Van Uc estuary. Mac Dang Dung was born in 1483, a grandson of Mac Binh. He worked as a fisherman in his youth, was of large stature, and had a reputation as a wrestler. But he also received an education and passed an exam for military officers. As noted previously, he received an appointment in the palace guard in 1508. The details of his career in royal service during the reigns of Le Tuan and Le Dinh are unknown, except that he received promotions and obtained titles of nobility. He is reported to have secretly attended the Do Son exorcism in 1511, supposedly rendering it void.

During the fighting between the two major Thanh Hoa families that broke out in the capital in 1517, Mac Dang Dung was in command of soldiers stationed south of Dong Kinh on the road to Thanh Hoa. When Tran Chan expelled Nguyen Hoang Du from the capital he sent a message to Mac Dang Dung instructing him to prevent Nguyen Hoang Du from returning to Thanh Hoa. Mac Dang Dung ignored this message and let Nguyen Hoang Du pass. This was his first major step on the political stage. If Trinh Tuy and Nguyen Hoang Du remained occupied with each other in Thanh Hoa, the only person standing between Mac Dang Dung and the 17-year-old king, Le Y, was Tran Chan. Mac Dang Dung moved rapidly to gain ascendancy over the royal court.

Mac Dang Dung endeavored to occupy the moral high ground and to gain followers at court with two long missives addressed to the king in late 1517. They are full of classical allusions and express fully developed analyses of the political problems facing the country. One of them denounced seditious superstition that thrived on popular ignorance and called for the death of a magician who had stirred up a large following in the east. The other denounced the unprincipled ambitions of great nobles and called for the death of Le Quang Do, a grand duke of the royal family who had joined Tran Cao. With these statements, Mac Dang Dung appealed to scholars and to Le loyalists, two important groups that overlapped.

The bracing effect of Mac Dang Dung's influence quickly spread through officialdom and gave a brief moment of confidence to the royal court during the first half of 1518. The capital examination that had been scheduled for 1517 and that had been cancelled due to warfare was now held. But the respite from warfare was short. In mid 1518, Tran Chan, the only plausible rival to Mac Dang Dung, was arrested for treason and killed. His followers in the region west and north of Dong Kinh quickly mobilized their soldiers and marched on the capital. Dong Kinh was left deserted as Le Y and his court fled across the Red River. In the turmoil of shifting the king from place to place, Mac Dang Dung vied with others to control the royal itinerary, even resorting to murder. The king sent a plea for help to Nguyen Hoang Du, but Nguyen Hoang Du did not stir. Instead, Trinh Tuy came marching from Thanh Hoa to join forces with Tran Chan's people.

Trinh Tuy was aflame with the idea of proclaiming another king, but his deeds were even more bungled than had been those of his elder brother Trinh Duy San in 1516. First, he proclaimed as king Le Bang, a fourth-generation descendent of Le Khac Xuong, Le Tu Thanh's elder brother and third son of Le Nguyen Long. Then, for reasons no longer apparent, he discarded Le Bang and instead proclaimed as king Le Do, a younger half-brother of Le Bang. Le Do and Le Bang had the same mother but Le Do's father was a commoner. Despite scraping the bottom of the royal barrel, Trinh Tuy rallied a credible threat to Le Y's court. This finally aroused Nguyen Hoang Du to lead his men up from Thanh Hoa to attack Trinh Tuy and his allies. Defeated, Nguyen Hoang Du returned to Thanh Hoa nearly as quickly as he had come and died soon after.

By early 1519, Le Y and his court were established at Bo De, directly across the Red River from Dong Kinh and Mac Dang Dung was in command of all royal soldiers. Trinh Tuy attempted to attack across the river on floating bridges but was repulsed. There followed three months of drought, which allowed raiders from the mountains to roam the lowlands on horseback for plunder. When the rains finally came in mid summer, miring the raiders in mud and sending them back into the mountains, the soldiers of the two Le kings once again concentrated on each other. Mac Dang Dung attacked, captured and killed Le Do, and sent Trinh Tuy, along with his followers, fleeing to Thanh Hoa.

In late autumn, Le Y and his court returned to Dong Kinh. With the elimination of any imminent threat, Mac Dang Dung spent the next two years building up his military strength while his allies at court endeavored to re-establish an appearance of normal government. Chief among these allies was Pham Gia Mo (b. 1476), a graduate of the 1505 examination who was Minister of Rites. Pham Gia Mo came from the same district as Mac Dang Dung and was also related to him by marriage. In 1520, the educational system was placed back on schedule by holding a capital examination. In 1521, a stele was finally erected to commemorate the graduates of the 1514 examination. The official assigned to prepare the inscription wrote an essay that eulogized the efforts of civil officials to do what was right for the people amidst all the turmoil and fighting during the preceding years. It may have seemed to him that public affairs were finally on a positive trajectory, particularly when, in the autumn of that year, Mac Dang Dung successfully attacked Tran Cung and eliminated the remnants of Tran Cao's rebellion. However, it was but an interlude before the next major shock in the death throes of the Le dynasty.

Le Y, now over 20 years old, began to bridle against the authority of Mac Dang Dung. Nobles and scholars who feared that Mac Dang Dung would bring an end to the dynasty gathered around him and even managed to imprison some of Mac Dang Dung's followers. In mid 1522, a series of events suddenly revealed accumulated tensions. First, there was a great hubbub in the royal palaces when "bandits" set off fires. Then, a rebellion materialized in the districts across the river from the capital involving members of the nobility. Mac Dang Dung no sooner suppressed this than Le Y fled from the capital to take refuge in Tran Chan's old stronghold northwest of the capital. There he mobilized local military units and appealed to Trinh Tuy at Tay Do for help. Mac Dang Dung sent an army against him but its commander was captured.

Mac Dang Dung then announced that Le Y had been kidnapped by rebels and raised Le Y's 15-year-old brother, Le Xuan, to the throne. In his haste to leave Dong Kinh, Le Y had forgotten to take his brother and his mother along with him. Mac Dang Dung's next step was to abandon the capital and bring Le Xuan and his mother to a fortified camp at Gia Loc district, fifty kilometers east of Dong Kinh, about ten kilometers south of the modern city of Hai Duong. Here he awaited events secure in his home territory.

Le Y returned to Dong Kinh, rallied his followers, and issued another appeal to Trinh Tuy for help. Court officials now had to choose which side to be on. Many were unimpressed with Le Y's prospects for overcoming Mac Dang Dung and hastened to join Le Xuan's court. There followed weeks of fighting between partisans of the two courts that sent soldiers chasing one another through large areas of the plain. Mac Dang Dung's men slowly gained the upper hand and finally invaded the palaces at Dong Kinh, forcing Le Y to flee. Dong Kinh once again became a battleground and Le Y established his headquarters on the western edge of the city.

Trinh Tuy finally arrived with a large army. Suspicion of Trinh Tuy among Le Y's followers had spread during the three months it had taken Trinh Tuy to appear after Le Y's first appeal for help. Convinced that he was in danger of being dethroned and using poor judgment, Le Y killed the general sent ahead by Trinh Tuy to meet with him and had his head delivered to Trinh Tuy's camp. Enraged, Trinh Tuy captured Le Y and returned to Thanh Hoa. By the end of 1522, Mac Dang Dung had pacified the Red River plain.

In 1523 and 1524 there was another effort to regain an appearance of normalcy at Dong Kinh. Provinces in the Red River plain sent their scholars for the scheduled capital examination in 1523, a census was taken of households and fields in 1524, and the Ministry of Rites compiled a list of 113 spirit shrines in the country. Mac Dang Dung's brother, Mac Quyet, led an army to Thanh Hoa that defeated Trinh Tuy and pursued him into the mountains. In 1525, Mac

Dang Dung led a large army into the mountains of Thanh Hoa. Trinh Tuy escaped and was not heard of again, but Le Y and his followers, including a number of relatively prominent scholars, were captured and brought back to Dong Kinh. Le Y was demoted, and a proclamation trumpeted the fact that the country was finally united under Le Xuan.

Officials who had thrown their lot in with Le Y during his Thanh Hoa sojourn now fled into hiding, committed suicide, were captured and killed, or submitted to Le Xuan and begged for forgiveness. One official apparently received mercy because he was famous for his sense of humor; he was sent to take a post in Quang Nam on the far southern frontier where he died soon after. Another official, Nguyen Mau, was spared through the intervention of Pham Gia Mo, who had followed Mac Dang Dung since 1519. Pham Gia Mo had high regard for Nguyen Mau's ability and integrity despite the differences in their political loyalties. In 1526, the scheduled capital examination was held and Nguyen Mau led efforts to fill the vacancies in officialdom.

It was after Le Y was captured and returned to Dong Kinh that the direction of events became clear, and the largest number of deaths for Le loyalists is recorded in 1525 and 1526. Four nobles attempted to flee to the Ming border but were captured and killed. Five scholars were involved in organizing an unsuccessful uprising in their home districts northeast of Dong Kinh and committed suicide or were executed. Mac Dang Dung forcibly summoned three scholars to court. One leaped into a river and drowned en route to the capital. The other two appeared before Mac Dang Dung but were executed after one spit in Mac Dang Dung's face and the other threw a rock at Mac Dang Dung. At the end of 1526, Le Y was unobtrusively killed. This dynastic transition was the least homicidal of any yet recorded since the founding of Thang Long more than five hundred years before.

With Thanh Hoa quiet, there would be no heroes marching north to keep the Le dynasty alive. Mac Dang Dung was the master of the country. But how does one change the ruling house? The way that Mac Dang Dung answered this question combined ruthlessness with tact. He withdrew to his home village at Co Trai. In the fourth month of 1527 he received a delegation of nobles who bore notice of his promotion from grand duke to prince and conferred upon him items of princely regalia. In the fifth month, he journeyed to the capital where he called on the king, who offered him a poem about the Duke of Zhou assisting his young king in antiquity, the last pitiful throb of Le royal hope. After only six days in Dong Kinh, Mac Dang Dung went back to Co Trai. In the sixth month he returned to the capital amidst great public acclaim. He went to court to receive the royal proclamation in which Le Xuan yielded the throne to him. After a small flutter of resistance among the scholars called on to draft the proclamation, it was done. A few months later, Le Xuan and his mother went the way of Le Y.

The manner in which the Le dynasty collapsed revealed the vital connection it had to Thanh Hoa. The leadership of Le Loi and Le Tu Thanh were individual achievements that rose above the raw martial exuberance of Thanh Hoa and its hinterland, an exuberance that found a pivot at the Tay Do fortress and an outlet in the newly acquired southern territories. The Le dynasty was the banner under which the lords of Thanh Hoa claimed access to Dong Kinh and the resources of the Red River plain. Mac Dang Dung led a response to this claim. He and his successors endeavored to turn Thanh Hoa from a royal sanctuary into just another province. Their eventual failure would be due not only to events in Thanh Hoa but also to the material and human resources of the long southern coast.

The early Mac dynasty

From the 1530s there began an era of warfare among Vietnamese speakers that would last until the 1670s. There were two major phases of fighting. The first phase went to the end of the sixteenth century and was a struggle between the Red River plain and the southern provinces under the leadership of men from Thanh Hoa. The second phase, in the seventeenth century, is discussed in the next chapter and had to do with a struggle between the emerging south and the "old world" of the north. The first phase brought a successful conclusion to the two-century-long struggle of Thanh Hoa to gain dominance over the Red River plain.

Much of the information that remains from this time is concerned with warfare and the politics of dynastic competition. But there are also three other stories. One is the story of educated people. All competitors for ascendancy continued to hold examinations in which scholars were given an opportunity to enter government service; some of these scholars have become important figures in Vietnamese literary and intellectual history. The second story is one of drought, flood, pestilence, epidemics, famine, and corpses piling up in the countryside as dikes broke, irrigation systems became dysfunctional, rice granaries were not maintained, medical systems broke down, men were taken from the rice fields to the battlefields, and crops failed or were not harvested. This vision of rural misery must be balanced with indications of peace and prosperity when large construction projects were undertaken in villages on the Red River plain that were related to the third story about money and religion. The men and women who made fortunes bringing weapons and uniforms and food to the armies invested their surplus capital in Buddhist temples, village community halls (*dinh*), and spirit shrines. Old temples were repaired or rebuilt and new deities and cults appeared as wealthy individuals endeavored to ensure the maintenance of their ancestral cults and to obtain divine protection for themselves and their property by patronizing centers of popular religion.

For twenty years the Mac dynasty was stable, peaceful, enjoyed good leadership, and established a foundation for prosperity. In 1532, the court annalist recorded that merchants and travelers stopped carrying weapons to protect themselves from bandits, nocturnal thieves and robbers ceased, and water buffaloes were allowed to graze freely without being penned at night for security: "Items dropped on the roads were not stolen, and outer doors were not barred; there were many years of plenty, and the country was rather peaceful." Even though in later decades warfare made its rounds, judging from inscriptions that record the repair, renovation, or construction of village halls and temples, large parts of the Red River plain continued to benefit from Mac government into the 1590s.

The few officials who were determined to resist Mac Dang Dung had already met their fates in 1525 and 1526 in the wake of Le Y's capture. After Mac Dang Dung took the throne in 1527, members of the Le royal family and of families closely allied with it, along with officials whose sense of loyalty to the Le was finally insurmountable, fled into the mountains, took refuge in neighboring kingdoms, or changed their names and withdrew into the obscurity of village life. The number of these people has not been recorded, but judging from indications of continuity at court it is unlikely to have been very significant. Two famous suicides were recorded. Thieu Quy Linh, returning from diplomatic work in China and finding a new dynasty in Dong Kinh, departed in retirement to his home in Thanh Hoa; on the way he leapt from a bridge and drowned. A scholar named Nguyen Thieu Tri, who had served Le Tu Thanh and had retired to his home in the foothills northwest of Dong Kinh, was so angry about his eldest son serving the Mac that in 1533 at the age of 92 he killed his son then cut his own throat.

The vast majority of officials navigated the dynastic change successfully. Mac Dang Dung made it easy for them to do this by maintaining the structure of government that had been established by Le Tu Thanh. He quenched apprehensions among officials by preserving the laws and regulations of the Le dynasty and by continuing its system of education and administration that was the basis for their careers. During the twenty-two capital examinations held under the Mac from 1529 to 1592, a total of 484 men were graduated, an average of twenty-two graduates per exam. Drawing upon candidates almost exclusively from the Red River plain, the Mac rate of producing scholars is not as impressive as that of Le Tu Thanh's reign, but it compares favorably with subsequent eras and is far greater than the forty-five graduates of the seven exams held by the reconstituted Le court in Thanh Hoa from 1554 to 1592, an average of fewer than six and a half graduates per exam.

The most famous literatus of the sixteenth century is Nguyen Binh Khiem (1491–1586). He was born into the erudite world of palace scholars during Le Tu Thanh's reign. His father was a prominent teacher and his mother was an ambitious and highly educated daughter of a senior court official. Abandoned by his mother when he was a child, Nguyen Binh Khiem was raised by his father. He went to study with Luong Dac Bang, a graduate of the 1499 capital exam from Hoang Hoa district in the lower plain of the Ma River in Thanh Hoa. The Luong family first became prominent at court in late Tran times. Branches of the family existed in China; Le Loi had executed an ancestor of Luong Dac Bang for siding with the Ming. Luong Dac Bang had an illustrious career at the Le court, but he died fairly early after entrusting his son Luong Huu Khanh into Nguyen Binh Khiem's care.

Luong Huu Khanh became one of Nguyen Binh Khiem's most outstanding students. He entered the capital exam of 1538 but quit the competition when although earning the highest honor it was denied to him because his family was from Thanh Hoa. He thereafter went to Thanh Hoa to join the reconstituted Le court and ably served the Le restoration movement until his death in 1573. According to one story, he left for Thanh Hoa in chagrin after failing to gain the hand of Nguyen Binh Khiem's eldest daughter in marriage due to his poverty. Following his father's death, Luong Huu Khanh's family had fallen on hard times, and his mother worked in a Dong Kinh market. He lacked the necessary resources to initiate marriage rites. Nguyen Binh Khiem instead gave his daughter in marriage to Pham Dao, son of a prominent official at the Mac court.

During the years of Le collapse and the rise of Mac Dang Dung, Nguyen Binh Khiem eschewed public life and spent his time teaching. In 1535, he finally competed in the examinations, won the highest honors, and entered officialdom. In 1542, shortly after the death of Mac Dang Dung, he retired to his home village in Vinh Bao district in Hai Phong, about twenty-five kilometers west of Co Trai, the home village of the Mac family. According to one story, he retired after unsuccessfully requesting the deaths of corrupt officials. There is no evidence for this, but, for Le historians who wanted to portray the Mac as an illegitimate regime, it put him in the protesting role made famous by Chu An at the dissipated court of Tran Hao nearly two centuries before. In fact, he retired to avoid being implicated in the intrigues of his infamous son-in-law Pham Dao.

Nguyen Binh Khiem built a school in his home village that became a gathering place for students from all parts of the country. Consequently, he was probably the most informed person in the country through the network of his students and their families. Mac officials regularly consulted him. He was famous for his mastery of the numerological method for consulting the *Classic of Changes* (*Yijing*) that had been devised by the Song scholar Shao Yong (1011–1077), and many tales survive about his ability to predict the future. He wrote prophetic works that are still consulted today, and he is often called the Vietnamese Nostradamus.

His most prominent student was Phung Khac Khoan (1528–1613), who went to Thanh Hoa to join the Le restoration movement in the early 1550s after a succession dispute had broken the momentum of Mac leadership. Phung Khac Khoan served the Le court for many years before eventually passing the Thanh Hoa exam of 1580; his subsequent diplomatic work and his poetry earned him honor in his lifetime and the esteem of later generations. Nguyen Binh Khiem and Phung Khac Khoan wrote poetry reflecting the views of intellectuals living in an age of warfare. Phung Khac Khoan expressed an ambition to achieve personal acclaim and an expectation that a time of peace would eventually enable educated people to make a better world. In contrast, Nguyen Binh Khiem expressed a self-effacing renunciation of worldly ambitions and a perception of human affairs being caught in cyclic forces beyond human will.

Nguyen Binh Khiem's poetry is often conflated and compared with the poetry of Nguyen Trai because, like Doan Van Kham in the eleventh century, they both elaborated the contrasting themes of service to one's country and of withdrawal for personal cultivation. While Nguyen Trai's poems praise the joys of retirement, they remain tied to a sense of duty to serve the public good. Nguyen Binh Khiem's poetry, however, is less concerned with public service and more at peace with the quiet country life. Both men lived in times of violence and change, but while Nguyen Trai experienced military victory and political achievements, Nguyen Binh Khiem witnessed a land caught in military and political deadlock. Their shared interest in both public service and eremitic withdrawal and their exploration of these themes in both literary and vernacular poetry inked terrain that inspired Vietnamese writers for centuries. The poetry of these men was laden with standard clichés and well-worn allusions to ancient texts, which appeared not only in poems written in Literary Chinese but also in vernacular Vietnamese, showing that classical idioms had entered the high-register vernacular of educated people. Their vernacular poems also displayed aphorisms and turns of phrase derived from popular oral culture.

Another man who is generally considered to have been a student of Nguyen Binh Khiem and who achieved a literary reputation is Nguyen Du, the son of Nguyen Tuong Phieu, an official who graduated in the 1496 capital examination. He was from the eastern part of the Red River plain, in Gia Loc district, south of the modern city of Hai Duong, where Mac Dang Dung temporarily fortified a royal residence for Le Xuan in 1522. After passing a regional exam, Nguyen Du received appointment as a district magistrate but retired after one year. He is famous for initiating in Vietnam a new genre of fiction writing modeled on the collection of stories entitled *Jian Deng Xin Hua* (New Tales by Lamplight) by the Ming writer Qu You (1341–1427). Nguyen Du wrote *Truyen Ky Man Luc* (Record of Strange Tales), which was reportedly revised by Nguyen Binh Khiem. Some of the stories in this collection are taken directly from Qu You, others are more original, but all in some way follow the theme of human encounters with ghosts, demons, and deities. Written in Literary Chinese, *Truyen Ky Man Luc* was subsequently translated into the vernacular and inspired many similar works in later centuries.

Interest in this kind of writing resonated with a strong current in popular culture at that time. According to a 1589 inscription, the Mac court promoted "the restoration of Buddhism," an indication that Buddhism had been relatively neglected in the fifteenth century after the fall of the Tran dynasty. The Mac era was a time of very active building and renovation of Buddhist temples in the Red River plain that expressed a revival of Tran dynasty architectural features and decorative arts, including statuary. The Mac also encouraged popular religious cults, which heightened interest in interaction between the realm of human beings and the realm of divine and demonic beings.

References to the Jade Emperor are first recorded among the Vietnamese at this time as presiding over a celestial court of deities who were sometimes incarnated as human beings. A collection of over one thousand biographies of deities who were the objects of local spirit cults was assembled in the 1570s, a time when the fortunes of war gave the Mac an era of relative ascendancy. One such deity was the Princess Lieu Hanh, a daughter of the Jade Emperor who was supposedly born among humans in the mid sixteenth century at Van Cat in Vu Ban district, about fifteen kilometers southwest of the modern city of Nam Dinh, on the road to Thanh Hoa. This place was a frequent wartime headquarters and stopping place along the invasion route followed by armies marching both north and south between the "two capitals" of Dong Kinh and Tay Do. A wide range of stories from the sublime to the demonic are told about Lieu Hanh's sojourn among humans before she eventually returned to her celestial abode. She is still considered to be a key figure in the pantheon of "Holy Mothers" who preside over a host of spirits available to mediums and sorcerers. Her major temples today are located on the invasion routes between Thanh Hoa and the Red River plain. Evidence indicates that her cult appeared and flourished among women who accumulated wealth in the markets that served the armies of that time.

Biographies of heavenly beings were compiled to textually authenticate them as the official protector spirits of villages (*thanh hoang*) and to obtain the recognition of their cults by governing authorities. The worship of these deities was conducted in the village community halls (*dinh*) that were built in great numbers during Mac times. Although the earliest surviving *dinh* date from the sixteenth century, they existed before and began to assume the characteristics and functions for which they are known in modern times from the fifteenth century when officials reorganized the administrative and ritual life of villages away from Buddhist temples. This effort by educated people to strengthen Confucian ethical norms among villagers gained unprecedented force after the chaos of the Tran Cao uprising and the subsequent years of fighting. Mac Dang Dung enforced an era of relative peace and prosperity in which village life was rebuilt. The *dinh* became the center of village administration and of court-sanctioned cults devoted to local protector deities. It became a ritual center dominated by men in contrast to the Buddhist temples where women were prominent and where, in the Red River plain, adjacent "mother houses" were frequently built for the worship of female deities.

Records from the reign of Le Tu Thanh and from Mac times indicate that Buddhist temples and *dinh* were often built with money contributed by people who sought to have the ritual observance of their death anniversaries conducted in those places. Laws were published by royal courts enforcing the obligations of those responsible for conducting these observances after the deaths of the bene-factors. Temples and *dinh* were a favored investment for those who accumulated money in the markets. It not only gained them public recognition, prestige, and the assurance of being remembered after their deaths, it also was the surest way to put surplus wealth out of the reach of thieves, swindlers, and tax collectors. The great surge of construction in the sixteenth century reveals an overflow of wealth from the markets. This is reflected in the attention given to coinage by both dynastic contenders. Beginning in the 1530s, coins were cast both by the Mac and by the Le in Thanh Hoa. While Le coins were traditional copper, and are likely to have been manufactured in China, the Mac cast coins of zinc and iron, giving them a distinctive color and heft.

The era of Mac prosperity was brief, for the men of Thanh Hoa and of the hinterland that they commanded were unwilling to submit to the new dynasty. The war that ensued brought decades of grief to people in all parts of the country and finally restored Thanh Hoa's dominance at Dong Kinh under the banner of the Le dynasty.

Outbreak of the Seventy Years War

The Le restoration movement was initially led by Nguyen Kim, a son of Nguyen Hoang Du who was briefly a major figure in the turmoil following Tran Cao's uprising in 1516. In 1529, shortly after Mac Dang Dung took the throne,

Nguyen Kim assembled his family and retainers and went to Laos where he submitted to King Photisarath (r. 1520–1548), during whose reign the kingdom of Lan Xang, based along the Mekong River at Luang Prabang and Vientiane, enjoyed an era of power, peace, and prosperity. King Photisarath accepted Nguyen Kim as a vassal and assigned him territory in the region of Sam Nua at the headwaters of the Ma and Chu Rivers, which flow down to the sea through Thanh Hoa. The Mac suppressed Le loyalist uprisings in Thanh Hoa in 1530 and 1531, but survivors found refuge with Nguyen Kim. In 1533, Nguyen Kim proclaimed Le Duy Ninh, an 18-year-old son of Le Y, as king. King Photisarath acknowledged this claim and allocated resources to support it. Envoys were sent to the Ming court to denounce Mac Dang Dung as a usurper and to request aid in restoring the legitimate dynasty.

The Ming emperor Zhu Houcong (r. 1521–1567), like his predecessor Zhu Houzhao (r. 1505–1521), was not very interested in government affairs. Imperial administration was enfeebled by neglect, corruption, and intrigue. The question of whether the Le or the Mac were the legitimate rulers of the vassal state of An Nam was ignored until 1537 when officials prepared to send missions to tributary states to announce the birth of an heir apparent and there had to be a decision about to whom the announcement should be addressed. Some officials argued in favor of the Le and drew up plans for an expedition to suppress the Mac. Other officials argued in favor of the Mac, citing interpretations of dynastic policy toward small tributary states, the cost of such an expedition, and the Mongol threat on the northern border. Although the emperor was inclined to favor the Le, war preparations were kept in abeyance as border officials were divided in their opinions and court officials were indecisive. Finally, the Ming conceived a compromise solution according to which there would be no expedition if the Mac would recognize the Le as suzerain. Mac Dang Dung's rejection of this demand triggered the expeditionary project, and by mid 1540 an army of over 110,000 soldiers had assembled on the border. Despite this, both sides were looking for a way to avoid war. The Mac worried about the growing Le threat in Thanh Hoa. The Ming worried about Altan Khan (1507–1582), the Mongol leader who was beginning to pose a serious problem on their northern frontier. Mac envoys met with Ming officials and worked out an accommodation.

Near the end of 1540, Mac Dang Dung and over forty of his officials and family members crawled on their hands and knees across the border bareheaded, barefooted, and with ropes tied around their necks symbolizing surrender. Mac Dang Dung presented tribute and administrative records to the commander of the Ming army; he yielded a few parcels of border territory and begged to be allowed to submit peacefully. The Ming army was withdrawn and within a year the Ming court issued a proclamation recognizing the Mac as administrators of their territory, albeit at a lower status in the scheme of tributary relationships than had previously existed for the Le. The proclamation declared that it was not clear whether or not the aspiring king in Thanh Hoa was really a descendent of the Le royal family, but if this should eventually be proven to be true, the Le would be allowed to administer Thanh Hoa Province.

By the time this proclamation was issued in late 1541, Mac Dang Dung had died. Historians later denounced his diplomatic settlement with Ming as an act of servile capitulation. However, given the context of events, it was an astute way to exploit the contradictions among Ming policymakers and a small price to pay for Ming recognition and for peace on the northern border. Nguyen Kim was beginning to send soldiers into the lowlands of Thanh Hoa and Nghe An and the Mac needed to concentrate their resources in that direction.

One of those who gathered around Nguyen Kim in the Laotian uplands was Trinh Kiem. He was from Vinh Loc district in Thanh Hoa, not far from Tay Do. Some scholars have speculated that he was related to the family of Trinh Duy San and Trinh Tuy, which was prominent in the uproars that ensued upon Tran Cao's uprising in 1516, but there is no evidence of this. He reportedly grew up in poverty and herded buffaloes in his youth, which does not suggest membership in a prominent family. Nguyen Kim discovered that Trinh Kiem was good at leading soldiers and made him his son-in-law through marriage to his eldest daughter Ngoc Bao. It was Trinh Kiem who, during a famine in 1539, led an army out of the mountains and struck the first blow in what became a long war by defeating a Mac army in Tho Xuan district along the lower Chu River in Thanh Hoa.

The Mac had initially placed Thanh Hoa in the hands of a eunuch from that province named Duong Chap Nhat. In 1532, an ambitious nobleman from Thanh Hoa named Le Phi Thua had persuaded the Mac court to divide Thanh Hoa and create for him a second command. In 1537, he had gone over to Nguyen Kim. His arrogance was insufferable and Nguyen Kim had him strangled four years later. But his defection added to the turmoil in the province, which gained momentum with Trinh Kiem's victory in 1539. By 1542, Nguyen Kim's men were attacking into both Thanh Hoa and Nghe An. In 1543, Duong Chap Nhat was besieged at Tay Do and surrendered, after which Nguyen Kim gained control of all Thanh Hoa. In 1545, Nguyen Kim was ready to attack into the Red River plain. While camped near Hoa Lu in Yen Mo district, Ninh Binh Province, he was invited to dine with Duong Chap Nhat, who poisoned him before fleeing back to the Mac.

With Nguyen Kim's death, Trinh Kiem became the leader of the Le camp. He was a competent general who repeatedly demonstrated his battlefield prowess during the next quarter-century. He was also a ruthless politician who was determined to eliminate all rivals within the Le restoration movement. He secured the death of Nguyen Kim's eldest son, Nguyen Uong, in circumstances that have not been recorded. Nguyen Kim's other son, Nguyen Hoang (1525–1613), benefited from the counsel of his mother's elder brother Nguyen U Di, who had raised him during his father's sojourn in Laos, and feigned insanity to deflect Trinh Kiem's suspicious eye. In 1546, Trinh Kiem gained the submission of all the provinces south of Thanh Hoa and the situation shifted rapidly in his favor as the Mac fell into a prolonged succession dispute.

Mac Dang Dung had apparently endeavored to establish a dynastic system modeled on the Tran by raising his son Mac Dang Doanh to be king in 1530 while he became the senior king. When Mac Dang Doanh died in 1540, his eldest son Mac Phuc Hai replaced him as king. But when Mac Dang Dung died a year later and Mac Phuc Hai might have replaced him as senior king, Mac Phuc Hai had no adult son to make king. Then, when Mac Phuc Hai died in 1546, a dispute erupted over the succession. Mac Phuc Hai had an infant son named Mac Phuc Nguyen, who, following the practice of primogeniture, held first claim on the throne. However, a general named Pham Tu Nghi argued that, considering the perilous situation in Thanh Hoa, the dynasty could not afford to have a child king. He championed the cause of Mac Chinh Trung, a younger son of Mac Dang Dung, and attracted a large following in the home region of the Mac family.

Opposed to him was the Mac court in Dong Kinh led by Mac Dang Doanh's third son Mac Kinh Dien, who stood up on behalf of his small nephew Mac Phuc Nguyen. Pham Dao, Nguyen Binh Khiem's son-in-law, was among those favoring Mac Phuc Nguyen. He was on very close terms with Mac Kinh Dien because his mother had been Mac Kinh Dien's wet nurse and was credited with saving him from a sickly infancy. Mac Kinh Dien fought Pham Tu Nghi for five years in the eastern plains and along the northern coast until capturing and beheading him in 1551. Mac Chinh Trung fled across the Ming border for refuge. These events provoked border problems and led to years of discussions with Ming envoys. As if this were not enough trouble for the Mac court, Pham Dao's schemes brought further difficulties, fulfilling the apprehensions that had led to his father-in-law Nguyen Binh Khiem's retirement a few years earlier.

While Mac Kinh Dien was busy with Pham Tu Nghi, a feud developed between Pham Dao's family and the family of Le Ba Ly, the Mac general in command of the army facing Thanh Hoa and the most senior Mac commander after Mac Kinh Dien. Le Ba Ly was originally from Thanh Hoa but he maintained a residence in the same village near Dong Kinh that was the home village of Pham Dao. For unrecorded reasons, the two families nurtured enmity against one another. Pham Dao denounced Le Ba Ly as a traitor at court and obtained a

246 / A history of the Vietnamese

royal order for his arrest. However, Le Ba Ly had many friends and allies. He happened to be the father-in-law of Nguyen Quyen, son of Nguyen Thien, who was the Minister of Personnel and a senior member of the court. Nguyen Thien, an examination graduate of 1532, had been a classmate of Nguyen Binh Khiem, and Nguyen Quyen had been Nguyen Binh Khiem's student. In 1550, when Pham Dao's influence proved insurmountable at court, Le Ba Ly, Nguyen Thien, and other prominent men along with their families and retainers went to Thanh Hoa and submitted to the Le, leaving the southern border defenseless. Pham Dao's baleful manipulations continued until 1562 when, accused of treachery, he was finally killed by the Mac.

In 1551, Trinh Kiem sent Le Ba Ly and others into the Red River plain against Dong Kinh. The Mac court fled to the safety of the eastern plains as Mac Kinh Dien guarded the capital until the Le forces withdrew. Thereafter, the two sides concentrated upon recruiting, training, arming, and organizing their armies. Finally, in 1555, Mac Kinh Dien led a large army up the Ma River against Trinh Kiem. A short distance downriver from his headquarters near Tay Do, Trinh Kiem ambushed and defeated the Mac. In 1557, Mac Kinh Dien again invaded Thanh Hoa and was again defeated. Trinh Kiem followed up this victory by pursuing the Mac army into Ninh Binh Province in the Red River plain. There, he defeated it again in a battle from which Mac Kinh Dien barely escaped with his life. A Mac seaborne invasion of Nghe An drew Trinh Kiem back south, but, after defeating it, Trinh Kiem renewed his invasion of the Red River plain. In a major battle on the Giao Thuy River in Truc Ninh district, Nam Dinh Province, he suffered a serious defeat near the end of the year and returned to Thanh Hoa to rebuild his forces. After the battles of 1557, both sides were exhausted and needed time to rebuild their armies.

During the course of these battles, both Le Ba Ly and Nguyen Thien had died, whether in battle or of natural causes is not recorded. Nguyen Thien's son, Nguyen Quyen, retained a sense of loyalty to the Mac despite the family feud that had taken him into the Le camp. With his father and father-in-law both dead, he was susceptible to an appeal from his former teacher Nguyen Binh Khiem, who sent him a poem and then arranged to meet him, facilitating his return to the Mac camp. Nguyen Quyen was a gifted military leader and became one of the most celebrated of the Mac generals.

During this time, Trinh Kiem resolved a small dynastic question. King Le Duy Ninh had died in 1548 and was succeeded by his son Le Duy Huyen. When Le Duy Huyen died without an heir in 1556, Trinh Kiem was said to have consulted Phung Khac Khoan about what to do. The dilemma was supposedly about whether or not to declare the Le family line to be dead, possibly opening the way for Trinh Kiem to claim the throne. According to a story recorded later,

Phung Khac Khoan sent a relative to seek the counsel of his teacher Nguyen Binh Khiem, whose reply indicated that when a crop fails, one should plant seeds obtained from earlier harvests. Trinh Kiem subsequently found Le Duy Bang, a fifth-generation descendent of Le Loi's second eldest brother, and made him king. In fact, Trinh Kiem had little practical alternative to this, for his leadership was based on loyalty to the Le and any effort to change that would have provoked an uproar among his followers.

The idea of consulting Nguyen Binh Khiem was later used to explain how another quasi-dynastic question was resolved at that time. The mother of Nguyen Kim's son Nguyen Hoang was from a locality near Nguyen Binh Khiem's home village. According to this story, she was concerned for the future of her son and sent an emissary to consult Nguyen Binh Khiem, whose reply indicated that Nguyen Hoang should go into the south beyond Ngang Pass. In 1558, Nguyen Hoang's sister, Ngoc Bao, persuaded her husband, Trinh Kiem, to appoint Nguyen Hoang as governor of Thuan Hoa, which encompassed the modern provinces of Quang Binh, Quang Tri, and Thua Thien. He departed with his maternal uncle and mentor Nguyen U Di, along with a large entourage of family members and retainers and made his headquarters near the modern town of Quang Tri, thus initiating the fortunes of his family in the south. In fact, Trinh Kiem's appointment of Nguyen Hoang to Thuan Hoa was an obvious solution to the perplexity of what to do with him. He was the leader of the Nguyen family, which still held the loyalty of many people in Thanh Hoa. Furthermore, Mac agents were becoming increasingly active along the southern coast and the Nguyen entourage would assist to keep that frontier in the Le camp.

During the following decade the fortunes of war shifted from side to side as Trinh Kiem and Mac Kinh Dien repeatedly met in battle. For a few years, Trinh Kiem kept the Mac on the defensive with extended raids that penetrated into nearly every part of the Mac territories, in both the uplands and the plains. This prompted the Mac to build a long defensive rampart west of Dong Kinh in 1560 to block the points at which Le forces were issuing from the mountains. In 1561, Mac Kinh Dien campaigned for six months in Thanh Hoa with some success. In 1562, Trinh Kiem occupied the southern part of the Red River plain for three months to collect the rice harvest; during that time he built a fortress in Ung Hoa district about forty kilometers south of Dong Kinh to shield his activities. He continued to campaign each year in this region. By 1565 he had built up such a position of strength there that Mac Kinh Dien decided to avoid direct battle and instead embarked an army and attacked into Thanh Hoa by sea, winning a major victory over Le forces in Hau Loc district and forcing Trinh Kiem to return to Thanh Hoa, after which the Mac army re-embarked and returned to Dong Kinh. For three more years, Trinh Kiem continued to conduct annual raids into the lower Red River plain, but he was growing ill and weak and during his final two campaigns had to be carried in a litter.

With news of Trinh Kiem's failing health, Nguyen Hoang traveled from Thuan Hoa in 1569 to pay his respects and to renew the anti-Mac alliance. According to surviving accounts, the two brothers-in-law enjoyed an amicable reunion. Before returning south in early 1570, Nguyen Hoang obtained an additional appointment as governor of Quang Nam, thereby giving him authority over all the southern territories. Within days of Nguyen Hoang's departure from Thanh Hoa, Trinh Kiem died. Several years of tumult within the Trinh family ensued.

Before his death, Trinh Kiem announced that his eldest son Trinh Coi would be leader in his stead. However, Trinh Coi had a reputation for wine and women, for excessive pride, and for lack of personal discipline. Within a few weeks of Trinh Kiem's death, many of his prominent followers abandoned Trinh Coi and instead gathered around Trinh Kiem's second son, Trinh Tung. Within three months of their father's death, the brothers were at war with each other. Mac Kinh Dien quickly took advantage of this by advancing his armies into Thanh Hoa. Trinh Coi surrendered to him while Trinh Tung resisted. Mac Kinh Dien took possession of the Thanh Hoa lowlands while Trinh Tung defended the uplands and harassed the Mac with nighttime raids. Amidst the fighting, much of the lowland population fled to the hills, no harvest was taken, famine spread, and many starved to death. At the end of the year, after eight months of campaigning, Mac Kinh Dien withdrew from Thanh Hoa for lack of food.

In 1571, Mac Kinh Dien advanced to Nghe An. During the previous year, Mac agents had recruited and organized an army in Thuan Hoa and the Mac were aiming to recover the southern frontier from which to build a second battlefront against Thanh Hoa. However, Nguyen Hoang defeated the Mac forces in Thuan Hoa and Trinh Tung forced Mac armies to withdraw from Nghe An. During this year of fighting in Thuan Hoa and Nghe An, Trinh Tung tried to resettle the refugee population of Thanh Hoa back into the lowlands but failed to obtain a rice crop, so Thanh Hoa endured a second year of famine.

In 1572, Mac Kinh Dien again marched through Thanh Hoa and advanced into Nghe An. At the same time, a Mac army arrived in Thuan Hoa by sea and rallied many of the people there. Trinh Tung met the Mac invasion with scorched earth and sent an army to Nghe An. There was no harvest in Nghe An. Famine and an epidemic carried away over half the population, and large numbers of survivors fled from the province. Nguyen Hoang defeated the Mac army in Thuan Hoa, and Mac Kinh Dien withdrew back to the north.

Meanwhile, resistance to Trinh Tung formed among members of the Le royal family led by a prince named Le Cap De. Near the end of the year, after the military campaigns had subsided, Trinh Tung seized and killed Le Cap De. This prompted the king, Le Duy Bang, to flee to Nghe An with his four eldest sons. Trinh Tung then raised Le Duy Bang's fifth son, Le Duy Dam, to the throne. In 1573, Le Duy Bang was captured and killed and a Mac attack on Thanh Hoa was repulsed. Trinh Tung remained preoccupied with rivals, however, and in 1574 he suppressed a group of dissidents within the Trinh family. In that year he also sent an army to repulse Mac forces that had arrived in Nghe An by sea.

Beginning in 1575 and continuing for seven years, the Mac conducted annual invasions of Thanh Hoa. Mac Kinh Dien led the first five of these, until his death in 1580. After the death of King Mac Phuc Hai in 1546, Mac Kinh Dien had led Mac armies in the field while his youngest brother Mac Don Nhung kept order at the court of the child king Mac Phuc Nguyen. When Mac Phuc Nguyen died of smallpox in 1561 and was succeeded by his infant son Mac Mau Hop, Mac Don Nhung continued to lead the court as regent while Mac Kinh Dien attended to the war. During the campaigns of the 1570s, Nguyen Binh Khiem's former student Nguyen Quyen emerged as Mac Kinh Dien's most able lieutenant. In those years, Nguyen Quyen typically invaded Nghe An while Mac Kinh Dien invaded Thanh Hoa. This was the apex of Mac military fortunes. Mac armies dominated the lowlands of Thanh Hoa and Nghe An during the fighting seasons. Those provinces suffered endemic famine, and Trinh Tung was constantly on the defensive. Nevertheless, in major battles when Mac Kinh Dien endeavored to destroy Trinh Tung, he was invariably defeated and forced to withdraw. Nguyen Quyen achieved some battlefield successes in Nghe An during these years, and this contributed to his reputation as a great general.

The Le restoration

After Mac Kinh Dien's death in 1580, the Mac military position steadily weakened. Trinh Tung's decisive defeat of the 1581 Mac invasion of Thanh Hoa was a turning point after which he gradually shifted from defense to offense. The last Mac effort to invade Thanh Hoa was repulsed in 1583. In that year, Trinh Tung made his first raid into the Red River plain, in Ninh Binh Province to collect rice, and the Mac general opposing him defected to the Le. Thereafter, the populations of Nghe An and Thanh Hoa lived in peace and slowly restored a more regular existence.

In these years Mac Mau Hop came of age and his faltering influence was increasingly felt at the Mac court. He was an unlucky man with little evidence of talent for government. He had been struck by lightning in 1578 and temporarily paralyzed, and in 1581 he had suffered from a brief spell of blindness. In 1582 he built a pleasure palace that was no sooner completed than it burned down. He repeatedly moved in and out of the capital, spending much time at the Mac family estate in Co Trai, far from the battlefields. There is a story that in 1585 he heard that Nguyen Binh Khiem was on his deathbed and sent someone to ask the dying sage for advice. Nguyen Binh Khiem reportedly foretold the fading fortunes of the Mac dynasty by indicating that the Mac family would be able to find refuge for a few generations in the upland valley of Cao Bang on the Ming border. Whether this message was thought to have given Mac Mau Hop fear or comfort is not recorded, but his subsequent actions were erratic and self-destructive.

Trinh Tung conducted regular raids and patrols in Ninh Binh Province, immediately north of the Thanh Hoa border in the southwestern corner of the Red River plain. He lacked water transport, so he looked for a way to gain access to Dong Kinh from the mountains without having to cross major rivers. In 1585 he led a large reconnaissance force through the mountains to enter the lowlands northwest of Dong Kinh in the region of the modern city of Son Tay. This route was difficult and impractical. He thereafter concentrated his attention on northern Ninh Binh Province in the districts of Nho Quan and Gia Vien. From there he could ascend the Boi River to Lac Thuy district, Hoa Binh Province, and pass northward through the uplands to emerge into the Red River plain about forty kilometers southwest of Dong Kinh at My Duc district, Ha Tay Province. He was inactive in 1586 because of massive floods, drought, then unseasonable rains, and, finally, a palace fire that brought death to his mother. In 1587, however, he marched his men along the route to Dong Kinh via My Duc district. He defeated a Mac army that mobilized to block his way into the lowlands and gathered plunder before returning to Thanh Hoa. In 1588, he raided through Ninh Binh amidst drought, crop failure, and famine. The famine continued into 1589 and people scattered in search of food.

In that year, Mac Don Nhung, Mac Kinh Dien's youngest brother, who had overseen the Mac court since the late 1540s, concentrated his dynasty's resources for an invasion of Thanh Hoa. He led a huge Mac army to the border where, in the Battle of Tam Diep, it was ambushed and dispersed by Trinh Tung. Trinh Tung counted over one thousand Mac dead. He captured some six hundred Mac soldiers whom he fed and released, now confident that the Mac family was in decline. The year 1590 was quiet as both sides rebuilt their armies and prepared for the next battle.

In 1591, Trinh Tung mobilized a great host and marched from Tay Do to northern Ninh Binh then north through Lac Thuy district. However, rather than emerge into the lowlands at My Duc district as he had done in 1587, he continued through the uplands, cutting his way through the wilderness for over ten days, to debouch from the mountains directly west of, and only twenty kilometers away from, Dong Kinh. Mac Mau Hop personally accompanied the Mac armies as they concentrated against the invaders. In a climactic battle three days before the lunar new year of 1592, the Mac were defeated and fell back. Trinh Tung's armies surged forward to envelop Dong Kinh. On the sixth day of the new lunar year, Trinh Tung took the capital after very bitter fighting during which the renowned Mac general Nguyen Quyen was captured and left to die in prison. Mac survivors fled to the north bank of the Red River where Mac Mau Hop relocated his court at Bo De.

Lacking any means for crossing the river, Trinh Tung occupied himself during the next several months with extending his control over localities near the capital and with building floating bridges for crossing the river. During this lull in the fighting both sides held capital examinations in accordance with the academic calendar. The Mac at Bo De graduated seventeen men and the Le at Tay Do graduated three. The regular working of these exams despite the disruptions of war shows that the educational and administrative system established a century earlier had become ingrained in public life.

At this time, Mac Mau Hop's capacity for folly was fully revealed. His queen was a daughter of Nguyen Quyen. She had a younger sister named Nguyen Thi Nien who was the wife of Bui Van Khue, one of the few remaining senior Mac generals. Bui Van Khue had been prominent in many battles and he had fought stubbornly in defense of Dong Kinh. Nguyen Thi Nien sometimes visited her sister in the royal palace. Mac Mau Hop became so enchanted with her that he plotted to kill Bui Van Khue in order to have her. When Nguyen Thi Nien learned of this, she informed her husband. They withdrew with their retainers to Bui Van Khue's home estates near Hoa Lu in Ninh Binh Province. Bui Van Khue sent word to Tay Do that he wished to submit to the Le. There followed a series of battles in which Mac forces endeavored to prevent his submission to the Le and Le forces sought to render him aid. During the course of these battles, Bui Van Khue gained possession of large numbers of Mac boats, which gave Trinh Tung the capability of crossing the Red River. Many Mac generals and officials submitted to the Le as Trinh Tung crossed to the north bank. Mac Mau Hop fled while abdicating in favor of his son Mac Toan, but both he and his son were captured and killed.

Trinh Tung pursued the retreating Mac armies into the eastern part of the plain. Mac Kinh Chi, the eldest son of Mac Kinh Dien, rallied Mac forces at the strategic site of Chi Linh and began to push back. He constructed a rampart along the Thai Binh River, which flows through the modern city of Hai Duong. After weeks of fruitless efforts to break through the Mac defenses, Trinh Tung withdrew to Dong Kinh at the end of the year to organize reinforcements. A few weeks later, early in 1593, he returned to the offensive, broke through the Mac lines, captured Mac Kinh Chi along with ten Mac nobles, and beheaded them all. Fifty-four Mac officials were taken into custody and brought back to Dong Kinh.

Two months later, Mac Kinh Cung, the seventh son of Mac Kinh Dien, rallied surviving Mac soldiers and people from all parts of the Red River plain and proclaimed himself king. He briefly established his headquarters at Bo De before Trinh Tung crossed the river on floating bridges and pushed back his followers. It became clear that most of the people in the Red River plain remained loyal to the Mac and were prepared to assist them. Trinh Tung could pacify the western edge of the plain on the right bank of the river, but Mac followers were busy building defensive walls to protect the east. Hoping to change the political atmosphere, Trinh Tung brought King Le Duy Dam from Thanh Hoa and enthroned him at the battle-ravaged capital in a newly built palace. The restoration of the Le dynasty was proclaimed, but the Mac were far from subdued.

It was at this time that the far southern provinces of Thuan Hoa and Quang Nam added their full weight to the contest as Nguyen Hoang arrived with ships, soldiers, elephants, horses, cannon, rice, and treasure. After leading his entourage south in 1558, Nguyen Hoang established a reputation for maintaining well-disciplined and up-to-date military forces while governing with a light hand, encouraging agriculture, sericulture, commerce, and a level of private wealth significantly higher than was possible in the north. The international port at Hoi An attracted Chinese, Japanese, and Portuguese merchants. Rice was plentiful. Sugar and silk were exported for manufactured goods from Japan, including ceramics, utensils, weapons, and armor. Hoi An was a convenient port of call for the Portuguese between Malacca and Macau; European artillery and musketry were quickly mastered. A discernible contrast between northern poverty and southern prosperity became fixed in Vietnamese regional perceptions. Consequently, the theme of northern tax collectors arriving with their demands eventually became a focus for southern resentment.

In addition to his relative wealth, Nguyen Hoang had the benefit of a new kind of Vietnamese population in the south, people who had learned to rely on their own resources and initiative to a degree not possible in the north. For several generations this had already been a place of exiled criminals, fugitives, refugees, adventurers, and pioneers, and of Chams acculturating to Vietnamese ways of life. The land was rich and productive. Nguyen Hoang obtained a generous portion of the surplus without being oppressive. The relative freedom enjoyed by the civil population was protected by the strict regime he designed for his soldiers under the command of trusted lieutenants in his close-knit entourage. Any challenge to his authority was quickly subdued. But beyond that he interfered very little in the lives of the people he ruled so long as they tendered him sufficient revenue and conscripts.

While Trinh Kiem regarded Nguyen Hoang with equanimity, Trinh Tung was less secure. In the early 1570s, amidst Mac invasions and struggles with rivals both in his own family and in the Le royal family, Trinh Tung viewed Nguyen Hoang with mistrust. There is evidence that he secretly encouraged Mac partisans in Thuan Hoa to attack Nguyen Hoang. Nguyen Hoang never gave any public indication of knowing about this. He benefited from the art of dissembling learned from his maternal uncle Nguyen U Di. The moment of anxiety passed as Trinh Tung established himself and both he and Nguyen Hoang accepted the need for a working relationship.

The year 1586 was a troubled year for Trinh Tung with floods, drought, and hunger in Thanh Hoa that led to cancellation of the examination scheduled for that year and precluded any military operations; furthermore, his mother, Nguyen Hoang's sister, died in a Tay Do fire. Whether it was his needy circumstances or the removal of his mother's restraining hand or both, Trinh Tung for the first time sent an "inspector general" to investigate the tax base and to collect revenue in Nguyen Hoang's jurisdiction. Nguyen Hoang ignored the implication that he had been neglecting his administrative duties and warmly welcomed the official. There was no system for registering fields and wealth in the south comparable to what was standard practice in the north, so Nguyen Hoang persuaded Trinh Tung's tax collector that it was unnecessary to calculate the amount due but that he would simply pay a negotiated amount. The amount he was willing to pay was generous enough that the official was satisfied, and they parted amicably. Thereafter, as Trinh Tung pressed his attacks into the Red River plain he was sustained by annual contributions of treasure from Nguyen Hoang.

When Trinh Tung announced the restoration of the Le dynasty in Dong Kinh in early summer of 1593, Nguyen Hoang arrived to pay his respects to the king, but also to bring his military assets to bear upon the conquest of the Red River plain. He went directly into battle, applying his cannon to demolish Mac defensive walls and providing the breakthrough that led to a series of successful battles that pushed Mac Kinh Cung out of the lowlands and into the northern border province of Lang Son. For the next two years, major battles continued not only in the mountains of Lang Son and of Thai Nguyen but also in many parts of the lowlands, particularly in the east and south where loyalty to the Mac remained strong.

During these years the Red River plain suffered from famine during which it is recorded that one-third of the people in the eastern plain perished. In early 1596, a large Mac army emerged from the mountains into the eastern plain but was defeated and Mac leaders withdrew to the northern border valley of Cao Bang. The famine continued for a third year in 1596 and annalists recorded that more than half the people in the plain died. Uprisings subsided but great disorder prevailed with armed bands of desperate people roving at will, burning, looting, and killing. According to the annalist, large bands numbered from three to four thousand and small bands numbered from seven to eight hundred.

Ming border officials reported on the uproar and, in 1596, the Ming court sent a committee to investigate. Mac officers told the Ming that the Le family had died out and that the Trinh had usurped power. A large delegation that included King Le Duy Dam, Nguyen Hoang, and Phung Khac Khoan traveled from Dong Kinh to the border and argued the case for the Le. The Ming court was fully occupied with the Japanese invasion of Korea and had no intention of getting involved in the situation. Nevertheless, whatever it did would have an effect either to confirm or to deny the relationship it already had with the Mac. Ming officials were not prepared to make a decision to change the status quo, so they temporized, sending the Le delegation away with hopes for further talks while accepting tribute from the Mac in exchange for confirming their version of events.

In early 1597, the Mac ambushed a Le delegation on its way to the border and seized the gold and silver it was bearing as tribute. Shortly after this, the Ming, seeking to maintain a show of impartiality, sent an envoy to Dong Kinh and invited the Le to attend a conference at the border. Once again, the king, Nguyen Hoang, and Phung Khac Khoan went to meet with the Ming officials, which resulted in Phung Khac Khoan being invited to go to the Ming capital to make the Le case at the imperial court. His erudition and poetic prowess were reported to have made a favorable impression on the emperor, but at the end of 1598 he arrived back at Dong Kinh in disappointment, for the emperor decided that for the time being he would grant equal recognition to both the Mac and the Le. This allowed Ming to enjoy the competition between Mac and Le tribute offerings while continuing to avoid any final decision. Many Ming border officials were sympathetic with the Mac, with whom they had long-standing relations. The Ming dynasty was already in the early stages of decline and collapse, but its dual recognition of the Vietnamese rivals helped the Mac to survive in Cao Bang for another seventy years.

Meanwhile, crops continued to fail in 1597, 1598, and 1599, with endemic famine amidst continued unrest and uprisings in the Red River plain. In 1597, Mac partisans set fires in the capital and an army of Mac supporters gained temporary control of the eastern plain until scattered in battle. In 1598, several Le armies pushed into the mountains but could not penetrate the Mac stronghold in Cao Bang. Trinh Tung's soldiers were getting old and efforts were made during these years to recruit new soldiers in Thanh Hoa and Nghe An to fill vacant ranks and to allow veterans to retire.

Despite continued hostilities with Mac partisans, those fighting under the Le banner were gradually gaining control of the Red River plain, and Trinh Tung was looking into the future. In 1599, he received a princely title that raised his status above all others at court save the king. When the king died soon after, Trinh Tung set aside the crown prince, considering him to be "without intelligence," and raised to the throne a younger prince named Le Duy Tan, for whom he became the regent. Trinh Tung thereby ensured his continued domination of the Le court.

A remaining question for Trinh Tung was what to do about his uncle Nguyen Hoang and about government in the far southern territories. He wanted to keep Nguyen Hoang close at hand under his surveillance and to gain more direct control over the south. Nguyen Hoang, however, was looking for a way to return south without provoking a confrontation with his nephew. He had arrived from the south several years before in the heat of battle and the excitement of the Le restoration. Now, with the Trinh solidly entrenched at Dong Kinh, his family had no scope for its ambitions except in the south. But lacking royal assent, which he understood would never be given, he could not return south without putting himself in a state of rebellion. He was 75 years old. Trinh Tung apparently hoped that in time the Nguyen family could be destroyed after Nguyen Hoang's death. Meanwhile, Nguyen Hoang resided with his men in an encampment outside the capital near the river where his boats were kept. He had been assigned a fief there, and Trinh Tung claimed to covet his counsel in governing the country.

At mid summer in 1600 three of Trinh Tung's generals, who were stationed with their troops along the lower Red River south of Dong Kinh, rebelled. Nguyen Hoang requested permission to attack them, which was readily granted. Burning his encampment, he embarked with his men, passed through the rebels, gained the coast, and returned to Thuan Hoa. Trinh historians believed that Nguyen Hoang instigated the rebellion as a cover for his departure. There is no direct evidence for this, but he is likely to have been in communication with the rebels, for they commanded the exact route he needed to depart from the Red River plain. Their complicity in his escape may not have arisen from his instigation. They may have believed that assisting him to return to the south would earn them an ally in that quarter. The uprising of these generals was a more general signal for Mac partisans to rise up in the east and for Mac Kinh Cung to emerge from the mountains. Mac forces converged on the capital. Trinh Trang sent men in pursuit of Nguyen Hoang, but when he saw that Nguyen Hoang had eluded him, he hastened to Tay Do with the king in fear that Nguyen Hoang intended to seize Thanh Hoa. Mac Kinh Cung entered Dong Kinh. Seeing that Nguyen Hoang had disappeared into the south, Trinh Tung mobilized soldiers from

Thanh Hoa and marched back to Dong Kinh. After several months of fighting, he defeated the Mac armies and Mac Dinh Cung withdrew back into the mountains.

Nguyen Hoang did everything he could to make it easy for his nephew to let him go in peace. He left behind a son and a grandson as pledges of his loyalty and explained that he had hastened south to ensure the security of the frontier. Trinh Tung sent a letter to Nguyen Hoang complaining of his behavior and demanding the payment of taxes. In reply, Nguyen Hoang proposed a covenant of peace and sent a daughter to marry Trinh Tung's son Trinh Trang, thereby renewing the family connection for another generation. Neither of these men wanted war with the other. Trinh Tung was still occupied with the Mac and Nguyen Hoang needed time to organize his domain before his death. A quarter-century later, their sons would bring the family quarrel to the battlefield.

The events of the sixteenth century reveal that no resolution of differences between Thanh Hoa and the Red River plain was possible without war. There was no negotiation and no reconciliation. The matter was settled by conquest and coercion. There were two kings in the land and, despite the circulation of merchants and scholars and side-shifting commanders, there was no basis for common ground. There was no center to hold the country together. There was even a linguistic dimension to this separation. The language spoken in lowland Nghe An today remains closer to dialects spoken in the adjacent mountains than to standard lowland Vietnamese. In the sixteenth century, this was probably also true of Thanh Hoa.

Educated Vietnamese later proposed the idea that sixteenth-century intellectuals constituted a cultural center that affirmed a single country despite the clash of regions and dynasties. The stories of how Trinh Kiem, Nguyen Hoang, and Mac Mau Hop all consulted Nguyen Binh Khiem at critical moments in the fortunes of their families have served this affirmation. Instead of being united in loyalty to one king, the Vietnamese were united in following the advice of one sage. In the absence of a king whom all were willing to serve, a sage announced the fates of the combatants and thereby the fate of the country. The superficial impression that Nguyen Binh Khiem was a voice from the center of a unifying Vietnamese cultural authority ignores the fact that his advice confirmed later generations in sundered realms.

According to one popular myth, Nguyen Binh Khiem and Phung Khac Khoan, exemplars, respectively, of Mac and Le intellectuals, were half-brothers, born of the same mother. Stories about Nguyen Binh Khiem's mother emphasize her ambition to give birth to a king and her chagrin at not marrying Mac Dang Dung. A clairvoyant, she reportedly abandoned Nguyen Binh Khiem in his childhood after realizing that he would not be a king. Vietnamese still savor the improbable idea that she became the mother of Phung Khac Khoan. This provides a common mother, albeit attenuated, for the realms of Mac and Le. As noted in previous chapters, the potency of one's mother's family was a theme entrenched in Vietnamese political thought for centuries. What is more certain than this myth is that, despite close family relationships between the Trinh and the Nguyen, when Nguyen Hoang sped down the coast in 1600, his men mending their cracking oars with silken cords to outrun their Trinh pursuers, he was inaugurating an age of separation that would last for two centuries.

6 THE FIFTY YEARS WAR

The north

For seven weeks in late 1618 and early 1619, sky gazers around the world watched what came to be called "the great comet of 1618." Europeans called it "the angry star" because of the remarkable length and reddish hue of its tail and because it was visible even during daylight. Astronomers, astrologers, and doomsayers in all parts of Europe wrote about it, whether as an interesting natural phenomenon or as a portent of calamity. The comet prompted such a degree of popular fear and agitation that King James I of England penned a poem to remind his subjects that, although it may well be a divine sign, there is no way to know what it means, for human thought cannot penetrate the purpose of God.

Vietnamese also watched this comet, and the recorded reactions to it in the two Vietnamese realms show that northerners and southerners were on different paths of historical experience. Southerners may have felt wonderment, if not fear, as they viewed the comet but made no recorded connection between it and public affairs; they simply noted it as a celestial event. Men in the north, however, viewed it as the climax of a series of heavenly warnings that public affairs were in disorder.

Celestial phenomena had been cited as omens at dynastic courts in China and Vietnam for centuries. Sometimes, an omen implying criticism of government policy was written into the record by later historians to express their judgment of events. In 1618 at Dong Kinh, however, the comet brought to a climax recorded discussions about the problems of government that had been accumulating during the previous eight years. During that time, officials from all regions of the northern realm addressed missives to Trinh Tung describing problems and proposing reforms. In these years, Trinh Tung was beset with serious difficulties. He had spent his life leading the fight against the Mac family to restore the Le dynasty and was baffled by any problem that could not be solved with soldiers.

After Nguyen Hoang's departure for the south in 1600, Trinh Tung continued to encounter resistance, sometimes passive and sometimes active, from the population of the Red River plain. This was encouraged by the continuing Mac threat based in the mountain valley of Cao Bang. For two years, the outbreak of warfare accompanying Nguyen Hoang's departure kept Trinh Tung fully occupied with battling his enemies. When Trinh Tung had hastened with the king to Thanh Hoa in fear that Nguyen Hoang was planning to seize that province, Mac Kinh Cung emerged from the northern mountains, rallied wide support in the lowlands, and gained possession of Dong Kinh. Within a month, Trinh Tung had expelled the Mac from the capital and from most territories west of the Red River, but his armies were unsuccessful in penetrating beyond the river to the east and south until the following year when Mac Kinh Cung was dislodged from his family's home region near modern Hai Phong and pressed back into the mountains. Not until autumn of 1601 did Trinh Tung consider the capital sufficiently safe to bring the king back from Tay Do.

With a disaffected and potentially rebellious population in the Red River plain and an active enemy based nearby in the mountains, Trinh Tung relied upon soldiers recruited in Thanh Hoa and Nghe An to enforce his authority. This was in effect a military occupation of the Red River plain by men from the southern provinces, but the burden of heavy military conscription in Thanh Hoa and Nghe An provoked distress and unrest even there. Furthermore, the bounty in men and treasure that Nguyen Hoang had provided from the far south during the 1590s was no longer available. Trinh Tung was paralyzed by the magnitude of his problems. Meanwhile, as the years passed, the question of his successor came to the fore but resisted resolution.

In 1610, Trinh Tung was 61 years old. In that year, he received two urgent recommendations from Le Bat Tu (1563–1627), a senior official from Thanh Hoa, the Trinh homeland, who had gained literary distinction in the 1598 examination. First, Trinh Tung must name a successor to take command of the military and to stabilize the loyalty of the people in Thanh Hoa and Nghe An. And second, he must destroy the Mac and Nguyen separatists who held the northern and southern borderlands. Le Bat Tu argued that the military was presently in excellent condition with experienced officers, well-trained men, thousands of boats, and hundreds of elephants. However, it was doing nothing but maintaining the security of the capital, enabling rebels to nurture their strength in remote places. He foresaw that continued inaction would wear away the readiness of the soldiers and lead to trouble in the future, and he cited historical precedents from the Tang dynasty for emphasis.

That Trinh Tung's heir was still undesignated in 1610 shows that this was a complicated matter. Trinh Tung had nineteen sons. His eldest son died young.

His second son, Trinh Trang, was already 34 years old, had held the rank of grand duke since 1598, and had accumulated years of experience leading soldiers. However, his third son, Trinh Xuan (d. 1623), also had ambitions, was virtually the same age as Trinh Trang (1576–1657), also a grand duke, and moreover had allies in the Le royal family as well as in the Trinh family. Trinh Tung could not find a way to resolve the issue. Within two years of Le Bat Tu's advice, he indicated his preference by conferring the position of "grand teacher" (*thai pho*) on Trinh Trang and the lesser position of "grand protector" (*thai bao*) on Trinh Xuan. But this did not put an end to intrigue and uncertainty. The competition between the brothers and their followers could not be dispelled.

As for military operations, the insecurity of the regime immobilized the thousands of soldiers from Thanh Hoa and Nghe An who were stationed in the capital and in other administrative centers. Nearly all the martial energy of the Trinh was absorbed in simply maintaining control of the large but disaffected population of the Red River plain. Not until 1613 was an army, commanded by Trinh Trang, sent to secure the mountainous eastern coastal province bordering Ming China. The emphasis upon military occupation and control enabled corruption and abuse, and it hindered civil officials from developing what they regarded as normal administration.

In 1612, Pham Tran (b. 1567, a graduate of the Mac exam of 1592 who then shifted to serve the Le) and Nguyen Duy Thi (1572–1652, a graduate of 1598), both officials in the Censorate and both from the Red River plain, addressed a long memorandum to Trinh Tung describing how the population was oppressed and impoverished by corruption. After an introductory passage affirming that rulers must care for the people and nurture their happiness, they observed that "the righteous will" of the ruler was not being followed by "those who implement policy," who "are diligent only in being heartless and cruel and in competing to live in luxury." According to the memorandum:

> Those in charge of a district bring misery to the people of that district, and those in charge of a village bring misery to the people of that village. They harass the people in every possible way, neglecting no method of oppression, which is why the sons and daughters of our country lack clothing, why there are no feasts with singing, why poverty makes wedding ceremonies impossible, why the living are nowhere nurtured and the dying are nowhere comforted. The means for obtaining daily food and the necessities of life are lacking everywhere. The poor and lowly are like bugs in the grass, unable to live like human beings.

The two authors of the memorandum believed that this pitiful situation was the cause of natural disasters indicating heaven's judgment against bad government:

> Because of these conditions, Heaven and Earth are affected and reveal to
> us that the will of Heaven above is not in agreement with our human
> affairs, for the calamity of successive floods exceeding what is normal is
> certainly related to current government affairs. How can we not be afraid
> and mend our ways considering that these woes in the natural world are a
> result of crimes among human beings?

Apparently acting in response to a perception of the problem analyzed in this
memorandum, in the following year Trinh Tung sent officials out to all jurisdictions to investigate "the misery of the people." He also cancelled corvée obligations during three years so that debtors who were wandering about could go
home and make their living. This measure implies that excessive requisitioning of
labor was driving peasants off their land. Peasants were being forced to sell or to
mortgage their land to pay their taxes or to meet living expenses when taken
from field work to provide public labor, apparently for the soldiers whose
garrisons functioned as local government authority.

In 1615, an elderly official from the Red River plain named Nguyen Le (1543–
1619, a graduate of the Mac exam of 1568 who shifted to serve the Le), then serving
as Minister of Justice, submitted to Trinh Tung a list of eight "evil practices" that
required reform. Trinh Tung praised and rewarded him for this initiative, but no
record has survived of what the eight items were or of what, if anything, Trinh Tung
did in response to them. Up until this point, voices calling for reform came from men
of the Red River plain, presumably reflecting the effects of the military regime
imposed on that region. In the following year, Trinh Tung received a report about
troubles affecting his ability to maintain the strength of his armies.

In late autumn of 1616, a procedure to conscript soldiers from Thanh Hoa
provoked a memorandum from two high officials, both from Thanh Hoa: Le Bat
Tu and Luu Dinh Chat (b. 1566, a graduate of the 1607 exam). They reminded
Trinh Tung that, "for the past five or six years, during the season for growing
crops, there has been drought and the farmers have lost hope. This year, as rice
ripened for the autumn harvest, again there was a great drought everywhere,
making two droughts in one year. With disaster coming again and again, the
villagers are resentful." Le Bat Tu and Luu Dinh Chat then deliver the punch line
that was becoming a common refrain in these years: "Surely this is related to
current government affairs." Such criticism of public policy, even from men
representing the home recruiting grounds of the Trinh, reveals how widespread
the perception of misgovernment had grown. The two officials recommended
that the round of conscription in Thanh Hoa be cancelled. Trinh Tung's reaction
to this memorandum is not known.

In 1617 there were unseasonable storms and floods. Insects infested fields near
the mountains that had escaped the floods, and the autumn harvest was lost.

Early in 1618, Trinh Tung roused himself to action in the way he knew best, by sending soldiers against his enemies. He dispatched armies into the northern mountains against the Mac, led jointly by his two sons, Trinh Trang and Trinh Xuan. The Mac avoided large battles and fighting continued inconclusively for several weeks until an epidemic swept the Trinh camps as the summer rains began. There was a great loss of men and horses, and the brothers returned in disarray. There followed a series of signs and wonders. An avalanche was reported on Mount Dong Co in Thanh Hoa where the mountain spirit resided in whose name the Trinh performed their annual oath of loyalty. Two odd stars were observed in the night sky. Then there was successively a yellow rain, a black rain, and a rain that tasted like sweet wine. Finally, the comet appeared, stimulating a rush of memoranda expressing consternation.

The first missive was from three officials who came from all parts of the Trinh realm. Pham Tran, who had co-authored the memorandum of 1612, was from the Red River plain. Le Bat Tu, who had submitted recommendations in 1610 and had co-authored the memorandum of 1616, was from Thanh Hoa. Ngo Tri Hoa (1565–1626, a graduate of the 1592 Le exam) was from Nghe An. These men noted the strange happenings of the previous months followed by the comet's appearance and concluded that all these unusual events "are surely related to current government affairs." They itemized a list of reforms that included restraining bullies, forbidding petty harassment of the people, forbidding luxurious living, and suppressing thieves and bandits. Also on the list was "to practice virtue in order to beseech Heaven's mandate," a remarkable proposal implying that the regime had either lost or was in danger of losing its legitimacy to rule.

This was followed by an appeal to Trinh Tung from Luu Dinh Chat, the other co-author of the 1616 memorandum about conscription in Thanh Hoa. There were apparently those who claimed that the various celestial signs were auspicious, for Luu Dinh Chat argued against this. He wrote that although the black and yellow rains were definitely bad omens, some avoided saying so and instead claimed that they were signs of good luck:

> Heaven has surely displayed admonitions but we have failed to wake up. So, now for weeks we see this comet in the southeastern sky. Everyone can see it and everyone is afraid. Truly this is not an insignificant sign. Does not our lack of virtue display shortcomings sufficient to provoke such a sign? Government policies are not implemented as in times past. Orders and instructions from those wielding power are not in accord with benevolence but are busy with cruelty and evil, scraping away the people's livelihood. The sound of the people sighing and groaning is enough to move Heaven to warn us with this unusual omen. Those who rule, seeing this, must examine themselves. I humbly request that

> Heaven's rebuke be taken to heart, that the powerless people be given
> love and care, that whatever harms and hinders their welfare be elimin-
> ated, and that sound policies be adopted toward them.

Luu Dinh Chat pointedly concluded: "The generals must be ordered to stop their
brazen appropriation of the country's wealth so that the source of the country's
strength can be renewed." This was not a new analysis. But Trinh Tung was in an
impossible position. He relied on his generals to maintain his power while being
given to understand that their depredations were ruining the country. He made
no recorded response to this appeal.

Discussion then spread to senior officials more generally. "Court officials"
submitted a memorial to the king that recited the signs and wonders, the
desperate condition of the country, and the need for reform. It was recorded
that the king made no reply. Finally, "court officials" addressed to Trinh Tung a
long itemization of abusive government practices that explicitly placed the blame
on the subordination of civil administration to military domination and even
implied that treasonous conspiracies were afoot:

> When we see strange signs appear successively like this, is it not certain
> that those in authority have yet to mend their virtue, that there is disorder
> in government affairs, that there are those who are scheming with evil
> intent? ... evil men go in and out of the inner palaces inciting turmoil ...
> illegal appointments are made ... tax collectors compete in their oppressive
> exactions ... false charges are made to imprison people and to seize their
> possessions ... men are illegally conscripted and military duty is excessively
> harsh ... Dynastic laws and regulations exist from past times decreeing that
> generals are to supervise only soldiers and not civilians, but now military
> officers specialize in supervising the people, taking their possessions,
> killing them, seizing them to be soldiers, and using them as their personal
> servants ... taking taxes at exorbitant rates ... they scheme with local
> officials to investigate and litigate ... they set up unlawful customs stations
> on roads and waterways. We beg a proclamation to the generals to urgently
> command them to stop this behavior. As for those who secretly have evil
> intentions, they are conspirators outside of the law.

The mention of conspiracy was not without substance.

As if punctuating the outpouring of anxious criticism provoked by the comet, fire
destroyed an entire district of the capital at the beginning of the 1619 lunar year. But
the accumulation of tensions within the regime was fully revealed when late in the
spring of that year an attempt was made on Trinh Tung's life. He was ambushed as
he returned to his palace from watching a boat race on the river. At a crossroads,
someone shot a firearm at him. His parasol bearer fell, but he was unharmed. The
would-be assassin was quickly captured and identified as a retainer of Trinh Xuan.

Further investigation revealed that Le Duy Tan, the 31-year-old king, had plotted with Trinh Xuan to kill Trinh Tung. The king hoped to remove Trinh Tung's suffocating hand from his royal aspirations, while Trinh Xuan hoped to remove the benefit of his father's favor from his fraternal rival, Trinh Trang.

The man who fired the shot was executed. The king was forced to commit suicide and was replaced with his 12-year-old son, Le Duy Ky, a grandson of Trinh Tung. Unwilling to order the execution of his own son, Trinh Tung imprisoned Trinh Xuan, but later allowed him to be released. Trinh Xuan had influential allies.

Trinh Tung was 70 years old in 1619. He lived for another four years, but he increasingly relinquished authority into the hands Trinh Trang. Meanwhile, Trinh Xuan endeavored to keep the succession question alive and assembled a large armed following. As Trinh Tung lay dying in 1623, Trinh Xuan led his men into the capital, chased away the palace guards, and took possession of his barely conscious father. He sent Trinh Tung, carried in a hammock, to his headquarters outside of the city as his men looted the capital of its valuables and set it afire.

Trinh Tung's younger full brother, Trinh Do, had been a prominent and active member of Trinh Tung's entourage. Hearing of what Trinh Xuan had done, Trinh Do saw an opportunity for himself. He sent his son, Trinh Khai, to intercept those carrying Trinh Tung and to bring his dying brother to his own house. His plan was apparently to separately summon the disputing brothers in the name of their father and put them to death, thus opening a path to power for his own son. Trinh Khai met with Trinh Xuan and persuaded him that Trinh Tung wanted to confer highest authority upon him. Trinh Xuan carelessly walked into the trap and was killed. Trinh Trang, however, was warned by an official, and he instead secured the young king, summoned all the men loyal to him, and set out for Thanh Hoa, understanding the logic of the regime that whoever controlled Thanh Hoa would prevail.

Trinh Do and his son were hastening, with Trinh Tung being carried along, in pursuit of some now obscure errand on the southwestern edge of the capital when the old man died. They abandoned the corpse beside the road. A eunuch picked it up and hastened with it by boat to join Trinh Trang, who gave his father a proper burial. Realizing his folly, Trinh Do hastened with his son to make peace with Trinh Trang, who forgave them.

As Trinh Trang concentrated his forces in Thanh Hoa, Mac Kinh Cung's nephew, Mac Kinh Khoan, emerged from the mountains, rallied thousands of recruits from throughout the Red River plain, and marched on Dong Kinh, camping just across the river at Bo De and making common cause with the group of nobles and officials who had supported Trinh Xuan. But within a month Trinh Trang had defeated his enemies. Mac Kinh Khoan's daughter led a valiant but suicidal rearguard attack to enable her father to make his escape back to Cao Bang. Two years later, Trinh Trang sent one of his sons to invade the Mac territory. Mac Kinh Cung was captured and killed. Mac Kinh Khoan begged to submit, was forgiven, and assigned to govern Cao Bang. After another two years, Trinh Trang was ready to lead his soldiers against the Nguyen in the south.

Trinh Trang became known for opening the way for an era of civil administration and relative prosperity in the villages. Many educated men trusted him. The official who warned him against Trinh Do was Luu Dinh Chat, a co-author of the 1616 appeal to cancel conscription in Thanh Hoa and the author of the 1618 argument against military interference in local government. Amidst the uncertainties of the events provoked by his brother's attempt to kidnap his dying father, Trinh Trang was advised by Nguyen Danh The (1572–1645, a graduate of 1595), who was from a locality near Dong Kinh. Trinh Trang's ideas about government were influenced by the agendas for reform that had accumulated in the time of the comet.

Some of the agrarian distress due to natural calamities recorded in the early seventeenth century may plausibly be attributed to what has been called "the little ice age," an era of relatively colder weather whose effects were especially felt in the early seventeenth century, a time when even the River Thames froze in winter giving Londoners the pleasure of annual "frost fairs" on the ice. However, misgovernment due to military rule was a salient factor in writings from that time. The situation was further aggravated by the prolonged stalemate between Trinh Trang and Trinh Xuan that prevented resolution of the leadership question. Trinh Tung's great achievement had been to restore the Le dynasty to Dong Kinh, but in his later years, in the seventh, eighth, and ninth decades of his life, he was irresolute and incapable of surmounting the contradiction of having restored a dynasty over a population in which loyalty to another dynasty remained strong. This contradiction could be dispelled only with the passing of time.

The south

In contrast, Trinh Tung's uncle, Nguyen Hoang, spent his last years enjoying the adventure of building a new realm. Descriptions of his return to the south in 1600 after an absence of eight years abound with celebrations and expressions of joy. During the remaining thirteen years of his life, he traveled, he built temples, he expanded his border southward, he received streams of emigrants fleeing famine in the north, and he established the rudiments of government.

In 1601, during the course of his travels, he was particularly taken with a hill on the Perfume River that runs through the modern city of Hue, which did not yet exist at that time. The hill looked to him like the head of a dragon turning to look back at its mother in the mountains. He enjoyed sitting at the top of the hill and viewing the scenery, but he was dismayed to discover a sandy trench that had been dug along one side of it. When he inquired about this, local people told a story about the ninth-century Tang general Gao Pian who had brought an end to the violence of the Nan Zhao War in the 860s. Gao Pian was famous for excavating places that, according to geomantic ideas, were likely to give rise to a king, thereby "cutting the dragon vein" that could nurture sovereignty. Geomancers believed that supernatural currents of energy flowed as if in veins through the earth from the Tibetan highlands down to the sea. Dragons symbolized sovereign power, so these currents were called "dragon veins." If one rearranged the terrain to "cut" the "dragon vein," then this flow of power would drain away and be lost. Rulers were careful to cut the dragon veins in their realm to ensure that no rival king would arise. According to one story, the rise of the Ly dynasty was possible because a Buddhist monk had restored the terrain and built a temple at a place where Gao Pian had cut a dragon vein, the place that became Ly Cong Uan's birthplace.

According to the tale reportedly given to Nguyen Hoang in 1601, the sandy trench had been dug by Gao Pian to cut the "dragon vein" that gave this place the potency to nurture a new kingdom. It is unlikely that Gao Pian ever traveled so far south, but possibly at some time in the past a general leading soldiers from the north against Chams had performed the geomantic surgery, inspired by the same thinking that had motivated Gao Pian. Gao Pian was thought to have introduced the study of terrain and geomancy into the Vietnamese lands, and many books of geography among the Vietnamese were attributed to him. Stories about him cutting "dragon veins" and about how a clever monk had repaired one of his geomantic excavations to enable the appearance of the Ly dynasty were well known among Vietnamese.

After hearing the story about the hill on the Perfume River, Nguyen Hoang was reportedly visited in a dream by a goddess who prophesied that a great lord would come and build a temple at this place and that consequently a new and enduring kingdom would be established. The name of the goddess was Thien Mu, meaning "heavenly mother." Nguyen Hoang accordingly built a temple on the hill, probably on the ruins of an earlier Cham temple. It was ostensibly "Buddhist," following a common practice of domesticating spirits by placing them under the Buddha's authority. The temple was rebuilt many times through the centuries. It still remains today as the Thien Mu Temple at Hue. Its distinctive tower was built in the mid nineteenth century by a king who was an eleventh-generation descendent of Nguyen Hoang.

At this time, Nguyen Hoang's headquarters were at Ai Tu, on the Quang Tri River around fifty kilometers northwest of the Perfume River; the basin of the

Perfume River was a major place of settlement that often held Nguyen Hoang's attention. In 1602, near the coast in modern Phu Vang district, where the Perfume River ends, he built a temple on the ruins of a previous temple and named it Sung Hoa. This became a thriving center of culture for several generations.

Also in 1602, Nguyen Hoang made his first visit to Quang Nam. He was reportedly exhilarated by the view down the coast southward from Hai Van Pass. He built a headquarters for governing his southern territories at modern Dien Ban, which commanded the waterways connecting the Bay of Da Nang with the Thu Bon River. The port of Hoi An lay near the mouth of the Thu Bon River, and it was already a lively entrepôt attracting Chinese, Japanese, and Portuguese merchants. Nguyen Hoang built a storehouse and a Buddhist temple at Dien Ban and assigned his sixth son and designated heir, Nguyen Phuc Nguyen, to be in command there.

On his 1602 trip to Quang Nam, Nguyen Hoang also met with Tran Duc Hoa (dates of birth and death are unknown; he was active c. 1600–1630), who was in command of the southern frontier in modern Binh Dinh Province. Tran Duc Hoa's father had served there before him, and the family had kept watch over the southern border during the years that Nguyen Hoang had been in the north. Tran Duc Hoa had a reputation for being well educated, an astute governor, a keen discerner of character, and utterly loyal to the Nguyen. When, a few years later, an ambitious and erudite man from Thanh Hoa named Dao Duy Tu decided to seek his fortune in the south, he entered the service of Tran Duc Hoa as the first step in what became an illustrious career in government.

Nguyen Hoang continued to take an interest in his southern territories. In 1604 he organized local administrative districts in Quang Nam, and in 1607 he build a Buddhist temple at the old Cham capital of Tra Kieu. In 1611, news of border problems with Chams prompted him to send an army to seize control of the basin of the Da Rang River in modern Phu Yen Province and to organize local administration for settlers there, thereby advancing the border southward from Cu Mong Pass to Ca Pass.

In 1608, a large influx of refugees from famine in the north arrived. They were likely settled in the basin of the Nhat Le River in modern Quang Binh Province, for in the following year Nguyen Hoang built a Buddhist temple there, at Le Thuy.

Nguyen Hoang's final years were serene in comparison with those of his nephew Trinh Tung. When he died in 1613 at the age of 88, his 51-year-old sixth son, Nguyen Phuc Nguyen, assumed authority without incident and was the first to distinguish the family surname as Nguyen Phuc, thereby setting the ruling lineage apart from other prominent families in the south with the Nguyen surname.

In his youth, Nguyen Phuc Nguyen had already shown himself to be a daring and able leader. In 1585, at the age of 22, he had earned the praise of his father by taking ten war boats out to sea and sinking two of five large pirate ships commanded by a Japanese who had been ravaging the coasts. When Nguyen Hoang went north in 1592, he had taken with him the three of his five elder sons then still living, leaving Nguyen Phuc Nguyen to keep watch over the south in his absence. When Nguyen Hoang returned to the south eight years later, none of his sons returned with him, two having died in battle and one having been left with Trinh Tung as a pledge of good faith. Nguyen Phuc Nguyen was seasoned with many years of experience in command by the time of his father's death.

During the years that officials were complaining of misgovernment and human distress in the north, Nguyen Phuc Nguyen was occupied with improvising a relatively simple yet versatile system of government for a land of diverse locales and peoples. He also nurtured an international seaport that attracted trade from many lands. His eldest son and heir, Nguyen Phuc Ky (d. 1632), was sent to govern at Dien Ban in Quang Nam. Portuguese ships on the route connecting Goa, Malacca, Macau, and Japan regularly arrived for commerce at the nearby port of Hoi An, where settled communities of Chinese and Japanese merchants already existed. Hoi An became known as a well-regulated port with reasonable duties, easy relations with local people, and where goods were available from Japan, China, Cambodia, Siam, the islands of Southeast Asia, and the local region. Jesuits based at Macau established the first Christian mission among Vietnamese in Quang Nam in 1615, and in 1618 they opened a second mission in modern Binh Dinh Province. Nguyen Phuc Nguyen held to a policy of good relations with foreigners, understanding that trade generated wealth. He was also careful to maintain trust with the Portuguese because this facilitated access to European military technology, particularly artillery and musketry.

Nguyen Phuc Nguyen did not have the dilemma of civil versus military control of government that agitated scholars in the north. Nor did he have the bitter legacy of civil war with one region having conquered another that aggravated this dilemma for Trinh Tung. Village governance in the north, and particularly in the Red River plain, had been decisively affected by the reforms in civil administration implemented during the reign of Le Tu Thanh over a century before and subsequently strengthened by Mac Dang Dung and his successors. The 1618 memoranda submitted to Trinh Tung referred to this in terms of "dynastic laws and regulations" that had been established in the past, according to which military officers had authority over soldiers only and not over the civilian population. This principle of keeping military and civilian authority separate had been superseded by the violence and contradictions in political loyalties that characterized the Le restoration in the Red River plain.

Le Tu Thanh's mode of civil government never extended to the southern frontier. There, Vietnamese speakers developed a form of social and political life that was closely related to the maintenance of garrisons, and the Nguyen Phuc family relied upon the military chain of command to provide the basic structure of their government. All able-bodied men were expected to be soldiers. The populations in the major areas of settlement were mobilized to produce taxes and conscripts for the military. There was no officially recognized civilian population. Instead, all loyal subjects were "military people." Farmers were also soldiers who trained and could be called to duty at any time. Craftsmen of all kinds were simply soldiers with specialized occupations. Relatively few men were members of full-time military units, stationed on the frontiers or at naval bases along the coasts, and even these were required to be married, to live with their wives and children, and to be involved at least part-time in some economic endeavor. The exceptions to this were the élite units serving full-time as the palace guard.

The Nguyen Phuc rulers were most immediately concerned with the region in which the central government was located, from the northern border at the Gianh River to Hai Van Pass. This region was known as Thuan Hoa (the modern provinces of Quang Binh, Quang Tri, and Thua Thien). Aside from the basin of the Gianh River, which remained a battleground for decades, there were three main river basins that could support agriculture. The largest was the furthest south, the basin of the Perfume River where the modern city of Hue is located. Just north of this was the basin of the Quang Tri and Ben Hai Rivers. The Nguyen Phuc headquarters was located here until 1626, when it was moved further south into the basin of the Perfume River as the Trinh wars began. Between this place and the Gianh River was the basin of the Nhat Le River, where the modern city of Dong Hoi is located. This was the strategic "choke point" between the mountains and the sea where major battles between the Trinh and Nguyen would be fought. Much of the attention of the Nguyen Phuc leaders in the first half of the seventeenth century was aimed at building up a large, well-organized population in Thuan Hoa as a bulwark against northern invasions.

To the south, beyond Hai Van Pass, Quang Nam, with the port of Hoi An, with abundant rice fields and with mines of gold and other metals, was a secondary focus of attention as a nearby source of manpower and wealth. The two regions of Thuan Hoa and Quang Nam, often referred to as Thuan-Quang, made up the heartland of the realm. Regions further south were mostly left to the vicissitudes of local officers so long as border security was maintained and surplus resources in cash, commodities, and manpower were produced by way of taxation and conscription. Although initially all territories south of Thuan Hoa were considered as part of Quang Nam, the jurisdictions that became the modern provinces of Quang Ngai, Binh Dinh, and Phu Yen gradually developed their own administrative identities as settlements of Vietnamese speakers grew. Binh Dinh, with the modern city of Qui Nhon, was the most important of these because it had been the southernmost garrison on the Cham border already for a century and a half, because of its good seaport, and because it was the terminus of a trade route going west through the uplands to the Mekong River and beyond.

The term used to designate administrative centers was initially the word for "garrison" (*dinh*, a southern vernacular pronunciation of *doanh*, a Sino-Vietnamese word for "garrison"). The meaning of this word expanded in the south to mean a military headquarters, a place of government authority, and, combined with the word for "first" or "primary" (*chinh*), the capital or site of the ruler's residence (*chinh dinh*). These etymological shifts reflected changes in the practice of government as Nguyen Hoang organized a land of frontier garrisons into a separate country.

In 1614, Nguyen Phuc Nguyen established four offices with administrative responsibilities that reveal a garrison model of government to rule the country. Three of these, the so-called "three offices" (*tam ty*), were concerned with public governance, while one of them served the extended household of the ruling family. Two of the "three offices" were charged with collecting taxes and organizing the transport and distribution of supplies and provisions to military units. The Office of the Guard (Lenh Su Ty) was concerned with units on duty in the capital and in the districts nearest to it. The Office of the Garrisons (Tuong Than Lai Ty) was responsible for supply to military units stationed in the provinces. A third office, the Office of the Commissioners (Xa Sai Ty), was responsible for administering courts of justice among populations where litigation was not subject to martial law. The fourth office, of the Inner Court (Noi Lenh Su Ty), was established to serve the ruling family and the highest levels of its entourage by supplying tax revenue and commodities from throughout the realm.

These offices operated in four jurisdictions that overlapped geographically but served four different classes of people. In the capital district, local administration was entirely in the hands of the Office of the Guard. There were no civil courts of law because the capital district was essentially a garrison under military discipline. In districts further from the capital, throughout Thuan Hoa and at strategic points further south, the Office of the Guard continued to be responsible for military units while the Office of Commissioners staffed courts of law for people not inside the system of military command. The Office of the Garrisons was responsible for military affairs outside of the places under control of the Guard, and it ensured supplies and trained conscripts for the Guard. The Office of

Commissioners was more prominent in areas more distant from the capital, where non-military and non-Vietnamese people constituted more of the population. The Office of the Inner Court went everywhere to collect goods and provisions directly for the ruler, his family, and his favorites.

In 1615, Nguyen Phuc Nguyen began to organize his lands into prefectures and districts. Local magistrates were assisted by clerks who investigated and kept records about residents, by officials in charge of education, and by ritual experts who conducted ceremonies and sacrifices at temples and shrines. While magistrates collected fees for village festivals and other miscellaneous local expenses, officials from the offices of the central government collected the head tax in cash and the field tax in rice. This was different from taxation in the north, which relied upon village officials to collect taxes.

In the north, taxation was such an onerous subject of contention and negotiation between villages and higher authorities that finally, in the 1660s, the system was simplified so that villages were communally subject to a fixed and unchanging rate, which, by the early eighteenth century, created an entirely new set of problems. In the south, however, taxpayers paid directly to the central government, not to village authorities, and their assessments were subject to triennial re-evaluations based on their property, age, health, social status, and other criteria, such as the part of the country in which they resided. Thus, the southern tax system was much more sensitive to the actual circumstances of the population than was the case in the north.

To some extent this reflects the fact that local populations in the south were constantly changing as people moved about and settled in new areas. This complicated the ownership of land with disputes involving local officials and individual residents. Consequently, in 1618, Nguyen Phuc Nguyen sent officials to survey and register the ownership of fields throughout the land, aiming to put an end to litigation over land ownership and to establish the basis for collecting field taxes.

A year earlier, in 1617, Nguyen Phuc Nguyen opened a bureau in the Office of the Inner Court to supervise gold, silver, and iron mines; to collect customs duties on merchant boats from Guangdong, Fujian, and Japan; and to control commodities of trade such as fragrant oils, honey, beeswax, elephant tusks, rattan mats, lacquer and lacquer paintings, aromatic wood, caulking resin, and wire of brass and steel. Nguyen Phuc Nguyen paid close attention to markets and trade. One of the features of situating the central government in the basin of the Quang Tri River was that it was at the eastern terminus of a well-worn route west along the Cam Lo River through the mountains to the Mekong River where the modern Lao town of Savannakhet is located; this became colonial route 9 along which major battles were fought during the period 1968–1971. When Lao bandits were making the route unsafe for merchants in 1621, Nguyen Phuc Nguyen's response was to collaborate with a group of merchants to lure the bandits into an ambush. In the following year, a garrison was established on this route to provide security for trade.

During the first quarter of the seventeenth century, the Trinh and Nguyen domains moved in different directions. While the Trinh were constricted with insoluble problems in the north, the Nguyen found themselves in a world of expanding possibilities. The Jesuit missionaries who arrived at this time perceived two hostile countries. They called the northern country Tonkin and the southern country Cochinchina, according to the usage of the Portuguese on whose ships they sailed. Tonkin was the European pronunciation of the northern capital, Dong Kinh, but Cochinchina derived from the wider world of maritime commerce.

The Portuguese obtained the term Cochinchina from the Malays, who had picked it up from the Arabs, who apparently coined the name in the early fifteenth century when Ming fleets sailed to India, Arabia, and Africa. At that time, the Ming used the ancient term Giao Chi for Vietnam, pronounced *Jiaozhi* in Mandarin Chinese and *Kawci* in Arabic. The Arabs used the term *Kawci min Cin* (Kawci of China) to indicate that this was a place near China. In Malay, *min* was absorbed into a nasalization of the second syllable of *Kawci*. When they received the name from the Malays, the Portuguese considered that the name Cochinchina was meant to distinguish this place from the Cochin that they knew on the western coast of India. What is probably most significant about this rather tortuous etymological path is that, although in the early fifteenth century the term initially appeared in reference to the north, which is where the Vietnamese were at that time, the Vietnamese place known by this name to the maritime world in the early seventeenth century was in the south. While northern rulers never learned the benefits to be derived from encouraging foreign trade, the southern rulers instinctively understood and wholeheartedly welcomed it.

For the Trinh who ruled the north, the Nguyen south was simply a rebellious province governed by a family of renegades. It could have no name separate from or equivalent to the realm of the Le dynasty. On the other hand, the terminology by which southerners distinguished between the north and the south eventually affected the vocabulary of all Vietnamese speakers. During the Le–Mac wars of the sixteenth century, Le partisans referred to themselves as those on the "inside," thereby indicating that they were in the center of authority with the legitimate king. By contrast, they referred to the Mac as being on the "outside," meaning in a state of rebellion. While this terminology was not continued in the north after the Le restoration, it shifted to a new context among those who went south with Nguyen Hoang. Southerners called their land the "Inside" (Dang

Trong) and the north they called the "Outside" (Dang Ngoai), for they considered that the Trinh were in a state of rebellion since they held the Le kings as virtual prisoners.

Nguyen Khoa Chiem (1659–1736), a southerner writing in the early eighteenth century about events a century earlier, recorded a poem that he claimed circulated after Trinh Tung had killed King Le Duy Tan in 1619. The poem assumes that Trinh Xuan had plotted to kill his father because he wanted to restore supreme authority to the king; yet it also suggests that Trinh Xuan's parricidal scheme is evidence that his family, a family of usurpers, is doomed. The poem reflects a southern perspective on the events in Dong Kinh:

> Pity the sad fate of the Le King;
> In evil times, men see omens and portents.
> Few brave men help the royal court,
> But many hands give aid to usurpation.
> If Trinh Xuan had planned for certain success
> The king would not have had to regret.
> As for that son and father seeking to destroy each other:
> It is clear that Heaven's favor has abandoned the Trinh family.

The poet's voice is from the "inside," professing allegiance to the king. It condemns the Trinh as "outside" of Heaven's favor because the Trinh have usurped royal authority. This ostensibly virtuous attitude was cheap in the south, where no Le king existed to interfere, even theoretically, with the ambitions of the Nguyen Phuc family.

The terminology of the south being "inside" and the north being "outside" was eventually generalized to all Vietnamese when southerners took over the whole country at the beginning of the nineteenth century. Today, when speaking of traveling in their narrowly vertical country, Vietnamese say they are going "into the south" (*vao nam*) and "out to the north" (*ra bac*), rhetorical vestiges of the two hundred years during which Vietnamese inhabited two countries.

War begins

During the 1620s the sons of Trinh Tung and Nguyen Hoang commenced a war that continued for fifty years and ended in stalemate. The exigencies of this war led to fundamental changes in both the north and the south, with the Trinh regime expanding its base of support to include the people of the Red River plain and the Nguyen regime expanding the reach of its armies into the Mekong region to become involved in Cambodian affairs. Also, during the first half of the seventeenth century, Europeans joined Chinese and Japanese as important participants in foreign trade, and Jesuits introduced a new religion from Europe that was accepted by many thousands of Vietnamese in both the south and the north.

Trinh Trang's resolution of the succession crisis at Dong Kinh in 1623 and his relatively successful invasion of Cao Bang to subdue the Mac in 1625 produced a sense of momentum that led naturally to an invasion of the south. Trinh Trang's eagerness to extend his hand into the south was demonstrated already in 1620, after his father's failing health opened opportunities for him to exercise greater authority. In that year he conspired with two sons of Nguyen Hoang, Nguyen Hiep and Nguyen Trach, to overthrow their elder brother, Nguyen Phuc Nguyen. Trinh Trang sent one of his younger brothers with a small army of 5,000 men to the border to divert Nguyen Phuc Nguyen's attention, enabling Nguyen Hiep and Nguyen Trach to mobilize their forces. Nguyen Tuyen, a son of Nguyen Hoang's deceased eldest son, who was Nguyen Phuc Nguyen's most able commander, learned of the plot and took precautions. When the rebellious brothers fortified Ai Tu, where Nguyen Hoang had resided from 1558 to 1570, Nguyen Tuyen attacked and captured them. They died in prison, and the Trinh army returned north without battle.

Trinh Trang was married to a daughter of Nguyen Hoang named Nguyen Ngoc Tu (d. 1631). In 1623, after the succession uproar in Dong Kinh and the deaths of Trinh Xuan and Trinh Tung, she wrote a letter to her brother Nguyen Phuc Nguyen and entrusted it to Nguyen Cuu Kieu, a high official at the Le court who opposed the Trinh and was resolved to flee into the south. When he arrived in the south he told a dramatic story of being trapped at the Gianh River by pursuing Trinh soldiers, but in answer to his prayers a water buffalo appeared and carried him swimming across to the other side, allowing him to escape. Nguyen Cuu Kieu became a loyal servant of the Nguyen Phuc family, served as an able military commander, and died of battle wounds in 1656 at the age of 58. He married a daughter of Nguyen Phuc Nguyen and founded the Nguyen Cuu family, which produced talented southern generals in every generation for the next two centuries. The letter he delivered in 1623 apparently contained information about political events in the north occasioned by the death of Trinh Tung.

The news of Trinh Tung's death was cause for celebration in the south. Nguyen Phuc Nguyen ordered three cannon volleys and three shouts of joy at his court. One of those at court that day was Nguyen Huu Dat (1603–1681). He was the son of a general, well educated, and had received a court appointment while still in his teens. Already showing the irrepressible personality for which he would be known throughout his illustrious career, he reacted to the volleys and shouts by bursting out in a loud voice, "What is all this for? Why don't we take the chance to invade the north?" Nguyen Phuc Nguyen instructed the young man's father to take him aside and explain to him that it would not be right to take advantage of kinsmen in mourning.

Nguyen Phuc Nguyen realized that Trinh Trang was intent upon war. He readied his soldiers but maintained a purely defensive posture, rejecting the advice of generals who wanted to march north. He was determined to avoid any gratuitous provocation, despite Trinh Trang's rising crescendo of demands. In 1624, he sent away Trinh Trang's tax collectors with the excuse that harvests had failed for several years. In 1626, he moved his court further south, from the Ai Tu area to the modern district of Huong Dien, in the northern part of the Perfume River basin. He was 64 years old and was relying increasingly upon his younger brother Nguyen Khe (1588–1646) for attending to details. In that year, Trinh armies began to assemble on the border and Trinh envoys arrived with a royal edict demanding taxes and summoning Nguyen Phuc Nguyen to the Le court. This reportedly provoked great indignation among Nguyen Phuc Nguyen's followers, who were eager for war. He was said to have calmed them by saying that, although the Trinh sought to provoke hatred, he would not trouble himself with earning ridicule by replying in kind. He sent the northern envoys away with the message: "Do not pursue a petty feud." He did not welcome war, but neither did he shrink from it when it came.

At the beginning of 1627, Trinh envoys demanded that Nguyen Phuc Nguyen send a son to the Le court with thirty bull elephants and thirty large ocean-going ships, supposedly to bear tribute to the Ming. They also conveyed a request that the children of Nguyen Hiep and Nguyen Trach, the deceased rebels, be sent to stay with their aunt, the wife of Trinh Trang. Nguyen Phuc Nguyen understood that war was now imminent. He replied that the elephants and ships were beyond the normal tribute schedule, that all the children were busy preparing weapons to defend the border, and, implying a threat, that his family would come to pay their respects to the king in a few years, which would be soon enough.

By this time, Trinh Trang had placed the palace women and his treasury in Tay Do for safekeeping and was already moving south, King Le Duy Ky in tow, with a large fleet, while the bulk of his army marched by land. He issued a long proclamation accusing the Nguyen of rebellion and announcing his punitive expedition against them. The Jesuit Alexandre de Rhodes (1593–1660) observed the expedition as it went down the coast. He described an advance guard of two hundred ships filled with soldiers followed by twenty-four large ships bearing the headquarters staff and the royal retinue. Five hundred boats carrying provisions brought up the rear. Three hundred elephants bearing artillery accompanied the land force. De Rhodes estimated the total number of men in the expedition, both on land and on sea, at two hundred thousand. Most were probably recruits from the Red River plain with likely no more than one-quarter of the number from Thanh Hoa and Nghe An. Many men from Thanh Hoa and Nghe An would have been left at Dong Kinh to ensure security while Trinh Trang was away in the south.

This war among Vietnamese broke out in the context of Ming dynastic weakness. In the early seventeenth century, the empire to the north was steadily declining and about to collapse. Trinh Trang understood that there was no danger of a Ming threat materializing on his northern border to take advantage of his being preoccupied with war in the south. The significance of this is clear from the fact that the Trinh ceased the war as soon as the nascent Qing dynasty was firmly established later in the century.

The Trinh campaign of 1627 lasted several weeks in the spring of the year. There was heavy fighting around the mouth of the Nhat Le River both on land and on water until a southern elephant charge somewhat pushed back the northerners. Nguyen Huu Dat, the youth who had cried out for war in 1623, was in the midst of the southern effort, and he played on Trinh insecurities by forging a letter that was passed to Trinh Trang implying that members of his family were plotting against him at Dong Kinh. Trinh Trang's nerve broke, and he rushed back north with his army following after. This turned to his advantage as he learned while on the way back that Mac Kinh Khoan had led his men out of the mountains and was moving through the waters of the Red River plain with large numbers of boats, once again rallying the people of the plain still loyal to his family. Trinh Trang's sudden appearance with his army marching north out of Thanh Hoa sent Mac Kinh Khoan fleeing back to Cao Bang.

After the Trinh retreat, the governor at Qui Nhon, Tran Duc Hoa, came to congratulate Nguyen Phuc Nguyen, to whom he introduced his son-in-law Dao Duy Tu. Dao Duy Tu (1572–1634) became Nguyen Phuc Nguyen's most prominent advisor during the next few years. His ideas about defending the south from the north, both militarily and diplomatically, shaped the southern attitude toward the northern threat. He was from a Thanh Hoa family of musicians and theatrical performers but had devoted himself to study. In 1625 he went to seek his fortune in the south. Hearing of Tran Duc Hoa's reputation, he sought and obtained service in the entourage of this venerable and highly respected governor. He wrote and sang vernacular poetry, which reportedly won him the attention of Tran Duc Hoa, who gave him a daughter in marriage. Nguyen Phuc Nguyen was quick to perceive that Dao Duy Tu was a man of unusual qualities: erudite in both literary and military matters, wise, and utterly loyal to the southern cause.

Dao Duy Tu was a breath of fresh air for Nguyen Phuc Nguyen. He had come of age during the final years of fighting between the Le partisans and the Mac during the 1590s and had watched the Trinh fight their way into power from their stronghold of Thanh Hoa. He spent many years studying the dynastic histories and classical literature, but he was blocked from seeking a government career because his father was an entertainer, a profession despised by the northern scholars. When he went south, he was in some sense going home, to a place where his abilities were appreciated and to a culture of public service that valued ability over ancestry.

Dao Duy Tu was one of the first poets to write long vernacular poems in the "six-eight" (*luc-bat*) mode, which became increasingly popular thereafter and is commonly regarded as a typical Vietnamese form of poetry, easy to memorize and to recite or sing because of its complicated but regular tonal and rhyme scheme. The poem that he wrote and supposedly sang to catch the attention of Tran Duc Hoa, and which Tran Duc Hoa passed to Nguyen Phuc Nguyen by way of introducing him, was a "six-eight" work in 136 lines about the third-century general Zhuge Liang, who spent many years in study and thought before becoming the most brilliant strategist of his generation. Zhuge Liang was prominent in the battles of the "Three Kingdoms" era that followed the collapse of the Han dynasty in the third century CE. Many southerners came to regard Dao Duy Tu as a Zhuge Liang in their own time.

Dao Duy Tu is widely thought to have introduced theater into the south, and his poetry is distinctive for its musicality, its exuberant joy in nature, and the absence of the weary cyclicity, eremitism, veneration of the past, and preoccupation with poverty and disappointment that had come to characterize northern poetry. He wrote a 332-line "six-eight" poem in praise of the Nguyen rulers and can easily be considered as the first southern poet. His more immediate contribution to the south, however, lay in his analysis of how to respond to the diplomatic and military challenges from the north, for Trinh Trang was fixed on a policy of quelling the south to complete the Le dynasty restoration.

After the failure of his southern campaign and the brief reappearance of the Mac ghost, Trinh Trang was faced with the familiar problems of natural calamities, rural distress, misgovernment, and fear of treachery. There was drought and famine in 1629 and there were floods and famine in 1630 when even the capital was inundated. In 1631 there were devastating storms with destructive winds and deadly hailstones accompanied by fires and floods in the capital. Furthermore, signs and wonders accumulated from year to year. An investigation revealed that most military commanders were corrupt and habitually abused the people and that the worst of this was in Thanh Hoa, the regime's homeland. Another investigation revealed that two high ministers had been playing a profitable scheme of appointing large numbers of corrupt officials who were seizing land in their jurisdictions and oppressing the people.

Amidst these problems, Trinh Trang endeavored to identify men he could trust and who knew how to govern. He promoted those who had stood with him during the crisis of 1623, and he turned to the examination system to bring new talent into government. In the capital examination of 1628, sixteen of the eighteen passing candidates were from the Red River plain. One of them was Pham Cong Tru (1602–1675), from the eastern part of the plain that had once been the Mac stronghold. Pham Cong Tru became the foremost scholar and statesman of his generation, and under his leadership a major reform of government was implemented at mid century. This became possible because of his close personal relationship with Trinh Trang's son and heir, Trinh Tac (d. 1682).

The date of Trinh Tac's birth is unrecorded, but he was given the rank of grand duke in 1614, which is likely to have been conferred sometime between the ages of 7 and 12. In 1631, he was put in command of the southern border jurisdictions of Nghe An and Bo Chinh, an important assignment that showed he had earned his father's confidence. During the next fifty years, Trinh Tac, through many vicissitudes, implemented changes that eventually brought men from the Red River plain into the center of government and eased the generals from Thanh Hoa and Nghe An out of the arena of decision-making.

Meanwhile, after 1627, both sides prepared for the next campaign. Realizing that the south was stronger than he had expected, Trinh Trang needed time to overcome his difficulties and to assemble a larger military force. He also wanted to strengthen his argument with his brother-in-law Nguyen Phuc Nguyen. In 1629 he had a royal appointment sent to confirm Nguyen Phuc Nguyen as governor of the southern territories while at the same time summoning him to bring soldiers to help suppress the Mac in Cao Bang. His thinking was that in the unlikely event that the appointment and summons were accepted and obeyed then it would be easy to dispose of the southern leader as he came north, but if the appointment was rejected then he would be clearly justified in pursuing the war since the south would unambiguously be in a state of rebellion against the king.

When the royal appointment arrived in the south, Nguyen Phuc Nguyen heard two conflicting opinions. Men who were nervous about the accusation of rebelling against the Le dynasty advised that since the appointment was from the king there was no way it could be refused. Men who were ready to throw over the Le monarchy countered: "We have our own kingdom here. Why do we need this appointment?"

Dao Duy Tu's view was focused on practicalities. He saw that the Trinh were trying to ensnare the southerners with a royal edict and that refusing it would certainly elicit another invasion from the north, for which the south was not prepared. There had been a major mobilization of men into the military during

1628, but no definite steps for defending the northern border had yet been taken. Furthermore, a Cham invasion of Phu Yen was just then drawing attention to the southern border. Dao Duy Tu advised to pretend to accept the appointment in order to buy time for preparing border defenses and then find a way to return it. This is what Nguyen Phuc Nguyen did.

The apparent acceptance of the royal appointment elicited a northern request to forward taxes from the southern territories. Nguyen Phuc Nguyen was inclined to meet this demand, believing that the south was so small and weak compared with the north that the best way was simply to pay the north off. Dao Duy Tu disagreed, reportedly saying: "Times are changing. This land is no longer part of the royal domain. Here you are the lord. Build walls to keep the northerners out."

Dao Duy Tu and southern mobilization

Dao Duy Tu traveled throughout the Nhat Le River basin to study the terrain. The river collects water flowing from the mountains that is caught behind a large stretch of coastal sand dunes sixty kilometers long and, on average, five kilometers wide, oriented from southeast to northwest. The river flows north and enters the sea where the dunes narrow and end. Much of the basin is swampy and subject to inundation, but the northern third of it, where the mountain slopes are less than ten kilometers from the coast, comprises the historic choke point that had made this a borderland for centuries.

In 1630 and 1631, two walls were built across the northern part of the Nhat Le River basin. One wall reached the coast at the mouth of the river. It was initially known as "the wall of the teacher" (Truong Thay), in reference to Dao Duy Tu. Later generations called it the Wall of Dong Hoi, after the name of the city now located there. A second wall was roughly parallel to the first wall and around twelve kilometers further south. It was called the Wall of Truong Duc, which might be translated as "the long 'heave ho' wall," bringing to mind that virtually the entire able-bodied male population of the southern realm was mobilized to construct these walls. These walls were around six meters high with cannon mounted every twelve to twenty meters. A third line of fortifications, called the Wall of Truong Sa, or "the long sand wall," was built facing the sea along the crest of the dunes between the other two walls. An iron chain was prepared for stretching across the mouth of the Nhat Le River to block enemy ships in time of battle. Finally, the Dinh Muoi fortress was built in the middle of the rectangle formed by the walls and the mountains.

With this system of fortifications materializing, Nguyen Phuc Nguyen, taking Dao Duy Tu's advice, sent an envoy to the north bearing a chest containing treasure and a hidden compartment in which was placed the royal edict and a coded message meaning "the appointment is not accepted." Southern historians recorded a long interview that the envoy supposedly had with Trinh Trang in which he cleverly countered all the northern arguments against the south and after which he managed to get away back to the south before the secret compartment was discovered.

At this time, the death of Trinh Trang's wife, Nguyen Ngoc Tu, daughter of Nguyen Hoang and sister of Nguyen Phuc Nguyen, removed a living link between the Trinh and Nguyen Phuc families. She had been an active presence in Dong Kinh society, patronizing Buddhism and building at least one temple. The death of Nguyen Phuc Nguyen's wife occurred around the same time. She exemplified another significant family connection of that time. She was a daughter of the renowned Mac prince and general Mac Kinh Dien. After the death of her father in 1580, she had been taken as a child to the south by an uncle, Mac Canh Huong. She was an aunt of Mac Kinh Khoan, who in the 1620s and 1630s led the Mac family and who, after his brief submission to the Le court in 1625, continued to harass Trinh Trang from his stronghold in Cao Bang.

Mac Canh Huong's service in the entourage of Nguyen Hoang from the 1580s on suggests the complexity of Nguyen Hoang's political calculations. Nguyen Hoang was an enemy of the Mac in his commitment to restore the Le dynasty, but he was an ally of the Mac against the ascendance of the Trinh. A son of Mac Canh Huong was married to a daughter of Nguyen Phuc Nguyen and had been adopted into the Nguyen Phuc lineage with the name Nguyen Phuc Vinh. He was a good general and led the army that successfully expelled the Cham invaders from Phu Yen in 1629. The Mac remained a worrisome but increasingly minor threat to the Trinh until the 1660s, capable of distracting raids whenever Trinh armies marched south. However, if some kind of implicit anti-Trinh alliance existed between the Mac and the Nguyen Phuc, conditions were never sufficiently favorable to enable it to materialize.

During the course of constructing the walls, Dao Duy Tu met a young military officer who so impressed him that he made him his son-in-law and introduced him to Nguyen Phuc Nguyen. This young man, Nguyen Huu Tien (1601–1666), was given an important command and became known for training his men to a remarkably high level of skill and discipline. He became one of the two southern generals to especially gain fame in the battles of the next thirty years. The other general was Nguyen Huu Dat, the young man who had called for war in 1623 and had participated in the battles of 1627.

The emplacement of so many cannons on the Nhat Le walls as well as the arming of ships with cannons required a large and reliable supply of artillery. In 1627, a Portuguese named Manuel Tavares Bocarro had established a gun foundry in Macau that for the next half-century produced cannons sold in many parts of Asia. Nguyen Phuc Nguyen purchased Bocarro cannons, but he needed more. In 1631, using methods learned from the Portuguese, a foundry for making guns and cannons was constructed near the walls, and the people of two villages were assigned to acquire the skills necessary for working there. One administrator, thirteen supervisors, and eighty-six workers were assigned to work at the foundry.

In 1632, Dao Duy Tu supervised a reform of procedures for mobilizing human and material resources that was ostensibly based on the late fifteenth-century model of King Le Tu Thanh, who had scheduled census registrations for taxation and conscription at six-year intervals and literary exams at three-year intervals. Population registers were to be kept up to date to facilitate a major military conscription every six years and a smaller mobilization during the intermediate third years. The country was organized into ten mobilization districts. Five of these were in Thuan Hoa, two were in modern Quang Nam, one in Quang Ngai, one in Binh Dinh, and one in Phu Yen. This may indicate the relative size of populations in these regions, but it surely indicates that the Thuan Hoa population was more militarized than those of areas further south. Three of the five districts in Thuan Hoa were in modern Quang Binh Province, namely the Nhat Le River basin and the territory north to the border. From this it is clear that the strategic border region was heavily populated with military settlements and may have provided around three-tenths of all conscripts.

Each district had a designated assembly point, and, during the years of major mobilizations, men with education could report to these places to take a one-day, two-part literary examination to measure ability in writing poetry and prose. Local magistrates gave a preliminary evaluation of these exams and judges in the Office of Commissioners decided the final results. The best candidates were exempted for five years (until the next large mobilization) from the head tax to allow them to continue their studies and to seek recommendations for government service. There was also an examination simply on ability to write classical characters, and from those who took this exam men were chosen to work as clerks in the "three offices." If there were still vacancies to be filled in the "three offices," they could be filled with men who contributed certain amounts of cash or rice and who presumably were in a position to assist in securing provisions for the military.

While some form of field tax was implemented to collect rice, this appears to have been done according to a relatively flexible method for supplying military units handled by the Offices of the Guard and of the Garrisons, for no specific information about this survives. It is probable that some rice was obtained by purchase rather than outright taxation. The main form of taxation was based upon the regularly updated population registers and was a head tax in cash levied on all male inhabitants. The head tax was based on the eight categories in which people were registered: active-duty soldiers, reserve soldiers, civilians, elderly (over 50 years old), disabled, mercenaries, indigent, and deserters. The tax rates were variable depending upon whether one was registered in Thuan Hoa or in the jurisdictions further south and whether one was classified as "primary," meaning a full citizen, or as a "guest," which apparently meant a relatively new settler who was still in the process of establishing a new life.

In general the head tax for "guests" was around one-half to two-thirds the amount levied on "primary" taxpayers. There was no tax on indigent or deserting "guests," probably indicating that such people did not exist in any significant number if at all. It is a mystery how the tax levy recorded for deserters was enforced, unless it was treated as a payment allowing one to be registered out of that category. The rates for "guests" were a bit lower in Thuan Hoa than in the southern regions, perhaps indicating that refugees and settlers arriving from the north were encouraged to settle there. The rates for "primary" taxpayers show minor variations for the two jurisdictions, except for mercenaries who in the southern regions were taxed significantly higher than in Thuan Hoa and who, while constituting only one category in Thuan Hoa, were separated into three categories with different rates further south. This may indicate that "mercenaries" were more numerous in the south where military units were organized comprised of Chams, uplanders, and eventually Khmers and Chinese. Soldiers, both active duty and reserve, had the highest tax rates, indicating that, far from being a fiscal liability, military men and their families were integrated into the productive economy. The level of discriminating detail displayed in the head tax schedule suggests that the authorities were concerned to ensure that the rates were an appropriate and workable compromise between the government's desire to maximize revenue and the taxpayer's ability to pay.

Within a few years, Dao Duy Tu's initiatives had affected nearly every aspect of Nguyen Phuc Nguyen's government. He also successfully discouraged policies of which he did not approve. For example, in 1632, Nguyen Phuc Nguyen wanted to establish government monopolies for luxury goods such as pepper, bird nests, and other southern exotica. Such monopolies were standard in the north. Dao Duy Tu, however, felt that this would distract government with unnecessary opportunities for corruption and would stifle commerce that could more profitably be taxed. He made his point by appearing in court dressed as a merchant. Nguyen Phuc Nguyen reportedly understood his point and abandoned the idea.

In just a few years, Dao Duy Tu's leadership had reorganized southern military and fiscal operations to channel human and material resources into a system of fortifications that protected the Nguyen Phuc realm from northern attacks during the remainder of the war. His unusual combination of abilities, unable to be exercised in the intellectually and socially constrained north, were appreciated and utilized in the south.

Trinh mobilization

In 1632, Nguyen Phuc Nguyen's eldest son and heir, Nguyen Phuc Ky, who had been governing the southern territories from Dien Ban in Quang Nam since 1614, died. Nguyen Phuc Nguyen, now 70 years old, immediately designated his second son, Nguyen Phuc Lan, as his heir, keeping him at his side while sending his third son, Nguyen Anh (d. 1635), to replace Nguyen Phuc Ky at Dien Ban. Nguyen Anh coveted the family inheritance and began to plot with Trinh Trang to coordinate an attempt to seize power with a northern invasion.

To facilitate his conspiracy, Nguyen Anh wanted to obtain command of the border region. He won over to his side the ranking civil official there and, by spreading false rumors, succeeded in having the prince in charge of the border dismissed and having himself named to replace him. But he was off on an extended hunting expedition when his father wanted to confer with him about his new appointment. This demonstration of disrespect and indiscipline so angered Nguyen Phuc Nguyen that he appointed another prince to the northern border instead. Despite this setback, Nguyen Anh continued his plans, evaluating the new commander on the border as likely to be timid in battle, which he imagined would offer an opportunity for his plans to prevail.

In late 1633, after twice sending out officials to examine the performance and loyalty of local administrators and, when necessary, appointing new men whom he trusted, Trinh Trang led his armies south and, for the first time, saw the walls. He hesitated to attack until his supposed ally, Nguyen Anh, showed his hand. However, the southern forces were vigilant and Nguyen Anh had no opportunity to implement his plot. Trinh Trang fired his cannons giving the prearranged signal to Nguyen Anh, but there was no response. In early 1634, as Trinh Trang paused in indecision, Nguyen Huu Dat led a southern attack that sent the Trinh army fleeing back north.

Both countries were absorbed in their internal affairs for several years after this. In 1634, Trinh Trang was 58 years old. He increasingly relied upon his son Trinh Tac, already around 40 years old. Both men were concerned to cultivate the loyalty of people in the Red River plain where most of the human and material resources of their realm were located. They aimed to do this by bringing literati families who had served the Mac into the government and following their ideas about how to govern. These families had been squeezed into poverty after the Le restoration but had maintained a tradition of learning and were respected by local people.

One such family was the Vu lineage, which traced its ancestry back to a ninth-century Tang governor who had settled near the modern city of Hai Duong. Five brothers in this family, great grandsons of a man who had risen to high position at the Mac court in the sixteenth century, enjoyed public careers and prospered under the patronage of Trinh Tac. One of the brothers, Vu Duy Chi, became Trinh Tac's closest friend and confidant. Pham Cong Tru, the scholar-official mentioned above as a close associate of Trinh Tac and the leading literatus of his generation, came from the same area as the Vu in the eastern plain, as did many other literati who rose to eminence in the mid seventeenth century.

Trinh Tung had been chiefly concerned with military matters and gave little attention to the examination system. During his time, relatively few candidates were selected at the triennial capital exam, only enough to staff the royal court and to attend to diplomatic relations with Ming. During the eleven examinations during the thirty years from the Le restoration in 1592 until the death of Trinh Tung in 1623, sixty-eight men had graduated.

During the next eleven examinations, held during the time Trinh Trang was in power, there were 150 graduates. Six of these eleven exams were held during times of war, when an average of only eight men were graduated in each exam. During the five exams held in years of peace, an average of twenty-one men were graduated in each exam.

The six exams held during the celebrated Vinh Tho and Canh Tri reign periods (1658–1671), which marked the ascendance of men from the Red River plain and the apogee of Trinh Tac's rule, saw 104 men selected, despite one of these exams, in 1667, yielding only three graduates during a time of intense conflict among officials.

The Trinh had two constituencies during these years. One was the generals and their associates from Thanh Hoa and Nghe An who were determined to pursue the war against the south. Victory in the south would offer them prospects for enrichment in a conquered land. The other constituency was the literati officials and their allies in the Red River plain. They were in a position to mobilize the men and wealth of their region that was necessary to continue the war, thereby earning a place for themselves in Trinh government. Yet, they saw no long-term benefit for themselves in continuing a war that nurtured the prerogatives and aspirations of the Thanh Hoa and Nghe An warriors. While the warriors saw the restoration of the Le dynasty as a purely military matter of subordinating separatists, the literati understood the restoration as a process of rebuilding the kind of government that had been established by King Le Tu Thanh in the late fifteenth century. This was not simply a regional contest. Each constituency had allies in the other camp, and Trinh Tac spent most of his life balancing the interests of the two groups while leaning his weight toward the literati at critical times.

After the expedition to the south in 1633–1634 ended in fiasco, the Trinh were confronted with the familiar problems of drought and famine. In 1638 another effort to subdue the Mac in Cao Bang ended in defeat. It was nearly a decade before the Trinh were in a position to attempt a new attack on the south. Meanwhile, as a signal to men in the Red River plain that their loyalty to the regime would be rewarded, a 79-year-old man, Nguyen Thuc (1555–1637), from the vicinity of Dong Kinh, who had graduated in the exam of 1595 and had served the regime faithfully for decades, was in 1634 honored as an "elder of the country," and when he died three years later he was given an especially high posthumous title. The examinations in 1637 and 1640 together selected forty-two men, many of whom would play prominent roles in reorienting the government during the next three decades.

The direction of this reorientation is apparent from edicts promulgated at this time. In 1635 a proclamation of twelve articles was aimed at corruption in the judiciary. In 1639, an edict restored a 1503 law forbidding excessive confiscation of property as compensation in litigation. This law specified that compensation could be taken only from property belonging to the person at fault along with his wife and children. If this was not enough, the law could obtain additional compensation from the person's parents and siblings, but the whole family lineage or the entire village could not be held responsible for compensation. This edict reveals a kind of judicial abuse, against which it was aimed, that had apparently become prevalent, and it also shows a vision of returning to the model of relatively benevolent government that had been envisioned by Le Tu Thanh. Also in 1639, another proclamation of twelve articles was published urging officials to follow the law, to serve dutifully, and to win the affection of the people. What in 1618 had been ineffectual cries for justice by comet watchers was now embedded in official government policy.

In 1642, Trinh Trang sent four of his sons to the four major administrative jurisdictions of the Red River plain to wipe out bandits and to adjudicate accumulated litigation. Assigned to each prince was a literati-official. The team sent to the southern part of the plain containing the strategic routes linking Dong Kinh with Thanh Hoa was Trinh Tac and Pham Cong Tru. This exercise in bringing order and justice to the Red River plain was apparently intended to stabilize administration while mobilizing men and material for a new expedition into the south, which was scheduled for the following year.

Although the participation of literati in government was being encouraged and the examination system was becoming a focus of access to public careers, the general level of learning and erudition had greatly deteriorated since the Le restoration in 1592. The Mac had maintained an educational level comparable to what had been achieved under Le Tu Thanh, but the Trinh, preoccupied with war and with their entourage of warlords, gave no particular attention to learning and simply made passive use of the examination system as a source of the few men needed to draft edicts and maintain relations with the Ming. Some of these men made themselves useful in other ways, for example by actively assisting Trinh Trang in the succession struggle, although others of them were penalized for having been too close to King Le Duy Tan or to Trinh Xuan.

There are many anecdotes recorded in the eighteenth century about the low level of learning in the seventeenth century and of how this was demonstrated during capital examinations. Discipline was not enforced in the examination yard so that candidates consulted among themselves about how to respond to questions, resulting in many identical answers. Those thought to be most erudite among the candidates took the lead in composing answers that were copied by others but were sometimes ludicrous with error. The examining officials often failed to recognize mistakes and passed exams based on trivial or random considerations.

A famous example of the low level of learning at this time was the story of Nguyen Minh Triet (1578–1672), from Chi Linh in the Red River plain, who spent decades in study and took the exam of 1631 at the age of 53. His exam was so erudite that none of the examiners could read it. Finally, it was discovered that a woman known as Le Phi, who had once passed a Mac examination in Cao Bang disguised as a man and was subsequently captured during the Trinh attack on Cao Bang in 1625, was able to read the exam. She was employed as a teacher of the palace women.

One of the palace women who may have benefited from Le Phi's learning was a daughter of Trinh Trang named Trinh Thi Ngoc Truc. She had been married to an uncle of King Le Duy Ky, but in 1630 her father imprisoned her husband so that she could be made Le Duy Ky's queen. The king, whose mother had been a daughter of Trinh Tung, was 23 years old at that time. King Le Duy Ky was known as a well-educated and intelligent man with a great devotion to Buddhism, a particular dislike of being king, and a lack of discipline over the kinds of people he allowed into his palace. In 1643, he was able to escape his royal tasks when allowed to raise his 14-year-old son Le Duy Huu to the throne. He is known to have traveled extensively to visit Buddhist temples. But his son died in 1649, and he was forced to return to the palace and to be king once again.

Queen Trinh Thi Ngoc Truc and the palace instructress Le Phi were both fervent Buddhists. Both took nun's vows in their later years, and in the 1640s Trinh Thi Ngoc Truc endowed fields and money to rebuild the But Thap Temple, several kilometers east of Dong Kinh. These women may also have been concerned about the problems of education in their time. A Han–Nom (Literary Chinese–vernacular Vietnamese) dictionary entitled *Chi Nam Ngoc Am* (Explanation of the South's Pearly Sounds) was published at a Buddhist temple in Dong Kinh, possibly in 1641. Some evidence encourages the conjecture that it was compiled under the supervision or patronage of Trinh Thi Ngoc Truc. According to the prefaces to the dictionary, it was prepared as an aid for students to master the literary language in order to pass the examinations. It was written in "six-eight" prosody making it easy to memorize. Furthermore, it paired Han literary expressions with vernacular equivalents that were mostly written in forms of Nom based on single Han characters used for their pronunciation rather than in the more common compound forms of Nom that combined elements of two Han characters to indicate meaning as well as pronunciation.

This dictionary reveals that Nom was used as a pedagogical tool for mastering Han. The prefaces argue that complex Nom characters were too difficult for students to learn, since their semantic elements already required mastery of Han in order to be understood. The dictionary was meant to address the pedagogical problem of how to provide students with an accessible form of Nom that could be used as a step into Han. The compiler expects resistance to more simplified forms of Nom and admonishes readers not to laugh at them, for using them will assist students to be successful. The arguments in the prefaces of this dictionary imply a solution to an apparent pedagogical crisis. Nom writing, which according to some traditional thinking was simply a means of amusement for retired scholars, was being reformed to be a more effective aid for teaching Han. This apparently lies behind the temporary shift toward simpler forms that Nom scholars have perceived in seventeenth-century texts. It was a response to the decline of education after the Mac had been expelled from Dong Kinh.

In the 1630s, both the Nguyen Phuc and the Trinh adjusted their policies of domestic governance to more efficiently mobilize their populations for war. Southerners organized to defend their northern border. In the north, people from the Red River plain were brought into the government and used to establish a regime of civil administration capable of mobilizing men and rice, while the warrior clans of Thanh Hoa and Nghe An were diverted from their occupation of the old Mac kingdom to focus on overrunning the separatists in the south.

Christianity

In 1651, Alexandre de Rhodes, already mentioned in connection with Trinh Trang's 1627 expedition against the south, published a Vietnamese–Portuguese–Latin dictionary in Rome. It is the first dictionary to use a Romanized transcription of the Vietnamese language. Because of this, Alexandre de Rhodes is commonly thought to have invented the Vietnamese alphabet, but in fact it was initially devised by Portuguese and subsequently adopted by the Jesuits as an aid for language learning. Alexandre de Rhodes, from Avignon in France, was one of the early Jesuit missionaries to work among the Vietnamese. After spending a year and a half in the south for language study, in 1627 he entered the north, where he remained for three years before being expelled. After spending a decade in Macau, he returned to the south for five years (1640–1645) and then departed, arriving in Rome in 1649.

Alexandre de Rhodes introduced knowledge of northern Vietnam to Europeans with his 1651 account of the "Kingdom of Tonkin," published in Italian in 1650, in French in 1651, and in Latin in 1652. Accounts of the north by other Jesuits followed shortly. Joseph Tissanier (1618–1688), who resided in the north during the years 1658–1663, published an account in French in 1663. In the same year, Giovanni Filippo de Marini (1608–1677), who served in the north during 1647–1658, published an account in Italian, of which a translation into French was published in 1666. An account of the south by Christoforo Borri (1583–1632), who lived in Binh Dinh Province from 1618 to 1622, was published in Italian in 1631 and within two years had been translated into Latin, French, English, Dutch, and German. Alexandre de Rhodes wrote an account of the mission in the south published in French in 1652. Behind these accounts were the experiences of dozens of Jesuits who lived in the two Vietnamese realms during the first half of the seventeenth century.

The beginning of Christianity among Vietnamese is commonly associated with the missionaries who wrote accounts in European languages, and especially with Alexandre de Rhodes because of his dictionary and also because of his Latin–Vietnamese catechism published at Rome in 1658. However, the man who probably had the greatest long-term impact on early Vietnamese Christianity has not been much remembered outside of Vietnam. Geronimo Maiorica (1589–1656), originally from Naples, spent four years, 1619–1623, in Goa before proceeding to Macau. After a brief time in Makassar in 1624, he arrived in southern Vietnam about the same time as Alexandre de Rhodes and spent four years in language study before returning to Macau in 1628–1630. After a failed attempt to establish a mission in Champa, he went to Dong Kinh in 1631. In 1632 he went to Nghe An and spent the next eighteen years in the area of the modern city of Vinh, relatively distant from Dong Kinh and the vicissitudes of court politics. There he nurtured one of the most successful of the early Christian missions, which by 1634 numbered twenty-six churches and over 4,000 Christians. By 1647, he reported fifty-three churches with Christians from over seventy villages. When he departed Nghe An in 1650, he estimated that there were approximately 40,000 Christians in the province. From Nghe An he went to Dong Kinh, where he resided until his death, serving as head of the mission in the north. The Christian community that he served in Nghe An has remained to this day.

A common misperception created by Alexandre de Rhodes' dictionary is that Christian missionaries used alphabetic writing in their proselytizing work. The alphabet was used by the Jesuits to study Vietnamese and by Vietnamese catechists to study Latin, and also both Europeans and Vietnamese wrote some alphabetic works for the education of new missionaries or for personal reasons. However, the writings for use in the daily life of the Christian communities were in Nom, and Geronimo Maiorica, during his years in Nghe An, produced a large literature in Nom about saints' lives, the sacraments, biblical stories about Jesus, practical morality, liturgical aids to worship, and devotional exercises. These have been used through generations of Vietnamese Christians into contemporary times.

The use of Nom by Christians is one aspect of the development of Nom in the seventeenth and eighteenth centuries that has received little attention by modern scholars. But, during the last quarter of the twentieth century, dictionaries compiled by Christians, Vu Van Kinh and Father Tran Van Kiem, have pioneered the development of modern Nom studies. These scholars included texts attributed to Maiorica among the source materials for their dictionaries.

The relative success of Christian proselytizing among Vietnamese, with a Jesuit estimate of 250,000 Christians in the north alone by 1655, was part of a more general religious ferment at this time, which was also expressed in the flourishing of Buddhism, Daoism, and spirit cults. Buddhists published many Nom texts at temples in the seventeenth and eighteenth centuries containing stories about Buddhas and bodhisattvas, translations of sutras, and instructions for performing rituals. King Le Duy Ky and the royal family patronized Buddhist temples, large numbers of which were built, rebuilt, or repaired in the seventeenth century. This was also the time when spirit pantheons appeared or were elaborated with hierarchies of spirits to be called on by mediums during séances. In response, a Buddhist sect known as the "School of the Inner Religion" specialized in subordinating popular spirits to the Buddha's authority. Daoists likewise wrote texts claiming popular spirits for their tradition. The pantheon of the "holy mothers" appeared contemporaneous with veneration of Mary the "holy mother" of Jesus by Christians. It was a time of lively religious activity that was either stimulated by the appearance of Christianity or, at least, in which Christians participated.

One the Jesuits' assets that recommended them to Vietnamese rulers was the mathematical and astronomical learning that some of them possessed and that enabled them to predict eclipses and to keep calendars more accurately than local specialists. Foreknowledge of eclipses and an accurate keeping of calendars were an important demonstration of a ruler's competence to govern, and European ability in this area of expertise was appreciated. In 1627, Trinh Trang was especially pleased with the gift of a clock from Alexandre de Rhodes. Jesuits also gained favor because of their medical knowledge and were often summoned by rulers to attend to the sick in their palaces.

European missionaries and Vietnamese Christians suffered periodic episodes of persecution led by local authorities or leaders of other religious traditions. Nevertheless, they mostly enjoyed the forbearance, if not the favor, of rulers during these years because they were viewed as a means of eliciting the assistance of European powers in the continuing struggle between north and south. In the south, relations with the Portuguese and Macau were firmly established by the time war broke out in the 1620s. Southerners quickly mastered Portuguese expertise in gunnery, both in manufacture and in use, including the skill of firing cannon on ships at sea. The Trinh turned to the enemy of the Portuguese, the Dutch.

Maritime trade

While Western accounts feature the activities of European merchants in the two Vietnamese countries during the seventeenth century, Chinese, and for a time Japanese, merchants were more important in the overall economy of foreign trade for both the north and the south. Europeans joined a system of maritime trade that had its own Asian tempo. In the early seventeenth century, a peaceful Japan, recently unified under the Tokugawa Shogunate, drove this tempo with a surging market for silk and large amounts of copper coins and silver specie to pay for the silk.

At the same time, Ming China, the main source of silk, was not only in decline but had prohibited trade with Japan. Consequently, Chinese and Japanese merchants gathered in Vietnamese ports where Chinese silk was exchanged for precious metals from Japan. As the Manchu conquest disordered China and the availability of Chinese silk fell, Vietnamese silk began to enter the market and became an increasingly large part of the trade. Large profits could be made, and the Portuguese and Dutch endeavored to join this trade. For their part, Vietnamese rulers in wartime valued trade with Europeans as a means of gaining access to European-style cannons and muskets, which were superior to the weapons previously available from Chinese manufacturers.

Northern and southern Vietnamese policies toward foreign merchants were very different. In the north, foreign trade was primarily a government monopoly, so merchants had to deal with an array of mandarins and eunuchs who imposed duties, fees, and bribes for their own enrichment as well as that of their lords. Furthermore, unlike Hoi An, which was near the sea at a place where sea-going ships could anchor and which was allowed to prosper without excessive government intervention, doing business in the north meant getting to Dong Kinh, where the governing authorities were located, and this in itself was a complicated task.

Ships could not ascend the main branches of the Red River because the currents flowed too fast. Rather, they entered the plain at the Thai Binh estuary and anchored in the Thai Binh River at a place in modern Tien Lang district. From here, merchandise was transferred to river boats and taken upriver. At the junction of the Thai Binh and Red Rivers lay Pho Hien, the modern town of Hung Yen. Here a customs station controlled all traffic passing upriver. Many foreign merchants resided and maintained warehouses at Pho Hien, going to Dong Kinh only to transact business. The community of Chinese merchants was particularly large at Pho Hien, where they even built temples. Europeans also maintained residences here, for obtaining permission to reside permanently at Dong Kinh was a special mark of favor by the Trinh authorities. Consequently, in order to even arrive at the place of business in Dong Kinh, foreign merchants had to run the gauntlet of two groups of predatory officials, one at the Thai Binh estuary and one at Pho Hien. And once in Dong Kinh, one still had to be ready with gifts for the highest authorities before actual business could be conducted. The Trinh authorities were in general disdainful of merchants. This may have been partly due to a Confucian prejudice against the merchant class, but it was more fundamentally due to a vigilant and avaricious Trinh policy of preventing any class of people from accumulating wealth. Foreign merchants submitted to the difficulties of doing business in the north in the seventeenth century only because the profits to be gained from selling Vietnamese silk in Japan were so high.

The southern rulers were more dependent upon and eager for foreign trade than were the Trinh. The port of Hoi An was more accessible to maritime routes than was the north, it offered a greater array of merchandise, it was basically a free port without duties, and it was governed with a sense of order based on market principles. Nguyen Hoang actively solicited foreign merchants. For example, during the first decade of the seventeenth century he repeatedly sent letters to the ruler of Japan to encourage Japanese investment in trade with his country. He even formally adopted a Japanese envoy to give his contact with the Japanese ruler the aura of a family relationship.

At that time, the Tokugawa Shogunate was seeking to sort out pirates from merchants by issuing "red seal" documents to ship masters who would then benefit from the protection of official recognition. The "red seal" trade was most active during the rule of Nguyen Phuc Nguyen (1613–1635). In 1635, it was discontinued and, thereafter, Chinese and European merchants handled most of the trade with Japan. During the time of Nguyen Phuc Nguyen, over 32 percent of all "red seal" ships registered for Southeast Asian ports went to Hoi An, sixty out of a total of 185 ships. By comparison, only twenty-eight went to northern Vietnam, thirty-one to Siam, thirty-one to the Philippines, twenty-four to Cambodia, and one to Champa. Trade with Hoi An amounted to around one-fourth of all Japanese foreign trade in these years.

While he did not attempt to monopolize trade, Nguyen Phuc Nguyen nevertheless participated in it, even marrying one of his daughters to a Japanese merchant. Major exports from Hoi An to Japan were silk, sugar, pepper, rattan, calambac, deerskins, and precious wood. Imports were ceramics, utensils, swords, armor, silver, and copper. Much of the copper was in the form of old coins no longer officially accepted in Japan, which arrived in large quantities during the 1620s and 1630s. Copper coins from Japan were an especially important item of trade at that time. Those of inferior quality were melted down to make cannon while the rest entered the cash economy. Behind the "red seal" ships, Chinese and European merchants also participated in the trade between Japan and Hoi An. When the "red seal" system was abandoned in 1635 and Japanese ships could no longer officially participate in the silk trade, the Portuguese and Dutch were quick to pick up the slack.

Large Chinese and Japanese communities developed at Hoi An and built up the culture of the port with Buddhist temples and Christian churches. The early Jesuit missionaries, who first entered the Vietnamese-speaking world at Hoi An in the 1610s, were assisted by Japanese Christians who arrived to escape persecution in Japan or who had become part of the Jesuit organization based at Macau. Ten kilometers upriver from Hoi An lay Dien Ban, the Nguyen Phuc headquarters for governing their southern territories and for overseeing foreign trade. The Hoi An/ Dien Ban area and the region of Qui Nhon, the second most important seaport on the southern coast, were the first places for Jesuits to reside, learn Vietnamese, and begin to proselytize.

The Hoi An market was part of a relatively monetized economy by Asian standards at that time. The significance of money in the southern economy is reflected in the tax policy, which relied upon the head tax in cash rather than upon the collection of rice, which was the main form of taxation in the north. Unlike in the north, where foreign trade mainly benefited high-ranking officials and their clients, commerce was an important part of southern life and many people of all classes profited from it. The regime benefited from this both by participating in it and by encouraging ordinary people to do so, not by taxing commerce per se but by insisting that taxpayers produce cash.

One reason that a tax on rice was not an important source of tax revenue in the south was that not very much rice was grown there. Much land was planted with mulberry trees and sugar cane to supply silk and sugar for the Hoi An market. Rice was imported from Cambodia to meet local needs. When the Cambodian king forbade the export of rice in 1637 because of a poor harvest, a serious famine resulted in Thuan Hoa, forcing the government to distribute rice from its storehouses. According to annalists, only Thuan Hoa was affected by this, probably indicating the large military population there.

The port of Hoi An was a point of concentration for goods from the mountains, the coasts, the sea, and from islands and coasts across the sea. While in the north foreign trade affected a relatively small part of the population, in the south many local economies, and also economies beyond the Nguyen Phuc domain, were mobilized to support the market demand at Hoi An. The wealth generated by this was critically important to the Nguyen Phuc, for it enabled them to buy modern weapons needed to defend the northern border, particularly cannon, muskets, and gunpowder. The Portuguese were prime suppliers of these items and enjoyed a special relationship with the Nguyen government in the south from its beginning.

When, early in the century, the Dutch sailed into Asian waters and attempted to trade at Hoi An, Portuguese envoys from Macau demanded of local authorities that they be excluded. The southern Vietnamese rulers were sufficiently solicitous of good relations with the Portuguese that they complied, though the exclusion was not always strictly enforced if the Portuguese happened not to be noticing. The Dutch and Portuguese were in a state of war during the first half of the seventeenth century.

Since 1568, the Dutch had been at war with Spain in a struggle that, after eighty years, eventually led to recognition of Dutch independence in 1648. From 1580 to 1640, Portugal was united with Spain under the Spanish Bourbon monarchy and thus was an enemy of the Dutch. Furthermore, the initial Dutch goal in going to Asia was to monopolize the Moluccan Spice Islands, which at the beginning of the seventeenth century were held by the Portuguese. The Dutch seized the Portuguese fort at Ambon in the Spice Islands in 1605. It was there that in 1623 they executed ten Englishmen along with one Portuguese and nine Japanese, the so-called Amboina Massacre that poisoned Dutch–English relations for decades but achieved for the Dutch a long-lasting dominance of the Spice Island trade. In addition to these factors was that the Dutch were Protestant Christians who, in the ongoing wars of Reformation versus Counter-Reformation in Europe, were enemies of the Catholic Iberians. Consequently, the Dutch in Asia attacked the Spanish and Portuguese at every opportunity.

The Portuguese and Spanish had pioneered European trade with Japan, but in 1600 a Dutch ship sent to attack the Portuguese and Spanish in Asia arrived in Japan and thereafter the Dutch became increasingly important participants in the Japanese trade, establishing a trading station in 1609 and breaking the Iberian monopoly on European trade with Japan. In 1619, the Dutch established their Asian headquarters at Batavia, modern Jakarta, on the island of Java, located to keep a firm grip on the Spice Islands and to take advantage of the westerly winds along the direct route across the Indian Ocean from the southern tip of Africa to the Sunda Strait separating the islands of Java and Sumatra, thereby avoiding the Portuguese bases at Goa and Malacca. This route was called the "roaring forties" because of the strong westerly winds that blew along forty degrees latitude. From 1624 to 1662, the Dutch maintained a strong presence on the island of Formosa. They frequently attacked the Portuguese at Macau and at Malacca. In 1641, they finally seized Malacca.

Considering that an amicable and satisfactory relationship had already existed between the Portuguese and the southern Vietnamese rulers before the appearance of the Dutch, it is not surprising that the Vietnamese absorbed from the Portuguese a certain suspicion and wariness toward the Dutch. The Portuguese at Hoi An did all they could to prejudice the southern Vietnamese rulers against the Dutch. For their part, the Dutch perceived with distaste the close relationship between their Iberian enemy and the southern Vietnamese authorities and were inclined toward a jaundiced view of the southern realm. The first Dutch attempt to do business at Hoi An was in the context of potential enmity.

Dutch sailors had already been killed along the southern Vietnamese coast when in 1601 Dutch merchants arrived at Hoi An to negotiate an agreement to open trading relations. A rumor that they were about to be ambushed provoked the nervous Dutchmen to flee, plundering and burning a village on their way out to sea. A second attempt to open trade relations in 1613 also ended in failure with a Dutch merchant being killed. During the next two decades, ships sent by the Dutch to Hoi An never arrived, either because of the distraction of attacking Portuguese shipping or because the crews refused to go there, fearful about their safety.

In 1632, a Portuguese ship that had been seized by the Dutch drifted ashore near Hoi An. Nguyen Phuc Nguyen sent the Dutch survivors to Batavia on a Chinese ship with an invitation to trade at Hoi An. However, during the next two years, Dutch efforts to trade at Hoi An were thwarted by Portuguese and Japanese competition, and the salvageable goods from three Dutch ships wrecked on the southern Vietnamese coast were confiscated. Dutch demands for compensation were refused by the Vietnamese authorities, and Dutch expectations of benefiting from the end of "red seal" shipping in 1635 were dashed by the decision of the Japanese merchant community in Hoi An to do business with the Chinese rather than with them. Subsequently, the Dutch abandoned further attempts to do business at Hoi An, deciding to go to the north instead.

Understanding the close relationship between the Portuguese and the southerners and the enmity between the Portuguese and the Dutch, Trinh Trang warmly welcomed the Dutch when they first arrived at Dong Kinh in 1637. He permitted the Dutch to reside at the capital and lost no time in initiating discussions to elicit Dutch naval participation in his next expedition against the south. A group of Dutchmen thereafter resided at Dong Kinh. Some of them took Vietnamese wives whose local knowledge enabled them to profit from fluctuations in the supply of silk. During their first few years at Dong Kinh, the Dutch enjoyed the fruits of Trinh Trang's benevolence, inspired by an expectation of Dutch military assistance against the south. The Dutch were spared the worst of extortionate practices and happily found that the price of silk in the north was around half the price in the south, where it was not so plentiful, allowing them to make huge profits in Japan.

Hendrik Baron was among the early employees of the Dutch East Indies Company assigned to reside at Dong Kinh. He learned Vietnamese and continued to work at Dong Kinh until his death in 1664. His son, Samuel Baron, born of a Vietnamese mother, grew up in Dong Kinh but was sent to Europe in 1659. In the 1670s Samuel Baron returned to Asia with the English East India Company and subsequently spent several years trading at Dong Kinh. In 1685 he wrote "A Description of the Kingdom of Tonkin" that was eventually published in 1732 at London. Baron's account, reflecting conditions in the late 1670s and early 1680s, after the end of the Trinh–Nguyen wars, portrays the Trinh government as viewing foreign merchants primarily as targets for extortion. The difficulties in doing business that he describes led to the departure of all European commercial enterprises from the north by the end of the century. The era of European trade with the north was an aspect of the Trinh search for arms and allies in wartime.

New leaders in an old war

After the Trinh army withdrew north in early 1634, there was a change of leadership in the south. Dao Duy Tu died later that year, and Nguyen Phuc Nguyen died a year after that. His son, Nguyen Phuc Lan, was 35 years old when he came to power in 1635. He was assisted by an uncle, Nguyen Khe, by a cousin, Nguyen Tuyen, and by his full brother, Nguyen An, all capable and loyal men. When Nguyen Anh, the royal brother whose schemes had failed to benefit from the Trinh invasion of 1633, openly rebelled, he was captured and killed after a battle that left many dead. Nguyen Phuc Lan moved the site of his government a bit further south, into what today is the northern fringe of the modern city of Hue.

Nguyen Phuc Lan viewed the northern border with relative complacency, and events in 1640 tended to confirm this attitude. Nguyen Khac Liet, the Trinh commander in charge of Northern Bo Chinh, on the northern bank of the Gianh River, which served as the border between the two realms, was apparently overly excited by his position on the border and, some years before, had begun to play a traitor's game by secretly pledging allegiance to Nguyen Phuc Lan. However, his arrogant behavior subsequently lost him the trust of both Trinh Trang and Nguyen Phuc Lan. When his activities began to stir unrest in Southern Bo Chinh, on the southern bank of the Gianh River, Nguyen Phuc Lan consulted with his generals. Following the advice of Nguyen Huu Dat, a letter was sent to Trinh Trang reporting Nguyen Khac Liet's treachery and pretending that his offer to serve Nguyen Phuc Lan had been refused. The idea was that if Trinh Trang sent a force to arrest Nguyen Khac Liet, the Nguyen would call on his previous pledge of allegiance to facilitate the movement of Nguyen forces across the river. Whichever way he turned, Nguyen Khac Liet would be easily eliminated, either by the southerners or by the northerners.

When a northern army approached to arrest Nguyen Khac Liet, the southerners attacked across the river and sent him fleeing into its arms. He was taken north and starved to death in prison. Meanwhile, the southerners gained control of Northern Bo Chinh. When Trinh Trang requested the return of this territory, Nguyen Phuc Lan agreed, having succeeded in establishing a new measure of peace along the riverine border.

In the wake of these events, a certain noble at Nguyen Phuc Lan's court cited the ancient sages and Trinh perfidy to advocate a more aggressive policy toward the north. Nguyen Phuc Lan responded by calling the man a fawner and dismissed him. Yet, two years later, when he decided that he wanted to attack the north, he found that his "boat soldiers" were not in a state of readiness, so he instituted a program of intense training for them. As it turned out, Trinh Trang was a step ahead of him.

In the dry season of 1643–1644, a large Trinh expedition marched and sailed south. Trinh Tac and Pham Cong Tru led the van. Trinh Trang and the king came with the main body of troops. The northern army brushed aside southern forces in Southern Bo Chinh and advanced to the wall at Dong Hoi, but northern efforts to break through the wall were repulsed. When the hot summer weather arrived, an epidemic ravaged the northern camp and the Trinh army withdrew. The Dutch also participated in this campaign, having arranged with Trinh Trang to join in combined action against the south.

The hostile Dutch attitude toward the south had hardened after two of their ships en route from Formosa to Batavia were shipwrecked on the southern Vietnamese coast in late 1641. All salvageable merchandise was confiscated and the eighty-two survivors were detained and placed under the supervision of the Japanese community in Hoi An.

Early the next year, the commander of a Dutch ship sailing to Batavia with a Trinh envoy was persuaded by the envoy to stop at Da Nang Bay to seize hostages. He seized over 100 people. Then, hearing about the Dutchmen held at Hoi An, he tried to negotiate an exchange with a local official. Thinking he had an agreement, he released the people he had seized, but he kept the Nguyen official and the official's Japanese interpreter pending release of the Dutchmen. The Vietnamese authorities then refused to release the Dutchmen until not only the official and the interpreter were released but also the northern envoy was handed over. Worried about rumors of approaching Vietnamese war galleys, the Dutch weighed anchor and sailed off to Batavia.

Apparently seeking to appear conciliatory, the Nguyen Phuc authorities allowed fifty of the Dutch hostages to board an unarmed ship and sail for Batavia. However, the Portuguese attacked the boat at sea and all the Dutchmen perished except for fourteen who washed up on the Cham coast where they were enslaved. One of them escaped to Cambodia from where he made his way to Batavia. The friendly gesture of releasing the fifty men was lost on the Dutch authorities at Batavia, who were determined on revenge for what they considered to be southern Vietnamese hostility toward them.

Thinking that the Trinh were planning to campaign against the southerners in 1642, in that year the Dutch sent five ships with over 200 sailors and soldiers to raid the coast and seize hostages before joining the northern army at the border. In Quang Ngai, they burned down several hundred houses, as well as a rice granary, and seized dozens of captives. At Cu Lao Cham, an island off the coast near Hoi An, a Dutch foray was repulsed with heavy losses. After this, Dutch demands for the release of their men were ignored and the Dutch killed some of their hostages before sailing north. Discovering that there was no Trinh campaign that year, the Dutch met with northern authorities to plan for a campaign the following year.

In early 1643, five Dutch ships arrived in northern Vietnam from Formosa to coordinate with the Trinh campaign, but the Trinh forces were not scheduled to depart for the south until later in the year. The Dutch commander would not wait, but agreed to leave one ship to go with the Trinh expedition, and then departed for Batavia. Contrary winds forced back two of the Dutch ships, so three Dutch ships were available to accompany the Trinh campaign.

Learning of this, the authorities at Batavia ordered three ships under the command of Pieter Baeck to sail from the Straits of Malacca to the Gianh River border on a schedule to arrive at the time of the expected campaign. Meanwhile, the Trinh army was already encamped at the border. The three Dutch ships that had joined the Trinh earlier in the year were in the vicinity but inactive. Pieter Baeck was instructed to place these ships under his authority and to coordinate with the Trinh battle plans.

Southerners at coastal watchtowers sighted Pieter Baeck's ships as they sailed north. Nguyen Phuc Lan's 25-year-old son and heir, Nguyen Phuc Tan, went in pursuit of them with sixty war galleys and engaged them in battle. The sounds of the battle from across the water were audible in the Trinh camp. The Dutch flagship caught fire and blew up when its powder magazine ignited. The other two Dutch ships were heavily damaged and escaped with difficulty. Pieter Baeck and one of the other Dutch captains were among those killed.

The Dutch briefly attempted to blockade Hoi An in 1644. Various efforts were made to mediate the release of the fourteen Dutchmen remaining in custody there, including an initiative by Alexandre de Rhodes, who happened to be in Hoi An at that time. However, the Dutch authorities had grown weary of their frustrations along the southern Vietnamese coast and gave no more attention to the matter until a brief effort at making peace was made with Nguyen Phuc Lan's successor in 1651.

The Dutch embarrassment from their defeat in the 1643 battle with the southern Vietnamese was contemporaneous with similar misadventures in Cambodia. Their consequent loss of prestige affected their trading operations in northern Vietnam, where they suddenly began to suffer in unprecedented ways from the depredations of greedy eunuchs and officials and to find that competition from Chinese merchants began to squeeze their portion of the silk market. From then on, the Dutch stayed clear of any further military alliance with the Trinh.

The Trinh followed up their disappointing southern adventure of 1643–1644 with an unsuccessful attack on Cao Bang led by Trinh Tac. Trinh Trang, then 68 years old, was beginning to lose his health and, in 1645, officially delegated decision-making powers to Trinh Tac. Trinh Tac then established his own court to govern the country. Two of his brothers led a rebellion against him in that year resulting in a battle that raged through the streets of Dong Kinh and left, according to Dutch estimates, some 4,000 people dead. Trinh Tac's rivals were captured and killed. Pham Cong Tru emerged as Trinh Tac's chief advisor on non-military matters, and his Confucian education was almost immediately apparent in edicts exhorting officials to be honest and not to oppress the people with unlawful extortions. Another edict forbad anonymous letters that bewitched and confused the people, suggesting that treason was finding many forms of expression. The next few years were relatively uneventful as Trinh Tac prepared for another propitious time to send his soldiers south.

In the south, the most salient piece of surviving information from this time is that in 1646 it was decreed that a new literary examination was to be held every nine years. The exam was for three days and consisted of three parts: (1) writing a type of poetic prose written in alternating four-six syllable lines; (2) writing the *phu* mode of rhythmic prose; and (3) writing prose essays on the classical books. At the same time, a system of ranks and appointments for graduates of this exam was put in place. In 1647, thirty-one men were selected as a result of the first such exam.

The widow of Nguyen Phuc Lan's elder brother, who had died in 1631, was known as Lady Tong. She was both beautiful and a clever conversationalist. In 1639 she had gained entry to Nguyen Phuc Lan's palace over the objections of some of his advisors who worried about her father who had turned coat and fled to the north. Nguyen Phuc Lan's younger brother, Prince Trung, became involved with her and fell into a conspiracy facilitated by her father to assist a northern invasion. The conspiracy was uncovered and Prince Trung died in prison. But the Trinh invasion of 1648 that arose in the context of this intrigue was the most serious test of southern defenses yet.

The Trinh broke through the first wall and took the fortress of Dinh Muoi, which was the center of the southern defense system. The northerners were breaking through the second wall when their offensive stalled. Truong Phuc Phan was in command of the section of the wall that was crumbling before the northern advance. His father had come south with Nguyen Hoang and by this time he was an old man. His son Truong Phuc Hung stood beside him as he sat calmly atop the wall under his parasol of authority directing the southern defense. His confident demeanor reportedly appeared to his troops as if he were a deity, which inspired them to greater effort. A female spy provided important information that helped to time a southern counterattack. Nguyen Huu Dat, in the midst of the battle, raised his eyes to the sky and observed in the clouds signs of southern victory. Nguyen Huu Tien shifted the fortunes of battle with a nighttime attack of one hundred bull elephants. Nguyen Phuc Lan was dying and had given command of the armies to his heir Nguyen Phuc Tan. The southern defenses were stretched to their limit, but they held, and the northern armies were pushed back and forced to return north. Nguyen Phuc Lan died within a day of reviewing his victorious troops.

Nguyen Phuc Tan was 28 years old when he assumed supreme authority after this grueling battle. His leadership during the next four decades continued the tradition of astute rule that had been established by his predecessors. Neither he nor his opponent in the north, Trinh Tac, was committed to a war begun by their fathers. Both eventually understood that there was no benefit from warring upon each other, but the forces producing the war were too strong to be halted immediately. In both the north and the south were many men who harbored dreams of conquest. After the fighting of 1648, the nature of the war shifted. Until then, it was a war of northern campaigns against the south. In the 1650s, as Trinh Trang slowly sank toward the grave and as challenges to Trinh Tac's authority continued to stir up from within the Trinh family, the south invaded the north, moving the war into a new phase during which fundamental changes occurred in both the north and the south that eventually led to an end of hostilities.

During the 1620s, 1630s, and 1640s, the north had attacked the south as often and with as much vigor as it was capable of doing. During the same time, the southerners had evaluated their relative inferiority in men and resources and had prepared defenses that were equal to the northern challenge. Despite the drama of war, fundamental changes in society, economy, and culture were taking place in both the north and the south that focused the north inward and the south outward. The sheer size of the population in the Red River plain kept Trinh attention upon the task of socializing large numbers of people to respond to authority. Meanwhile, the southerners were awakening to the beckoning possibilities of the Mekong frontier.

The far south

As described in earlier chapters, the Vietnamese had experienced centuries of contact, both hostile and peaceful, with the Chams and related upland peoples who spoke languages affiliated with the Malay peoples of the coasts and islands of Southeast Asia. By the seventeenth century, there had been much mingling of Chams and Viets along the southern coast. Although many Chams had fled further south, into the mountains, or into the sea with each advance of Vietnamese conquest, many others had chosen to remain, took Vietnamese names, adopted Vietnamese habits, and over time became Vietnamese. Cham soldiers served in Vietnamese armies and were led by Cham officers. The army sent by Nguyen Hoang to conquer Phu Yen in 1611 had been commanded by a Cham general.

For forty years after 1611, the Cham population of Phu Yen continued to elicit efforts by Cham kings to retake this rich province. Phu Yen lay in the coastal plain of the Da Rang River, which drained a large part of the adjacent uplands and was the last region suitable for large-scale agriculture before passing through relatively arid, semi-desert lands on the way to the Mekong River plain. Confined to a dry coastal strip, Cham leaders struggled to redefine their authority.

In 1613, the Cham king had withdrawn his capital from Phan Rang to Phan Ri, which was futher south, possibly seeking greater distance from the

Vietnamese threat, but just as likely in response to tension between Hindu and Muslim Chams. The Muslims appear to have been dominant at modern Nha Trang, the last Cham seaport. In 1622, a Hindu king was killed and replaced by a Muslim king, who chased off visiting Jesuits, attacked Dutch ships, and provoked bitter fighting between Cham Hindus and Cham Muslims. This strife attracted the participation of neighboring upland peoples in modern Lam Dong Province. The Churu, Ede, and Jarai were ethno-linguistically related to the Chams and for centuries had been part of the larger political, economic, and cultural world of the Chams. They were neither Hindu nor Muslim. Their societies were matrilineal and matrilocal. Women initiated marriage, men joined the families of their wives, and children inherited property through mothers. These peoples intermarried among themselves and also with the Chams.

As the coastal Cham population declined and was increasingly limited to the sandy lands that faced southeastward to the sea, the role of the uplanders in Cham political life increased. In 1627, a Churu chieftain known as Po Ramo subdued both Hindu and Muslim factions and forced peace between the two Cham communities. He was originally from Don Duong district near the modern city of Dalat. He ruled from the Phan Rang basin and built dams and canals to nurture agriculture in that region. He still had the seaport at Nha Trang and for a quarter-century presided over a small surge of prosperity among the Chams. His three principal wives were daughters of a previous king, of an Ede chieftain, and of Nguyen Phuc Nguyen. Although for two decades his leadership went far toward stabilizing the Cham–Viet border at Ca Pass, he could not stay clear of continuing tensions between the Cham and Vietnamese communities in Phu Yen.

In 1651, Po Ramo was wounded in Phu Yen during an outbreak of hostilities between Chams and Viets. He died of his wounds. Po Nraup, one of his half-brothers, a son of his Churu mother and a Cham father, took authority and went on the offensive, attacking Phu Yen and driving Vietnamese soldiers and officials out of that province.

Nguyen Phuc Tan sent an army of three thousand men under the command of a Cham general known as Hung Loc. Hung Loc not only retook Phu Yen, but he also continued his advance to Nha Trang. He captured Po Nraup and forced him to cede all territories north of the Phan Rang River. Po Nraup died shortly after this, and in the turmoil of Vietnamese conquest a son and a grandson of Po Ramo were successively but briefly appointed as vassal kings by the Vietnamese until a measure of calm was restored under a Cham lord named Po Sot, who, from 1659 to 1692, governed at Phan Ri. The Chams, deprived of a seaport and of good agricultural land, went through another major demographic adjustment as many Muslims took the upland road from Nha Trang across the Central Highlands to the Mekong and beyond to Siam, where they settled at Ayutthia.

The new border placed the modern province of Khanh Hoa, where Nha Trang is located, under Vietnamese administration. Po Sot presided over the last semblance of a Cham kingdom before Cham kings were reduced to being administrators of a minority people in a Vietnamese kingdom.

The seventeenth century also saw the first Vietnamese contact with the Khmers of Cambodia and with the Siamese, whose rising influence over Cambodia elicited Vietnamese interest in Khmer royal politics. At that time, Cambodia included the entire lower plain of the Mekong River. The western provinces of Cambodia were increasingly subject to Siamese power. At the same time, the Vietnamese, allied with immigrant Chinese, established a sphere of action in the eastern Cambodian provinces.

Around two centuries earlier, Khmer kings had abandoned Angkor, which was located to govern an agricultural empire that included large parts of modern Thailand. They shifted to sites on or near the Mekong River with access to the sea and a new source of wealth that was based on international trade. In the late fifteenth century, Siam achieved a new level of regional ascendancy under the leadership of Naresuan (reigned 1590–1605). When they could no longer resist the Siamese, Khmer kings solicited military assistance from the communities of foreigners who had gathered in their kingdom attracted by trade: Chinese, Japanese, Malays, Chams, Portuguese, and Spanish, but to no avail. In the first decade of the seventeenth century, Cambodia was reduced to the status of a Siamese vassal. However, in 1618, Chei Chéttha II became king of Cambodia and, with Siam under threat from Burma, he repudiated Siamese vassalage in a way that elicited the beginning of Vietnamese involvement in Cambodian affairs.

Chei Chéttha II turned to Nguyen Phuc Nguyen for assistance in resisting the Siamese. It seemed to be a good idea because there was no common border with the Vietnamese and the antagonism between the Trinh and the Nguyen promised to keep them busy with each other. Nguyen Phuc Nguyen married his second daughter Ngoc Van to Chei Chéttha II. With her went an entourage of around 1,000 Vietnamese, including soldiers to serve as bodyguards and a Vietnamese official to serve as resident ambassador. In 1622, the Vietnamese participated in a naval battle that defeated a Siamese invasion. A community of Vietnamese began to form at the Khmer capital.

In 1623, Nguyen Phuc Nguyen asked Chei Chéttha II for the authority to collect taxes at Prei Nokor and Kampong Krabei. These were adjacent settlements that were the economic and administrative centers of the easternmost Khmer province, in the basin of the Daung Nay (Vietnamese Dong Nai) River on the Cham frontier. Khmer histories affirm that Chei Chéttha II agreed to this as a temporary arrangement of five years, supposedly to give his ally some consideration for the assistance against Siam in the previous year. Khmer historians may have interpolated the idea of a five-year term for this arrangement to support later requests by Khmer kings that the Vietnamese return the privileges they had been granted, but this does not take into account that a population of Chinese and Vietnamese traders and adventurers was already accumulating in the basin of the Dong Nai River.

Prei Nokor was a Chinese commercial center on the site of modern Cholon ("big market"), the Chinese district of modern Saigon. A Chinese population of merchants was already established there. It was situated to take advantage of waterways connecting the eastern part of the Mekong plain with access to the sea via the Sai Gon and Dong Nai Rivers. Kampong Krabei (Vietnamese Ben Nghe) was on the Sai Gon River, on the site of modern Saigon, and was primarily an administrative center. A Vietnamese garrison was established there, and officials were assigned to collect revenue, to report events in the region, and to keep some measure of order among the Chinese and Vietnamese population, which included banished criminals, fugitives, and vagabonds as well as merchants and agriculturalists. The Vietnamese called the Kampong Krabei garrison by the name Gia Dinh.

When Chei Chéttha II died in 1627, his eldest son reigned for five years as Srei Thoamareachea I. However, Chei Chéttha II's younger full brother Barom Reachea exercised great authority as the "second king" (*opphayoreach*). Vietnamese envoys arrived bearing gifts and requested that Ngoc Van, Chei Chéttha II's Vietnamese widow, be elevated to the rank of "queen mother," the highest position for a woman at court. She had given birth to a daughter but had no sons. In consideration of the importance that the Khmer court gave to the Vietnamese alliance, this request was granted. With the envoys came 500 Vietnamese soldiers to reinforce her bodyguard.

In 1632, Srei Thoamareachea I provoked a war with his uncle Barom Reachea by indulging in an affair with Barom Reachea's wife. Srei Thoamareachea I had encouraged a large influx of Chinese residents during his years as king and they supplied him with troops in the struggle with his uncle. For his part, Barom Reachea's forces included a contingent of Portuguese. Srei Thoamareachea I was defeated, killed, and replaced by a younger brother, Ang Tong Reachea. However, Barom Reachea was the actual ruler. Shortly after, as Nguyen Phuc Nguyen was preoccupied with his northern border and with his approaching death, Barom Reachea requested that the Vietnamese evacuate Prei Nokor and Kampong Krabei. This request was withdrawn after the intercession of the Vietnamese "queen mother," Ngoc Van. In the late 1630s, the Dutch established a trading station in Cambodia, introducing a new source of tension into the kingdom in the form of Dutch–Portuguese hostility that was prone to erupt in violence.

When Ang Tong Reachea died in 1640, Barom Reachea placed his own son on the throne as Botum Reachea I. A son of Chei Chéttha II refused to accept this, however, and in 1642, with the support of Ngoc Van, he killed his uncle Barom Reachea and his cousin Botum Reachea I, along with many members of their family and officials who had supported them; he then took the throne as Reameathipadei I. He married a Muslim, identified in some texts as Malay and in others as Cham, and converted to Islam (taking the title Sultan Ibrahim), thereby gaining the support of the Malay and Cham communities and their military forces. He took the side of the Portuguese against the Dutch, which led to a brief war with the Dutch that ended with their expulsion.

Vietnamese merchants became more active in Cambodia at this time, particularly in buying rice needed to supply the heavily militarized population among the walls on their northern frontier. Ngoc Van preserved her high position as "queen mother" with her own palace and entourage. She continued to deflect tentative Khmer efforts to regain Prei Nokor and Kampong Krabei. Two of Barom Reachea's sons, Ang So and Ang Tan, who had escaped the homicidal inauguration of Reameathipadei I's reign, found safety in her entourage, as did her grandson, Srei Chei Chét, the son of her daughter and of Botum Reachea I. These princes were determined to avenge the deaths of their fathers.

In 1658, as King Narai of Siam made a show of preparing to invade from the west, Ang So led a rebellion against Reameathipadei I. Ang So easily raised support from the Buddhist leaders who were alienated from the Muslim king, but Reameathipadei I raised a large army that included Malays, Chams, some 150–200 men from the Vietnamese garrison, and the ships of Europeans that happened to be in Cambodia at the time, including the Dutch (who meanwhile had made peace with Reameathipadei I and had regained a trading station in the country), the English and, briefly, the Spanish and the Danes. Having endeavored during previous years to keep the peace between Reameathipadei I and the princes whose fathers he had killed, the Vietnamese queen mother Ngoc Van was caught in the middle. Nevertheless, when the rebellion began to fail and Ang So appealed to her, she sent a request to Nguyen Phuc Tan for help.

At that time, Nguyen Phuc Tan was engaged in a prolonged invasion of the north that had begun three years before. He was determined that the Gia Dinh garrison not be disturbed, for it was an important source of wealth and supplies. Other than that, he was not concerned about who would rule Cambodia, but he saw an opportunity to launch an expedition for plunder to supply his armies in the north and to degrade the potential of Khmer kings to oppose his policies in the future. In late 1658, he sent a fleet with around 3,000 well-trained and disciplined men down the coast and up the Mekong. Its sudden appearance in the heart of the Khmer kingdom gave Reameathipadei I little time to prepare for the river battle that ensued. Reameathipadei I was captured, and the Vietnamese systematically looted the capital of Oudong, loading around one hundred boats with plunder, including gold, silver, various weapons, and 1,600 pieces of artillery. They also obtained eight hundred elephants and even more horses. Among the assets the Vietnamese found in Cambodia was a Portuguese cannon maker named Jean de la Croix. When they departed Cambodia in spring of 1659, the Vietnamese took this man with them and set him to work in their gun foundries.

When he understood that the Vietnamese had come on a looting expedition, Ang So resisted them and, when the Vietnamese had left, he proclaimed himself king as Barom Reachea VIII. Nguyen Phuc Tan sent Reameathipadei I back to Cambodia as his vassal, but he died along the way. An army of Cham and Malay Muslims rose up against Barom Reachea VIII, who was a devout Buddhist, but were defeated and took refuge with King Narai of Siam. Barom Reachea VIII gave particular preference to the Chinese community in Cambodia. In 1667, a large group of Chinese, reportedly over 3,000, arrived from Taiwan. In a surprise attack that had the approval of Barom Reachea VIII, the Chinese set upon the one to two thousand Vietnamese who resided near the capital, killing most of them, capturing some, and sending the survivors fleeing north. The Chinese then set upon the Dutch, seizing their property, killing many and expelling the rest. Thus, the Chinese removed their two largest competitors for control of the local economy. Barom Reachea VIII proclaimed an end to relations with the Vietnamese and prohibited them from entering his kingdom. This had no effect upon the Vietnamese garrison at Gia Dinh, which remained as before.

Barom Reachea VIII was killed in 1672 by his nephew, Srei Chei Chét, who appears to have had no greater motive than an urgent desire to be king. The regicide's uncle, Ang Tan, who was the "second king," feared for his own life and fled to the court of Nguyen Phuc Tan, leaving behind his wife, a prominent princess, as well as his nephew and adopted son, Ang Nan, the son of a deceased younger brother, who reportedly had been Barom Reachea VIII's designated heir. When Srei Chei Chét attempted to make Ang Tan's wife his queen, she had him killed and, following her advice, the royal court sent for the eldest son of Barom Reachea VIII, who had meanwhile become a forest monk, and enthroned him as Kèv Fa II.

Rivalry between Kèv Fa II and Ang Nan quickly spun out of control. Kèv Fa II made a show of calling in the Siamese to pacify Ang Nan. In 1674, Ang Nan departed to seek assistance from the Vietnamese. On the way, he met Ang Tan accompanied by the second Vietnamese expedition to Cambodia. Unlike the first expedition of 1658, which had essentially been for plunder, this expedition was prepared to undertake an extended campaign on behalf of Ang Nan. Nguyen

Phuc Tan wanted not only to safeguard the Vietnamese position at Gia Dinh and to gain the benefits of trade with Cambodia, but also to counter Siamese influence by nurturing the ambitions of friendly Khmer princes.

Initial Vietnamese victories sent Kèv Fa II to the Siamese border, but the sudden death of Ang Tan left the pro-Vietnamese faction of the Khmer royal family in the less-experienced hands of Ang Nan. Siamese assistance reinvigorated Kèv Fa II's cause, and soon Kèv Fa II counterattacked against the Vietnamese and their Cambodian allies. Vietnamese reinforcements arrived and the fighting continued. When Kèv Fa II died in 1677, his half-brother became king as Chei Chéttha III. Meanwhile, Ang Nan had proclaimed himself the "second king." The result of this turmoil was the partitioning of the kingdom between Chei Chéttha III in the north and west, supported by Siam, and Ang Nan in the east and south, supported by the Vietnamese. The wars that ensued between Chei Chéttha III and Ang Nan continued beyond Nguyen Phuc Tan's lifetime and entrenched the Siamese and the Vietnamese as regular participants in Khmer politics.

Vietnamese involvement in Cambodian affairs started with the calculations of a Khmer king, Chei Chéttha II, who viewed the Vietnamese as a relatively non-threatening ally against Siamese domination. Granting Nguyen Phuc Nguyen's request to collect revenue at Prei Nokor and Kampong Krabei, on the far eastern edge of the kingdom, where Chinese and Vietnamese had already begun to settle, was a plausible means to keep interested and involved a distant ally distracted by more serious matters elsewhere. Nguyen Phuc Nguyen's daughter, Ngoc Van, anchored a Vietnamese presence at the heart of the Khmer kingdom for forty years. She exercised her skill in navigating Khmer royal politics and in promoting the interests of her family until the first Vietnamese expedition in 1658, after which she is no longer mentioned in any surviving records.

In the 1670s, with the end of the Trinh wars and with appeals for intervention by Khmer princes, Nguyen Phuc Tan analyzed a frontier problem without precedent in Vietnamese historical experience. Until then, Vietnamese frontiers had always been mountain passes or rivers or places where the ever-present western mountains ran out into the sea. But here there were no western mountains, no mountain passes, no transverse rivers, nothing but a vast deltaic plain through which the branches of a great river flowed out to the sea. The first moves, made by Nguyen Phuc Nguyen, were methods of establishing relationships and influence that had been traditional with upland chieftains: a marriage alliance and the arrival of Vietnamese settlers and soldiers. In 1658, Nguyen Phuc Tan had exercised another mode of action that had been used for centuries with the Chams: an expedition to temporarily seize and plunder the capital of a neighboring kingdom. In the 1670s, however, Nguyen Phuc Tan began to view the situation in a new way.

The Khmer monarchy was located in the midst of a vast plain, for which the Dong Nai and Sai Gon River basin was like an antechamber for the Vietnamese. The only means of transport were up the branches of the Mekong that came together at the center of the kingdom before branching off to the "Great Lake" (Tonle Sap) and upriver to Laos. Siam stood watching just beyond. There was no terrain to barricade a border against enemies, nor was Cambodia like Champa, a relatively vulnerable and isolated neighbor that could be kept weak by periodically looting its capital. The characteristic circumstances of this new kind of frontier were clearly apparent by 1674 when the Khmer royal family was split into pro-Siamese and pro-Vietnamese factions. Nguyen Phuc Tan saw that rival Khmer princes would define the Siamese and Vietnamese spheres of influence in their country and that the next necessary step on his southern border was to ally with a Khmer prince and to cultivate clients in the Khmer royal family.

Thus, by the 1670s, the Cham kingdom had been deprived of its last major seaport and pushed into a relatively arid corner, and the Khmer kingdom had been partitioned into two realms under rival kings, one a vassal of Siam and the other a vassal of the Vietnamese. Furthermore, the Vietnamese had established a position at modern Saigon and Cholon that would never be relinquished and that was destined to become the largest of all Vietnamese cities.

Nguyen Phuc Tan, Trinh Tac, and the Nghe An campaign

During the three decades of the 1650s, 1660s, and 1670s, Trinh Tac in the north and Nguyen Phuc Tan in the south made decisions that moved the two Vietnamese countries beyond the military impasse that became increasingly apparent in those years. They were both strong leaders who took a detailed interest in government and who had definite ideas about priorities. While Trinh Tac was occupied with internal tensions that had become embedded in his realm, Nguyen Phuc Tan considered how best to maintain the expansionary energy of his realm.

Following the war of 1648, Trinh Tac became increasingly preoccupied with intrigues and conspiracies stimulated by Trinh Trang's failing health. Although Trinh Tac was by now the chief decision-maker at Dong Kinh, his aging father continued to hold his own court with his own circle of powerful favorites, some of whom harbored extravagant ambitions. Trinh Tac also had enemies among the princes of his own family who sought to undermine his authority by manipulating the people in Trinh Trang's entourage. The premature death of the young king, Le Duy Huu, in 1649 may have been related to a conspiracy against Trinh Tac, for Dutchmen arriving at Dong Kinh in that year reported that Trinh Tac had poisoned both an uncle and the young king. Eunuchs were particularly prominent among Trinh Trang's confidants. They held high military and civil positions and were in control of the lucrative silk industry. In 1652, when Trinh Trang's health temporarily worsened, a conspiracy was uncovered that was led by a eunuch and included court officials, Japanese merchants, and a sorcerer, all of whom were close to Trinh Trang.

While Trinh Tac waited apprehensively through his father's declining years, Nguyen Phuc Tan gloried in his victorious army and dreamed of new adventures. He quickly established a reputation for his knowledge of ancient history, for paying close attention to matters of government, and for maintaining a disciplined style of life. When a beautiful female singer arrived from the north and gained entrance to his palace, he was reminded of an episode in antiquity where just such a woman from the land of an enemy had brought down a kingdom. He ordered that she be taken out of the palace and killed.

In 1653, he organized a massive military exercise in the Hue region with nearly 400 war boats and 20,000 men. In military matters, he was listening to two generals. Nguyen Huu Tien, the son-in-law and protégé of Dao Duy Tu, was calm, methodical, and relied upon strict discipline and careful planning. Nguyen Huu Dat was a brilliant strategist who favored feints and ambushes and liked to sow confusion among northern leaders by sending letters to arouse their fear of treason. Nguyen Huu Dat was arguing for an invasion of the north, something that had been on his mind since 1623 when he had blurted it out at Nguyen Phuc Nguyen's court on the occasion of Trinh Tung's death. Nguyen Phuc Tan was inclined to agree but wanted the steadier hand of Nguyen Huu Tien in command. There was rivalry between the two generals. In early 1655, Nguyen Phuc Tan resolved the question of command by reporting a poem recited to him by a divine being in a dream that contained classical allusions indicating that Nguyen Huu Tien should have seniority over Nguyen Huu Dat.

In 1655, the two generals embarked on an invasion of the north. They were partnered in a two-headed command, in which Nguyen Huu Dat's ideas set the battlefield agenda and in which Nguyen Huu Tien had the final word. During the first four years, so long as the southerners enjoyed success, this partnership was harmonious. However, after the death of Trinh Trang and after Trinh Tac had taken a firm grip on authority at Dong Kinh and was able to organize the superior resources of the Red River plain, the southerners began to suffer loses and the two generals began to quarrel.

During 1655, the southerners advanced steadily into Nghe An. The northern commanders suffered defeat after defeat and, by mid summer, were recalled to Dong Kinh, demoted, and replaced by new senior officers arriving with reinforcements. However, the southerners continued to advance, reaching the Lam River, the lowland portion of the Ca River, which flows through the modern city of Vinh. The situation became so critical for the northerners that in autumn Trinh Tac himself arrived with more reinforcements. He spent three months on the battlefield and managed to push the southerners back somewhat. When he returned north near the end of the year, he left his younger brother Trinh Toan (d. 1674) in command.

In early 1656, the southerners returned to the offensive, sending their navy up the Lam River and consolidating their control of the southern bank of the river while threatening to cross to the northern bank. At mid year, Trinh Tac sent his eldest son, Trinh Can, with a new army. There followed several months of dismay and confusion among Trinh officers as Trinh Can established a head-quarters separate from Trinh Toan and received most of the supplies and men being sent south. Trinh Toan was popular among the soldiers, but his elder brother, Trinh Tac, did not trust him. Trinh Tac feared that Trinh Toan's influ-ence in the army posed a threat to himself. Trinh Can was stable, cautious, and level headed, while Trinh Toan was noted for an excitable temperament with flashes of inspiration. Many officers were devoted to him and found it hard to swallow the realization that he was being pushed aside. Meanwhile, the southern generals were receiving messages not only from the Mac in Cao Bang but also from prominent leaders in the Red River plain, promising to rise up and attack the Trinh when the southerners crossed the Lam River.

Nevertheless, the soldiers accumulating under Trinh Can's command halted the southern advance at the Lam River. In mid 1656, Nguyen Phuc Tan met with his generals and was told by Nguyen Huu Dat that new recruits arriving from the south lacked training and discipline and were alienating the population of Nghe An. Nguyen Huu Dat recommended that the southerners fortify their position on the southern bank of the Lam River, consolidate their gains, discipline their men, and await a new opportunity to advance.

In early 1657, Trinh Trang finally died. Tac had the situation well in hand and there was no succession disturbance in Dong Kinh. However, when Trinh Toan was subsequently recalled and imprisoned at the capital, many northern officers defected to the south. Southern efforts to establish a structure of regular govern-ment in Nghe An south of the Lam River began to bear fruit in 1658 as educated men from that region were recruited to administer villages, capture criminals, dispense justice, and to collect rice and other taxes to supply the southern armies. When local people expressed uneasiness about the new regime, men were sent out to explain matters to them and to win them over to the southern cause. Unknown numbers of people were recruited, or possibly coerced, to go south, where they were resettled in the more southerly Nguyen Phuc territories.

The southern advance reached its furthest extent in 1658 with heavy fighting around Vinh and even a southern foray through the mountains with the collaboration of an upland chieftain that briefly threatened Quynh Luu near the northern border of Nghe An. However, by the end of the year, Trinh Can had fended off the southern attacks and had gained an important victory at Huong Son district in the foothills that anchored his defense of the Lam River. From this time on, the southern position became increasingly difficult to maintain as Trinh Tac ruled with a confidence that had not been possible during the lifetime of his father.

At the beginning of 1658, Trinh Tac initiated a new era in northern government with the proclamation of the Vinh Tho reign period. He put Pham Cong Tru and other literati officials from the Red River plain at the center of decision-making with the mandate to reform government according to their ideas. They had been educated to regard the Hong Duc government of Le Tu Thanh as the model for good government. The examination scheduled for 1655 had been postponed because of the military emergency of that year, and when it was held in 1656 only six men were selected. However, examinations were held in 1658 and in 1659 with twenty-two men being selected in each of those years. The prospects of many literati families in the Red River plain that had suffered for their service to the Mac began to rise from this time. The legislation of the Vinh Tho era (1658–1662) covered nearly every aspect of government: population registers; taxation; conscription; legal tender; internal customs stations; roads and dikes; education; examinations; administrative appointments; judicial procedures; public sacrifices; and public morality. Some legislation specifically addressed the recruitment of soldiers in Thanh Hoa and Nghe An, including their landholding rights and tax obligations.

By 1659, Trinh Tac was in a position to push back at the southerners. He treated Nguyen Huu Dat to a taste of his own style of intrigue by sending him gifts and a letter inviting him to defect. Nguyen Huu Dat immediately informed Nguyen Phuc Tan, who trusted him completely, but rumors among southern officers in Nghe An about Nguyen Huu Dat being in secret communication with the enemy began to circulate. When a spy arrived at Nguyen Huu Dat's headquarters and reported on conditions in the north, Nguyen Huu Dat sent him back across enemy lines without first having him report to Nguyen Huu Tien. This irritated Nguyen Huu Tien and increased suspicion of Nguyen Huu Dat among his colleagues. Nguyen Huu Dat reacted to these doubts about his loyalty by feigning "illness" and withdrawing into inaction. Amidst the discord in the southern camps, many northern officers and men who had previously defected to the south went back to rejoin the northern forces, and soldiers recruited by the southerners in Nghe An also began to defect. Trinh agents circulated among the villagers in the territory occupied by the southerners spreading discontent.

The southern armies had remained mostly inactive during 1659 and early 1660, immobilized by dissention and declining morale. In mid 1660, Nguyen Huu Tien launched an offensive without informing Nguyen Huu Dat. Nguyen Huu Dat, hearing of it after it had begun, quickly brought his armies into the battle, and the southerners gained a foothold on the northern bank of the Lam River. At that point, Nguyen Phuc Tan met with his generals to evaluate the situation. There were voices urging a continuation of the offensive, but Nguyen Phuc Tan had had enough. He told his generals that their men were weary and homesick and that supplying an advance beyond the Lam River would be very difficult. He ordered them to return to the southern bank of the river and fortify their positions. Shortly after this, Trinh Can took the offensive, striking across the river and gaining victories.

As Trinh Can advanced, the men who had been recruited from Nghe An into the southern armies began a stampede of desertion to join the northerners. A debate among the southern generals over what to do about this broke whatever cooperative spirit yet existed between Nguyen Huu Tien, who favored capital punishment for these deserters, and Nguyen Huu Dat, who argued for clemency. Under constant pressure from Trinh Can's attacks, Nguyen Huu Tien decided to retreat and did so without informing Nguyen Huu Dat, leaving him in an exposed position. Nguyen Huu Dat was nevertheless quick to realize what was happening and joined the southern withdrawal. The northern armies followed and arrived at the Gianh River by the end of 1660. In early 1661, Trinh Can traveled to Dong Kinh for a hero's welcome.

It is hard to avoid the conclusion that by 1659 Nguyen Phuc Tan was no longer interested in conquering the north. He may have been able to dispel the dissention among his generals, rally the morale of his soldiers, and solve the supply problems of an advancing army. Many of his officers clearly felt that this was possible. However, he chose to see it differently. He allowed his armies to remain inactive for a year and a half at a critical point in the war. When his generals crossed the Lam River, he brought them back. When they retreated to the Gianh River, there is no indication that he was unhappy with them. He did not punish his defeated generals, which was standard practice in the north. He immediately set Nguyen Huu Dat to work building a new wall ten kilometers north of the existing system of walls. He was content to keep the northerners out. He apparently did not want to govern the north with its deep-seated regional rivalries and its relative poverty. And, perhaps most important of all, he preferred not to have the headache of playing nursemaid to a monarchy that could neither be abandoned nor be allowed to grow up. In the south, he was free to be the lord of his own kingdom. If he wanted adventure, the far south could provide plenty of that. The two Vietnamese realms no longer shared a common context of political ambition. The Nghe An war had taught Nguyen Phuc Tan that con-quering the north would not be worth the trouble.

After successfully concluding a difficult war to expel an invader that had lasted for six years, Trinh Tac could not resist enthusiasm for another effort to break through the southern walls. In late 1661, Trinh Can led his men across the Gianh River and, after heavy fighting, took Nguyen Huu Dat's new wall. However, he could not break through the Dong Hoi Wall at the mouth of the Nhat Le River. A southern counterattack in early 1662 sent him retreating back north. There-after, the border was quiet for ten years.

Nguyen Phuc Tan did not let down his guard toward the north. After with-drawal of the northern army in 1661, he sent Nguyen Huu Tien and Nguyen Huu Dat to build a new wall a short distance north of the Dong Hoi Wall, called the Tran Ninh Wall, which blocked the coastal plain and was a northern extension of the existing system of walls. It was designed to prevent northern land and sea forces from joining to concentrate at the mouth of the Nhat Le River. In subsequent years, he gave detailed attention to the recruitment of soldiers and to organizing countrywide military mobilizations for training pur-poses. He instituted a regime of daily shooting practice for his gunners and musketeers. In 1669, he extended his regulations on recruitment and training to the new territories seized from Champa during the previous decade, the modern province of Khanh Hoa and beyond to the Phan Rang River. Also at this time, he realized that much new land had been opened up for cultivation but was producing no tax revenue. He established an Agricultural Office to survey fields, establish ownership, and levy taxes.

The last battle

Meanwhile, in the north, Trinh Tac and his literati advisors embarked on the most ambitious effort to reform government since the time of Le Tu Thanh, two centuries before. King Le Duy Ky died in late 1662. Trinh Tac selected one of Le Duy Ky's sons, 10-year-old Le Duy Vu, to sit upon the throne. The years of Le Duy Vu's reign, known as the Canh Tri reign period (1663–1671), became, after Le Tu Thanh's Hong Duc era, the most celebrated time of good government in the historiography of Vietnamese Confucianists. The same kinds of laws, edicts, rules, and regulations about examinations, appointments, promotions, demo-tions, administrative and judicial procedures, corruption, abuse, public morality, population registers, taxation, conscription, etc. were promulgated during the Canh Tri period as had been routine during the reign of Le Tu Thanh. The difference was that the Canh Tri period lacked a king like Le Tu Thanh and lasted only one-quarter as long as that king's reign. Instead of a king there was a hard-bitten though somewhat enlightened warlord, Trinh Tac, and a gathering of aspiring administrators shepherded by a group of old scholar-officials led by Pham Cong Tru. There was no firm hand holding the system in place by force of personality. Consequently, the bureaucratic procedures formulated at this time simply became an arena for factional conflict over control of policy. The warriors of Thanh Hoa and Nghe An were not to be so easily pushed aside by the "poor but erudite" scholars of the Red River plain.

The test of wills was not simply between military and civil officials but rather among civil officials with different backgrounds and experiences. On one side were those who had been closely involved with the armies during the Nghe An campaign, most, but not all of them, from Nghe An and Thanh Hoa. These favored continuation of the war in the south. On the other side were those who had spent the war in villages mobilizing men and rice for the southern battle-fields, most, but not all of them, from the Red River plain. These were ready to end the conflict with the south. The question of continuing the war was not necessarily the most important issue, but it came to stand for two conflicting views of how the country should be governed.

The event that ignited the matter was the appointment of Pham Cong Tru's son, Pham Cong Kiem, to a high provincial post in 1665. Some considered him to be unqualified for the position, and, when his father retired three years later and was no longer able to protect him, he was dismissed for incompetence. It is not clear whether he was in fact incompetent or if he was a victim of intrigue. In seeking his dismissal in 1665, high officials of the military faction were hoping to unravel the position of his father and those associated with him. Trinh Tac could not allow this to happen, nor yet could he afford to give too much offense to the men representing the view of his soldiers. Trinh Tac sought to finesse the matter by charging those who had called for Pham Cong Kiem's dismissal with relatively minor violations of bureaucratic protocol and demoting them out of the top echelon of the court hierarchy. During the following year, administrative discipline was tightened and bureaucratic litigation was regulated as Trinh Tac sought to keep both groups engaged in his government.

Regional examinations had become a scandal and already in 1664 new rules had been issued to stop rampant cheating. In the regional examinations of 1666, particular attention was given to candidates from Mo Trach, the home district of the Vu family that was closely allied with Trinh Tac and which had been famously successful in previous examinations. There had been so many recent graduates from Mo Trach that accusations of chicanery were rife. Nevertheless, despite all manner of precaution, men from this district were disproportionately successful in 1666. This could mean that this district enjoyed excellent educational opportunities or it could mean that being connected to the Trinh family trumped the most thorough efforts to prevent corruption. It was natural that the struggle for control of policy spread to the examination system, which afforded access to government positions. The effect of this was to immobilize the capital examination of 1667, in which only three men graduated.

By this time, those demoted in 1665 were being promoted again as prospects for a military solution to the Cao Bang problem materialized. In early 1667, diplomatic contact was established with the new Qing dynasty in China. Since the Mac had been protected in Cao Bang by their status as a Ming vassal, Trinh Tac wagered that the Qing would acquiesce to their demise. In autumn of 1667 a large Trinh army conquered Cao Bang, sending the last of the Mac leaders, Mac Kinh Vu, fleeing to the Qing. However, to Trinh dismay, the Qing decided that any Ming vassal also belonged to them, and in 1669 the Trinh were ordered to restore Cao Bang to Mac Kinh Vu. Not until 1677, when Mac Kinh Vu joined the rebellion of Wu Sangui in Yunnan against the Qing were the Trinh allowed to occupy Cao Bang, thus finally bringing an end to the long political career of the Mac family, though as late as 1715 Trinh officials in Cao Bang still found it necessary to hunt down a man causing unrest by claiming to be a descendent of the Mac, and in 1719 special instructions were issued to ensure security in that sensitive border province.

The successful expedition to Cao Bang in 1667 did much to raise the prospects of those arguing for a new invasion of the south. Pham Cong Tru retired in 1668, and officials close to the military regained high positions. Three years of drought delayed preparations, but in 1671 soldiers from the Red River plain were being mobilized and trained. In 1672 the Trinh armies moved south. Trinh Tac, Trinh Can, and the new king, 12-year-old Le Duy Hoi, all accompanied the expedition.

The southern army that waited at the walls was under the command of Nguyen Phuc Tan's 20-year-old fourth son, Prince Hiep, a brilliant, monkish youth who had already earned the respect of military commanders two and three times his age. Nguyen Huu Tien had died in 1666, murmuring his chagrin at not living to see the downfall of the Trinh. Nguyen Huu Dat was 69 years old and placed in command of a new, strategically sited fortification called Sa Phu, "sand port," on the dunes overlooking the southern bank of the Nhat Le River mouth. According to southern historians, there was a pre-battle parley between the armies in which the old arguments were recited about which side was more loyal to the Le dynasty, the southern view being that the Trinh were keeping the Le kings as prisoners while the northerners accused the Nguyen of being in rebellion. By now this was a very tiresome argument, and it was the last time for it to be heard.

The Wall of Tran Ninh, erected ten years before in front of the pre-existing network of walls, became the focus of battle. The Trinh were breaking through this wall and were on the verge of overrunning it when Prince Hiep ordered Nguyen Huu Dat to move his men across the river to reinforce it. Nguyen Huu Dat went forward at night, his men bearing torches and planks to repair the walls before an expected dawn attack. Prince Hiep moved up to Sa Phu and from there directed a water battle denying the northern fleet entrance into the river. Meanwhile, Nguyen Huu Dat stopped the northern advance at the Wall of Tran Ninh. The Trinh were forced to withdraw. It was the last battle in this Fifty Years War.

After victory celebrations, Prince Hiep, refusing any contact with women, entered a temple to devote himself to the Buddha. He liked to go out and preach about the Buddha to the common people. In 1675, at the age of 23, he died, a shooting star of a hero.

Trinh Tac was determined to have done with this fruitless war. In 1673, he recalled Pham Cong Tru out of retirement and began to systematically demote or remove those who disagreed with him. When the capital examination of that year graduated only five men amidst factional conflict, he ordered a special exam to be held in which thirty men were selected. By early 1674 he had outmaneuvered his opponents in the arena of bureaucratic appointments, and they resorted to the only asset they had left, the soldiers from Thanh Hoa and Nghe An who were stationed in the capital as the palace guard. In the summer of 1674, incited by officials from those provinces who had many years of service but had been recently dismissed, the guardsmen mutinied. They demolished Pham Cong Tru's house, killed Nguyen Quoc Trinh, one of Trinh Tac's most trusted advisors, and demanded the release of Trinh Toan, Trinh Tac's younger brother, who had been popular among the soldiers and had lived in confinement since the death of his father in 1657.

Trinh Tac responded to this challenge with characteristic alacrity and guile. Trinh Toan was given poison. Cash was distributed to the guardsmen. Their ringleaders were discreetly seized and executed. The officials who had stirred up the episode were reinstated for a few months until matters settled down and then they were dismissed for the last time. Most significantly, Trinh Tac officially conferred the dignity of leadership upon Trinh Can, taking himself out of the limelight. The edict proclaiming the elevation of Trinh Can praised his military achievements but, unlike every such kind of edict in the past, did not mention the necessity of pacifying the south to complete the restoration of the Le dynasty. The war policy was finally abandoned. When he died in 1675 at the age of 76, Pham Cong Tru had the satisfaction of having contributed to a major reform of government. When Trinh Tac died in 1682, he had the satisfaction of having engineered the first peaceful succession of power from one generation to the next in his family since the beginning of its fortunes more than a century before. His own prolonged accession had been marked by a battle with two of his brothers in 1645, by conspiracies in 1649 and 1652, and by his pre-emptive arrest of Trinh Toan when Trinh Trang finally died in 1657.

The Canh Tri era produced one piece of legislation that had a long-term effect on village politics and agrarian affairs, particularly in the Red River plain. In the Hong Duc era, Le Tu Thanh had instituted a sexennial registration of land ownership as the basis for taxation on fields. The periodic revision was intended to take account of changes in land ownership, but it was a labor-intensive and often litigious procedure that required relatively large numbers of officials and clerks with sufficient authority to conduct the necessary investigations and to assemble the required paperwork. It was a product of Le Tu Thanh's unusual interest in administration and his charismatic hands-on approach to government. This system apparently continued in some form through the years of Mac rule. It was able to function as long as the power of the central state had the ability to reach into the villages and to compel the cooperation of village leaders.

The disorders accompanying the Le restoration led to the breakdown of the sexennial registration system. During the decades of Trinh military occupation of the Red River plain, agrarian taxes were collected in a relatively unsystematic, ad hoc manner. Military authorities often ignored tax laws with arbitrary confiscations, and different officials sometimes competed to obtain revenue from the same source. The disaffection of the rural population combined with an absence of rational government to create a gap between village authorities and the state. Trinh Tac and his entourage of literati endeavored to revive rural administration, including the sexennial registration system. But, the administrative capacity of the state was unequal to the task. Provincial and district officials lacked the manpower and expertise to penetrate the details of village property arrangements, while village leaders had learned how to dissemble in their relations with higher authorities.

Canh Tri was not Hong Duc, and Canh Tri legislation on agrarian taxation displays the superficiality of Canh Tri achievements in comparison with those of Hong Duc. In 1664, in what became known as the "equal rule" (binh le), or Stabilization Act, a survey of land and registration of ownership was initiated throughout the country. It was completed five years later and became the basis for taxation from that time on. There would be no revisions. Changes in land ownership thereafter would not be taken into account.

In practice, what this meant was that local leaders became responsible for the collective assessment of their village. Instead of going into the villages to collect taxes from individual taxpayers, district magistrates now stood at the village gate and received what was due from the hands of village leaders. This measure reflects the relative weakening of central administration in comparison with the times of Le Tu Thanh and the Mac. It also reflects the relative strengthening of the autonomy of village leaders and of their authority within the villages. The well-known aphorism that "the law of the king stops at the village gate" dates from this time and reflects the Canh Tri compromise between villages and tax collectors enacted by the Stabilization Act. The long-term impracticality of this measure became glaringly apparent half a century later and subsequent efforts to remedy its shortcomings led to decades of unrest and uprisings in the eighteenth century.

A famous proclamation of the Canh Tri era is the 47-article "Edict to Explain Civilizing Instructions" issued in 1663, commonly interpreted as a major initiative to enforce Confucian moral behavior. It systematically presents a list of exhortations and prohibitions that had been regularly issued in more piecemeal form since the fifteenth century and would continue to be issued into the nineteenth century. Updated versions would appear in the late twentieth century. This edict, and all the others like it, encouraged thought about public morality and gave authorities a legal basis for their efforts to keep people involved in productive work rather than letting them waste time on gambling, cockfighting, playing chess, pornography, singing, dancing, lewd festivals, worshipping evil spirits, sitting around in temples, or following strange religions. Nevertheless, such edicts never put an end to these things.

Perhaps more successful were the rules for following a Confucian model of family life with ancestral veneration, marriage rites, mourning regulations, and a hierarchy of deference, which provided a blueprint for aspiring patriarchs and families ambitious to gain favor with the rulers. Against the efforts of Confucian officials to promulgate their values should be set the prospering of spirit cults, the building and repair of Buddhist temples, and the spread of Christianity, all of which were salient features of Vietnamese society in the seventeenth century.

The most important work of the Canh Tri people, so far as surviving knowledge about the Vietnamese past is concerned, was in writing history. Pham Cong Tru supervised a continuation of the fifteenth-century work of Ngo Si Lien through the reign of Le Duy Ky in 1662, just before the beginning of the Canh Tri era. Thirty years later, Le Hy (1646–1702), who began his career by passing the capital examination of 1664 as a teenager, supervised the addition of thirteen additional years to 1675, covering Canh Tri (1663–1671) and the short reign of Le Duy Hoi that followed (1672–1675), which in effect carried the account through to Pham Cong Tru's death and included the victory of Trinh Tac over the war party and the formal transfer of power to Trinh Can. This work was printed with woodblocks in 1697, and is known today as the Chinh Hoa Edition of the *Complete Book of the History of Great Viet*. The writing of official histories was traditionally defined by the rise and fall of dynasties. For Pham Cong Tru and Le Hy and their colleagues, however, the dynastic idea was no longer of historical importance. For them, it was as if they lived in a time when educated men had found solid footing after many years of war and turmoil and were able to celebrate the ascendancy of their pacific approach to government over the vainglorious aims and violent means of warriors.

Nguyen Phuc Tan and Trinh Tac were the architects of two countries that would subsequently go their separate ways for another century. Their predecessors had remained entangled in each other's ambitions, unable to entirely let go of one another. But these two men understood that there was enough for them to do without trying to rule the other's country too.

Trinh Tac had to do something about the disconnection of his regime from the majority of its population and the habits of intrigue that made leadership in his family so precarious. Victory in the south would simply feed the power and ambition of the most undisciplined elements of his regime, producing endless problems. Ending hostilities with the south enabled him to concentrate on the more urgent priority of building a government administration that would no longer fear popular disaffection. The north was turning inward.

Nguyen Huu Dat, whose whole life had been dedicated to fighting the Trinh, died in 1681 at the age of 78. His spirit was still alive a few months later, shortly before Trinh Tac's death, when rumors reached the south that the Trinh had gone off to fight rebels and had left Dong Kinh unprotected. Voices were raised at Nguyen Phuc Tan's court proposing that it was an excellent time to attack the north. Against this exuberant prospect, Nguyen Phuc Tan decided that not enough men and supplies were available for such an adventure. It was the last recorded discussion of such an idea at Nguyen Phuc Tan's court. Sometime during the Nghe An campaign, perhaps in 1658, the year of the expedition to Cambodia, Nguyen Phuc Tan lost interest in conquering the north. He began to look south. Effort was more likely to yield benefit on the relatively open Mekong frontier than on the densely populated and fiercely defended plains in the north. When Nguyen Phuc Tan died in 1687, the situation he had helped to create by encouraging warfare among Khmer princes was moving rapidly toward a major geo-political shift on the Vietnamese southern frontier. The south was turning outward.

7 THE SOUTH AND THE NORTH DIVERGE

Relations with Cambodia

When Nguyen Phuc Tan died in 1687, his 39-year-old second son, Nguyen Phuc Tran, came to power and shifted the seat of government to Phu Xuan, the modern city of Hue. Nguyen Phuc Tran's elder brother, Nguyen Phuc Tan's designated heir, had died three years before. Nguyen Phuc Tran's short four-year rule shows him to have been an uninspiring leader and a poor judge of character. No sooner had he assumed command than the far south began to slip out of his control, and the people he sent to deal with it were famous failures.

Nguyen Phuc Tan had left a situation on the southern frontier that was unstable but full of promise. The two kings of Cambodia, the "first king" Chei Chéttha III and the "second king" Ang Nan, had been in a more or less continual state of war since the 1670s, with Siamese troops intervening on behalf of Chei Chéttha III and Vietnamese troops intervening on behalf of Ang Nan. Cambodia was partitioned between the two Khmer princes with Ang Nan's territories generally coinciding with the parts of the country that would eventually become Vietnamese.

In 1679, a new element was added with the arrival of a fleet of the Ming navy that had been pushed out of Chinese seaports by the Qing Manchu conquerors. This fleet had been operating in the South China Sea for many years and already had contacts among Chinese merchants at Hoi An and other Vietnamese ports, including Prei Nokor (modern Cholon). When over fifty ships with some three thousand men, along with their families, arrived at Da Nang Bay and neighboring anchorages, Nguyen Phuc Tan directed them to the Mekong frontier. One group under Chen Shangchuan settled at Bien Hoa on the Dong Nai River, not far from Prei Nokor. A second group under Yang Yandi settled at modern My Tho on the northern bank of the northernmost arm of the Mekong River, accessible to Prei Nokor via canals and the Vam Co river system that drains a vast swampy region between the Dong Nai/Sai Gon River basin and the Mekong plain. Prei Nokor, located between the two settlements and protected by the Vietnamese garrison at Kampong Krabei (Saigon), rapidly developed from this time and became a major port city that attracted merchants from many Asian and European countries. The Ming settlers maintained armies that in the 1680s began to participate in the Cambodian civil wars in support of Ang Nan. Chen Shangchuan was particularly active in this regard.

Nguyen Phuc Tan had assembled the structure of loyalties holding together the Vietnamese, the Chinese, and the Khmer followers of Ang Nan. After his death, the court at Phu Xuan was unable to maintain this structure, and it began to disintegrate. Furthermore, just at this time, the death of King Narai in Siam produced a major political change there, which drew Siamese attention away from Cambodia for a time. In 1688, Yang Yandi, the Ming leader at My Tho, was murdered by his lieutenant Huang Jin, who then built fortifications, trained soldiers, preyed on shipping, and was rumored to harbor the ambition of seizing control of all Cambodia. In response to this, Chei Chéttha III increased his military forces and displayed indications of preparing for war. Ang Nan, alarmed, appealed to Phu Xuan for help.

Nguyen Phuc Tran was persuaded by corrupt schemers to give command of his army to a man without military ability. In 1689, this man succeeded in capturing and killing Huang Jin, and then, with Chen Shangchuan leading the vanguard, he proceeded to attack Chei Chéttha III. However, according to a story recorded by Vietnamese historians, he fell into the wiles of a beautiful woman, Chei Chéttha III's envoy, and, making peace with Chei Chéttha III, he withdrew his army back to Kampong Krabei, becoming the laughing stock of his generals. Hearing of this, Nguyen Phuc Tran dismissed the commander and replaced him with Nguyen Huu Hao, a son of the famous general Nguyen Huu Dat. In 1690, once again the Vietnamese and Chinese forces, along with Ang Nan's Khmers, advanced against Chei Chéttha III. And once again Chei Chéttha III's seductive envoy made a laughing stock of the Vietnamese commander by persuading him to withdraw his army and wait for gifts that never came. Nguyen Phuc Tran dismissed Nguyen Huu Hao. Shortly after, in early 1691, Nguyen Phuc Tran fell ill and died with affairs on the Mekong frontier in such disarray that Ang Nan killed himself in despair. Ang Nan's 10-year-old son, Ang Im, whose mother was Chinese, lived under the protection of Chen Shangchuan. Such was the situation when Nguyen Phuc Tran's eldest son, Nguyen Phuc Chu, came to power.

Although only 16 years old when he began to rule, Nguyen Phuc Chu quickly established a reputation for intelligence, modesty, and effective leadership. In 1694 he was confronted by a conspiracy of cousins, sons of Nguyen Phuc Tan's deceased eldest son, who believed they represented the "senior line" of the family and thus had the right to exercise power. Without hesitation he seized and executed the conspirators and their followers. Nguyen Phuc Chu governed for thirty-four years, sired 146 children, and added to his grandfather's legacy of making astute and far-sighted decisions. His first test was the disordered situation on the southern frontier. The incompetence of the men sent by his father, and then his father's death, apparently emboldened the Cham king, Po Sot, to seize the Phan Rang region in defiance of Phu Xuan's authority. Before dealing with the Khmer situation, Nguyen Phuc Chu had to first respond to the Chams.

The man selected to go south was another son of Nguyen Huu Dat, a younger brother of the hapless Nguyen Huu Hao named Nguyen Huu Canh. In 1693, Nguyen Huu Canh captured Po Sot. The Cham kingdom was reorganized into the province of Binh Thuan (the modern provinces of Binh Thuan and Ninh Thuan). Vietnamese officials were sent to administer the major coastal population centers at Phan Rang, Phan Ri, and Phan Thiet. A Cham noble led some five thousand Cham Muslims to join the Cham Muslim community in Cambodia. Many Chams moved into the uplands and joined the Churu, Ede, and Jarai peoples there.

Po Sot died shortly after, in captivity, but a younger brother of his named Po Saktiray Depatih (known to the Vietnamese as Ke Ba Tu) was appointed as an "aboriginal king" by the Vietnamese to govern the Cham population that remained. In late 1693 and early 1694, a Cham noble and a Chinese claiming magical powers rallied an uprising among the Chams, but, after twice besieging Phan Rang, they were driven off and fled for refuge in Cambodia.

Thereafter, until his death in 1727, Po Saktiray Depatih maintained peaceful relations between the Chams of Binh Thuan and the Vietnamese court at Phu Xuan, sending tribute as required while endeavoring to shield the Chams from the authority of Vietnamese administrators. The Vietnamese agreed to return all the prisoners and plunder they had taken from Champa in the recent campaign. For their part, the Chams were charged with an annual tribute of 2 bull elephants, 20 head of cattle, 6 elephant tusks, 10 rhinoceros horns, 500 measures of cloth, 50 measures of honey, 200 measures of dried fish, 400 measures of salt-encrusted sand for making an alkaline solution used for washing hair, 500 bamboo mats, 200 ebony trees, and 1 long boat.

In 1712 Po Saktiray Depatih obtained a "five-point treaty" with the Vietnamese that, at least in theory, remained in effect until the abolition of the Cham "aboriginal kingship" in 1832. According to this treaty, the Cham king had sole jurisdiction over litigation among Chams, while litigation between Chams and Vietnamese was to be jointly decided by Cham and Vietnamese officials. Other provisions required that merchants moving through Cham territory to trade with the upland peoples register with Cham officials and that Vietnamese authorities were not to oppress or abuse Chams. Chams were supposedly required to adopt the Vietnamese style of clothing, though it is not known to what extent this was enforced. With most Muslim Chams having fled to Cambodia, those remaining in Binh Thuan mainly followed the Hindu tradition in Cham culture. A separate and distinctive population also appeared in subsequent generations from Cham–Viet intermarriage that combined features of both Cham and Vietnamese culture.

In 1714, Po Saktiray Depatih traveled with his family and entourage to attend a vegetarian feast celebrating the completion of a major construction project at Thien Mu Temple in Phu Xuan. Later that year, he requested permission to erect a new building where his administration of the Cham people could be conducted. His request was approved and he received from the Vietnamese court an architectural plan for his magistracy. After his death, members of his family succeeded him for several generations.

Nguyen Phuc Chu presided over the demise of Champa as a vassal kingdom and its incorporation into the structure of Vietnamese government. This eliminated the "Cham gap" that had separated the Vietnamese settlements in the Dong Nai and Sai Gon River basin from the rest of the country and unambiguously advanced the Vietnamese border to this "antechamber" of the Mekong plain. This may have been what prompted Nguyen Phuc Chu to take an elevated title for himself in 1693 as "lord of the kingdom" (*quoc chua*) and two years later to build a temple to venerate the spirits of his predecessors.

The poorly led expeditions sent to Cambodia by Nguyen Phuc Tran diminished Vietnamese prestige in the region, and Chei Chéttha III exploited this in 1696 when he invited Ang Im, the 15-year-old son of his deceased cousin and old enemy Ang Nan, to come to his court at Oudong. Ang Im accepted the invitation and was married to one of Chei Chéttha III's daughters. The war that had divided the Khmers since the 1670s was seemingly at an end.

Building on the experience of erasing the Cham kingdom and establishing the province of Thuan Thanh, Nguyen Phuc Chu proceded in 1698 to establish the province of Gia Dinh in the basin of the Dong Nai and Sai Gon Rivers. The headquarters of the province was at Saigon. People were recruited from the provinces in the north and sent to augment the Vietnamese population there. Many of these were landless peasants and those without an apparent means of livelihood.

According to missionary accounts, around 10 percent of the Vietnamese population in Gia Dinh by the beginning of the eighteenth century was Christian. That Christians were a discernible element in the Gia Dinh population can be inferred from an order sent to Gia Dinh administrators in 1699 to expel all Christians and European missionaries, an order which seems not to have been enforced. To any extent that it might have been enforced, such a ban would have served only to send more Vietnamese settlers into marginal lands of the Mekong plain. Vietnamese Christians were attracted to this frontier because of the greater freedom there amidst the cultural diversity of Chinese, Khmers, and Chams. Many Khmer communities with their own leaders continued to exist in Gia Dinh. There were also Cham communities, although at that time most of the Chams outside of Binh Thuan had settled under the protection of the Khmer king.

The Chinese population of Gia Dinh was changing with the older Ming immigrants congregating at Cholon and more recent Qing immigrants gathering at Bien Hoa. The Ming Chinese population at My Tho was beyond the administrative jurisdiction of Gia Dinh, but nevertheless remained closely allied with the Vietnamese authorities at Saigon. Chen Shangchuan, who commanded Chinese military forces, was stationed at an advanced position upriver from My Tho, near where the northern branch of the Mekong begins to split into several channels on its way to the sea. His post was at Vinh Long, between the two main branches of the Mekong, in a position to observe all riverine traffic in or out of Cambodia. One of his assignments was to safeguard Chinese and Vietnamese trade on the river.

Chei Chéttha III responded to the fait accompli of Nguyen Phuc Chu's annexation of Gia Dinh by making military preparations and, according to Chen Shangchuan's reports, interfering with trade. Nguyen Phuc Chu immediately initiated military operations. In 1700, Chen Shangchuan led the vanguard of an expedition commanded by Nguyen Huu Canh, who seized the Khmer capital and forced Chei Chéttha III to flee. Chei Chéttha III's son-in-law, Ang Im, the teenage son of Ang Nan who had been raised by his Chinese mother under the protection of Chen Shangchuan before joining the Khmer royal court in 1696, first resisted the Phu Xuan forces on behalf of his father-in-law, and then submitted to Nguyen Huu Canh, allowing himself to be made king of Cambodia by the Vietnamese. Within weeks, however, Nguyen Huu Canh died, the Phu Xuan forces withdrew, and Chei Chéttha III returned to the throne.

In the years that followed, Chei Chéttha III yielded increasing authority into the hands of his son, who ruled as Srei Thoamareachea II and who elicited Siamese intervention against Ang Im, now supported by the Vietnamese. In 1705, Nguyen Phuc Chu sent an expedition to push back the Siamese and to advance Ang Im's cause. Thereafter, Srei Thoamareachea II and Ang Im revived the wars of their fathers, Chei Chéttha III and Ang Nan, which had lasted from the 1670s to the 1690s. Interventions in this struggle by Siam and Phu Xuan became routine during the first half of the eighteenth century, with Siam and Phu Xuan both annexing parts of the Cambodian kingdom as the price of assistance to their respective protégés.

One small aspect of the 1705 Vietnamese expedition involved an English outpost that had been established in 1702 on the island of Con Dao, about ninety kilometers off the southern mouth of the Mekong River. Nguyen Phuc Chu apparently tolerated this in expectation that the English would conform to his policies toward Cambodia. But when the English indicated an interest in trading with Cambodia and a large Cambodian delegation arrived at Con Dao, Vietnamese authorities at Gia Dinh were instructed to eliminate this potential source of interference in Phu Xuan's policy toward Cambodia. Shortly before the 1705 expedition, the English and Khmers on Con Dao were massacred by Macassarese mercenaries of the English and by Vietnamese residing on the island. The Vietnamese governor at Gia Dinh apparently instigated this event, for he arrived immediately after with soldiers to take possession of the island.

The Ming people who had settled at Bien Hoa and My Tho under the authority of the fleet commanders in 1679 were the most organized of a large migration of refugees from the Qing conquest of China into the Mekong region. Among this migration was a man from Guangdong named Mo Jiu (1655–1735) who insinuated himself into the entourage of Chei Chéttha III and received from him an appointment in the province of Peam (at the modern Vietnamese city of Ha Tien), on the Gulf of Siam, where Khmer, Vietnamese, Chinese, and Malay merchants gathered. He opened a gambling house and became exceedingly wealthy. This place was a gateway from the sea into the Khmer kingdom that did not rely upon the Mekong River. Amidst the confusions of the Khmer kingdom in those years, Mo Jiu established himself as ruler of the western coast of the Mekong's deltaic plain, comprised of territories around the modern cities of Ha Tien, Rach Gia, and Ca Mau, as well as the large island of Phu Quoc, all of which at that time came to be known as Ha Tien to the Vietnamese.

As his patron Chei Chéttha III faded from the scene and the Sino-Vietnamese presence grew along the Mekong, Mo Jiu did not find Srei Thoamareachea II to be a reliable suzerain. In 1708, he submitted to Nguyen Phuc Chu and received an appointment to govern Ha Tien as a Vietnamese territory. Thereafter, he cooperated with Phu Xuan in the complex game of politics along the main arms of the Mekong River that involved Khmers, Siamese, Vietnamese, Chinese, Chams, and also a community of nearly three thousand Laotians who had found refuge with Chei Chéttha III in 1691 after fleeing a power struggle in their country. In just a few years of Nguyen Phuc Chu's rule, Phu Xuan's strategic position had dramatically improved with the annexations of Gia Dinh and Ha Tien, territories that anchored the eastern and western ends of a future Khmer–Viet deltaic border.

Nguyen Cuu Van, the leader of the 1705 expedition, subsequently served for many years as governor of Gia Dinh. He asserted personal ownership over much land in territories to the southwest and northwest of Saigon. Directly to the west is a vast swampy region unsuitable for agriculture. His lands to the southwest, in modern Tien Giang Province west of My Tho, were vulnerable to Khmer attack so he built a defensive wall from the West Vam Co River to the northern branch of the Mekong River. His practice of forcing settlers on his land into a serf-like status was imitated by other locally powerful men and provoked sufficient unrest that it was reported to Nguyen Phuc Chu in 1711. Nguyen Phuc Chu admonished Nguyen Cuu Van to stop enslaving people and ordered him to institute a policy of distributing land to the landless and allowing them three years of exemption from taxation. This measure reportedly calmed the situation, but the practice of powerful men claiming vast lands worked by landless peasants became characteristic of Vietnamese settlement in the Mekong plain.

Later that same year, Nguyen Cuu Van and Chen Shangchuan reported that Srei Thoamareachea II was reinforcing his position in Cambodia with large numbers of troops arriving from Siam. Nguyen Phuc Chu instructed them to maintain vigilance, but he chose to postpone action until absolutely necessary, understanding that the passing of time and the arrival of increasing numbers of Vietnamese settlers would strengthen his position.

Finally, in late 1714, Srei Thoamareachea II, reinforced with a Siamese army, besieged Ang Im, probably at Srei Santhor, about forty kilometers north of Phnom Penh, where his father's headquarters had often been located. With Ang Im and his Khmer followers was a military force recruited from the Laotian community in Cambodia, which allied with him against the Siamese. However, Ang Im's enemies outnumbered him four to one, so he called to Gia Dinh for help. Chen Shangchuan again led the way for Phu Xuan armies to advance upriver and seize the Khmer capital. Srei Thoamareachea II fled to Siam and the Vietnamese proclaimed Ang Im as King of Cambodia. Ang Im and his son Ang Chi reigned as kings of Cambodia from then until 1737. In the 1720s they fended off several Siamese invasions with Phu Xuan's assistance. Chen Shangchuan died in 1715 but his son Chen Dading continued to loyally serve Phu Xuan's interests.

Politics and government in the south

Nguyen Phuc Chu was concerned with much more than the Mekong frontier. In 1697 and again in 1714 he fought brief wars with upland chieftains who threatened to cut the Cam Lo Road west from Quang Tri to the Mekong, a route not only important commercially but also militarily because of its proximity to the northern border. In 1700, he inspected the northern wall complex and embarked on a two-year project to repair and renovate it. A year later he ordered a map to be made of the entire country. Ten years later, the northern walls were repaired once again and a survey was conducted of roads and beaches in the border region. In 1713, another inspection of the walls on the northern border was made. Despite the seeming peace with the north, Nguyen Phuc Chu was taking nothing for granted. In 1715 he sent two Fujianese merchants into the north as spies to evaluate Trinh military preparedness.

Military affairs took precedence over all other public concerns. Nguyen Phuc Chu scheduled mobilizations of conscripts for military service on a five-year cycle. In 1707, he issued a detailed edict with twenty-two articles on military conscription. In 1708 there were thirteen assembly points for organizing conscripts, five in Thuan Hoa, two in Quang Nam, and one each in Quang Ngai, Binh Dinh, Phu Yen, Khanh Hoa, Thuan Thanh, and Gia Dinh. Nguyen Phuc Chu halted the 1713 call-up when he learned that his officials were unlawfully harassing people and acquiring personal fortunes by selling exemptions. In addition to paying close attention to the system for acquiring soldiers, he emphasized military training. In 1696, he began an annual event for his officials to practice shooting muskets. In 1701, he inspected a center for training soldiers in how to shoot guns. In 1700 he opened a school for performing horses and two years later held an examination of his generals in horsemanship. He also instituted a new program for training elephants for battle. In 1703 a new kind of crossbow was introduced and it became all the rage to acquire one and to learn how to shoot it. Elaborate naval and land exercises were regularly held to simulate battlefield conditions and to sharpen military skills.

Nguyen Phuc Chu also gave close attention to education and to the system of examinations for filling public positions. Literary examinations were regularly held on a six-year schedule. There were five categories of achievement and appointments were accordingly made to provincial or district offices, to oversee education, or to work in one of the three "offices" of the central government (ty). One of the categories that produced officials for the three "offices" was facility in the Chinese spoken language, which reveals the importance of the Chinese communities in the country.

The basic curriculum of literary examinations in the south was well established by the end of the seventeenth century and continued through the eighteenth century. Unlike the curriculum in the north, which was more academic and emphasized skill in traditional poetic forms, the southern curriculum included practical skills and new literary forms. The first level of achievement was to demonstrate skill in a distich rhythmic prose of alternating four- and six-syllable lines (tu-luc), a distinctive feature of southern exams. The second level was to write compositions in the *phu* rhyming prose that had been part of the

Vietnamese curriculum since Tran times. The third level was the standard composition about the meaning of classical texts. The fourth level changed through the years from tests in mathematics for calculating taxes and market duties, to questions about case law for judging litigation in the late seventeenth century, to dissertations on public policy by the mid eighteenth century. Students who successfully completed the fourth level were qualified for appointments in government offices.

A new departure commonly thought to have appeared in Vietnamese literature during the eighteenth century is an appreciation of women and of their point of view, which was usually a complaint against Heaven for the hard life that women had to lead. The earliest example of this kind of literature comes from Nguyen Phuc Chu's wife, Nguyen Kinh Phi (d. 1714), who wrote four poems lamenting the transience of her fading beauty and blaming Heaven for "robbing" her of her youth. After her death, Nguyen Phuc Chu wrote four poems in response, lamenting her death and accusing Heaven of "hating" his wife. In the poems of both poets, readers are admonished not to "laugh" at such sentiments, for they express feelings that all people experience. The mention of laughter reveals that this kind of poetry exceeded existing conventions and was intentionally provocative. By the end of the century, the theme of a woman's "complaint" against Heaven would not only be acceptable in literature but it would also be used by men to voice their feelings at a time when a man's voice was not considered appropriate to express complaints without suggesting an inclination to rebel against political authority.

Nguyen Phuc Chu aspired to have his realm recognized by the Qing, thus gaining imperial acknowledgment that he no longer owed allegiance to the Le dynasty. In 1702, he sent a letter to the Qing court requesting appointment as a vassal separate from the Le. The Qing rejected the request, replying that the Le dynasty yet reigned and thus remained the Qing vassal for that part of the world. A separate Vietnamese kingdom could not penetrate the Qing system of vassalage. Nguyen Phuc Chu nevertheless expressed his aspirations with a new seal in 1709 inscribed: "The Nguyen Lord Eternally Guarding the Kingdom of Great Viet."

The economic development of the Mekong during the first decade of the eighteenth century led to an expansion of coastal shipping. The transport of rice from the Mekong to the northern provinces, particularly Thuan Hoa with its large military population on guard at the northern border, was a critical concern of the Phu Xuan government. It had been subject to a system of conscripting boat owners and requiring them to transport rice twice a year in exchange for tax exemptions and allowances for expenses. However, as the coastal economy grew, boat owners balked at this arrangement because opportunities for private business were so much more lucrative than government service. Consequently, a major shift in government policy was initiated in 1714 under the leadership of an official named Nguyen Khoa Chiem, by which the government abandoned the system of commandeering transport and instead simply joined the market by purchasing rice with cash at prevailing rates while establishing a new tax scheme on private shipping. This monetizing of the rice economy began to affect the supply of money, which was already shrinking due to the decreasing availability of coins from China and Japan, and within a few decades became a factor contributing to serious fiscal problems.

Nguyen Phuc Chu died in 1725 and was succeeded by his 30-year-old eldest son, Nguyen Phuc Tru. During his thirteen years of rule, Nguyen Phuc Tru did not show as much personal engagement with government as did his father, but rather relied upon the senior members of his entourage to handle affairs. Three families that were particularly prominent at this time were the Nguyen Cuu, the Nguyen Khoa, and the Truong Phuc.

Nguyen Cuu Kieu, the man who had fled to the south in 1623 with a letter from Trinh Trang's wife to her brother Nguyen Phuc Nguyen, was the founder of the Nguyen Cuu family. Nguyen Cuu Van, who had led the 1705 expedition to Cambodia and served for many years thereafter as the governor of Gia Dinh, was a grandson of Nguyen Cuu Kieu. He was prominent in opening up land to Vietnamese settlement west of My Tho, between the Mekong and West Vam Co Rivers. In 1715, Nguyen Cuu Chiem, a son of Nguyen Cuu Van, became governor of Gia Dinh and inherited lands that his father had possessed along the East Vam Co River, northwest of Saigon in the region of modern Tay Ninh, which, during the next two decades, he opened up to Vietnamese settlement. He was still the governor at Gia Dinh in the 1730s when another round of fighting led to the annexation of more territory.

The Nguyen Khoa family traced its ancestry to a man who had come south with Nguyen Hoang in 1558. In the early eighteenth century, the most prominent person of this family was Nguyen Khoa Chiem, who made his mark both in administration and in literature. He was the official who had monetized the system of coastal rice transport in 1714. He also wrote a book that he entitled *Stories about the Achievements of the Southern Court* (*Nam Trieu Cong Nghiep Dien Chi*), a book now commonly referred to as *Stories about the Founding of the Country of Viet Nam* (*Viet Nam Khai Quoc Chi Truyen*), which is an anecdotal history of the south from the time of Nguyen Hoang through the time of Nguyen Phuc Tan (mid sixteenth century to the end of the seventeenth century).

Nguyen Khoa Chiem's second son, Nguyen Khoa Dang, became a prominent official at Phu Xuan in the 1720s. Nguyen Khoa Dang was famous for being utterly honest and very strict in the performance of his official duties. He was an excellent judge and many stories were told of how he decided difficult cases. He was greatly trusted by Nguyen Phuc Chu, who appointed him to many difficult assignments, including supervision of the treasury and of the "meat ration" for members of the Nguyen Phuc family and of other prominent families at court. Perhaps his enthusiasm for doing the right thing was too exuberant for Phu Xuan. He earned the enmity of powerful families at court by persuading Nguyen Phuc Chu to require that they pay back all the money they had "borrowed" from the treasury. Shortly after the death of Nguyen Phuc Chu in 1725, a cousin of Nguyen Cuu Van accused Nguyen Khoa Dang of treason and he was put to death, only 35 years old, unprotected by Nguyen Phuc Tru.

Another family that, like the Nguyen Cuu family, was prominent both at the Phu Xuan court and in Gia Dinh, was descended from Truong Phuc Phan, who had gained fame during the Trinh invasion of 1648 by calmly directing the defense of the last wall amidst desperate fighting. One of his grandsons had been governor at Gia Dinh during the episode of eliminating the English base on Con Dao Island. In 1731, Nguyen Phuc Tru appointed another member of this family, Truong Phuc Vinh, to be "controller" in overall command of the Mekong River plain. This was a new position. It was made amidst a new crisis in the far south and a perception that government authority there had become too decentralized with Nguyen Cuu Chiem at Gia Dinh, Mo Jiu at Ha Tien, and Chen Dading, son of Chen Shangchuan, at My Tho. Truong Phuc Vinh was eager to rebuild the fortunes of his family on this frontier. The situation that he faced in 1731 arose from events within the Laotian community in Cambodia, which had supported Ang Im against the Siamese in 1714 and continued to support Ang Im's son, Ang Chi, who was then reigning as king.

The Laotian community was centered along the Mekong River north of Phnom Penh, west of modern Tay Ninh Province where Nguyen Cuu Chiem's private lands were. In 1731, a leader of this community, seemingly without the approval of Ang Chi, mobilized his followers, along with many Khmers, and began to attack down the East Vam Co River toward Gia Dinh. Nguyen Cuu Chiem successfully fended them off, but, after news of this arrived at Phu Xuan, Truong Phuc Vinh was sent to take command of the situation. By the time he had arrived, the Lao–Khmer forces had shifted to attack toward My Tho along the West Vam Co River. Truong Phuc Vinh sent Nguyen Cuu Chiem and Chen Dading to repulse them. Ang Chi, fearing reprisals, sent a letter of submission to Truong Phuc Vinh and ceded the My Tho and Vinh Long regions to Phu Xuan. Truong Phuc Vinh thereafter occupied himself with conscripting labor to open lacquer plantations in Gia Dinh.

However, in the following year, the Laotians mobilized more attacks in the Vinh Long and My Tho areas. Truong Phuc Vinh accused Ang Chi of supporting the Laotians and prepared to attack up the Mekong River. Finding himself in an impossible situation and learning of Truong Phuc Vinh's desire for wealth, Ang Chi sent a large sum of money to Truong Phuc Vinh as a bribe to stop any military action against him. Truong Phuc Vinh accepted the bribe. He then hoped to remove Chen Dading's authority in My Tho and Vinh Long by ordering him to attack while withdrawing his own forces back to Gia Dinh, meanwhile reporting to Phu Xuan that Chen Dading had refused his order to advance. Chen Dading's advance up the Mekong gave Ang Chi an opportunity to mobilize his Khmer followers and wipe out the Laotian "rebels." But when he learned of Truong Phuc Vinh's treachery, Chen Dading went immediately to Phu Xuan to plead his case. However, the influence of the Truong Phuc family was so strong that he was summarily imprisoned. He died before Nguyen Cuu Chiem was able to inform Nguyen Phuc Tru of Chen Dading's innocence. Nguyen Cuu Chiem was rewarded for uncovering the affair with land in Vinh Long, and Truong Phuc Vinh was dismissed.

The formal annexation of the My Tho and Vinh Long territories was accomplished under somewhat odd circumstances. Ang Chi considered himself allied with Phu Xuan against his rival, Srei Thoamareachea II, who was allied with Siam. He was also allied with the Laotian community in Cambodia against Siam. However, the Laotians proved to be a wild card and, for reasons unknown but that may simply have been a lust for plunder, a certain Lao leader, called Sa Tot in Vietnamese records, initiated a war with the Vietnamese. Under duress from all sides, Ang Chi used what capital he had available in territorial claims and treasure to forestall Vietnamese invasions until finding a chance to eliminate the Laotians. Vietnamese authority had already extended into many areas of the My Tho and Vinh Long regions. The events of 1731 and 1732 resulted in making official the penetration of Vietnamese settlement into the Mekong's northerly downriver territories.

Aside from these acquisitions on the Gia Dinh frontier, indications of administrative energy during Nguyen Phuc Tru's years appear to have been aimed at seeking an appearance of uniformity. For example, in 1733 he ordered that clocks be put in all administrative centers and coastal watch stations to coordinate the timing of government activities and related events. The edict proclaiming this innovation included a detailed description of the clocks that were to be used, their manufacture, and their various functions.

Other innovations came early in Nguyen Phuc Tru's rule. In 1726, he issued two edicts to instruct the people how to live proper, civilized lives. He emphasized the merit of his family in founding the country and the gratitude for this that should encourage an industrious and productive spirit among the people. Gambling, corrupt litigation, and efforts to avoid census takers and military

conscription were specifically forbidden. This appears to have been an exhortation for human behaviour to be as correct, morally, as clocks could be in telling
time. Also in 1726, a new system of administration was set up for jurisdictions
along the western upland frontier from the northern border all the way down to
the Mekong plain. It appears to have created an administrative border zone
between lowland Viets and uplanders and to have defined more clearly a boundary between the two populations.

Nguyen Phuc Khoat, the first southern king

In 1738, Nguyen Phuc Tru died and was succeeded by his 25-year-old eldest son
Nguyen Phuc Khoat. He ruled for twenty-seven years during a time when the
Trinh were beset by vast, prolonged rebellions in the north and the southerners
annexed the remaining territories in the Mekong plain that would become
Vietnamese. He presided with vigor and imagination over the last era of peace
and prosperity for the southerners before the outbreak of the Thirty Years War.
He is most noted for claiming royal status, thereby casting aside any vestige of
subordination to the Le dynasty and openly affirming the political independence
of the south.

In 1744, after a series of auspicious signs and the ritual of his officials three
times requesting him to take the throne, Nguyen Phuc Khoat proclaimed himself
a king, issued a new seal inscribed with "King of the Realm," and published an
edict announcing a "change to the new." All of his predecessors were known by
the title of "duke" (quan cong). He was the first to be known as "king" (vuong).
There had been a well-known prophesy in the south that the Nguyen family
would "return to the royal capital" after eight generations. Nguyen Phuc Khoat
was in the eighth generation from Nguyen Hoang, and by making Phu Xuan a
royal capital he fulfilled this prophesy. The government offices at Phu Xuan
were, at least superficially, reorganized under the "Six Ministries" and the other
administrative units that had been used at Dong Kinh since the time of Le Tu
Thanh. The hierarchy of titles, clothing regulations for officials, court ritual, and
the provincial administrative system were all reformed to be in accord with what
were understood as royal practice. The only compromise with respect to complete sovereignty was that official paperwork was still dated using Le dynasty
reign years to avoid diplomatic problems with the Qing imperial court. In 1754,
a major project to construct palaces and gardens was initiated to make Phu Xuan
look more like a royal capital.

Nguyen Phuc Khoat continued the attention to education displayed by his
predecessors. In 1740, he revised the literary examinations. Success at the first

three of four levels of achievement, covering four-six distich prose, *phu* rhyming prose, and a prose composition on classical texts, respectively, earned various tax and corvée exemptions. The fourth and highest level required a dissertation in response to a question about public policy and success at this level earned an appointment at a provincial or district government office.

One of the graduates of this 1740 examination was Nguyen Cu Trinh (1716–1767). He became one the most famous scholar-officials during the time of Nguyen Phuc Khoat. His ancestors had left Nghe An for the south in the early sixteenth century. His father was Nguyen Dang De (1668–1727), a graduate of the 1701 examination who had a distinguished career under Nguyen Phuc Chu and authored the edicts on civilized behavior at the beginning of Nguyen Phuc Tru's rule. A cousin of Nguyen Cu Trinh, Nguyen Dang Thinh (1693–1755), a graduate of the 1721 exam, was known for his erudition, was entrusted with the drafting of all edicts, and became the teacher of Nguyen Phuc Khoat. Nguyen Cu Trinh's exceptionally astute administrative work is an indication of the quality of men who entered government through the educational system at this time, which provides a partial explanation for the achievements of Nguyen Phuc Khoat's reign.

Nguyen Cu Trinh was known for good manners, which probably contributed to his rapid rise at Phu Xuan. He already held a high court position when Nguyen Phuc Khoat proclaimed himself king in 1744. In 1750, he was made governor of Quang Ngai Province at a time when conditions there were in disarray and government authority was in danger of unraveling. Since Nguyen Phuc Khoat's accession, the long southern coast and the Mekong plain gave frequent cause for concern, despite initiatives to maintain communications and to strengthen administration.

No sooner had Nguyen Phuc Tru died in 1738 than a Siamese army expelled Ang Chi, the pro-Vietnamese king of Cambodia, and reinstalled Srei Thoamareachea II on the Khmer throne. Ang Chi fled to Gia Dinh. This was immediately followed by a Khmer attack on Ha Tien. Mo Jiu, the governor of Ha Tien, had died in 1735 and had been replaced by his son, Mac Thien Tu (Chinese: Mo Tianci; also known as Mo Tianxi, Vietnamese Mac Thien Tich; 1710–1780). Mac Thien Tu responded to the Khmer attack with such vigor that his men outran their supplies, but his wife organized the wives of his men to bring up supplies, which enabled him to decisively defeat the Khmers.

When Truong Phuc Vinh was discredited and dismissed in 1632 as "controller" with overall command in the Mekong region, a man named Nguyen Huu Doan was appointed to replace him. Thereafter, Nguyen Huu Doan's competent leadership stabilized the Vietnamese position in the Mekong plain. In 1741 he established nine new storehouses in Gia Dinh as part of a general reorganization of storehouses throughout the country that was designed to reduce the level of corruption in storehouse administration. In 1746, he sent soldiers to put down an uprising among the Chams in Binh Thuan to the north. Shortly after this he suppressed an attempt by Qing merchants to take over Bien Hoa. This was no sooner settled than the Khmer monarchy fell open for contestation.

In 1747, the death of Srei Thoamareachea II provoked a new round of fighting in the Mekong plain among his potential successors. Amidst this turmoil, a Khmer army seized and plundered My Tho. Nguyen Huu Doan replied to this with an advance up the Mekong River to the Khmer capital where he made Ang Chi king, but Ang Chi was soon driven out and died shortly after. Eventually, a son of Srei Thoamareachea II emerged as the new king, known as Chei Chéttha IV. Nguyen Huu Doan was content to let matters calm down and concentrated on establishing a system of roads and ferry crossings to facilitate communication and transport in the Mekong plain. This became the southernmost extension of the first land road with ferry crossings that was then being built from the northern border to Gia Dinh.

All the problems that could be expected in frontier jurisdictions seem to have accumulated with particular virulence in Quang Ngai. Although not very far from Phu Xuan, and despite, or maybe because of, being commonly treated as a backwater of Quang Nam, Vietnamese settlers in Quang Ngai had developed an adversarial attitude toward government authority. Unlike neighboring provinces, Quang Ngai had no easy access into the mountains, which stood, in the expression of the time, like a "stone wall" in the west. One particular mountain was named "Stone Wall Mountain." The province extended from north to south for about one hundred kilometers, but the coastal plain was relatively narrow, on average ten to fifteen kilometers wide, and the mountains were never out of sight.

Nguyen Cu Trinh's report on the conditions he found in Quang Ngai when he arrived in 1750 is a list of problems: corrupt officials; bullies and bandits everywhere; poor communication; a sparse and scattered population; stubborn, ungovernable people living in misery; soldiers living in neglect; and chronic attacks from upland peoples, called "stone wall barbarians." His analysis was that the first priority was to take care of the soldiers and to improve the morale of the people.

A year later, he submitted a follow-up report with a more detailed analysis of the situation and with recommendations for improvement. He thought that excessive taxes, legal fees levied by corrupt officials, and demands to provide supplies for garrisons and to care for elephants were impoverishing the people in the province. Local officials were busying themselves with raising money by making arrests, conducting interrogations, and seeking bribes. He recommended that taxes be collected by provincial authorities and thus taken out of the hands of local magistrates; that magistrates be paid salaries and be promoted, demoted, or dismissed based on evaluations of their honesty; that the large population of vagabonds be sorted out to distinguish good people fleeing oppressive taxation from troublemakers, and that those simply seeking a livelihood be allowed to settle where they wished; and, finally, that people be required to carry identification papers to clearly distinguish honest citizens from people wandering around stealing chickens and horses and disturbing the peace.

Nguyen Cu Trinh was in Quang Ngai only three years. It is unknown to what extent he was able to implement his recommendations, but he did considerably improve conditions in the province. He brought available military forces to a high level of training and, using both force and conciliation, ended the depredations of the "stone wall barbarians." Beyond that, he composed a vernacular work that could be performed on stage that was aimed at raising the morale of the people in Quang Ngai and at giving them a vocabulary to increase their cultural and political awareness. The work is a dialogue between a Buddhist monk and a Buddhist nun called *Sai Vai* (Monk and Nun). It is an entertaining, racy, and at times almost pornographic work in easily memorized six-eight vernacular verse. It includes humorous critiques both of Buddhist meditational practice and of Confucian ideas about good government and it ends with a rallying cry against the "stone wall barbarians." The *Sai Vai* was a brilliant way to catch the attention of a dispirited population and give them a laugh while providing an education in the rhetoric of civilized behavior and good government. Another gift of Nguyen Cu Trinh to the people of Quang Ngai was a set of poems praising the "ten most scenic places" in the province, which was a traditional way of putting a locality on the literary map. It might be thought that he pacified the province with theater and literature.

With his exceptional abilities, Nguyen Cu Trinh was given the most difficult assignments. In early 1753, he was sent to administer the northern border region. This followed reports in 1752 that corruption among officials there was causing unrest among the people, which invited Trinh intervention. At that time, the Trinh were requesting permission of Phu Xuan to move their armies through the border region to attack a rebel Le prince who had taken refuge in Laos. Nguyen Cu Trinh dismissed the corrupt officials, raised the level of vigilance on the border, and wrote a reply to the Trinh denying their request. After only eight months on the northern border he had settled matters there. He was immediately reassigned to the southern frontier where turmoil in the Khmer royal family was creating new opportunities.

Nguyen Cu Trinh was sent south to be Nguyen Huu Doan's successor as "controller" in the Mekong region, but the territory over which he was given authority extended up the coast as far as Nha Trang to give him greater resources for dealing with the Cambodian situation. There was supposedly a rumor that Chei Chéttha IV, the king of Cambodia, was in league with the Trinh, and there were suspicions that the border flap Nguyen Cu Trinh encountered in the north was connected with events in Cambodia. The implausibility of this rumor may suggest that it was recorded by way of justifying Nguyen Cu Trinh's assignment, but given the embattled view that the southerners had of both frontiers it is not unlikely that such a rumor could easily have gained currency at that time.

Nguyen Phuc Khoat heard news of confusion at the Khmer capital and decided to simply move in and overwhelm the contestants for power there. In late 1753, Nguyen Cu Trinh was ordered to Gia Dinh where he was to prepare an expedition against Cambodia. In mid 1754 he launched an attack upriver from My Tho toward the Khmer capital. The Cham community in Cambodia found itself in the middle of this campaign and rallied to Nguyen Cu Trinh, providing him with scouts and guides. During the course of this campaign, which continued for two years, a front-line Vietnamese general ordered the Chams to relocate, and then, apparently seeing little value in protecting his "barbarian" allies, he withdrew to My Tho as a Khmer army attacked the Cham refugees, numbering some five thousand men and women. Nguyen Cu Trinh, alerted to the situation, came to the rescue of the Chams and escorted them to safety, out of the battle zone to the northwest of Saigon. He then replaced the apparently racist general with a man who incorporated Cham soldiers into his vanguard and renewed the offensive against the Khmers.

Chei Chéttha IV had been in the midst of murderous intrigues among the Khmer princes and members of his court when the Vietnamese attack was launched. He eventually fled to Ha Tien and found refuge with Mac Thien Tu. In 1756, Mac Thien Tu relayed a message from Chei Chéttha IV to Nguyen Cu Trinh begging to submit and offering to pay tribute due for the preceding three years and to hand over two Khmer territories along the two branches of the Mekong River from the modern cities of Vinh Long and Can Tho upriver to the vicinity of Chau Doc, on the modern Khmer–Viet border. Nguyen Phuc Khoat was not inclined to accept this offer of submission from Chei Chéttha IV, not believing that he would keep his word. Nguyen Cu Trinh then sent a letter to Nguyen Phuc Khoat that reveals the quality of his thought:

> We use military force to exterminate enemies and to expand our control
> of territory. Now Chei Chéttha IV shows an attitude of repentance and
> submission, and he offers us land. If we persist in doubting him, he will
> surely run away and nothing will have been achieved. From Gia Dinh to
> Phnom Penh the way is far and difficult with rivers and forests. It will not
> be easy to run him down. If we want to expand our territory, we should
> take the two places he offers to us before we do anything else, so that they

will definitely be ours. If we toss away what is near in search of what is far, I fear that there will be difficulties that our soldiers cannot overcome. Although it is easy to take territory, it is not so easy to truly hold it. In the past, our occupation of these territories in this region has been slow, step-by-step. In fact, the land we now occupy does not have enough settlers and soldiers. The Chams are good soldiers and the Khmers fear them. We should give the Chams land and support them, using barbarians against barbarians. I recommend that we forgive Chei Chéttha IV, take the two regions he has offered to us, inspect them, build fortifications, establish garrisons, settle people, make a border, and soon we will have the whole region.

Nguyen Phuc Khoat found nothing wrong with this argument and accordingly made peace with Chei Chéttha IV.

One year later, in 1757, Chei Chéttha IV died. Two men who endeavored to succeed him were successively murdered. Vietnamese armies were again mobilized to intervene. Once again, Mac Thien Tu provided the solution for settling matters by proposing that a Khmer prince who had found refuge with him be made king of Cambodia. Nguyen Phuc Khoat agreed to this on condition that all remaining downriver Khmer territories, in the region of modern Tra Vinh and Soc Trang, were to be ceded to the Vietnamese. On this basis, Nguyen Cu Trinh and Mac Thien Tu marched to the Khmer capital and enthroned a grandson of one of Chei Chéttha IV's second cousins as Outeireachea III, who reigned thereafter until 1775. As part of the final settlement, Outeireachea III ceded more territories along the borders of Ha Tien to Mac Thien Tu, who then passed them along to Phu Xuan. With this, the Khmer–Viet border was drawn more or less as it exists today.

Nguyen Cu Trinh remained in the south until 1765. He and Mac Thien Tu were well-educated men who became famous for their friendship. Both loved poetry and Nguyen Cu Trinh contributed to an anthology of poems praising the "ten most scenic places" in Ha Tien. Nguyen Cu Trinh's leadership was a critical factor in stabilizing a Khmer–Viet border that would thereafter stand the test of time.

It was during Nguyen Cu Trinh's service in the south, in 1751, that envoys are recorded from the "Water Chieftain" and the "Fire Chieftain" of the Central Highlands in the vicinity of modern Buon Ma Thuot. Vietnamese historians considered these men to be descendents of the Cham king defeated by Le Tu Thanh in 1471 and recorded tribute and trading relationships with them since the time Phu Yen had been added to Vietnamese territory in the early seventeenth century, for access to their lands was up the Da Rang River that flowed into the sea at Phu Yen. According to southern annalists, Vietnamese traded silks, hats, brass pots, iron pans, and ceramics for beeswax, deer antlers, bear gall, stallions, and bull elephants. Trade with the Laotian kingdom via the Cam Lo Road west from Quang Tri continued to be important as well. In 1761, Laotian envoys arrived in Phu Xuan to demonstrate their interest in maintaining this trade.

Information recorded in the time of Nguyen Phuc Khoat also gives details about the maritime frontier. In 1754, a Vietnamese ship on its way to the Hoang Sa Islands (Paracel Islands) was blown off course by a storm and shipwrecked on Hainan Island. Qing magistrates sent the survivors back to Phu Xuan, and Nguyen Phuc Khoat wrote a letter of thanks to the Qing authorities. This episode was the occasion for Vietnamese historians to record information about Vietnamese activities on offshore islands. According to them, each year, since the beginning of Nguyen rule in the south, around seventy people were assigned to sail to the Hoang Sa Islands in the third lunar month to collect sea products and to return in the eighth lunar month. The trip normally took three days each way. The passage also mentions that Vietnamese regularly visited the Truong Sa Islands (Spratley Islands), describing them as over 130 islets, some with fresh water, spread over a huge distance. The products collected from the islands included shellfish, sea ginseng, tortoise shell, and many kinds of sea turtles.

However impressive the achievements of Nguyen Phuc Khoat's reign may appear, failure to find any solution to a deepening fiscal conundrum also characterized his time. The basic problem was that the southern economy was increasingly monetized just as money was increasingly scarce. This led to a shift of coinage from copper to zinc, which led to inflation and the erosion of both the private economy and government finances.

In the seventeenth century, trade with China and Japan produced an abundance of copper coins, which met the needs of the economy. By the early eighteenth century, however, this supply declined and the price of copper rapidly rose relative to silver, which became more abundant from South America via Manila. Chinese copper became expensive, and Japan began to limit the export of copper coins in the early eighteenth century. The first indication of this problem in the annals comes in 1724 with an edict forbidding the casting of tin, lead, or iron coins or the melting down of copper coins unless they were chipped, cracked, or worn away. Apparently, not only were people melting down copper coins because their actual value was higher than their face value, but there was also private minting of non-copper coins. The edict appears to have been an effort to maintain copper as legal tender despite the market forces that were replacing copper with cheaper materials. In the following year, copper coins were cast and distributed to soldiers. The annal explains that this was necessary because people were melting down copper coins and making them scarce.

The first indication of inflation comes from 1741 when Nguyen Phuc Khoat ordered an examination of tax receipts for rice and salt during the preceding three years to see if the tax rate was correct in reference to expenses. It was at that time that he became concerned about corruption in storehouses and instituted a new system of control for storehouses to maintain stricter supervision of them and to prevent officials from abusing their access to these sites of non-monetary wealth. The scarcity of copper coinage finally led to the casting of zinc coins in 1746. These coins were one-third to half the weight of copper coins and their face value was more than twice their real value. In 1748, an edict prescribed punishments for those refusing to use these new coins. Before long, private foundries were producing as many of these coins as the government was supplying, and inflation became a very serious matter. Indications of government efforts to keep up with inflation are frequent in the 1750s. In 1753, Nguyen Phuc Khoat ordered a calculation and analysis of revenues and expenditures during the preceding six years. In 1758, officials were sent to adjust tax rates in Phu Yen because revenue from that province was not consistent with rising revenues from neighboring jurisdictions; perhaps officials in Phu Yen were trying to benefit from inflation while pretending it was not happening.

In 1755, custom duties on foreign ships were increased. European ships were assessed at the highest rate. Ships from Macau and Japan were assessed at half the European rate. Ships from Guangdong and Shanghai were assessed at three-quarters the Macau and Japanese rate, and those from Fujian, Siam, and Manila at two-thirds the Guangdong and Shanghai rate. The effect of inflation on foreign trade was disastrous. Whereas in the 1740s sixty to eighty foreign ships called at Hoi An each year, by the early 1770s the number was down at ten to fifteen.

The inflationary squeeze that developed during Nguyen Phuc Khoat's time tore the vitality out of the southern economy and, by the mid 1760s, brought to the verge of poverty a country that for the preceding two centuries had been mostly prosperous. The failure to solve this economic crisis led to a collapse of political leaderhip in the 1760s that contributed to the outbreak of the Thirty Years War. At the time of his death in 1765, Nguyen Phuc Khoat's designated heir was his 33-year-old second son, Nguyen Phuc Con. However, a member of the powerful Truong Phuc family named Truong Phuc Loan, a brother of Nguyen Phuc Khoat's mother, had insinuated himself into an impregnable position at court. Nguyen Phuc Con was imprisoned and killed as Truong Phuc Loan brought to the throne Nguyen Phuc Khoat's sixteenth son, 11-year-old Nguyen Phuc Thuan. Truong Phuc Loan thereafter maintained power with an entourage of homicidal sycophants. He was greedy for riches and spent much time with food, wine, and women. However, he was an incompetent ruler, and it was not long before the country began to drift into disorder.

In the Phu Xuan era, the southerners established a new country extending from the Gianh River to the Gulf of Siam. The Nguyen Phuc family gradually abandoned its pose of loyalty to a dynasty held hostage by its Trinh enemy. After generations of acting as an independent monarchy, the Nguyen Phuc openly claimed that status. Under Nguyen Phuc Khoat, Phu Xuan's wealth and power overwhelmed Cambodia, was felt among chieftains in the Central Highlands, extended to the Laotian kingdom on the mid Mekong, and echoed across the sea. That Phu Xuan was destined to collapse so suddenly within a few years of Nguyen Phuc Khoat's death was not foreseen by anyone during his lifetime.

The helplessness of the Nguyen Phuc family under the machinations of Truong Phuc Loan is difficult to explain without an understanding of what can begin to happen at a royal court suffering financial woes and where greed and intrigue become the everyday style of life. By the 1760s, Phu Xuan was not a garrison, or the headquarters of a regional lord, or the center of administration for an aspiring monarchy. It had become a royal court and was consequently the arena of king-making ambitions modeled on the Trinh in the north. In 1765, Truong Phuc Loan aspired to be for the Nguyen Phuc what the Trinh were for the Le. However, unlike the Trinh, he lacked a strong regional base from which to dominate the rest of the country, and he was bereft of political acuity. His adventure as lord of the palace did not last long.

Misgovernment in the north

In Samuel Baron's words, written in the 1680s and later published in London as "A Description of the Kingdom of Tonqueen,"

> the city of Ke Cho is the metropolis of Tonkin … and may, for its capaciousness, be compared with many cities in Asia, and superior to most for populousness, especially on the first and fifteenth day of their new moon, being their market days … when the people from the adjacent villages flock thither with their trade, in such numbers, as is almost incredible; several of the streets, though broad and spacious, are then so crowded that one finds enough to do if he can sometimes advance through the multitude a hundred paces in half an hour.

The vernacular term *ke cho* means "people in the market." Thang Long, Dong Kinh, and other classical terms for the capital did not enjoy popular currency. From at least the seventeenth century, the capital was known to the people who lived there as Ke Cho, the place where large numbers of people gathered on the bi-monthly market days.

In the seventeenth century, Europeans also knew the city as Ke Cho. The city was no longer a royal capital of kings who ruled. Kings now sat powerless in the solitude of their palaces while in a separate palace complex in the southern part of the city sat the lords who ruled with their garrison of thousands of soldiers from Thanh Hoa and Nghe An. The reforms of the Vinh Tho and Canh Tri eras (1658–1671) had brought men from the Red River plain into the government, but their efforts to harness the agrarian resources of this potentially rich land were ad hoc and constrained by the limitations of Trinh leadership.

The Trinh conundrum was that they dared not dispense with the Le dynasty because it was in the name of that dynasty that they had been able to establish relations with first the Ming and then the Qing Empires to the north. Furthermore, without the Le dynasty, the Trinh would have no credible claim over the southerners. Even though efforts to enforce that claim had lapsed in the 1670s, the Trinh were not prepared to relinquish it altogether. But having to live with the fuss and bother of a royal court that by its nature was a magnet for seditious loyalties and a natural seedbed of opposition kept Trinh nerves stretched taut. The Le court was a reminder of unfulfilled ambition and a threat of disloyalty and insubordination. The Trinh and their supporters inhabited an institutionalized contradiction, which made it difficult to resist the lazy pleasures of enjoying power and easy to avoid the headache of government. Trinh Tac's successors displayed a range of qualities and achievements, from flawed efforts to solve problems to irresponsible self-indulgence.

While political and administrative life crept along in a shadow of perplexity, the bi-monthly surge of people into and out of the city demonstrated the living, pulsing energy of the country. Powerful eunuchs were able to put their hands on the profits of foreign merchants, but the thousands of peasants and artisans who regularly did business in the streets of Ke Cho inhabited another world where an inattentive government fumbled and failed to find a grip. The entrepreneurial energy expressed by these "people in the market" had its own tempo arising from the aspirations of thousands of people inhabiting many hundreds of villages, and government administrators could not keep pace with it. Trinh efforts to maintain control of the Red River countryside without resorting to soldiers did not succeed.

The lively international commerce of the early seventeenth century was in steep decline by the 1670s. With the end of their wars against the Nguyen and the Mac, the Trinh interest in foreign trade faded. The Dutch began to lose money and in 1671 abandoned their formerly lucrative shipments of silk directly to Japan and thereafter sent all their Tonkin trade to Batavia to be reshipped from there. The English arrived in 1672 and competed with the Dutch for what was left of the market. In the 1680s and 1690s, Trinh Can badgered the Dutch for difficult-to-obtain gifts, sometimes confiscated their property or imprisoned them, and insisted that they continue to buy raw silk that was no longer in demand anywhere. The English never made any profits in Tonkin and finally left in 1697. Even Chinese merchants were departing in large numbers during these years. The Dutch finally sailed away, never to return, in 1700.

The French appeared in the late 1660s and for several years maintained a residence at Pho Hien. However, this was not a commercial venture so much as a new missionary initiative. The Jesuits were expelled in 1663 during the Confucianizing exuberance of the Canh Tri period. The Paris Society of Foreign Missions had been established in the 1650s with Papal blessing as a French-led alternative to the Jesuits, whose activities in Asia, with their headquarters in Macau, were dependent upon Portuguese transport and tended to operate within the confines of Portuguese interests. Alexandre de Rhodes, as much French as he was Jesuit, had a role in initiating this new organization. The Paris Society was comprised of "secular" priests, not members of religious orders such as the Jesuits, Franciscans, Dominicans, and Augustinians who had pioneered Christian proselytization in Asia. The Society ostensibly aimed to train native clergy to be under the direct guidance of Rome rather than to be partisans of any particular religious order. Yet, the Society lent itself to Asian adventures sponsored by the French crown, particularly in Siam, where a scheme to convert the monarchy led to a short-lived French military intervention in the 1680s.

In Tonkin, the Society began its operations clandestinely in collaboration with the newly formed French East India Company. Once the missionaries of the Society discovered that they were able to operate among the Vietnamese under these conditions, the Jesuits returned via Macau, and soon Dominicans also arrived from Manila. This new wave of European missionaries established contact with the Vietnamese Christian communities that had grown up under Jesuit tutelage in earlier decades. Despite initial tension between Vietnamese Christian leaders who favored different groups of missionaries, and despite disputes between the Jesuits and the Society about how best to train a native clergy, and, also, despite periodic persecutions of Christians by Vietnamese authorities, the Christian missionary effort spread through the villages of the Red River plain. By the time of Trinh Can's death in 1709, forty-seven European missionaries are recorded as having gone to serve in Tonkin: eighteen Jesuits, fourteen members of the Society, ten Dominicans, one Augustinian, and four others. During the same time, the missionaries of the Society ordained twenty-eight native priests and the Jesuits ordained four. The Society and the various religious orders were also conducting missionary work in the south at a similar level of activity.

Trinh Can's date of birth is unknown, but he was most probably born in the 1620s. He had spent 25 years as his father's right-hand man. During the

27 years that he ruled after the death of Trinh Tac, he showed himself to be secretive, scheming, greedy, reliant upon a small circle of cronies, passive, and unimaginative. He was already an old man at this time. He outlived three designated heirs and was finally succeeded by a great grandson. His years in power were filled with cyclic recurrences of the "same old" problems: drought, flood, and famine; border disputes with Qing; corruption in the examination halls; confusion in the courts of law; and bitter feuds among his officials.

Whatever Vinh Tho and Canh Tri administrators had achieved with regard to agrarian affairs in the late 1650s and early 1660s was lost amidst recurring disasters beginning in the early 1680s. Dikes broke with distressing frequency. Famine was endemic. Europeans reported outbreaks of cannibalism. In 1694, Trinh soldiers attacked and destroyed an entire village after it had become a major center of brigandage that threatened communication between the capital and Thanh Hoa. Officials were sent to investigate "the misery of the people" but without any indication of action taken to alleviate the situation. Inspectors were repeatedly sent out to the provinces to clean up courts of law that had become "clogged" with unresolved litigation. Routine exhortations for officials to be honest were repeated again and again. Regional examinations were famous for chaos and corruption, and in 1696 there was a major scandal in the capital exam despite repeated efforts to "reform" the system. In the same year, the proscription of Christianity was reaffirmed while noting that during the preceding thirty-three years it had had no effect. Qing immigrants were spreading their style of dress and haircut among the people, so this was forbidden. A form of gambling became such a rage that it was forbidden. Officials who refused to serve under the supervision of eunuchs were summarily dismissed. Negotiations with Qing over border issues were entangled in the politics of Trinh Can's court. In two separate cases, honest officials who had been dismissed arbitrarily or as a result of being on the losing side of a feud among officials turned to teaching and established reputations for producing many famous students.

One of Trinh Can's especial favorites was Le Hy, the scholar who supervised completion of the court history published in 1697. Le Hy was also a corrupt man who did not shrink from homicide in his feuds with other officials. In 1696 he obtained the death of an official with whom he had nurtured enmity and who had sabotaged a scheme for Le Hy's son to cheat on a regional exam. Described as cunning and naturally suspicious of others, Le Hy was a specialist in false accusations that derailed the careers of his enemies. A popular saying was recorded that went: "The greedy chant prayers to Le Hy; the whole world is as sad as can be."

When Le Hy died in 1702, some of his enemies managed to regain positions at the Trinh court. One of these was Nguyen Quan Nho (1638–1709), a Canh Tri graduate who retained some of the idealism of those years. Returning to the capital from his home in Thanh Hoa, he reported to Trinh Can that not only was Thanh Hoa suffering from famine but also that military commanders there were abusive and oppressive. He appealed for more enlightened policies toward the common people. Trinh Can listened to him.

Trinh Can's designated heir, a grandson, died in the following year, and Nguyen Quan Nho along with other officials of his ilk prevailed upon Trinh Can to elevate an 18-year-old great grandson, Trinh Cuong, to be his heir. This provoked resistance among the eunuchs and generals, who turned to their allies within the Trinh family. In 1704, two grandsons of Trinh Can, sons of an earlier but deceased heir, were executed after plotting a coup against Trinh Cuong. Resistance to Trinh Cuong from Trinh kinsmen continued for several years. The contention over Trinh Cuong's appointment may have also spread to the royal family, which could explain why, in 1705, Trinh Can deposed the 45-year-old king, Le Duy Cap, and replaced him with his 26-year-old son, Le Duy Duong.

Trinh Cuong's reforms

When Trinh Can died in 1709, Trinh Cuong, then 24 years old, came to power surrounded by men keen to reform the government. One of Trinh Cuong's first acts was to reissue "the six teachings" that had been promulgated in the late 1670s, just before Trinh Tac's death: (1) great lords must not rely upon coercion to have their way; (2) military officers must constantly train and drill their men and must not be heartless and cruel toward the people; (3) civil officials must be honest and industrious; (4) court ministers must be loyal and without guile; (5) soldiers must follow orders; (6) the people must do their best to know the difference between right and wrong. These "teachings" were an echo of the idealism of the Hong Duc and Canh Tri eras. That they were again announced at this time is an indication that the undesirable behaviors they addressed were still very much in evidence. The small quiver of idealism expressed in Trinh Cuong's accession to power and reflected in the recycling of these "teachings" was probably based on Trinh Cuong's susceptibility to the influence of a group of officials inclined toward the rhetoric of good government. These officials apparently found their step up into power in alliance with Trinh Cuong's mother, a woman who had achieved high status among the palace women.

Trinh Cuong's twenty years of rule displayed a flurry of legislation aimed at the country's problems. Yet, the disconnection between government authority and a population in distress paradoxically increased. The literati families in the Red River plain that had been mobilized by Trinh Tac, with a few notable exeptions, simply added a new level of corruption and oppression between the Trinh regime and village agriculturalists. Trinh Cuong's reforms produced little more than opportunities for new forms of abuse. Meanwhile, rural impoverishment continued unabated while Trinh treatment of the Le kings eroded the moral authority of the regime.

If one were to take at face value the busy concern with which Trinh Cuong and his small circle of advisors appeared to have addressed government affairs, it would seem to have been a time of relatively enlightened rule motivated by strong feelings of benevolence toward the common people. Trinh Cuong was an intelligent man who appears to have taken to heart the task of sorting out the mess in which he found the country. However, he and his advisors found no way to translate ostensibly good intentions into real achievements. Whatever they tried to do got lost somewhere between plan and implementation. Furthermore, the gap that had always existed between the Trinh regime and the people of the Red River plain, instead of being mended, was being filled by a new class of locally produced rapacious officials and "notables." Beneath the veneer of fine rhetoric and legislative activism, the regime continued down the path of corruption, factional intrigue, and virulently oppressive taxation. Trinh Cuong's reputation as a reformer has been enhanced among historians by comparison with the disasters that followed.

Trinh Cuong's closest advisors were Le Anh Tuan (1671–1734), a graduate of 1694, and Nguyen Cong Hang (1680–1732), a graduate of 1700. Both were from localities near the capital. They had supported Trinh Cuong's elevation during Trinh Can's final years. According to an anecdote, Trinh Cuong was in the habit of summoning these men in the dead of night to discuss problems and policies over tea. However, their ideas did not fare well in the light of day. They were the architects of Trinh Cuong's reforms. They also found ways to abuse their power and made many enemies. After Trinh Cuong's death, they met untimely ends when their enemies were ascendant.

Trinh Cuong's reforms were not entirely hollow. They did have an effect on the country, even if not what was apparently intended, and they became a point of reference for legislative initiatives later in the century. Furthermore, they concentrated on the most intractable sector of Trinh government: land tenure and rural taxation. A detailed look at these measures reveals why Trinh Cuong's so-called reforms were unsuccessful. It was a case of palace theory encountering the stubborn reality of a countryside where an ineffective central authority had to compromise every measure with the most predatory elements of rural society.

The breakdown of dikes and devastating floods had become common in Trinh Can's later years. Consequently, one of the first measures taken by Trinh Cuong was to take the responsibility for dike maintenance out of the hands of provincial officials and to centralize the supervision of dikes from the capital. While this was intended to eliminate provincial corruption of dike management, it was no guarantee against corruption at the central government level. Furthermore, this removed supervisory responsibility from people closest to the dikes and placed it in hands at some distance away. This measure does not seem to have significantly affected the frequency of dike breaches, even for dikes in the immediate vicinity of the capital. Just a few months before Trinh Cuong's death in 1729, there were serious dike failures with floods along the Red River. Floodwaters broke through a dike directly across the river from Ke Cho, washing away a palace that Trinh Cuong had built for his mother only two years before. In 1725, the collapse of dikes in Hai Duong, east of the capital, had produced the unusual calamity of seawater invading the rice fields. The example of dike management is an indication of the quality of Trinh Cuong's reforms. They did not improve administration so much as reallocate opportunities for the personal enrichment of officials.

Famines are recorded in 1713, 1721, 1724, 1726, and 1728. In 1721, famine created such panic in the capital that special police units were deployed to keep order in the streets as dying peasants invaded the capital. In 1715, an epidemic ravaged Nghe An, prompting authorities to make prayers to Buddha for deliverance. Missionary accounts from this time attest to the utter misery of the rural population. Farmers lived on the edge of starvation. Taxation and conscription pushed large numbers of people to flee, leaving empty villages and abandoned fields. Wealthy notables and predatory mandarins accumulated land. Trinh Cuong spent vast sums on new palaces and gardens. His eunuchs were everywhere seeking ways to fill their pockets.

In 1711, Trinh Cuong's advisors noted the basic outline of the rural problem. Powerful families had accumulated land into big estates worked by fugitives and refugees who thereby had escaped from village tax and conscription registers. Many villages stood deserted, and a large part of the rural population had disappeared from administrative oversight. There was no prospect of changing the general dynamic of this situation. Trinh Cuong's advisors understood that they could not stop people from leaving their villages and seeking their livelihoods elsewhere. All they could propose was that when people did move to another place they were supposed to register with the authorities in that place to be included in the rolls for taxation and conscription.

They were also concerned about the common fields that were meant to support landless widows and widowers, childless elderly people, the disabled, and soldiers. There was a perception that village common fields were not being allocated properly, so Trinh Cuong's advisors proposed to conduct a survey of these fields every six years to make sure that they were sufficient to meet the demands placed on them. The main concern here, however, was not with the landless, the elderly, or the disabled, but with the soldiers, and the soldiers in question were men from Thanh Hoa and Nghe An who were garrisoned in the Red River plain. Men in the Red River plain were conscripted as soldiers in times of emergency or for periodic training, or for rotational duty in the northern border provinces, but they were not maintained as part of the regular, standing military force in the lowlands. In 1722, this was changed, and men from the Red River plain were integrated into the regular standing army. As part of this new scheme, the common fields in the villages of the Red River plain were reassigned for the support of soldiers from the Red River plain. Although this provided some temporary relief to local populations that no longer had to allocate land to support soldiers from other provinces, in the long term it created a new class of villagers with military training who would turn against the Trinh during the rebellions that broke out in the 1730s.

A common means by which local officials accumulated wealth at the expense of villagers was through litigation in courts of law that resulted in the penalty of confiscation, either of land or of other forms of property. The abuses of this procedure had been entrenched in village life for centuries, but they had reached such a level of virulence that Trinh Cuong's advisors took note of them in 1715 by ordering a triennial inspection of confiscations to ensure that they were appropriate, not too much or too little. This measure neither ended the practice nor did it ensure an end to abuse. It simply brought the central authorities into the picture and gave them opportunities to participate in managing this method of transferring wealth from villagers to government officials.

In 1716, Trinh Cuong's advisors began to discuss what to do about the Stabilization Act that had been implemented in the 1660s by the Canh Tri reformers to fix a final, definitive survey of village land ownership as the basis for taxation. This survey, made when there was little difference between landowners and village populations, produced a set of census registers that were also used for the conscription of laborers and soldiers when needed. Since the brunt of military service was borne by men from Thanh Hoa and Nghe An, the conscription of men from the Red River plain was not a high priority for routine administration and could be accomplished when needed on an ad hoc basis. However, by the time of Trinh Cuong, this was changing, and the idea of incorporating men from the Red River plain into the regular standing army was growing. In order to accomplish this, an up-to-date census of village populations would have to be taken. The first step in the minds of Trinh Cuong's advisors was to distinguish between surveys of land ownership and census registers. They regarded these as different issues and began to make plans for both a survey of land ownership and a census of the population as separate procedures.

The record of land ownership that had been produced by the Stabilization Act was absurdly out of date, which increasingly distorted the tax burden. Villages were taxed according to rates that had been calculated half a century earlier. This was not a problem for villages that had grown or become wealthier, but, for the more typical villages that had fallen on difficult times and seen much of their land go into the untaxed hands of powerful families, this made their tax burden oppressively out of proportion to available resources. Meanwhile, rich land-owners were not bearing an equitable share of the tax burden. In 1619, a field survey to record land ownership for purposes of taxation was ordered so that "the rich will bear their proportional share of the tax burden and the poor will not be oppressed." But a survey of land ownership would not help to administer labor and military conscription or the head tax and the public service fees levied to support local shrines, temples, dikes, bridges, storehouses, and examination halls, so in 1722 the first of what were to be triennial censuses was taken.

The census of 1722 resulted in a redrawing of the administrative maps and became the basis for the new system of conscripting soldiers from the Red River plain into the standing army. It was also the basis for new tax legislation announced in 1723, which was supposedly based on the "Tang dynasty model." The main source for field taxes was on the common lands that were mostly apportioned to the families of men serving on active military duty. Private land was taxed at less than half the rate of common land, and the private land of officials was exempt from taxation altogether. The head tax, which in the past had been levied according to a schedule of variable rates, was simplified to a fixed rate for all men eligible for military service, with students and the elderly paying half the regular rate. The public service fees were likewise simplified to a fixed rate to be paid by all men eligible for military service. Fields were designated for the support of schools. Furthermore, a school tax was added to the head tax in the Red River plain and to the public service fee in Thanh Hoa and Nghe An; the school tax in Nghe An was half that in the Red River plain, and in Thanh Hoa it was less yet than that. Other innovations to the tax system were duties on the sale of cinnamon bark and of bronze. Inspection stations on the rivers taxed boats at the rate of one-fortieth the value of merchandise they carried. A special tax scheme was established for salt makers, who were exempt from regular taxation.

The new tax policy was modified as soon as it encountered reality. In 1724, the head tax was abolished in Thanh Hoa and Nghe An, and the land tax rates in those provinces were reduced by half. In the Red River plain, the schedule of tax rates was reduced "in accordance with local conditions." When a drought ruined the rice harvest, taxes were reduced even further. In an effort to find new sources of revenue, a survey was ordered of land that had appeared as a result of changes in the courses of rivers, and a new tax was levied on the sale of fruits and vegetables.

Plans were made for the second triennial census in 1725, but this census apparently never materialized as problems overwhelmed Trinh Cuong's advisors.

In 1725, all unpaid taxes were forgiven and Nguyen Cong Hang was assigned to personally tour the countryside to sort out the mess. The survey of fields had produced a great snarl of disputes over ownership of land and over access to water that was made available from dikes and dams. The policy of conscripting soldiers from the Red River plain into the regular army resulted in large numbers of men fleeing their villages to avoid military service. The only government initiative recorded this year was to issue rules on how much property various grades of officials were allowed to possess, which gave the Trinh regime an opportunity to appropriate what it decided was the excess property of officials, basically skimming off its share of what local authorities had acquired. The regime also issued an invitation to villagers to speak up in praise or blame of local magistrates, thus acknowledging a certain concern about popular opinion.

Thereafter, the initiatives taken to survey land ownership and to establish a system of taxation were overwhelmed by the poverty of rural life and by the culture of corruption that had become endemic to officialdom. In 1727, new rules for collecting taxes were published. It is unclear what exactly they were, but they were ostensibly meant to remedy the "chaos" of existing practice. In 1728, the rate of taxation on land was increased, and there were new rules for allotting common land to the families of soldiers. Trinh Cuong died the following year without having solved the agrarian problems that seemed to occupy so much of his advisors' attention.

Trinh Cuong's advisors also made innovations in education and the examination system during the 1720s. The curriculum for military examinations was published in 1721. Designed to produce officers, it included the study of Sunzi, an ancient author on "the art of war," and the demonstration of skill in horsemanship, in the use of shield and sword, and in handling knives. The focus of concern about literary examinations was directed at the regional exams and the procedure for students to gain access to regional exams. The same questions were being used in regional exams year after year and were well known to students, so in 1711 officials were directed to change the questions for each exam. But this did not end the chicanery. In 1720, the setting of regional examination questions was taken out of the hands of provincial officials altogether and was thereafter to be done in the capital. In 1722, new regulations for the conduct of regional examinations were issued. The most significant departure from previous practice had to do with the pre-exams that determined the eligibility of students to advance to the provincial-level regional exams.

Pre-exams had previously been held at the village level under the supervision of district magistrates, but they were now to be conducted at the district level under the supervision of provincial education officers. One effect was that the quotas for students who could pass were now set at the district level rather than at the village level, so whereas before every village could theoretically be represented at the regional exam, this was no longer the case, and there was greater opportunity for notoriously corrupt provincial education officials to determine the results. Another innovation was that, while those who passed the pre-exams had before been sorted into two categories of achievement, "completely good," and "less good," with the "less good" having to wait for the next regional exam, now a third intermediate category of "rather good" was inserted into the scheme and allowed to advance directly to the regional exam. There were two effects of this. One was that the "rather good" category became a fast track for favorite candidates of education officials and the other was that large numbers of aspiring students began to collect in the "less good" category, waiting for their chance to advance to the regional exam. The abuses occasioned by the "rather good" track led to this category being abolished in 1741, but in 1750 it was reinstituted to normalize a growing practice of people buying their way into the regional exam.

The principal administrative innovation of this time was the institution in 1718 of the Six Sessions (Luc Phien). There had been up to three sessions prior to this, but they were simply part of the Trinh military command structure and were in charge of handling the finances of the land army, the naval forces, and the headquarters. Now, sessions directly under the authority of the Trinh lord were established as part of the civil government to handle the finances of each of the Six Ministries (Luc Bo). In practice, the Six Sessions took over the functions of the Six Ministries, although the Six Ministries continued to exist with certain appellate duties, at least in theory. In practice, the Six Sessions were a new level of authority over the entire system of government located at the "court" of the Trinh lord. This authority was based upon the control of revenue. This may appear to have tightened the chain of command from the Trinh lord to the various offices of government, but it also inserted another layer of officialdom at the top of the system that offered excellent opportunities to favored officials for cultivating power and for personal enrichment. At the same time, another layer of fiscal administration was added with the formation of the Six Treasuries (Luc Cung). The flow of tax revenue was redirected from the Ministry of Finance to the Six Treasuries, which were attached to the Six Sessions. While the creation of the Six Sessions and Six Treasuries may superficially appear to have been a means for the Trinh lord to centralize his control over the government, it also opened the stream of tax revenues to the hands of more officials in the lord's inner circle of favorites.

The formation of the Six Sessions and the Six Treasuries was shortly followed, in 1720, by a reform in the hierarchy of appointments, ostensibly modeled on the Hong Duc official registry, although, in the words of the annalist, "the importance of positions was not the same." At the time of this reform, the group of officials closest to Trinh Cuong were recognized for their service during the preceding ten years. Nguyen Cong Hang and Le Anh Tuan, along with three others, were given top honors. Nine men received lesser awards. The administrative innovations of 1718 were apparently related to the ascendance of this group of officials. Pensions for retired officials were also established at this time. Two years later, a new set of regulations for making appointments to government offices was published.

Most of the reforming zeal of these years was directed at organizing access to public revenues. Other aspects of government, for example the administration of justice, were ignored. In 1723, following a routine established in the time of Trinh Can, officials were sent out to clear up the backlog of litigation in the provinces. This was yet another opportunity for squeezing money into official-dom through fees, fines, and confiscations.

The first peacetime conscription of soldiers from the Red River plain was initiated in 1721. In the following year, these men were integrated into regular military units along with men from Thanh Hoa and Nghe An. Among other things, this was part of an effort to remove the army from the politics of the Trinh family. In 1722, Trinh Cuong began to retire members of the Trinh family out of military positions because he did not want disaffected kinsmen with military commands. He was also worried about problems on the Qing border and felt the need to bring the manpower of the Red River plain into the equation of frontier security. In 1724, soldiers from the northern jurisdictions of the plain began to be rotated for service in Cao Bang. In 1726, at a time of unrest in Cao Bang, ten thousand freshly recruited men from the Red River plain were mobilized to the capital for training and drill.

Security issues on the northern border were a chronic source of concern. In 1714, a campaign against pirates along the coastal border with Qing was launched. In 1715, Nguyen Cong Hang went to Cao Bang to deal with unrest occasioned by someone claiming to be a descendent of the Mac. In 1717, the large numbers of men from Qing gathering in the northern mountains to work in the gold, silver, copper, zinc, and iron mines so worried Trinh Cuong that he decreed their number should be limited to three hundred. Vietnamese officials resisted taking assignments in the northern border provinces. Those appointed to serve there were in the habit of staying in the capital and pretending to fulfill their duties at a distance. In 1712, Trinh Cuong forced officials appointed to the northern border provinces to actually go there. These officials then apparently discovered the opportunities for personal enrichment available in these relatively remote but productive regions. Their style of administration resulted in large numbers of people fleeing across the border to live under the Qing. When this became apparent in 1720, Trinh Cuong decided there were too many officials in the border provinces and ordered that their number be reduced.

One year earlier, Trinh Cuong reportedly had become concerned about the quality of officials in the provinces and issued an edict charging them with five priorities: suppression of bandits, prosecution of criminals, repair of dikes and roads, vigilance at border gates, and maintenance of military discipline. Additional charges were issued specifically for Cao Bang that included border defense and keeping in readiness post stations for sending dispatches. None of these priorities had anything directly to do with governing the people.

The only indication of interest in moral behavior comes from an edict in 1720 exhorting students to learn propriety, righteousness, loyalty, and trustworthiness; forbidding marriage among people in the same family; forbidding clothing and material possessions beyond one's station in life, evil habits that wasted one's assets, superstitious practices, and a lazy playboy lifestyle; and advocating moderation and thriftiness. It appears that this exhortation was aimed at people seeking to enter officialdom through the examination system and not at the population in general. The qualities featured in this exhortation are primarily about how one appears in society and indicate a certain bottom line for maintaining a plausible public reputation.

Despite his seeming susceptibility to a group of scholars, Trinh Cuong also made use of eunuchs, sending them to govern provinces and to supervise building projects, among other assignments. He was also impervious to the opinions of his literati advisors when dealing with the issue of succession in both the Trinh and the Le families. In 1727, Trinh Cuong named his eldest son Trinh Giang as his heir, despite Nguyen Cong Hang and Le Anh Tuan arguing that Trinh Giang was stupid and unequal to the task of governing the country. In the same year, he also demoted the Le crown prince, Le Duy Tuong, whose mother was not from the Trinh family, and replaced him with a younger brother, Le Duy Phuong, whose mother was a Trinh woman. Then, in 1729, shortly before he died, Trinh Cuong forced the king, Le Duy Duong, to abdicate in favor of Le Duy Phuong. So, Trinh Cuong left an heir who lacked the confidence of his closest advisors and a royal family with an upstart king and a recently deposed king and crown prince.

Trinh Giang and the collapse of government

During the early years of Trinh Giang's rule, the literati enemies of Nguyen Cong Hang and Le Anh Tuan gradually gained influence amidst chaotic efforts to deal with a deepening agrarian crisis. The first question Trinh Giang had for his officials in 1730 was to explain why tax revenues were decreasing. The answer was that impoverished peasants were wandering away from their villages to escape taxation, causing unpaid back taxes to accumulate. Officials counted 527 villages that had been deserted. Two solutions to this problem were proposed. One was simply to find ways of moderating the tax burden. To this end, the head tax was abolished in Thanh Hoa and Nghe An, and it was reduced in the Red River plain for people who provided labor for maintaining the dikes. The tax on private land was reduced, and customs stations on the rivers were abolished except for two at the capital. Furthermore, the triennial census, which was the basis for the head tax and public service fees, was rescheduled for twelve-year intervals, thus putting into the relatively distant future any revision for this source of popular aggravation.

The other solution was to compel people to return to the villages where they were registered and pay their taxes there. An idea here was that people who had left their villages to escape taxation were doing financially better than those who remained at home, and so they should accordingly pay their tax at a higher rate. Villages whose people went back to pay their taxes were rewarded, while villages whose people did not go back were punished. Nguyen Cong Hang was put in charge of a group of officials sent out to implement this plan to reconcentrate people in their home villages. The results of this were not recorded, but it is unlikely to have been very successful, if at all. Just at this time the dikes downriver from the capital broke and a devastating flood inundated nine districts.

In 1731, an official from the coastal region of the Red River plain (modern Thai Binh Province) named Bui Si Tiem (b. 1690) submitted a ten-point analysis of what was wrong in the country. It so infuriated Trinh Giang that Bui Si Tiem was dismissed and sent back to his home village. It nevertheless offers a glimpse into how one man viewed the situation. Le Duy Duong, the king that Trinh Cuong had forced to abdicate two years earlier, had just died, and Bui Si Tiem claimed that the manner in which he had been treated had damaged public morale. Another point was the need to reform the education and examination system to select men who could think and not just memorize passages. Several points had to do with officialdom. There were too many officials for too few people, and they were ignorant of how people lived, corrupt, hungry for bribes, oppressive, and abusive. Taxation was too heavy, and the administration of conscription for labor and military service caused unnecessary misery. Finally, there was a lack of supervision over foreign workers in the mines of the northern mountains. This last point implies that Qing miners were in some way contributing to the mood of popular disaffection as well as compromising the border.

In 1732, Nguyen Hieu (1674–1735), from Thanh Hoa and an examination graduate of 1700, emerged as Trinh Giang's principal advisor. Nguyen Cong Hang and Le Anh Tuan were exiled to posts in the mountains. Nguyen Cong

Hang was killed almost immediately. Le Anh Tuan was killed two years later. In addition to this coup at the top of officialdom, there was another intervention into the royal family. The king, Le Duy Phuong, was deposed and replaced with his elder brother, Le Duy Tuong. When Le Duy Tuong died three years later, Le Duy Phuong was killed, and a younger brother named Le Duy Thin was made king. Le Duy Thin was a cousin of Trinh Giang on his mother's side and the eleventh son of Le Duy Duong. The only substantive administrative act this year was to abolish all taxes on "earth products" such as tin, iron, lumber, lacquer, silk, tea, flowers, salt, fish, and shrimp, ostensibly because the taxes on these items were causing people to stop supplying them.

Strangely enough, in this year Trinh Giang imagined that the kingdom was in such a state of peace and prosperity that music was needed to celebrate. He began to have musicians accompany him wherever he went through the streets, playing the music of Ming and Qing composers. On the other hand, a traveler at an inn in Bat Trang, a village specializing in ceramics a short distance downriver from Ke Cho, thoughtlessly tossed a torch into a hole in the ground, causing the eruption of a huge flame that burned for a month. This gave rise to a rumor of imminent war that spread throughout the country.

In 1733, following the recommendation of Nguyen Hieu, the policy of conscripting soldiers for the regular army from the Red River plain was discontinued. Nguyen Hieu, perhaps reflecting the prejudice of his home province, Thanh Hoa, claimed that the men recruited from the Red River plain were poor soldiers, being mainly orphans and youths who loitered around the markets, and that the cost of maintaining them was too high. He was particularly opposed to the policy established ten years earlier of allotting to them common land, which he argued brought misery to villagers. Three years later, all men from the Red River plain serving in the army were dismissed, and the regime went back to relying on their levies from Thanh Hoa and Nghe An. One effect of this was to fill the villages of the Red River plain with men who had learned military drills and had been trained in the use of weapons.

In 1735, Nguyen Hieu died while trying to adjust taxes in villages where the population had scattered from floodwaters when the dikes again broke downriver from the capital. Thereafter, eunuchs gained dominance over Trinh Giang under the leadership of Hoang Cong Phu, who did not shrink from homicide to eliminate rivals and to advance his allies. In 1736, as an epidemic spread death through the countryside, Hoang Cong Phu instituted the practice of selling appointments in officialdom as a means of raising money. Trinh Giang was busy building temples and improving the roads and dikes in his mother's home district, several kilometers east of Ke Cho. The transport of lumber and stone from Thanh Hoa kept large numbers of farmers from working their fields.

In 1736 Hoang Cong Phu persuaded Trinh Giang to change the traditional location of the palace examination from the king's palace to his own. He then manipulated the results to give unusually high honors to Trinh Tue (b. 1704), a protégé of his who was a member of the branch of the Trinh family that had remained in Thanh Hoa. Trinh Tue thereafter received high appointments and was a loyal ally of Hoang Cong Phu. The appointment of military men to high civil positions in 1737 provoked dismay and laughter, but more serious than this was that the northern border provinces began to pull away from Trinh authority, that bands of bandits began to "swarm up like bees" across the countryside, and that a ragged army of peasants from the upper plains gathered on Mount Tam Dao, about fifty kilometers north of the capital, where they gave battle to Trinh army units.

People began to bury their valuables and to hoard food. Inhabitants of the capital fled into the countryside. More ominous still was that, in 1738, Le Duy Mat (d. 1770), a brother of the king, along with several other Le princes and a group of disaffected officials, failing in a plot to unseat the Trinh, fled to the uplands of Thanh Hoa and raised the flag of revolt. The effect of this was like a signal igniting insurrection nearly everywhere. What followed was a year in which the eunuchs, led by Hoang Cong Phu, endeavored to use the crisis to advance their power, while Trinh efforts to raise solders gave fresh impetus to rebellion. And then, Trinh Giang, at his wit's end while looking for ways to subdue the rebels, suffered a nervous breakdown.

In 1739, the status of eunuchs was raised to be equal to that of the regular military and civil officials. The number of eunuchs at this time is not known, but missionary accounts estimated their population in Ke Cho at four to five hundred in the 1680s. There is likely to have been even more of them fifty years later. Trinh Tue was by now the leader of a group of officials who were willing to cooperate with the eunuchs. Meanwhile, Hoang Cong Phu was occupying himself with building a palace in his home village a short distance northeast of the capital.

The most urgent military problem seemed to have been the spread of disorder coming out of the northern border provinces, so military units were ordered to set up defensive positions to protect the lowlands from rebels coming from these provinces. Efforts to pacify the border provinces included allying with Nung chieftains, forgiving unpaid taxes, reducing taxes on merchants doing business in these provinces, and forbidding the forced sale of lumber on credit, which seemed to be a particular grievance in the border areas.

Trinh Giang insisted on calling up the soldiers from the Red River plain who had been previously demobilized, despite strenuous objections from many of his officials who predicted that this would simply add to the uproar. The result was as the objecting officials feared. Rebellion gained momentum daily. Trinh Giang organized militia units in villages still under his command, but the distribution of weapons to men in these units became a means of supply for the rebels. He proclaimed a tax amnesty, but it was too late to have any calming effect. He called for more soldiers from Thanh Hoa and Nghe An. He began to suffer from panic attacks and could no longer endure noise, reportedly after being struck by a thunderbolt. He retreated to an underground chamber and refused to emerge; government affairs were left in the hands of Hoang Cong Phu and Trinh Tue.

In 1736, Trinh Giang had made his younger full brother, Trinh Doanh, the commander of all military forces. As the Trinh situation deteriorated in 1739, men who were concerned and dismayed began to look to him for leadership. They gathered around his mother and the leaders of her family, who encouraged him to act. His reluctance to openly oppose his brother was finally overcome when one of those urging him forward, an official from a western suburb of Hanoi named Nguyen Cong Thai, who had recruited a large militia force from that place, prevailed upon the king to call upon Trinh Doanh to step forward.

On the day designated for "opening the government" to begin official business following the lunar new year in 1740, Trinh Doanh with soldiers loyal to him and Nguyen Cong Thai with his militia moved against the eunuchs, who had their own military force. There was a battle in the capital. Trinh Doanh prevailed, and there was a slaughter of eunuchs as Hoang Cong Phu, Trinh Tue, and other prominent men in their group fled. Trinh Giang lived until 1761, under what conditions is not known.

Trinh Doanh and the age of rebellion

Trinh Doanh was only 21 years old when he assumed power. He demonstrated a competence and a decisiveness that enabled the Trinh family to survive as lords of the palace for another generation. But most of his 27 years of rule were devoted first to surviving more than a decade of widespread rebellions and then to sorting out the chaos produced by those rebellions. His entourage included people who had been pushed aside by Trinh Giang for their criticisms of Trinh government, such as Bui Si Tiem, whose ten-point analysis of problems in 1731 had earned him dismissal. When Trinh Doanh took over at the beginning of 1740, he issued a fifteen-point blueprint for action that reflected the views of such people.

First and foremost was a determination to suppress the ranks of eunuchs. This did not mean that eunuchs were to be utterly eradicated, but rather that their status would be reduced to what it had been before 1739, as personal servants of the ruler and not a third group at court equal to men who had earned their positions through literary examinations and military leadership. In fact, Trinh Doanh benefited from the abilities of several eunuchs who were effective administrators and successful generals.

Next were provisions to sort out and dismiss corrupt and incompetent officials. A favorite form of official abuse was false accusations leading to corrupt litigation and the confiscation of property. This was specifically forbidden. Trinh Doanh's followers were keen to refurbish the image of officialdom from the shabby practices that had become endemic during previous decades. This intent, of course, would not escape the feuds, personal animosities, and intrigues that had characterized government in the past, but, amidst the emergency conditions of the 1740s, a certain level of competence was enforced by circumstances. Nevertheless, within weeks of issuing these good intentions, Trinh Doanh was dispensing honors, tax exemptions, and appointments in officialdom to those contributing money and rice to fight the rebels.

The generals were also to undergo an evaluation of their abilities to determine whether they deserved rewards or punishments. By the end of the year, a new group of generals appeared who had risen rapidly through the ranks from the level of common soldiers as a result of their ability. Hastening this phenomenon were multiple defeats in battle in which many Trinh generals were captured or lost their lives. As for the common soldiers, they were promised more fields to support their families. Merchants were placated by abolishing customs stations at ferry crossings and by forbidding price fixing and the forcible sale of merchandise. Peasants were given an amnesty on all land and head taxes. The land tax in Thanh Hoa and Nghe An was entirely discontinued. Furthermore, all of Trinh Giang's and Hoang Cong Phu's construction projects were halted. Instead, workers were sent to repair dikes. Finally, tax revenues were to go through the Ministry of Finance instead of through the Six Sessions. It appears that tax revenues being directed through the Six Sessions had a way of disappearing.

In this year, major rebellions expanded from the northern border provinces and consumed every part of the Red River plain. The capital was an island of Trinh authority with a tenuous lifeline to Thanh Hoa and Nghe An. Recruitment of soldiers in these southern provinces was increased from one-fifth of the men available for conscription to one-third. Trinh Doanh also made an appeal for volunteers from the families of loyal officials. There was such a rush of disorderly recruits into the capital that undisciplined soldiers began acting as gangs of bandits. Trinh Doanh moved quickly to establish disipline over this mob, rejecting many undesirables and putting the rest into a regimen of training and drill. He also mobilized militia forces from localities near the capital. Bells and gongs from temples were seized and melted down to make weapons, and people contributing bronze and lead were given official appointments. With copper coins being melted down for weaponry, soldiers were paid in silver, causing the value of silver to drop, resulting in efforts to fix the value of silver.

The greatest center of rebellion was in the old Mac territory of Hai Duong in the eastern part of the plain. The most prominent rebel leader at this time was a man named Nguyen Tuyen. Many battles were fought along the lower Red River as Trinh Doanh tried to prevent rebel forces from moving into this region, which was critical for water communication between Thanh Hoa and the capital. At one point, as he was occupied with rebel forces downriver, rebel armies from Hai Duong moved in behind him and threatened the capital. Desperate action from Trinh generals in the capital forced the rebel armies to move back.

Probably because Trinh Giang had made him king, Le Duy Thin was forced to abdicate, becoming "senior king" until his death in 1759. A nephew of his, 24-year-old Le Duy Dieu, was made king. He was the eldest son of Le Duy Tuong, the king who had died in 1735. Le Duy Dieu was king for a record forty-six years, and the short reign of his grandson, Le Duy Khiem, would mark the end of the Le dynasty in the 1780s.

In 1741, Le Duy Mat was pressing upon the capital from the northwest while Nguyen Tuyen advanced from the southeast. When Nguyen Tuyen died, other rebel leaders quickly took his place. Because of the fighting, there were no harvests in the Red River plain and famine spread through the land. So many soldiers were deserting to return to their villages that Trinh Doanh announced preferential treatment for villages if none of their soldiers deserted. Rice was transported from Thanh Hoa and Nghe An, and more soldiers were recruited from those provinces. The soldiers from Thanh Hoa and Nghe An, realizing their importance to the regime, demanded the right to collect taxes from villages in the Red River plain. When this was denied, they rioted and demolished the estate of one of Trinh Doanh's high officials. Trinh Doanh sdzed and punished the ringleaders of this affair, but the soldiers continued to be volatile and prone to disorder. At that time, an official survey concluded that 1,730 villages in the Red River plain had been abandoned and 1,961 had been partially abandoned. Trinh Doanh took these abandoned lands to settle soldiers in a system of military colonies (don dien). At the same time, he changed the means of providing salaries for officials from calculating the tax on a certain number of taxpayers to calculating the tax obtained from a certain amount of land. This encouraged officials to get land back into production.

Famine continued through 1742 and spread into Thanh Hoa. The only information recorded in this year was focused on Thanh Hoa, where Trinh Doanh battled with Le Duy Mat and finally forced him into the uplands of Lang Chanh district. Trinh Doanh raised land taxes and increased the conscription of soldiers in Thanh Hoa during this year.

The year 1743 saw fighting nearly everywhere, including the border province of Lang Son, and especially in the eastern plains where a new rebel leader named Nguyen Huu Cau had risen to prominence. Trinh Doanh managed to besiege him at Do Son on the coast by the end of the year. The year 1744 began ominously when a strange huge fish, described as one hundred meters long and with a head like an elephant, was observed swimming up the Red River to the limit of saltwater, about thirty kilometers south of the capital, then turning and going back out to sea. Shortly after, Nguyen Huu Cau broke the siege of Do Son and advanced upriver to the northeastern part of the plain. Meanwhile, another rebel leader, Nguyen Danh Phuong, had gained control of the territories north and northwest of the capital, and a third major rebel leader, Hoang Cong Chat, was holding fast in the region downriver from the capital. The following year did not see much change except that Nguyen Huu Cau was driven further east into Yen Quang Province, Mac partisans attacking south out of Cao Bang were repulsed, and Hoang Cong Chat managed to capture and kill a Trinh governor.

During the next five years, to 1750, the battlefield situation gradually changed but without a clear indication of any side gaining an advantage. Nguyen Huu Cau built up his position in the eastern plains. He developed a navy and obtained rice from abroad to distribute to the starving people of that region. He spread his authority throughout the districts east of the capital, reportedly winning popularity by shielding villagers from rapacious Trinh officials. Nguyen Danh Phuong retained control of the region northwest of the capital. Hoang Cong Chat shifted his base of operations from the south to the northeastern part of the plain. Meanwhile, in 1749, Le Duy Mat emerged from the Thanh Hoa uplands to attack into the region south of the capital.

The most significant piece of information about Trinh Doanh from these years is that he began to take a strong interest in the problems of government. Perhaps he decided that the best way to counter the appeal of rebel leaders was to provide a plausible alternative. He published measures to improve the courts of law, to end the abuses of corvée service, to allow militiamen time off to work in their fields, to forgive unpaid taxes in the capital region, to reinstitute the salt tax, to stabilize the agrarian situation in Thanh Hoa that was under stress from conscripting so many soldiers, and to postpone taxes on private property in Thanh Hoa and Nghe An. In 1750, he published a twelve-point manifesto that shows a modicum of normal government to have been restored in areas under his control. The manifesto covers the familiar ground of behavior expected of all classes of people: great lords, high ministers, military commanders, censors, nobles, judicial commissioners, magistrates, soldiers, and common people. This manifesto is in itself not remarkable, but the fact that it was issued at this time shows that

Trinh Doanh had moved out of the phase of emergency management and was now thinking of how to establish a regular system of administration.

The examination system received close attention from Trinh Doanh and his advisors during the early years of his rule. The class of men aspiring to gain status through participation in this system was not only large but also influential in forming public opinion. The few men who gained entry to the palace examination were but a tiny minority of all those who received some social capital from their participation in the exams that preceded it, from the district pre-exam through the provincial regional exam and on to the capital exam. There was intense pressure on this system of examinations, not only from aspiring students, but also from the officials in charge of administering them, who endeavored to ensure the success of students from families with whom they were allied or of their own protégés.

In 1741, the "rather good" category of achievement for pre-exams and regional exams was abolished. But without this convenient track into the regional exams, corruption became even more open and rampant as powerful families used their money and influence to affect the outcome of exams. In 1743, the regional exams in Nghe An were so chaotic that a riot erupted in the middle of the exam and students destroyed the examination place. In 1747, Trinh Doanh ordered an investigation of abuses in the regional exams and subsequently reinstated the "rather good" stream. He also reduced district quotas for entry to the regional exams, thereby giving more power to provincial educational officers. At the same time, a way was opened for wealthy but poorly educated students to buy admission to part of the regional exam and thereby gain a certain status. Aside from the mainstream of literary examinations, there were more specialized academic evaluations. For example, in 1762, clerks and accountants were recruited into government service with examinations in writing and mathematics, resulting in 978 men selected for writing and 120 selected for math.

In 1750, the need for revenue led to a new scheme in which students of at least 10 years old could buy tickets to skip the pre-exam and to enroll in the regional exam, which in itself conferred a coveted social status. Furthermore, they were allowed to have substitutes take the exam for them. If the student showed sufficient academic ability by the time of the next exam, he could compete with the possibility of being promoted to the capital exam. This practice was motivated by a need to raise money and a desire to bring wealthy families into officialdom. But the result was to make marketplaces out of the regional examinations. In 1751 there was such disorder and scandal in the regional exams that Trinh Doanh stepped in and annulled the results of over two hundred successful candidates who were not even students. Virtually all of the education officials in charge of the exams that year were demoted or dismissed, but corruption of the examination system continued unabated. In 1765, according to a new rule, admission tickets to the regional examinations were openly sold without any conditions.

Another cycle of Trinh misgovernment

In early 1751, the battlefield situation changed dramatically. Both Nguyen Huu Cau and Nguyen Danh Phuong were captured and killed after heavy fighting. Hoang Cong Chat was driven into the mountains of Hung Hoa. Le Duy Mat was pushed into the mountains of Nghe An and eventually forced up the Ca River to the Xieng Khouang plateau of Laos where he and his followers established a small domain. Both Hoang Cong Chat and Le Duy Mat would survive in their mountain fortresses for nearly two more decades, but they were never again active in the lowlands. The years of rebellion were coming to an end.

By mid 1751, Nhu Dinh Toan (1703–1774), a graduate of the 1736 examination, from an area east of the capital, was assigned to draw up plans for rebuilding a system of administration. He announced nine basic principles that predictably echoed the ideals of the Hong Duc and Canh Tri eras. In more specific terms, he proposed that the Six Sessions, the Six Ministries, the Six Departments, the Six Courts, the Censorate, as well as the provincial and district officials, should all bear their respective responsibilities. He observed that, in actual fact, the Six Sessions, under direct Trinh control, decided everything while the other offices, in the royal domain, did nothing, and many high officials and prominent nobles did as they pleased. Two new offices were to be established to collect taxes in the Red River plain. For good measure, the 1663 "Edict to Explain Civilizing Instructions" was reissued.

In 1752, remaining rebel bands in the lowlands were tracked down and pacified, and officials were sent to return scattered refugees to their villages and fields. In 1753, soldiers from the Red River plain were released to bring abandoned fields back under cultivation. In these years, Trinh Doanh held daily meetings with his highest officials to discuss the details of restoring calm to the country. He is reported to have admonished his Censorate and provincial judicial officers: "All I get from you is trivia! I know there are many bad things going on. You must report them to me so that something can be done about them."

Two authors writing in the 1740s, during the rebellions, have been remembered for new literary departures. Dang Tran Con (1710–1745) wrote a long poem entitled *Chinh Phu Ngam Khuc* (Song of a Soldier's Wife), a lament in the voice of a woman whose husband had gone off to war, leaving her to mourn the passing of her years in loneliness. This work was written in Literary Chinese. Several later writers wrote translations of it in vernacular Nom. The most popular vernacular version today is attributed to Phan Huy Ich (1750–1822), written in the early nineteenth century.

The second author was Doan Thi Diem (1705–1748), the daughter of a teacher. She wrote poetry and prose in Literary Chinese. Her work expressed the perspective of an educated woman who considered herself to be, and was, the intellectual equal of men. Among her works is *Truyen Ky Tan Pha* (New Collection of Marvelous Stories), which includes her version of the earthly life of the woman who became the popular goddess Lieu Hanh, emphasizing Lieu Hanh's erudition as a mark of her divinity. Both Dang Tran Con and Doan Thi Diem gave impetus to the literary trend of using the voice of a woman to comment on social and political affairs. The literary conceit of intelligent and complaining women appeared amidst turmoil that tended to discredit the existing political leadership of men.

By 1754, conditions were thought to have become sufficiently normal that the king was allowed to take a day excursion by boat on the Red River. In that year, taxation was reinstituted in the northern border provinces and officials reported that the village populations in the lowlands had been stabilized and fields had been restored to cultivation. Thereafter, the rural situation returned to the familiar cycle of subsistence: a good harvest, then famine and misery, and then waiting for the next good harvest. A drought in 1755 put taxes into arrears, clogged the courts of law with litigation over land, which was the only asset in poverty-stricken villages, and caused soldiers from Thanh Hoa and Nghe An to desert their units and return home to care for their families. Initiatives to reform judicial procedures were made in 1758 and again in 1762, but courts of law were as chronic a source of dismay as were the vicissitudes of agriculture. In 1757 there were floods, epidemics, and a famine. In 1759, there was drought, insects, and famine. In 1761 there was drought. In 1762 there was a rural epidemic. In 1765 there was drought and an epidemic. In 1766 there were broken dikes and floods.

Trinh agrarian policy remained at the level of ad hoc reactions to these events. In 1755, all unpaid taxes in the Red River plain were forgiven, and the Nghe An land tax rate was reduced. In 1756, the Six Sessions were found to be incompetent at collecting the land tax so this task was put into the hands of a eunuch. In 1757, military colonies (*don dien*) were abolished and their land was returned to village leaders. In 1762, Thanh Hoa and Nghe An were subject to a new census for conscripting soldiers. In 1765, an edict admonished powerful families to stop harassing the farmers. In 1766, soldiers were sent to suppress an outbreak of rural banditry in the region northwest of the capital.

Commercial policy in these years was aimed at limiting excessive exactions at customs stations that hindered the movement of goods and discouraged merchants. Copper coins were again being cast. Communities of Qing merchants existed at Mong Cai on the coast at the Qing border, at the old port of Van Don, and in Nghe An at Quynh Luu and at Vinh. In 1764, the Qing people in these communities were forbidden to mix with the local population and required to stay in their own quarters.

Christianity was routinely proscribed along with various forms of undesirable behavior such as gambling. The number of Christians nevertheless continued to grow. During the fifty years from the beginning of Trinh Cuong's rule in 1709 through Trinh Doanh's rule in the 1760s, eighty-six European missionaries are recorded as having served among the northern Vietnamese and 111 northern Vietnamese were ordained as priests. Major concentrations of Christian communities developed in Nghe An, in the coastal area south of Ke Cho at modern Phat Diem, and in the region east of Ke Cho at Ke Sat and neighboring areas of the Hai Duong plain. The missionaries tried to keep Christians out of the rebellions of the 1730s and 1740s but were not always successful in doing so. Their accounts describe the grinding misery of rural life. Christian soldiers served in the military during those years, being allowed to swear an oath of loyalty to the Trinh in the name of the Christian god rather than of the traditional mountain spirit.

In the mid 1750s, Trinh Doanh's interest in the examination system extended to conducting continuing evaluations of the officials who had emerged from that system and who, in peacetime, were taking greater roles in government administration. In 1756, he assigned Le Quy Don (1726–1784), a graduate of 1752 from the coastal region of modern Thai Binh Province, to examine all officials and make recommendations for promotions and demotions. Le Quy Don was a relatively erudite man, which may explain the confidence placed in him by Trinh Doanh. He was also a clever self-promoter and did not neglect opportunities to advance the careers of men in his debt or to derail the careers of men he did not like. In 1762, Trinh Doanh established a privy council (*bi thu cac*) and put Le Quy Don in charge of it along with an older official named Nguyen Ba Lan (1701–1786), a graduate of 1731. Shortly after, Le Quy Don departed as envoy to China. When he returned in 1765, however, he made himself so ridiculous by ostensibly announcing his errors while in fact publicly praising himself that Trinh Doanh dismissed him into early retirement.

In 1767, Trinh Doanh died and was succeeded by his eldest son Trinh Sam. Trinh Sam had been designated as heir fourteen years earlier when he was a teenager. At the time of his elevation, Ngo Thi Si (1725–1780), an official who had been brought into officialdom in 1756 when Le Quy Don was ascendant, was in the northern mountains with a group of subordinates. He had been sent by Trinh Doanh to bring the mining operations there under control. All the profits from the mines were going to Qing businessmen across the border and Ke Cho administrators were stymied in their efforts to collect taxes. It is typical of Trinh Sam's rule that, upon his coming to power, Ngo Thi Si and his colleagues were recalled to the capital and no further effort was taken to deal with the perennial problem of the mines along the Qing border. Trinh Sam called Le Quy Don back from retirement, and, during the next fifteen years, Le Quy Don and Ngo Thi Si were prominent in a group of officials who worked closely with eunuchs to maintain a modicum of public order while attending to Trinh Sam's wishes and their own enrichment.

Trinh Sam bore lifelong resentment against the Le family, being incurably jealous of its royal status. He had grown up with the crown prince, Le Duy Vi, and the two young men nurtured a deep hatred of one another. Le Duy Vi resented Trinh domination of the royal family, and Trinh Sam was consumed with an impossible desire for the throne. The personal animus between the two came to a head in 1769 when Trinh Sam deposed and imprisoned Le Duy Vi, replacing him as crown prince with a younger brother, Le Duy Can. This happened shortly after the death of the old rebel Hoang Cong Chat in the mountains of Hung Hoa and an expedition that decisively defeated his son, thus putting to an end that group of diehards from the rebellions of two decades before. The only remaining holdout from that era was Le Duy Mat, the prince who had established himself on the Xieng Khouang plateau of Laos.

One of the main things that occupied Trinh Sam's attention after he came to power was his determination to put an end to Le Duy Mat. In fact, when Trinh Doanh died in 1767, Le Duy Mat decided to test the new Trinh ruler by leading his men out of the mountains to attack him. Trinh armies drove him back into the mountains and from then on were urged forward by Trinh Sam with orders to destroy this prince who for thirty years had flourished the banner of Le resistance to the Trinh. In 1770, Le Duy Mat's stronghold finally fell and he took his own life.

In 1771, Trinh Sam killed Le Duy Vi and imprisoned Le Duy Vi's three sons. The eldest of these sons, Le Duy Khiem, a future king, was then 6 years old. Trinh Sam continued to look for new ways to humiliate the royal family, and he found a willing henchman for this endeavor in Le Quy Don. Le Quy Don had been rising in Trinh Sam's esteem as a result of his passing along a percentage of the wealth that he was accumulating through bribery and corruption. In 1771, Le Quy Don was in the Censorate and was cultivating eunuchs close to Trinh Sam by giving them positions of supervision over officials. He managed to insinuate himself into the confidence of Pham Huy Dinh, a eunuch who was a great favorite of Trinh Sam. Together they embarked on various corrupt schemes. Le Quy Don began to use the position of immunity conferred by his alliance with the eunuchs to penalize officials who were close to the king. Within a short time he was able to sufficiently intimidate officials to stop them from attending the bi-monthly sessions of the royal court on the first and fifteenth days of the lunar month. This gave immense satisfaction to Trinh Sam, whose passion for demeaning the royal court was insatiable.

By the early 1770s, when events in the south began to open new possibilities, Trinh government at Ke Cho had survived an age of insurrection without having seriously addressed its causes. The inability of rebel leaders to unite and Trinh Doanh's persistence gave the Trinh regime an opportunity to be renewed. However, instead of renewal, once the rebellions had been calmed, the Trinh simply returned to the conundrums that had been at the heart of their political problems from the very beginning: a dependence upon soldiers from the southern provinces to rule a sullen and impoverished population in the Red River plain and an inability to escape from doubts about the Trinh right to exercise power on behalf of the Le dynasty. Trinh Tac had addressed the first of these problems by bringing the literati of the Red River plain into his government. But the long-term effect of this was simply to burden the agriculturalists of the Red River plain with a new class of predators. The northern Vietnamese had not been able to find a way out of this impasse. The impetus for a new age would come from the southerners. The relative passivity of the northerners during the Thirty Years War that broke out in the 1770s revealed an exhaustion of hope that came from generations of oppression, poverty, and despair.

8 THE THIRTY YEARS WAR

The rise of Qui Nhon

In the 1770s, war broke out among the Vietnamese. The immediate cause was an uprising in Binh Dinh Province against the misgovernment of Truong Phuc Loan. People in Binh Dinh had for generations borne the brunt of demands for soldiers, supplies, and transport to sustain Nguyen Phuc policy in the Mekong plain as well as in the mountainous hinterlands. When an ascendant Siam began to challenge the Vietnamese position in Cambodia and the court at Phu Xuan could not rise above a morass of corruption and incompetence, a new political force emerged in Binh Dinh.

In 1767, Burmese invaders seized Ayutthia, the capital of Siam. A provincial Siamese governor named Taksin subsequently expelled the invaders and reigned as king for fourteen years (1768–1782). Taksin's father, a Teochow Chinese, had made a career as a Siamese tax collector while also being active in the Chinese merchant community of Siam. Taksin had spent part of his youth doing business in Cambodia and reportedly learned to speak both Khmer and Vietnamese. He launched his bid to become king of Siam from Chanthaburi, on the southeastern coast of Siam near the Cambodian border. His familiarity with Cambodia may explain his desire to reduce this Siamese neighbor to vassalage. His means of accomplishing this was to champion the cause of a Khmer prince who came to be known as Chei Chéttha V, the son of Chei Chéttha IV, a former king who had died in 1757.

The king of Cambodia in the 1760s was Outeireachea III. The Vietnamese had placed him on the Khmer throne in 1758 through the intervention of Mac Thien Tu, the lord of Ha Tien. Consequently, Outeireachea III was closely allied with Mac Thien Tu and the Vietnamese. As early as 1768, Taksin sent military forces by sea and seized some territory on the Cambodian coast around Kampot, only about forty kilometers northwest of Ha Tien, but Outeireachea III refused his demand to pay tribute. In 1769, Siamese and Khmer forces supporting Chei

Chéttha V attacked Outeireachea III and, at the same time, a Teochow Chinese serving as Taksin's agent conspired with some members of Mac Thien Tu's family against him. Both the attack and the conspiracy failed.

Mac Thien Tu held a strong position on the Khmer–Viet coast, which, rather than the overland route, was Taksin's chosen approach to the Khmer capital. Taksin decided that in order to prevail against Outeireachea III, he would first have to deal with Mac Thien Tu. In 1770, several hundred Khmers and Malays who were allied with Taksin, led by a turncoat from Mac Thien Tu's army, assaulted Ha Tien by sea. Mac Thien Tu defeated this challenge but it provoked great disorder in his domain. Some Ha Tien Chinese were interested in doing business with the half-Teochow Siamese king and were ready to throw off their allegiance to Phu Xuan. In this same year, people in the Central Highlands, emboldened by Phu Xuan's inattention or by Taksin's agents or by both, emerged from the mountains to plunder Quang Ngai, spreading fear and confusion along the coast from Quang Nam to Phu Yen.

In 1771, Taksin arrived by sea with a large army. He seized Ha Tien and marched to the Khmer capital at Oudong, where he enthroned Chei Chéttha V. Mac Thien Tu and Outeireachea III fled to Saigon. At the same time as Taksin was putting his candidate on the Cambodian throne, whether by coincidence or by design, a man named Nguyen Nhac, supported by uplanders, Chams, Chinese merchants, and Vietnamese peasants established himself at An Khe on the main east–west trade route through the Central Highlands that connected the port of Qui Nhon with northern Cambodia and the Siamese capital. He raised a flag of rebellion and thereby initiated the Thirty Years War.

The Mekong plain was alive with battles between Khmer armies and their Siamese and Vietnamese allies as a large Vietnamese expeditionary force was mobilized at Saigon in late 1771 and early 1772. By mid 1772, this force had advanced up the Mekong and restored Outeireachea III to his throne. Taksin withdrew his soldiers to the coast and returned to Siam. Thereafter, he relied upon the disorder that began to spread among the Vietnamese to serve his interests in Cambodia.

In early 1773, Nguyen Nhac seized Qui Nhon. He claimed descent from Ho Quy Ly. A paternal ancestor had been taken as a prisoner of war by the southerners during the fighting in Nghe An during the 1650s and was settled on the upland frontier of Binh Dinh Province at a village named Tay Son ("west mountain"). His surname was changed to Nguyen, the most common surname in the south for displaced people seeking to identify with the new ruling house. Nguyen Nhac traveled widely as an itinerant betel merchant and tax collector, which gave him first-hand knowledge of conditions in many regions. According to Nguyen historians, he had a weakness for gambling and had a habit of using tax revenue to pay his gambling debts. When this was brought to light by higher authorities, he fled to the mountains and organized a rebellion. But there was more to his uprising than this, for he mobilized upland peoples from the Central Highlands and he also drew upon Cham symbols of kingship to rally large numbers of Chams. He furthermore gained the support of the Chinese merchant community at the port of Qui Nhon. Tay Son and An Khe were connected to Chinese merchant communities not only in Qui Nhon on the coast but also in Cambodia and at the Siamese capital further west. Nguyen Nhac's seizure of Qui Nhon made him a major figure in the political world of the Vietnamese-speaking peoples. He would rule from Qui Nhon until his death in 1793.

Nguyen Nhac benefited from a popular attribution of all the country's woes to the perfidy of Truong Phuc Loan and his usurpation of the authority of the legitimate Nguyen Phuc royal house. He had no trouble finding recruits for his armies. He used unusual tactics to unnerve his enemies, simple tricks like having his men hiss and rattle their weapons when attacking. He organized shock troops with especially tall men who were sent into battle with Qing haircuts, naked with gold and silver paper pasted to their bodies as offerings to the gods, and inebriated to the point of being eager to die. Phu Xuan soldiers, led by incompetent cronies of Truong Phuc Loan, fled from Nguyen Nhac's armies. By the end of 1773, Nguyen Nhac's men had advanced south all the way to the border of Gia Dinh and north to the border of Quang Nam.

Nguyen Cuu Dat, a scion of the redoubtable Nguyen Cuu family that had already served the Nguyen Phuc with distinction for a century and a half, repulsed Nguyen Nhac's attacks into Quang Nam. In early 1774, the Phu Xuan armies based at Gia Dinh pushed north and retook all the territories up to the mountainous terrain at Ca Pass on the southern border of Phu Yen Province. But within a few weeks the situation changed dramatically when Trinh Sam decided to march south.

Despite a famine in Nghe An, Trinh Sam could not resist taking advantage of the troubles besetting the old enemies of his family in the south. He recalled from retirement a eunuch with a reputation for competence, Hoang Ngu Phuc (d. 1775), and put him in command of an expedition into the south. When he crossed the Gianh River in autumn of 1774, Hoang Ngu Phuc announced that he was coming to help put down Nguyen Nhac's rebellion. He met with Nguyen Phuc envoys, and they assured him that this was not necessary. But one of the envoys, wanting to unseat Truong Phuc Loan, secretly encouraged him to continue his march south. All of the best military officers in the southern army were in Quang Nam resisting Nguyen Nhac. Officers facing the Trinh army were timid or incompetent. Furthermore, Thuan Hoa was in the grip of famine. A shipment of rice sent from Ha Tien by Mac Thien Tu had been captured by

Nguyen Nhac's men. People in Thuan Hoa were dying and there were reports of cannibalism. When the Trinh army arrived at the Tran Ninh Wall, the southern soldiers opened the gates and fled.

As Hoang Ngu Phuc took possession of the abandoned system of walls, he issued another message saying that he had come not only to deliver the southerners from Nguyen Nhac's rebellion but also to relieve them of the usurping despot Truong Phuc Loan. He called upon the southerners to deliver Truong Phuc Loan into his hands. A group of Nguyen Phuc princes and Nguyen Cuu Phap, another member of the Nguyen Cuu family, gathered the nerve to seize Truong Phuc Loan and deliver him to Hoang Ngu Phuc. Hoang Ngu Phuc continued his advance south as the 20-year-old ruler, Nguyen Phuc Thuan, and a band of princes who rallied around him, desperately attempted to organize resistance to the Trinh advance. In the last month of 1774, Hoang Ngu Phuc entered Phu Xuan and the Nguyen Phuc leaders fled to Quang Nam.

Within weeks, the forces of Nguyen Nhac were moving north to take advantage of Phu Xuan's fall. Two Chinese merchants, Tap Dinh and Ly Tai, had joined Nguyen Nhac when he seized Qui Nhon in 1773 and had raised shipborne armies that included Qing pirates. These men led Nguyen Nhac's naval forces to blockade Hoi An at the mouth of the Thu Bon River as Nguyen Nhac's land forces marched north along the foothills then downriver to meet them. The Nguyen Phuc were defeated and looked for ways to escape. Nguyen Phuc Thuan named a nephew, Nguyen Phuc Duong, son of a crown prince who had died in 1760, to be crown prince and left him in command of the soldiers that remained in Quang Nam, while he and as many as could get away embarked for Gia Dinh. A boat carrying the Nguyen Phuc generals was lost in a storm, but a boat carrying Nguyen Phuc Thuan and Nguyen Phuc Anh, the fourteen-year-old son of Nguyen Phuc Con, Nguyen Phuc Khoat's designated heir, whom Truong Phuc Loan had killed in 1765, arrived at Nha Trang and was welcomed by loyal officials there before continuing the journey to Gia Dinh.

Nguyen Nhac captured Nguyen Phuc Duong in Quang Nam shortly before Hoang Ngu Phuc advanced from the north and pushed him back out of the province. Tap Dinh, defeated by the Trinh, fled to Guangdong where he was killed by Qing authorities, who regarded him as a pirate. Ly Tai followed Nguyen Nhac back to Qui Nhon. Nguyen Phuc Duong urged Nguyen Nhac to unite with Nguyen Phuc Thuan at Gia Dinh against the Trinh, but Nguyen Nhac had an idea of proclaiming Nguyen Phuc Duong as king to rally the southerners against the Trinh. Nguyen Phuc Duong refused to cooperate with this scheme, and for a few months in mid 1775 Nguyen Nhac's fortunes appeared to be in decline as Trinh armies arrived at the northern border of Quang Ngai and Nguyen Phuc armies retook Phu Yen, just south of Qui Nhon. Ly Tai, thinking that Nguyen Nhac was not treating him with sufficient regard, defected to the Nguyen Phuc forces in Phu Yen.

Under attack from the Nguyen Phuc armies in Phu Yen to the south and with the Trinh army threatening to advance into Quang Ngai to the north, Nguyen Nhac sent treasure to Hoang Ngu Phuc requesting to submit. He viewed the Trinh, far from their line of supply and in unfamiliar territory, as a less dangerous foe than the Nguyen Phuc. Hoang Ngu Phuc sent one of his generals, Nguyen Huu Chinh, to meet with Nguyen Nhac, to accept his submission, and to appoint him to lead the vanguard against the Nguyen Phuc.

Within a few weeks, the situation dramatically changed when an epidemic wasted the Trinh army in Quang Nam. Hoang Ngu Phuc withdrew to Phu Xuan and died shortly after. The Trinh abandoned Quang Nam, settled down to govern Thuan Hoa, and thereafter posed no threat of advancing further south. Nguyen Nhac marched north and retook Quang Nam from Nguyen Phuc partisans who had risen up when the Trinh withdrew. At the same time, Nguyen Nhac's younger brother Nguyen Hue attacked south into Phu Yen and put Nguyen Phuc forces there on the defensive.

Nguyen Nhac moved quickly to take advantage of this turn of affairs. At the beginning of 1776, he sent another younger brother, Nguyen Lu, with a large seaborne expedition to Gia Dinh. Nguyen Lu seized Saigon. One Nguyen Phuc official, Bui Huu Le, was captured and subsequently became famous for bitterly scolding one of Nguyen Lu's generals to his face, which so infuriated his captors that they killed and ate him.

Buoyed by the victories in Quang Nam and in Gia Dinh, Nguyen Nhac, in the spring of 1776, proclaimed himself King of Tay Son at Cha Ban, the old Cham capital of Vijaya, around twenty-five kilometers northwest of Qui Nhon, near the modern town of An Nhon. Here, he would reign for the next seventeen years. But only two months later, the Nguyen Phuc general at My Tho, Do Thanh Nhan, retook Saigon, sending Nguyen Lu fleeing back to Qui Nhon. During the next year, from mid 1776 to mid 1777, Nguyen Phuc politics at Saigon unraveled when Ly Tai arrived from Phu Yen and a feud broke out between him and Do Thanh Nhan. When Nguyen Phuc Duong arrived in Saigon after escaping from Nguyen Nhac, Ly Tai promoted his claim to be king and forced Nguyen Phuc Thuan to yield. At My Tho, Do Thanh Nhan (d. 1781) and Nguyen Phuc Anh remained attached to Nguyen Phuc Thuan, the "senior king."

During the fighting with Nguyen Lu earlier in the year, Nguyen Phuc Thuan had called upon the Cambodian king for assistance. In the previous year, 1775, Outeireachea III had made peace with Taksin's candidate for the Khmer throne, Chei Chéttha V. Chei Chéttha V became king and Outeireachea III went into retirement. In 1776, Chei Chéttha V refused Nguyen Phuc Thuan's appeal. Later in the year, Nguyen Phuc Anh led a brief raiding expedition up the Mekong to punish him for this. Although only 14 years old, he had organized his own army, and he began to show unusual qualities of leadership.

After five years of fighting, two Vietnamese regimes had become three. The northerners had taken Thuan Hoa but were incapable of moving any further south. Nguyen Nhac's regime was ascendant from Hai Van Pass in the north to the Binh Thuan dry zone in the south. Remnants of the Nguyen Phuc family and their followers desperately endeavored to build a new center of power at Saigon. This was not a war between northerners and southerners. For the most part, the northerners were passive observers in this war, handicapped by poor leadership, dysfunctional government, and a demoralized population. This became a war between two groups of southerners based at Qui Nhon and at Saigon. The importance of Saigon became increasingly apparent as the years of war accumulated. In the earlier phases of the war, control of Saigon was the prize of battle.

Resurgence of the Nguyen Phuc and decline of the Trinh

In the spring of 1777, Nguyen Nhac sent Nguyen Hue to Saigon with a large seaborne expedition. In a six-month campaign, Nguyen Hue defeated all the Nguyen Phuc armies, including those of Mac Thien Tu and reinforcements from Phu Yen. Nguyen Phuc Thuan, Nguyen Phuc Duong, and most of the Nguyen Phuc princes were captured and killed, as was Ly Tai. Mac Thien Tu fled to Siam. Nguyen Phuc Anh escaped through many vicissitudes to the island of Tho Chu, 150 kilometers into the sea west of the Ca Mau peninsula. For a short time he found refuge at a Christian seminary in Ha Tien directed by a French missionary named Pierre Pigneau (1741–1799, later known as Pigneau de Behaine and, in Vietnamese, Ba Da Loc). Pierre Pigneau spent the rest of his life devoted to Nguyen Phuc Anh's cause. Shortly after Nguyen Hue had returned to Qui Nhon in the autumn of 1777, Nguyen Phuc Anh rallied men in Gia Dinh loyal to his family. By the end of the year, with the assistance of Do Thanh Nhan and others, he had retaken Saigon.

During the first half of 1778, Nguyen Phuc Anh repulsed all Tay Son efforts to regain Saigon. During the second half of the year, he was busy building military bases and sea-going warships. In 1779, he established an administrative structure to govern the major population centers in the Mekong plain. In this year, he also intervened in Cambodia to establish a regime that was friendly to him. Outeireachea III had died in 1777. In 1778, Chei Chéttha V, as a Siamese vassal, had conscripted an army and sent it to join Taksin's invasion of Laos. This provoked distress, unrest, and, finally, rebellion. In 1779, Nguyen Phuc Anh sent

Do Thanh Nhan with an army to place Ang Eng, a 5-year-old son of Out-eireachea III, on the throne. Chei Chéttha V was killed, and a pro-Vietnamese nobleman named Mou was appointed to serve as regent for the young king.

In 1780, Nguyen Phuc Anh, at the age of 18, proclaimed himself king at Saigon. His authority extended north into the province of Phu Yen and west to his vassal in Cambodia. In a domain of rivers and coasts, shipbuilding continued to be a priority, and a new design of two-level galleys began to be produced at Saigon, with rowers in the bottom level and soldiers on the upper level. Do Thanh Nhan invented innovative means of attacking in swampy terrain while pacifying Khmer resistance in Tra Vinh. Do Thanh Nhan's successes and the trust that Nguyen Phuc Anh placed in him made him a target of jealousy, and it may have been that his popularity among the soldiers began to threaten Nguyen Phuc Anh's sense of security. Whether with reason or not, in spring of 1781 Do Thanh Nhan was accused of disloyalty and killed. A subsequent uprising led by men loyal to him was put down with hard fighting. Shortly after, Nguyen Phuc Anh sent a large army north to join the battles in Phu Yen. With it went some eighty war boats, two of them of European design. This was the high point of Nguyen Phuc Anh's fortunes before many years of tribulation and exile.

Since proclaiming himself king in 1776, Nguyen Nhac had been frustrated in his efforts to destroy the Nguyen Phuc. He was not able to concentrate his attention on his southern enemy because he remained uncertain about his northern enemy, with whom he maintained an uneasy truce. During these years, his base of power was in the three provinces of Binh Dinh, Quang Ngai, and Quang Nam. His southern border in Phu Yen was in perpetual contestation, while the border between Quang Nam and Thuan Hoa needed constant vigilance, for the Trinh frequently sent raids into Quang Nam to test Tay Son readiness and to collect rice. This situation began to change in 1781 and 1782 as a result of events related to the failing health and death of Trinh Sam.

In the late 1770s and early 1780s, there was a series of droughts and nearly constant famine conditions in the north. Taxes were regularly excused due to rural hunger. Meanwhile the same old agrarian problems continued to appear with corruption drying up tax revenue and unsuccessful efforts to repopulate abandoned fields. In 1776, the taxes of over half of all registered fields were assigned to officials in lieu of salaries. Officials wanted to change salaries from fields to cash, but cash was unavailable. In this year, the government appears to have given up on any effort to even think about village conditions. The requirement that provincial officials make an annual report on the welfare of the common people was discontinued with the argument that it was a troublesome procedure that wasted time and produced no results. Yet, in 1779, as famine conditions became difficult to ignore, an edict went out for officials to investigate the living conditions of the people, but there is no indication of any result. Northerners had learned to live with misgovernment.

Despite his inability to address real problems, Trinh Sam could not shake away his desire to be king. In 1777 he sent an envoy to Qing reporting that the Le dynasty was extinct and requesting recognition of himself as king. The envoy was so disturbed by his mission that after departing he burned his documents and took poison. In these years, Ngo Thi Si and especially Le Quy Don pandered to Trinh Sam's whims. Le Quy Don and his disreputable son became notorious for corruption. The son was briefly imprisoned in 1775 when he was caught cheating in the capital examination. In 1776, Le Quy Don spent several months in Thuan Hoa, assigned to inspect and report on conditions there. In 1777 he was sent to inspect the tax registers in Thanh Hoa. In 1778, Trinh Sam ignored public denunciations of Le Quy Don and his son for corruption. In 1779, Le Quy Don suffered a brief embarrassment when his corrupt dealings with an upland chieftain in the northern mountains provoked an uprising. The fact was that an important source of wealth for Trinh Sam was from corrupt officials like Le Quy Don.

In 1780, Trinh Sam demoted his eldest son Trinh Khai and instead named as his heir Trinh Cau, a sickly infant son of his favorite concubine. Trinh Cau's mother was closely allied with the family of Hoang Ngu Phuc, the famous, now deceased, general. There were rumors that Hoang Ngu Phuc's grandson, Hoang Dinh Bao, was her lover and that he planned to murder the child and seize power for himself. Nguyen Khai was imprisoned when he was discovered to be in a plot against Hoang Dinh Bao. Le Quy Don and members of his clique were busy on behalf of Hoang Dinh Bao. For two years, this situation drifted along with both Trinh Sam and Trinh Cau incapacitated by illness.

When Trinh Sam died in autumn of 1782, the Thanh Hoa and Nghe An soldiers stationed in Ke Cho killed Hoang Dinh Bao, discarded Trinh Cau, and released Trinh Khai from prison, making him lord of the palace. When the élite prisons were opened to release Trinh Khai, three grandsons of the king were also released. They had been imprisoned in 1769 along with their father, former crown prince Le Duy Vi, Trinh Sam's childhood nemesis. Le Duy Vi had been replaced as crown prince by a younger brother, and then killed two years later. In early 1783, the soldiers raised the eldest of Le Duy Vi's sons, 18-year-old Le Duy Khiem, to be the crown prince, deposing a younger brother of Le Duy Vi who had been selected by Trinh Sam.

One member of the Hoang Dinh Bao faction was Nguyen Huu Chinh, a protégé of Hoang Ngu Phuc who was then in command of Nghe An Province. With his enemies gaining power at Ke Cho, he was in a vulnerable position, so he decided to flee south and join Nguyen Nhac. He had been Hoang Ngu Phuc's envoy to Nguyen Nhac in 1775 and the two men reportedly had gotten along well on that occasion. He now advised Nguyen Nhac that it would be a propitious time to take Thuan Hoa.

Meanwhile, at Ke Cho, the Thanh Hoa and Nghe An soldiers, having tasted power, began to dominate and terrorize public life with riots and homicides. In 1784, Trinh Khai made a secret plan to raise soldiers from the Red River plain to pacify the Thanh Hoa and Nghe An men, but he was stymied when word of it leaked out. Efforts to placate the soldiers failed. They established a regime of pillaging that began to replace any semblance of normal government. In 1785, Bui Huy Bich (1744–1802), a graduate of 1769 from the capital, tried to encourage greater soberness among the arrogant soldiers by giving more visibility to the king, Le Duy Dieu. He did this by making large events of the public sessions of the royal court on the first and fifteenth days of the lunar month, which Le Quy Don, on behalf of Trinh Sam, had sabotaged more than a decade earlier. But the theater of ritual was no substitute for military discipline.

The Trinh reliance upon the soldiers from Thanh Hoa and Nghe An, which for generations had been the source of Trinh strength, had now become the source of Trinh weakness. Leadership at Ke Cho was at an impasse, and a foe was now gathering new strength in the south.

Tay Son ascendancy and division

King Taksin of Siam was not reconciled to the ascendant position gained by the Vietnamese in Cambodia when Ang Eng was placed on the throne with Mou as regent in 1779. In 1780, he took an accusation of conspiracy as reason to kill fifty-three high-ranking Vietnamese refugees in Siam, including Mac Thien Tu and a son of Nguyen Phuc Khoat. During the winter dry season of 1781–1782, he sent General Chakri to attack the Vietnamese and their Khmer allies in Cambodia. In the midst of this campaign, Taksin was deposed in a coup. Chakri met with the Vietnamese generals and negotiated an end to hostilities, then hastened back to Siam where he was crowned king. This was the beginning of an alliance between Chakri and Nguyen Phuc Anh that would continue for twenty years, until the end of the Vietnamese wars.

Shortly after the return of the Vietnamese army from Cambodia in spring of 1782, Nguyen Nhac and Nguyen Hue arrived with several hundred ships and thousands of men at the Can Gio estuary, the main entrance to the Sai Gon and Dong Nai Rivers. As the Tay Son forces fought their way upriver their progress was reportedly resisted the longest by a European-style ship commanded by a Frenchman whose name was recorded by the Vietnamese as Man Hoe

(Manuel). This man was a French adventurer who had been introduced to Nguyen Phuc Anh by Pierre Pigneau. He perished with his ship, and the Tay Son took Saigon. As Tay Son armies moved against Nguyen Phuc Anh at My Tho, Nguyen Phuc armies from the northern coast arrived and attacked the Tay Son from the other direction. During the battle that ensued, troops under the command of generals from the Chinese community in Cholon managed to kill a kinsman of Nguyen Nhac, which so enraged him that he slaughtered some ten thousand members of the Chinese community – men, women, and children – filling the rivers with their corpses. Nguyen Phuc Anh was soon forced to flee to Phu Quoc Island, off the coast of Ha Tien, where he sent a request to Chakri of Siam for help.

Nguyen Nhac and Nguyen Hue returned to Qui Nhon at mid summer. In the autumn, Nguyen Phuc Anh fought his way back to retake Saigon. For six months he feverishly prepared for the expected Tay Son counterattack while also mobilizing a Khmer army from Cambodia. Nguyen Hue and Nguyen Lu returned to the offensive in spring 1783, arriving at Gia Dinh with a large seaborne army. Nguyen Phuc Anh's allied Khmer–Viet armies were defeated, and he eventually found refuge again on Phu Quoc Island.

Nguyen Phuc Anh's appeal to Chakri was answered in autumn 1783 with Siamese armies moving through Cambodia to attack the Tay Son. The pro-Vietnamese regent, Mou, was killed by his enemies and replaced by a pro-Siamese regent, Ben, who ceded Cambodia's western provinces to Siam and sent the young king, Ang Eng, to Bangkok for safekeeping. A younger brother of Mou named Ten mobilized his followers and joined the Tay Son resistance against the advance of the Siamese. A second Siamese force arrived by sea at Ha Tien. Tay Son and Siamese armies confronted each other and fought several battles in the region of Sa Dec until the Siamese were forced to withdraw in late 1783. The Tay Son advanced to Phnom Penh where they placed Ten in power. The pro-Vietnamese Khmer had found new patrons in the Tay Son. Meanwhile, Siamese forces remained in Cambodia to support Ben at Oudong. Nguyen Phuc Anh and what survived of his entourage found refuge at Chakri's court in the new Siamese capital of Bangkok.

In mid 1784 a large Siamese expedition set out against the Tay Son both by land and by sea. The Siamese defeated the Tay Son at Sa Dec and continued downriver toward My Tho, the gateway to Saigon. Nguyen Phuc Anh complained to the Siamese generals that their men were plundering the local people and giving him a bad name. The Siamese generals seem not to have paid him any heed, nor to have availed themselves of his local knowledge. Ignorant of tidal currents in the lower Mekong, they fell into a Tay Son ambush as they prepared to attack My Tho by river. In the last lunar month of the year, at what became known as the Battle of Rach Gam–Xoai Mut, Nguyen Hue defeated the Siamese expedition and sent it fleeing back the way it had come.

Nguyen Phuc Anh was once again reduced to being an offshore wanderer. By late spring 1785 he had found refuge in Siam. He built a settlement outside of Bangkok and rallied his scattered followers. Within a few months several thousand men had gathered under his command. For the next year he served as a loyal ally of Chakri while sending spies to stay informed of conditions in Gia Dinh. He led his army against Burmese invaders, reportedly making use of "fire-spewing pipes." When Malay invaders threatened the Siamese south, he sent men to help repulse them. After two years of exile in Siam, a falling out among the Tay Son leaders gave him the opportunity he needed to return to Gia Dinh.

During 1785, the north was plagued with continual rain, insect infestations, pirates ravaging the coast of Yen Quang (modern Quang Ninh), soaring rice prices, famine, and starvation. At Ke Cho, Trinh Khai watched helplessly as the soldiers from Thanh Hoa and Nghe An strutted around the capital and intimidated government officials. In Thuan Hoa, the Trinh governor was uninterested in military matters. He spent his time building a personal fortune from commercial ventures while letting border defense lapse.

After Tay Son forces had gained control of Gia Dinh and expelled Nguyen Phuc Anh into Siamese exile, and after news from the north indicated that the Trinh were in trouble, Nguyen Nhac decided to act on Nguyen Huu Chinh's advice to seize Thuan Hoa and thereby reassemble the old Nguyen Phuc domain under his hand. In summer of 1786, Nguyen Nhac sent Nguyen Hue into Thuan Hoa. Nguyen Huu Chinh and Vo Van Nham commanded land forces and Nguyen Lu commanded naval forces. Treachery among the Trinh generals assisted their advance, and Thuan Hoa was taken with relative ease.

Nguyen Hue then made a decision that would have far-reaching consequences. Nguyen Huu Chinh and other northerners were urging him to march on Ke Cho, pointing out that government in the north was in disarray. Without consulting his elder brother, Nguyen Hue left Nguyen Lu at Phu Xuan and continued north, announcing that he intended "to exterminate the Trinh and restore the Le." Meeting little resistance along the way, he arrived at Ke Cho in less than a month. Trinh Khai fled and took his own life as the southerners suppressed the disorderly soldiers in the capital.

Nguyen Hue went to see the king. Le Duy Dieu was known as a kindhearted and even-tempered man. He was now 70 years old and in poor health. He endeavored to placate Nguyen Hue by giving him one of his daughters in marriage. And then he suddenly died. Le Duy Khiem, the 21-year-old crown prince, was raised to the throne. Shortly after, as Le Duy Dieu was being buried in Thanh Hoa, Nguyen Nhac appeared, angry about his younger brother's insubordinate northern adventure.

Nguyen Nhac considered involvement in northern affairs to be a great mistake and saw no value in the north except as a place to plunder, and plundering is what he and his men proceeded to do. But most of all, Nguyen Nhac did not like Nguyen Hue acting on his own initiative. For his part, Nguyen Hue was beginning to see beyond his brother's provincial perspective and to chafe at his brother's efforts to keep him in line. He also understood that the north was a difficult place to govern and that he needed a base in the south.

The two brothers quarreled, then raced back south to mobilize their followers and test their clashing ambitions on the battlefield. Nguyen Nhac called on his army in Gia Dinh to march north to assist him. Nguyen Hue ambushed it in Phu Yen and forced it to surrender. The two brothers fought for several months in their home province of Binh Dinh. Nguyen Hue besieged Nguyen Nhac in his capital of Cha Ban, but the brothers had exhausted each other, and, in early 1787, negotiated a peace, partitioning the Tay Son realm. Nguyen Hue received Thuan Hoa and northern Quang Nam. He went to Phu Xuan and proclaimed himself "the king that pacifies the north." Nguyen Nhac proclaimed himself "emperor of the center" at Cha Ban and sent Nguyen Lu to hold Gia Dinh.

The fighting among the Tay Son brothers gave Nguyen Phuc Anh the opportunity he had been waiting for. By early 1787, his agents were already active along the coasts of Ha Tien, Rach Gia, and Ca Mau. In early autumn, he and his men slipped away from Siam by sea. He established himself on the island of Hon Tre off the Rach Gia coast. The Tay Son governor of the lands along the western Vietnamese coast submitted to him, as did a Qing pirate on Con Dao Island. Within weeks he had gained the submission of all the territory south of the lower branch of the Mekong.

A premature seaborne attack up the Sai Gon River failed, but it frightened Nguyen Lu into fleeing back to Qui Nhon, where he died shortly after. However, several Tay Son generals remained at their posts and continued to resist. Ten, the Khmer ally of the Tay Son, joined them against Nguyen Phuc Anh. Ten's enemy, the pro-Siamese Ben, came into the fray on Nguyen Phuc Anh's side. By the end of the year, Nguyen Phuc Anh had captured Ten and sent him to Siam.

In the spring of 1788, Nguyen Phuc Anh's battlefield victories were gaining momentum and Tay Son units began to surrender to him. By summer, Nguyen Phuc Anh was organizing law and tax regimes in the areas under his control, and by autumn he had retaken Saigon and was busy setting up a new structure of government. At that time, Nguyen Hue was preparing another major initiative in the north, where his ambitions were focused. This, with the shrinking of Nguyen

Nhac's sphere of action to his provincial domain and Nguyen Lu's incapacity, had opened the way for Nguyen Phuc Anh's return from Siam.

Nguyen Hue, the Quang Trung emperor

When Nguyen Nhac and Nguyen Hue had hastened south to fight each other in late 1786, Nguyen Huu Chinh remained in Nghe An. Nguyen Hue retained his family as hostages and expected him to watch the north for him. At Ke Cho, different groups of partisans gathered behind Trinh Bong, a younger brother of Trinh Khai, and Trinh Le, their uncle. The king took the side of Trinh Bong and Trinh Le was driven out. Trinh Bong was lazy and lacked political sense, but among his supporters were men who were determined to re-establish Trinh dominance over the monarchy. The king was erudite, even bookish, but inexperienced in politics. He wanted to assert the right of his dynasty to rule but was unsure about how to do this. When it became clear that Trinh Bong was preparing to attack his palace, he summoned Nguyen Huu Chinh from Nghe An.

Nguyen Huu Chinh marched north, defeating a Trinh army sent against him in Thanh Hoa. He took control of the capital and sent Trinh Bong and his partisans fleeing. He began to assume the old role of the Trinh lords. The king was unhappy but found no way to do anything about it. By summer 1787, Nguyen Hue had returned to Phu Xuan from fighting with his elder brother. He interpreted Nguyen Huu Chinh's activities at Ke Cho as insubordination. He was also wary of people he knew to have been close to his elder brother, and Nguyen Huu Chinh was such a person. He sent Vo Van Nham to occupy Nghe An and summoned Nguyen Huu Chinh. Nguyen Huu Chinh did not come, being in the midst of a series of campaigns against his enemies in the north, including Trinh Bong, whom he finally drove across the Qing border. The king sent a royal uncle and an elderly scholar who had been Nguyen Huu Chinh's teacher on a fool's errand to demand that Nguyen Hue evacuate Nghe An. Nguyen Hue drowned both of these men in a river and ordered Vo Van Nham to march north against Nguyen Huu Chinh.

In late 1787, Vo Van Nham defeated Nguyen Huu Chinh in Thanh Hoa and advanced to occupy Ke Cho. He captured and killed Nguyen Huu Chinh, but the king escaped into the countryside where several leaders rallied armies in his support. As Vo Van Nham was busy fighting these armies, he got himself into a feud with a subordinate general, Ngo Van So. Ngo Van So reported to Nguyen Hue that Vo Van Nham was disloyal. Nguyen Hue was inclined to believe this because Vo Van Nham was a brother-in-law of Nguyen Nhac, with whom he had just been fighting. Nguyen Hue, riding hard with a cavalry unit, suddenly appeared at Ke Cho in summer 1788. Vo Van Nham protested his innocence but Nguyen Hue reportedly replied: "Even if you are innocent, you still made me worry, and that is already a crime." He killed Vo Van Nham and replaced him with Ngo Van So. He met with government officials at the capital and left affairs in charge of men he trusted. Realizing that more soldiers were needed to control the north, he returned to Phu Xuan to raise new armies.

While the king was wandering about the countryside with his partisans, his mother had gone to the Le dynasty's suzerain in the north and asked for help. The governor general of the "two Guangs" (i.e. Guangdong and Guangxi, the southernmost provinces of the Qing Empire), Sun Shiyi, was eager to gain martial glory, and he strongly pressed the Qing court to approve action. The Qianlong emperor (r. 1735–1796) was not interested in territorial expansion in the south, but, taking his duty as an overlord seriously, he approved a limited expedition to support Le dynasty forces in taking back their capital.

When he heard that an army had been mobilized from Qing border provinces and was about to enter the country, King Le Duy Khiem sent envoys to meet with the Qing commanders as they marched to Ke Cho. In autumn 1788 the Qing army occupied Ke Cho and Ngo Van So withdrew to Thanh Hoa. Le Duy Khiem was restored to his palace, where he fruitlessly urged the Qing to advance against Nguyen Hue. The Qing remained inactive, having achieved their objective of returning their vassal king to his throne.

The Qing court did not want what they considered to be a small operation to expand into a large commitment, and, furthermore, there were doubts among informed Qing officials about the future of the Le dynasty. Qing authorities were in the process of preparing to withdraw when, at the time of the 1789 lunar new year celebration, Nguyen Hue suddenly burst upon them. Having proclaimed himself emperor in Phu Xuan, he rushed his armies north and pushed the Qing troops into and across the Red River.

The scholars assisting Nguyen Hue quickly negotiated peace with the Qing court, sending apologies, tribute, and appropriate words of submission. As part of the settlement, Nguyen Hue was to attend Emperor Qianlong's eightieth birthday celebration in 1790. According to Vietnamese historians, a maternal kinsman of Nguyen Hue named Pham Cong Tri, who looked very much like him, went in his place, pretending to be him. Although Qing officials learned of the ruse, they kept quiet about it to avoid embarrassment and any further involvement in Vietnamese affairs.

What is known about Nguyen Hue makes it very unlikely that he would have been able to observe the strict ritual and protocol at the Qing imperial court without producing some unseemly outburst. This, as much as the pleasure of tricking the suzerain, lay behind the decision to send a double. Also, Nguyen Hue lacked the trust in his subordinates that would be necessary for him to be absent for several months. While Nguyen Phuc Anh spent years crafting a complex administrative structure and carefully building up his strength at Saigon, Nguyen Hue, during the four brief years of his reign, left the details of government to his entourage of officials and gave his attention to plans for a new capital and for invading the Qing Empire.

Nguyen Hue ruled from Phu Xuan. He began to build a new capital in Nghe An, near the modern city of Vinh, halfway between Phu Xuan and Ke Cho, but it was never completed. No administrative reforms or indications of efforts to address the usual problems of government are attributed to him aside from the same old recycled measures that had been announced for generations. The regime of law and taxation that kept public order and produced revenue was left in the hands of the class of scholar-officials who had attended to these matters for the Trinh. Some officials remained loyal to the Le and refused to serve the new emperor, but there was no lack of those who welcomed the opportunities of the time. Nguyen Hue was not particularly concerned with administering the flow of tax revenue because he obtained a steady source of wealth from the many Qing pirates whom he incorporated into his navy and who preyed upon shipping in the South China Sea.

The only seemingly significant change from past practice was to use vernacular Vietnamese writing (Nom) rather than the Literary Chinese (Han) in education, administration, and in official documents. No definite evidence of this has survived, because Nguyen Phuc Anh supposedly destroyed all such materials in the early nineteenth century. Yet, there is no reason to doubt that such a change did occur, for Nom writing was an aspect of new trends in literature during the eighteenth century.

The first major work in Nom using double-seven-six-eight (*luc bat song that*) prosody dates from the 1790s in Ke Cho. This is the *Cung Oan Ngam Khuc* (Complaint from the Harem) of Nguyen Gia Thieu (1741–1798). Nguyen Gia Thieu was a grandson of Trinh Cuong who feigned madness when Nguyen Hue expelled the Trinh from Ke Cho. He wrote many poems, but is most noted for his "Complaint," which is written in the voice of a woman who was brought to the royal palace, spent a few glorious moments with the king, and then was left to spend the rest of her life in loneliness as a harem inmate, complaining bitterly against Heaven for her fate. The unresolved anger of this work is quite different from the *Song of a Soldier's Wife* written earlier in the century by Dang Tran Con, in which the wife's complaint is soothed and released in a final passage anticipating the return of the husband as a hero.

The use of Nom was probably congenial to Nguyen Hue because of his educational and career background. He may have studied with the teacher of

Nguyen Nhac, a man named Truong Van Hien who had fled from Phu Xuan after Truong Phuc Loan had killed his elder brother. Nguyen Hue surely had at least a rudimentary knowledge of Han, but Nom was more than likely used for communicating information and instructions among the officers of his armies, and commanding soldiers was what he knew and did best. Any effort to shift from Han to Nom in education and government, however, could not have achieved any significant result in the few years that Nguyen Hue ostensibly ruled.

The character of Nguyen Hue's mind is revealed in his plan to attack the Qing Empire. Rather than focusing his attention upon his implacable foe at Saigon, he dreamed of annexing the two Qing provinces of Guangxi and Guangdong. His career reveals a perpetual search for new battlefields. He had sent armies to plunder Laos in 1790 and 1791. He had defeated one Qing army, and this made him think that he could defeat others. Planning to attack the north was more interesting to him than worrying about old enemies in the south, whom he had defeated in the past and whom he was convinced could easily be defeated again. Furthermore, his attention was drawn north by the fleets of Qing pirates who filled his ports with plunder. The inability of Qing officials to police the coasts of Guangdong and Guangxi was an indication to him that he could easily take those provinces. He died in mid 1792 at the age of 40; at that time he was constructing large ships to transport war elephants to Guangdong and had sent envoys to the Qing court with requests for marriage to an imperial princess and for possession of the two provinces. When news of his death reached the envoys, they burned their documents and returned.

Nguyen Hue, also known by his imperial title of Quang Trung, became a famous hero in the accounts of later historians despite the brevity of his reign. This is because of his battlefield prowess in defeating a Siamese army in the south and a Chinese army in the north. However, his brilliance on the battlefield was not matched by his ability to govern. Unlike the men who became founders of dynasties, he had no mind for the details of administration. While Nguyen Hue won battles and dreamed of future conquests in the north, Nguyen Phuc Anh occupied himself with laying the foundation for a new country in the south.

Nguyen Phuc Anh at Saigon

In 1792, Nguyen Hue's 11-year-old son, Nguyen Toan, was placed on the throne at Phu Xuan, and Bui Dac Tuyen, Nguyen Toan's maternal uncle, ruled as regent. Although Nguyen Toan's court was thereafter troubled with factional intrigues, for a decade it was a headquarters for marshaling resistance to the northward advance of Nguyen Phuc Anh's armies, which by this time were on the move and threatening Nguyen Nhac at Cha Ban.

After retaking Saigon for the final time in autumn 1788, Nguyen Phuc Anh spent nearly two years establishing an administration to govern the peoples of Gia Dinh and building up his military forces. One of his first and most enduring concerns was the lawlessness endemic to the Gia Dinh frontier, particularly after more than a decade of war. Even before retaking Saigon, as his armies were advancing, he emphasized his prohibition on raping and plundering by beheading two offenders. In mid 1789 he sent men to punish bandits, bullies, and officials who were oppressing people at My Tho and Vinh Long. Shortly after this, he published harsh punishments for robbers, particularly for soldiers who robbed. In following years he repeatedly sent out soldiers to suppress bandits. People suffered not only from human predators. In 1789, rewards were posted for the death or capture of a tiger that was preying on a village near Bien Hoa, north of Saigon. On the other hand, to help restore a more normal agrarian life, water buffalo were sent to the My Tho area because so many of these useful animals had been killed in that strategic region during the wars.

Even more than suppressing lawlessness, Nguyen Phuc Anh sought to encourage a law-abiding and productive mode of life. Gambling was forbidden among the Vietnamese, although it was allowed and taxed among the Chinese. Sorcery and séances were discouraged because they took attention away from the real world, where Nguyen Phuc Anh was marshaling resources. Men were urged to work and not to cultivate lazy habits. Men with an inclination to study were encouraged with exemptions from corvée and military conscription.

Nguyen Phuc Anh published an amnesty for those who had ignored his summons to contribute manpower and supplies when he first returned from Siam in 1787. While he accepted those who had rallied to him in autumn of 1787 when he was at Long Xuyen, those who waited to rally behind him until after his advance to Vinh Long in early summer 1788, only four months before he retook Saigon, were punished for their tardiness. He later published an amnesty for "good people" who, being unfamiliar with all the new laws he was publishing, found themselves in trouble. He established a granary in Saigon to feed the stream of refugees from the north coming to join him. He kept a sharp eye on public morale and repeatedly solicited comments and ideas from both subordinates and common people.

His first recorded act upon retaking Saigon was to establish a court where he regularly discussed public affairs with the leaders of his entourage. There was apparently a disorderly chorus of comments about what needed to be done, for one month later he issued rules for the proper way to make comments and complaints. Perhaps these rules inhibited open discussion, so a few weeks later he announced a policy to encourage people to freely voice their ideas, asserting that no one would be punished for bad ideas. Shortly after that, a "suggestion box" was set out to facilitate the flow of thought. In spring 1790, Nguyen Phuc Anh assigned scribes the task of writing down everything that was said in his presence. He was said to have given close attention to all details of government.

Within days of retaking Saigon he sent officials out to all the administrative jurisdictions to check the tax and conscription records. He then immediately announced a tax policy and established three ministries to deal with the appointment of civil officials, with military affairs, and with the courts of law. He also established a Han Lam Academy to prepare his edicts. In 1789, a system of local government offices was established and many appointments were made to fill them. Particular attention was given to measures for the encouragement of agriculture and to regularizing local governance. Any locality with at least forty Vietnamese was required to have a "leader" to be responsible for dealing with government authorities.

A Tay Son general unable to escape north had sought refuge with the Khmers in the lower Mekong plain. In early 1789 he was forced to surrender, along with an army of around 1,500 Khmers that had been allied with the Tay Son. The Khmer soldiers were allowed to join Nguyen Phuc Anh's command on condition of contributing a certain amount of rice. Khmer officials were then appointed to govern the Khmer population in the regions of modern Tra Vinh and Can Tho. Displaced Khmers were given rice to settle down as agriculturalists in that region.

Lawless Vietnamese coveting Khmer land provoked a brief uprising among the Khmers in late 1789. In 1791, Nguyen Phuc Anh decreed that Vietnamese were not to seize land from Khmers. Khmers were to keep their land and Vietnamese were to open up new land for cultivation, of which there was "plenty available." For their part, Khmers did not have the right to open up new land. The Vietnamese and Khmers were to keep "separate" from each other. This problem did not go away, however, and in 1798 Nguyen Phuc Anh sent officials to prevent Vietnamese from taking land away from the Khmers and instead to send them to open up uncultivated land.

Nguyen Phuc Anh appointed Chinese to govern the Chinese communities that had developed from the Ming immigrants of the previous century, of which there were five, for people from Guangdong, Fujian, Hainan, Shanghai, and the Teochow. These Chinese communities had their own regulations for registering people for taxation and military conscription and were integrated into the Vietnamese style of administration. More recent "sojourners" from Qing were less adapted to local society and Nguyen Phuc Anh kept close watch on their relatively more predatory economic activities, in particular their penchant for loaning money to Vietnamese settlers at exorbitant interest rates resulting in the enslavement of wives and children. In mid 1791, laws against such interest rates were published.

Customs duties for merchant ships of the five Chinese communities were fixed with the highest rates being placed on the ships of Guangdong and Shanghai (3,300 strings of cash), then Fujian (2,400 strings), Teochow (1,200 strings), and Hainan (650 strings). Chinese merchants who brought iron, zinc, and sulphur, all being important for military purposes, were exempt from duties and received an allotment of rice, but they were required to sell their goods to the government. Severe punishments were published against ship owners smuggling goods out of Gia Dinh. Currency regulations were published enforcing the acceptance of chipped or worn coins so long as they could still be kept on strings. The price of sugar was regulated to encourage European merchants to bring weapons in trade.

The management of military manpower was Nguyen Phuc Anh's most critical concern. In early 1789 men were required to register for conscription. Those who had served in the Tay Son armies but failed to register were subject to the penalty of death. Parents were allowed to keep one son at home to care for them. Severe punishments for draft dodgers and deserters extended to their families, and rewards were posted for those providing information about the whereabouts of these fugitives. Soldiers were warned against bothering people or harassing merchants and were forbidden to carry their weapons unless they were on duty. Entertainers could not be enrolled in the ranks because Nguyen Phuc Anh believed their presence in the army would damage martial valor, although they were allowed to perform for soldiers under certain restrictions.

In addition to regular units, there were also local militia units. In 1790, regulations for establishing peasant-soldier settlements (*don dien*) were published and incentives were posted for officials to organize such settlements in the Vam Co region west of Saigon. Initially, conscription mobilizations were scheduled at three-year intervals, but as battlefield activity accelerated during the 1790s they became annual procedures. With an infusion of men into the military, Nguyen Phuc Anh organized instruction for his officers in training, discipline, supply, and battlefield behavior.

Nguyen Phuc Anh gave particular attention to the system of supply for his men. Rice granaries were established and, throughout the succeeding years of warfare, provisions for building new granaries and for moving rice to the battle-fronts were an integral part of planning troop movements. Nguyen Phuc Anh's victories rested in large part upon his mastery of the problems of supply. In order to move rice and men and supplies, ships were necessary, and shipbuilding was a constant and urgent priority. No sooner had Saigon been retaken in 1788 than Nguyen Phuc Anh sent soldiers to cut lumber and transport it down to the shipyards. Instructions for maintaining the supply of lumber for the shipyards are mentioned repeatedly during succeeding years. The Gia Dinh shipbuilding industry, at Saigon and at My Tho, became very large in the 1790s, producing hundreds of ships with innovative designs that came to be coveted by rulers and merchants in neighboring countries.

Con Dao Island was used for breeding and raising horses, which were then transported to Gia Dinh and trained for the battlefield. Blacksmiths, gunsmiths, and metalworkers of all kinds were put under the supervision of officials and mobilized to produce weapons. Men were sent to Guangdong to buy chemicals for military purposes, and weapons were bought in markets throughout the region, including Portuguese Macau and Goa and Dutch Batavia. A reliable source of weapons was the Sultanate of Johore, where Mahmud Shaz III (r. 1761–1811) maintained a friendly relationship with Nguyen Phuc Anh and kept a market well stocked with guns, bullets, sulphur, and saltpeter. During the 1790s, Nguyen Phuc Anh repeatedly sent men to buy war materials from him.

During his years of exile, Nguyen Phuc Anh had entrusted his eldest son, Prince Canh, to the French missionary Pierre Pigneau. Pigneau proposed to go to France and negotiate a treaty with the French government on behalf of Nguyen Phuc Anh and thereby obtain military assistance for his cause. Prince Canh and two of Nguyen Phuc Anh's officers accompanied Pigneau to demonstrate the legitimacy of the mission. After spending most of 1787 in Paris, Pigneau secured a treaty, which proved to be worthless as the French government was bankrupt and on the verge of revolution. Pigneau and Prince Canh arrived in French Pondicherry, on the coast of India, in spring of 1788. Realizing that the French authorities were not going to honor the treaty, Pigneau spent the next year raising funds and recruiting deserters from the French navy. He purchased two merchant vessels, armed them, and filled them with military supplies. Manned by fewer than one hundred French deserters, along with a few Portuguese and Asian volunteers, these ships arrived at Saigon in summer 1789.

Most of the Frenchmen who arrived at this time left within two or three years, disappointed by the lack of opportunity for monetary enrichment and disgusted by what they viewed as Nguyen Phuc Anh's inaction. Among the few who remained longer were about a dozen naval officers. The French were the smallest group among the diverse collection of non-Vietnamese to be found in Nguyen Phuc Anh's armies in the 1790s: Chinese, Chams, Ede, Malays, Khmers, Siamese, Laotians, and Portuguese. The French exercised little, if any, influence over Nguyen Phuc Anh's government or battle plans. But they did contribute to the training and organization of some military units, particularly in the navy.

Four officers who arrived with Pigneau drilled the navy in battle formations. In the early years, they frequently sailed with Nguyen Phuc Anh's fleets in command of ships and sometimes provided battlefield leadership. They were Jean Marie Dayot (1759–1809), Jean Baptiste Chaigneau (1769–1832), Philippe Vannier (1762–1842), and Godefroy de Forsans (d. 1811). Dayot was particularly active in naval affairs. With the assistance of his brother, he drafted maps of the Vietnamese coast. He departed in 1795 when Nguyen Phuc Anh humiliated him for having accidentally run his ship aground. Chaigneau and Vannier became Vietnamized, established local families, and remained in Nguyen Phuc Anh's service after the end of the war. Less is known about Forsans, but he remained in Vietnam until his death.

Another Frenchman who served Nguyen Phuc Anh was Olivier de Puymanel (1768–1799). He did not arrive with Pigneau but had deserted from a French warship visiting Con Dao Island shortly before the return of Pigneau and Prince Canh. He was trained as a construction engineer. In 1790 he supervised the construction of the citadel at Saigon following the most recent European ideas in fortification. Théodore Lebrun (at Saigon 1790–1791), another officer who had deserted from the French fleet, assisted in drawing up plans for the city and the citadel, but he became disgruntled and left after a year. Puymanel remained and also drilled Nguyen Phuc Nguyen's land soldiers in infantry formations and tactics and trained them in the use of mobile artillery. He frequently traveled to buy weapons in various regional ports and died in Malacca, only 31 years old. Laurent Barizy (1769–1802), a friend of Puymanel's who entered Nguyen Phuc Anh's service in 1793, spent most of his time buying military supplies in Malacca, Manila, and Batavia.

The role of Pierre Pigneau and the small group of French naval officers was a palpable ingredient in Nguyen Phuc Anh's ultimate success because of their contributions to organizing and drilling both naval and land forces, their expertise in constructing fortifications, their efforts to obtain supplies of up-to-date weapons, and their occasional leadership in battle. However, they were but a small part of what became a huge military organization that included thousands of men from several countries. Their role is testimony to Nguyen Phuc Anh's ability to understand and to make use of them more than it is of any French influence on him, which, in any case, is meaningless and anachronistic in that time and place. Very few of the Frenchmen who arrived in Saigon remained after 1792. Most of those who did became personally loyal to Nguyen Phuc Anh, established families with Vietnamese wives, and intended to remain among the Vietnamese for the rest of their lives.

Nguyen Phuc Anh understood how to maximize the assets of Saigon as an international seaport with a rich agricultural hinterland and a shipbuilding industry. Within a few years he mastered the Saigon region with an efficient civil government capable of organizing and supplying large expeditionary forces.

Having experienced many defeats, he was unimpressed with the outcome of any single battle. His was a long-term vision that he pursued with method and persistence.

From Saigon to Dien Khanh

Unlike traditional Vietnamese warfare in northern Vietnam that was conducted during the winter dry season when north winds blew from the continent into the sea, Nguyen Phuc Anh's campaigns were organized to catch the south winds that blew from the sea from late spring into autumn. His basic strategy was to move north by sea with the winds, landing troops and supplies to support the advance of land armies. When the winds changed he would return to Saigon with his fleet and leave land forces in defensive positions to hold off the enemy until the following year when the south winds returned.

Nguyen Phuc Anh's first experiment with this type of warfare was in 1790 when he ordered an advance up the coast into Binh Thuan. This was a dry region that produced little rice. There were no important harbors. The Cham population was concentrated here and had provided strong support to Nguyen Nhac. After initial success in marching north through Binh Thuan, Nguyen Phuc Anh's generals floundered in confusion when Nguyen Nhac counterattacked. By the end of the year, Nguyen Phuc Anh had withdrawn his forces back to their starting point at Ba Ria.

During the following year, Nguyen Phuc Anh concentrated upon rebuilding the morale of his officers after the dismaying Binh Thuan campaign. He also strengthened his military forces, dealt with a drought, spread propaganda in the north, and nurtured his alliance with Siam. This was the first year that the conscription procedure among Vietnamese was made annual. New army units were organized with volunteers from the Chinese communities. Military colonies (*don dien*) were established among the Chinese at Long Xuyen, among the Khmers at Can Tho, and among the Vietnamese at Ba Ria. Lumber was brought from Cambodia to the My Tho shipyard and some one hundred ships were built. The Saigon shipyard was building ships that could carry twenty-six to thirty-six cannon and over three hundred men.

Rice was purchased in Siam to alleviate near famine conditions caused by drought, and measures were taken to keep local rice from being hoarded or made into wine. People continued to arrive from the north, and they had to be examined to sort out loyal people from spies. Meanwhile spies were sent into the north to inspect conditions there and to spread songs of nostalgia for the Nguyen Phuc and of anticipation for the south wind that would bring the

Nguyen Phuc back to power. Literary examinations were held to test knowledge of history and the ability to think about current events. Those who achieved the best grades were assigned to teach in government schools. Others received tax and conscription exemptions and were assigned to continue their studies. Shrines were built for the souls of those who had perished in battle.

The Laotian king had captured some of Nguyen Hue's soldiers, banners, and drums during Nguyen Hue's expedition into Laos of this year. He sent these to his Siamese overlord, who forwarded them to Nguyen Phuc Anh. Nguyen Phuc Anh sent an envoy to Chakri at Bangkok conveying his appreciation. The envoy was also instructed to explain to Chakri that, although there were bound to be tensions and unfortunate events along the Khmer–Viet border, Nguyen Phuc Anh regarded Cambodia as a Siamese vassal and would refer all matters regarding Cambodia to him. The two kings throughout their reigns maintained a plausible appearance of trust.

In 1792, Nguyen Phuc Anh waited until his spies reported a large enemy fleet at Qui Nhon, Nguyen Nhac's harbor. He sent his fleet, which captured the enemy ships and briefly occupied Qui Nhon before returning to Saigon. During this operation, his land soldiers advanced as far as Phan Rang before turning back to Ba Ria when the winds changed. Cham leaders in Binh Thuan pledged loyalty to Nguyen Phuc Anh, and a good harvest brought an end to the famine laws. News from the north was also encouraging. After Nguyen Hue's death, tension between Nguyen Nhac and the leaders at Phu Xuan had prevented Nguyen Nhac from attending his brother's funerary rites.

In 1791 and 1792, the relationship between Nguyen Phuc Anh and Pierre Pigneau was nearly broken over the issue of Pigneau's role as teacher and mentor of Prince Canh. Nguyen Phuc Anh was dismayed by his son's fidelity to his Christian education in rejecting certain features of local culture, in particular the veneration of his ancestors. He consequently relieved Pigneau of his responsibilities as Prince Canh's teacher. He was also impatient with Pigneau's incessant urgings to attack the Tay Son before he considered the time to be propitious. At one point, Pigneau threatened to leave. By 1793, however, after much discussion between the two men, mutual accommodations opened the way for reconciliation. Pigneau was reinstated as Prince Canh's mentor, Prince Canh emerged from adolescence and became more tolerant of local practices, and Nguyen Phuc Anh was ready to move north.

Nguyen Phuc Anh's south wind campaign of 1793 was a success that greatly advanced his battlefield position. In preparation for it, early in the year he issued an edict calling on the people to abandon lazy habits and work hard to serve the country. He also issued a call for special efforts against thieves and bandits. He then began to mobilize his soldiers, including an army of Khmers and an army recruited from upland peoples. Families of soldiers, including the Khmers, received tax exemptions. Qing, Siamese, and French were serving in the fleet along with the Vietnamese.

In the fifth lunar month, with a strong south wind, Nguyen Phuc Anh took his fleet up the coast and seized Nha Trang, where he was joined by his land armies. His land and sea forces then advanced through Phu Yen and, after heavy fighting, captured strategic positions around Cha Ban, Nguyen Nhac's capital, and the seaport of Qui Nhon. While his armies were occupied with taking the surrender of enemy soldiers and with collecting weapons at Cha Ban and Qui Nhon, Nguyen Phuc Anh took his fleet north to Quang Ngai where he rallied supporters from among the local population and fought several battles against armies from Phu Xuan seeking to come to Nguyen Nhac's assistance.

As the winds began to change, Nguyen Phuc Anh withdrew his forces to Phu Yen. He then mobilized some four thousand men from Binh Thuan to build a fortress at Dien Khanh, under the supervision of Olivier de Puymanel. Dien Khanh, about fifteen kilometers west of Nha Trang, is the modern capital of Khanh Hoa Province. It is strategically located to guard the way south out of the Nha Trang region. A system of post houses and storehouses in Binh Thuan linking Gia Dinh with Dien Khanh was established. Nguyen Phuc Anh was determined to defend Dien Khanh at all costs.

Leadership among Nguyen Phuc Anh's enemies weakened as a result of the 1793 battles. Nguyen Nhac died, reportedly in a fit of chagrin because his generals did not follow his commands during the battles around his capital. His son and heir, Nguyen Bao, immediately began to quarrel with the leaders at Phu Xuan. But the building of the Dien Khanh fortress gave these men a target against which they could unite, at least temporarily. The fighting of the next two years was basically an unsuccessful effort by the Phu Xuan generals to seize Dien Khanh. Nguyen Phuc Anh had succeeded in shifting the focus of battle to a place of his choosing.

During the 1793–1794 dry season, virtually all of Nguyen Phuc Anh's activities were oriented toward strengthening Dien Khanh. Ships and weapons were being produced as fast as possible. Militia units were organized in Binh Thuan and in the region of Dien Khanh. Men from Quang Ngai who had rallied during the 1793 fighting were organized into an army. Dien Khanh was reinforced not only with Vietnamese soldiers but also with units of Khmers, Siamese, and Malays. Cham soldiers at Dien Khanh were released to serve in their home province of Binh Thuan as supply troops. A Cham leader who supported the Tay Son was captured and killed. Vietnamese settlers were assigned to work the fields that had been abandoned by Chams in Binh Thuan. Amidst all of this, Nguyen Phuc Anh arranged to sell rice to Siam to alleviate a famine there.

When, in spring 1794, a large Tay Son army marched into Phu Yen, forcing his men to retreat, Nguyen Phuc Anh hastened rice and men to Dien Khanh. Shortly after, the Tay Son advanced to attack Dien Khanh. By this time the south wind allowed Nguyen Phuc Anh to set sail with his fleet. News of this led to the Tay Son withdrawing back to Phu Yen. Nguyen Phuc Anh advanced to Phu Yen, fought many battles there, and also sent seaborne forces to disrupt Tay Son communications in Quang Ngai. Reinforcements were summoned to the Phu Yen battlefront as he visited Dien Khanh and ordered repairs to the fortress. The Siamese soldiers at Dien Khanh were allowed to return to their country. Officials in Saigon were instructed to issue them their pay as they passed through. Before returning to Saigon, Nguyen Phuc Anh endeavored to resolve problems caused by sending Vietnamese to cultivate former Cham lands in Binh Thuan. He ordered Vietnamese officials to consult with Cham officials to adjudicate boundary disputes fairly so that the two peoples could live together in peace.

Shortly after the winds changed to the north in late 1794, the Tay Son returned to the offensive. As they fought their way south through Phu Yen and to the walls of Dien Khanh, Nguyen Phuc Anh rushed supplies and reinforcements to Vo Tanh, the commander at Dien Khanh. By the end of the year, after heavy fighting, the Tay Son armies had Dien Khanh under siege and were advancing into Binh Thuan.

Within a few weeks, by early 1795, the Tay Son had pushed all the way to Ba Ria. An army of 1,500 Khmers was organized in Tra Vinh and, along with other Gia Dinh militia and reserve units, was ordered forward. The Tay Son forces were pushed back. Meanwhile, Nguyen Phuc Anh was with his fleet, filled with supplies and troops, waiting for the winds to change. When they did, he sailed to Nha Trang to disembark an army to relieve Dien Khanh, then continued to Phu Yen to disembark another army to block the Tay Son from escaping back north. During the next four months, fighting raged from Binh Thuan to Phu Yen. Defeated in Binh Thuan, Tay Son forces withdrew and joined the armies besieging Dien Khanh. At the same time, an army of uplanders helped Nguyen Phuc Anh to obtain an important victory in Phu Yen.

Meanwhile, in Phu Xuan, murderous feuds broke into the open. A general named Vo Van Dung killed the regent, Bui Dac Tuyen. The general besieging Dien Khanh, Tran Quang Dieu, was a supporter of Bui Dac Tuyen, so Vo Van Dung sent agents to kill him. Before this could come to pass, the siege of Dien Khanh was broken when a Tay Son deserter revealed a mountain path that allowed a unit of Saigon soldiers to pry open the Tay Son position. The Tay Son armies fled north as their generals raced back to Phu Xuan to join the struggle for power. Eventually, Phu Xuan leadership was reorganized as a coalition of four powerful generals, each of whom desired supremacy. Two of these generals were Vo Van Dung and Tran Quang Dieu. Nguyen Toan, the young king, was powerless.

For three years, the war had centered on Dien Khanh, a fortress built at a place chosen by Nguyen Phuc Anh as his first step up the coast from Saigon. The failure of his enemies to take Dien Khanh and their lack of unity made it possible for him to advance the focus of warfare further north into Binh Dinh.

From Dien Khanh to Binh Dinh

After breaking the nine-month siege of Dien Khanh, Nguyen Phuc Anh spent 1796 reorganizing his armies, making new appointments, inspecting agriculture, holding a literary examination, building ships, buying weapons, training horses, conscripting soldiers, and admonishing his generals, who were wasting their spare time on gambling and cockfights. When the south winds arrived in 1797, he seized the port of Qui Nhon and then advanced to Quang Nam. While some of his generals attacked up the Thu Bon River to Hoi An and Dien Ban, he disembarked in Da Nang Bay and attacked up toward Hai Van Pass. Troops raised in Quang Ngai joined his armies and fighting raged from Phu Yen to Quang Nam for three months until the winds changed and Nguyen Phuc Anh returned to Saigon.

Nguyen Phuc Anh spent the last months of the year 1797 dealing with Chams who had been serving with the Tay Son armies and had returned to Binh Thuan, provoking uprisings and unrest. Siamese troops assisted in calming this problem, perhaps in return for Vietnamese troops helping to suppress an uprising of minority peoples in Cambodia a short time before. At this time, discussions were initiated to coordinate Siamese and Lao troops with Nguyen Phuc Anh's future campaigns by having them march over the mountains and down the Ca River valley into Nghe An to threaten the Tay Son from behind. A diplomatic initiative was also taken to cultivate good will with the Qing Empire. Qing pirates captured from the Tay Son fleets were sent into the custody of Qing authorities in Guangdong.

In 1798, Nguyen Phuc Anh bought weapons, built ships, reorganized supply lines, mobilized and trained soldiers, reinforced his front-line units at Dien Khanh and Ca Pass, and dealt with the problem of deserting soldiers by imprisoning their families. In early 1799 he was laying plans for another south wind campaign. He published thirty-six articles on military discipline, which give an indication of the serious expectations he had for upcoming operations, for they had much to say about behavior in time of battlefield victories, behavior toward prisoners, and behavior toward the civilian population of newly occupied areas.

Nguyen Phuc Anh had several talented generals, but by this time none of them had been with him longer than Le Van Duyet (1764–1832). Le Van Duyet was originally from Quang Ngai, where Nguyen Cu Trinh had served in the early 1750s, a place known for poverty and lawlessness. He was reportedly born without genitals and began his career as a eunuch at Phu Xuan. He first appears in Nguyen Phuc Anh's entourage in the late 1770s, during the years of fighting and fleeing from the Tay Son armies in Gia Dinh. He was known to be austere and humorless, often prickly with colleagues and always strict toward subordinates. Yet, through the years, he assembled a large "family" of talented men whom he adopted as sons, and he was utterly devoted to Nguyen Phuc Anh. Although Le Van Duyet had served prominently in previous campaigns, in 1799 he emerged as a versatile and reliable commander whom Nguyen Phuc Anh would increasingly rely upon in the final years of war.

In late spring of 1799, Nguyen Phuc Anh sailed with his war fleet, followed by his supply fleet, to Nha Trang. After consulting with Prince Canh, who was in command at Dien Khanh, he ordered his land forces to march north through Phu Yen toward Cha Ban. Nguyen Phuc Anh sailed ahead and seized the port of Qui Nhon, assisted by dissention among the Tay Son generals there. He then sent Le Van Duyet to northern Binh Dinh Province to block Tay Son armies marching south. Le Van Duyet rallied Ede chieftains in the mountains to assist in barring the passes leading from Quang Ngai into Binh Dinh. The Tay Son armies came through the passes in two columns. One of the columns dissolved in panic when a forward scout shouted "*nai!*" upon seeing a herd of deer. *Nai* is the word for "deer," but it was also northern slang for soldiers from Gia Dinh, deriving from the Dong Nai ("deer field") River where Vietnamese first began to settle in the Mekong region. Soldiers following the scout picked up the cry of "*Nai! Nai!*" This filled the column with fear of an ambush and provoked a stampede to the rear. The Tay Son soldiers were no longer as fearsome as they had been twenty-five years before.

Meanwhile, Nguyen Phuc Anh defeated a Tay Son fleet as his land forces advanced and took Nguyen Nhac's old capital, Cha Ban, near the modern city of An Nhon. In this campaign, a Vietnamese general leading a force of Khmers with Siamese officers rallied upland peoples to assist along the mountain flanks. It was at this time that the province received its modern name, as Nguyen Phuc Anh called it Binh Dinh, meaning "pacified" or "put in order" or "set right."

Nguyen Phuc Anh spent over three months in Binh Dinh, collecting rice, organizing supplies, recruiting soldiers, appointing administrators, fixing taxes, selecting students, seeking out those who had remained loyal, honoring the dead, building storehouses, organizing post stations, and positioning his soldiers, including a force of ten thousand Siamese. Over one thousand men from Binh

Dinh were selected for their "strength and quickness" and trained to handle artillery. Pierre Pigneau, who accompanied Prince Canh on this campaign, died of dysentery in Binh Dinh during this time. Nguyen Phuc Anh brought his body back to Saigon and gave him a burial with honor.

The Tay Son generals continued their feuds. Two of them, the erstwhile enemies Vo Van Dung and Tran Quang Dieu, were now yoked together on the southern border of Quang Ngai, making plans to march south when the winds changed. At Saigon, Nguyen Phuc Anh was occupied with building ships, mobilizing metalworkers to produce weapons, tracking down bandits, and raising more soldiers, including an army of five thousand Khmers. Meanwhile, the Tay Son armies advanced, enveloped, and besieged Cha Ban in early 1800. Vo Tanh, Nguyen Phuc Anh's commander at Cha Ban, had been left with orders to resist until the south wind brought reinforcements. Once again, as in 1795 at Dien Khanh, Vo Tanh found himself in command of the pivot in Nguyen Phuc Anh's strategic position and under siege.

After suppressing a Cham uprising in the Phan Rang area and mobilizing Khmers to pacify marauding uplanders north of Saigon, Nguyen Phuc Anh started his land forces marching north and prepared to sail as soon as the winds changed. Ships bearing rice sent by his ally, Chakri of Siam, joined his supply fleet. At the beginning of summer, Nguyen Phuc Anh arrived at Nha Trang and met with his land forces at Dien Khanh before sending them forward into Phu Yen, which for months had been disturbed by Tay Son forays and one of his generals who had turned traitor. When he received word that the King of Cambodia had sent an army of five thousand men and ten elephants, Nguyen Phuc Anh instructed Prince Canh at Saigon to send the Khmers north.

Phu Yen was in a state of seemingly irremediable disorder with detachments of Tay Son troops, bands of traitors, large numbers of deserters, camps of the sick and wounded, and demoralized soldiers resisting discipline. Most of Nguyen Phuc Anh's generals wanted to withdraw, citing enemy strength and sinking morale. Time was passing. If something were not done soon, the winds would change, and they would be blown back to Saigon leaving Vo Tanh behind and a trail of confusion.

Nguyen Phuc Anh refused to accept this impasse. News arrived that his Lao allies were attacking into Nghe An assisted by the uplanders of that province. He turned to Le Van Duyet and ordered him to advance. Le Van Duyet pushed forward into Binh Dinh and reached the Tay Son siege walls, but could go no further. Nevertheless, Nguyen Phuc Anh's ships seized a Tay Son supply fleet on the northern coast of Binh Dinh and, shortly after, captured a fleet of Qing pirates in Tay Son service.

At this point, Nguyen Phuc Anh made a fateful decision. This year, he would not return south with the north wind. The greatest problem this posed was how to maintain the rice supply to his armies during the winter. He sent an urgent message to Saigon to build more ships to carry that year's harvest north before the winds shifted. Then he ordered that a system of transporting rice north by land be established. He finally solved the problem by mobilizing great numbers of small fishing boats to carry rice north, hugging the coast amidst contrary winds. He then ordered up more soldiers from Saigon.

In late 1800, Le Van Duyet, guided by allies among upland peoples, shifted behind the backs of Vo Tanh's besiegers and broke into the lowlands of Binh Dinh. A few weeks later, in early 1801, Le Van Duyet used fireships to seize the port of Qui Nhon. These victories dramatically changed the battlefield situation in Nguyen Phuc Anh's favor, significantly strengthening his position in Binh Dinh. Just at that moment, news arrived that Prince Canh had died of smallpox. How Nguyen Phuc Anh was affected by this news is not known, but he then made another fateful decision. It was as if the death of his son in Saigon somehow turned him away from that place, which had been his temporary home for many years, and sent him back toward his ancestral home where he had spent his youth. He decided to leave behind the turmoil in Phu Yen and the ensnarled armies in Binh Dinh and instead to proceed north to take Phu Xuan.

A new peace

Sending word to his Laotian allies to renew their attacks, he sailed to Hoi An, landing troops to join with local men from Quang Ngai and Quang Nam who rallied to his banner. After collecting rice in Quang Nam and capturing more Qing pirates at sea, he sailed to Da Nang Bay and advanced to Phu Xuan. Tay Son forces offered little resistance as Phu Xuan fell and Nguyen Toan fled to the north. Nguyen Phuc Anh secured the old border at the Gianh River as his Lao and uplander allies attacked Nghe An and Thanh Hoa. It was now summer 1801, and just as Nguyen Phuc Anh paused to savor his victory, word came that Vo Tanh, out of provisions, had committed suicide, and Cha Ban had fallen to the Tay Son generals, Vo Van Dung and Tran Quang Dieu. This Tay Son victory was nearly meaningless, however, for the focus of war had shifted further north and the Tay Son army in Binh Dinh, although large and still potent, was little more than the residue from an earlier phase of fighting.

During the last half of 1801, Nguyen Phuc Anh prepared for an expected counterattack from Nguyen Toan in the north, began to form a government at Phu Xuan, and arranged for the supply of his armies. Le Van Duyet was ordered to contain the Tay Son army in Binh Dinh while the walls at Dong Hoi were repaired and garrisoned. A few battles were fought with Tay Son forces around the Gianh River, followed by another Laotian thrust into Nghe An. The Cam Lo Road to Laos was mapped and garrisoned. Naval forces captured more Qing pirates.

In Thuan Hoa, Nguyen Phuc Anh searched for descendents of the "old honor roll of 1558," which enumerated all those who had come south with Nguyen Hoang in that year. He found 469 people. He repaired the tombs of his ancestors that had been despoiled by Nguyen Hue. He also dug up and exposed Nguyen Hue's corpse and executed thirty-one of Nguyen Hue's descendents and generals. He began to spend more time reading history books and discussing them with scholars, pondering his own place in history.

Nguyen Toan had spent this time mobilizing an army in the north. Near the end of the year, after the rains had stopped, he appeared at the border along with a fleet of more than one hundred Qing pirate ships. Nguyen Phuc Anh took up his position at the walls as his ancestors had done in the past. The battle that ensued in the early weeks of 1802 was a ghostly echo of the seventeenth-century campaigns. Nguyen Toan advanced to the Tran Ninh Wall where southern gunners inflicted high casualties on his men. When Nguyen Phuc Anh's fleet captured twenty of the Qing pirate ships and turned back the rest, Nguyen Toan began to retreat. Nguyen Phuc Anh sent his ships to the Gianh River, where they captured Nguyen Toan's supply fleet and prevented most of his army from crossing the river. A Siamese army of five thousand men with allied Laotians appeared from the mountains in Nghe An and hastened Nguyen Toan's flight back to Ke Cho.

Nguyen Phuc Anh returned to Phu Xuan, repaired the palaces, rested his soldiers, and waited for the fighting in Binh Dinh to end. Many of his soldiers were from Thuan Hoa and had traveled to Saigon years before to join his armies. He now allowed these men to visit their families. Sick and wounded soldiers from Gia Dinh were sent home, and families of Gia Dinh soldiers still on duty in Thuan Hoa were instructed to write letters to give them news of home. Nguyen Phuc Anh continued his reading of history and his discussions with scholars. He understood that he was on the verge of an unprecedented situation and he wanted the perspective of educated men.

Binh Dinh fell in late spring. The Tay Son generals with around three thousand of their men escaped into the mountains and tried to return north. Very few of them succeeded in reaching their goal as Nguyen Phuc Anh ordered his men into the valleys of Quang Nam and Thuan Hoa to block their way and sent messages to alert his Siamese and Laotian allies to watch for them.

Shortly after receiving news of victory in Binh Dinh, Nguyen Phuc Anh raised for discussion the question of whether the Le dynasty was dead or alive.

Everyone agreed that it was dead. Having already proclaimed himself king, Nguyen Phuc Anh now took the last step in proclaiming sovereignty by abandoning the Le reign title for marking years and publishing his own reign title, Gia Long, thereby founding the Nguyen dynasty. Accompanying this was a flurry of conferring ranks of nobility and of appointing a host of officials. Gifts and honors were given to the Khmer and Siamese generals and they were sent home with their men. Envoys were sent to Qing to hand over captured pirates.

In mid summer 1802, Nguyen Phuc Anh issued an edict to the people in the north, urging them to render assistance and warning them against lawlessness. He issued another edict to his men with instructions about the treatment of prisoners and civilians with strict orders to maintain discipline. He then set out with his fleet and army for the north. He arrived at Vinh in Nghe An without encountering any resistance. He spent a few days there reorganizing his supply system before proceeding to Thanh Hoa, again without encountering any resistance. In Thanh Hoa, he visited the Le dynastic ancestral shrine and received a hospitable welcome from members of the Le family. With Le Van Duyet leading the advance, he entered Ke Cho without a battle only thirty days after departing Phu Xuan. Nguyen Toan and his followers fled the city but were quickly captured.

Nguyen Phuc Anh spent less than four months at Ke Cho, establishing order in the north, conscripting soldiers, issuing rules and regulations, appointing officials, establishing an ancestral shrine for the Trinh family, and sending envoys to Qing. In autumn, he sent his soldiers back south and returned to Phu Xuan. There, he presided over Nguyen Toan's death and inaugurated the first government to rule all of the Vietnamese-speaking peoples from the Qing border in the north to the Gulf of Siam in the south.

The thirty years of warfare at the end of the eighteenth century produced the country of Vietnam as we see it on the map today. What is notable is that northerners, including the people of Thanh Hoa and Nghe An, played hardly any role at all in these events. By the 1770s, the Le–Trinh regime, and northern society generally, was so worn down by the accumulated effects of flawed efforts to govern during the course of two centuries that there was no energy to contribute to the great upsurge of disorder breaking out in the south. The most that could be accomplished was to occupy Thuan Hoa for a few years while the southerners battled among themselves. The north had become a place where dynastic dreams died, whether of the Mac, the Le, the Trinh, or those of Nguyen Hue and his heir. The miserable effects of war, misgovernment, and hunger had turned northern villagers inward to the small details of subsistence. Peasants developed a crust of indifference toward the ambitions of aspiring lords and kings. Events in Ke Cho did not echo through the countryside. After the Le kings and Trinh lords were gone, northerners simply waited for the outcome to be decided elsewhere. During the Thirty Years War, the north went from being the seat of kings to a provincial backwater.

Thuan Hoa was of symbolic and geographic importance as a place where the Nguyen Phuc rulers had created a royal court and guarded the south for several generations. However, once the Nguyen Phuc family had been displaced from Phu Xuan, Thuan Hoa was disconnected from those who subsequently assumed power there. Nguyen Hue and his heir used Phu Xuan as an expedient, a place to stand before taking the next step. The political loyalties of Thuan Hoa people, for the most part, remained with the Nguyen Phuc family, whose fortunes had come to depend upon a different region.

The Thirty Years War was basically a contest between two parts of the southern frontier, Binh Dinh and Gia Dinh. The most desperate fighting took place in and between these two places. Even after the outcome of the war was no longer in doubt, the men of Binh Dinh continued to fight to the end. From the perspective of more than two centuries, why this was the case is not readily apparent. What was there about Binh Dinh that led so many men to fight so valiantly for it? The answer to this question lies in the career of Nguyen Nhac, who was content to rule this place for two decades.

Unlike the other two main figures of this time, Nguyen Hue and Nguyen Phuc Anh, Nguyen Nhac had no ambition to rule distant places. He represented the perspective of those frontiersmen who resisted any centralized government over all Vietnamese speakers, who simply wanted to be left alone to enjoy their small part of the world. This was a provincial perspective in comparison with the outlook of men who studied history and had ideas about building a large kingdom. Nguyen Hue began to pull away from Nguyen Nhac's view of the word as he came into contact with the educated men of the north who saw in him a potential founder of a new dynasty. Nguyen Phuc Anh, for his part, was educated as a high-ranking member of a royal family that aimed to rule all Vietnamese. Nguyen Nhac did not care about all of that. The tension between him and Nguyen Hue, and those who ruled in Phu Xuan after Nguyen Hue's death, was about his resistance to the pan-Vietnamese idea. His viewpoint may appear to be stupidly myopic to those who today assume that all Vietnamese naturally belong in one country. But this was not an extravagant idea in that time, after generations of separation between north and south. For many people in Nguyen Nhac's time, the idea that all Vietnamese should be joined in one country appeared to be no more inevitable than that they should be separated into two or three, or even more, separate countries. Nguyen Nhac and those who picked up his banner in Binh Dinh resisted Nguyen Phuc Anh because he represented the threat of an organizing and homogenizing unity that would squeeze away their provincial way of life.

Nguyen Phuc Anh is among the most astute and persistent leaders in Vietnam-ese history. He was a shrewd judge of character and knew how to use different kinds of men. He had a vision that enabled him to form successful alliances with neighboring rulers. He instinctively understood the basics of government and the importance of paying attention to detail. Yet, without a place like Saigon in which to exercise his abilities, he is unlikely to have achieved what he did. At least as important as his qualities of leadership was the dynamic world of Gia Dinh. Saigon was an international seaport where merchants from many lands gathered. The cultural diversity of the Mekong plain with Vietnamese, Chinese, Khmer, Cham, Malay, Siamese, Laotian, European, and upland peoples all present or coming and going made it a place of encounter and creativity. Naval power was a critical ingredient of Nguyen Phuc Anh's success. While the Tay Son navy was composed of ships seized and sailed by pirates, the shipyards of Saigon and My Tho produced the most modern navy of any Asian country at that time. The rise of the south that brought the Thirty Years War to an end was the rise of Saigon and of the large view of the world that had developed there.

9 THE NGUYEN DYNASTY

Between north and south

The country that appeared at the beginning of the nineteenth century stretching from the southern border of China to the eastern border of Cambodia had never existed before. The name Vietnam can be found in some earlier Vietnamese texts, and the Qing court used this name when recognizing the new country as a vassal kingdom, but it was not commonly used until the twentieth century. The Qing continued to routinely refer to this place as An Nam, a name that dated from the Tang dynasty and that later became the French name for the central part of the country.

In 1802, Vietnamese envoys to the Qing court were instructed to propose Nam Viet as the name of their new country. The message sent with the envoys cited the ancient kingdom of Nam Viet founded by Zhao To in Guangdong and Guangxi at the beginning of the Han dynasty as an auspicious precedent because it had pacified and civilized all the southern territories. Furthermore, the message gave the name a new contemporary meaning as representing the unification of all the Vietnamese lands: "Now, the South (Nam) has been swept of rebels and the whole realm of Viet has been restored to normalcy." The Qing court, however, objected to the name Nam Viet for the very same reason proposed in its favor by the Vietnamese. In imperial historiography, contrary to Vietnamese historical tradition, Zhao To's kingdom was an inauspicious rather than an auspicious precedent because it had rebelled against the Han dynasty. Arguments about the name shuttled between Hue and Beijing for nearly a year before the Qing court finally turned the name to Viet Nam, thereby avoiding the unpropitious connotation of insubordination and separatism in the name Nam Viet. The name Vietnam eventually entered popular usage with the spread of alphabetic literacy and nationalist ideas in the 1910s, 1920s, and 1930s.

Nguyen Phuc Anh, subsequently remembered by his dynastic name of Gia Long, established his court at Hue, old Phu Xuan, where his ancestors had ruled since the seventeenth century. Putting the central government at Hue is under-standable, considering the ruling family's long and illustrious association with this place, and it is even plausible as being more or less equidistant from the two main centers of population and economy in the plains of the Red and Mekong Rivers. However, Hue suffered from disadvantages that crippled the efforts of kings to govern the new country. Hanoi was around 650 kilometers to the north and Saigon was around 900 kilometers to the south. For a majority of people in the country, either Hanoi or Saigon was the administrative and economic center that governed public life. Experience eventually showed that a ruler had to have a firm grip on one of these places in order to be able to control the other. Sitting at Hue, rulers had difficulty controlling either the north or the south.

Hue was previously well situated to guard the northern border of the southern domain, but that border no longer existed. Furthermore, it was located in a narrow, relatively isolated, coastal strip without a seaport. Nguyen Phuc Anh's military campaigns had shown the importance of shipping and access to the sea for establishing his new regime, but, after gaining success, he turned away from the sea and chose to place his court near the tombs of his ancestors. Hue was masked from the sea behind the shifting sands of dunes and the shallow currents of lagoons. Da Nang Bay became the main point of access for Hue to the sea, but it was sixty kilometers south over a major mountain pass. The old seaport of Hoi An, even further south, was no longer usable because the Thu Bon River had silted up by the end of the eighteenth century.

The disconnection of Hue from the rest of the country became increasingly obvious as time went on. The main population centers, in the plains of the Red and Mekong Rivers, could not be easily governed from this place given the speed of communication at that time. Historians have faulted the Nguyen dynasty of the nineteenth century for its rigid and unimaginative response to changing conditions, but the passivity of leadership at Hue during this time also reflected the palace-bound routines and limited perspectives of men in a quiet corner of the country while in the northern and southern plains people were experiencing dramatic encounters with the forces of a new age. Gia Long's successor, Minh Mang, ruling from 1820 to 1840, understood the problem and endeavored to centralize the dynastic system, but his ambition to enforce unity led to rebellion and confrontation with Siam. His successors, overwhelmed by court politics and befuddled by unprecedented seaborne threats, stiffened into spectators at the palace windows.

Gia Long understood that the peoples of his newly conquered realm needed time to put behind them not only the wars of recent decades but also the sense of separation that had been enforced for generations at the walls in the Nhat Le River basin. He ruled with a relatively light touch. He governed as he had learned to do at Saigon during wartime, with a strict assertion of his authority combined with pragmatic improvisation and a reluctance to act without careful preparation and the assurance of success. Furthermore, in the urgent pressures of wartime he came to understand the strengths and weaknesses of his top-ranking generals, and he learned to delegate authority to them if not to entirely trust them. The two most capable of his generals were Nguyen Van Thanh (1757–1817) and Le Van Duyet. They were in the midst of the hardest fighting during the last years of the war, often being yoked together in collegial command of critical campaigns. Yet, they were very different from each other, and they disliked one another.

Nguyen Van Thanh's ancestors came from the northern border region of the old Nguyen domain, in modern Quang Binh Province, but he grew up in Gia Dinh. His father was a general in the Gia Dinh army who died fighting the Tay Son in the mid 1770s. Nguyen Van Thanh was well educated in both literary and military studies. He began his career on his father's staff and, after his father's death, entered the circle of Nguyen Phuc Anh's closest retainers. In 1802, Gia Long made him his viceroy at Hanoi with responsibility for governing the old Trinh domain. This appointment was ostensibly made because his education and political cunning made him suitable for dealing with the large number of literati in the north, many of whom retained lingering loyalties to the Le dynasty. He was susceptible to pride and ambition.

Le Van Duyet's ancestors were peasants from Quang Ngai Province. He grew up in the vicinity of My Tho on the Mekong River. Reportedly born without genitals, he entered royal service as a eunuch and was with Nguyen Phuc Anh in 1780 when he was proclaimed king at Gia Dinh. Like Nguyen Van Thanh, he followed Nguyen Phuc Anh into Siamese exile and survived many perilous adventures. Without literary pretensions, he often dressed as a peasant, was informal, brusque, and even rude, in his manners. His entourage of adopted sons included Chinese merchants and members of upland minorities. He enjoyed cockfighting, southern folk theater, and he worshipped local goddesses. After 1802, he became Gia Long's most trusted man in the far south and eventually occupied the post of viceroy at Saigon with responsibility for the volatile Khmer frontier. He was known for being utterly loyal to Gia Long.

According to a famous anecdote, on the eve of battle in 1800, Nguyen Van Thanh offered Le Van Duyet a cup of wine, saying, "Let us drink to give us strength." But Le Van Duyet refused, saying, "Only those who are afraid borrow strength from wine. As for me, I see nothing to be afraid of, so what use have I for wine?" Embarrassed, Nguyen Van Thanh thereafter nurtured resentment against Le Van Duyet. Whatever truth may be in this anecdote, the two men came to represent conflicting tendencies in Gia Long's entourage. Nguyen Van Thanh eventually found himself among erudite northerners who were seeking a point of entry into the Hue court. Le Van Duyet remained among a diverse population of southerners who were devoted to Gia Long but content to have as little to do with Hue as possible.

In 1810, Nguyen Van Thanh requested to be replaced as viceroy at Hanoi in order to mourn the death of his mother. This enabled him to reside at Hue where he was soon among Gia Long's closest advisors. Nguyen Van Thanh occasionally submitted confidential messages to Gia Long proposing various measures that he considered to be propitious. His ideas tended to be astute and timely, and Gia Long generally followed his advice. With one such message in 1812, he proposed four courses of action, to all of which Gia Long indicated his assent. The four priorities addressed by his message were major issues during Gia Long's reign: publishing a unified code of law; selecting Confucianists for high office; pacifying the Cambodian border; and selecting a crown prince to safeguard the succession.

In 1811, Gia Long had assigned Nguyen Van Thanh to work on sorting out the codes of law being applied in different parts of the country. In 1812, what came to be called the Gia Long Code was issued. Modern scholars have dilated about the extent to which this code simply copied provisions from the Qing dynastic law code, often expressing surprise that Gia Long did not make more use of the Le Code that had developed at Hanoi since the fifteenth century, which presumably was more resonant with local practice than the code that had developed in China. French colonial administrators were particularly critical of the Gia Long Code, not only because it was so different from their own practice of law but also because they were inclined to romanticize the Le Code and what they perceived as indigenous Vietnamese culture as a way of justifying their efforts to eradicate Chinese influence among the Vietnamese.

Gia Long saw the matter quite differently. For him, the Le Code did not represent the legal experience of the Vietnamese people. It represented the practice of Vietnamese in the north. His ancestors had ruled the south for two centuries without any explicit reference to the Le Code. There is no evidence that civil law was ever standardized in the south. In fact, there is very little evidence of concern for standardizing civil law in the south at all. The reason for this is that southern society developed under the pattern of military authority prevailing at frontier garrisons. The application of law in the south depended on the vicissitudes of contact with non-Vietnamese peoples, local conditions in places distant from the central government, and the educational level and personal predilections of relatively unsupervised officials. Many Vietnamese chose to live in the south exactly to put distance between themselves and the kind of society adjudicated by the Le Code in the north. Any attempt to enforce the Le Code in the south, however appropriate it might seem to later scholars, would have been anachronistic and unacceptable to southerners in Gia Long's time, for whom the habits of governance in the north represented the oppressive practice of what for generations had been their enemy.

At the same time, any legal system designed in the south would have been unacceptable to northerners. In northern eyes, southerners had turned away from a properly ordered society and were naturally lawless. Nguyen Van Thanh and Gia Long resolved the conundrum by importing the Qing Code while adding and subtracting particular provisions to make it a feasible framework for legal practice among all Vietnamese. The word "framework" is important, for the Gia Long Code was never strictly or uniformly applied. Hundreds of edicts were subsequently published to supplement the code, connecting it to conditions existing in the country. Legal practice followed a variety of regional administrative adaptations. The Gia Long Code gave a gloss of unity over a new country without a common sense of law.

The reason that it was possible to adapt the Qing Code was that legal ideas and practices among the Chinese and Vietnamese were not excessively dissimilar, at least in theory and to a large extent even in practice. Furthermore, Gia Long's judicial administration was neither adequately staffed with qualified officials nor sufficiently concerned with a systematic application of law as to be able to strictly implement the code. This helped to ensure that potential points of dissonance between provisions in the code and the actual practice of law did not generate unsolvable problems. Nguyen Van Thanh's years of administrative experience at Hanoi among the northern scholars probably turned his mind to the Qing Code as an admirable solution to the legal morass in the country that would be acceptable to northerners who valued their membership in the larger East Asian world and would also be unobjectionable to southerners for whom law was of little interest.

Nguyen Van Thanh's idea to appoint more Confucianists to high positions was designed to appeal to the northern scholars, who made up the bulk of Confucianists in the country. Gia Long had encouraged the allegiance and participation in government of educated northerners from the beginning of his reign, but while this was readily implemented in the viceroyalty at Hanoi, the central court at Hue remained populated mostly by southerners who had earned their positions through wartime service. Most of these southerners were experienced soldiers with mediocre educations and little, if any, interest in Confucianism. Le Van Duyet was a prominent example of such a man.

Gia Long understood the tensions between the northern men with their classical educations and his loyal entourage of pragmatic southerners, but he was not eager to open opportunities for these tensions to disturb his government.

Consequently, he promoted education and appointed men of trust and talent wherever he found them, but he did not establish a system of literary exams at the capital nor did he particularly aim to promote the ambitions of northern scholars.

In 1807, in response to a proposal from Nguyen Van Thanh, Gia Long opened regional literary exams at four locations in the Red River plain plus one each in Thanh Hoa and Nghe An. A total of sixty-two men were selected at these exams. Those who entered officialdom after excelling in this exam did so in the northern viceroyalty. Thereafter, Gia Long followed the practice of his ancestors in holding exams at the regional level every six years. He never instituted a capital-level exam because "peace had but recently been established and literary study was still weak." In 1813, regional exams were expanded to include the southern provinces. Surviving information about the results of these exams and about the regional exams of 1819 is sketchy and incomplete. However, some details of the notorious 1819 exam at Saigon were recorded. When students were on the verge of rioting because the questions were too difficult, the examiners gave them easier questions. Then, there were accusations that one candidate had concealed the fact that he was in mourning in order to take the exam and that another candidate had hired a substitute to take the exam for him. Disciplinary action was taken against both the offending candidates and the examiners.

Gia Long's relative lack of interest in establishing an examination system is in contrast to the practice of previous founders of new regimes in the north, such as Le Loi and Trinh Tung, who held examinations even before achieving success on the battlefield. It is also in contrast to the Mac, who maintained an examination schedule amidst the disorders of civil war. The explanation for this is that in the south a literary education had never been the means for advancing a public career to the extent that it had become in the north. Aside from the fact that Gia Long viewed education primarily from a southern perspective as the acquisition of practical skills, he was not in a hurry to force southerners into academic contests with northerners, which could only exacerbate regional friction.

Literature

Gia Long's reign became famous in Vietnamese literary history because of three poets who have remained popular to the present time. One of them, Nguyen Du (1765–1820), came from a prominent family from Nghi Xuan district in Nghe An, near the coast just south of the Ca River. His father, Nguyen Nghiem (1708–1775), was a laureate of the 1731 literary examination and had served the Le–Trinh regime as both a civil administrator and a military commander. His elder brother, Nguyen Khan (born in the 1740s), a laureate of the 1760 examination, was active in the mid 1780s attempting to assist the Le–Trinh regime in putting down the mutinous soldiers at Ke Cho and in resisting Nguyen Huu Chinh.

Nguyen Du, orphaned at age 12, passed the regional examination of 1784 at age 19 and thereafter assisted his brother until they were overwhelmed by the Tay Son and forced to flee. His brother fled up the Red River into the mountains where he died. Nguyen Du returned to his home district and avoided serving the Tay Son, spending his time hunting in the Hong Mountains in the south of Nghi Xuan district. It was said that his footprints could be found nearly everywhere on the "ninety-nine" peaks of this region that rise up amidst rice fields near the sea. He finally returned to public service when he was summoned by Gia Long in 1802 and was appointed to a post in a prefecture near Hanoi. He served a short time before asking for and obtaining sick leave. But his taste for reclusion could not be enjoyed for long, because his reputation for erudition was too great. In 1806, he was summoned to Hue and appointed to the Secretariat. In 1809, he was given a post in Quang Binh Province, a short distance north of Hue, which contained the border walls built in the seventeenth century. According to his biographer, "he was frequently humiliated by his superiors and consequently writhed in frustration." He was nevertheless selected to lead an embassy to the Qing court in 1813 because of his mastery of classical learning.

Nguyen Du's journey to the imperial capital at Beijing proved to be a large event in his life, for it inspired him to write two works of poetry that were widely circulated when he returned. He had a reputation as a good poet and for being especially good at writing poetry in the vernacular. One of the works he brought back from his trip to Beijing was a collection of poems in the classical language entitled *Travels in the North*, which followed a well-worn tradition of envoys to the north writing poetry about their experiences and feelings while on the road. The second work was a novel in the vernacular six-eight mode of poetry. In the twentieth century, when literary critics began to think about "national litera-ture," this work was raised to the status of "the masterpiece of Vietnamese literature" and is relatively well known today among English-speaking peoples as *The Tale of Kieu* (the Vietnamese title is *Kim Van Kieu*).

Despite his literary reputation, and despite his willingness to continue serving the reigning dynasty, Nguyen Du was not comfortable at the Hue court. According to his biographer, he was "haughty and conceited, but outwardly respectful, and was speechless with fear in the king's presence." Gia Long was reported to have chided him for his silent demeanor by reminding him that he had been treated well and entrusted with important tasks and in return owed his sovereign the benefit of his thoughts. Perhaps Gia Long identified the problem when, in the course of his gentle reprimand to Nguyen Du, he observed that the royal court "employs people on the basis of their talent without any regard to distinguishing between north and south." The fact that he mentioned this point is a good indication that it was a sensitive issue. Nguyen Du, a northerner, may well have felt that he was intellectually superior to his southern colleagues and supervisors, and this may have been the source of his taciturnity. He was nevertheless highly valued by the rulers. He was on the verge of departing on another mission to the Qing court in 1820 when he died. Gia Long's son and successor, Minh Mang, honored him at his death, and two of his sons subsequently enjoyed successful careers in officialdom.

The Tale of Kieu is a vernacular poetic translation of a Qing prose novel that Nguyen Du apparently encountered while on his 1813 diplomatic mission. Inspired by events during the disorders attending the fall of the Ming and the rise of the Qing in the seventeenth century, the Qing novel is in a romantic genre of "good boy" meets "good girl": they fall in love, then great tribulations separate them until they are reunited in an ostensibly happy ending. Nguyen Du's work is a relatively faithful translation of the Qing original, but what distinguishes it is his superb prosodic artistry, which displays a great knowledge of classical erudition yet cast into deliciously memorable vernacular poetry. A century later, the desire of Vietnamese and non-Vietnamese alike to put their finger on the essence of Vietnamese cultural identity found a plausible target in *The Tale of Kieu*, but setting aside the exuberance of modern nationalism, it also had meaning for the time in which it was written.

The Tale of Kieu came from an orphaned, educated northerner raised among people loyal to the Le dynasty. Then, after years of rustic retirement to avoid serving a rebel regime, he decided to serve a new "southern" dynasty. The plot borrowed from the Qing novel provided ample scope for Nguyen Du to explore the vicissitudes of idealism and tragedy; good intentions gone awry; compromises between virtue and profligacy; the breaking of faith and the joy of redemption; the search for the comfort of human love, of religion, of obedience to those with a claim on one's loyalty, and of doing what is right. The comedic reconciliation at the end of the tale, seemingly contrived by appeal to abstract moral values, is nevertheless an affirmation of family solidarity despite the random violence of a world twisted with corruption and war. The story is also an answer to the question about injustice visited upon women found in the eighteenth-century works by Dang Tran Con (*Song of a Soldier's Wife*) and Nguyen Gia Thieu (*Complaint from the Harem*). Like these works, *The Tale of Kieu* is about how women must suffer for their beauty and talent, but it goes beyond Dang Tran Con's simplistic resolution as well as Nguyen Gia Thieu's unresolved anger. It is a more nuanced and complicated exposition of the ambiguities and contradictions encountered by people in real-life situations. It reflects the climate of thought during the reign of Gia Long when, after centuries of separation and three decades of bitter warfare, a king had managed to enforce peace and the possibility of some kind of unprecedented unity among Vietnamese speakers. Nguyen Du persevered amidst the frustrations provoked by his less educated southern overseers because he believed that a dysfunctional Confucian family was still better than no family at all.

Another literary figure of this time whose reputation has been burnished by modern scholars is Ho Xuan Huong, a poetess who skillfully combined erudition with bawdiness in poems expressing a woman's critical view of men scrambling up the ladder of success in a Confucian society. Most of what is written about her that cannot be gleaned from her poems has arisen from conjecture, for very little information about her actual life has survived. Pham Dinh Ho (1768–1839), known for his collections of anecdotes, was apparently acquainted with Ho Xuan Huong, for he wrote about her poems and that she enjoyed a literary reputation in Hanoi during the reign of Gia Long. It is generally believed that she came from a prominent literati family of Quynh Luu district in northern Nghe An Province. Different theories have been advanced to link her to one or another branch of this family, either the Ho Phi branch or the Ho Si branch. Both branches produced respectable scholars in the eighteenth century who served in missions to the Qing court. One of these, Ho Si Dong (1739–1785), imagined by some to have been an elder half-brother of Ho Xuan Huong, passed the capital exam of 1772 and ended his career, as did the elder brother of Nguyen Du, struggling on behalf of the Le–Trinh leaders against mutinous soldiers and the Tay Son.

By the time of Ho Xuan Huong's birth, her family was established in Hanoi on the shore of West Lake. Her father died when she was small and her mother, a "second wife," remarried. Despite her lack of parental care, she received a good education, probably through the attentions of elder siblings or other members of her extended family. While still young, she was twice married and twice widowed as a "second wife" to older men who were local magistrates. Thereafter, she remained single and established a reputation in the literary circles of Hanoi with her poetry. Her poems reveal an intelligent and strong-minded woman with little patience for the authority of men. Recently, she has been celebrated as an early example of a liberated woman in Vietnam. However that may be, her poems were written from her experience and for people in her time. Judging from Pham Dinh Ho's mention of her, she was appreciated in the Hanoi literary world of her own generation. The cultural scene in Hanoi during Gia Long's reign is significant not only as the context of Ho Xuan Huong's poetry, but also for revealing an aspect of social and political history in early nineteenth-century Vietnam that would have long-term effects.

One feature of Gia Long's reign was the large population of unemployed educated northerners who gathered at Hanoi on the fringe of the viceroyal government. Most of these men received an income from lands owned by their families. Many of them were waiting for opportunities to be employed in officialdom. Many others had no such expectations but simply enjoyed the lifestyle available in Hanoi. In 1807, 1813, and 1819, when regional exams were held in the north, the city was crowded with aspiring graduates. As in times past, there were famous teachers, hundreds of students, and merchants selling books and writing supplies. But something had changed from earlier times.

After 1789, for the first time in centuries, there was no king residing in the city. The country was in the hands of the southerners. The sons of northern literati families, who for generations had been educated for government service, accumulated in Hanoi with time on their hands and money in their pockets. During the 1790s and 1810s, the culture of the Le royal court shifted from the palaces into the city streets and was transformed in response to the large numbers of northern scholars who were without access to, if not alienated from, the rulers at Hue and, consequently, without career prospects.

It was at this time that the style of singing that had developed among the women of the royal court passed into the tea and wine shops of Hanoi, giving rise to "tally songs" (*ca tru*) or "happy girl songs" (*hat a dao*). The customers purchased tokens or "tallies" which they gave to their favorite singers. The women sang while beating castanet-style with sticks upon a small wooden sound box, being accompanied by a musician with a long-necked three-stringed lute. Customers took turns beating a small drum. The ability to beat the drum correctly and in such a way as to express appreciation for the singer at appropriate parts of the song was a highly prized skill. Books were written to instruct potential customers in how to beat the drum. In some establishments, a house critic measured the drummer's skill by adding pebbles to a basket and the drummer would have to pay accordingly to ransom the pebbles out of the basket before departing for the night. Girls with less talent for singing danced to the music or served drinks to the customers.

Two streets in Hanoi became famous for tally songs. Each street was under the jurisdiction of a village outside of the city that specialized in managing these places of entertainment. The youth of these villages were taught from an early age how to sing, dance, or play the lute. Tally song inns continued to be popular even during the era of French colonial rule. In the mid 1950s the new revolutionary government proscribed this form of music on the basis that it manifested the decadence of the old feudal order, but since the 1990s it has been revived as a distinctive vestige of "national culture."

Ho Xuan Huong lived in Hanoi during the time that tally songs became fashionable among educated northern men with the luxury of spending their time in the city. Her poetry playfully uses double entendre and a woman's perspective to satirize male sexual prowess as but a tedious demonstration of powerlessness in public affairs. Her poems were directed at an audience of men who could feel the sting of her prosodic skill.

Nguyen Cong Tru (1778–1859) was a poet from this time who eventually escaped from the realm of uselessness inhabited by many northern literati. He was from the same district as Nguyen Du, Nghi Xuan in Nghe An. Nothing has been recorded about his family background, but he did obtain a good education, which suggests that he may have come from an obscure family of local magistrates and teachers or that he may have been a peasant whose intelligence earned the patronage of a magistrate or teacher. His biographer notes that he was proud and headstrong from the time of his youth, an observation that may have been colored by the vicissitudes of his later career as an official in the 1820s, 1830s, and 1840s. During those years, he experienced several turns of fortune with promotions and demotions resulting from his combination of an independent spirit with irrefutable talent. A certain strength of mind was already apparent in 1803 when, at the age of 25, he presented Gia Long with a ten-point petition during a royal visit to Nghe An. The contents of his petition have not been recorded but it was written in response to Gia Long publicly soliciting the opinions of local people after witnessing the distressing poverty of the region.

When regional examinations were held for northerners in 1807 and 1813, Nguyen Cong Tru is said to have tried but failed. He finally obtained success in the examination of 1819 and thereafter embarked on what became a colorful but distinguished career during which he gained fame for reclaiming land on the coast of the Red River plain as well as for serving on the Cambodian border. He retired in 1848 and lived as a hermit in a Buddhist temple on a mountain. In 1859, at the age of 82, he requested to return to government service to help against the French invaders, but died shortly after leaving his mountain retreat.

Nguyen Cong Tru was apparently among the customers of the tally song establishments in Hanoi during Gia Long's reign, for he wrote many songs for women to sing in this style as well as instructions for how to express appreciation for their singing with the drum. His biographer, writing in 1910, noted that the songs he wrote were still popular. His poetry is full of optimism and the enjoyment of life amidst troubles and setbacks. He was one northerner who overcame the disorientation of the royal court being relocated into the south and found scope for his abilities in service to a new country.

Siam and the question of Khmer vassalage

The third point in Nguyen Van Thanh's message of 1812 had to do with the situation on the Cambodian border, which had just erupted into a new crisis. The competition between the Siamese and Vietnamese for control of Cambodia was in abeyance during the lifetime of Gia Long's wartime ally, King Chakri, known posthumously as Rama I. Rama I kept a tight grip on his Khmer vassal and Gia Long did nothing to contradict this. In 1799, Bangkok had called up a Khmer army and sent it with Siamese and Laotian armies to assist Gia Long against his Tay Son enemies during the final campaigns of the Vietnamese wars. But, when the commander of the Khmer army returned with what appeared to be an excessively friendly attitude toward the Vietnamese, he was exiled to Bangkok.

The Khmer king Ang Eng had died in 1796, and was succeeded by his 7-year-old eldest son, Ang Chan. A Khmer regent governed Cambodia under Siamese supervision. In 1806, the regent died, and Ang Chan, then 16 years old, was crowned in Bangkok before being sent to the Khmer throne in Oudong. The presence of a crowned king in Cambodia along with increasing slack in the Siamese presence during Rama I's declining years opened a possibility for Ang Chan and the Khmer royal court to claim a larger measure of autonomy.

After Rama I's death in 1809, the new Siamese king, Rama II, aiming to exercise his ascendancy in Cambodia, sought to undermine Ang Chan's position. He affirmed the finality of the Siamese annexation of the Khmer provinces of Battambang and Siem Reap in the northwest and looked for ways to extend Siamese influence into the adjacent provinces of Pursat and Kompong Svay. The governor of Kompong Svay, a man named Moeung, was close to the Siamese and had been forced to flee to Bangkok in 1808 when he refused to acknowledge Ang Chan's authority, an event that reportedly angered Rama II.

In 1810, Rama II sent Moeung back to his post in Kompong Svay, but Moeung still refused to swear allegiance to Ang Chan. When Ang Chan had Moeung assassinated, Rama II decided to teach the young Khmer king a lesson by engineering a rebellion led by Ang Chan's younger brother, Ang Snguon. Early in the year 1812, Ang Snguon stood up against his elder brother in Pursat, about 130 kilometers northwest of Oudong, where a Siamese army arrived to champion his cause. Ang Chan, unwilling to bow to Siamese efforts to weaken his authority and to deprive him of territory, but lacking the military strength to challenge Siam, sent envoys to Gia Dinh requesting Vietnamese assistance. The old story of feuding Khmer princes and Siamese–Vietnamese contention was about to begin again.

Unable to stand up to the Siamese advance, Ang Chan fled to Gia Dinh at the beginning of 1813. Gia Long, no longer confined by the scruples of friendship toward his deceased wartime ally, Rama I, took time to mobilize a large army and placed it under the command of Le Van Duyet. In late spring of 1813, Le Van Duyet escorted Ang Chan into Cambodia but allowed the Siamese time to withdraw. The Siamese were unprepared to oppose such a large Vietnamese force and acquiesced in the Vietnamese restoration of Ang Chan. Ang Snguon took refuge in Bangkok. Le Van Duyet built strong defenses for Phnom Penh, where he installed Ang Chan with a Vietnamese garrison, then withdrew his army back into Vietnam. Rama II had overplayed his hand in Cambodia and provoked into reality a situation that he had been determined to avoid. Gia Long was characteristically decisive and planned carefully for success.

Gia Long enforced his authority as Ang Chan's suzerain with the principle of maintaining boundaries between peoples. When Siamese envoys arrived by sea at Hue in 1815 and requested permission to return to Bangkok via Cambodia to pay their respects to the Khmer king, Gia Long refused, determined to offer no opportunity for Siamese intrigue to germinate. Later in the year, when he learned that large numbers of Vietnamese fugitives and adventurers were going to Cambodia and causing trouble, he instructed Ang Chan to expel all Vietnamese back into Vietnam except for soldiers assigned to garrison duty and merchants with passports. At the end of the year, when he learned that a Khmer officer had provoked a border incident with the Siamese, Gia Long instructed Ang Chan to punish him. In 1818, Gia Long ordered officials to encourage Chams, Chinese, and Khmers to settle on uninhabited land in the Mekong plain and to prevent Vietnamese from bothering them.

Gia Long's policy toward Cambodia was to minimize interference in Khmer affairs and to encourage a sense of well being among the Khmer people while maintaining the upper hand in regard to Siam. In late 1818, in response to Khmer complaints about the Vietnamese official serving as "protector" at Phnom Penh, Gia Long replaced the man, saying, "The government must be in harmony with the feelings of the people. If the [Khmer] people do not want something, it cannot be forced on them. If something is forced on them, we will provoke hatred on the border." Such high-sounding sentiments did not always translate from the court at Hue to Vietnamese administrators in the Mekong plain, but they had been typical of Gia Long's attitude toward governing the diverse populations of the south and of government in general since the 1780s. He never showed interest in changing the way people lived so long as they were obedient to him and did not harm others.

Dynastic discipline

The fourth issue raised by Nguyen Van Thanh in 1812 proved to be his undoing. This was the succession question. Gia Long's three eldest sons were already dead. The choice of crown prince was between My Duong, the eldest son of former Crown Prince Canh, who was in his teens and was Gia Long's eldest grandson, and Gia Long's fourth son, Minh Mang (1791–1840), already in his twenties. Gia Long was inclined toward Minh Mang because of his maturity and the fact that he was not likely to be manipulated by others. He considered that those who favored My Duong were looking for an opportunity to influence a youthful king. Nguyen Van Thanh, for reasons that can only be conjectured, decided to pose publicly as an advocate for My Duong. Apparently, he was led astray by his past experience in submitting proposals to Gia Long and having them approved, as well as by his well-known fondness for wine.

In 1815, Nguyen Van Thanh announced to a group of officials whom he had invited to his house for drinks that "The kid will be named crown prince; I am about to petition the king about it." Informants reported the remark to Gia Long. Shortly after, an official reported to Le Van Duyet that Nguyen Van Thanh's son was making conspiratorial moves to ensure that My Duong would follow his grandfather on the throne. Le Van Duyet immediately alerted Gia Long. In 1816, Nguyen Van Thanh was arrested. Shortly after, a conspiracy to rally a rebellion around Le Duy Hoan, the senior member of the formerly royal Le family, was uncovered, and Nguyen Van Thanh and his son were implicated as having previously given encouragement to the conspirators. In 1817, Nguyen Van Thanh drank poison and his son was executed. Thus ended the old feud between Nguyen Van Thanh and Le Van Duyet.

The supposed conspiracies of Nguyen Van Thanh and his son to engineer the appointment of My Duong as crown prince and to champion the restoration of the Le dynasty may have been more smoke than fire, but even smoke is a sign of something. Behind Nguyen Van Thanh's support of My Duong and the suspicions of his pro-Le sympathies lay his susceptibility to the sensitivities of northerners and his efforts to soften southern attitudes toward northerners at the Hue court. This was demonstrated in 1811 when he argued on behalf of Dang Tran Thuong.

Dang Tran Thuong (d. 1816) was from the Hanoi area. His family had held prestigious positions under the Le dynasty. He was well educated and ambitious. Unwilling to serve the Tay Son, in 1794 he fled by sea to Saigon and joined Nguyen Phuc Anh, who quickly learned to appreciate his skill as an administrator and as a leader of soldiers. He was in the forefront of many battles during the final years of the war and was assigned to serve with Nguyen Van Thanh at Hanoi when the war ended. In 1805, he recommended fourteen northern scholars for service at the Hue court. In 1809 he was summoned from Hanoi to Hue to take charge of the Ministry of War. During his service at Hanoi, a group of officials had been charged with compiling biographical information about prominent deceased northerners in order to prepare a register of those worthy of being posthumously honored by the Hue court. When indications of widespread fraud began to surface, motivated by northerners seeking to revise family records to burnish their credentials with the new dynasty, a full investigation was set in motion.

Among the facts that came to light was that Dang Tran Thuong had revised information about Hoang Ngu Phuc, the Trinh general who had invaded the south and expelled the Nguyen Phuc from Hue in 1774–1775. Dang Tran Thuong erased the posthumous titles granted to Hoang Ngu Phuc by the Trinh and added Hoang Ngu Phuc's name to the register being compiled for honors at the Hue court. A long and contentious argument broke out between those affirming that Dang Tran Thuong deserved death and those favoring clemency on account of previous merit. Nguyen Van Thanh, who had worked with Dang Tran Thuong in Hanoi for several years, was at the head of those speaking for clemency. Gia Long finally decided that, considering how Hoang Ngu Phuc's southern campaign had affected not only his family but him personally, any effort to rehabilitate the man's name was unacceptable and deserved death. Nguyen Van Thanh was fined for arguing on Dang Tran Thuong's behalf.

Dang Tran Thuong was imprisoned, but in 1813 Gia Long lifted his death sentence and released him, yet he was not allowed to leave Hue. In 1816, after the arrest of Nguyen Van Thanh, new charges of corruption were brought against Dang Tran Thuong dating from the time he had served in Hanoi. This prompted him to deliver a drunken rant against Gia Long, after which he was seized and hung. The angry words that earned him the belated execution of his death sentence were not recorded. They escaped from the disappointed ambitions of a talented man and the whispering world of suppressed northern resentment toward a regime of southerners. That it ever entered Dang Tran Thuong's mind to rehabilitate the memory of Hoang Ngu Phuc at Gia Long's court is a remarkable indication of the blind intensity of northern feelings.

Gia Long dealt with court politics in a manner similar to that in which he had conducted his armies during the war. He was not hasty, yet he was decisive. He strictly enforced norms of obedience and trusted his enemies to eventually bring about their own downfall. Predictably, the most serious intrigues that he faced were related to tensions between northerners and southerners, particularly to efforts by northerners to reshape the central government toward their regional interests and the vigilance of southerners to prevent this.

Relations with the Khmer vassal

One of Gia Long's final decisions would have a long-term effect on Khmer–Viet relations. In 1819, Gia Long decided to dig what became the Vinh Te and Vinh An Canals. Gia Long's stated intention was to benefit Cambodia by creating a more convenient water route from the Khmer capital to the sea and to benefit Vietnam by completing an inland water route connecting all administrative centers in the Mekong plain. The Vinh Te Canal would link Ha Tien, on the Gulf of Siam, with Chau Doc, on the southern branch of the Mekong River. The Vinh An Canal extended the Vinh Te Canal to the northern branch of the Mekong River with access to Vinh Long, My Tho, Saigon, and Bien Hoa. Plans for the canals were prepared in consultation with Ang Chan, and workers from both countries were mobilized for the task, reportedly five thousand Khmers and five thousand Vietnamese, along with five hundred Vietnamese soldiers. The Khmer and Vietnamese workers were organized and supervised by officials of their own countries. Gia Long ordered that every worker, both Khmer and Vietnamese, was to receive a monthly allotment of rice and a cash salary. He acknowledged that it would be hard labor but that the benefit for future generations would be great. Gia Long completed arrangements for work on the canals in late 1819, shortly before his death, and construction began after the new year holiday.

By late spring 1820, with the work about one-third completed, reports that the workers were suffering from the effects of hard labor prompted Minh Mang, the new king at Hue, to issue an appeal to the Khmer king and his officials encouraging them to persevere in the common task. At the same time he gave orders to distribute medicine to sick workers and to issue money and cloth to the families of workers who died on the job. He also ordered that the scale of the remaining work be temporarily reduced to allow passage for small boats only. That summer, when the monsoon rains arrived, an epidemic spread among the workers and into the neighboring population. The Hue court sent instructions for prayers to be made, medicine to be distributed, and burial costs to be paid at public expense. According to a Khmer source, bad working conditions were exacerbated for the Khmer by the arrogant and unsympathetic attitude of Vietnamese officials, producing dissention among the Khmer officials in charge of the workforce; this led many Khmer laborers to abandon the project and to return to their villages. In fact, soon after the coming of the summer rains, the project was suspended and all workers were sent back to their homes.

The digging of these canals had commenced as the Hue court was distracted by the death of one king and the accession of another. Local Vietnamese officials nevertheless already had prior experience mobilizing thousands of workers for canal work and organizing logistics for food, housing, and equipment. For example, in early 1819, around twenty thousand people had been mobilized for canal work in the Saigon and My Tho areas. Cambodian officials had no comparable prior experience and expected the Vietnamese to take responsibility for problems. The canals were eventually completed during the springtime dry seasons of 1823 and 1824 with a workforce of around fifty thousand men in 1823 and twenty-five thousand in 1824, two-thirds of which in both years was comprised of Vietnamese militiamen with Khmer laborers constituting the rest. Today, the Vinh Te Canal marks the border between Cambodia and Vietnam.

In autumn of 1820, a Khmer Buddhist monk named Ke, in the region of Ba Phnom east of the Mekong River, initiated a rebellion against King Ang Chan. Ba Phnom is in the center of a triangle formed by Phnom Penh, Chau Doc, and Tay Ninh, being about seventy kilometers from each of these places. Cambodian historians have commonly assumed that this uprising was an anti-Vietnamese revolt provoked by conditions at the canal worksite. Ba Phnom is rather far away and across the Mekong River from the worksite. Khmer workers were mostly mobilized from the modern provinces of Kampot and Takeo, directly adjacent to the worksite south of the Mekong River, judging from French reports of memories among peasants in those areas later in the century. Consequently, Khmer workers returning to their villages were unlikely to have gone anywhere near Ba Phnom. With Ang Chan's attention focused on the worksite, however, it was an opportune time for Ke to initiate his uprising.

Ke appears to have been motivated by Ang Chan's reliance upon Chams at least as much as he was by his hatred of Vietnamese. Ke was unhappy about Ang Chan showing favor to a Muslim Cham leader named Tuan Pha, who had become one of Ang Chan's trusted subordinates. Muslim Cham communities had been established in areas near Ba Phnom for several generations and friction between them and the Buddhist Khmers was in the background of Ke's uprising. Instead of leading his followers across the Mekong River to the canal worksite where he could presumably have mobilized disaffected Khmer workers, Ke advanced in the opposite direction and ravaged the region of Tay Ninh, far from the canal, which was inhabited by Chams and Vietnamese.

The Vietnamese garrison at Gia Dinh was unsuccessful against Ke, but Le Van Duyet soon arrived with soldiers from the north and pushed the rebel army back into Cambodia. Ke then led his followers to attack Phnom Penh. Ang Chan sent Tuan Pha against the rebels, but several Khmer generals defected to Ke and Tuan Pha was repulsed. Within a matter of weeks, Le Van Duyet led a Vietnamese army up the Mekong and joined with Ang Chan's army, comprised mainly of Chams and Chinese, to utterly defeat the uprising, killing Ke in battle. By the end of the year, Le Van Duyet took his army back to Vietnam, leaving a 700-man garrison at Phnom Penh. Ang Chan had become a docile Vietnamese vassal. So long as Le Van Duyet lived, the Siamese made no attempt to challenge this state of affairs. After the Cambodian campaign of 1820, Le Van Duyet served as the viceroy at Saigon until his death, twelve years later.

During Gia Long's reign, Le Van Duyet had specialized in crises requiring military responses. Aside from Cambodia, two other areas had occupied much of his attention. Depredations of the "stone wall" people in Quang Ngai, which had absorbed Nguyen Cu Trinh's attention in the 1750s, became chronic after the wars. Le Van Duyet carried out major operations in Quang Ngai Province four times between 1803 and 1815. He finally arranged a defensive system of walls and garrisons facing the mountains that extended from Quang Nam Province through Quang Ngai to Binh Dinh Province.

Le Van Duyet spent several months during 1819 in Nghe An and Thanh Hoa, where reports of banditry and insubordination had accumulated. He reported that misgovernment by incompetent, corrupt, and oppressive local officials had led to peasants fleeing from their villages and soldiers rising in mutiny. After consulting with Gia Long, he appointed new officials, forgave unpaid taxes, reduced corvée obligations, and thereby restored order. Some places required military action against bandits and small armies of disaffected fugitives. As much as possible, Le Van Duyet made use of local military leadership. He was also willing to incorporate surrendered rebels into his military units. His method of pacification was based on winning the cooperation of local people and appears to have been mostly successful. After this assignment, Le Van Duyet oversaw the accession of Gia Long's successor at Hue before traveling south to deal with the Cambodian uprising.

Minh Mang's centralizing policies

Gia Long's confidence in his fourth son as a man with his own mind was well placed. Minh Mang was an intelligent and active ruler with definite ideas about how to govern. Unlike his successors, historians have never viewed him as being manipulated by others. On the other hand, My Duong, the royal grandson who had been championed by Nguyen Van Thanh in 1815, was turned into an embarrassment, whether justly or through trickery is unknown. In 1824, he and his mother were charged with incest. His mother was put to death, and he was banished from the royal family.

Minh Mang was a child during the final years of his father's wars, came of age as Hue was being built into a royal capital, and became king at age 30. He had received an excellent education with the most erudite of teachers. He was a relatively disciplined man with a lively interest in government and a strong sense of responsibility for ruling his country. On the other hand, he lacked the practical experience of his father. He also lacked his father's toleration of administrative heterogeneity and cultural diversity. Gia Long had the benefit of subordinates with whose strengths and weaknesses he was familiar through years of military campaigns. He had created his government from his wartime entourage and for the most part it operated as an extension of his personality. Minh Mang entered an existing structure of authority and eventually came to see some of the men who had served his father as obstacles to his more strictly bureaucratic style of rule. Minh Mang was a strong and decisive leader. But he was also ethno-culturally intolerant, which limited his capacity to devise successful policies in the Mekong plain.

Historians have tended to see Minh Mang as a centralizer because he elimin-ated the northern and southern viceroyalties and tried to organize a single administrative system for the whole country. His policies revealed a desire for uniformity in government, in religion, in culture, and even in apparel. For example, during the seventeenth and eighteenth centuries, silk was relatively more available for common use in the south than in the north, and silk trousers became everyday wear for both men and women. In the north, however, cotton skirts similar to the Burmese *longyi* were widely worn, especially by women. Minh Mang promoted a policy of encouraging northerners to adopt what southerners, in an 1828 court discussion, considered to be more "proper" attire. However, he instructed officials to enforce the new dress code slowly and cautioned them against expecting to change "in a day" the manner of dress that had been customary in the north for "six or seven hundred years."

One of Minh Mang's first concerns was to establish a source of new men who had not served his father, men who could be shaped by his own style of authority. As Vietnamese rulers had done for generations, he turned to the literary examination system. He instituted the capital examination in 1822, which conferred the doctoral degree (*tien si*) for the first time since the last capital examination held under the Le dynasty in 1787, thirty-five years before. When this did not produce many graduates, in 1829 he began to award a second-rank degree, which can be called a junior doctor (*pho bang*), to make men with good, if not excellent, educational achievement available for administrative appointments. Whether by design or not, thirty-five of the thirty-six men who received the doctoral degree in the first four examinations (1822, 1826, 1829, and 1832) were from the north, that is from Nghe An and jurisdictions to the north. Six of the eight junior doctors in the years 1829 and 1832 were also from the north. In the two remaining examinations during Minh Mang's reign, 1835 and 1838, thirteen of twenty-one doctors and six of twelve junior doctors were from the north.

Overall, in the six examinations during Minh Mang's reign, forty-eight of fifty-seven doctors and twelve of twenty junior doctors were from the north. For the first four examinations, the proportion of examination graduates from the north was overwhelming. More graduates began to appear from the south near the end of Minh Mang's reign. To some extent these results can be attributed to the relatively more developed tradition of study and scholarship in the north, but they also show that Minh Mang was prepared to open government service to educated northerners.

Nevertheless, the number of graduates is not impressive when compared with the fifteenth and sixteenth centuries. To fill administrative positions, many graduates of regional examinations were taken directly into government service, and non-literary roads to appointment remained alive, particularly in the south. During Minh Mang's reign, over seven hundred men graduated from regional examinations, but only around 10 percent of these came from the south. The potential of the educational and examination systems to unify the country with a large cadre of officials shaped by a common curriculum and a common career path was not realized to any significant degree. The reason for this was that regional differences continued to present serious obstacles to a unifying educational system. Education meant different things to northerners and southerners. Beginning in the 1830s, capital examination graduates started to appear from the Hue region, comprised of the modern provinces of Quang Binh, Quang Tri, Thua Thien, and, to a lesser extent, Quang Nam. But graduates from further south were extremely rare. During Minh Mang's, Thieu Tri's, and Tu Duc's reigns, only two doctors and five junior doctors came from Quang Ngai, four doctors and two junior doctors came from Binh Dinh, and three doctors and one junior doctor came from Gia Dinh in the Mekong plain. There were no graduates from Phu Yen, Khanh Hoa, or Binh Thuan.

After the examination of 1856, the French navy occupied Gia Dinh, but even before that there is no evidence of success in incorporating the provinces south of the Hue region into the examination system. Aside from people in provinces close to the royal court, southerners showed little interest in the kind of literary education required to enter the examinations. In the south, relatively abundant land, a market culture of entrepreneurship, and a tradition of military service provided appealing alternatives to years of study.

Minh Mang did not initiate any significant reform of the agrarian regime or the tax system. Rather, he adjusted policies in various localities in response to changing conditions, aiming at a general appearance of uniformity. An almost continual rustling of unrest and popular disaffection drew attention to the ongoing task of pacification and emphasized the difficulty of governing distant places from Hue. Minh Mang responded with major administrative initiatives, by which he endeavored to establish a system of authority throughout the country that was directly responsive to him. There may have been no reason why eventually such a government based at Hue could not have been effective. But, given the legacies of regional separatisms and the distance of Hue from major population centers, more time would have been needed to achieve this than was available to Gia Long's heirs.

In 1831, Minh Mang abolished the viceroyalty at Hanoi and reorganized northern provinces to be more directly under the authority of the Hue royal court. In announcing this change, he cited fifteen reasons, all of which indicated the greater efficiency to be obtained by removing a level of government between the royal court and provincial officials. Five of the fifteen points had to do with expectations of more effective military responses to unrest, banditry, and rebellion in local jurisdictions. Nine of the points referred to inefficiencies and irregularities, waste of time and manpower, and lack of transparency between the court and the provinces that were characteristic of the viceroyalty. One point aimed at liberating local feeling from the big mix of a regional jurisdiction. Demonstrating this point at a sub-provincial level, the lowland districts south of the Ca River in Nghe An were at this time separated to form Ha Tinh Province. A number of other adjustments to provincial boundaries in the north were implemented.

The end of the Hanoi viceroyalty did not mean the end of administrative posts between Hue and the provinces. The viceroyalty was replaced with a structure of jurisdictions that were mostly comprised of two neighboring provinces, which provided a more direct link between local government and the royal court. At the same time, a separate system of military commands under the Ministry of War was organized at the sub-provincial level, which gave Hue an administrative path to localities that bypassed provincial government. The reforms implemented at this time extended to all jurisdictions north of Hue, including Quang Tri and Quang Binh. They came after several years during which the role of the Hanoi viceroyalty had been gradually diminished, and they were achieved without difficulty. Minh Mang's effort to implement similar reforms in the south, however, was not as uneventful.

During the 1820s, Le Van Duyet, the viceroy at Saigon, presided over the Mekong plain, including the Khmer protectorate, as if it were his private domain. He had no discernible disloyal design, but his style of governance, although harmonious with local conditions, was at odds with Minh Mang's unifying aims.

Le Van Duyet followed Gia Long's policy of keeping the various ethnic, religious, and social groups in the south separate from each other and allowing each group to follow its own way of life so long as it did not threaten public order. These groups were Khmers, Chams, Chinese, and upland minorities, but also different kinds of Vietnamese, such as Christians, former rebels, and prisoners from northern jurisdictions suffering banishment. Le Van Duyet cultivated the trust and loyalty of all these groups. He protected a French missionary who entered the country illegally, he encouraged exiled criminals to integrate into normal society, he shielded Khmer and Cham communities from encroaching Vietnamese, he allowed Chinese and Vietnamese businessmen to prosper, he supervised the Khmer king and watched the Siamese border with discreet vigilance. But, by the late 1820s, he was in his mid sixties and beginning to tire. His popularity among the people in the far south persuaded Minh Mang to keep him at his post while meanwhile reducing his authority by replacing his men with officials sent from Hue.

In 1828, one of Le Van Duyet's senior administrators was reassigned to the north, where he was promptly accused of corruption and imprisoned. He was replaced by one of Minh Mang's trusted officers. The inability of Le Van Duyet to control the appointments in his jurisdiction and to protect his men, as he had been able to do in previous years, indicated the beginning of a shift in the relationship between him and the king. The Vietnamese protector at the Khmer royal court was a man recommended by Le Van Duyet. When the protector died in 1829, however, Minh Mang ignored Le Van Duyet's recommendation and instead appointed two of his officials from Hue to supervise the Cambodian protectorate. In 1831, Minh Mang replaced the military commander at Saigon, and Le Van Duyet's army units were reassigned to places further north. By the time of Le Van Duyet's death in 1832, officials sent from Hue, unfamiliar with and intolerant of local conditions, were provoking widespread disaffection and agitation among the various populations in the Mekong plain.

Immediately upon Le Van Duyet's death, the southern viceroyalty was abolished and replaced with an administrative scheme similar to what had been implemented in the north the previous year. The "Six Provinces" (Luc Tinh) of the Mekong plain (Bien Hoa; Gia Dinh/Saigon; Dinh Tuong/My Tho; Vinh Long; An Giang/Chau Doc; and Ha Tien) were reorganized and paired with supervising officials assigned to two provinces. If he had left it at that, Minh Mang may have had as peaceful a transition to his centralization policy as there had been in the north. But Minh Mang took the opportunity to unleash pent-up frustrations with what he perceived as problems that had been enabled by Le Van Duyet's regime in the far south. Without delay he moved decisively to privilege Vietnamese over other ethnic groups, to prohibit Christianity, to harden the penal regime on banished criminals, to increase surveillance of Chinese business activities, and to posthumously proclaim Le Van Duyet to have been a traitor.

Even this may not have provoked more than minor disorders if Le Van Duyet's regime had not been a critical factor in providing an escape valve for internal unrest and in keeping the peace with Siam. Minh Mang's high-handed move into the south was accompanied by major domestic rebellions and war with Siam. When applied to the far south, Minh Mang's passion for uniformity led him into confrontations that brought an end to Gia Long's era of tolerating differences. Minh Mang established strict, even harsh, policies toward local officials, toward Christians, and toward Cambodians that his weak successors were unable to change except under duress. His reign was followed by an era of spreading disorder that left men at the Hue court as spectators to the collapse of dynastic authority. By suppressing the south, Minh Mang attacked its awareness of the outside world that could have been an asset when the European threat materialized shortly after his death. Instead, his policies provoked internal discord and created opportunities for foreign powers.

Background to Le Van Khoi's rebellion

When Le Van Duyet pacified Nghe An and Thanh Hoa in 1819, he acquired armies of surrendered rebels and bandits who swore loyalty to him and to the king at Hue. When he went south in 1820 to deal with the Cambodian uprising and to thereafter be viceroy at Saigon, these armies went with him. One of the men he acquired in Thanh Hoa was a charismatic and capable officer named Be Van Khoi (d. 1834) who was originally from the northern mountain province of Cao Bang. In 1787, when he was a child, his father, a local leader in Cao Bang, had been killed in fighting between feuding officials taking opposite sides in the breakdown of Trinh rule. Be Van Khoi apparently had a mixed career first as a bandit chief and then as a military officer under the Hanoi viceroy. He eventually established himself in Thanh Hoa, where he took the name Nguyen Huu Khoi. In 1819, Le Van Duyet adopted him into his entourage, and he changed his name to Le Van Khoi. Le Van Khoi became a trusted subordinate of Le Van Duyet in the Saigon viceroyalty during the 1820s.

The pardoned insurgents from Nghe An and Thanh Hoa were organized into peasant militias in the Mekong plain. There was also a population of banished criminals from the north that had been accumulating since the beginning of Gia Long's reign. Many of them brought their families with them into exile and were assigned to open up new agricultural land. In 1824, Le Van Duyet remitted their sentences and accorded them a status similar to the pardoned insurgents from

Nghe An and Thanh Hoa. Nguyen Van Cham, previously banished from a district near Hanoi, became a leader of militia units composed of these men. Furthermore, a military unit was made up of men from the Red River plain who had failed to register for military conscription and who accepted a term of service in the south to restore their legal status. Because of the ongoing unrest and failures of government in the north, the population of men serving terms of exile in the far south was continually replenished by new arrivals. Many such men sought to build new lives by joining one of these militia organizations. Le Van Duyet gave lawless and unlucky men from the north a second chance.

In 1832, after Le Van Duyet's death, Minh Mang revoked Le Van Duyet's policy of clemency toward banished northerners and returned them to the status of criminals. They were uprooted and sent to remote places on the Cambodian border. This provoked resistance and antagonism among all the northerners who had found opportunities for new lives under Le Van Duyet. The groups of militia made up of former northern lawbreakers were in the forefront of the rebellion that broke out in May of 1833, led by Le Van Khoi.

The Chinese were another target of Minh Mang's frustration with Le Van Duyet's regime. Minh Mang believed that Chinese merchants were illegally exporting rice from Saigon, which drove up the price of rice in the country. There is evidence that Vietnamese merchants were involved in the contraband rice trade as well as the Chinese, but Minh Mang placed the onus of this problem upon the Chinese. That Chinese maintained close relationships with their Chinese homeland and with Chinese communities elsewhere in Southeast Asia stimulated Minh Mang's doubts about their loyalty and trustworthiness. Minh Mang was keen to bring the Chinese population and its considerable wealth under the control of Hue. The unsympathetic, even harsh, attitude of newly appointed Hue officials toward the Chinese ensured that, when rebellion came in 1833, the Chinese were active participants. Luu Tin was a prominent leader in the rebellion. A Chinese merchant born in Hoi An, he had traveled in China, was a prominent leader of the Chinese in Saigon, and, like Le Van Khoi, had become an adopted son of Le Van Duyet.

Christians were also active in this rebellion. Christians had been a relatively large part of the Vietnamese population in the Mekong plain from the seventeenth century. Le Van Duyet's protection of Christians was at odds with Minh Mang's great antipathy toward them. Minh Mang believed that Christians subverted public morality, engaged in despicable practices, and invited European aggression. His attitude toward Christianity was formed first of all by his disgust with the lack of respect that Christians expressed for "Buddha and ancestors," two objects of veneration upon which the authority of his dynasty had been built, and by his reading of stories from the Christian Bible, which he considered irrational and ridiculous. He lived in a time when virulently anti-Christian propaganda was being circulated among Vietnamese officials. He both encouraged and was influenced by writings that described the mixing of men and women in churches during worship and practices that led to public fornication and the seduction of women and girls. He was upset about rumors that Christians used human eyeballs to make medicine. But what most worried him were writings that claimed to prove how the Christian religion was a means for Europeans to take over foreign countries. He praised the Tokugawa policy of exterminating Christianity in Japan.

Despite his view of Christianity, Minh Mang respected the merit of the three Frenchmen who had served in the entourage of his father and who remained in Vietnam as dynastic servants in the early years of his reign. Jean Marie Despiau had worked in the medical service since 1795, and Minh Mang sent him to Macau to obtain smallpox vaccine to inoculate members of the royal family. Jean Baptiste Chaigneau and Philippe Vannier had married Vietnamese women, established families at Hue, and held positions at the royal court. Chaigneau returned from a visit to France in 1820 with an appointment as diplomatic representative from the French court to Hue, which greatly complicated his position in Minh Mang's service.

In late 1824, shortly after Despiau's death, Chaigneau and Vannier departed Hue and returned to France for good. They left Hue just months after the British had seized Rangoon during the so-called First Anglo-Burmese War, an event that particularly aroused Minh Mang's perception of Europeans as aggressive and dangerous. The British founding of Singapore in 1819 had caught Minh Mang's frowning attention; then efforts by the Burmese king Bogyidaw (r. 1819–1837) to enforce his authority over vassals on the borders of British India elicited an invasion that led to British annexation of Arakan and Tenasserim, creating a common Anglo-Siamese border. Minh Mang's reaction to events in Burma was a decisive turning away from contact with Europeans and a determination to eradicate the European religion. In 1825, Minh Mang prohibited European missionaries from entering the country. At the beginning of 1833, he published an edict against Christianity, calling on officials to destroy churches, to arrest Christian leaders, to send European missionaries to Hue, and to persuade Christians to abandon their religion. Four months later, the southern rebellion began.

The rebellion was also related to Siamese policy. Gia Long had ruled during a time when Europeans were occupied with the Napoleonic Wars and Siam was confronted with a rampant Burma. During Minh Mang's reign, Siam was freed from the Burmese threat by the rise of British India and, obtaining a treaty of non-aggression with the British, King Rama III (r. 1824–1851) reoriented his armies to embark on more active policies along his eastern borders. Minh Mang's first encounter with these policies was in Laos during the late 1820s.

At that time, three Lao realms professing allegiance to Siam existed along the Mekong River. The most important was Lan Sang, ruled from Vientiane, which extended along both banks of the middle Mekong and included most of what is now northeast Thailand. Champassak in the south on the Cambodian border and Luang Prabang in the northern mountains were of lesser importance. The ruler of Lan Sang, Chao Anou (1767–1829), rebelled against Rama III in 1827 after a series of personal humiliations and Siamese violations of existing protocols. The final provocation was a Siamese campaign to brand the Lao people west of the Mekong River, thereby claiming them as Siamese subjects with no obligations to Chao Anou.

Defeated in battle, Chao Anou fled to the Nghe An border and begged for refuge from Minh Mang. Minh Mang gave him temporary shelter while insisting that he would have to return to his Siamese suzerain. In 1828 a small Vietnamese force escorted him back to Vientiane. He was subsequently captured by the Siamese and died in captivity. Minh Mang was determined to avoid getting involved with the Siamese over Laotian affairs in the Mekong plain. However, when the ruler of Xieng Khouang (Siang Khuang) on the plateau upriver from Nghe An, threatened by enemies allied with the Siamese, came and submitted to him, Minh Mang readily sent soldiers to assert Vietnamese sovereignty in the mountains. The Siamese acquiesced to this, being occupied with relocating the lowland Lao population from the left to the right bank of the Mekong River. Taking their cue from Xieng Khouang, the various mountain lords further south also submitted to Hue. Amidst these events, Siamese troops threatened Vietnamese outposts on the Cam Lo Road that extended from Quang Tri across the mountains to the Mekong and a Siamese officer murdered three Vietnamese envoys in southern Laos, which gave rise to strong anti-Siamese sentiments among Vietnamese officials and soured diplomatic exchanges between Bangkok and Hue. Minh Mang nevertheless benefited from the Siamese suppression of lowland Lao by gaining ascendancy in the adjacent mountains with a minimum of effort and without provoking war with Siam.

The effect of Minh Mang's changes in governance and in administrative personnel in the south after the death of Le Van Duyet gave rise to great unease among the various marginal peoples there, not only northern exiles, Christians, and Chinese, but also Chams, Khmers, and other ethnic minorities. In 1832, at the same time that the Saigon viceroyalty was abolished, Minh Mang dissolved the Cham tributary kingdom in Binh Thanh, just to the north of the Mekong plain. Minh Mang's men in Cambodia soon alienated the Khmers with their

424 / A history of the Vietnamese

ignorance of and lack of respect for local custom, and the Siamese were quick to take note.

As if he wanted to make sure to alienate every possible group in the region, Minh Mang aimed a direct attack upon the old established Vietnamese population of Gia Dinh by opening investigations into Le Van Duyet's rule and posthumously charging him with corruption and sedition. This official smearing of Le Van Duyet's memory was too much for local Vietnamese. It clearly showed that Minh Mang was determined, by any means, to break the spirits of the southerners.

Minh Mang's haste to seize the upper hand in the far south was in some measure motivated by his perception that Rama III had designs on the Cambodian protectorate. That he chose to employ the certainty of hard measures rather than chancing the possibility of mobilizing the willing support of such a diverse population may have been due to what some have described as his wary, mistrustful personality. His mode of leadership tended toward unyielding enforcement of ostensibly logical policies and did not include the flexible toleration of differences or the low-key charisma that had been characteristic of his father.

Nevertheless, Le Van Khoi may not have dared to challenge Minh Mang had it not been for events in the north that encouraged him to imagine a prospect of restoring the Le dynasty. When the last Le king, Le Duy Khiem, had died in China in 1804, Gia Long sent the senior member of the Le family in Vietnam, Le Duy Hoan, to escort his remains from the Qing border to Thanh Hoa Province, where the Le family maintained its ancestral tombs. Le Duy Hoan apparently harbored no illusions of dynastic restoration, but in 1816 he allowed himself to be used by a group of conspirators seeking to mobilize the north against Hue. He was arrested and executed in 1817. At that time, his infant son, Le Duy Luong (1814–1833), was taken by a member of his father's entourage into the mountains of what is now Hoa Binh Province, located between the uplands of Thanh Hoa and Hanoi, where he was given refuge by a prominent family surnamed Quach. The Quach were leaders among the upland communities that would be called Muong a century later, where loyalties to the Le dynasty remained alive.

The Quach were surely encouraged in their disaffection from Hue by the rebellion led by Phan Ba Vanh in the coastal regions of what are now Nam Dinh, Thai Binh, and Hai Phong Provinces. For the better part of a year in 1826 and 1827, Phan Ba Vanh led armies estimated at more than five thousand men and defeated Hue forces until men were mobilized against him from throughout the Red River plain, Thanh Hoa, and Nghe An. When he was finally captured and executed, survivors of his armies fled, and many of them took refuge in the uplands. Phan Ba Vanh's rebellion revealed that there were thousands of

Vietnamese in the north who were willing to follow a rebel against Hue. And his ability to defeat royal armies in the lowlands for over half a year demonstrated slack in Hue's ability to mobilize and coordinate soldiers in the north. Throughout the months of Phan Ba Vanh's rebellion, Minh Mang's frustration was expressed with sharp demands upon his commanders that they end the affair without delay. His sense of threat was sufficiently alert that in 1831 he sent officials to Binh Dinh and Gia Dinh to capture over one hundred surviving descendents of the Tay Son brothers. Twenty-nine of these were sentenced to death, and forty were exiled, enslaved, or assigned as soldiers. The rest, mainly women and children, were released.

In the spring of 1832, soldiers on the upland frontier of Nghe An killed their officers, burned down their outposts, seized weapons, and marched north through the mountains, apparently to join the Quach who, according to information at the Hue court, had plotted with the mutineers in the name of Le Duy Luong. Unable to capture Le Duy Luong, Minh Mang executed a brother of his who had been in prison since the arrest of their father, sixteen years before.

In the spring of 1833, Le Duy Luong was proclaimed king in the uplands of Hoa Binh Province. Many men from Thanh Hoa, Nghe An, and the Red River plain rallied to him, and leaders of the Quach family led armies into the plains west and south of Hanoi and gained victories. For several weeks, local militiamen defected to the rebels as royal commanders mobilized their forces. By mid summer, Le Duy Luong's partisans had been pushed back into the mountains, and, at the end of summer, he was captured and beheaded. Minh Mang subsequently forcibly removed surviving members of the Le family from Thanh Hoa and resettled them in provinces south of Hue. Although the Le Duy Luong uprising was relatively brief, it was enough to inspire an echoing uprising in the south.

Le Van Khoi's rebellion and war with Siam

In the spring of 1833, Le Van Khoi was being investigated by Minh Mang's officials for irregularities in supplying lumber to shipyards when news arrived that Le Duy Luong had been proclaimed king and that two or three provinces in the north had already come under his control. Le Van Khoi reportedly received a message from Le Duy Luong calling on him to rise against the Hue monarchy. If he did in fact receive such a message, it implies that he had been in some kind of prior contact with Le Duy Luong's group. Two months after the outbreak of Le Duy Luong's uprising in the north, at a time when Le Duy Luong's armies appeared to be building momentum and just prior to suffering defeats, Le Van

Khoi mobilized a large following and killed the upper echelon of Minh Mang's officials at Saigon. Within a few days, men at the other provincial centers in the Mekong plain killed or drove off Hue officials and recognized Le Van Khoi's authority.

Le Van Khoi's immediate entourage was mostly comprised of Le Van Duyet's old circle of officials, including officers of the militia organizations of former insurgents from Thanh Hoa and Nghe An, the men with whom Le Van Khoi had come south under Le Van Duyet's leadership more than ten years earlier. Christians, Chinese, and other minority groups, as well as mainstream local Vietnamese, also rallied to him. For about three months, as Minh Mang was suppressing Le Duy Luong in the north, Le Van Khoi and his followers were ascendant in the south.

Minh Mang viewed the southern uprising as the outcome of a long-standing problem related to Le Van Duyet's heterodox regime. He announced that Le Van Duyet had neglected the law and ignored social discipline, had not encouraged righteous behavior, allowed many illegalities and tolerated evil customs, such as gambling and lasciviousness among his officials. Consequently, the southerners had become arrogant, lazy, and rebellious. He was particularly concerned about the many surrendered rebels and banished criminals from the north who filled the southern militia units. He cautioned his generals that these men were not a rabble but were experienced soldiers and desperate outlaws. Meanwhile, he ordered that members of Le Van Khoi's family in Cao Bang be seized. Fourteen people were arrested, including a brother and two sons of Le Van Khoi. The fact that these relatives of Le Van Khoi were found in Cao Bang shows that the family was part of a network of contacts that stretched from the northernmost to the southernmost parts of the country. The significance of this lay not only in the resonance between the Le Duy Luong and Le Van Khoi uprisings, but also in the rebellion of Nong Van Van, which erupted at this same time in the mountains north of Tuyen Quang, just west of Cao Bang.

Nong Van Van was a local chieftain of this region. He was also the elder brother of Le Van Khoi's wife. For the better part of the next two years, he led armies of several thousands and dominated most of the upland territory east of the Red River as far as the Qing border, comprising the modern provinces of Ha Giang, Tuyen Quang, Cao Bang, Bac Can, Thai Nguyen, and Lang Son. As Minh Mang's armies gradually pacified these mountain jurisdictions during 1834, Nong Van Van sought refuge across the border, but Qing officials, alerted by Minh Mang, refused him asylum. In the spring of 1835, he was finally cornered in a thick forest where he perished when royal troops set the trees afire in a strong wind.

The Le Duy Luong, Le Van Khoi, and Nong Van Van uprisings were in some degree coordinated by contacts among the rebel leaders. But they were also coordinated with the plans of Rama III of Siam, who, after subduing the lowland Lao, was determined to wrest Cambodia away from Minh Mang. Le Van Khoi, after his initial success, and while waiting for the inevitable arrival of Hue's armies, sent a messenger to Rama III, supposedly asking for Siamese assistance. The content of his message is no longer known, but it may have been primarily to inform Rama III about events at Saigon and to indicate that the time for action had arrived. Within weeks, Siamese armies appeared at several strategic points along the western borders of Vietnam. Siamese military demonstrations occurred on the Xieng Khouang frontier of Nghe An, where the 1832 mutiny had occurred, on the western border of Ha Tien, and on the Cam Lo Road that crossed the mountains to Quang Tri, only a short distance north of Hue. These operations were intended to divert Minh Mang's attention from Cambodia, where the main Siamese invasion occurred.

In autumn of 1833, tens of thousands of Siamese soldiers marched into Cambodia along both shores of the Tonle Sap to rendezvous with a seaborne expedition moving up the Vinh Te Canal from Ha Tien to the Mekong River. King Ang Chan escaped downriver where the situation among the Vietnamese had by then dramatically changed in Minh Mang's favor as a result of the actions of Thai Cong Trieu.

Thai Cong Trieu was a man from the Hue area whom Le Van Duyet had learned to trust. In 1830, at Le Van Duyet's request, he was made second-in-command of all military forces in the south. When Minh Mang reorganized the south, Thai Cong Trieu became the senior military officer. He maintained good relations with local people while retaining his loyalty to Hue. When Le Van Khoi and his followers made their bid for power, he chose to go with them rather than be killed. He became the commander of the rebel army that took control of the provincial centers at My Tho, Vinh Long, Chau Doc, and Ha Tien. Le Van Khoi and his closest associates occupied themselves at Saigon and Bien Hoa. When seaborne armies from Hue began to appear at the mouths of southern rivers, Thai Cong Trieu was in the Chau Doc area on the Cambodian frontier. He sent a message to Truong Minh Giang (d. 1841), commander of the Hue forces, affirming his loyalty to Minh Mang despite having been coerced into joining the rebels. He then assisted men loyal to Hue who had survived the rebellion and had gone into hiding to expel Le Van Khoi's partisans and to reassert royal government in Ha Tien, Chau Doc, Vinh Long, and My Tho. From My Tho he advanced his men toward Saigon in coordination with Truong Minh Giang. Thai Cong Trieu's role in the events of 1833 was crucial for minimizing the effects of Le Van Khoi's rebellion and for enabling Truong Minh Giang to concentrate his forces against the Siamese.

Le Van Khoi and several thousand of his most fervent followers, mainly Christians, banished militiamen, and Chinese, took refuge in the huge Saigon fortress that had been renovated by Le Van Duyet and was stocked with enough weaponry and provisions to withstand a long siege. Le Van Khoi died in early 1834 from an eruption of tumors. Nguyen Van Cham, leader of the banished militiamen, thereafter exercised command among the besieged. The fortress held out for another year and a half. In autumn of 1835, it fell. Five hundred and fifty-four ringleaders and their families were beheaded on the spot. One thousand two hundred and seventy-eight people, being lower-ranking rebels and their families, were seized alive and later killed, buried in a large common grave. Six hundred and sixty-six of those killed were reportedly Christians. Six persons, including Nguyen Van Cham, the Chinese leader Luu Tin, a French missionary named Joseph Marchand, and one of Le Van Khoi's sons, were taken to Hue and publicly executed. The Saigon fortress was demolished. Meanwhile, Minh Mang's attention had moved on to the Siamese in Cambodia.

Truong Minh Giang was from the Saigon region, had passed the 1819 regional exam, and, despite his youth, had risen to the top echelon of Minh Mang's court during the 1820s. In 1833, Minh Mang chose him to be in charge of settling matters in the south and dealing with the Siamese in Cambodia. He spent the eight remaining years of his life on this assignment, gaining a reputation for severity among the Khmer and for competence among the Vietnamese.

By the time that Truong Minh Giang was able to turn his attention from Saigon in late 1833, the Siamese had already advanced into the region of the Vinh Te Canal between Ha Tien and Chau Doc, and Ang Chan and his court had arrived in Vinh Long seeking protection from the invaders. The Siamese brought along from Bangkok two of Ang Chan's younger brothers, Ang Im and Ang Duong, to assist with their plan of occupying all of Cambodia. In a series of battles in late 1833 and early 1834, Truong Minh Giang forced the Siamese out of Cambodia. As the Siamese withdrew back along the two shores of the Tonle Sap, they plundered and destroyed habitations and forced the able-bodied population to move west under their control. Great numbers of elderly people were left to fend for themselves and died in the ravaged countryside. Truong Minh Giang restored Ang Chan to Phnom Penh. However, the country was devastated with a large part of the population deported to Siamese territory and much of the countryside laid waste. The Siamese occupation had been brief but destructive. Rama III had not been prepared for such a sudden confrontation with large Vietnamese armies so had simply done his best to degrade the assets of the Khmer protectorate.

Ang Chan died in 1835. There was no prince to manage the relationship between the Vietnamese suzerains and the Khmer people as successfully as he had done. He had no sons, but he had four daughters. His eldest daughter favored the Siamese, as did her two uncles in Bangkok, Ang Im and Ang Duong.

The Vietnamese could think of nothing better than to hail Ang Chan's second daughter, Ang Mei, as the Queen of Cambodia. However, Ang Mei had no political ability and exerted no discernible influence on public affairs. The task of government fell upon Truong Minh Giang, who was subject to the instructions of Minh Mang. Minh Mang decided to simply extend to Cambodia the administrative reforms that he had already implemented in Hanoi and Saigon, which amounted to the annexation of Cambodia behind the façade of Ang Mei's royal court. In 1836, Truong Minh Giang reorganized local Khmer jurisdictions, appointed Vietnamese officials to oversee the Khmer governors of provinces, and established garrisons of Khmer and Vietnamese soldiers at strategic locations.

In 1836, Rama III built up his military forces in Battambang and Siem Reap, the parts of northwestern Cambodia that had already been annexed by Siam. The Khmer princes, Ang Im and Ang Duong, were sent to the frontier to rally support for the Siamese among the Khmer. During the next three years, the Siamese General Bodin and Truong Minh Giang endeavored to destabilize each other's positions with intrigues, raids, and uprisings.

In 1839, Truong Minh Giang succeeded in persuading Ang Im, the elder of the two princes, to come over to the Vietnamese side. Ang Im's expectation of being made king by the Vietnamese was disabused when he was unceremoniously hustled off to Hue. Rama III returned Ang Duong to Bangkok for safekeeping, proclaimed him the King of Cambodia, and prepared for war. Truong Minh Giang sent Ang Mei, along with her two younger sisters, to Saigon. He killed her anti-Vietnamese elder sister to remove what had become a magnet for pro-Siamese conspiracies. In 1840, Bodin launched a general offensive. At the same time, Siamese agents inspired uprisings among the Khmer downriver in Vietnamese territory. After nearly two years of fighting, the new Vietnamese king, Thieu Tri, was persuaded to redeploy out of Cambodia in order to concentrate upon the disorders in the rear of his armies. Thieu Tri ordered Truong Minh Giang to withdraw, blaming him for having been unable to prevent the situation from reaching such an impasse. When he arrived at Chau Doc in the autumn of 1841, having retreated completely out of Cambodia, Truong Minh Giang, overwhelmed with a sense of failure, stopped eating and died of chagrin, less than a year after the death of Minh Mang.

Thieu Tri and the French navy

In 1838, when it seemed that he had prevailed over the last echoes of the Le dynasty, had perfectly unified the country, and had achieved his ambitions in Cambodia, Minh Mang celebrated by renaming his realm Dai Nam, "Great

South." Barely three years later, he died after a fall from a horse, amidst a war with Siam that would erase what he thought he had achieved in Cambodia. Minh Mang's death also came during the Opium War of 1839–1842, in which a British expeditionary force humbled Qing China and obtained possession of Hong Kong, thereby opening a new era when European warships began to appear regularly in Vietnamese coastal waters. During the short reign of Minh Mang's son and successor, Thieu Tri (r. 1840–1847), the Siamese in Cambodia and the Europeans offshore pulled the attention of the Hue court in two directions.

Thieu Tri, Minh Mang's eldest son, was born in 1807. He was well educated, highly cultured, and intelligent. He was also reluctant to change his father's policies except under duress. He lacked the strength of mind to see beyond immediate problems, and he was vulnerable to the schemes of ambitious officials. The main features of his reign were ending the Siamese war, continuing the anti-Christian measures begun by Minh Mang, albeit without the use of capital punishment, and suffering humiliating confrontations with the French navy.

A salient consideration that had led to Truong Minh Giang's recall from Cambodia in 1841 was a Siamese-inspired rebellion among the downriver Khmer population centered in the modern province of Tra Vinh, the deltaic region lying between the two main branches of the Mekong River. For nine months, beginning in spring 1841, a charismatic Khmer named Lam Sam led large armies that also included some Chinese and Vietnamese. Hue forces gradually pressed Lam Sam's army against the coast where he built defensive walls. In the last month of the year his position was overrun, and he was captured and killed. A Siamese offensive into Vietnam intended to coordinate with Lam Sam was repulsed. Lam Sam's uprising was a typical feature of Siamese–Vietnamese warfare in the 1830s and 1840s as each side endeavored to rally Khmer partisans to distract the other from the main battlefront.

Lam Sam's rebellion was but the most spectacular of several Khmer uprisings in the lower Mekong during the 1840s. These uprisings, like the Le Duy Luong uprising, Nong Van Van's rebellion among the minority peoples in the northern border provinces, and to some extent even Le Van Khoi's rebellion, were part of a countrywide reaction to Minh Mang's effort to propagate and discipline a stricter sense of Vietnamese cultural identity by promoting Confucian education, eradicating Christianity, and erasing ethnic minorities. Minh Mang abandoned the policy of Gia Long and Le Van Duyet that discouraged Vietnamese from trespassing into territories inhabited by other ethnic groups. Instead, he promoted a policy of assimilating ethnic minorities. For example, in the south, Khmer and Vietnamese villages were combined into single jurisdictions, Vietnamese villages were established in localities previously reserved for Khmer, and Khmer were pressured to attend Vietnamese schools and to speak Vietnamese.

Similar policies were established among upland minorities. The Chinese were a special problem, and Minh Mang moved more cautiously and with less effect toward abolishing Chinese communal organizations. Thieu Tri continued Minh Mang's assimilating policies.

The Vietnamese withdrawal from Cambodia that had sunk Truong Minh Giang in despair did not indicate any renunciation of Hue's ambitions in Cambodia but was simply a tactical response to the Siamese offensive and the emergency of Lam Sam's revolt. After Lam Sam's movement had been suppressed and the Siamese offensive was spent, the Vietnamese rebuilt their armies and supply lines and pushed back across the border into the Khmer provinces adjacent to the Vinh Te Canal, after which the war lapsed into an extended lull.

Khmer leaders wanted to find a way to make peace between the Siamese and Vietnamese so that foreign armies would depart and a monarchy acceptable to both sides could regain a measure of autonomy. Ang Duong, the Siamese candidate for the Cambodian throne, was at Oudong under the watchful eyes of the Siamese general Bodin. Ang Mei, Ang Duong's niece, whom the Vietnamese had poised as Queen of Cambodia in 1835, and Ang Im, Ang Duong's elder brother, who had fallen into Vietnamese hands in 1839, were in Vietnamese custody at Saigon. Confidential messages passed among these people seeking some way to negotiate an end to the war and a restoration of the Khmer monarchy. While Ang Mei sought conciliation between Ang Duong and the Vietnamese, Thieu Tri, revealing a typical Vietnamese concern with territorial control, favored a partition of Cambodia with Ang Duong and Ang Im reigning as kings in their respective pro-Siamese and pro-Vietnamese domains. The Siamese opposed the idea of partition, being determined to gain control over all of Cambodia.

Ang Im's death in 1843 inspired Rama III to renew the war. Thinking to capitalize on Ang Duong's unassailable claim to the throne, he hastily ordered an offensive against the Vietnamese. A Siamese attack by sea at Kampot was intended to coordinate with a Khmer offensive downriver led by Ang Duong. However, poor communication and misunderstandings resulted in the Siamese expedition re-embarking and returning to Bangkok, leaving Ang Duong to face the Vietnamese alone. The Vietnamese advanced, sending Ang Duong's army upriver in retreat. Bodin moved his forces downriver to secure Phnom Penh. He then called out thousands of Khmers in forced labor to build lines of fortifications to protect Phnom Penh. The Khmers were suffering from chronic famine caused by wartime conditions, and Bodin's sense of urgency drove him to harsh usage of the Khmers, which provoked anti-Siamese sentiments among local Khmer leaders. After uncovering and suppressing a pro-Vietnamese plot against Ang Duong led by the governors of Baphnom (Svay Rieng) and Prey Veng, located near the Vietnamese border north of the Mekong River, Bodin went to Bangkok to confer with Rama III.

Taking advantage of Bodin's absence from Cambodia, a group of Khmer nobles, encouraged by the Vietnamese, conspired against Ang Duong. When he learned of the conspiracy, Ang Duong quickly arrested eight of the conspirators; four others escaped to Vietnam. Exasperated by this indication of Khmer support for the Vietnamese, Rama III sent Bodin back to Cambodia with reinforcements and instructions to expel the Vietnamese from there. However, before Bodin could bring his armies into position, the Vietnamese attacked upriver in the autumn of 1845, breaking through the Siamese fortifications and taking Phnom Penh. After months of fighting, a battle line was stabilized between Phnom Penh and Oudong, and the war settled into a stalemate.

Peace negotiations began in early 1846 and continued for over a year. An agreement was finally ratified in late spring of 1847. All fortifications were demolished, Siamese and Vietnamese armies withdrew from the country, prisoners and hostages were exchanged, and Ang Duong supplied a message to Hue that could be interpreted by the Vietnamese as submission. But the outcome of the war favored the Siamese, who emphasized this by annexing two more provinces in northern Cambodia, Preah Vihear and Stung Treng. Ang Duong reigned under close Siamese supervision until 1860 and has been remembered for his efforts to rebuild his war-ravaged kingdom.

Thieu Tri's acquiescence to the loss of the Cambodian protectorate, albeit veiled by the fiction of joint Siamese–Vietnamese suzerainty, reflected not only his relatively pacific temperament but also his deep concern, even anger, aroused by the threatening appearance of French warships. French naval officers demanded the release of imprisoned missionaries and the abolition of Minh Mang's anti-Christian edicts. Between 1833 and 1838, Minh Mang had executed ten European missionaries, six Frenchmen sent by the Paris Society for Foreign Missions, three Spanish Dominicans from Manila, and one Franciscan. During that same time many Vietnamese Christian leaders were also killed, churches were demolished, and unknown numbers of Christians were deported to remote upland areas. With the outbreak of the Opium War in 1839 and the landing of an army from British India in Guangdong, Minh Mang suspended further executions of Europeans and sent envoys to Dutch Batavia, to Penang where many Vietnamese Christians attended a French seminary, to Calcutta to meet with the authorities of British India, and then on to Paris and London. He apparently wanted to establish contact with the increasingly aggressive Europeans in the region and to evaluate the extent to which the Sino-British War would affect the security of his country. The envoys to Europe returned to Hue after Minh Mang's death, and this diplomatic initiative was bereft of results.

Thieu Tri upheld Minh Mang's prohibition of Christianity and several Vietnamese Christian leaders were put to death. Although European missionaries were imprisoned and condemned to death during Thieu Tri's reign, none of them was executed. Thieu Tri lived in a world that had suddenly changed from that of his father.

After the Opium War, the French navy began to patrol Asian waters in search of a permanent base from which to spread the influence of France. Although Tahiti was taken in 1843, it was too far away to serve any Asian purpose. A French scheme to build a naval base on the island of Basilan in the Philippines was thwarted in 1845 by Spanish and British objections. Meanwhile, French naval officers were guests in Spanish Manila, Dutch Batavia, British Singapore and Hong Kong, and Portuguese Macau. In early 1843, a French naval captain, learning in Macau that five French missionaries were imprisoned in Hue under sentences of death, took his warship to Da Nang Bay on his own authority and, after a week of negotiation and threats, obtained the release of the five men. This fixed in Thieu Tri's mind a connection between Christian missionaries and foreign warships.

Two months after this episode, Admiral Jean Baptiste Cécille arrived in Asian waters from France in command of a new French fleet. He spent a few weeks in Da Nang Bay arguing fruitlessly with local mandarins about his request for a cession of territory for a naval base and about the persecution of Christians. His argument that the French would protect the Vietnamese from the British gained no traction among Vietnamese officials, who were instructed to hasten the departure of the uninvited visitors.

Dominique Lefèbvre (1810–1865), a French missionary, was imprisoned at Hue under a sentence of death when the American Commodore John Percival stopped at Da Nang in May 1845 during his three-year circumnavigation of the globe aboard the venerable USS *Constitution*. Hearing of the ship's presence, Lefèbvre managed to send a message to the Americans pleading for deliverance. Percival failed to gain Lefèbvre's release despite taking hostage three Vietnamese officials and seizing three Vietnamese boats. After two weeks had passed without achieving any result, Percival released the hostages and the boats, and then sailed off. Four years later, the US consul at Singapore traveled to Da Nang to deliver a formal apology for this episode and to convey the US government's disavowal of Percival's actions.

Meanwhile, within a week of Percival's departure from Da Nang, a French warship arrived with a letter from Admiral Cécille demanding Lefèbvre's release. Thieu Tri, heavily engaged in Cambodia and worried about the affair with the previously unknown Americans and its possible connection with the sudden appearance of the French warship, complied, and Lefèbvre was allowed to depart. After a sojourn in Singapore, Lefèbvre, in 1846, attempted to enter the port of Saigon clandestinely but was caught and eventually sent to Hue. In the spring of 1847, while occupied with the final arrangements for concluding the treaty of peace in Cambodia and not wanting any further complication with the French, Thieu Tri sent Lefèbvre to Singapore. Unaware of this, Cécille sent two warships to Da Nang with a letter demanding Lefèbvre's release and an end to the persecution of Christians.

After three weeks, failures of communication between the French naval officers and local Vietnamese officials led to a battle in which the French sank five Vietnamese warships and destroyed the harbor forts with artillery fire. The French then sailed off. The Vietnamese officially recorded 40 sailors dead, 90 wounded, and 104 missing. The French recorded one dead and one wounded. Behind this outbreak of violence was deep mutual suspicion. For example, in fear of being taken hostage, the Vietnamese refused the French demand to deliver a message from Hue aboard their ships, while the French, fearing an ambush, refused the Vietnamese demand to come ashore to receive the message. The French appear to have initiated hostilities when their nerves broke as Vietnamese warships continued to arrive in the harbor. A few days after this battle, the persistent Lefèbvre successfully entered the country by the Mekong River and conducted his missionary work in hiding for the next twelve years until the French seized Saigon.

Thieu Tri was deeply disturbed by the Da Nang battle, not only because of the loss of men and material but also from a sense of impending doom unless he could find a way to manage the threat posed by the French navy. He became grim and prone to anger. For several days, the smallest irritation would cause him to erupt. Guardsmen falling asleep on duty at night, an official who dared to argue with him, another official who made errors in preparing a document, all were punished with eighty to a hundred strokes of the cane. Thieu Tri asked Truong Dang Que (1794–1864), his most trusted official, "These Western ships come for only two basic reasons: they want us to abolish the edicts against Christianity and they want to trade. We can accommodate trade, but what about Christianity – can we allow it?" Having just disengaged from the Cambodian confrontation with Siam, he was looking for a way out of the seeming impasse with Western navies. He was particularly concerned because of the geography of his country having such an extensive coastline and being susceptible to being cut in half at its narrow center. But the location of Hue was also a problem, being vulnerable to the sea but far from the reservoirs of manpower and resources needed to defend it.

Truong Dang Que was from Quang Ngai. Although his father had served the Tay Son, he was able to enter royal service at Hue after passing the 1819 regional examination. He rose rapidly to the top of court appointments under Minh

Mang and in 1845 emerged as the most powerful minister at Thieu Tri's court. He reportedly answered Thieu Tri's question, with more brevity than clarity, by saying: "They started this, and we cannot expect them to be reasonable."

Thieu Tri sensed that such an uncompromising attitude would not go far, but he could not see a way forward. He was sufficiently intelligent to analyze the situation with care and passionate enough to be thoroughly engaged with the problem, but it was easy for him to postpone making decisions. According to the *True Records of the Great South* (*Dai Nam Thuc Luc*), he reportedly said:

> The Westerners are cunning. If we abolish our laws against Christianity, the British will hear of it and demand that we abolish our laws against opium. The Westerners are wolves: there is no way to satisfy them! What can we do when everything must be according to their demands? More-over, Christianity is a false religion and its harm to us has reached the level of foreign relations and has opened the door to war. Opium is an anesthetic, and it utterly ruins human lives. These two things are both strictly forbidden and we will publicly affirm this so that it will be known in the history written by future generations ... The Westerners are not simply one country. For example, the Dutch we never see and when they send messages to us they are not from a king but from some strange authority that we cannot understand. But the French, although we have released them from prison many times, despite forbidding them to enter our country, and we thereby deserve their thanks, still they sprout more desperate schemes. Let us wait for the return of our traveling officials, and we can ask them about French intentions. If this enemy has some aggressive idea, Saigon and Hai Phong will also be places of danger, not only Da Nang.

With a strong orientation toward the opinions of moralistic historians in the future, such was Thieu Tri's prophetic but ultimately passive frame of mind when, half a year later, in the autumn of 1847, two British warships appeared at Da Nang with proposals for a commercial treaty. The British were hoping to contrast their friendly demeanor with the truculent impression left by the French. But Thieu Tri would have none of it. Despite amicable greetings between the British and local officials, the ships left empty-handed. While Thieu Tri under-stood the French to be champions of Christianity, he understood the British to be champions of opium. The idea of bending under foreign pressure to succumb to either of these two calamities filled Thieu Tri with rage. Thieu Tri had been in poor health for a month already. A few days after the British departed, he died at the age of 41, according to some reports, of apoplexy.

Mention of traveling officials refers to an established practice of regularly sending men to Manila, Singapore, Hong Kong, and Batavia to buy merchandise for the court and to collect news. Information about the outside world was not lacking at Hue. What was lacking was leadership capable of processing and acting on information. Minh Mang had built a centralized structure of authority at Hue, but his successors, erudite prisoners of palace life, tended to rely upon the initiative of experienced officials. The chief priority for the most ambitious and successful of senior officials was to ensure their continued exercise of power. Thieu Tri's weak, hesitating leadership opened space for such men.

Tu Duc's accession and incapacity to rule

Until 1845, two men shared influence at the top of Thieu Tri's court, Truong Dang Que and Nguyen Dang Tuan (1772–1845). Nguyen Dang Tuan was from Quang Binh, a short distance north of Hue. Both Nguyen Dang Tuan and Truong Dang Que had been prominent in implementing the administrative reforms and in suppressing the rebellions during Minh Mang's reign. They also administered the examination system to diminish the dominance of northern scholars in favor of men from the south. While the percentage of junior doctors from the north declined only slightly from the reign of Minh Mang to the reign of Thieu Tri, from 60 percent to 58 percent, the percentage of northern doctors fell from 85 percent in Minh Mang's reign to 54 percent in Thieu Tri's reign. Nguyen Dang Tuan and Truong Dang Que led a southern reaction to northern success in Minh Mang's examinations. The examinations were not simply objective measures of ability but were an aspect of administrative policy and of regional politics.

After Nguyen Dang Tuan's death in 1845, Truong Dang Que gained a dominant position at court. His management of the succession upon Thieu Tri's death greatly weakened the monarchy. Thieu Tri's two eldest sons were born only one hundred days apart in 1829. The eldest, Hong Bao, was Thieu Tri's designated heir. Thieu Tri had conferred upon him duties and titles giving him precedence over his slightly younger brother, Hong Nham, including a dynastic ceremony upon the birth of Hong Bao's first son in 1845. However, Hong Bao's mother had died when he was 9 and Nguyen Dang Tuan had been his chief protector at court. Nguyen Dang Tuan's son, Nguyen Dang Giai, was unable to compete with Truong Dang Que in court politics after the death of his father and spent years on an assignment to analyze the system of dikes in the Red River plain. Consequently, Hong Bao was nearly bereft of allies in the palace and in officialdom.

Truong Dang Que favored Hong Nham because he was more malleable to his purposes. Hong Nham suffered a bout of smallpox in 1845 that was said to have left him sterile. Exceedingly erudite, he was sickly and less assertive than Hong Bao. But his mother was a dominant figure in the inner palace. Truong Dang Que or one of his assistants altered or forged Thieu Tri's deathbed testament to designate Hong Nham over Hong Bao as heir. Truong Dang Que moved quickly to proclaim Hong Nham king, subsequently known by his dynastic title as Tu Duc. In this way, Truong Dang Que was able to maintain his dominant position at court, albeit at the expense of peace in the royal family, many members of which were disturbed by the denial of Hong Bao's claim to the throne. Meanwhile, Hong Bao was not reconciled to Truong Dang Que's coup and began searching for ways to undo it.

Some sources suggest that when Thieu Tri died there were other claimants to the throne besides his two eldest sons, for example Gia Long's eldest grandson My Duong, who had been considered by some as a rival to Minh Mang and who had been disgraced in 1824. During Thieu Tri's reign there was strong sentiment among members of the royal family to restore My Duong to his princely status, but he was not a plausible candidate for the throne in 1847. When he died in 1849, however, his family was reinstated into royalty under the leadership of his eldest son Le Chung, who was entrusted with the duty of maintaining the ancestral cult of his famous grandfather, Prince Canh. In consideration of the youth of Thieu Tri's sons, there were reportedly some arguments in favor of Prince Kien An (1795–1849), a younger full brother of Minh Mang. Despite one of his junior wives being a niece of Le Van Khoi, he had a reputation as a competent and loyal stalwart of the royal family. There may have been discreet talk, but certainly no action, on his behalf.

Hong Bao was kept in Hue under strict observation. Nevertheless, contacts with French missionaries on his behalf were made, leading Christians to believe that he favored their cause when in fact he may simply have been searching for a way to escape from Hue. In 1851, a scheme to smuggle him out of the country to Singapore was uncovered and he was imprisoned. What the scheme was about is obscure but it was said that he had planned to rally foreign support to claim what he considered to be his inheritance. In 1854, further intrigues led to his suicide in prison, whether voluntary or forced is unknown, but rumors spread by his partisans that it was a case of fratricide gained currency and this greatly diminished Tu Duc's reputation. The Hong Bao affair followed Tu Duc throughout his reign and kept him on the moral defensive. Twelve years later, in 1866, a conspiracy to place Hong Bao's son on the throne was uncovered.

Tu Duc became king under the handicaps of being widely viewed as a usurper and of being unable to have children. If he had been a strong ruler he could certainly have overcome these problems. But his erudition could not make up for his timidity. The passion with which he penned commentaries on ancient history turned to inarticulate fear and hatred when faced in his own time with the spreading disorder of his government and the military might of France.

During the early years of Tu Duc's reign, Truong Dang Que continued to use the examination system in favor of the south, but he also particularly opened the system to candidates from Nghe An and Ha Tinh, discriminating between those provinces and Thanh Hoa, which bordered the Red River plain further north. Before moving to Quang Ngai, Truong Dang Que's ancestors had been established in Ha Tinh, but to what extent any lingering sense of identification with that region influenced his policies is unknown. In any case, the rise of scholar families from Nghe An and Ha Tinh became a phenomenon of Tu Duc's reign.

For example, during the exams held under Minh Mang and Thieu Tri, 56 percent of graduating doctors were from Thanh Hoa and the Red River plain, while in the five exams held under Tu Duc before the beginning of the French conquest in 1858, only 39 percent of graduating doctors were from those places. At the same time, while only 15 percent of graduating doctors under Minh Mang and Thieu Tri were from the Nghe An and Ha Tinh region, 26 percent of the graduating doctors in Tu Duc's first five exams were from those two provinces. During the same time, the graduating doctors from places further south increased from 29 percent to 35 percent. This trend continued during the remaining exams held during Tu Duc's reign, between 1862 and 1880, when the number of graduates from the northernmost region remained fairly steady while those from Nghe An and Ha Tinh increased at the expense of the south: 42 percent for Thanh Hoa and the Red River plain, 30 percent for Nghe An and Ha Tinh, and 27 percent for the south.

During Tu Duc's reign, men from Nghe An and Ha Tinh became relatively more prominent in officialdom. Rather than identifying with the dynasty to the same extent as officials from places further south, they tended to be more committed to the abstract ideals of their Confucian education. In comparison, scholars from Thanh Hoa and the Red River plain were more diverse and more susceptible to a perfunctory and somewhat cynical obedience to Hue. None of the Nguyen kings was successful in using the examination system to unify officialdom. The system was an arena for the negotiation of personal and regional aspirations.

During the first ten years of Tu Duc's reign, while he was in his twenties and before the beginning of the French invasion, unrest and rebellion became endemic in many parts of the country, particularly in the north. A large number of royal officials were kept employed with chasing insurgents. The most famous rebel from this time is Cao Ba Quat (1809–1855). He was from a highly educated family in the Hanoi area. He passed the regional exam in 1831, but, although he quickly gained a reputation for erudition and poetic skill, his lack of regard for rules and regulations prevented him from gaining the doctoral degree at the capital examinations. When he somehow managed to gain an appointment as a regional examination grader at Hue in 1841, he revised the exam essays of some candidates who were acquaintances of his to give them a pass. When this was discovered, only Thieu Tri's clemency kept him from the penalty of death. Two years later, Thieu Tri gave him a chance to rehabilitate himself with an assignment to go on a mission to Batavia, and thereafter he was posted as an education officer near Hanoi, a position that he considered to be an insult to his ability.

In 1854, Cao Ba Quat joined with a Le dynasty pretender named Le Duy Cu and openly rebelled. For five months he and his associates spread havoc in Son Tay Province, west and north of Hanoi, until he was killed by musket fire during a battle. Le Duy Cu was not captured until the summer of 1855. Meanwhile, in early 1855, two of Cao Ba Quat's former students were captured and killed when they led an uprising in Hung Yen Province, a short distance downriver from Hanoi. Later in the year, five of his disciples were captured in the Hanoi area and sentenced to death for their subversive activities.

In 1859, when French forces were landing in the south, a son and a nephew of Cao Ba Quat were captured and killed while following one of the Le pretenders that proliferated in the north during the 1850s and 1860s. Le pretenders and men of Cao Ba Quat's caliber were only the most prominent among the rebel leaders that sprang up at this time. In addition to "rebels" there were even more leaders of bandits and fugitives who were active not only in the north but also in other parts of the country. Furthermore, in 1850 the Taiping Rebellion, which ravaged Qing China for two decades, broke out in Guangxi, just across the northern border. The human debris of that great disorder spilled over into the northern mountains of Vietnam. Qing rebel leaders gained control of large parts of the northern uplands and became allies of local outlaws.

According to the *True Records of the Great South*, three months after Cao Ba Quat's death, Tu Duc reportedly made a lengthy analysis of the problems in the north. From his perspective, Cao Ba Quat had opened a floodgate of unrest in the north: "Suddenly last year, because of that wayward official Cao Ba Quat, plots to incite the people to rise in rebellion were like the noise of many gathering mosquitoes becoming claps of thunder. At first they disturbed only hamlets and villages, but then they struck whole districts and provinces." The young king, who never ventured far from his palace, tried to understand what was going on in the north and concluded that there were five reasons for the outbreak of rebellions.

The first reason was misgovernment by local officials:

> Our court has often given generous assistance to the people with great expense to our treasury, but local officials, following their custom, greedily take the money for themselves no matter what the occasion, thereby

defeating our generosity, and so royal favor does not reach down to the people; the people are full of resentment, they become careless of life, and desperately rush down the path of destruction without knowing what they are doing. Rebellion arises naturally not just because of the incitement of violent and cruel men, but more truly because of bad, greedy, heartless officials.

The second reason was the poor quality of royal soldiers: "Soldiers are only concerned with satisfying their service contract with their villages. They are not properly trained and, without discipline, they become discontented and commit evil deeds."

The third reason was the selfish ignorance of villagers that left them vulnerable to rabble-rousers:

Common people compete among themselves and are untrustworthy. They seek personal advantage and disdain righteousness. They encourage each other to gather in the markets to drink, gamble, and play around. Fortune-tellers mislead them and lying bullies victimize them. One cup of wine makes a gang of bandits. One idle word can provoke a battle. When they are defeated it is too late for them.

The fourth reason was the gangsters who were nurtured in the households of the wealthy: "Among rural notables and village worthies, every wealthy house has servants, sixty to a hundred men, among whom accumulate hooligans with plenty of weapons. Local people are coerced to do their bidding and even local officials fear to report their lawless behavior, so higher authorities do not know what is going on in the villages."

The fifth reason was the dense population in villages and their maze-like intersecting roads and paths, which enabled fugitives to escape and hide.

These five considerations apparently represented the best thought at the Hue court about how to explain the northern disorders. What they reveal is a lack of effective government. Tu Duc, or whoever wrote the analysis, appears to understand the structural problem of governing the Red River plain from Hue: "I want to establish a policy to maintain lasting order, but evil rises from the people, and I can but guess about unforeseen affairs so far away." Yet, rather than addressing the problems with concrete measures, the analysis ends with a weak moral appeal for officials to work harder. The analysis and the conclusion are characteristic of Tu Duc's intellectual perspicuity and practical incompetence. When he understood the problem, he could think of nothing better than to pass responsibility for plans and action to his officials.

The five-point analysis reveals corrupt magistrates, disaffected soldiers, and local bullies, phenomena that had been typical of Vietnamese villages for centuries. Yet the scale of dysfunctional government was apparently excessive, tempting desperate or alienated people into open rebellion. The repeated appearance of Le dynasty pretenders indicates, more than sixty years after the end of the Le dynasty, the inability of the Hue court to firmly establish its legitimacy among the people in the north. This inability was a failure to overcome the physical and mental distance between Hanoi and Hue. More prosaically, it was a failure to provide a modicum of security and justice.

Meanwhile, the Hue court returned to Minh Mang's anti-Christian policy of the 1830s, thereby attracting the attention of the French navy and of Louis Napoleon's government in Paris. Among the most prominent of Truong Dang Que's collaborators was Nguyen Tri Phuong (1800–1873), from the Hue region, who specialized in military affairs. He had traveled to Manila and Singapore in the early 1830s, had assisted in putting down the Le Van Khoi rebellion, was prominent in the Siamese war of the 1840s, and spent much of the 1850s in Saigon suppressing southern unrest, watching the Siamese, and securing the Cambodian border. After the 1847 Battle of Da Nang, his attitude toward the French became hostile, and he accordingly became a determined foe of Christianity. Under his influence and the influence of other officials with similar views, including Truong Dang Que, the persecution of Christians gained new life after the death of Thieu Tri. In 1848, an edict prescribed death for foreign missionaries and banishment or imprisonment for Vietnamese Christians. In 1851, the death penalty was extended to Vietnamese clergy. Within the next year, two French missionaries were beheaded in the north, and the execution of Vietnamese priests was resumed.

The threat from Europe

The French navy was increasingly active along the Chinese coast in the early 1850s, collaborating and competing with the British and the Americans for treaty privileges and territorial concessions. But it was not until the end of the Crimean War in 1856 that Louis Napoleon was prepared to initiate a policy toward Vietnam. The British had obtained a commercial treaty with Siam in 1855, and Louis Napoleon sent Charles de Montigny (1805–1868) to Bangkok to obtain a similar treaty. Montigny had gone out to the Chinese coast with the French navy as a member of a diplomatic mission in 1843. He subsequently spent the rest of his career in the French diplomatic service in China, serving as the first French consul in Shanghai (1848–1853) and later as consul at Tientsin (1863–1868). He was experienced in Chinese affairs but had little knowledge of Siam, Cambodia, and Vietnam, the countries placed on his 1856 itinerary. His

Vietnamese agenda was to obtain a treaty protecting Christians and to open the country to trade.

The plan was for Montigny to appear in Vietnamese waters with a naval escort that would support his negotiations with a show of force. However, poor coordination between Montigny and the navy resulted in Montigny's ship arriving four months after the navy had come and gone. The first of two naval vessels assigned to meet Montigny at Da Nang, a new steam-powered warship, arrived at Da Nang in September 1856. Waiting for Montigny, the ship's captain was frustrated by the cold welcome he received from local officials. Feeling threatened by what he interpreted as Vietnamese military preparations, he bombarded and demolished the harbor forts. By the time Montigny arrived in early 1857, the navy had long since departed and the Vietnamese were uninterested in talking with him.

When the French warship had first arrived at Da Nang in September 1856, local officials reported to Hue that the French captain threatened that if the Vietnamese king did not agree to negotiate a treaty with the soon-to-arrive French envoy, it would be reported to the British navy, which would then arrive with unpleasant consequences for the Vietnamese. If this report was correct, it reveals an interesting use of the British by the French for making threats, suggesting that the French lacked confidence in their own reputation. In response to this news, Hue ordered that military units be put on the alert and that patrols be maintained to watch for any additional ships. If the French should attempt to sneak ashore, the intruders were to be confronted, "so that they will know that we are prepared."

A few days later, news reached Hue that the French had bombarded and destroyed the harbor fortresses. Tu Duc was reportedly upset by this and said:

> The provincial officials did not know how to be prepared. Reading their report makes it sound like they were only a few feeble people in a situation beyond their means. Considering that this one Western ship was beneath our forts and that a ship can contain but a certain number of shells and furthermore that it must shoot them slowly and deliberately, how could the shells from this ship have come down like rain as claimed in the report? Furthermore, our soldiers were at higher elevations with strong fortifications. How could this ship destroy every one of our emplacements but we could not shoot the ship? Surely our troops did not have the heart to fight with the enemy, so they schemed in fear to simply save their lives.

This reaction to the Da Nang action contains four points of interest. First, Tu Duc had no understanding of the technical disparity between modern Western warships and Vietnamese coastal batteries. Second, he did not know the difference between giving a command and ensuring that it was executed. Third, he was easily distracted from the reality of a situation by quibbles over the use of a metaphor, in this case his objection to mention of French shells coming down like rain. Finally, and most tellingly, he was fully prepared to attribute cowardice to his own soldiers. His scolding comments echo the analysis of northern insurgency recorded two years before. Trouble comes from the bad performance of officials and soldiers. It did not occur to him that failure could be caused by anything other than people not correctly performing their duties.

Unlike Japanese leaders, who quickly understood the threat posed by Western navies and who were willing to accept revolutionary change in order to respond to it, Vietnamese leaders phlegmatically watched an increasingly rampant French fleet materialize off their coasts during the course of nearly two decades. Finding themselves in a world dominated by military technology and organization beyond what they possessed, Vietnamese leaders took comfort in being members of a civilized world led by China. Like Japan, Vietnam was vulnerable to hostile sea power. But unlike Japanese leaders, who even after more than two centuries of peace had retained the samurai's sensitivity to military affairs, Vietnamese rulers, like their counterparts in China, were educated in literature, history, and philosophy. What appeared to be plausible for China, however, did not hold for Vietnam. Vietnam lacked the vast hinterland that enabled China to project an air of sovereignty despite the loss of control over its coasts.

On the eve of the French conquest, leaders at Hue faced an impasse. The moral values on which they believed their society was built did not let them agree to legalize either Christianity or opium. Yet, accepting the treaty demands of the Western powers whose warships threatened their harbors meant opening their country both to Christianity and to opium. Expectations of being able to prevail in this confrontation may appear unrealistic from the perspective of later events, but these men had no choice but to resist as best they could, for they were not prepared to change their fundamental view of what it meant to be civilized.

After Montigny's visit to Da Nang, a new anti-Christian edict was published and a fresh wave of persecution passed through Vietnamese Christian communities. In July of 1857, a Spanish missionary was executed in northern Vietnam. Dominicans based in Manila maintained an active mission in the Red River plain. Little more than a year later, a joint Franco-Spanish expedition was prepared to forcibly open the country.

The issue of Christianity in motivating French and Spanish military action against Vietnam, while superficially apparent, was not fundamental. Christianity had been a discernible part of Vietnamese society for over three hundred years before the French conquest. Vietnamese rulers had attempted to discourage Christianity from time to time when urged on by their Confucian advisors, but

Christians were largely integrated into normal society. For example, in the seventeenth and eighteenth centuries, Christian soldiers in the north were allowed to take their oaths of loyalty in the name of their own religion rather than in the name of the traditional mountain spirit. Relations between communities of Christians and non-Christians were overwhelmingly peaceful.

The virulence of the anti-Christian policy initiated by Minh Mang, while built upon conventional Confucian views, more immediately expressed fear of European imperial intentions. It arose at the time of the First Anglo-Burmese War (1824–1826) and was accompanied by a wave of anti-Christian propaganda in Vietnam that was unprecedented in associating Christianity with European imperialism. The participation of Christians in Le Van Khoi's uprising confirmed the Hue court in a view of Christians as disloyal and prone to rebellion. Furthermore, Christianity offended Minh Mang's passion for enforcing uniformity in all aspects of his country's life. By the time that decades of anti-Christian propaganda and persecution had developed into the outbreaks of violence between Christians and non-Christians of the 1860s, 1870s, and 1880s, during the years of French conquest, the association of Christians with French aggression had hardened in the minds of many royal officials and of others educated to be influenced by them.

When missionaries were the only Frenchmen in Vietnam, their importance to French policy appeared much larger than it actually was. The significance of Christianity for drawing French imperial interest toward Vietnam wore off within weeks of the landing of the Franco-Spanish expeditionary forces at Da Nang near the end of summer in 1858. In the calculations of Louis Napoleon and his chief advisors, the religious question was a convenient explanation to rally Spanish participation and public support for military action in Vietnam, but economic and political considerations were more fundamental. Men with little patience for religion built French Indochina. Naval officers led the way in their search for an Asian seaport and a river route to the back door of China to gain an advantage over the British, who policed China's front doors. The British seizure of lower Burma in the Second Anglo-Burmese War of 1852–1853 aroused French fears of the British gaining the Chinese back door through Burma and of failure to compete for colonial territories. The new Prussian navy began to appear in Asian waters by the mid 1850s and provoked apprehensions of another competitor.

In the late 1870s and early 1880s, under the Third Republic, industrialists and merchants became the driving force for expanding the colonial holdings in Vietnam. Then, beginning in the mid 1880s, colonial administrators began to pursue a vision of building a modern Asian state to demonstrate the imperial genius of France. By the turn of the twentieth century, the creative energy of the

French to initiate change in Vietnam had been mostly spent. Aside from a great surge of investment in the 1920s, French rule in Vietnam would thereafter be a holding operation as initiative for change shifted to the Vietnamese.

At the beginning of the nineteenth century, the new country of Vietnam appeared in a world of great and constant change. In the 1820s and 1830s, Minh Mang endeavored to centralize his authority over all Vietnamese and to establish his realm as a major regional power, imagining that seaborne threats could be kept at bay. In the 1840s and 1850s, however, the imperial powers of Europe gained momentum, riding their superior technology, their military discipline, and their visions of great achievements. At the same time, Vietnam slipped into a ferment of insubordination without effective leadership. Tu Duc was isolated from disturbing events, never traveled far from his palace, and had no policy aside from avoiding change. What ensued for the Hue monarchy was a painful process of being forced to accept change. By the late 1880s, Vietnamese kings had become functionaries of a colonial regime.

10 THE FRENCH CONQUEST

The Treaty of Saigon, 1862

French rule in Vietnam was established over a period of fifty years through a process that had several phases. Between 1857 and 1862, the French decision to launch an expedition against Vietnam was made and implemented, resulting in the Treaty of Saigon, which granted France possession of the region surrounding Saigon. Between 1862 and 1874, Vietnamese efforts to negotiate a French departure failed as the naval officers who governed at Saigon annexed the rest of the Mekong plain to create the colony of Cochinchina. They also established a protectorate over Cambodia and sent an expedition up the Mekong, which determined that this was not a feasible route to China.

Consequently, French interest shifted to northern Vietnam and the Red River route to Yunnan, leading to a rapid conquest of the Red River plain in 1873. This, however, was quickly disavowed by the new Third Republic government of France, still reeling over the disaster of the Franco-Prussian War and the civil war between the Paris Communards and the National Guard. With the Treaty of 1874, France evacuated the Red River plain but established a loose "protectorate" over the Hue monarchy with joint Franco-Vietnamese customs stations at Hanoi, Hai Phong, and Qui Nhon.

In the early 1880s, rising commercial and industrial interests in France superseded the agenda of the navy. Furthermore, a great spasm of competition among European imperial powers for colonial territories led to a firm French determination to ensure the exclusion of potential British or German interference in Vietnam. The French government decided to take possession of the entire country. In 1883, the French occupied Hue and forced the Vietnamese monarchy to accept their "protection."

During the next twelve years, France gained control of northern Vietnam through a series of events that involved a war with China and a committed program of pacification. A brief war with Siam in 1893 enabled France to establish a protectorate over Laos. Efforts to put in order the administrative and financial arrangements for governing the pacified and protected territories were repeatedly initiated from the mid 1880s to the mid 1890s as a cadre of colonial officials with visions of an Asian colonial state accumulated in Saigon, Hue, and Hanoi.

During the governor generalship of Paul Doumer (1897–1902), French Indochina was organized on a fiscal and administrative basis that would endure with minor adjustments to the end of French rule in 1945. As a strategic bloc directed from Hanoi, Indochina without the French has in some respects continued into more recent times. Doumer, a prominent figure in French politics, created a regime of taxation, public works, centralized government, scientific investigation, and scholarly inquiry that defined the French colonial achievement among the Vietnamese. The inability of later governor generals to significantly change this regime defined the ultimate failure of the French to adjust to the consequences of their rule among the Vietnamese.

The events culminating in Paul Doumer's term as governor general of French Indochina were initiated forty years earlier in the summer of 1857. In the wake of the fiasco of Montigny's mission a few months earlier, Louis Napoleon, Emperor of France, convened a commission to study the question of policy toward Vietnam. Members of the commission included representatives of the navy, the Foreign Ministry, and the Ministries of Agriculture, Commerce, and Public Works. Their report recommended intervention to achieve three goals. The primary consideration was a strongly felt need to be part of the European presence in Asia. The British, Dutch, Portuguese, Russians, and Spanish were all established in Asia. Participation with the British in the Crimean War demonstrated that France had emerged from its post-Napoleonic caution and could seek its place in the constellation of European powers. The British, who had tutored French foreign policy since Waterloo, were distracted in 1857 by rebellion in India and the outbreak of the Arrow War in Guangdong. The British showed no particular interest in Vietnam, so Vietnam was an appropriate place for the French to focus their attention. It was thought to be especially important for the navy to establish a secure base for its Asian operations, and Vietnam was admirably located in the center of Eastern Asia.

The secondary consideration was economic. There was a perceived need to secure stable sources of commodities such as cotton, silk, sugar, rice, and coffee. Vietnam offered a place accessible by many seaports where a great range of products could be obtained. Furthermore, it offered opportunities for emerging French industries to market their manufactured goods.

The final consideration was the religious question, which was pressed upon the commission by representatives of the missionaries. Ensuring the security of French missionaries and of Vietnamese Christians was viewed as a moral argument for intervention that would elicit the approval of the Catholic Church and would be useful for generating positive public opinion more generally. Louis Napoleon had cultivated the support of the Church in his rise to power and was inclined to pose as its protector.

Louis Napoleon endorsed the commission's recommendation. It happened that he was in the midst of plans to send an expeditionary force to join the British in an attack on China to force the revision of treaties that had been signed in the 1840s after the Opium War. Leonard Victor Joseph Charner (1797–1869) commanded the French naval forces to be engaged in China, and Pierre Louis Charles Rigault de Genouilly (1807–1873) was in command of one of the divisions of the French fleet. Rigault de Genouilly had commanded one of the French warships that bombarded Da Nang in April 1847, had served with distinction in the Crimean War, and was a strong advocate of attacking Vietnam to secure an Asian naval base. His assignment in 1857 included command of naval operations to be undertaken in Vietnamese waters.

In late summer of 1857, French and Spanish representatives in Macau received news that in July a Spanish Dominican missionary had been publicly executed in Nam Dinh, south of Hanoi. Spanish authorities, learning of the prospect for French action against Vietnam, volunteered to add a contingent of Spanish-led Filipino troops. By the end of the year, the governments in Paris and Madrid had agreed on a joint expedition.

After the British and French expedition had forced the Qing government to sign the Treaties of Tientsin in June 1858, Rigault de Genouilly was released from Charner's command and directed to rendezvous with a Spanish flotilla off Hainan Island and to commence operations against Vietnam. On August 31 the Franco-Spanish expedition entered the Bay of Da Nang with fourteen ships, including five transports. There were around two thousand French troops, many of them Africans, and five hundred Spanish-led Filipinos; another five hundred Filipinos eventually arrived from Manila.

The invaders quickly secured the harbor forts and established a beachhead. Mount Tra, a massif nearly seven hundred meters high, rises on the southeastern side of the bay. It forms a peninsula attached to the mainland by a narrow strip of land. The French placed an observation post on its peak, which enabled them to observe troop movements throughout the region. Between Mount Tra and the mouth of the Thu Bon River, thirty kilometers to the south, the hinterland is crisscrossed with waterways and footpaths. It was in this territory that most of the fighting between the Vietnamese and the Franco-Spanish forces took place during the next several months.

The Vietnamese mobilized thousands of soldiers against the invaders but could not dislodge them. After four months, Tu Duc analyzed the gloomy situation of his army under six headings. According to him, the enemy was superior to Vietnamese troops in the gathering of intelligence, in communications, in the quality of equipment, in mobility, in tactical versatility, and in morale. Tu Duc's conclusion, predictably, was to exhort his officials to try harder.

In early 1859, Nguyen Tri Phuong arrived in the field and Vietnamese forces began to record some successes in repulsing enemy attacks. By this time Rigault de Genouilly had turned his attention away from Quang Nam and was preparing to strike Saigon. The French commander realized that the initial idea of trying to reach Hue was futile. There was no plausible way to access Hue directly by sea and his forces were not sufficient for a major land operation against the large numbers of Vietnamese soldiers that had been mobilized against him in Quang Nam.

Missionaries argued for shifting operations to the Red River plain where they promised the support of a large population of Christians. The Spanish strongly supported this idea because all of their missionaries were in the north. However, Rigault de Genouilly had already been disabused of illusory missionary expectations of local people rising up in support of the invaders. Although Tu Duc attributed the superior intelligence of his enemy to the spying activities of Vietnamese Christians, Rigault de Genouilly evaluated the information he received from missionary sources as unreliable. The French commander quarreled with the missionaries and turned his back on them. Ignoring the protests of his Spanish allies, he decided to leave a garrison at Da Nang and with two-thirds of his men, fewer than two thousand soldiers, seized Saigon in February 1859.

Two months later, leaving a garrison at Saigon, Rigault de Genouilly returned to Da Nang with most of his men. Reinforced by one thousand troops from France, he endeavored for the next several months to negotiate with the Vietnamese, but nothing was achieved. In the summer of 1860, cholera and typhus spread among the expeditionary force at Da Nang, particularly among the reinforcements fresh from France, and the Spanish were increasingly disenchanted with the operation. There was no prospect of further reinforcements because Louis Napoleon had suddenly entered a war against Austria in northern Italy. This war ended in a matter of weeks but it thoroughly diverted the emperor's attention to European affairs and involved complications with Prussia and Britain. Furthermore, any resources that Paris could spare for Asia were absorbed by the renewal of hostilities in northern China following Qing disavowal of the Treaties of Tientsin.

A new French expeditionary force arrived in Asia in 1860 to operate jointly with British forces in northern China. In March 1860 the Franco-Spanish garrison at Da Nang was terminated. Spanish units returned to Manila and French units joined the expedition to China. Rigault de Genouilly had returned to

France in October 1859 where he argued successfully for the retention of Saigon. During the summer of 1860, while Franco-British forces were engaged in China, Nguyen Tri Phuong invested Saigon with around twelve thousand Vietnamese troops, severing it from the outside world. A small Franco-Spanish garrison of fewer than one thousand men held on, most being Senegalese and Filipino soldiers. After the conclusion of the Chinese war in late 1860, French forces became available to relieve the Saigon garrison.

In February 1861, Admiral Charner arrived in Saigon with reinforcements of around 2,500 men. During the preceding six months, Nguyen Tri Phuong had built a large fortress at Ky Hoa designed to prevent the invaders from breaking out of Saigon. In what became known as the Battle of Ky Hoa, Charner attacked and demolished this fortress. He then fought through the canal system connecting Cholon with the Mekong and seized My Tho.

In November, Charner was replaced by Louis Adolphe Bonard (1805–1867), whose prior naval career had included action in Tahiti and the governorship of French Guiana in South America. Bonard expanded French-held territory to include Bien Hoa in December 1861 and Vinh Long in March 1862. In June 1862, a delegation from Hue negotiated the Treaty of Saigon with him, by which Tu Duc ended his anti-Christian policy, agreed to pay an indemnity, and recognized French possession of the three provinces of Bien Hoa, Gia Dinh, and Dinh Tuong, comprising all of the plain north of the Mekong River. The small Spanish contingent at Saigon departed for Manila a year later when the treaty was ratified at Hue; Spanish bitterness over having gained nothing from the affair soured relations between Paris and Madrid for several years thereafter.

The leader of the Vietnamese delegation that negotiated the Treaty of Saigon was Phan Thanh Gian (1796–1867). Of modest ancestry from Vinh Long Province, he was awarded the doctoral degree in 1826, the only man from the Mekong plain to attain this honor prior to 1856. He served as an envoy to the Qing court in the 1830s and became a prominent associate of Truong Dang Que at Tu Duc's court in the 1850s. In 1862, he was the prime spokesman for a realist appraisal that resistance to the French was hopeless and that diplomacy was the only feasible path to take.

The Treaty of Saigon became the basis on which subsequent Franco-Vietnamese relations were contested and expanded. In addition to granting sovereignty over three provinces to France, it also granted religious freedom to Catholics. The Hue court had allowed Phan Thanh Gian to negotiate the treaty under duress, for another Le pretender had appeared in the north at the head of a serious rebellion. Tu Duc understood that he could not fight the French in the south and the rebels in the north at the same time.

Formation of French Cochinchina

The inability to pacify the Red River plain and to eradicate the appeal of Le dynastic pretenders was a great weakness of the Hue monarchy and prevented concentration of the country's resources against the French at Saigon. The Le Duy Cu rebellion of 1854–1855 in which Cao Ba Quat had played a part was followed by a series of rebellions led by men claiming to fight for restoration of the Le dynasty. There were two main centers of disaffection with the Nguyen dynasty. One was in the province of Son Tay northwest of Hanoi, adjacent to the uplands inhabited by people later called Muong, among whom loyalty to the Le remained strong. The other was along the coast from the Chinese border to the southernmost estuaries of the Red River south of Nam Dinh, with particular strength in the old Mac homeland in the region of the modern city of Hai Phong, which at that time was not yet a city or seaport of significance.

A series of rebellions associated with a Le pretender named Le Duy Minh emerged from this coastal region from 1857 into the 1860s. Although Le Duy Minh was captured and executed more than once, new Le Duy Minhs continued to appear, demonstrating that a pattern of insurrection had become institutionalized with interchangeable men. The story line of these rebellions held that Le Duy Minh was aboard a European ship off the coast; he and his generals arrived in small boats, gathered armies of Christians and Le dynasty enthusiasts from the peasant population and were assisted by Vietnamese and Chinese pirates whose boats penetrated deep into the deltaic river system. The first inkling of this story is dated in Vietnamese records to the autumn of 1857. At that time, French naval craft were poking about the coast seeking information about the death of the Spanish Dominican missionary who had been executed the previous July. Alienated and lawless elements in the Red River plain apparently combined the old narrative of restoring the Le with a new narrative of European intervention to protect the Christians. The Sino-Vietnamese pirate world was quick to join these narratives as Nguyen dynasty authority receded from the coast.

In 1861 and 1862, just as Charner and Bonard were expanding their grip on the Saigon region, an especially spectacular outbreak of insurrection led by a Le Duy Minh occurred in the north. The French identified this Le Duy Minh as someone they knew by the name of Pierre Le Duy Phung, who in his youth had been educated at the French missionary school in Penang. He had political ambitions and as early as 1855 had unsuccessfully lobbied the French navy for assistance in igniting a rebellion against Hue. He accompanied Rigault de Genouilly's expedition to Da Nang as an interpreter. When the French shifted to the south rather than the north, he disappeared. He reappeared as Le Duy

Minh and by late 1861 had mobilized an army said to number twenty thousand men from the coastal provinces of the Red River plain. In early 1862 he appealed to Saigon for aid. The Spanish officers were eager to support him but Bonard said no and opted instead to accept Hue's offer to negotiate peace, albeit taking advantage of the situation in the north to obtain his treaty objectives. Tu Duc submitted to the Treaty of Saigon just as the rebel army was preparing to attack Hanoi. He was thereafter able to concentrate enough soldiers against the rebels to abate the emergency. A year later, in the summer of 1863, the Hue court recorded that Le Duy Minh had fled into the sea but that his followers were still numerous. Small armies continued to claim adherence to the cause of Le Duy Minh as late as 1867.

Tu Duc was careful to observe the provisions of the Treaty of Saigon. He withdrew his soldiers and officials from the three provinces ceded to France and abandoned his anti-Christian policies. Some local resistance to the French emerged in relatively remote districts south and west of Saigon, but it was suppressed within a year, and thereafter the newly acquired French territories were relatively calm. Tu Duc did not encourage anti-French activities, being occupied with the rebellion in the north and wanting to give no excuse for further trouble with France. He was nevertheless not reconciled to the loss of the three southern provinces and, in the spring of 1863, shortly after ratifying the Treaty of Saigon, he sent a delegation led by Phan Thanh Gian to France to negotiate a new treaty directly with the government at Paris.

Louis Napoleon was then fully occupied with his intervention in Mexico and showed indications of being tempted by Phan Thanh Gian's offer of generous commercial and financial concessions if the three provinces were returned. Phan Thanh Gian returned to Vietnam in 1864 with a draft treaty containing these provisions, albeit granting to France an enclave at Saigon. Vietnamese hopes were dashed a year later when word arrived that Louis Napoleon had decided to retain the 1862 treaty.

Meanwhile, Tu Duc was buffeted by indignation among educated Vietnamese over the Treaty of Saigon, particularly in the north where literati were strongly anti-Christian and anti-foreign. Details of the treaty spread among the thousands of men who gathered for the 1864 regional examinations. Riots erupted in the examination yards of Hanoi, Nam Dinh, and Hue. One of Tu Duc's royal cousins gathered a large following, including most of the four thousand examination candidates at Hue, and plotted to unseat Tu Duc, punish Phan Thanh Gian, and massacre the Christians. This conspiracy was foiled, but outrage continued unabated.

After the untimely death of Tu Duc's imprisoned brother, Hong Bao, in 1854, a faction of the royal family continued to view Hong Bao's lineage as the legitimate line of succession to the throne. In August of 1866, the son-in-law of one of Tu Duc's uncles organized an attempt to unseat Tu Duc and to replace him with Hong Bao's son. Leaders of this coup attempt accused Tu Duc of being incapable of resisting the French and of wasting resources on the building of his own elaborate tomb complex. The conspirators mobilized the workers at the tomb construction site along with some military units and penetrated into the royal throne room before being subdued. All members of Hong Bao's family were subsequently killed.

During this time, the French at Saigon were led by a senior career naval officer named Pierre Paul Marie de La Grandière (1807–1876). His governorship, from October 1863 to April 1868, was the longest of all the naval officers who presided at Saigon during the 1860s and 1870s, the so-called "era of the admirals" in the history of French Indochina. La Grandière acted decisively to stabilize the French position at Saigon and to expand French influence up the Mekong. Among his initial priorities was to gain a firm grip on the Khmer monarchy.

When, in 1859, the Franco-Spanish expedition seized Saigon and the Vietnamese were concentrating their military resources there, King Ang Duong took the opportunity to attack Vietnam. His idea, as expressed to French missionaries in Cambodia, was to ally with France against Vietnam, although the missionaries did not encourage him in this and the French officers at Saigon ignored him. In 1860, his Khmer and Chinese military units overran Vietnamese border outposts. He encouraged the Khmer governor of the Vietnamese jurisdiction at Soc Trang, near the sea just south of the western arm of the Mekong, to rebel, but his army was unable to force its way downriver to assist this uprising and the Vietnamese quickly subdued it. When Ang Duong died in December 1860, Siam, which did not want war with France, pressed his son and successor, Norodom, to make peace.

After the Treaty of Saigon was ratified in 1863, Bonard, in one of his last official acts, obtained from Norodom a treaty of protectorate that contradicted Cambodia's existing relationship of vassalage with Siam. During the next four years, La Grandière orchestrated matters between Saigon, Phnom Penh, Bangkok, and Paris to eventually gain the approval of his superiors, the acquiescence of the Siamese, and the approbation of Norodom to the assertion of French suzerainty over Cambodia. In 1866, he sent an expedition up the Mekong River to explore the possibilities of using it as a route to China. In 1867, he seized the three remaining Vietnamese provinces in the Mekong plain: Vinh Long, An Giang, and Ha Tien. Phan Thanh Gian, then serving as governor of these provinces, deemed resistance to be futile and the annexation was peaceful. The only notable casualty of the operation was Phan Thanh Gian himself, who committed suicide in acknowledgment of the failure of his policy of peaceful negotiation with the French. His death enabled Tu Duc to use him as a scapegoat for the loss of the south and he was posthumously denounced at Hue.

By 1868, when he returned to France, La Grandière had established the Colony of Cochinchina and the Protectorate of Cambodia as the foundation upon which French Indochina would subsequently be built. Plans for building and administering the City of Saigon were formalized and a cadre of young naval officers embarked on experiments in administering the indigenous populations, some of them learning Vietnamese, Chinese, and Khmer. At the same time, French-speaking Vietnamese graduates of mission schools, local Christians, and other Vietnamese adapted quickly to French rule and the opportunities it provided for achieving a range of goals from personal advancement to visions of a new Vietnam in the modern world. Finally, a non-military colonial population began to accumulate in Saigon and Cholon, comprised of people mainly from France but also from other European countries, from India, and from China, attracted by economic opportunities. Saigon was open for business as an international seaport and quickly became known for the export of rice.

The Treaty of 1874

During the late 1860s and early 1870s, Tu Duc, having lost possession of what had become French Cochinchina in the south, also lost control over the upland hinterland of the Red River plain, while his authority in the lowlands shrank to a few garrisoned administrative centers, primarily Hanoi, Son Tay, Bac Ninh, Hai Duong, Hon Gai, Nam Dinh, and Ninh Binh. Adding to the long-term trend of increasing insubordination and insurrection that characterized Tu Duc's entire reign was the turmoil and disaffection among officialdom produced by Tu Duc's effort to end his anti-Christian policy in accordance with the Treaty of Saigon. Anti-Christian sentiment was strong in officialdom and Christians were vulnerable targets for anger over loss of the south. Tu Duc's efforts to avoid further complications with the French by enforcing religious provisions of the treaty led to a diminution of respect for him among local officials who viewed Christians as French partisans. The exam riots of 1864 and the coup attempt of 1866 were but the most visible demonstrations of growing dissatisfaction with his leadership. In 1866 and again in 1868, Tu Duc disciplined officials in Nghe An and Ha Tinh for their anti-Christian activities. Similar but less publicized episodes of punishing officials and calming tensions between Christians and local officials occurred with increasing frequency in the Red River plain.

Meanwhile, the leaders of upland peoples in the northern mountains slipped out of Hue's control. Many of them allied with private Chinese armies that crossed the border from Guangxi. The most important of these armies was led by Liu Yongfu (1837–1917), a Hakka Chinese from Guangxi who grew up in poverty and came of age in the 1850s when the Taiping Rebellion erupted in Guangxi and spread north into the Yangtze River basin. He joined elements of the rebel movement that remained in Guangxi and rose to a position of leadership. After the death of the Taiping leader in 1864, Qing forces gradually reasserted their control over the territories held by insurgents, and some local strongmen in the south led their followers across the Sino-Vietnamese border to seek their fortunes in the uplands of northern Vietnam, where opium and precious metals were produced. Most of these men rallied under the yellow flags of Huang Chungying (d. 1876). Huang Chungying allied himself with the chieftains of the upland minority peoples and established a reputation for being in defiance of both Qing and Hue authorities.

Liu Yongfu's army, flying black flags, was smaller but more disciplined than the yellow flag army. He impressed Vietnamese officials by defeating an array of rebellious local chieftains and obtained a commission from Hue to pacify the uplands. In 1868, he expelled Huang Chungying from Lao Cai, on the Red River at the Yunnan border. The Qing general sent at the request of Hue to subdue the yellow flag army was impressed by this, and Liu Yongfu subsequently received a Qing commission to assist in suppressing Huang Chungying. Huang Chungying was eventually defeated and killed by a combined Sino-Vietnamese operation in which Liu Yongfu played a prominent part during 1875–1876. Meanwhile, Liu Yongfu, based at Lao Cai, gained control of the lucrative commerce on the Red River between Yunnan and Hanoi. In the late 1870s, he established a secondary base of operations at Hung Hoa to protect the Red River from remnants of the yellow flag forces who had moved west into Laos as well as from the red and striped banner forces comprised of rebels in Yunnan that shifted into northern Laos after being defeated by Qing armies.

In the early 1870s, a French merchant adventurer named Jean Dupuis (1829–1912) appeared in the midst of the relatively lawless situation in northern Vietnam and provoked an episode that demonstrated the impotence of the Hue court and revealed contradictions between French authorities in Saigon and the new republican government in Paris. Dupuis had gone to China in 1861 to seek his fortune in trade. In 1868 he met members of the French Mekong River expedition as they made their way from the upper Mekong in Yunnan to the coast at Shanghai. From them he learned of the likelihood that the Red River was navigable from Yunnan to the sea. In 1869, he traveled to Yunnan and took orders for an arms shipment from the Qing officials then engaged in fighting a

rebellion in that province. In 1871, he revisited Yunnan and reconnoitered part-
way down the Red River to verify that it was navigable all the way to the
lowlands.

At the beginning of 1872, he was in Paris. Although the new Third Republic
government was just emerging from the disorders of the Franco-Prussian War
and the suppression of the Communards, he obtained permission from the
Ministry of War to purchase a consignment of arms to sell to China. Also, the
Ministry of the Navy promised to send a letter to Cochinchina authorizing
assistance to facilitate his travel from Saigon to Hue in order to obtain Vietnamese approval to traverse the Red River. He was soon back in Asia where in Hong
Kong he assembled a small flotilla and a force of around 175 men, twenty-five of
them Europeans and the rest Asian, mostly Chinese. When the arms shipment
arrived from Europe, he went to Saigon where a letter from Paris on his behalf
was waiting. The governor was absent, but the presiding official passed him to a
naval captain about to depart on a survey of the Vietnamese coast. The captain
advised Dupuis to forget about going to Hue, for, in his view, dealing with the
officials at the Vietnamese court was nothing but an aggravating waste of time.
He advised Dupuis to simply take his shipment up the Red River, assuring him
that Vietnamese authorities would not be able to stop him. Dupuis took this
advice and hastened back to Hong Kong. A few weeks later he and his flotilla
rendezvoused with the captain who showed him how to get into the Red River
from the sea. In December, he arrived at Hanoi.

Vietnamese authorities were taken aback by the appearance of this small but
well-armed force and could not prevent Dupuis from fortifying a district in
Hanoi with the support of the Chinese merchant community. Leaving most of
his men at Hanoi, Dupuis proceeding upriver with part of his cargo. He arrived
in Yunnan, delivered his merchandise, and was back in Hanoi by April with a
shipment of precious metals along with 150 Qing soldiers provided by the
governor of Yunnan. He was arranging to return to Yunnan with a shipment
of salt when Nguyen Tri Phuong arrived to take charge of the situation in Hanoi.
Nguyen Tri Phuong stiffened the resistance of Vietnamese officials to Dupuis'
seemingly uncontrollable activities. Dupuis set himself in defiance of the Vietnamese government, and a state of hostilities ensued between him and Nguyen
Tri Phuong. Tu Duc sent an appeal to Saigon, complaining that Dupuis was
lawlessly violating existing agreements.

Marie Jules Dupré (1813–1881) was the governor at Saigon from 1871 to
1874. He was a career naval officer who had participated in the earliest phase of
French operations at Saigon and was an ardent exponent of expanding French
control over all of Vietnam. At the same time, he was under strict instructions
from the government in Paris to avoid any expansion of French involvement in

Vietnamese affairs. The government of the Third Republic, still suffering the effects of defeat by Prussia and of the ensuing civil war in the streets of Paris, had no appetite for new colonial adventures. Dupré was caught between his instructions and his personal inclinations. Not wanting to ruin his career by being insubordinate, he sent a message to Dupuis instructing him to submit to the Vietnamese authorities. Dupuis cleverly replied that if the French did not seize the Red River route to China then the British, or the Germans, or even the Chinese would move in. The prospect of this so frightened Dupré that he sent money to sustain Dupuis and decided to depute someone he could trust to sort out the confrontation in Hanoi. He turned to a young naval officer named Marie Joseph François Garnier (1839–1873).

Garnier had been on the staff of Admiral Charner and had subsequently served as the administrator of Cholon under Bonard and La Grandière. It was at Garnier's urging that the Mekong expedition was initiated in 1866. He was a member of the expedition and assumed command of it when the leader died in Yunnan. His outstanding qualities of leadership, despite his youth, were demonstrated in bringing the expedition out through China from Yunnan via the Yangtze River. His encounter with Dupuis at that time alerted Dupuis to the idea of opening trade with Yunnan on the Red River. Garnier returned to France and fought in the Franco-Prussian War. In the summer of 1873, he was honeymooning in China when he received an urgent summons from Dupré. He arrived in Saigon in August and, after conferring with Dupré, was soon on his way to Hanoi with 170 men. What passed between Dupré and Garnier is not exactly clear, but presumably they entertained expectations similar to those expressed by the captain who had advised Dupuis and guided him into the Red River the previous year. A common opinion among the French in Cochinchina was that the Vietnamese were incapable of any serious resistance. As for Paris, Dupré apparently gambled that the attitude of the metropolitan government could be moved by a fait accompli.

Tu Duc and Nguyen Tri Phuong imagined that Garnier had arrived to escort Dupuis out of the country by force. Instead, Garnier allied with Dupuis and began to issue commands contradicting the public announcements of Nguyen Tri Phuong. Events moved quickly to a military confrontation. In addition to the few French troops who had arrived with Garnier, Dupuis had about 500 men under arms with up-to-date weapons, including the 150 Qing soldiers from Yunnan as well as men he recruited from the local Chinese community and deserters from the Qing army that had entered the country from Guangxi to suppress the yellow banner forces. In the Hanoi citadel, Nguyen Tri Phuong had around seven thousand soldiers, but their weapons were outdated. In late November, Garnier attacked the citadel and it quickly fell. Nguyen Tri Phuong was wounded and died.

During the next three weeks, Garnier's men raced on river steamboats from one place to another and easily took possession of nearly all the Vietnamese administrative centers in the Red River plain between Hanoi and the sea. Although the Spanish missionaries held aloof, most French missionaries cooperated with Garnier, and many Vietnamese Christians assisted the French with supply and reconnaissance, as auxiliary militia, and in setting up local administrations. While French missionaries and Vietnamese Christians were prominent in assisting Garnier, they constituted a relatively small minority of the Vietnamese who rallied in support of the invaders. The reservoir of dissidents who had provided manpower to the series of Le pretenders in previous years also responded to Garnier.

Hoang Ta Viem (1820–1909), the husband of one of Minh Mang's daughters, was in command of the Vietnamese fortress at Son Tay, about forty kilometers upriver from Hanoi. Another senior Vietnamese official in the region was Ton That Thuyet (1839–1913), a descendent of the seventeenth-century ruler Nguyen Phuc Tan, who was rising to the top echelon of influence at Tu Duc's court. These two men called upon Liu Yongfu for help. Hoang Ta Viem had previously established a close and friendly relationship with Liu Yongfu. Liu Yongfu moved his men downriver and was in the vicinity of Hanoi by mid December. The yellow flag forces, not yet subdued, were inclined to support the French against the black flags, but were too slow to have any effect on the situation. Considering that the black flag soldiers were his most serious adversaries, Garnier was determined to demonstrate his mastery over them at the earliest opportunity. When they appeared at the western gates of Hanoi, Garnier impetuously led a sally against them, but was ambushed and killed.

Saigon had just been linked to Paris by undersea cable, and news of Garnier's activities quickly reached men in the metropolitan government and they directed Dupré to put an end to the affair. Dupré's gamble had failed. There was no way for him to temporize, to let events take their course, to wait for the surface mails to shuttle across the seas, giving time for a fait accompli to gain momentum. His instructions from Paris to stop Garnier were unmistakable and promised disgrace if he did not immediately comply. He turned to a young naval officer and colonial administrator with a reputation as a serious scholar of Vietnamese culture, Paul Louis Felix Philastre (1837–1902).

Philastre had arrived in Vietnam with Charner in 1861. He was soon fluent in Vietnamese and learned to read Chinese characters. Dupré sent him north with authority to terminate the French adventure on the Red River. He arrived in Hanoi shortly after Garnier's death and moved quickly to restore Tu Duc's officials to their posts and to redeploy the French soldiers back to Cochinchina. He sent Dupuis packing with a strong rebuke. A new agreement was subsequently negotiated, known as the Treaty of 1874, which superseded the 1862 Treaty of Saigon.

The Treaty of 1874 appeared to stabilize and deepen the Franco-Vietnamese relationship, but in fact it became a source of misunderstanding and frustration to both sides. The Vietnamese obtained the French evacuation of the north, which was Tu Duc's main concern. For their part, the French obtained formal Vietnamese acknowledgment of their 1867 annexation of the three western provinces of Cochinchina, which Hue had previously refused to grant. The freedom of missionaries and the protection of Christians were guaranteed. Although some local magistrates countenanced a wave of reprisals against the Christians who had supported Garnier's brief conquest in the north, Tu Duc discouraged this because he wanted to provide no excuse for the return of French soldiers. The most serious anti-Christian activities occurred not in the Red River plain but in Nghe An and Ha Tinh, where a large Christian population had existed since the early seventeenth century and where the Confucian-educated literati were particularly anti-Christian and anti-French. Ton That Thuyet was eventually sent to calm those two provinces.

Post-treaty disorder in the north

With the Treaty of 1874, the French appeared to have gained what Dupuis had initially sought. Treaty provisions opened the Red River, as well as the ports of Qui Nhon, Hanoi, and Hai Phong, to international commerce. French consuls were to be stationed in these ports with judicial prerogatives over any litigation involving Europeans and with the authority to issue travel passes to Europeans, countersigned by Vietnamese officials. Joint Franco-Vietnamese customs houses were to be set up in these ports and were governed by arrangements specified in a commercial treaty concluded a few months later. These commercial aspects of the treaty were never implemented to the satisfaction of either party. On the Red River between Son Tay and Lao Cai, after expulsion of the yellow flags in 1875, Liu Yongfu was in control and levied substantial fees without regard for any other authority, whether Vietnamese, Chinese, or French. There was relatively little commercial activity in Hanoi or Qui Nhon.

Hai Phong, however, was a different matter. Hai Phong did not exist as a place of any significance until this time. It was situated to control access into the Red River plain from the sea, and it had the added advantage of being located near the coal mines of Hon Gai. Within six months of Hai Phong being opened to trade under the new treaty, the population of Chinese there increased from zero to six thousand. Soon there was a regular steamship service between Hong Kong and Hai Phong. Rice and coal began to flow out of the new port. The excessive export of rice led to a steep rise in its price and to famine conditions in the hinterland. Vietnamese officials did not know how to administer the burgeoning port city and could not control the activities of Chinese merchants. They wanted to fix the price of rice and to limit its export. The French wanted an open market. Mutual aggravation ensued.

More serious than this were the 1874 treaty provisions on diplomatic and military matters. The French deemed that they had obtained the equivalent of a protectorate over Vietnam with a resident chargé d'affaires at Hue and articles asserting that Vietnam did not recognize the suzerainty of any third country and that Vietnam would subordinate its foreign policy to French supervision. The French believed that this ended Qing sovereignty over Vietnam and were indignant when Vietnam continued to send regular tribute missions to China and to rely on Qing assistance against the yellow flags. The French were inclined to view this as violating an article in the treaty specifying that, in case of internal disorder, Vietnam would call upon France for assistance. Some Frenchmen were exercised about the suppression of the yellow flags by joint Sino-Vietnamese operations in 1875 and 1876 because they viewed the yellow flags as a potential pro-French force. When a man claiming to be a descendent of the Ly dynasty of the eleventh and twelfth centuries came across the Sino-Vietnamese border in 1877 with an army of several thousand, some French were incensed when Tu Duc called upon the Qing rather than the French for help. In 1879, Qing forces captured the pretender and carried him back to China for execution.

Also troubling to many of the French was that the British interpreted the Treaty of 1874 as implying in principle the residence of consuls from other countries in the Vietnamese port cities, and that these consuls would have jurisdiction over judicial affairs concerning their people, thus dismissing French pretensions of having an exclusive relationship with the Vietnamese court as its protector. The French were concerned to make good their control of Vietnam before other countries could enter the situation. For his part, Tu Duc still dreamed of negotiating the withdrawal of the French and, in 1878, used the occasion of sending a delegation to an international exposition in France for a vain attempt to reopen the matter with Paris. A Vietnamese diplomatic mission to Siam was thwarted when the Siamese, fearing the French, refused to receive it. Not so timorous were the Spanish, who in 1880 negotiated a commercial treaty with Hue, raising French apprehensions that the British and Germans would not be far behind. Frustration with the state of Franco-Vietnamese affairs in the late 1870s was mostly confined to a group of Frenchmen in Cochinchina and their friends in Paris who were committed to colonial expansion for reasons of commerce and of competition with other imperial powers. The Paris government at this time was absorbed in domestic politics and gave little attention to the provisions of the Treaty of 1874. The admirals governing at Saigon during this time, stung by the Garnier affair, were loath to go down that road again. They professed contentment with Cochinchina and Cambodia and saw nothing in the north but an ungovernable headache.

Local administration in many parts of the Red River plain never returned to a semblance of normal government after the Garnier affair. Hunger and banditry spread as village notables and wealthy families changed communal land into private land to enable them to participate in the export market for rice. Tu Duc attempted to enact a tax reform to obtain more revenue from privately held land but achieved little more than to further alienate influential men in the north. He initiated a plan to organize landless peasants into militia units and to settle them on vacant land in upland valleys. He wanted to increase the number of soldiers available to suppress bandits and to relieve the pressure on royal troops, but the effect of this, to the extent that it was implemented, was to increase the control of local officials over military resources. Tu Duc's efforts to govern the north were increasingly disconnected from the situation existing there. Vietnamese and Chinese pirates on the coasts and along the major rivers operated with impunity. They specialized in capturing women and children to sell into slavery in China. French coastal vessels were assigned to intercept them, and in 1877 the Hue court even proposed that France establish a fortress on Cat Ba Island, near Hai Phong, to suppress the slave trade, which was centered there. In conditions of increasing lawlessness, local communities, particularly those comprised of Christians under the leadership of missionaries, organized for self-defense.

French administration in rural Cochinchina

Meanwhile, the situation in Cochinchina was developing very differently. Vietnamese administrators had abandoned the Mekong provinces, leaving the task of government completely in the hands of the French. A brief flurry of resistance to the French broke out after the Battle of Ky Hoa in early 1861, but faded away in 1863 when the Hue court ratified the Treaty of Saigon. The most famous leader of this resistance was Truong Dinh (1820–1864), a military officer who established his main base at Go Cong, about forty kilometers south of Saigon. French pacification operations were increasingly effective, and, in early 1864, Truong Dinh took his own life when he was betrayed and ambushed. Truong Dinh's reputation as an enemy of the French invaders was partly a result of him being celebrated in the writings of Nguyen Dinh Chieu (1822–1888), a blind scholar from the Saigon area who settled in Ben Tre, about seventy kilometers south of Saigon, where he wrote anti-French and anti-Christian poetry until his death.

The pattern of rural resistance to established authority that subsequently developed in Cochinchina pre-dated the French. It emerged from the cultural mix of Khmer, Chinese, and Vietnamese in the western provinces. Government had always been weak or non-existent in this remote region. The inhabitants typically sought to distance themselves from authority. There were few people who could read or write. Village organization was rudimentary at best. Family bonds were tenuous. Since the seventeenth century, armies of Khmers, Vietnamese, Siamese, and Chinese had passed through, sometimes without serious effect, sometimes giving a certain temporary ascendancy to one group or another, and sometimes with destruction and grief in their wakes. In the late eighteenth century, Nguyen Phuc Anh endeavored to stabilize the region by enforcing separation between the various groups and appointing Chinese, Khmers, and Vietnamese to each govern their own people. The building of the Vinh Te Canal between Ha Tien and Chau Doc in the 1820s superficially made a geographical border but it also created a venue for even greater contact among the various peoples.

Minh Mang's policy of ethnic assimilation removed administrative barriers between the different peoples. This was intended to Vietnamize the non-Vietnamese, but here, where the Vietnamese were not a majority, it led to strong Khmer and Chinese influence upon the Vietnamese. Le Van Khoi's rebellion and the subsequent wars involving Cambodia and Siam further destabilized government administration. The Lam Sam rebellion in the early 1840s rallied members of all three ethnic groups behind a man claiming religious rather than secular authority. When warfare ended in the late 1840s, ideas and practices from Theravada and Mahayana Buddhism, Daoist spiritualism, popular religious cults, secret societies, and the prowess of magicians, healers, sorcerers, diviners, and geomancers combined with millenarian expectations, creating a current of religious thought and action that continued through the twentieth century, periodically mobilized by charismatic personalities.

Remnants of the Lam Sam movement took refuge in the Seven Mountains (That Son) between Ha Tien and Chau Doc, just south of the Vinh Te Canal, which popular belief identified as a gateway to Heaven where deities appeared. Generations of religious leaders and their disciples have resided in these mountains to the present day. In times of social stress, healers believed to possess divine powers went through the region attracting followers. One such person appeared during the cholera epidemic of 1849. Arrested by Vietnamese authorities, he was forced to enter a traditional Buddhist monastery where he could be supervised. But his charisma overcame all who would restrain him and he soon went to the

Seven Mountains beyond the reach of government. Although he died shortly after, from among his followers there periodically appeared men who stimulated new episodes of millenarian enthusiasm that were directed toward the supernatural world and consequently did not acknowledge earthly authorities, whether Vietnamese magistrates or French administrators. Beginning in the late 1860s, those inclined to resist the French tended to join this reservoir of belief beyond secular law, from which they occasionally emerged in uprisings that were easily suppressed by the French. Being on the Cambodian border, these uprisings were sometimes related to similar movements among Khmers rebelling against authorities in Phnom Penh.

The enduring appeal of millenarian healers and magicians in Cochinchina was also related to two features of southern Vietnamese society that have been attributed by historians to the effects of French colonialism but that in fact predated the French. These are the relative weakness of village organization and the relative significance of a mobile landless population. Without the economic security of land or the social security of a village community, religious figures offered the promise of salvation and the comfort of mutual care in their entourages. Combined with European cultural influences felt during French colonial rule, these conditions eventually gave rise to new religions in the twentieth century.

From the very beginning of organized Vietnamese penetration into the Mekong plain, landless peasants working as virtual slaves for large landowners were a salient feature of Vietnamese settlement. As noted in a previous chapter, in 1711 Nguyen Phuc Chu admonished his officials at Saigon to stop enslaving peasants and to allocate land to them. The recording of such an event is typically an indication of a chronic condition rather than of a problem being solved. Efforts to mitigate the status of landless peasants are most evident in instructions to organize military colonies, in which case peasants were still in a disciplined structure of authority. Since land was plentiful, peasants who wanted to avoid serving a landlord or a military officer simply moved further south or west, giving rise to the pattern of large organized landholdings in the east where government authority was strongest, and a more miscellaneous situation among the Chinese, Khmer, and Vietnamese peasants of western Cochinchina, which was less developed economically and administratively.

One effect of French rule was to expand the regime of large estates into western Cochinchina in order to increase the export of rice, which produced more landless peasants. Village organizations were generally controlled by those with the most wealth, typically landlords, and they provided no plausible remedy for landlessness. French administrators in Cochinchina repeatedly commented upon the large population of landless peasants who marketed their labor, and they assumed that this was a result of their own policies. Some of the French were dismayed by the phenomenon while others considered it an inevitable phase in the necessary shift of Vietnamese society from village communalism toward individual freedom and responsibility.

French policy toward village government was to shift authority away from the group of wealthy and educated elders called notables, and to put it into the hands of someone they identified as the "mayor." In the past, this person was the representative of the notables, usually a younger man, chosen by them to implement their decisions. But the French considered him to be an equivalent of the mayor of a French town who represented the central government rather than the village. The French believed that the notables were primarily motivated to maintain their own economic advantages and that they could not be trusted to serve in a scheme of authority controlled by colonial administrators. Since many notables and those who spoke on their behalf supported the French regime, the status of the village notables became a controversial issue. The French were reluctant to cede administrative authority into the hands of men already established in positions of importance in local society for fear of not being able to exercise their authority unimpeded by local self-interest. Rather, they relied upon younger, less established, men to serve as village leaders. These men were expected to be more dependent upon the French than the village notables could be. However, as they received no salary and often had to use their own funds to carry out their duties, it was often difficult to find qualified men willing to serve in this position. The result was a general weakening of village government as the notables were disengaged from local decision-making and administrative authority was vested in men with relatively little influence in local society and with little incentive to perform their duties.

The collection of revenue did not at this time change dramatically from prior practice, except that it was collected more efficiently than in pre-French times. Eventually, in the 1880s, taxation would be changed from a collective village responsibility to the individual responsibility of each taxpayer. Not until the turn of the century would the French initiate the elaborate tax regime that became characteristic of their rule.

Law and language in Cochinchina

The French naval authorities in Cochinchina were perplexed most of all by efforts to administer justice. The pre-French legal system had been administered by magistrates with a relatively high level of educational achievement in the system of examinations used by the Hue court to staff officialdom. These men were not only conversant with the law code published by the founder of the dynasty in 1812 but also with the edicts, sub-statutes, and precedents that had developed around it and that made it practicable. With the arrival of the French, these men departed for the north. No one remained in French Cochinchina with the knowledge and experience necessary to apply the law.

The naval officers in Saigon initially decided to translate the Vietnamese law code into French, imagining that this would allow them to practice law in the manner to which the people were accustomed. An officer named Louis Gabriel Galderec Aubaret (1825–1894) was one of the first Frenchmen in Saigon to gain fluency in Vietnamese and the ability to read Chinese characters. His perception of the great gulf separating Vietnamese and French culture led him to believe that any effort by Frenchmen to govern Vietnamese was doomed to fail. Consequently, he had assisted Phan Thanh Gian on his trip to Paris in 1863 and helped to draft the treaty, never ratified, that provided for returning the hinterland of Saigon to the Vietnamese. He completed a translation of the law code in 1865, but, for one thing, the associated edicts and statutes were missing and, for another thing, unlike French law that specified all conceivable cases in some detail, this code was oriented toward general principles to be applied as deemed appropriate in individual cases by judges with years of local experience. The application of Vietnamese law depended more upon the discretion of magistrates than upon the letter of the law.

French administrators could make little sense of Aubaret's translation. The alternative was to simply apply French law, but Philastre, who terminated the Garnier affair in 1873, believed that rulers should learn the culture of the people they governed rather than vice versa. He argued the need for a more detailed translation of the Vietnamese law code and accordingly received authorization to produce it. Completed in 1875, Philastre's translation was erudite, meticulous, and included sub-statutes as well as Ming and Qing commentaries. Unfortunately, it would have taken a scholar to make use of it, and it proved to be no more practicable than Aubaret's translation had been. Meanwhile, the admirals experimented for two decades with various measures for administering justice until French law was extended to Cochinchina after the appointment of its first civilian governor in 1879.

Men like Aubaret and Philastre were disturbed by how young French officers with no Vietnamese language ability or knowledge of Vietnamese culture were governing Cochinchina through a cadre of Vietnamese translators of very uneven quality. One of their like-minded colleagues, Jean Baptiste Eliacin Luro (1837–1877), obtained authorization to open a school for trainees to give new arrivals from France an introduction to Cochinchinese administration. He designed a curriculum that included Vietnamese language, Chinese characters, and

introductions to Vietnamese culture, society, and government. The school operated from 1874 to 1878. Most Frenchmen considered the workload to be
excessive, and the school was closed after Luro's death from illness. Aubaret,
Philastre, and Luro were the most prominent of the naval officers serving in the
first generation of French administration in Cochinchina who learned to respect
Vietnamese culture. Men with similar views were an influential, and occasionally
dominant, minority in subsequent generations of colonial administration in
Indochina.

Some Vietnamese translators were poorly educated or more interested in
personal advancement than in government service. Yet, there were many other
Vietnamese, both Christians and non-Christians, who accepted French rule as
the way for their country to enter the new global realm of advanced technology.
They served not only as translators but also as journalists, scholars, administrators, and soldiers. One of the most famous of these was Petrus Truong Vinh
Ky (1837–1898), a Christian from Ben Tre in Vinh Long Province who studied
both Chinese and Latin in his youth. He attended mission schools in Phnom Penh
(1848–1851) and Penang (1851–1858), learning French and training to be a
priest. The death of his mother brought him back to Vietnam just as the French
invasion was beginning. In 1860 he sought refuge with the French in Saigon from
anti-Christian activists. He married the following year, and in 1862 he was
teaching in a school for translators. In 1863 he accompanied Phan Thanh Gian
to France as an interpreter and took the opportunity to also visit Spain, Portugal,
and Italy. He became a tireless advocate of Quoc Ngu, the Vietnamese alphabet.
He was involved in beginning the publication of the first Quoc Ngu newspaper in
1865, *Gia Dinh Bao*, and within a few years was serving as its editor. He headed
the school for translators in the late 1860s and in 1871 became the principal of a
school for teachers. He taught Vietnamese and Chinese in Luro's school for
trainees in the mid 1870s and served French administrators in various capacities
during the 1870s and 1880s. His greatest contribution, however, was in the
development of Quoc Ngu from a relatively rudimentary tool for transcription
into a means for writing the contemporary spoken vernacular. He translated
many works from Chinese and Vietnamese character writing (Han and Nom)
into Quoc Ngu. He believed that Vietnamese could fully express their experience
of the world in vernacular writing; he wrote and published many works in Quoc
Ngu, not only about history, literature, and morality but also about grammar
and pedagogy.

Paulus Huynh Tinh Cua (1834–1907) was another man who contributed to
the development of Quoc Ngu. He was from Ba Ria, on the coast east of Saigon.
He joined French service in 1861 and, like Truong Vinh Ky, went to France with
Phan Thanh Gian and was an editor of *Gia Dinh Bao*. He was a prolific writer

and produced a large body of articles and essays in the vernacular. Truong Vinh Ky and Huynh Tinh Cua were but the two most prominent among a large number of Vietnamese in Saigon who were dedicated to vernacular writing and whose works became the basis for the great awakening that occurred in the early twentieth century of Vietnamese thought about the modern world.

The naval officers who governed Cochinchina in the 1860s and 1870s were determined to eradicate the use of character writing, which they considered to represent all the backward attachments to China that impeded their aim of bringing progress to the Vietnamese. Although they were unable to completely dispense with character writing for many years because of the degree to which it was ingrained in the minds of educated Vietnamese, they strove to educate a new generation of students in the Vietnamese alphabet and in French. In the 1860s there were false starts, including an unsuccessful program to send teenage Vietnamese boys to Catholic schools in France. In the 1870s, a system of provincial primary schools in Quoc Ngu and in French was established with a secondary school at Saigon in French. Educational policy provoked prolonged controversies over language, with some arguing that only French should be allowed and that Quoc Ngu should be discouraged because it was a potential language of resistance to French. Others argued that you could not eradicate the vernacular language and that Quoc Ngu should be used as an alphabetic step for students into French.

Behind this difference of opinion lay a larger theoretical issue in the minds of French colonialists, commonly referred to as a choice between assimilation, turning Vietnam into an Asiatic France, and association, nurturing a version of Vietnamese culture that could be associated with the French endeavor to bring Vietnam into the modern world. In the jargon of the time, the French called this task a "civilizing mission." However, they did not understand this in the way of more recent generations as expressing the idea that the Vietnamese were not civilized. Most French administrators who accumulated years of experience among the Vietnamese and who learned to speak Vietnamese had no doubt but that the Vietnamese were already a civilized people with their own history, literature, philosophies, religions, and patterns for organizing families, communities, and government. What the "civilizing mission" meant for them was to teach the Vietnamese how to enjoy the benefits of up-to-date technology, medical science, modern industrial and agricultural production, communications, transportation, and the liberation of individual creativity from the stifling hand of dead tradition. This idealistic task was often corrupted by arrogance, racism, and greed, but French colonial rule cannot be judged as more virulent and corrupt than the regimes that had governed the Vietnamese in earlier ages. It was based, as all regimes in the past had been, upon the power to coerce and the corruptions of human nature. But it was also based upon the ideal of helping the Vietnamese to overcome the backwardness that had enabled the French invaders to prevail.

The rhetoric of assimilation and association went through several phases of debate and understanding in French colonial thought, but would not have any discernible significance for Vietnamese until the second decade of the twentieth century when the French began to take into account the Vietnamese response to the colonial relationship. The contradiction between assimilation and association continued to the very end of the French efforts to maintain their ascendancy over the Vietnamese. This was also the contradiction found in French politics and government in France between the urge to enforce centralized uniformity and the appreciation for distinctive characteristics of regional identities.

In general, Cochinchina in the 1860s and 1870s enjoyed relative peace and security. Although French administration was in a process of adaptation to local conditions, it nevertheless provided a measure of calm and prosperity in great contrast to the disturbed conditions in the Red River plain. The export of rice from Cochinchina rose from around 50,000 tons annually in the early 1860s to 320,000 tons annually by 1877. Land grants designed to increase rice production led to the growth of the landlord class but at the same time provided employment for peasants. Cochinchina became the only part of Vietnam to be ruled as a direct colony subject to French law. Its economy was organized toward the international seaport of Saigon-Cholon where entrepreneurial ambitions and a cosmopolitan urban culture grew. The quarter-century of subordination to Hue, from the suppression of Le Van Khoi to the French invasion, was anomalous in the history of Saigon. Life in southern Vietnam under the French resonated with the earlier era of power and prosperity in the late eighteenth and early nineteenth centuries under Nguyen Phuc Anh/Gia Long and Le Van Duyet. Southern Vietnamese were part of the wider world while Vietnamese in the north suffered the effects of isolation, poverty, insecurity, and governmental breakdown.

The Sino-French War

By the end of the 1870s, the number of Frenchmen, both in Cochinchina and in France, who had given up on hopes of establishing a working relationship with Tu Duc was growing rapidly. Furthermore, the lack of effective authority in the north aroused French fears of intervention by China or by another European power. Advocates of colonial expansion were determined to establish French control over the Red River route to Yunnan. But any new French initiative would require the full support of Paris. Such support began to develop in the late 1870s as new industrial, commercial, and colonial interests began to be felt in parliament after the monarchists were defeated in 1877. The resistance of the naval officers in Saigon to these new interests, which they believed would push aside their priorities, led in 1879 to the appointment of the first civilian governor of Cochinchina, Charles Le Myre de Vilers (1833–1918).

The rise of republican politicians in parliament at this time produced a major shift in French policy toward colonial expansion in Vietnam. Their anticlericalism, partly derived from the Church's support of monarchy, made them uninterested in and sometimes hostile to the missionaries. But they wanted to restore France as a great European power and believed that the acquisition of a colonial empire would go far toward erasing the humiliating defeat in the Prussian War of 1870–1871. There were, however, two major tendencies among the republicans. The Radical Republicans supported colonial expansion so long as it did not interfere with their agenda of major domestic reforms. The Opportunist Republicans were less ideologically committed to effecting social change and were more interested in international affairs. They favored gradualist domestic policies that seized opportunities for, but did not force, reform. They were also more susceptible to seizing opportunities for colonial expansion. Such an opportunity presented itself in Vietnam.

Major figures among the Opportunist Republicans served as prime ministers during the early 1880s when the decisions were made that pushed forward the conquest of Vietnam: Léon Gambetta (1838–1882), Charles Louis de Saulces de Freycinet (1828–1923), and Jules François Camille Ferry (1832–1893). Gambetta was closely associated with the deputy representing Cochinchina in Parliament, Jules Blancsubé, who was also the Mayor of Saigon and an advocate of taking northern Vietnam. These men were at the forefront of a growing chorus of politicians, government officials, businessmen, geographical societies, chambers of commerce, and propagandists such as Jean Dupuis, the merchant adventurer who had been expelled from Hanoi by the navy in 1874. One firm proponent of action in Vietnam was Jean Bernard Jauréguiberry (1815–1887), a distinguished admiral who as a captain had led the first French landing at Saigon in 1859. In the autumn of 1879, as Minister of the Navy and of Colonies, he proposed that a large expeditionary force be sent to northern Vietnam. This plan was too ambitious at that time and it languished. But the idea remained alive, and, in early 1882, Le Myre de Vilers was authorized to send a military detachment to Hanoi for the purpose of opening up the Red River to commerce. In effect, the first step in the new French policy was to challenge Liu Yongfu.

Le Myre de Vilers turned to Henri Laurent Rivière (1827–1883), a career naval officer with literary ambitions who had been recently posted to Saigon as commander of the Cochinchina naval division. When Rivière seized Hanoi citadel with around five hundred men in April 1882, China mobilized an army across the Sino-Vietnamese border. The French minister to China was so alarmed that he negotiated an agreement for a Sino-French partition of northern Vietnam. There followed nearly a year of inaction as Le Myre de Vilers shrank from confrontation with China, Rivière sat in Hanoi working on his novel, and the politicians in Paris were occupied with changing governments. When he became prime minister for the second time, in February 1883, Ferry discarded the draft treaty of partition with China and ordered Rivière to proceed.

A few months earlier, in the autumn of 1882, Le Myre de Vilers had been replaced by Charles Antoine François Thomson (1845–1898), a former secretary of Gambetta with an uncompromising attitude toward implementing the conquest of Vietnam. Ly Myre de Vilers had shown more interest in the internal administration of Cochinchina than in being involved with the "Tonkin Question." Derived from Dong Kinh, the old name of Hanoi, Tonkin became colonial terminology for the Red River plain.

In addition to affirming French law and implementing civilian government in Cochinchina, Le Myre de Vilers was interested in expanding the possibilities of Franco-Vietnamese cooperation. He started a program to send young Vietnamese on visits to France, he established the Alliance Français in Saigon, he opened procedures for Vietnamese to gain French citizenship, and he instituted the Colonial Council of Cochinchina, partly appointed and partly elected, which included Vietnamese representatives. Thomson continued these policies but at the same time moved aggressively in Tonkin.

In March 1883, roused from his pen, Rivière led his few hundred men to seize the coal mines at Hon Gai, the port at Hai Phong, and the fortress at Nam Dinh, thereby opening up the Red River plain for further French operations from the sea. Within weeks, Qing military intervention recommenced in the northern mountains, and Liu Yongfu moved downriver to confront the French. In May, Liu Yongfu's men killed Rivière in an ambush near Hanoi. Unlike the death of Garnier a decade earlier, Rivière's death provoked a great outburst of French enthusiasm for continuing the intervention, and the French Parliament voted for money and soldiers for the conquest of Vietnam.

Thousands of French and Chinese reinforcements poured into northern Vietnam during the summer and autumn of 1883. A Qing army from Guangxi moved down into the lowlands and occupied Bac Ninh, about thirty kilometers northeast of Hanoi. Vietnamese military units under the command of Hoang Ta Viem rallied at the Son Tay fortress, about thirty kilometers northwest of Hanoi on the Red River, where they were joined by Liu Yongfu and Qing military units from Yunnan. In December, Son Tay fell to the French. When the French moved against Bac Ninh in March of 1884, the Guangxi army, suffering from poor leadership and lack of discipline, offered minimal resistance before escaping north into the mountains. Hoang Ta Viem and Liu Yongfu had meanwhile withdrawn to Hung Hoa, on the Red River about thirty kilometers northwest of Son Tay. In April, French forces concentrated against Hung Hoa, bombarding it with artillery and threatening to encircle it. Liu Yongfu escaped upriver with his men and the Qing Yunnanese soldiers while Hoang Ta Viem fled with his Vietnamese forces south through the mountains to Thanh Hoa.

On the basis of these French victories, pacifist elements in the Qing government gained a brief ascendancy and in May negotiated an agreement with French diplomats at Tientsin in northern China. The Tientsin Accord provided for Chinese recognition of a French protectorate over Vietnam and withdrawal of Chinese soldiers from Vietnam. But differing French and Chinese views about the schedule for withdrawal of Qing troops led to a military encounter in June when French troops moving north to occupy the border at Lang Son struck Qing outposts. This episode stiffened bellicose spirits in both Paris and Beijing, and the war was subsequently renewed.

By October of 1884, the Quangxi army was threatening to re-emerge from the mountains into the plains. In a series of battles, the French pushed back toward Lang Son. Then, after weeks of preparation, in a two-week campaign in early February 1885, the French took Lang Son and Qing forces withdrew to the border. Meanwhile, Liu Yongfu and Qing units from Yunnan had besieged the French garrison at Tuyen Quang, which the French had seized from Liu Yongfu the previous June. Tuyen Quang was isolated in the mountains about one hundred kilometers northwest of Hanoi. The small French garrison, comprised of four hundred legionnaires and two hundred Vietnamese troops, was nearly overwhelmed before French reinforcements defeated the besiegers after hard fighting in early March.

The French reinforcements for Tuyen Quang included units withdrawn from Lang Son. The French commander left at Lang Son lost his nerve in late March and ordered a panicked withdrawal that enabled the Chinese to reoccupy Lang Son. The news of this retreat from Lang Son provoked a political crisis in Paris, where the colonial adventure was suddenly vulnerable to critics. The Radical Republicans, led by George Benjamin Clemenceau (1841–1929), who was later famous as prime minister during and after the First World War, denounced Prime Minister Ferry in Parliament. Ferry was voted out of office and his political career was ended. A surge of anti-colonial sentiment swept away the influence of the colonial lobby. Heated parliamentary debates over colonial policy continued for months, and in December of 1885 an appropriations bill to finance operations in Vietnam passed by only four votes.

Meanwhile, war with China was quickly concluded on the basis of the Tientsin Accord of the previous year. China was also ready for peace, mainly as a result of French naval operations along the Chinese coast that had blockaded the movement of rice from southern China, causing a food shortage in northern China. Liu Yongfu evacuated northern Vietnam with the Qing forces, ending his Vietnamese career but beginning a new career in the Qing army.

With the end of the Sino-French War in early summer of 1885, the French began to give serious thought to organizing their newly won protectorate over the court at Hue. During the preceding two years, while enthusiasm for colonial expansion prevailed in Paris following the death of Rivière and while French attention was fixed upon China, the royal court at Hue was divided between those interested in working with the French and those aiming to resist the French. Not until hopes and apprehensions of Qing intervention were extinguished did the situation in Hue shift toward a definite resolution.

The French take Hue

King Tu Duc died in July 1883. During the last year of his life, whatever authority he still may have had was ebbing away as Rivière waited in Hanoi, new Qing armies crossed the border, and Vietnamese officials in the north prepared to resist the French despite their king's passivity. Tu Duc seldom stirred from his palace unless to visit the gardens built at his nearby tomb. Unable to command the respect of his officials, he could not avoid relying upon men whom he did not trust. He faded into a shadow of impotent fear. Prominent members of the royal family and senior officials at Hue pulled in various directions in pursuit of personal interests or clashing policy agendas.

The French chargé d'affaires at Hue, Pierre Paul Rheinart (1840–1902), was relatively sympathetic toward the Vietnamese. He thought that Rivière had exceeded his instructions and created an unnecessarily adversarial situation in the north. He gave strong encouragement to those among the Vietnamese who were inclined to view cooperation with the French as the best available alternative.

Tran Tien Thanh (1813–1883) was the most senior of the officials who favored this view. He was from the Hue area and had earned his doctoral degree in 1838. He had been a close associate of Phan Thanh Gian, with whom he had traveled to France in 1864. He was a respected academician. He understood that resisting France was not a viable option.

Ton That Thuyet, the prince who had played a prominent role in the Garnier affair of 1873, had risen steadily thereafter to become the senior military official at court. He stepped into the role of commanding general that had been occupied by Nguyen Tri Phuong, who had died during the Garnier affair. He was irreconcilably anti-French and was determined to resist any further assertion of French authority at Hue.

The third man who emerged into prominence at Tu Duc's death was Nguyen Van Tuong (1810–1886). His eagerness to insinuate himself into the center of power was already evident when he registered for the 1841 regional examination at Hue with the royal surname Nguyen Phuc. He may have wished to divert attention from his real ancestry for, according to some accounts, his father had been a rebel. Thieu Tri punished him with a term of banishment for *lèse-majesté*. His next recorded appearance is in 1856, during Tu Duc's reign, as a district magistrate in his home province of Quang Tri, a short distance north of Hue. His jurisdiction was along the upland frontier of the Cam Lo Road that went over the mountains to Savannakhet on the Mekong River in Laos. This was an important military and commercial route where information from Siam was collected, merchants made profits, and relations with upland populations were chronically troubled. Nguyen Van Tuong came to the attention of the court in the 1850s because of his success in sorting out problems with minority peoples and in keeping open the flow of trade between Savannakhet and Quang Tri. For the rest of his life he remained the royal expert on this place and frequently returned to set things right.

He established a reputation for being competent and shrewd. When the examination riots broke out at Hue in 1864, Tu Duc put him in charge of the Hue police. In 1867 he went with a delegation to Saigon for talks with the French, and thereafter Tu Duc began to rely on him to handle French relations. In 1869 he was sent to the northern mountains to assist in combating the rebels and bandits that proliferated there. At times he worked as liaison with the Qing army that arrived at Hue's request. At other times he led soldiers on campaign. Nguyen Tri Phuong praised his ability and observed that he could not be motivated by the threat of demotion or the prospect of promotion, indicating that he was able to focus on the task at hand.

Nguyen Van Tuong was an earthy man of few words who made the most of whatever situation he encountered. He does not seem to have cared what others thought of him, apparently because he knew that Tu Duc needed him. When Tu Duc later asked him why the Qing soldiers were more successful than the Vietnamese soldiers, he replied: "Our soldiers are not used to the mountains and easily get sick; the Qing soldiers are used to the mountains and do not get sick." Tu Duc exploded in exasperation: "We have been fighting up there for four or five years, we are worn out, and still we have no success; what should we do?" Nguyen Van Tuong simply said: "We have done our best but it is not good enough." He did not spend time worrying about things he could not change.

During the Garnier affair of 1873, Nguyen Van Tuong was called to Hue and sent to Saigon to consult with the French. He traveled with Philastre to Hanoi, worked with him to settle matters there, and subsequently negotiated the Treaty of 1874. Tu Duc thereafter relied on him for advice on nearly all matters of consequence. In particular, all foreign relations were in his hands. By the time of Tu Duc's death, Nguyen Van Tuong was having an affair with Hoc Phi, Tu Duc's wife.

As Tu Duc lay dying in July 1883, he is said to have entrusted the succession to Tran Tien Thanh, Ton That Thuyet, and Nguyen Van Tuong. Childless, Tu Duc had adopted three of his nephews: Duc Duc (1852–1883), Dong Khanh (1864–1889), and Kien Phuc (1869–1884). Although Kien Phuc was the youngest, he appears to have been the most intelligent, and some accounts affirm that he was Tu Duc's choice. However, after Tu Duc's death, the three regents swore that on his deathbed the king had designated Duc Duc, the eldest, as his successor. There are indications that pressure from the palace women enforced this observance of primogeniture. Three senior women, known collectively as "The Three Chambers," were particularly powerful. These were Tu Duc's mother, Pham Thi Hang (1810–1902), his wife Hoc Phi, and a surviving consort of Thieu Tri. These women enforced a strict hierarchy among the palace women and any violation of the rule of seniority in succession to the throne would have serious repercussions on their control of the inner quarters.

Duc Duc was king for three days before being imprisoned and killed by the three regents. What led to this royal homicide remains a matter of conjecture, but something passed between Duc Duc and the regents that caused them to do away with him. The 31-year-old king may have made it clear that he did not want the tutelage of the three older men, and they were surely unwilling to give up the power to which they had grown accustomed under Tu Duc's weak rule.

Perhaps seeking to minimize any objections from "The Three Chambers," the regents passed over the two young surviving adopted nephews and brought to the throne Hiep Hoa (1847–1883), a 36-year-old younger half-brother of Tu Duc. A senior Censorate official named Phan Dinh Phung (1844–1895) dared to openly denounce the regents for their irregular handling of Tu Duc's succession. Ton That Thuyet arrested Phan Dinh Phung and sent him back to his home village in Ha Tinh Province. Phan Dinh Phung had obtained his doctoral degree only in 1877 but had risen quickly in the Censorate because of his reputation for rectitude. He later led an anti-French movement in his home district and subsequently was regarded by Vietnamese nationalists as a hero.

One month after the enthronement of Hiep Hoa, a French fleet landed troops and overran the forts guarding access to Hue from the sea. Nguyen Van Tuong hastened to sign what came to be called the Harmand Treaty, which met all French demands as defined by François Jules Harmand (1845–1921). Harmand was a naval physician who had played an enthusiastic role in the Garnier affair and subsequently shifted into diplomatic service. In the summer of 1883 he was empowered by Paris to obtain a protectorate treaty with Hue. The Harmand Treaty placed the Hue court under direct French supervision, annexed Binh Thuan to Cochinchina, and created a Tonkin governed by Vietnamese magistrates under the authority of resident French administrators. Thanh Hoa, Nghe An, and Ha Tinh were included in Tonkin and a French garrison was to be placed on the border between Tonkin and the territory still under the government of Hue, which the French called the Kingdom of Annam.

The Harmand Treaty shrank the territory under the direct governance of Hue to the provinces from Quang Binh in the north to Khanh Hoa in the south. The French were to have direct access to the rest of the country. Many politicians in France considered the Harmand Treaty inappropriately ambitious during a time of war with China. French leaders were reluctant to take responsibility for governing so much of the Vietnamese population before matters were settled with China. The Paris government never ratified the Harmand Treaty.

Meanwhile, King Hiep Hoa maintained an attitude of cooperating with the French and relied on Tran Tien Thanh for advice. On the other hand he detested Ton That Thuyet and Nguyen Van Tuong, primarily because they obstructed his authority. Although Ton That Thuyet and Nguyen Van Tuong were not on good terms personally, they were allied against anyone who threatened their respective spheres of dominance, which for Ton That Thuyet was the army and for Nguyen Van Tuong was the palace and the court. Ton That Thuyet realized that with Hiep Hoa as king it would be impossible to organize resistance to the French. He persuaded Nguyen Van Tuong to join him in a coup. In late November 1883, both Hiep Hoa and Tran Tien Thanh were put to death, and the two remaining regents then brought to the throne 14-year-old Kien Phuc. They expected that Kien Phuc's youth would ensure his compliance with their wishes.

During the false Sino-French peace after the signing of the Tientsin Accord in May 1884, the French ambassador to China, Jules Patenôtre des Noyers, arrived at Hue and presented a new treaty to Nguyen Van Tuong, which Nguyen Van Tuong readily signed. The Patenôtre Treaty, which became the basis of the subsequent colonial relationship, was essentially the same as the Harmand Treaty except that the four provinces that Harmand had detached to Cochinchina and Tonkin (Binh Thuan, Ha Tinh, Nghe An, and Thanh Hoa) were left in the Kingdom of Annam. In early June, on the occasion of signing this new treaty, the gold and silver seal of investiture given to Hue by Qing was melted down to symbolically bring an end to the centuries of Vietnamese vassalage to Chinese dynasties.

The young king, Kien Phuc, was known for his integrity and wisdom, which was his undoing. During the months following Kien Phuc's enthronement, Ton

That Thuyet, with the approbation of Nguyen Van Tuong, began to organize a private army, separate from the regular military forces, loyal to him personally. Ton That Thuyet continued to harbor the dream of attacking the French and driving them into the sea. Kien Phuc understood the folly of this and was an obstacle to Ton That Thuyet's plans. Furthermore, Kien Phuc was reportedly outraged over the illicit relationship between Nguyen Van Tuong and Hoc Phi. Accordingly, the two kingmakers resolved to be rid of him. At the end of July 1884, Kien Phuc died, plausibly of illness but more likely of poison. A 12-year-old half-brother of Kien Phuc named Ham Nghi (1872–1943) was placed on the throne. Ham Nghi was the pliant tool that Ton That Thuyet had been seeking. During the months that followed, as the Sino-French War ran its course, Ton That Thuyet stored weapons in the mountains and made plans to resist the French.

So long as the French were occupied with the Chinese war and made no further moves to assert their authority at Hue, the situation remained quiet. However, with the end of the Sino-French War in spring of 1885, the assignment of Philippe Marie Henri Roussel de Courcy (1827–1887) to begin implementing the Patenôtre Treaty ended the calm. De Courcy was a career army officer with a record of distinguished service in nearly every French war since the 1850s. But this was his first experience in Asia, and his blustering demeanor, devoid of nuance or of any sensitivity to local conditions, persuaded Ton That Thuyet that the time of decision had arrived.

In early July 1885, Ton That Thuyet launched a nighttime attack on the French garrison in Hue and used the ensuing confusion and panic to stampede the royal court out of the capital. The refugees gathered at the provincial capital of Quang Tri, around sixty kilometers north of Hue, and deliberated about what to do. Ton That Thuyet announced his plans to take the small king to the mountains and appealed for followers. However, he was trusted by very few, and, with so much royal blood on his hands, he did not inspire confidence among members of the royal family or the court. Most chose to follow Nguyen Van Tuong and Pham Thi Hang, Tu Duc's mother and the matriarch of the royal family, back to Hue where they submitted to the French. A few weeks later, the last surviving adopted nephew of Tu Duc and elder half-brother of Ham Nghi, Dong Khanh, was made king at Hue.

Meanwhile, Ton That Thuyet issued a proclamation in the name of King Ham Nghi calling on the Vietnamese to rise up against the French. He installed Ham Nghi in the mountainous wilderness near the Laotian border around ten kilometers south of the Ha Tinh–Quang Binh provincial boundary, leaving him in the care of his two sons. He then departed northward through the mountains on a journey to seek the help of China, from where he never returned. Along the way, he endeavored to stir up anti-French activity. Ton That Thuyet's schemes left a trail of misery and death.

Hoang Ta Viem, the royal son-in-law who had commanded Vietnamese forces in northern Vietnam since the 1860s and had collaborated with Liu Yongfu against the French during the Garnier and Rivière affairs and the dry-season battles of 1883–1884, had known Ton That Thuyet for many years and looked askance at what this man had done. He rallied members of the royal family and their entourages behind King Dong Khanh and, in late 1886, unsuccessfully endeavored to persuade Ham Nghi's keepers to come down from the mountains.

Ton That Thuyet's dramatic appeal to fight the French on behalf of a king in the mountains unleashed a rage of violence against Christians, the most vulnerable targets of anti-French enthusiasm. The number of Christians killed in the months that followed is unknown, but published estimates range from forty thousand to well over fifty thousand. Acts of resistance to the French appeared in many areas but were most persistent in the provinces north of Hue, particularly in Ha Tinh, Nghe An, and Thanh Hoa, where there were significant numbers of Christians and where a relatively large population of educated men had been alienated by Tu Duc's failures of leadership. Village scholars, having grown frustrated with palace-bound royal leadership, were exhilarated to be called on by a king who had taken to the countryside to resist the French.

During the autumn of 1885, the French army was greatly diminished by a cholera epidemic and did little more than attempt to protect endangered Christian communities. De Courcy considered Nguyen Van Tuong to be devious and exiled him to Tahiti where he soon died. In Paris, the French government was still digesting the shock of the so-called "Tonkin Affair" of the previous spring when French forces had retreated in panic from Lang Son, provoking a parliamentary crisis that had brought an end to the Ferry government and a hasty conclusion to the Sino-French War. There were heated debates over policy in Vietnam and approval for continued operations there was voted by a very narrow margin. General de Courcy was denounced for having unnecessarily provoked a dismaying situation with his excessive arrogance. Furthermore, in the summer of 1885, Governor General Thomson at Saigon, in his effort to enhance French authority in Cambodia, had managed to stimulate a brief but widespread anti-French uprising among the Khmers.

Formation of French Indochina

A new policy initiative was needed to sustain the colonial project in Vietnam. The man selected to implement this was Paul Bert (1833–1886), a man of science, professor of physiology, and staunch anti-cleric who entered politics as a follower of Gambetta, for whom he served as Minister of Education. He arrived at Hue in April 1886 in the midst of the military emergency, but he understood that the fundamental problem was political, not military. Turning against the tide of French colonial thought in Cochinchina, he established a new focus for colonial leadership to deal with the Hue court and the existing Vietnamese administration in Annam and Tonkin. A group of men who went to Vietnam with him became the first of those who served as resident supervisors of Vietnamese magistrates and who would eventually provide the expertise needed to establish the General Government of French Indochina. Bert succeeded in laying the basis for a working relationship between French and Vietnamese officials. He acknowledged the cultural norms of Vietnamese officialdom and provided for traditionally educated Vietnamese to continue to have careers in government service. Although he survived in Vietnam for only about six months, dying of dysentery in November, he was a major architect of French rule in Vietnam. He solidified a cooperative relationship with the royal family and opened the way for a new kind of colonial administrator for whom Hanoi became the seat of authority.

In the late 1880s and early 1890s, the French encountered two forms of resistance in the provinces north of Hue. First was the response to Ton That Thuyet's call to rally under King Ham Nghi's banner against the invaders. Educated men with positions of local prominence organized offensive operations and prepared defensive positions. In addition to resisting the French, three other more purely domestic factors were prominent in this fighting. One was the conflict between Christian and non-Christian Vietnamese, which became especially virulent in the context of French pacification efforts. Another was the difference of opinion among educated men about the merits of resistance. Most upper-echelon Vietnamese officials followed the thinking of the court at Hue that resistance to the French was not only hopeless but would simply bring death and misery to the people; furthermore, as they became aware of events in the wider world, they could see no plausible alternative to French rule. These people provided intelligence and propaganda, performed administrative tasks, and organized military units to assist the French.

A final aspect was regional and, to some extent, even dynastic. The ancestors of educated men in the north had served the Le dynasty for centuries. As late as the 1860s, major uprisings could be launched in the north on behalf of Le pretenders. The loyalty of these men was not to the "southern" Nguyen dynasty so much as to the ideals of their Confucian education, which they believed to be threatened by the French. This contrasted with educated men in provinces further south, for whom loyalty to the Nguyen dynasty was the foundation of political behavior. Once Paul Bert had made it clear that the French would discard neither the Nguyen dynasty nor the class of men educated to serve it, the path was open for literati of all regions to serve the French.

Ham Nghi was too young and passive to play any role in these events. He lived in a hut on a remote mountain, watched over by Ton That Thuyet's sons and half a dozen servants and guards. In late 1888, one of his guards and the local strongman who had been providing him food brought him out to the French, who sent him to a new life in Algeria. One of Ton That Thuyet's sons was killed in this episode and another son killed himself. By this time, the French had already subdued the major center of resistance in Thanh Hoa, at Ba Dinh. A few months later, the major center of resistance in the Red River plain, at Bai Say, was also overrun.

Thereafter, those still unreconciled to the French rallied behind Phan Dinh Phung, the Censorate official who had been escorted back to his village after denouncing Ton That Thuyet and the other regents for their irregular handling of succession to the throne after Tu Duc's death in July 1883. In the early 1890s he organized a small army in southern Ha Tinh. After many defeats, he was forced to take refuge in the mountains where he died in late 1895.

The second form of resistance was a greater problem for the French than these uprisings led by local scholars, for it came from a resistance to government of any kind that had been endemic for generations. The Trinh regime had never established a stable agrarian policy. From the early eighteenth century, rebellion was chronic among the people of the Red River plain. The Nguyen dynasty never achieved a complete pacification of the north. During Tu Duc's reign, there was a trend toward misgovernment, insubordination, and banditry, which accelerated with rebellions led by Le pretenders in the 1850s and 1860s and with the disorders of the Garnier and Rivière affairs and the Sino-French War in the 1870s and 1880s. Chinese adventurers and Qing armies had possessed much of the upland hinterland of the Red River plain since the 1860s, providing refuge, arms, and encouragement to Vietnamese fugitives. Chinese pirates prowled the coast, often assisted by Vietnamese outlaws, conducting a brisk business of kidnapping women and children to sell into slavery in China. By the late 1880s, the Red River plain had been without effective government for decades. Here, the French faced not organized resistance led by men who could be defeated or won over but rather an entire society that had grown accustomed to evading authority. Resistance to the French became a legitimizing tag for lawlessness in general.

An essential element of the French pacification effort was to secure the Sino-Vietnamese frontier, thereby breaking the connection between the Chinese and Vietnamese underworlds. It was also essential for the French to demonstrate to the Vietnamese that they had come to stay and that colonial rule was much preferable to anarchy. The question of how to do this was answered by Jean Marie Antoine de Lanessan (1843–1919). He was a naval physician in Cochinchina in the 1860s, and in the 1870s he became a professor of medicine before entering politics. He made an official visit to Vietnam in the late 1880s and took an interest in theories of colonialism. He believed that the only justifiable purpose of colonialism was to serve as the agent of change to bring defenseless, out-of-date countries up to the highest possible level of administrative order and technical efficiency. He was convinced that the only way to do this was by working through the existing structures of authority.

When he was named Governor General of Indochina in 1891, de Lanessan successfully used the royal court to strengthen the relationship between Vietnamese officials and the French. Dong Khanh had died of illness in 1889 and was succeeded as king by Thanh Thai (1879–1954), the 10-year-old son of Duc Duc. Although his father's murder in 1883 appears to have deprived him of a cheerful or trusting demeanor, Thanh Thai learned to play his assigned role in the French colonial order.

De Lanessan understood that the problem of pacifying the north was political as much as it was military. He reorganized military operations to be conducted in close collaboration with efforts to build a civil administration. His approach was implemented by two army officers who later gained fame in the history of the French army: Joseph Simon Gallieni (1849–1916), who served in Vietnam from 1892 to 1896, and Louis Hubert Gonzalve Lyautey (1854–1934), who served in Vietnam from 1894 to 1897. These men implemented what came to be known as the "oil spot" method of pacification, in which military operations moved forward incrementally no faster than the pace at which civil government could be stabilized. Whereas in 1888 French troops in Tonkin numbered 14,000 with 20,000 Vietnamese commanded by French officers, in 1894 the troop level had fallen to 5,000 French and 12,000 Vietnamese. By 1896, the pacification program was completed.

De Lanessan also initiated a series of events that forced Siam to cede control of Laos. When Siam resisted the movement of French military units into Laos in spring of 1893, French ships forced their way upriver from the Gulf of Siam to place the royal palace in Bangkok under their guns. The Siamese subsequently signed a treaty with France renouncing Laos east of the Mekong. In later treaties, in 1904 and 1907, Siam gave up two Laotian territories west of the Mekong, as well as the northwestern Cambodian provinces that had been annexed a century before. The modern borders of Thailand with Laos and Cambodia were thus drawn.

In the 1880s and 1890s, the British were consolidating their control over northern Burma. In 1896, a Franco-British treaty set the Mekong River as the boundary between British Burma and French Indochina. The territories that would make up French Indochina were thus defined by the mid 1890s. But the question of how they would be administered provoked a decade of conflict between the colonial government that had been developing since the 1860s in Saigon and the new corps of administrators at Hanoi.

Cochinchina, with its port of Saigon and capacity to export rice, was a consistent generator of revenue surplus, but the Cochinchinese system of government recycled most of the profits into the pockets of administrators and members of the French colon community. The nascent Indochinese government being established at Hanoi was saddled with the deficits created by efforts to pacify and govern a territory in which a stable system of administration and of taxation did not yet exist. The considerable French colon community in Saigon fiercely rejected the argument that Cochinchina should help to defray the expenses of the larger Indochinese project. The French in Saigon had developed an effective lobby to represent their interests in Paris. For all of his success in pacifying the north and asserting the Mekong as a western border, de Lanessan was powerless before the Saigon lobby in Paris. In 1894, he was abruptly recalled when his efforts to incorporate Saigon into the Indochinese budget failed to prevail over the entrenched political connections between Saigon and Paris.

Since the days of the admirals in Saigon, French people, however lowly their status in metropolitan French society may have been, found in Cochinchina a lordly lifestyle and a subservient population. They devised an administration that promoted their personal enrichment. The prospect of having to contribute surplus revenue to a budget covering all of Indochina was for them an unwelcome shock. The Saigon Frenchmen were represented in the Chamber of Deputies and had considerable influence in Paris. They fought stubbornly against the formation of a central Indochina government.

On the other hand, from the time of Paul Bert, administrators in Hanoi began to entertain the vision of a colonial government in which Cochinchina was simply one among several subordinate units. Beginning in 1887, efforts to achieve such a government were announced as the aim of French policy. Nevertheless, the French colons of Saigon managed to maintain their autonomy and to thwart any attempt to incorporate Cochinchina into a larger Indochina.

De Lanessan was replaced by Paul Armand Rousseau (1835–1896), an engineer and politician with a level of experience and seniority deemed sufficient to enable him to sort out the conflict of interests between Saigon and Hanoi. Rousseau continued the policies of de Lanessan and was soon in a stalemate with Saigon. He returned to Paris to obtain sufficient authority to bring Cochinchina under the budgetary and administrative authority of Hanoi. In declining health, he intended to resign but died in late 1896. Such was the situation when Paul Doumer (1857–1932) was appointed to be Governor General of Indochina in early 1897.

From a working-class background, raised by a widowed mother, Doumer excelled at his studies and was a mathematics teacher by the age of 20. He worked for a time in journalism and subsequently entered politics, becoming a specialist in financial affairs. By the early 1890s, he was the parliamentary expert on the Indochinese budget. He was Minister of Finance in the brief "radical" cabinet of Leon Bourgeois (November 1895 to April 1896). His efforts to use fiscal policy to effect social reform contributed to bringing down the Bourgeois government. He was strong-minded and decisive. With his knowledge of colonial budgets, it was convenient for his political enemies to send him out of their way to a difficult assignment in Indochina.

During his five-year term as governor general (1897–1902), Doumer established a structure of administration and a set of policies that none of his successors significantly altered. Despite the bitter opposition of Le Myre de Vilers, then serving as the Cochinchinese representative in the Chamber of Deputies, Doumer asserted Hanoi's authority over all five Indochinese jurisdictions: the protectorates of Tonkin, Annam, Cambodia, and Laos, and the colony of Cochinchina. Although Cochinchina retained many distinctive characteristics, being not a protectorate but rather a colony governed under French law, Doumer nevertheless brought it into the framework of a unified budget and of a single authority for government operations. Senior Residents were appointed to administer the four protectorates, but a Lieutenant Governor sat at Saigon.

The construction of an effective central government was one of Doumer's achievements. Behind this achievement was a balanced budget that for the first time made Indochina a generator of revenue, ending its financial dependency upon Paris. By 1899, a comprehensive tax regime began to produce large surpluses. In addition to land taxes, poll taxes, excise taxes, and an array of administrative fees, government monopolies were organized on salt, alcohol, and opium. The Bank of Indochina was opened in Hanoi to process revenue and expenditure. With a stable budget, Doumer was able to float large loans to initiate ambitious infrastructure projects for roads, railroads, bridges, canals, and harbors. In addition to administration, finance, and public works, culture and scholarship were also on his agenda. In 1900, he set up the French School of the Far East (École Française d'Extrême-Orient), which became a major center of academic research on Asia.

Doumer's activist leadership was controversial and provoked sharp criticism, but his achievements were relatively solid and enduring. He returned from Indochina to continue his political career in France, eventually becoming President in 1931. Paul Beau (1857–1927), a career diplomat who had been Minister to China, succeeded him in Indochina. Beau's term as governor general (1902–1907) was relatively calm and uneventful. After Doumer, there were no major problems to solve, and the Vietnamese reaction to what Doumer had done was not yet apparent.

During the four decades since the French had taken Saigon, French ambitions in Asia had struggled for fulfillment until Doumer established French Indochina in its definitive form. Two salient reasons appear to explain the failure of Vietnamese resistance to the French. First, there was a collapse of leadership. Tu Duc could not govern a country that he never knew or understood, being a bookish creature of the palace. He was unable either to maintain the domestic peace or to unite the country against a foreign threat. The north was already in a state of endemic rebellion before the French arrived. Then, the regicidal regency of Ton That Thuyet and Nguyen Van Tuong was the best that the Hue court could provide by way of leadership during the most critical phase of the French conquest. Neither Ton That Thuyet's reckless schemes nor Nguyen Van Tuong's palace intrigues inspired confidence. The alacrity with which the adult leaders of the royal family and its courtiers made peace with the French in 1885 revealed an absence of options.

The second, and more fundamental, reason for failure can be found in the larger context of the global situation in which European imperial powers were dominating Asia. The only exceptions to this were Japan, which successfully adapted to global changes, Siam, which survived as a semi-colony and convenient buffer between the British and the French, and China, which, although surrendering control of its seaports, had large continental territories where its own political development could continue. Vietnam did not have the samurai leadership of Japan that understood and solved the military problem. It did not have the benefit of a geographical position, as Siam did, that enabled it to enjoy a place of balance between two predatory powers. Nor did it have the vast hinterland of China in which it could sustain the semblance of an independent country. Considering Vietnam's vulnerable terrain and the structural limitations of a government at Hue, there is no apparent reason to think that more effective leadership could have responded successfully to the French challenge. The French conquest brought Vietnamese out of the mono-centric political and cultural focus upon China that had previously prevailed and into a larger world of potentially multi-polar relationships.

11 FRANCO-VIETNAMESE COLONIAL RELATIONS

Intellectuals respond to the colonial regime

By the turn of the century, many educated Vietnamese were endeavoring to think their way through the events of the French conquest, aiming to arrive at some vision of a future for themselves or for their country. Not all Vietnamese were concerned with ideas about a Vietnamese country. The uneducated and probably most of the educated, though it is impossible to estimate with any certainty how many, were chiefly concerned with the welfare of themselves and their families, and they had no definite sense of identification with a nation in the twentieth-century sense. Prior ideas about a Vietnamese country had been almost entirely focused upon the monarchy and upon the mandarinate as an extension of it, which became decreasingly plausible as French rule stabilized.

In Cochinchina, the process of colonial transformation was already into a second generation of Vietnamese for whom the Nguyen monarchy at Hue had no concrete presence in their lives. The traditional mandarinate did not exist for them and educational opportunities pointed toward reading and writing alpha-betically in the French and Vietnamese languages. Classical studies and character writing survived for a time in private schools, but soon faded away. Early twentieth-century responses to French rule in Cochinchina emerged with urban journalism, covert support of a monarch in exile, and rural millenarian movements.

In Annam and Tonkin, the mandarinate continued to exist, presided over by a king and staffed by men educated in character writing, and whose educational and career aspirations were defined by the civil service examination system. Although fewer and fewer men showed interest in the examinations and they were abolished after 1919, and although the greatest challenge to French coloni-alism would come with a later generation of people educated in French and Vietnamese, the ferment of ideas among the last generation to be educated in Literary Chinese characters demonstrated a deep intellectual engagement with the colonial situation arising from the Confucian curriculum that emphasized a commitment to public affairs.

Estimates of the number of men who entered the triennial examinations fall from around six thousand in the late nineteenth century to four thousand at the turn of the century to not many more than one thousand by the 1910s. Regional exam graduates staffed most mandarinal positions in the protectorates of Annam and Tonkin. During the eleven examinations held under French supervision, from 1889 to 1919, 83 doctorates and 107 junior doctorates were awarded. The impact of Paul Doumer's governorship is apparent in an analysis of these 190 men. Doumer detached the mandarins in Tonkin from the Hue court and put them under direct French supervision. Thereafter, the number of degrees awarded to people from Tonkin fell dramatically. In the five exams from 1889 to 1901, 34.2 percent of the higher degrees were awarded to men from Tonkin. However, only 12.9 percent of the higher degrees in the six subsequent exams were awarded to men from Tonkin. On the other hand, while men from the northern provinces of Annam (Thanh Hoa, Nghe An, and Ha Tinh, commonly referred to as Thanh-Nghe-Tinh) received 15.3 percent of the higher degrees through 1901, they received 53.8 percent of those awarded thereafter. The three provinces in the plains adjacent to Hue (Quang Binh, Quang Tri, and Thua Thien) increased their collective percentage more modestly, from 18 percent to 24.7 percent. In the provinces south of Hue, the number of higher graduates declined from 14.4 percent to 8.6 percent, a decline even sharper if calculated with the turn point at 1908 when uprisings broke out there.

The region that became pre-eminent in classical studies during the early years of French rule, the provinces of Nghe An and Ha Tinh, commonly referred to as Nghe-Tinh, produced people who responded to French rule with a degree of intellectual engagement and political activism that put them, in numbers dispro-portionate to other regions, at the forefront of national leadership when the colonial regime failed at mid century. From 1889 to 1919, 30 percent of all higher degrees in the country were awarded to men from Nghe-Tinh; calculating from 1904 to 1919, it was 40 percent. This region, in the plains of the Ca River, was already famous as a cradle of scholars. It was known for chronic poverty, which was widely presumed to have driven its young men to study in order to improve their prospects. During the French era, it was an overflowing reservoir of young men eager to see the world and susceptible to radical ideas about ending the colonial regime.

Nghe-Tinh was the center of anti-Christian agitation in the 1870s and 1880s and of the most persistent resistance to the French conquest into the 1890s. In the 1900s, many Nghe-Tinh people went into exile to Japan and China in search of a way to expel the French. During the First World War, men from Thanh-Nghe-Tinh made up over half of all Vietnamese that volunteered to go to France as soldiers or workers, with most of these being from Nghe-Tinh.

In the 1920s, Nghe-Tinh youth were a significant element among the Vietnamese who went to southern China to join anti-French groups associated with the Chinese communists and nationalists. More than a few Vietnamese communist leaders came from Nghe-Tinh, including Ho Chi Minh, and one of the three Vietnamese groups claiming to be a communist party in 1929–1930 was based there. The Nghe-Tinh soviet uprising in 1930–1931 was the largest episode of violent resistance to French rule during the first four decades of the twentieth century. The communist-led resistance to the French in the late 1940s and early 1950s was strongly supported by the populations of Thanh-Nghe-Tinh, and the government established in northern Vietnam after the departure of the French in 1954 included many people from these provinces.

One aspect of Thanh-Nghe-Tinh that was distinctive under French rule is that it was the least "supervised" of all Vietnamese regions. Making up "northern Annam," this region did not experience the degree of direct French rule that prevailed in Tonkin and, to an even greater extent, in Cochinchina. But neither did it experience the degree of royal authority that prevailed in southern Annam, for only in the nineteenth century had it become part of the Nguyen dynastic realm, and even then it never displayed a sense of connection or of loyalty to the Nguyen monarchy such as existed in the other coastal provinces that were governed by the protectorate regime at Hue. Thanh-Nghe-Tinh was in a relative backwater where the administrative energies radiating from Hanoi and Hue were not fully present. At the same time, many educated men of the region learned to combine their alienation from the protectorate regime with a sense of patriotic attachment to an idealized nation.

A fashionable current of thought among the Tonkin mandarins who worked in close proximity with the center of French authority at Hanoi was an interest in the "new learning" about the modern world that was flooding in from France. This interest remained vague and unfocused, however, because there seemed to be no way to incorporate it into the prevailing ideology and careerism of the mandarinate. A minor trend in Tonkin reacted against the "new learning" by proposing religion as the foundation of a strong future Vietnamese country. Kieu Oanh Mau (1854–1912), despite his checkered career in the Tonkin mandarinate, wrote and published books about Buddhism and popular religious cults. He claimed a spiritual heritage as the most potent Vietnamese asset amidst the tumults of the modern world. The French considered him harmless and allowed him to publish.

In general, mandarinal officials throughout Annam and Tonkin tended to become timeservers, primarily interested in maintaining the social position of their families. Ironically, this class of people had never been as powerful as it became under French rule. Unlike earlier generations of officials, who were often in delicate situations, having to mediate between volatile local interests and a distant, distracted, or weak central authority, twentieth-century magistrates were backed by the considerable coercive powers of an alert and modern colonial regime. Consequently, they espoused the Confucian social values of their education with unprecedented vehemence and effect. As time passed and the classical curriculum that was the ostensible source of their moral authority withered away, they were increasingly viewed by the younger generation as hypocritical guardians of a tradition that they had betrayed. This contradiction between assertions of authority based on tradition being enforced by a modern colonial regime became apparent earliest in southern Annam, where the Nguyen Phuc family had ruled for over three centuries and where mandarinal officials were connected and committed to the royal court at Hue to a relatively greater degree than were officials in Tonkin or northern Annam.

The royal court, however, was in various phases of disarray during the reign of Thanh Thai. He became king at the age of 10 in 1889 and grew to manhood leaving a trail of scandals that some nationalist historians have endeavored to portray as acts of resistance to French rule. A son of Duc Duc, who had been killed by the regents after only three days as king in 1883, Thanh Thai was intelligent, wary, and prone to licentious habits that often turned violent. His interest in being "modern" as displayed in cutting his hair, wearing Western suits, and driving cars made him acceptable to the French for several years. However, in 1906, a new French "high resident" in Hue began to take exception to Thanh Thai's behavior, and demonstrations of antagonism between the two men escalated. In early 1907, Thanh Thai publicly expressed a hope that Japan would expel the French from his country, and the French intercepted correspondence between him and anti-French exiles in China. He was promptly deposed, removed to confinement in the southern coastal resort town of Vung Tau, and replaced by his 8-year-old son.

The reign name assigned to the small new monarch, Duy Tan, is striking evidence that hopes for change were exceedingly widespread among Vietnamese at that time. Duy Tan, a classical expression, literally "to be attached to the new," is generally translated as "reformation," but in Vietnamese can also be glossed as *doi moi*, "to change to the new," which as the name for a recent government policy has been translated as "renovation." In 1907, apparently unbeknownst to the French, Duy Tan also happened to be the name of a secret organization dedicated to the expulsion of the French that already had followers in all of the Vietnamese territories. The leading figure in this organization was a regional exam graduate of 1900 from Nghe An named Phan Boi Chau

(1867–1940). By 1904, when he and a group of disaffected men from northern and southern Annam established the Duy Tan Society, he had already found a prince of the royal family willing to serve as an anti-French pretender to the throne. This was Cuong De (1882–1951), a fourth-generation descendent of Prince Canh, the eldest son of Gia Long who had died as crown prince. In 1907, when Thanh Thai expressed his hope for help from Japan, both Phan Boi Chau and Cuong De were in Tokyo with the same hope.

In the early 1900s, Phan Boi Chau and other educated Vietnamese concerned about the colonial situation were reading the writings of the Chinese reformers Kang Youwei (1858–1927) and Liang Qichao (1873–1929). In addition to elaborating ideas about constitutional monarchy and democracy, these men conveyed to readers of Literary Chinese descriptions of the Meiji reforms in Japan and the thought of European political and social philosophers. Liang Qichao, living in exile in Tokyo, was especially active as a translator of European writers and as a pioneer for using journalism for political propaganda. Phan Boi Chau met Liang Qichao in Tokyo and obtained from him advice as well as introductions to Japanese politicians, which for a few years made it plausible for anti-colonial Vietnamese to look hopefully to Japan. Japan's prestige as an Asian power was unsurpassed as a result of its defeats in war of first China and then Russia. Liang Qichao and his Japanese contacts advised Phan Boi Chau to send Vietnamese students to Japan as a first step.

By 1907, over one hundred Vietnamese boys had arrived in Japan to receive a modern education. More than half of these aspiring students came from Cochinchina and most of the expenses of this educational program came from landowners there. These men were wealthy and therefore able to finance Phan Boi Chau's activities. They were also dissatisfied with the French regime, both for its racism toward them and for how it facilitated the dominance of Chinese entrepreneurs in the local economy. Furthermore, feelings of loyalty to Cuong De were easily aroused among them because of local memories of Cuong De's ancestor Prince Canh, who had governed at Saigon until his death. Furthermore, Cochinchina tended to be alienated from the line of Minh Mang, which, after slandering the southern hero Le Van Duyet, had abandoned the far south to the French. During the next four decades, Cuong De's most faithful adherents were in Cochinchina. On the other hand, the most active partisans of Phan Boi Chau's program to forcibly expel the French were largely from his home region of northern Annam.

The activities of the Duy Tan Society were but the most adventurous aspect of a great ferment among educated Vietnamese inspired by Chinese authors and translators and by Japanese success in modernizing. Phan Boi Chau's emphasis upon seeking foreign assistance to overthrow the French was not shared by men who believed that the Vietnamese should rely upon themselves to supersede the colonial situation by learning from it. Prominent among these were three men from Quang Nam. Tran Quy Cap (1870–1908) and Huynh Thuc Khang (1876–1947) had both received doctoral degrees in the examination of 1904, but rather than pursuing a career in officialdom, they joined Phan Chu Trinh (1872–1926), recipient of a junior doctoral degree in 1901, and set themselves against the mandarinal regime, regarding it as an obstacle to the progress of their country. In 1905, these three men traveled through southern Annam, speaking against what they viewed as an outmoded educational and administrative system. As men who had passed the examinations at the highest level, their words carried weight. But this also earned them the hatred of men who inhabited the protectorate regime.

In 1906, Phan Chu Trinh went to Japan to see for himself the country in which Phan Boi Chau was placing his trust, but he returned to Vietnam with visions of making modern education available in his homeland rather than sending students to study abroad. He wrote a letter to Governor General Paul Beau vainly appealing for the French to discard the examination system, the monarchy, and the mandarinal structure of administration and instead to institute reforms to modernize the country.

In 1907, Phan Chu Trinh and like-minded men promoted the opening of schools, inspired by the writings and the example of Fukuzawa Yukichi (1835–1901), whose efforts to make modern education available to all Japanese had led to the founding of Keio University. These schools promoted literacy in the Vietnamese alphabet and spread information about history, literature, science, and hygiene. The best-known of these schools was the one established in Hanoi, the Tonkin Public School (Dong Kinh Nghia Thuc). For several months in late 1907 and early 1908, until closed down by the French, it bustled with classes, public lectures, publications, theatrical productions, and campaigns to "modernize," which could mean something as simple as cutting one's hair, a violation of the Confucian code of filial piety, or as complex as organizing business ventures, thereby entering the dangerous realm of the colonial economy. Similar schools were also set up in southern Annam, particularly in Quang Nam, the home province of Phan Chu Trinh and other prominent reformists.

There was an overlap of people involved in this educational movement from both those of Phan Chu Trinh's reformist persuasion and those more inclined toward Phan Boi Chau's advocacy of an armed uprising against the French. The more radical edge of these activities provoked the French to shut the Hanoi school, but not before a momentum of public awareness and conspiratorial schemes produced an outbreak of disorders in 1908 that led to a shift in the rhetoric of French colonial policy and in Vietnamese responses to it.

The 1908 disturbances and their sequel

In Quang Nam, the operations of Phan Boi Chau's Duy Tan Society, the modernizing schools inspired by Phan Chu Trinh, heavy French demands for corvée labor to exploit coal mines, the irresponsible behavior of Vietnamese magistrates, and a relatively large peasant population in distress all overlapped and, in March 1908, combined to initiate three months of disturbances that spread down the coast through Quang Ngai, Binh Dinh, and Phu Yen Provinces. Thousands of peasants attacked tax collectors and camped around administrative centers until dispersed by French soldiers with episodes of violence and loss of life.

In late June 1908, a conspiracy was put in motion to spark an insurrection by poisoning the French garrison in Hanoi; mutinous Vietnamese soldiers were to be mobilized and supported by Hoang Hoa Tham (1858–1913), the last survivor from the anti-French resistance who was ensconced in the mountains. Young men inspired by Phan Boi Chau and by the excitement generated around the Tonkin Public School initiated this event. The plot was poorly planned and the French quickly squelched it.

Hoang Hoa Tham (also known as De Tham) came from an upland family that had participated in the anti-Nguyen uprising led by Nong Van Van in the 1830s. He made his career among the mixture of Chinese and Vietnamese who followed Liu Yongfu in the 1870s and 1880s and negotiated an arrangement with the French in the late 1890s that allowed him to survive in the mountains of Yen The district north of Bac Giang, east of Thai Nguyen, and southwest of Lang Son, a region with very difficult terrain. His implication in the Hanoi poison plot led the French to move determinedly against him, which ended with his death in 1913.

Meanwhile, in Cochinchina, Gilbert Tran Chanh Chieu (1867–1919), a French citizen who was a Saigon newspaper editor and businessman, was arrested, along with many of his associates, when the French became aware of his activities on behalf of Phan Boi Chau. He had been the in-country contact for sending funds and students from Cochinchina to Phan Boi Chau in Japan. The French had informants among a group of wealthy Cochinchinese who traveled with aspiring students to meet with Phan Boi Chau in Japan in early 1908. Consequently, France pressured Japan to expel the Vietnamese, which was done in 1909. Phan Boi Chau went to southern China where he fruitlessly endeavored to buy arms for Hoang Hoa Tham. Cuong De spent several years traveling in China, Siam, Europe, and even made a brief clandestine visit to his supporters in Cochinchina in 1913. He returned to Japan during the First World War, from where he thereafter conducted ineffectual anti-French activities with frequent visits to China.

Paul Beau completed his term as governor general and departed Indochina in February 1908, just before the disturbances began. Louis Alphonse Bonhoure (1864–1909), a colonial functionary recently arrived from an assignment in French Guiana, was acting governor general during the troubles from February to September 1908, at which time he was replaced by Antony Wladislas Klobukowski (1855–1934). Klobukowski had started his career as a colonial administrator in Vietnam in the 1880s. He became a close associate of Paul Bert in 1886 and married Bert's daughter. Thereafter he served in a number of other colonial assignments but was sent back to Indochina in 1908 because of his prior experience there, his association with Paul Bert's success in establishing the protectorate regime, and his reputation for efficient administration.

In retrospect, it may appear that the most important aspect of the 1908 disturbances was the road not taken by French authorities, as if they were incapable of comprehending Phan Chu Trinh's critique of the mandarinate and of acting on it to promote a more modern administration. The inability of the French regime to abandon the mandarinate, despite its corruption, which was obvious even to the French, might plausibly be attributed to Klobukowski because of his prior investment in Bert's policy of relying upon this class of Vietnamese officials. However, Phan Chu Trinh and all other reformist scholars, along with a host of other prisoners, had already been sent to the Con Son Island penal colony before Klobukowski arrived in Indochina. For the French, the possibility of working with the reformists was never considered as an option. Like the tax and administrative regime established by Paul Doumer, the protectorate scheme established by Paul Bert was firmly fixed in the French idea of Indochina and never abandoned. Among the French was a paralyzing fear that any major restructuring of the colonial relationship could lead to the loss of a privileged position that had been achieved after decades of effort.

But while the dismissal of any questioning of existing policy was instinctive among the French in Indochina, matters looked differently from the vantage of Paris. There, in the wake of the events of 1908, a lively debate ensued among politicians over colonial policy in Indochina. The debate was focused on the merits of an associationist policy that would ostensibly promote the material well being of colonized people and open space for Vietnamese cultural development in "association" with the French colonial government. The idea of association was abstract and disconnected from colonial realities, but it was adopted as official policy and led to the appointment as governor general of a prominent politician, Albert Sarraut (1872–1962). Sarraut was from an influential family in the newspaper business and had the gift of speaking with persuasive eloquence. He served in Indochina from November 1911 to January 1914 and from January 1917 to May 1919. During his three-year absence for reasons of health, three successive colonial administrators took his place without distinguishing themselves in any discernible way. Consequently, the second decade of the twentieth century is generally known as the Sarraut era in Indochinese history. He inspired a significant effort to arouse Vietnamese enthusiasm for French rule.

Aside from minor initiatives in medical services and education, Sarraut's contribution to the history of Indochina lay in his promotion of a new formulation of Vietnamese tradition. He invited Vietnamese intellectuals to explore and define a Vietnamese culture that could exist in harmonious association with French rule. What this meant in practice was the cultivation of a narrowly Confucianized version of Vietnamese culture that stressed social order and obedience to hierarchy. As the examination system and character writing were abandoned, the Vietnamese alphabet was mobilized to create a new medium for cultural dissemination. Under Sarraut, the government of Indochina actively supported the publication of vernacular books and journals to develop the aura of a traditional Vietnamese identity that was indebted to French rule for its continued survival amidst the tumults of the modern world.

Frenchmen sympathetic with a conservative and romanticized vision of Vietnamese culture joined with groups of cooperative Vietnamese in organizations such as "The Association of Friends of Old Hue" and "The League of Friends of Annam" to propagate the theme of Franco-Vietnamese friendship among both educated Vietnamese and enlightened French colons. Sarraut's administration subsidized Vietnamese journals to promote a colonial version of Vietnamese tradition. For example, in the journal *Nam Phong* (South Wind), Pham Quynh (1892–1945) argued in 1918 that the example of French literature made it possible to identify Nguyen Du's *Kim Van Kieu* (The Tale of Kieu) as the masterpiece of Vietnamese literature and that until the coming of the French the significance of this work in Vietnamese culture had not been appreciated. This initiated a debate among Vietnamese in which, among other things, it was asserted that Pham Quynh adored this work because it romanced the virtues of a prostitute, of which in serving the French he was one.

In opening vernacular writing to the issue of cultural, and inevitably national, identity, Sarraut and his assistants wagered that the French could retain control of the discussion. Within a decade, however, they were proven wrong when in the mid 1920s a new generation of Vietnamese began to challenge the French version of Vietnamese identity. Nevertheless, the Confucianized version of Vietnamese tradition that was fostered during the Sarraut era became a major force in the thinking of later Vietnamese nationalists of all ideological persuasions. It linked in their minds an outmoded cultural tradition with a hated colonial regime, overtly manifested in the mandarins of the protectorate, and it gave a sharp edge to the need for a new vision of national society and culture.

Sarraut's rhetorical fervor for Franco-Vietnamese friendship was nestled in the wartime urgency of France fighting desperately year after year against German invaders. With most French and the best Vietnamese military units deployed to Europe, French administrators in Indochina perceived themselves to be vulnerable to the vicissitudes of endemic Vietnamese resistance. Despite this perception, the series of anti-French episodes that occurred during the Sarraut era demonstrate that the French regime was strong enough to easily dispose of any opposition and that anti-French movements were localized and disconnected from each other. The parade of events that unnerved the French during this time nevertheless reveals that the colonial regime had stimulated opposition from constituencies in nearly all parts of the Vietnamese realm.

Domestic ferment with Europe at war

In 1911, inspired by the Chinese revolution, Phan Boi Chau organized the Vietnamese Restoration Society (Viet Nam Quang Phuc Hoi) in southern China and endeavored to rebuild a network of activists in Tonkin. The only results of this were some assassinations and bombings in 1913, which attracted the attention of French security agents who pressured the new Chinese government to cease encouraging Phan Boi Chau's group. Phan Boi Chau subsequently spent three years, 1914–1917, in a Chinese jail.

Luong Ngoc Quyen (1890–1917), an early follower of Phan Boi Chau who had studied in Japan and was active in the Restoration Society, was arrested in Hong Kong in 1915 and extradited to Hanoi. Charged with complicity in a 1913 bomb attack, he was imprisoned at the Thai Nguyen Penitentiary, sixty-five kilometers north of Hanoi. The senior French official at Thai Nguyen had alienated local townspeople and soldiers in the Vietnamese garrison with his odious behavior. At the end of August 1917, the garrison mutinied, led by Vietnamese sergeants, who freed the prisoners, some of whom had been followers of Hoang Hoa Tham in the nearby mountains. The soldiers, prisoners, and local townspeople, led by Luong Ngoc Quyen and a sergeant named Trinh Van Can, hastily fortified Thai Nguyen but within a few days French forces retook the town after heavy fighting in which Luong Ngoc Quyen died. Large numbers of the Vietnamese resisters, including Trinh Van Can, escaped to the mountains where the last of them were cornered and eliminated during the following six months. This uprising was the most spectacular anti-colonial event with some connection, however indirect, to Phan Boi Chau's activities. It demonstrated that people of various classes could be provoked to unite against the French.

The construction of the Hanoi–Yunnan railroad brought distress to the people who lived along the line by demands for labor and supplies. In late 1914 and early 1915, inhabitants in the region of Yen Bay, about halfway between Hanoi and the Yunnan border, openly resisted French authority. They had no modern weapons and were soon subjugated. By this time, railroads had already been constructed between Hanoi and Lang Son on the Guangxi border of China and between Hanoi and Vinh. Railroads had also been completed between Hue and Da Nang and between Nha Trang and Saigon. Hue would be connected by rail to Vinh in 1927 and to Nha Trang in 1936. The development of the railroad network in Indochina introduced a new class of Vietnamese who worked to maintain and operate the lines and the trains. Many men returning from France after the First World War had acquired skills that led to their employment in the railroad system, as well as in shipyards, mines, and factories. The railroad system was a matter of pride for the French and, although it did not turn a profit until after completion of the Hanoi–Saigon connection in the late 1930s, it promoted economic growth and connectivity among the Vietnamese regions. It also aroused among Vietnamese an experience of travel and an awareness of wider horizons that contributed substance to nationalist ideas that were beginning to take form at this time.

In Cochinchina, popular movements based on the leadership of charismatic religious figures had produced a series of anti-French disturbances in the 1860s, 1870s, and 1880s. This tendency toward what has been called peasant politics in the guise of millenarian enthusiasm took strength from the large population of landless wage laborers in rural Cochinchina who existed in precarious economic conditions and from a rejection of the Buddhism espoused by the monks in richly endowed and officially sanctioned temples that prospered in towns and cities. The Seven Mountains region near the Vinh Te Canal on the Cambodian border in western Cochinchina was the center of a series of Khmer–Viet religious fermentations out of which individuals, who were believed to have powers of healing and magic, periodically emerged to organize and lead millennial uprisings against established authority. Western Cochinchina was a reservoir for mobilizing this volatile tradition of popular Buddhism and mass religious excitement that at times spread easily into eastern Cochinchina where power sat in Saigon.

At the same time, many secret societies in the large Chinese immigrant communities in Cochinchina, which are sometimes generally referred to as belonging to the Heaven and Earth Society, were being Vietnamized. These societies were organized for the purpose of mutual aid and often had a quasi-religious aspect. Built into these societies were patron–client relationships in which wealthier members looked after the welfare of the less fortunate in return for services and loyalty.

In the early 1910s, labor requirements for building roads and canals combined with a heavy tax regime to put pressure on the realms of both millennial sectarianism and mutual welfare secret societies. A young man named Phan Phat Sanh (1892–1916), who was conversant with both of these realms, attracted followers and made plans to brush aside the French with supernatural powers. Phan Phat Sanh was reportedly the son of a policeman in the Chinese city of Cholon; he studied mysticism, fortune telling, sorcery, geomancy, magic, and explosives in the Seven Mountains and at Kampot, a short distance across the Cambodian border, where he gained inspiration from an uprising that had occurred there in 1909. He proclaimed himself a Buddha and an emperor with the title Phan Xich Long (Phan the Red Dragon) and in March 1913 prepared to attack the centers of colonial government in Saigon. He was arrested and his bombs were discovered and defused. Nevertheless, some six hundred of his rural adherents invaded Saigon armed with amulets and primitive weapons. They were easily dispersed, but the French were unnerved by such bold, albeit ineffectual, defiance. By coincidence, it was at this same time that Cuong De was clandestinely visiting his wealthy landlord supporters in Cochinchina. He managed to get away ahead of French security agents, but the French associated the Phan Phat Sanh uproar with him and with the 1913 assassins and bomb throwers in Tonkin sent by Phan Boi Chau's Restoration Society. They neglected to address the causes of rural distress in Cochinchina that had put force behind Phan Phat Sanh's movement.

In the years that followed, conditions in Cochinchina were aggravated by coercive recruitment of men to serve in wartime France. Compared with northern Annam where large numbers of men freely volunteered, in Cochinchina there was little enthusiasm. Consequently, French authorities resorted to harsh measures, which simply added to popular resentment against them. When news about the siege of Verdun spread through rural Cochinchina in early 1916 along with hopeful rumors that the French were about to be defeated, a series of local uprisings culminated in a small invasion of Saigon by peasants intent upon breaking into the central prison where Phan Phat Sanh was incarcerated. As in 1913, these riots posed no serious threat to the French, but Phan Phat Sanh was executed as a precaution against future unrest. In the distinctive social, cultural, and economic situation of Cochinchina, popular religion and mutual aid societies continued to be important for the Vietnamese population most affected by direct French rule and within a few years would inspire the rise of new and enduring religions.

Meanwhile, the monarchy continued to figure in the anti-colonial schemes of some Vietnamese and became the focus of a plot that broke into the open a few weeks after the 1916 ripple of uprisings in Cochinchina. The 16-year-old King Duy Tan resented being supervised by his elderly regents and by the French who stood behind them and in 1915 caused concern in both groups by speaking out against what he viewed as French looting of his dynasty's ancestral treasures and French violations of the protectorate agreement. French authorities interpreted his outbursts as adolescent angst and aimed to calm him with a royal wedding ceremony in January 1916. But his attitude also reflected the views of some members of his retinue, and he remained susceptible to ideas for taking advantage of the European war to obtain concessions from the French.

One person with such ideas was Tran Cao Van (1866–1916). He was an educated man from a village near Dien Ban in Quang Nam who had a varied career in the 1880s and 1890s as keeper of a Daoist temple, geography teacher, geomancer, and participant in a minor anti-French uprising before retiring to the obscurity of his home village at the turn of the century. In 1908 he was arrested and sent to the penal colony on Con Son Island in the wake of the disturbances of that year. Released in 1913, he returned to Quang Nam and subsequently made contact with the Restoration Society network that extended into central Annam via Siam and linked activists with sympathizers among Vietnamese soldiers in garrisons extending from Hue to Quang Ngai.

In early 1916 there happened to be at Hue a large encampment of recruits being trained prior to embarkation for France. The news of war in Europe was bleak, and morale among the recruits was low. Arms and supplies were accumulating to accompany the men aboard ship. Tran Cao Van saw an opportunity to mobilize soldiers and recruits to initiate an uprising that might inspire Vietnamese in other parts of Indochina. He met clandestinely with Duy Tan, who agreed to play his part in the plan. However, in early May 1916 when Duy Tan fled the palace to join plotters in the mountains, the French had already learned of the scheme. Duy Tan was seized a few kilometers outside of Hue, and most Vietnamese soldiers were disarmed and confined. Tran Cao Van was executed with other leaders of the plot.

Duy Tan was sent, with his mother, wife, and sister, to join his father, the former king Thanh Thai, who had been living in confinement at Vung Tau since 1907. Later in 1916, the two former kings and their families were exiled to the island of Réunion in the Indian Ocean. Within days of Duy Tan's arrest, a new king was enthroned. This was Khai Dinh (1885–1925), a son of Dong Khanh, who had sat on the throne from 1885 to 1889. Like his father, he was a willing collaborator with the French, and from then the monarchy offered no further worry to colonial authorities.

The Indochina prison system tended to nurture anti-colonial activism because it brought together potentially disaffected people from all Vietnamese regions and encouraged a radical attitude toward the regime. The various prisons manifested a great variety of conditions depending upon time and place, upon the degree of isolation from the non-prison population, and upon the personal qualities of administrators. These factors were all part of the February 1918 disturbance on the Con Son Island penal colony. During the early years of the First World War when France was overwhelmed by a sense of emergency, a relatively lenient prison director had moderated the potential for insubordination by giving prisoners certain freedoms that included participation in the local island economy outside the prison walls. After the United States joined the Allies and the war began to turn against Germany, this man was replaced by a disabled veteran of the Battle of Verdun who instituted a more disciplined and harshly punitive regime. The reaction among prisoners against this change was easily repressed, but the briefly violent event demonstrated that prison populations lived in an overtly confrontational relationship with French authority where the colonial situation was devoid of euphemism and where Sarraut-style idealism could not penetrate.

A combination of abstract expressions of Franco-Vietnamese friendship and of an underworld of easily suppressed anti-colonial resistance characterized the years during which France was locked in a dire struggle with German invaders. The French had no capacity for administrative or economic initiative at this time and could do little more than resort to eloquent blandishments, of which Albert Sarraut was a master. For their part, the Vietnamese were incapable of any unified response to French rule and could do little more than respond to local grievances and episodic opportunities. However, after the war, Indochina bustled with a developing economy driven by the high tide of French investment; with a growing class of workers in mines, factories, shipyards, railroads, and plantations; with a vigorous expansion of vernacular journalism and publishing; with Vietnamese efforts to obtain greater participation in government; and with the emergence of a generation of youth that began to experiment with new forms of anti-colonial organization.

The beginning of Saigon politics

One of the publishing ventures subsidized by the Sarraut government was a French-language Saigon newspaper, *La Tribune Indigène*, begun in 1917, which soon became the mouthpiece of Bui Quang Chieu (1872–1945), a man from the Mekong delta who in the 1890s had studied in France and obtained a degree in agricultural engineering. From 1897 he was employed by the colonial government as an agricultural expert at various assignments in Indochina. He became a French citizen and eventually owned extensive Mekong ricelands. By the mid 1910s, he had developed a network of acquaintances among Vietnamese administrators, businessmen, landowners, and intellectuals who were keen to give substance to Sarraut's rhetoric. He was especially concerned to expand

Vietnamese involvement in economic enterprise as the basis of promoting participation in colonial politics. He was active in organizing mutual aid societies in which Vietnamese could pool their resources for business initiatives. One of his early collaborators had, at My Tho in 1915, built the first Vietnamese-owned rice mill to compete with the Chinese businesses that monopolized the rice trade.

Bui Quang Chieu believed that, fixated on the fossilized protectorate, the French were perpetuating lamentable aspects of traditional Vietnamese government. He called for an independent judiciary; for fewer, more professional, and better-paid administrators; and for the elimination of the large numbers of underlings who fed from the scraps of the regime. He also advocated opening the naturalization process for more Vietnamese to become citizens, thereby conferring rights enabling greater participation in public debate and politics, and he furthermore favored expanding the electorate for Vietnamese seats on the Cochinchina Colonial Council. However, these proposals did not interest Sarraut who, in his last years as governor general, gave more attention to laying a basis for modern higher education by abolishing the examination system and reopening the University of Hanoi, which had been closed during the disturbances of 1908.

In late summer 1919, shortly after Sarraut departed Indochina, an opportunity arose for Bui Quang Chieu to combine his economic and political goals when protests broke out against Chinese business monopolies in Saigon. Bui Quang Chieu and his friends called for a boycott of Chinese retail businesses, organized a commercial society that established the first Vietnamese-owned bank, and endeavored to open a congress for economic development in Cochinchina. Many French administrators were sympathetic, but they could not act against Chinese business without undermining the entire colonial economy. As for the Vietnamese, despite small bursts of enthusiasm, the task of displacing Chinese business was too monumental to even comprehend, and the boycott campaign faded away by the time a new governor general, Maurice Long (1866–1923), arrived in February 1920.

Long was a liberal politician who had supported Sarraut's ideas about developing Franco-Vietnamese cooperation. Although he proved to be a cautious administrator, he nevertheless did push forward a reform of the Cochinchina Colonial Council that increased Vietnamese representation from six to ten, increased French representation from twelve to fourteen, and expanded the number of Vietnamese eligible to vote from less than 2,000 to around 20,000.

The people gathered around Bui Quang Chieu's agenda, collectively known as Constitutionalists, included Nguyen Phan Long (1889–1960), who since 1920 had edited the newspaper *L'Écho Annamite*. After Bui Quang Chieu, he became the most prominent of the Constitutionalists. Although he had argued against the electoral reform on the basis that it would open politics to irresponsible people without social standing, he was ironically elected in the autumn 1922 election, the first to be held under the new law.

The Council had been established in the 1880s and was the center of power for French colons in Cochinchina. Vietnamese members of the Council, with few exceptions, had for decades simply followed the French and competed for the benefits of doing that. The 1922 reform, however, led to Constitutionalists winning seats on the Council and speaking out against the most notoriously corrupt practices of the administration. Their élitism and the opposition of French colons would confound their efforts to play a leading role in the emerging Vietnamese politics of the 1920s and 1930s, but during the years 1923–1926 they opened a door for the younger generation.

Other initiatives of Long were a minor expansion of opportunities for Vietnamese in colonial administration and a significant expansion of primary and secondary education in Cochinchina. Realizing that his government could not meet the demand for education, he allowed new private schools to open. However, the driving force of French policy in Indochina was now the flow of investment that became a flood after the 1922 Marseille Colonial Exposition.

Long was replaced not by a politician susceptible to Sarraut's thought but by a career colonial administrator fresh from over fifteen years' experience governing French colonies in Africa, Martial Henri Merlin (1860–1935). Merlin, governor general from August 1922 to April 1925, ended the era of Sarrautian idealism with a determination to enforce a disciplined calm to facilitate economic development. He revealed his priorities in 1924 when he rolled back Long's educational reforms, which he considered unnecessary. French colons welcomed his attitude, and during his tenure they pushed back at the dream of Franco-Vietnamese friendship that threatened their position of racial superiority. This exacerbated tensions as Constitutionalists publicly dissented in the Council, uncensored Francophone newspapers proliferated, and a new generation of Vietnamese came of age.

In the decade following the end of the First World War, investment in Indochina was more than fifteen times what it had been during the preceding three decades. As automobiles spread around the world, Indochinese rubber production increased by more than thirty times in the 1920s, and the number of workers on rubber plantations increased from fewer than 3,000 to more than 80,000. Coal production increased nearly 300 percent. The annual number of applications for mining licenses increased by a factor of thirty-five. By 1929, more than 85,000 people were employed in textile factories. Many new industries that manufactured goods for local consumption were developed. The export of rice doubled.

This happened to be the time when the first generation of Vietnamese students to be educated in French rather than in Literary Chinese became politically active. During the first half of the 1920s, members of this generation began to gather around the Constitutionalists in Saigon. They came to be known as the Jeune (young) Annam movement, which was more radical than the Constitutionalists but developed confidence in public activism under the patronage of prominent Constitutionalists. The most active Jeune Annam figure was Nguyen An Ninh (1900–1943), who in 1923 returned from three years of studying law in France to edit *La Cloche Fêlée*, a newspaper that vented his passionate opposition to the colonial regime.

The emergence of the Constitutionalists and the Jeune Annam activists occurred during a particularly notorious time in the government of Cochinchina under the leadership of Maurice Cognacq (1870–1949), governor from 1921 to 1926. Cognacq's circle of cronies included corrupt businessmen and professional thugs. His chief of police was the discredited administrator who had provoked the 1917 Thai Nguyen mutiny and who had subsequently made a fortune in the alcohol monopoly. Cognacq was prone to outrageous statements that exacerbated Franco-Vietnamese tensions.

As for Merlin, other than his reputation for dashing cold water on hopes inspired by Sarraut, he became most famously known for narrowly escaping unharmed from a bomb thrown in 1924 by a young Vietnamese during a banquet in the British concession at Guangzhou in southern China. He departed Indochina in April 1925, just before a series of events fundamentally altered the Franco-Vietnamese relationship.

In retrospect, it may be tempting to imagine that in the early 1920s there was a moment of opportunity for the French to follow up and build on the enthusiasm for Franco-Vietnamese collaboration elicited by Sarraut. It is plausibly true that this was the last time that political concessions might have turned Indochinese politics away from confrontation and stalemate. But, it is also true that the racist attitude of the French colons and the degree to which colonial administration served the interests of investment made such concessions very improbable. The Sarraut magic was not meant for real life, but before the hopes it inspired finally died, there was a brief but fateful resurgence of expectancy in 1925 when Alexandre Varenne (1870–1947) was appointed governor general.

Cochinchina and the new generation

A leftist coalition was elected to power in France in 1924. It included many politicians opposed to colonialism, which led in 1925 to the replacement of Merlin by Varenne, a Socialist politician who had expressed sympathy for Vietnamese aspirations. Although disowned by his own party for accepting the colonial appointment, Varenne believed that he should do what he could to apply his political beliefs to the Indochinese situation. However, between Merlin's departure in April and Varenne's arrival in November, a series of unprecedented events had begun to change the political atmosphere in Indochina, and Varenne was immobilized between Vietnamese hope and French colon fear.

The shift in French politics encouraged Phan Chu Trinh to return to Indochina after fourteen years of voluntary exile in France that had followed his release from prison in 1911. He arrived in Saigon in June 1925. Shortly after, Phan Boi Chau was arrested by French agents in China and brought to Hanoi to stand trial. Suddenly, the two major figures of the older generation who had chosen exile over living under French colonialism were back in the country. Fresh from the outside world, the venerable voices of Phan Chu Trinh, in public lectures, and Phan Boi Chau, speaking in his defense during his trial, woke many Vietnamese from the mental somnolence induced by living under the French regime.

In addition to these Vietnamese voices from the past, the dissonant voices of angry Frenchmen filled Saigon newspapers during the summer of 1925. André Malraux (1901–1976), a French writer accused of stealing antiquities while adventuring in Cambodia, conceived a repugnance for the colonial regime and, taking the side of his Vietnamese friends in the Jeune Annam movement, published a Saigon newspaper called *Indochine*, in which he denounced colonialism and engaged in a public feud with Governor Cognacq. The two men traded public insults until Cognacq managed to shut down Malraux's newspaper by intimidating the printers. This spectacle of verbal battle between Frenchmen inspired Vietnamese observers to imagine that times were changing, particularly since one of the combatants was the despised Cochinchinese governor.

While waiting for the new governor general to arrive, the French were also waiting and preparing for the death of King Khai Dinh, who had suffered from spinal tuberculosis for several years. His health declined rapidly from mid summer, and he died in early November. His 12-year-old heir, Bao Dai, was studying in Europe. The French decided to leave him in Europe to complete his studies and meanwhile to administer the protectorate without a king. The monarchy had already become an object of derision, not only among the reformists of the old generation like Phan Chu Trinh, but even more generally among the younger generation. Yet, the absence of a king in the country was unprecedented and gave edge to a sensation of passing into a new era.

Within two weeks of Khai Dinh's death, Varenne arrived in Saigon and was immediately pressured to respond to Vietnamese expectations by Nguyen Phan Long, who met with him and presented an itemization of reforms. Under countervailing pressure from the French colons, Varenne equivocated and proceeded to Hanoi where Phan Boi Chau had just been sentenced to life imprisonment with hard labor. Although Varenne decided to pardon the old foe of France and allow him to retire to Hue under house arrest, this did not dispel the hardening Vietnamese perception of the new governor general as unwilling or unable to initiate change, and disappointment rapidly spread.

Shortly after Varenne's arrival, Malraux began publishing a new newspaper called *Indochine Enchaîné*, in which he renewed his verbal duel with Cognacq. At the same time, Nguyen An Ninh restarted his *La Cloche Fêlée*, which earlier had ceased publication when he took a trip to France. He now became even more critical of the French regime than he had been before.

Nguyen Phan Long's *L'Écho Annamite* also registered chagrin at Varenne's pusillanimity, and Bui Quang Chieu, despairing of Varenne, went to France to present his plan for reform directly to the government in Paris. He called for basic civil liberties, expanded educational opportunities, administrative and judicial reforms, greater Vietnamese representation in government, extension to Indochina of French labor legislation, and suppression of the alcohol monopoly. Although he had friends among French politicians, Third Republic politics were too fragile to bear the weight of such a program of reform, particularly since the French colons in Indochina also had their allies among politicians in Paris and they were at the same time calling for the recall of Varenne because he was not firm enough toward the Vietnamese. Bui Quang Chieu's trip was in vain.

During the early weeks of 1926, Jeune Annam activists took up the cause of a Vietnamese journalist being prosecuted for exposing the abuse of workers from Tonkin and Annam at Cochinchina rubber plantations and rice farms. In late March, they organized a public rally in Saigon. Tracts were distributed that called for political action with rhetoric reminiscent of communist slogans in Europe, and Nguyen An Ninh gave a rousing speech. He and two of his associates were arrested a few days later. In subsequent weeks, *La Cloche Fêlée* serially published Karl Marx's *Communist Manifesto*. While Nguyen Phan Long and other Constitutionalists were dismayed by this radical turn, it propelled youth into a new politics of the streets.

A few days after the rally, Bui Quang Chieu returned from his trip to France and was met at the dockside by a crowd of Vietnamese showing their support for his agenda and a crowd of French people demonstrating against him. He scrambled away to avert an incident, and his later mild utterances discredited him among the younger generation.

Meanwhile, Phan Chu Trinh died. In early April, Jeune Annam organized a funeral procession through the streets of Saigon that included contingents of students from all over Cochinchina. The efforts of authorities to punish students for absenting classes and for wearing black armbands provoked an escalation of school boycotts as students expanded their mourning of Phan Chu Trinh to protest the harsh discipline and racist attitudes of their French teachers. Student activism spread from Saigon to other cities in Cochinchina and, to a lesser extent, in Annam and Tonkin. Unrest also spread to urban workers, who were emboldened to organize strikes to improve their salaries and working conditions.

Varenne restored a modicum of calm by enforcing public order, which included the expulsion of insubordinate students from their schools, and by sending Cognacq back to France, thereby removing what he viewed as a primary cause of the disturbances in Cochinchina. Malraux was also induced to return to France. The Jeune Annam movement had burst out of its Constitutionalist chrysalis but began to lose its coherence as members scattered in various directions, taking with them commitments to resist the colonial state that found many manifestations.

Some of the Jeune Annam activists with the means for travel went to France where they studied and gained experience in anti-colonial politics. Some of these returned to Indochina a few years later with commitments to communism in either its Stalinist or Trotskyist version. For a few, Paris was a stop on the way to Moscow and the embrace of the Third Communist International (Comintern), which promised world revolution. Young Vietnamese in France during the 1920s increasingly organized anti-colonial propaganda activities, sometimes with the support of sympathetic French people. Meanwhile, most Vietnamese of the new generation had to come to terms with the reality of living in Indochina.

By 1926, the role of newspapers in expanding the realm of commentary on public affairs had been clearly demonstrated. From then, a new generation of aspiring journalists expressed their political aims through investigative reporting to uncover corruption and abuse and through editorializing essays. Censorship was less strict in Cochinchina than it was in Annam and Tonkin. It was also less strict in the French language than in Vietnamese. Nevertheless, the emerging new generation created a great surge of publishing in the alphabetic vernacular throughout the Vietnamese regions of Indochina, not only of newspapers but also of journals, books, and pamphlets. For example, between 1923 and 1928 approximately sixty daily and weekly Vietnamese newspapers were started in Indochina. Many had a relatively short life-span due to financial and censorship problems, but they continued to appear. Journals that typically appeared monthly or bi-monthly were produced on a wide range of topics. In 1925 there were around thirty-five Vietnamese journals; by 1930 there were seventy-five. The rush of the new generation into vernacular alphabetic print was a major event. It was accompanied by an expansion of alphabetic literacy that in the 1930s enabled the emergence of new literary trends as well as the widespread dissemination of political programs that crossed the boundaries separating the three colonial jurisdictions of Vietnam.

After his release from prison and a trip to France, Nguyen An Ninh,withdrew to his home village of Hoc Mon, a short distance northwest of Saigon, where in 1928 he organized a secret revolutionary society with a network of adherents numbering a few hundred. Within months, French authorities uncovered his activities and he was returned to prison. His turn to the countryside appears to have been partly influenced by an anarchist dream of "returning to the people." But he was also influenced by a new religion that had appeared in Cochinchina.

The popular Buddhist millennialism and the mutual-aid secret societies that had contextualized the rural disturbances of 1913 and 1916 had not disappeared. Within ten years, the continuing distress of landless Cochinchinese peasants combined with the altruism of sympathetic Vietnamese landlords and civil servants to create the Cao Dai religion. Cao Dai combined aspects of several religious, philosophical, and literary traditions from both Asia and Europe based on messages received from the one deity that was believed to exist behind all religions. Cao Dai operated through a hierarchy modeled on the Roman Catholic Church and established communities that reified the landlord–tenant relationship into a fellowship of believers. It was loosely associated with a constellation of secret societies cum popular cults that were active in rural Cochinchina. It spread widely, organizing rural communities and building temples. Its leaders erected an impressive cathedral in Tay Ninh, around eighty kilometers northwest of Saigon.

Cao Dai was a model of Vietnamese banding together from various social classes to address problems exacerbated by the colonial state. Its concern for Vietnamizing rural society away from the economic exploitation of Chinese business and the administrative indifference of French officials overlapped to some extent with the aims of Constitutionalists. Nguyen Phan Long took a strong interest in the new religion. Although the very existence of Cao Dai expressed alienation from the colonial project, the French perceived no immediate threat to their authority and did not interfere with it.

The new generation in Tonkin and Annam

Activist members of the new generation in Tonkin, galvanized by the events of 1925–1926, gathered in Hanoi and were initially involved in publishing efforts. The level of French surveillance and censorship, however, stymied them, and in December 1927 they organized the Vietnamese Nationalist Party under the leadership of Nguyen Thai Hoc (1902–1930). This organization was modeled on the Chinese Nationalist Party, which for several years had been based in southern China. It was of necessity a clandestine party but, spreading rapidly to include adherents in nearly all parts of Tonkin, it was soon infiltrated by French agents.

In Annam, people imprisoned after the 1908 disturbances began to be released in the 1910s. At that time, some of them aimed to associate with Phan Boi Chau's Restoration Society, and they formed a clandestine organization, many members of which resided at Vinh in Nghe An, Phan Boi Chau's home province where his in-country contacts were thickest. Students, teachers, and other members of the new generation began to join in 1926. This organization changed its name several times through the years as it repeatedly redefined its aims and became progressively more radical. It is usually referred to either as Phuc Viet, one of its early names, to resonate with Phan Boi Chau's Restoration (Quang Phuc) Society or as Tan ("new") Viet, one of its last names. Because of Phan Boi Chau's influence, it had connections with exiles in China, which it maintained even after Phan Boi Chau's capture. By 1926 it was in contact with a group in southern China known as the Vietnamese Revolutionary Youth League, in which several of its younger members had become active, and in 1927 there was a failed effort to merge the two organizations.

The Youth League had been formed in 1925 as part of the extensive Comintern presence in Guangzhou to support the alliance between the Chinese Nationalist Party and the Chinese Communist Party in preparation for a joint expedition against the warlords who dominated central and northern China. Building on a group of young anti-French Vietnamese who had gathered in southern China and led by a Comintern agent later known as Ho Chi Minh (1890–1969), the Youth League was busy establishing networks in the Vietnamese regions of Indochina, disseminating propaganda, and clandestinely bringing young people to Guangzhou for training. Ho Chi Minh, originally from Nghe An, came to China at the end of 1924 after a year and a half in Moscow; prior to that, he had spent several years in France, where he had participated in the founding of the French Communist Party. The Youth League's earliest and strongest in-country connection was with the Vinh group, but, by 1927, it had also established a network in Cochinchina by tapping into what remained of the Jeune Annam movement. In 1927, the Youth League's activities were disrupted when civil war broke out between the Chinese Nationalists and the Chinese Communists, prompting Ho Chi Minh to flee back to Moscow.

By early 1928, the Youth League had leadership committees in all three Vietnamese regions and a central committee located in Hong Kong. During the next two years, the Hanoi committee began to follow an independent line. It was competing with Nguyen Thai Hoc's Nationalist Party for followers and by late 1929 had gained influence over that party's "leftist" wing. It was also susceptible to influences from within the Chinese Communist Party through its members in the local Chinese community and cross-border contacts. The rise of Li Lisan within the leadership of the Chinese party at this time contributed to the Hanoi committee's growing alienation from the Youth League's Central Committee, which appeared relatively passive in comparison with Li Lisan's efforts to promote a revolutionary upsurge. Furthermore, the 1928 Sixth Comintern Congress held in Moscow marked a shift toward greater emphasis on class struggle, an issue on which the Hanoi committee members considered that they were more correct than the Central Committee.

In 1929, the Youth League split into two competing communist parties, one based in Hanoi and the other with most of its strength in Cochinchina. In early 1930, Ho Chi Minh arrived in Hong Kong following his escape to Europe and a sojourn in the Vietnamese community of northeastern Siam. He summoned representatives from both parties and papered over the schism to form a united party to which the Tan Viet group of Annam subsequently adhered as well. Problems remained, however, and the Comintern was not satisfied with what Ho Chi Minh had achieved. Tran Phu (1904–1931), an early recruit of the Youth League from Ha Tinh who had meanwhile arrived from Moscow with fresh instructions, chaired the "first plenum" of the new party in October 1930 at which the Indochinese Communist Party was inaugurated as the Comintern arm for the French colonial state. After Comintern assignments in China, Ho Chi Minh suffered a brief imprisonment in Hong Kong, and then, in 1934, he again returned to Moscow, where he spent the next four years. While the formation of the Indochinese Communist Party was the work of exiles working in an international organization, much of its energy and capacity to operate inside the colonial state came from movements that grew up within Indochina: the Tan Viet of Annam, the Jeune Annam of Cochinchina, and the Nationalist Party of Tonkin.

What was apparent by the end of the 1920s was that Vietnamese were not confined to the colonial relationship. Young anti-colonial activists of both reformist and revolutionary persuasions traveled, lived, learned, organized or were being organized in China, France, and the Soviet Union, and they brought their new ideas and skills back to Indochina. Their parents' generation had been oppressed with a sense of having "lost" their country, which had been reinforced by Social Darwinist thought arriving via Chinese translations of European books. But this generation learned European languages and had knowledge and experience of parliamentary democracy, electoral politics, anarchism, print activism, Comintern communism, and Trotskyist communism, all of which contextualized the colonial relationship in a world of wider possibilities. In the 1920s, the French colonial authorities lost the attention of the younger generation of Vietnamese. In the early 1930s, the consequences of this forced the French regime into a defensive stance, from which it never regained the initiative.

Events in Cochinchina, driven by influences from France, had stimulated the politicization of young Vietnamese in the mid 1920s. However, it was in Tonkin and northern Annam, where French idealism was less plausible and where exposure to the political cultures of China was more compelling, that a fateful crossover into violence occurred.

During 1928, the Vietnamese Nationalist Party led by Nguyen Thai Hoc was expanding its organization among educated youth, workers, and soldiers in Tonkin. Nguyen Thai Hoc's ideological orientation was rather vaguely defined by the "three principles" – national unity, democracy, and social welfare – of the revolutionary leader who founded the Chinese Nationalist Party, Sun Yatsen (1866–1925), and by the French revolutionary motto of "liberty, equality, and solidarity." Despite efforts to maintain a clandestine profile, the arousal of eager but undisciplined revolutionaries severely challenged organizational control and created a vulnerability to French surveillance. Furthermore, the Tonkin committee of the Youth League was competing with the Vietnamese Nationalist Party for recruits. Negotiations to merge the two organizations failed because they could not agree on the issues of class-based politics and adherence to a foreign-led organization.

In February 1929, a rogue member of the Vietnamese Nationalist Party, seeking to prove his party's anti-colonial prowess to those tempted to join the Youth League, defied his party's instructions and assassinated a Frenchman, Hervé Bazin. Bazin was in charge of recruiting laborers from Tonkin, often through trickery or coercion, for plantations in Cochinchina and New Caledonia. His death provoked the French to arrest several hundred Nationalist Party members, including most of the central leadership. Several members of the Youth League were also swept up in the arrests, which continued throughout the year. Nguyen Thai Hoc escaped and tried to rebuild the party, but finally concluded that there was no time to do this and that an insurrection was the only way to stave off disaster.

This was also a critical time in the fortunes of Chinese and Vietnamese adherents of the Comintern. In December 1928, struggle over leadership of the Youth League in Cochinchina had resulted in homicide, the so-called Rue Barbier Affair, triggering a wave of arrests that crippled the southern committee of the Youth League. Furthermore, in 1929 the split in the Youth League broke open with the Hanoi-based committee responding to the Li Lisan leadership in the Chinese Communist Party.

The Chinese communists, endeavoring to survive Chinese Nationalist Party efforts to destroy them, were building military bases in remote places, which they called soviets. In 1929, hostilities erupted in Guangxi, just north of the border, between Chinese Nationalist forces and Chinese Communist forces. Defeated, the Chinese communists led by Deng Xiaoping withdrew upriver into the mountains north of the Cao Bang border where, from December 1929 to February 1930 they organized uprisings and formed soviets. These soviets, the Youjiang Soviet at Baise and the Zuojiang Soviet at Longzhou, existed for about six months, during the first half of 1930. Some Vietnamese who were residing in the area or serving with Chinese Communist forces were involved in these events.

At the same time, Ho Chi Minh was in Hong Kong bringing together the Youth League factions to form a united Vietnamese Communist Party. The unification of Vietnamese communist organizations simultaneous with the appearance of Chinese communist soviets on the Vietnamese border increased enthusiasm for action among party members in Tonkin and northern Annam. When French military forces were deployed to help suppress the Chinese soviets, Vietnamese communists were tempted to assist their Chinese allies by distracting French attention back to Indochina.

This temptation was particularly strong because the leader of the Chinese Communist Party at this time, Li Lisan, was advocating that communist parties throughout Asia should implement general uprisings. The central leadership of the Vietnamese Communist Party initially hesitated to follow the Li Lisan line because it seemed to be at odds with Comintern policy. But the line was also being conveyed to Vietnamese through Chinese Communist Party members among overseas Chinese in Indochina, particularly in Cochinchina. Furthermore, Vietnamese communists were unavoidably involved in the protests, strikes, and insurrections that broke out in the Vietnamese parts of Indochina at the beginning of 1930 and that continued for more than a year.

The unrest and violence of 1930–1931 arose first of all from the politicization of youth in the mid 1920s, which began a general shift in Vietnamese attitudes toward the French. Varenne's failure to surmount the colonial regime's resistance to change brought an end to the Sarraut dream. Aside from confirmed élitists, such as the Constitutionalists, and those attached to the Hue monarchy, Vietnamese increasingly lost interest in cooperating with the French. Instead of being a potential mentor or partner for developing structures of reform, self-government, and autonomy, the French had become an obstacle to the aspirations of young Vietnamese.

Consequently, Vietnamese inclined toward public activism, whether among workers or peasants, soldiers or intellectuals, having lost their respect for the French, and without alternate paths toward their goals, dared to stand up in demonstrations, strikes, and uprisings. In particular, labor unrest on plantations and factories grew in the late 1920s to reach a crescendo in 1930 with labor strikes throughout Vietnamese Indochina that mobilized hundreds, sometimes thousands, of workers at a time.

The soviets in Nghe-Tinh and western Cochinchina

Aside from the change in Vietnamese perceptions arising from the obduracy of the French regime that affected all Vietnamese regions, Tonkin was particularly responsive to developments in southern China that inspired Vietnamese efforts to build clandestine anti-colonial organizations modeled on the Chinese Communist and the Chinese Nationalist Parties. In late 1929, Nguyen Thai Hoc, the leader of the most volatile and vulnerable of these organizations, the Nationalist Party, was running on a very short fuse of desperation, barely keeping ahead of the arrests that were ruining his party even as he made plans for an insurrection.

The Nationalist Party was disintegrating under the pressure of French repression and the turning of some members toward the Communist Party when the uprising was triggered in early February 1930. A mutiny in the Vietnamese garrison at Yen Bay and uncoordinated uprisings around Tonkin were quickly suppressed. Nguyen Thai Hoc and most of his party's leadership were arrested and eventually executed. The French repression in Tonkin destroyed the Nationalist Party, although some members escaped into Chinese exile. The Communist Party in Tonkin was damaged but not destroyed. The demise of the Nationalist Party and the disturbance it produced in Tonkin were but a prelude to the most spectacular episode of anti-colonial action, which broke out at Vinh and its hinterland in the Nghe-Tinh region of northern Annam.

All three regional communist organizations that had been theoretically united following Ho Chi Minh's intervention at the beginning of 1930 were involved in organizing and leading the demonstrations and strikes that reached a crescendo in the month of April as the French bombed the Chinese soviets and exterminated the Nationalist Party in Tonkin. However, because of the repression in Cochinchina following the Rue Barbier Affair and in Tonkin following the Nguyen Thai Hoc uprising, and because vigilant protectorate magistrates had minimized communist influence in southern Annam, the only region in which the communist network was relatively strong and intact was northern Annam, in particular the region of Vinh where the Tan Viet movement had been active for several years and was most firmly embedded.

With Ho Chi Minh away on a Comintern assignment in Singapore and Bangkok to assist in organizing Malayan and Siamese communist parties, a group of leaders, most of whom were from the northern branch of the Vietnamese Communist Party, met in Hanoi in April 1930, calling themselves the "provisional central committee." This group, seemingly inspired by the Li Lisan line, the Chinese soviets across the border, the strikes and demonstrations, and the atmosphere of French repression in Tonkin, decided to organize an uprising in

Nghe-Tinh. Two men from Tonkin, Nguyen Phong Sac (1902–1931) and Nguyen Duc Canh (1908–1932), were assigned to go to Vinh and implement this plan.

Beginning in May, a campaign of peaceful demonstrations by peasants and workers was initiated in Nghe-Tinh against excessive taxation and the colonial salt monopoly. Within a few weeks, this campaign turned violent and local administration began to disintegrate. By September, Nguyen Duc Canh and Nguyen Phong Sac were organizing revolutionary governments in villages, which came to be called soviets. During the next six months approximately thirty soviets were organized in the Nghe-Tinh countryside. The manner in which these soviets were organized reflected the methods espoused and taught by the Chinese Communist Party about how to organize peasants. Efforts were also made to organize soviets in southern Annam in the regions of Dong Hoi, Quang Tri, and Quang Ngai but were unsuccessful.

It took the French nearly a year to put down what became known as the Nghe-Tinh Soviets. Not trusting their Vietnamese soldiers, they employed military units composed of upland minority groups and the French Foreign Legion. Even with aerial bombardment and a policy of pillage and slaughter, it took months for the French to begin to regain control of the Nghe-Tinh countryside. Meanwhile the "first plenum" of the Vietnamese Communist Party was convened in Hong Kong in October. Despite the events in Nghe-Tinh, this meeting was primarily occupied with putting the Comintern stamp on the new party, changing its name to the Indochinese Communist Party and sidelining Ho Chi Minh in favor of Tran Phu, who more faithfully espoused the ascendant Comintern line in favor of class struggle. At the same time, the plenum went on record as criticizing the Nghe-Tinh uprising and predicting its failure, this at a time when the Comintern was moving against Li Lisan and his policy of general uprisings.

When the "second plenum" was held at Saigon in March 1931, Tran Phu re-emphasized class struggle and the need to remove class enemies. The Nghe-Tinh Soviets, in the last phase of being destroyed and led by increasingly radical elements, translated this into a homicidal campaign against suspected informers, those without revolutionary enthusiasm, and the wealthy. In April and May, the top level of leadership in the soviets was arrested, including both Nguyen Phong Sac and Nguyen Duc Canh. Tran Phu was also arrested at this time in Saigon. By the end of summer the French had pacified Nghe-Tinh. By the end of the year, nearly all the leaders of the Indochinese Communist Party had been arrested or had fled, and the party was a shambles.

During the high tide of the Nghe-Tinh Soviet movement in late 1930, a less spectacular but, in the long term, more significant breakdown of colonial authority occurred in rural Cochinchina, particular in western districts such as Cao Lanh and Cho Moi where short-lived soviets were organized. Although French security forces maintained general ascendancy, this was the beginning of a gradual erosion of administrative control in parts of western Cochinchina that continued for the next quarter-century until the French colonial effort finally collapsed. Here, communist propaganda and organizing activities mixed with the millenarian tendencies revealed most recently in the disturbances of 1913 and 1916. In 1931 and 1932, the French arrested many communist activists in Cochinchina. Although a certain calm was restored, it was deceptive. The world-wide depression severely damaged the rice export market and the potential for political and religious excitement remained.

The French resort to the monarchy

For five years after the events of 1930–1931, the Franco-Vietnamese relationship was in a surface holding pattern while, beneath the calm, important changes were occurring among the Vietnamese. The governor generals during this time were men who had many years of administrative experience in Indochina and had risen to high positions under Sarraut in the 1910s. Pierre Marie Antoine Pasquier (1877–1934) had been serving in Indochina since the 1890s. He had written and lectured extensively about Vietnamese culture, about which he was well informed and with which he was sympathetic, and he had served as senior administrator at Hue from 1920 to 1927. When Varenne was recalled due to pressure from the French colon lobby in 1928, Pasquier was named governor general. After Pasquier's death in an airplane accident in 1934, Eugène Jean Louis René Robin (1872–1954) was appointed to succeed him. Robin had served as senior administrator of Tonkin from 1925 to 1930. Both Pasquier and Robin were conservative and held the trust of French people in Cochinchina. Their attitude toward the Vietnamese was paternalistic.

Pasquier sternly enforced the status quo while resorting to a recycling of old solutions for new problems. With Sarraut-like rhetoric, he spoke admiringly of a traditional Vietnamese culture and of France's duty to preserve it. While this was soothing to Vietnamese monarchists and conservatives, for many in the younger generation it was a bad dream from an oppressive past, the glorification of the worst features of their society, in particular the new colonial mandarinate and its combination of old-fashioned Confucian values with modern administrative coercive powers.

The traditional Vietnamese culture espoused by Pasquier was in large part a colonial invention based on aspects of Confucianism that enforced gender and age subordinations in family relations. It also fed from the aura of a venerable antiquity with which the French invested the dynastic routine at "old Hue." Having spent most of the 1920s overseeing the protectorate, Pasquier thought to renew Paul Bert's alliance with the monarchy as a way of regaining Vietnamese interest in the colonial project.

After the death of King Khai Dinh in 1925, when the French assumed direct control of the protectorate government at Hue, there was a series of proposals for reforming the monarchy. French colonial functionaries even drew up a draft for something like a constitutional monarchy. Pham Quynh, whose career began during Sarraut's time as editor of a journal promoting the kind of traditional culture espoused by Pasquier, was a prominent Vietnamese proponent of returning administrative responsibilities to the monarchy. Other Vietnamese, such as Nguyen Van Vinh (1882–1936), a journalist who started his career as a French apologist during Sarraut's time and became a translator of French literature into Vietnamese, subscribed to Phan Chu Trinh's disdain for the monarchy and urged the French to brush aside the protectorate in order to modernize the government.

The cabinet of royal ministers, although subdued by French supervision, was not utterly supine. The most influential minister was Nguyen Huu Bai (1863–1935). He was a Roman Catholic from Quang Tri who, educated by the Church, entered public service in 1884 when the Patenôtre protectorate treaty was put into effect. He became the leading minister at court during the reign of Khai Dinh (1916–1925). He welcomed Phan Boi Chau to Hue after his pardon in December 1925 and assured French authorities that no problems would ensue. But in the years that followed, the French were increasingly irritated by his requests to return Bao Dai from Europe and to re-establish the provisions of the Patenôtre Treaty, which the French had superseded in 1925. Beneath his loyalty to the French was a staunch regard for an autonomous Vietnamese administration. The French tended to interpret his attitude as out of date and as shielding the corruptions and irrationalities that they considered to be the worst features of Vietnamese magistrates.

One of Maurice Long's initiatives in 1920 was to establish an elected Vietnamese consultative council for Annam; Sarrault had established such a council for Tonkin in 1913. The electorate was extremely limited and the council's sphere of activity was severely restricted, but its profile was enhanced when Varenne redesigned the Tonkin and Annam councils as "representative chambers" in 1926. Council members began to add their voices to calls for a return to the Patenôtre Treaty being made by Nguyen Huu Bai and his ministerial colleagues.

The French resolution that something needed to be done about the monarchy was strengthened by the crisis of 1930–1931, and ideas about reform came to be focused on planning for Bao Dai's return from Europe. As would again be the case fifteen years later, the French turned to Bao Dai as a solution to their alienation from the Vietnamese. However, when Bao Dai arrived in Hue in September 1932, French caution and differing Vietnamese agendas imposed an inertia that was not broken for several months. Bao Dai, 20 years old and fresh from many years in Europe, was intelligent but indolent. Pham Quynh, 40 years old and a career propagandist for Franco-Vietnamese cooperation, was eager to modernize the monarchy and willingly negotiated between French sensibilities and Bao Dai's kingly aspirations. Nguyen Huu Bai, 70 years old and a lifelong veteran of protectorate politics, became stubborn and, with senior members of the royal family, did not want to let slip an opportunity for restoring a semblance of real authority to the protectorate.

Finally, in May 1933, Pasquier engineered a "coup" in which Nguyen Huu Bai and his elderly colleagues were retired and replaced in the royal council of ministers by younger men with Pham Quynh at their head. Despite the relatively minor administrative, legal, and educational innovations that would be implemented by the protectorate over the next few years, it was quickly apparent that the French had no intention of relinquishing any authority to the monarchy, and this contributed to the resignation of the Minister of the Interior, Ngo Dinh Diem (1901–1963), after less than three months in office.

Like Nguyen Huu Bai, Ngo Dinh Diem came from a family that had been Roman Catholic for many generations. His father had been a senior official at Thanh Thai's court and had retired to the countryside when Thanh Thai was deposed in 1907. Ngo Dinh Diem entered protectorate administration after graduating in 1921 from the School of Public Administration and Law in Hanoi, which prepared aspiring government officials in place of the abolished civil service examination system. His eldest brother had preceded him into officialdom and had married a daughter of Nguyen Huu Bai. Ngo Dinh Diem rapidly ascended the ranks of office due to his honesty and his effectiveness in governing rural areas, which impressed the French, and to the patronage of Nguyen Huu Bai that was based on family connections. His father's unhappy experience with French treatment of the monarchy in 1907 and Nguyen Huu Bai's belief that Pham Quynh was leading the monarchy deeper into the smothering French embrace was the context of Ngo Dinh Diem's disillusionment with the new cabinet. His rapid rise in protectorate politics ended with his decision to never again serve as a functionary of French rule. He spent the next decade in retirement under French surveillance.

The policy of reforming the monarchy lapsed with Pasquier's death in 1934. Robin, the new governor general, was not particularly interested in the monarchy. He was more concerned about what he viewed as the most fundamental problem in Indochina, the pauperization of the peasantry that was exacerbated by the effects of the worldwide depression. However, the economic structure of Indochina resisted change, and during his short tenure (1934–1936) there was no time to do more than talk. Furthermore, by the mid 1930s, politics in France were shifting to the left in response to the rise of fascism in Europe, bringing new uncertainties to colonial administrators.

Vietnamese politics and the Popular Front

During the prolonged suppression of the Vietnamese Nationalist Party and the Nghe-Tinh Soviets, Vietnamese students and young professionals in France organized protest demonstrations, resulting in many of their leaders being arrested and expelled back to Indochina or evading arrest and escaping back to Indochina. Most of these had participated in the Jeune Annam movement of the mid 1920s and had gone to France to avoid French measures against student unrest following Phan Chu Trinh's death in 1926. Many became communists while in France. Some adhered to the French Communist Party and a few of these returned to Vietnam via Moscow and the Comintern network. Others became followers of Leon Trotsky (1879–1940), the Bolshevik leader whom Stalin expelled from public life in 1927 and forced into exile in 1929. Trotsky opposed the bureaucratic and regimented version of state government and international revolution espoused by Stalin and the Comintern. He proposed a radical faith in the masses to ignite and sustain revolution in a less disciplined, more spontaneous, and more open-ended way than was the Stalinist style of strict obedience to party leaders. In the 1930s, Vietnamese Trotskyists became a driving force in Cochinchinese politics with their emphasis on propagandizing and organizing among workers in plantations, factories, shipyards, railyards, and arsenals.

Trotskyists first appeared in Cochinchina in 1932, just in time to experience the wave of arrests that snared Tran Phu and other communist leaders as the Nghe-Tinh Soviets were being shut down. Resistant to party discipline, Trotskyists tended toward the leadership of either Ta Thu Thau (1906–1945) or Ho Huu Tuong (1910–1980), both of whom had been politicized in France. While Ta Thu Thau was willing to cooperate with Stalinists to advance his political program, Ho Huu Tuong believed that the Indochinese Communist Party could not be trusted to place revolutionary priorities above either the national interests of the Soviet Union or the temptation to make alliances with class enemies.

Most Trotskyists maintained informal working relationships with each other while Ta Thu Thau was willing to do the same with Stalinists, which was facilitated by the disarray of the Stalinist party. By the end of 1932, the

Indochinese Communist Party had lost most of its leadership and no longer had a functioning network of command. Nguyen Van Tao (1908–1970), a member of the French Communist Party and an adherent of the Comintern, had been expelled from France in 1930 and became a close associate of Ta Thu Thau, as did Duong Bach Mai (1905–1964), who in 1932 arrived in Saigon from France via a three-year sojourn in Moscow. Ta Thu Thau was also willing to work with non-communist nationalists such as Tran Van Thach (1903–?), who was expelled from France with Nguyen Van Tao and eventually became a Trotskyist by the late 1930s, and with independent revolutionaries and anarchists such as Nguyen An Ninh. In the spring of 1933, elections to the Saigon Municipal Council provided a focus for cooperation.

The electorate for these elections was small and restricted to Vietnamese already having some connection to the colonial government. Nevertheless, Ta Thu Thau and his associates put forward a "workers' list" of candidates and briefly published a French-language newspaper called *La Lutte* (Struggle) to rally support for it. Two members of this Struggle Group, Tran Van Thach and Nguyen Van Tao, were elected. They were not allowed to take their council seats, but their election indicated a sense of alienation from the French regime felt even by Vietnamese most closely associated with it. The Vietnamese electorate was familiar with the racist discrimination, arrogance, and brutality that pervaded the colonial regime, and *La Lutte* aroused their intolerance of injustice. Furthermore, the Struggle Group spoke for a wider spectrum of the population than did other politically active Vietnamese. Previously, men closely associated with French interests had dominated Cochinchinese elections until the Constitutionalists rose to prominence in the mid 1920s as a kind of loyal opposition. But, Constitutionalists had limited appeal because of their élitism. Furthermore, in the early 1930s, they began to break into factions based on personality and generational change, with younger men believing that their senior colleagues had become susceptible to corruption and were too comfortable in the French embrace.

The Struggle Group disbanded after the election, but in the autumn of 1934, partly through the efforts of Nguyen An Ninh, it was reconstituted with an eye toward elections in 1935, and the newspaper *La Lutte* began to be published regularly. In the Cochinchina Colonial Council elections of March 1935, candidates supported by the Struggle Group received 17 percent of the vote, although none was elected. However, two months later, in the Saigon Municipal Council elections, four of six candidates on the "workers' list" were elected: Tran Van Thach, Nguyen Van Tao, Ta Thu Thau, and Duong Bach Mai. Of these, only Tran Van Thach, ostensibly not a communist, was allowed to take his seat.

By this time, the leftward shift of French politics was becoming palpable in Indochina. The French Communist Party began to cooperate with the French Socialist Party, and visiting parliamentary delegations included communists, who spoke in favor of labor legislation and an amnesty for political prisoners. In the summer of 1935, reflecting Stalin's concern about the rise of fascism, the Seventh Comintern Congress in Moscow called on communist parties to join with anti-fascists to form "popular front" governments. In the French elections of May 1936 a Popular Front government led by the French Socialist Party was voted into power. This government included many politicians who were critical of colonial policies and a parliamentary Committee of Inquiry was established with plans for fact-finding visits to the colonies.

Announcement of the Committee of Inquiry prompted a campaign to organize a congress in Saigon to formulate proposals to present to the committee when it arrived. Prominent leaders of this so-called "democracy movement" included members of the Struggle Group as well as Constitutionalists. However, when the Struggle Group began to organize "action committees" at localities throughout Cochinchina to select delegates to the Congress, many Constitutionalists abandoned the movement, believing that it was becoming too radical. The upsurge of activity surrounding the "action committees" and plans for the proposed congress unnerved colonial authorities. In September 1936 the French announced that the Committee of Inquiry would not come to Indochina after all and all further planning for the congress was banned.

In the same month, a new governor general arrived in Indochina. Joseph Jules Brévié (1889–1964) had just served for six years as Governor General of French West Africa. He had a reputation among colonial administrators as a liberal, which apparently recommended him to the Popular Front government. During his tenure, progressive labor legislation was enacted, amnesties released hundreds of political prisoners, and there was a general loosening of censorship and restrictions on political activity. The Indochinese Communist Party was revived by the release of prisoners, by new leadership arriving with fresh instructions from Moscow, and by the opportunity to openly operate as a legal organization. However, the popular front policy of the Comintern meant that the Indochinese Communist Party was now allied with the French colonial regime against the fascist threat, which seemed remote in Indochina, and this caused a certain amount of confusion and consternation in anti-colonial ranks. The rebuilding of party discipline under the watchful eye of the French Communist Party also brought an end to Stalinist participation in the Struggle Group.

The Struggle Group held together through the May 1937 Saigon Municipal Council elections, in which three of its members were elected: Ta Thu Thau, Nguyen Van Tao, and Duong Bach Mai. Thereafter, the Stalinists withdrew into the ranks of their own party. At this time, Stalinists established a strong position in Tonkin, where there were few Trotskyists. There, they were leaders in investigative journalism and labor organization.

In Cochinchina, the Trotskyists prospered during the Popular Front era of relatively open politics. In the Cochinchina Colonial Council elections of April 1939, the Trotskyist slate of candidates won 80 percent of the vote, defeating Constitutionalists, Stalinists, and others. Trotskyist electoral strength in the south reflected their flexible attitude toward authority and their emphasis on issues affecting the livelihood of large numbers of people. By the late 1930s, Vietnamese voters in Cochinchina had abandoned the Constitutionalists. Trotskyists were successful in elections not because voters favored communism but rather because their firm stand against the injustices of the colonial situation was popular.

New cultural patterns

Vietnamese history in the 1930s is much more than the story of communist activists, and not all members of the new generation were absorbed by politics. The events just narrated above were peripheral to fundamental changes taking place in scholarship, literature, society, and religion. The last decade without war until the 1990s, this was the most dynamic and creative era for the new generation in the full enthusiasm of youth.

Educated Vietnamese born after the turn of the twentieth century learned about the attributes of what was perceived as "modern" civilization as displayed by the major world powers and eagerly elaborated versions of this that became the basis for contemporary Vietnamese culture. Inevitably, the French were in varying degrees participants in this endeavor. Some Frenchmen and Eurasians with French citizenship assisted Vietnamese anti-colonialists and revolutionaries by providing legal cover for publishing and organizing activities. Others, on the precarious "ethical edge" of colonial life and thought, dedicated themselves to scholarship, education, medicine, and the arts with the willing collaboration of many Vietnamese.

Established at Hanoi in 1900, the French School of the Far East (École Française d'Extrême-Orient) was the center of French academic study of Asia. Many prominent members of the pioneering generation of French sinology spent periods of research and writing in Hanoi and worked on Vietnamese historical materials using up-to-date methods. They laid the basis for what became, in the independent Vietnam of recent decades, the academic fields of anthropology, ethnology, archaeology, art, geography, history, linguistics, music, philology, religion, and sociology. French people not directly associated with the School also produced important scholarship, most famously the Catholic priest Léopold Michel Cadière (1869–1955), who spent most of his life in Annam and published important studies on Vietnamese history and religion.

By the 1930s, young Vietnamese scholars who would have a lasting impact on academic work in Vietnam were beginning to emerge in the French School of the Far East. Two of the most prominent of these were Tran Van Giap (1902–1973) and Nguyen Van Huyen (1908–1975). After a period of study at the Sorbonne in Paris, Tran Van Giap collected and catalogued Han and Nom texts. His efforts made possible the establishment of the Institute of Han-Nom Studies, which is today the principal archive of character texts in Vietnam. Nguyen Van Huyen researched and wrote on many topics but had a strong and lasting influence on the study of anthropology, popular religion, and sociology. Another scholar whose academic writings have stood the test of time relatively well was Hoang Xuan Han (1900–1996). He was not affiliated with the School, but after studying at the Sorbonne in the early 1930s he returned to Indochina and published on history.

A slightly different case but with a more immediate effect on thought in his time was Tran Trong Kim (1883–1953). His career was in the French educational service, and his interests were oriented toward pedagogy. In the 1920s he published a history of Vietnam based on traditional historical materials that was subsequently used for decades as a classroom textbook. He also wrote a study of Confucianism that was published in several printings during the 1930s and 1940s. This book attempted to use philosophical ideas current in France to support Confucian family ethics. It became a bible for conservatives when the generation gap opened in the 1930s and during the Vichy regime of the early 1940s.

A significant effect of French ideas about language and ethnicity was the study of upland non-Vietnamese peoples and the categorization of them into various ethnic groups. This procedure would later assume great importance in an independent Vietnam when these peoples were organized as "ethnic minorities" and policies for integrating them into the state were developed. It was at this time that the peoples inhabiting the midlands of Thanh Hoa and Nghe An were classified as a Muong ethnic group separate from the Vietnamese.

The Frenchman who has been best remembered in post-colonial Vietnam is Alexandre Émile Jean Yersin (1863–1943), a Swiss-born medical doctor who went to Asia in the early 1890s with the Pasteur Institute. In 1894, at the Pasteur Institute in Hong Kong, he and his Japanese collaborator Shibasaburo Kitasato discovered the bacillus for bubonic plague. In 1895 he went to Nha Trang in Annam and established a laboratory for manufacturing plague serum. He became the first director of the medical school established in Hanoi in 1902, propagated the use of quinine against malaria, and experimented with rubber trees. He spent much of his life in Nha Trang where he was highly esteemed by the local people.

Another Frenchman who left a good reputation in Vietnam is Victor Tardieu (1870–1937). In 1925, he established the Indochina School of Fine Arts (École des Beaux-Arts d'Indochine) in Hanoi and, until his death, dedicated himself to training a new generation of Vietnamese artists. He disagreed with the prevailing French opinion that traditional Vietnamese arts could not rise above artisanship to become "fine art." He taught European painting techniques to his students but also encouraged them to develop their local traditions to produce what could be recognized as modern fine art. Two of his students had a lasting influence on Vietnamese art. Nguyen Phan Chanh (1892–1984) experimented in creating new effects with paint on silk, and Nguyen Gia Tri (1906–1993) applied abstractionism to traditional lacquer painting.

French music, opera, and theater exerted a strong influence upon the Vietnamese, especially in Saigon. A new form of opera called *cai luong* adapted French theatrical and musical influences to traditional forms of opera, including a mix of spoken and sung dialogue, and sometimes featured non-traditional instruments such as guitar, violin, and saxophone. French popular music found a receptive audience, especially among young Vietnamese, and Vietnamese songs began to appear that followed French styles of lyricism and melody, which were more rhythmic than traditional pentatonic music. The European spoken theater, without music or singing, was also adopted in Saigon (called *kich noi*).

Movie theaters made an appearance in Vietnamese cities during the 1920s. A small Vietnamese film industry began with silent films and was eventually producing sound films by the late 1930s. Most of the screen fare, however, came from France and Hollywood. The films of Buster Keaton and Charlie Chaplin were particularly popular in the 1920s and 1930s. Vietnamese newspapers began to carry cartoon strips that were sometimes modeled on popular movie characters and themes.

The arena of greatest contention between the old and the new in the 1930s was literature and journalism. A great rush of passion against the Confucian tradition of parents subordinating youth by arranged marriages blew open the generational gap and marked the beginning of what has become known as modern Vietnamese literature. Traditional Vietnamese literature was almost exclusively poetic. Consequently, the first significant shift in literary expression occurred in poetry.

The two most popular poets in the early French period, both from Tonkin, could do little more than express vexation at the contradiction between their classical education and the colonial situation. Nguyen Khuyen (1835–1909) received his doctoral degree in 1871 and thereafter served in officialdom until the crisis of 1885 when he retired and wrote poems expressing his refusal to accept office under the French protectorate. Tran Te Xuong (1870–1907), a famous failure in the higher levels of the examination system in the 1890s and 1900s, wrote with self-deprecating humor about the sense of uselessness he felt after investing many years studying an outmoded curriculum and being dependent upon his wife to support his family. Tan Da (1888–1939; real name: Nguyen Khac Hieu) is often viewed as a "transitional" poet who used metaphors to express his disgust toward French rule but also displayed a certain daring playfulness with language that pushed beyond prevailing conventions and suggested the influence of French poetry. In the 1930s, poets adapted the forms and spirit of twentieth-century French poetry to their own language. They turned away from oblique expressions of the well-worn colonial conundrum and experimented with free-verse forms to explore more personal and romantic expressions of freedom from social conventions.

Phan Khoi (1887–1959) had participated in the reformist movement led by Phan Chu Trinh in the 1900s. He was imprisoned for three years as a result of the 1908 disturbances and subsequently pursued a career as an editor and writer. In 1932 he published a poem entitled "Old Love," which criticized the practice of arranged marriage. This poem inspired what came to be called the New Poetry Movement, from which emerged the major poets of the twentieth century: The Lu (1907–1989), Luu Trong Lu (1912–1991), Ngo Xuan Dieu (1916–1985), Cu Huy Can (1919–2005), and Che Lan Vien (1920–1989). Although in the 1940s these men dramatically changed the content of their work to serve politics, in the 1930s they ventilated exuberant emotions of love, sadness, longing, and a full range of personal feelings that violated traditional poetic conventions and offended prevailing norms of expression.

In 1933, a circle of writers that included The Lu formed the Self-Strengthening Literary Group (Tu Luc Van Doan), led by Nguyen Tuong Tam (1905–1963; pen name: Nhat Linh). Nguyen Tuong Tam had received a high-school diploma in 1923, worked as a government clerk, briefly enrolled in the Hanoi medical school, then shifted to Tardieu's School of Fine Arts before going to France where he obtained a bachelor's degree in science. By 1932, he was working on the staff of a Saigon literary journal called *Mores*. The Literary Group included Tran Khanh Giu (1896–1947; pen name: Khai Hung) and two of Nguyen Tuong Tam's brothers: Nguyen Tuong Long (1907–1947; pen name: Hoang Dao) and Nguyen Tuong Vinh (1910–1942; pen name: Thach Lam). Novels published by these men aroused controversy with their depictions of traditional Confucian family practices as unjust, cruel, and destructive of decent human feelings.

Other writers opposed this kind of writing, viewing it as stories about people in upper-class families who could afford the luxury of romantic confusions and generational combat. Ngo Tat To (1894–1954) and Nguyen Cong Hoan (1903–1977) published novels with more "realistic" depictions of human suffering and social injustice. Perhaps the most popular writer to depict the raw side of colonial life was Vu Trong Phung (1912–1939). He combined investigative journalism and literature in a distinctive form of reportage that was clever, amusing, and instructive.

The publication of newspapers, journals, magazines, books, and pamphlets thrived in the 1930s as literacy in alphabetic Vietnamese spread. There were publications specializing in nearly every area of interest from fiction to various branches of science, economics, agriculture, medicine, hygiene, history, folklore, philosophy, and religion. Developing the written vernacular to write about totally new topics and in a form accessible to people of all classes produced major changes in vocabulary and syntax. The idea of a grammatical sentence and of coherent paragraphs introduced new structures of thought, logic, and argumentation to readers. The spread of alphabetic literacy was the most decisive event in the history of French Indochina. Vietnamese created their own sphere of print culture from which the French were excluded.

French security officers learned to monitor and understand the activities of communists, but the world of Buddhist and Cao Dai temples, secret societies, popular cults, peripatetic healers, and belief in messianic millenarianism was much more difficult to penetrate, particularly in Cochinchina where all of these phenomena existed in a potent and unstable mixture.

Most French administrators preferred to see Confucianism, rather than Buddhism, as the primary element in traditional Vietnamese culture because of its emphasis on hierarchy and social order. Buddhist monks tended to be involved in anti-colonial movements or to do little more than sit in their temples. Buddhists existed in an anarchic constellation of competing local and regional sects, often in conflation with popular spirit cults. The arcane and contentious world of doctrine inhabited by the most erudite monks was totally disconnected from the lives of lay people, of whom very few displayed any serious interest in the religion. For the most part, people calling themselves Buddhist subscribed to the Pure Land School that required little more than occasionally reciting a short prayer calling on the Amitabha Buddha for "good luck." For all of these reasons, Buddhism was in decline in the early twentieth century as Roman Catholicism, Confucianism, and even Cao Daism gained strength and coherence under the colonial regime.

Beginning in the 1920s, the influence of the Chinese monk Tai Xu (1890–1947) began to be felt in Vietnam. He had supported Sun Yatsen and the Chinese

Revolution of 1911 and thereafter established an association for Buddhists that promoted political activism. Although he represented a minority view among Chinese monks, his ideas spread widely among young Buddhists in eastern Asia. His advocacy of monks being involved in public affairs inspired a Cochinchinese monk named Vien Chieu (1898–1974), who in 1925 and 1926 participated in the campaign to grant amnesty to Phan Boi Chau and in the demonstrations provoked by Phan Chu Trinh's death. By then, Vien Chieu was already actively promoting a renovation of Buddhism under lay leadership and establishing his influence in urban temples experiencing prosperity from the developing colonial economy. In the late 1920s and early 1930s, Buddhist publications proliferated and a public debate in print ensued between Vien Chieu with others of his persuasion and the majority of monks who believed that Buddhism should not be mixed with politics. This debate revealed a new trend in southern Vietnamese Buddhism that would emerge as a major political movement in the 1960s.

Vien Chieu argued that Buddhism was atheist and that there was no immortality of the human soul. This point of view is perfectly plausible according to prominent philosophical traditions in Buddhism. However, it was controversial among monks because it denied fundamental assumptions that sustained popular forms of Mahayana Buddhism, particularly Pure Land, which believed in a Buddhist deity able to save one's soul for the Pure Land paradise. Vien Chieu rejected the Pure Land and the concept of an afterlife in general, which was also a plausible, if unpopular, position for a text-based monk to take against what was widely viewed by educated monks as a Buddhist version of popular religious cults. What was most controversial, however, was Vien Chieu's affirmation of the material world as "real," thereby rejecting the basic Buddhist doctrine that the material world is but an illusion. He equated the idea of an illusory world with a passive reluctance to improve the material existence of human beings and, thus, a rejection of political involvement to improve the "real world," to which he was committed.

Although Vien Chieu is commonly regarded as the most prominent figure in a Vietnamese "Buddhist revival," in the late 1930s he and many other monks left Buddhism to join the communists. His ideas nevertheless remained influential, particularly among younger monks. Furthermore, in rural Cochinchinese temples, his influence mingled easily with the popular millenarianism that was sustained by economic distress and lay waiting to be activated by a charismatic leader.

The "action committees" in rural Cochinchina organized by Struggle Group activists in 1936 did not cease to exist after the French banned the congress movement, of which they were ostensibly a first step. In varying degrees they continued to exist as unifying cooperative networks for pre-existing local mutual-aid organizations for youth, laborers, and women. These networks were susceptible to the influence of the Indochinese Communist Party. At this time the Cao Dai religion was also expanding its influence. Many Cao Dai leaders nurtured a loyalty to Cuong De, still living in Japanese exile. Consequently, after 1937, when Japan invaded China, they welcomed the prospect of Japan sweeping away the French. Their anticipation of an imminent French defeat spread through parts of rural Cochinchina where French administration had been in decline throughout the 1930s.

The decline of the colonial regime and its lapse into a defensive posture during the 1930s came from the failure of the French to establish a relationship with the Vietnamese that showed any plausible prospect of moving beyond the colonial relationship of master and subordinate. During the first four decades of the twentieth century, educated Vietnamese put a large measure of intellectual energy into engaging the modern world and planning for the future of their country. The French, however, were mentally inert and could not relax from their policeman's pose. They made no serious response to the ferment that their rule stimulated among the Vietnamese. This unimaginative attitude would remain fundamentally unchanged through fifteen years of war and political upheaval.

12 INDOCHINA AT WAR

The Japanese arrive

As the Sino-Japanese War raged just over the northern border and as war in Europe shifted from threat to reality, a fresh upsurge of religious excitement spread in western Cochinchina. In July of 1939, in a village near the Seven Mountains near the Khmer border, a sickly but charismatic young man named Huynh Phu So (1919–1947) claimed to be a Buddha and attracted large numbers of followers. By the summer of 1940, the resulting uproar prompted the French to take him into custody. After nearly a year of confinement in a Cholon psychiatric hospital, he was allowed to return to the countryside under house arrest. In 1942, the Japanese, who had meanwhile entered southern Indochina, gained possession of him and thereafter cultivated his following as a pro-Japanese force. This movement came to be known by the name of Huynh Phu So's home village, Hoa Hao. The Hoa Hao religion arose from the millenarian traditions of western Cochinchina, but instead of being an ephemeral movement as previous millenarian episodes had been, it gained coherence in the peculiar conditions of the Franco-Japanese wartime relationship.

The French Popular Front faded away during the course of 1938 and was replaced by a more conservative government that began to prepare for war. In August 1939, General George Catroux (1877–1969), the commander of French military forces in Indochina, replaced Brévié as governor general. Catroux had served in Indochina prior to the First World War and more recently had held colonial commands in Morocco, Algeria, and Syria. Within weeks of his appointment, the Indochina Communist Party was deprived of its legal status. Catroux focused on military preparations and enforced strict internal security, arresting many communists and other anti-colonial activists and confiscating their property.

With the German conquest of France and the formation of the collaborationist French government at Vichy in June of 1940, Indochina was at a crossroads. The

French fascists of Vichy were allied through Germany with Japan, and Japan lost no time in demanding access to Tonkin to ensure an end to supplies reaching their Chinese enemies via the port of Hai Phong and the railway line to Yunnan. It was quickly apparent that the continued existence of the French regime in Indochina required either effective anti-Japanese assistance or cooperation with the Japanese under the Vichy banner. The British in Singapore were already stretched to near breaking point and the Americans in Manila were not yet ready to shake off their isolationism. In July, as Japanese pressure on Indochina grew, Catroux was replaced by Admiral Jean Decoux (1884–1963), commander of the French navy in Asia. Decoux adhered to Vichy, thereby maximizing the possibility of preserving French rule in Indochina, albeit in alliance with Japan. Catroux departed to join the Free French forces being formed in opposition to Vichy by Charles de Gaulle, of whom Catroux was a close personal acquaintance.

Vichy diplomats in Tokyo reached an accord at the end of August 1940 by which Japan recognized French sovereignty in Indochina. In return, France recognized Japanese supremacy in eastern Asia and agreed to provide Japan with military access to Tonkin. Negotiating the details of this accord then commenced in Indochina between Japanese military authorities and Decoux's administration. In late September, an arrangement was reached allowing Japanese use of several airfields, the port of Hai Phong, the railroad lines connecting Hai Phong with Guangxi and Yunnan, as well as the right to station up to six thousand troops north of the Red River.

As the Franco-Japanese agreement was being finalized, impatient Japanese army officers on the Sino-Vietnamese border and aboard troop transports off the Tonkin coast, having grown accustomed to driving expansionary policies in China by presenting Tokyo with faits accomplis, launched operations without authorization. Japanese units briefly seized Lang Son, on the northern border, and Do Son, on the coast near Hai Phong. Senior officers quickly re-established the chain of command and restored Lang Son and Do Son to the French, but the Lang Son episode was not a purely Franco-Japanese affair.

Several hundred Vietnamese in China had been mobilized the previous year by Cuong De and accompanied the Japanese into Lang Son as an auxiliary force. They were joined by hundreds of local soldiers and civilians, including communists released from the Lang Son jail. When the Japanese withdrew back into China, this ad hoc anti-colonial accumulation of people, a mixture of Vietnamese and ethnic minorities of the border region, unsuccessfully resisted the return of French authority. Some of the survivors, led by local members of the Indochina Communist Party, went into the mountains west of Lang Son and for a few weeks contested French authority in the rugged Bac Son region where De Tham had maintained his lair in the 1890s and 1900s. This became known as the Bac

Son Uprising. Eventually, a small guerrilla base under communist leadership was established there that survived to the end of the Japanese war.

The Vichy submission to Japanese demands in Tonkin emboldened Siam, renamed Thailand in 1939, to demand that the French relinquish northern and western Cambodian provinces and Laotian provinces west of the Mekong. The leader of Thailand was Field Marshal Plaek Pibulsongkram (1897–1964), commonly known as Phibun, a Thai nationalist with fascist tendencies who dominated Thai politics from the 1930s into the 1950s. Phibun was shifting Thai foreign policy away from its deference to the British toward an accommodation with Japan and saw an opportunity to reclaim territories from the French.

Against the threat of Thai invasion, Decoux shifted his military forces into the south. The Indochinese Communist Party had a strong organization in parts of Cochinchina, particularly in the My Tho area. It had also infiltrated Vietnamese army units. Hoping to benefit from the Franco-Thai confrontation, the communists planned an uprising. Learning of this, the French disarmed and confined Vietnamese soldiers to their barracks and within a month overcame civilian insurrectionists with overwhelming force, killing and arresting thousands of people, including virtually the entire southern leadership of the Indochinese Communist Party. Among those arrested was the former reformist Buddhist monk, now communist, Vien Chieu. The debacle of this so-called Nam Ky Uprising dealt the Stalinist party in Cochinchina a severe blow from which its efforts to recover were slow and difficult. Meanwhile, in early 1941, Japan stepped into the Franco-Thai confrontation and forced the French to give up the territories coveted by Phibun.

The Moscow–Tokyo "nonaggression pact" signed in April 1941 and the German invasion of the Soviet Union in June 1941 removed Tokyo's concerns about Russian policy in Asia and encouraged Japanese ambitions to expand into the southern seas. As a first step, in July 1941, Japan forced Vichy to accept the integration of Indochina into the Japanese military system with the right to station planes, ships, and tens of thousands of troops throughout Indochina. This brought Singapore within range of Japanese bombers and provided a strategic commissary, communication, and transshipment base for operations against Burma, Malaya, the Dutch East Indies (Indonesia), and the Philippines.

The United States, unwilling to let pass this threat to all of southeastern Asia, was aroused into action. When Japan refused American demands to withdraw from Indochina, Japanese assets in the US were frozen and the US imposed a de facto embargo on the export of oil and other strategic goods to Japan. Subsequent Japanese–American negotiations simply led to a hardening of positions on both sides. With limited oil reserves, Japan urgently aimed to acquire the oilfields in the Dutch East Indies and prepared to attack the American, British, and Dutch possessions in Asia and the Pacific Ocean.

The new phase of war that broke out in December 1941 brought Indochina into the center of Japanese military activity. Decoux was soon forced to grant Japan access to the entire communication and transportation infrastructure of Indochina, to place the economic resources of Indochina at the disposal of Japan, and to allow the Japanese to monitor his administration. The Japanese were occupied with battlefields stretching from the Burmese–Indian border through Southeast Asia to the islands of the Pacific. The convenience of retaining the French to administer the strategic Indochinese transport and supply center overrode Japanese propaganda about Asia for the Asians. For their part, the French entertained the hope that the tide of war would eventually turn against the Japanese, at which time they would still be in possession of Indochina.

During the next three years, Decoux, cut off from Europe and forced to serve an alien imperial power, endeavored to rally the Vietnamese to his regime with a combination of Vichy fascism and Confucian paternalism that emphasized hard work, obedience to superiors, and concern for the welfare of subordinates. Vietnamese civil servants, upon whom the French were now increasingly reliant, were granted improvements in salary and promotion policies. Relatively liberal labor laws were enforced. Particular efforts were made to win the attention of youth by a major expansion of educational facilities and a lively program of sports and scouting. At the same time, French security agents were busy with a clandestine struggle to thwart Japanese cultivation of anti-French Vietnamese nationalists.

Cao Dai leaders were not shy about expressing their loyalty to Cuong De and his Japanese patrons. In 1941, the French deported Cao Dai leaders to the Comoros Islands and occupied the Cao Dai headquarters in Tay Ninh. This did not prevent remaining Cao Dai leaders from working closely with the Japanese, providing thousands of workers for Japanese installations and organizing paramilitary units with Japanese protection. In 1942, Japanese agents succeeded in plucking Huynh Phu So from French custody and thereafter used him to spread their influence and to organize paramilitary units among his followers in western Cochinchina.

Many educated Vietnamese drawn toward political activism were energized by the Japanese counterweight to the French regime and the prospect of eventual Japanese action against the French. A number of loosely connected semi-clandestine groups with this inclination had begun to develop in Tonkin during the Popular Front period. They aimed to draw upon a sense of connection to a more glorious Vietnamese past than could be expressed by the names Dai Nam (Great South) and Viet Nam (Viet South) that had come into usage during the

Nguyen dynasty, a dynasty that had failed to protect the country's independence. Instead, they identified with the name Dai Viet (Great Viet), which had been the official name of the kingdom from the tenth through the eighteenth centuries.

Four such groups emerged during the late 1930s. They were to some extent influenced by the writings of Nietzsche and the muscular nationalism of the Young Turks and of the fascism then rising in Europe and Japan. They rejected both the ineffectual idealism of parliamentary democracy and the dialectical materialism of the communists. An early group espoused a principle of "mutuality" (*ho tuong*) in human relations as the basis for a theory of "between idealism and materialism" (*duy tam trung vat*). Called the Dai Viet National Socialist Party (Dai Viet Quoc Xa Dang), it was strong among urban intellectuals in Hanoi and Hai Phong.

Another group was established by Truong Tu Anh (1914–1946), who came from Phu Yen to Hanoi in 1934 to study law and subsequently developed a philosophy of "the people's livelihood" (*chu nghia dan toc sinh ton*) that focused upon the economic welfare of the common people; this group was named the Dai Viet Nationalist Party (Dai Viet Quoc Dan Dang) and was strong in Bac Giang, between Hanoi and the Guangxi border.

Two other groups emerged from people associated with the Self-Strengthening Literary Group (Tu Luc Van Doan). One was called the Dai Viet Humanist Party (Dai Viet Duy Dan Dang) and eventually became strong in the Ninh Binh area south of Hanoi. The other was the Dai Viet True People (Dai Viet Dan Chinh) of Nguyen Tuong Tam, the leading figure of the Self-Strengthening Literary Group, which published a Hanoi newspaper and endeavored to publicize the shared ideas of Dai Viet activists.

In 1939–1940, some Dai Viet people went to China to join the military unit being formed by the Japanese under the auspices of Cuong De and participated in the Lang Son affair of September 1940. In 1942 and 1943, the French attempted to suppress Dai Viet activities and made many arrests. Although he was not directly involved with Dai Viet groups, Tran Trong Kim, the education expert, historian, and propagandist of Confucianism, was acquainted with some of their members, which prompted him to seek Japanese protection during a wave of French arrests in late 1943. In 1944, after the fall of Vichy France, the four Dai Viet groups in Tonkin joined in the Dai Viet National Alliance (Dai Viet Quoc Gia Lien Minh). Although to some extent intellectually compatible with Vichy philosophy, Dai Viet people were uncompromisingly opposed to French colonialism.

In Annam, Ngo Dinh Diem organized the Dai Viet Restoration Association (Dai Viet Phuc Hung Hoi) in 1942 and, with his four brothers, formed youth groups to mobilize both Catholic and non-Catholic nationalists. His eldest brother, Ngo Dinh Khoi, was a prominent Hue official. Ngo Dinh Khoi's son served on the staff of the ranking Japanese official in Hue. Ngo Dinh Khoi opposed Pham Quynh, the prime minister, for being too pro-French and was consequently dismissed from office. When the French moved to suppress the Restoration Association in the summer of 1944, Ngo Dinh Diem obtained Japanese protection to evade arrest.

The Dai Viet groups gained traction from the Japanese propaganda of Asia for the Asians. They searched the history of their own country for an Asian answer to the impasse of Western values that were discredited by colonial capitalism on the one hand and by the materialism of communist internationalism on the other hand. This was a purely Vietnamese response to the country's predicament in the twentieth century and continued to be an influential intellectual trend for another generation.

Formation of the Viet Minh

After the destruction of the Indochinese Communist Party in Cochinchina in November 1940, the center of party authority emerged in Tonkin under the direction of Truong Chinh (given name: Dang Xuan Khu, 1907–1988), who had joined the Youth League in the late 1920s, had spent six years in prison, and had worked as a legal journalist in Hanoi during the Popular Front period. This man had chosen his revolutionary name to celebrate the Long March (*truong chinh* in Vietnamese) that had been a defining event in the history of the Chinese Communist Party during the 1930s. Within a few months he was summoned to the Sino-Vietnamese border to join a new leadership group developing in southern China around Ho Chi Minh.

The Comintern released Ho Chi Minh to depart Moscow in late 1938 with a caravan bringing aid and advisors to the Chinese Communist Party in northwestern China at Yenan. From there he was sent south as an officer in the Red Army and assigned to administrative duties with joint Communist–Nationalist operations in the Hunan–Guangxi border region. Following the Japanese advance into Guangxi in the autumn of 1939, he went to Chongqing where the Nationalist government of Chiang Kai-shek (1887–1975) was located. There he consulted with Zhou Enlai (1898–1976), the representative of the Chinese Communist Party at Chiang Kai-shek's capital, and with local Vietnamese.

One important contact that he apparently made at this time was Ho Hoc Lam (d. 1942), a compatriot from Nghe An. Ho Hoc Lam had gone to Japan as a student with Phan Boi Chau. There he met Chiang Kai-shek, a fellow student, and formed a lifelong friendship with him. Ho Hoc Lam subsequently supported

Phan Boi Chau's activities in China and eventually became a general in the Chinese Nationalist Army. In 1936, Ho Hoc Lam, along with other Vietnamese émigrés in Nanjing, had formed an organization called the Vietnamese Independence League (Viet Nam Doc Loc Dong Minh Hoi). Although moribund, it was still officially recognized as an organization by the Nationalist government and, with Ho Hoc Lam's blessing, was available for future use by Ho Chi Minh.

In early 1940, Ho Chi Minh went to Kunming, the capital of Yunnan. The ruler of Yunnan was Long Yun (1883–1962), a sinicized member of the Yi (Lolo) Tibeto-Burman ethnic group, who had governed the province since 1927. The relationship between Chiang Kai-shek and Long Yun was difficult, but critical aid reached Chongqing through Yunnan via the Burma Road and the air link over the mountains from India. Kunming was also where the largest American air base in China was located, the home of the "Flying Tigers" of Claire Lee Chennault (1893–1958).

In Kunming, Ho Chi Minh met with two Vietnamese members of the Indochinese Communist Party just arrived from Hanoi, Pham Van Dong (1906–2000) and Vo Nguyen Giap (b. 1911). Pham Van Dong, originally from Quang Ngai, had a typical biography of being active in Revolutionary Youth and the founding of the Indochinese Communist Party with prison time in the 1930s. Vo Nguyen Giap, from Quang Binh, had been a secondary school classmate of Pham Van Dong and had subsequently graduated from the University of Hanoi and became a history teacher.

The meeting of Ho Chi Minh with these two men at Kunming in June 1940 prompted letters to the Comintern and the Chinese Communist Party soliciting aid, though there was little prospect of assistance from either potential source. News of the events in Lang Son and Bac Son prompted Ho Chi Minh and his accumulating associates to shift to Guilin, which was closer to military operations. Guilin was under the authority of Zhang Fakui (1896–1980), a Hakka Nationalist general with a certain reputation for military competence. In the wake of the unauthorized Japanese attack on Lang Son, Zhang Fakui was driving the Japanese out of Guangxi. Meanwhile, Vietnamese refugees from the Lang Son debacle were crossing the border into China.

In October 1940, Ho Chi Minh reactivated the Vietnamese Independence League, obtained documentation with the name Ho Chi Minh (previously he had used a series of cover names, the most well-known of which was Nguyen Ai Quoc), and went to Jingxi, in western Guangxi about one hundred kilometers from the Cao Bang border. Members of the Vietnamese Nationalist Party were recruiting refugees from Lang Son at Jingxi. Ho Chi Minh and his entourage went there to also take advantage of this recruiting opportunity. He made a local accord with the Vietnamese Nationalist Party at Jingxi, forming an alliance called the Vietnamese Liberation League (Viet Nam Gia Phong Dong Minh Hoi) but the relationship between the two groups was competitive and without trust.

From Jingxi, Ho Chi Minh established contact with Truong Chinh's committee in Tonkin. In May 1941, he convened what became known as the Eighth Plenum of the Indochinese Communist Party, subsequently called the Pac Bo Plenum. Pac Bo was a liaison base in the mountains just inside the Vietnamese border. This meeting established the Vietnamese Independence League, thereafter commonly known by the abbreviation Viet Minh, as a front organization for the Indochinese Communist Party to rally patriotic Vietnamese willing to fight for independence but not necessarily interested in fighting for a communist revolution.

After a year of supervising propaganda, training recruits, and establishing bases in Cao Bang, in August 1942 Ho Chi Minh set out for Chongqing to bring the Viet Minh to the attention of Allied representatives. Nationalist security agents arrested him near Jingxi because of the forged documentation he was carrying. By February 1943 he had been transferred to the prison at Liuzhou, a major center of Zhang Fakui's operations.

In Liuzhou, Zhang Fakui had gathered Vietnamese émigrés under an umbrella organization called the Vietnamese Revolutionary League (Viet Nam Cach Mang Dong Minh Hoi). The Revolutionary League included members of the Vietnamese Nationalist Party, the Dai Viet movement, and other smaller groups as well as unaffiliated individuals. Nguyen Hai Than (1879–1955) was chairman of the Revolutionary League. He was a veteran of Phan Boi Chau's operations and a long-term resident of China. He had been peripherally affiliated with Ho Chi Minh's Revolutionary Youth movement of the 1920s, but did not like its communist connection. He had also been associated with Ho Hoc Lam in the formation of the Vietnamese Independence League at Nanjing in 1936. A prominent figure in the Revolutionary League was Nguyen Tuong Tam, the former leader of the 1930s literary group turned Dai Viet activist. He had gone to China where he became a leader of the Vietnamese Nationalist Party. Another leading figure in the Revolutionary League was Vu Hong Khanh (1898–1993). He had fled to China during the failed uprising of the Nationalist Party in 1930. He became a general in the Chinese Nationalist army, established a good relationship with Long Yun in Yunnan, and had assembled a Nationalist Party base at Kunming.

Zhang Fakui's intention was to use the Revolutionary League to develop an intelligence operation in Indochina. Eventually, he learned of Ho Chi Minh's true identity and was authorized by Chongqing to make use of him. After being released from prison and demonstrating his ability to supply information, Ho Chi Minh was brought into a reorganized Revolutionary League in early 1944.

Finally, in August 1944, Zhang Fakui allowed Ho Chi Minh to leave Liuzhou, and he returned to Cao Bang.

During Ho Chi Minh's two years of confinement in Guangxi, his colleagues began to build military bases in the mountains north of Hanoi and initiated National Salvation Associations (Hoi Cuu Quoc) to expand their influence among peasants, workers, youth, women's organizations, and soldiers in Tonkin and Annam. Truong Chinh was particularly active in rallying intellectuals into the Viet Minh. In addition to a National Salvation Cultural Association (Hoi Van Hoa Cuu Quoc), he also formed two ostensibly non-communist parties as member organizations of the Viet Minh front: the Vietnamese Socialist Party (Viet Nam Xa Hoi Dang) and the Vietnamese Democratic Party (Viet Nam Dan Chu Dang).

The August Revolution

For Vietnamese in Tonkin and northern Annam, the winter of 1944–1945 was a time of famine with around one million people dying of starvation. The 1944 spring rice crop had been reduced by drought and insect infestation and the autumn crop had been reduced by a typhoon; however, by themselves these events would not have caused this famine. Another factor was a long-term trend of population growth and decline of rice production in northern Vietnamese provinces that made them dependent upon rice from Cochinchina. This was exacerbated during the war by the Japanese demand that land be shifted from rice to strategic commodities such as jute, hemp, ramie, cotton, peanuts, and castor oil seed; this mainly affected Tonkin where these items were best cultivated due to soil and climate. But even under these conditions a famine would not have occurred without more immediate factors related to the final year of the war.

After the Allied liberation of France and the fall of the Vichy French government in the summer of 1944, the French military command in Indochina expanded its clandestine contact with Free French forces and made plans for the anticipated defeat of Japan. The arrival of American forces in the Philippines raised the possibility that the Americans might land in Indochina, although it was becoming obvious to all that the main line of American attack was directly toward the Japanese islands. In the autumn of 1944, American bombers began to hit Vietnamese ports and railroads and the US navy began to sink coastal shipping. Consequently, the amount of rice that could be shipped from Cochinchina to the north in 1944 was much less than usual.

But even the American disruption of the transportation system would not have produced such a devastating famine if not for the policies of the two armies in

Indochina. The final phase of the war turned nervous allies into potential enemies. Most of the transportation system was reserved for military purposes and both the French and the Japanese stockpiled large amounts of rice that would normally have been available for the civilian market. Furthermore, because of the looming military and political uncertainties, the wartime economy was collapsing with large-scale inflation, speculation, and hoarding.

In the midst of the famine, the tensions between the French and Japanese were released in early March 1945 when the Japanese disarmed and interned the French. Although this is what the French had most feared, they had done little to prepare for it and it was a relatively quick and non-violent event. In just a few hours, the French colonial regime was brought to an end by a dying imperial power whose own life was draining away. General Tsuchihashi Yuitsu (1891–1975) planned and executed this action. He had served as a military attaché at the Japanese embassy in Paris in the late 1930s and had held various Southeast Asian commands during the war before being assigned to Indochina in 1944. He became the de facto governor general of Indochina and assigned senior Japanese diplomats to replace the ranking French administrators in Cochinchina, Annam, and Tonkin. At the same time, he proclaimed Vietnam to be independent and formed a royal government at Hue to which he could pass governing responsibilities as the war ended.

Some Vietnamese, especially among the Cao Dai, expected Tsuchihashi to replace Bao Dai with Cuong De, who was residing in Tokyo, but wartime conditions made travel for such an important person too risky, and, in any case, Tsuchihashi wanted to minimize disruption as the Japanese position was becoming more fragile. Pham Quynh was discarded as Bao Dai's prime minister, both because of his Francophile disposition and because Bao Dai did not like him. Ngo Dinh Diem was widely regarded as the strongest candidate to replace Pham Quynh, but his strong anti-French attitude had inhibited his relationship with Bao Dai, and Tsuchihashi turned to Tran Trong Kim. After seeking protection with the Japanese in 1943, Tran Trong Kim had spent a year in Singapore and then was transferred to Bangkok. He was now brought to Hue and installed as head of a quasi-independent royal government.

It took until early May for Tran Trong Kim to form his cabinet of ministers and to begin to provide leadership to the protectorate government in Tonkin and Annam. His government did not extend its authority over Cochinchina or major cities, although the Japanese finally approved of it doing so at the very end of the war. With its passive reliance on the Japanese, it was a factor in the evolving situation more by what it did not do than by anything it did do. It did not inhibit the activities of nationalist organizations, which began to operate with a freedom that had never existed before.

Although it did not exercise the substance of independence, Tran Trong Kim's government nevertheless accelerated the mood of independence by releasing political prisoners and replacing the institutional symbols and vocabulary of the colonial regime with Vietnamese versions, giving the country the name of Viet Nam, replacing the terms Tonkin, Annam, and Cochinchina with Bac Bo, Trung Bo, and Nam Bo (northern division, central division, and southern division), issuing a national flag and a national anthem, organizing national holidays to celebrate famous events and heroic people in Vietnamese history. Most of all, the charismatic Minister of Youth, Phan Anh (1912–1990), contributed to politicizing young people and preparing them to participate in revolutionary action. Originally from Ha Tinh, Phan Anh studied law in France and spent the war years in Hue writing for a youth publication. During his brief time as Minister of Youth, he traveled extensively, speaking to gatherings of youth and exciting them with patriotic fervor. On the other hand, in the final weeks before the Japanese surrender, Tran Trong Kim was immobilized by a cabinet crisis. For the most part, the protectorate administration facilitated rather than obstructed the draining away of its authority at war's end.

Meanwhile, the Indochinese Communist Party was quick to take advantage of the Japanese takeover in early March. By this time, the Americans had begun to bomb railroads and harbors in Indochina to impede Japanese transport and communications; some American planes were shot down, and Ho Chi Minh established contact with US officers in Kunming by way of returning surviving pilots who had come under the control of his people. It was a propitious time because the French internment had erased the Allied intelligence network in Indochina, and Ho Chi Minh was in a position to offer an alternative. American intelligence officers sent him back with a radioman and within weeks were parachuting supplies, equipment, and weapons trainers.

In the summer of 1945, Ho Chi Minh and his associates established a headquarters at Tan Trao, in Son Duong district of Tuyen Quang Province, less than two hundred kilometers northwest of Hanoi. Around seventy people from northern Indochina were summoned as delegates to a series of conferences held at Tan Trao in mid August, then urgently sent back to their localities as news of the unexpectedly sudden Japanese surrender spread through the Vietnamese population.

During the five months between the internment of the French and the Japanese surrender, the Indochinese Communist Party was not the only political organization to anticipate an opportunity. In late March 1945, the Dai Viet National Alliance that had been formed in 1944 reorganized for military action. Despite the Dai Viet affinity for the Japanese, the Japanese were preoccupied with their sinking fortunes and gave the Dai Viet little encouragement. Dai Viet activists nevertheless became discernible factors in certain localities of lowland Tonkin. Nguyen Tuong Tam briefly attempted to mobilize these Dai Viet elements until he decided that Japan was a dead end and, in the summer of 1945, returned to Guangxi where he again became active in the Nationalist Party. From its base in Yunnan, the Nationalist Party established a strong presence down the Red River toward Hanoi. Groups associated with the Revolutionary League in Guangxi became active in Quang Ninh Province along the coast and its hinterland adjacent to the Chinese border.

What distinguished the Indochinese Communist Party and the organizations it had gathered in the Viet Minh front from its rivals were the breadth and depth of its influence both regionally and socially, although in most cases this influence was diffuse and more of a potential capable of being awakened by circumstances than a structure for conveying instructions and directing responses. At the time of the Japanese surrender, the Indochinese Communist Party was but one element in a revolutionary situation far beyond its capacity to control. It gained power in Hanoi and elsewhere through the accumulation of initiatives by many groups, few of which were under its direct supervision but most of which were susceptible to its leadership.

Upon news of Tokyo's surrender, Japanese forces quickly withdrew from exposed outposts, concentrated near ports from where they expected to be repatriated, and assumed an attitude of armed passivity, minimizing contact with local administrators. The royal government at Hue was inert. The communist leaders prepared to move out of their mountain bases toward Hanoi. Meanwhile, in villages, towns, and cities across the country, activists banded together to absorb or overwhelm existing authorities in a burst of exhilaration at the absence of foreign rulers.

Already in the weeks before the Japanese surrender there were violent episodes between Viet Minh activists and rival groups such as the Nationalist Party and the Dai Viet, particularly in provinces with easy access to the Chinese border where the leaders of these groups were located. The Japanese surrender did not create a vacuum. It simply removed the external restraints on a Vietnamese political process that had been developing for a long time in underground organizations and in the minds of people. Four days after the Japanese surrender, Viet Minh activists, mainly members of the Democratic Party, seized control of Hanoi and delivered it into the hands of their leaders, who arrived from the mountains a few days later.

Vietnamese historians call this the August Revolution. An initial phase of chaotic, exuberant, often spontaneous and relatively non-violent seizing of power by local groups was soon followed by a second phase in which the communist leadership in Hanoi extended its authority throughout Tonkin and down the coast of Annam. In some areas rival groups retained control, such as the Nationalist Party upriver from Hanoi where they benefited from easy access to their base in Kunming and the protection of incoming Chinese troops from Yunnan. In other areas, particularly the further south one went, where the Viet Minh organization was progressively weaker, uprisings turned violent, as in Quang Ngai, or resulted in confrontation between rival groups claiming to be Viet Minh, as in Binh Dinh and Phu Yen. Agents of the new authorities in Hanoi were sent to sort out local issues and to eliminate people regarded as threats to the regime. Thousands were assassinated, including prominent Francophiles such as Bui Quang Chieu and Pham Quynh.

The revolution had come to Quang Ngai early and violently with the arrival of local communists released from prison in the central highlands after the French internment. By the time of the Japanese surrender, radical groups claiming affiliation with the Viet Minh were already in the process of spreading class struggle in rural areas. The provincial governor happened to be Ngo Dinh Diem's eldest brother Ngo Dinh Khoi, who had been appointed by Tran Trong Kim. In the high tide of the August Revolution, he was put to death, and his son with him. Quang Ngai was also the final resting place of Ta Thu Thau, who was seized and killed as he was making his way from Tonkin to Saigon.

Return of the French

Ho Chi Minh proclaimed Vietnamese independence and the Democratic Republic of Vietnam at a Hanoi rally on September 2, but already the attention of his new government was shifting from internal matters to the arrival of Allied troops, ostensibly to disarm and repatriate the Japanese. At the Potsdam conference in July, Allied leaders divided Indochina at the sixteenth parallel with British forces responsible for the south and Chinese Nationalist forces responsible for the north. The sixteenth parallel crosses the Vietnamese coast between Da Nang and Hoi An in Quang Nam Province.

Chiang Kai-shek took this allied assignment as an opportunity to settle matters with Long Yun, the leader of Yunnan whom he distrusted. He placed Long Yun in command of the Indochinese operation as a way of emptying Yunnan of Long Yun's troops. Lu Han (1895–1974), a cousin of Long Yun and a general in his army, was given charge of the Indochina operation, during which Chiang Kai-shek engineered the replacement of Long Yun by Lu Han, an affair that distracted Lu Han from events in Indochina. Accompanying the Chinese forces into northern Indochina were hundreds of Vietnamese anti-communist nationalists returning from exile, the most prominent of whom were Nguyen Tuong Tam and

Vu Hong Khanh of the Nationalist Party and Nguyen Hai Than with an assortment of people gathered in the Revolutionary League.

The Chinese understood that they could not push aside the new authorities in Hanoi without provoking a popular reaction that would endanger their mission. At the same time, they pressured Ho Chi Minh to incorporate into his government the anti-communist politicians who arrived in Hanoi with them. Within a few weeks of the September 2 declaration of independence, it became obvious to Ho Chi Minh that he and his communist colleagues would have to broaden their government to include large numbers of people not associated with the Viet Minh front. This was not only because of Chinese pressure to include members of the Nationalist Party and the Revolutionary League, but also because they could not entirely control the overwhelming popular response to the August Revolution. Practical problems of establishing a new system of government required the inclusion of many people outside of their organizational control. The Dai Viet groups, however, were outlawed from the start, ostensibly because of their association with the Japanese.

In November, the Indochinese Communist Party officially disbanded and went underground. Subsequent negotiations produced an arrangement by which seventy of the National Assembly seats to be filled in a January 1946 election were reserved for members of the Nationalist Party (allotted fifty seats) and the Revolutionary League (allotted twenty seats). These allotted seats amounted to about 20 percent of the Assembly. Furthermore, a cabinet was to be formed that included members from both of these non-Viet Minh groups. Ho Chi Minh was to be president of the new coalition government and Nguyen Hai Than was designated as vice president. This government came into existence in early 1946 just as the French, having returned to the south, were preparing to re-enter the north.

In August 1945 the Viet Minh organization in Cochinchina was mostly on paper and the Communist Party in Cochinchina was split and surrounded by rivals. The regional leadership committee could not agree on what to do, being divided into factions based in Can Tho and in Saigon, each of which sent representatives to Hanoi seeking approval. The leader of the Saigon faction was Tran Van Giau (1911–2010), a southerner who had followed a typical communist career with sojourns in Paris, in Moscow, and in Indochinese prisons. In addition to arguing with his fellow communists, Tran Van Giau had to negotiate with a constellation of religious, monarchist, and other groups that had been encouraged by the Japanese in the last months of the war.

After disarming the French in March, the Japanese had begun to arm paramilitary units attached to the Cao Dai and Hoa Hao religions. When Japan surrendered, these groups along with Catholics, Dai Viet activists, Trotskyists, and members of the Red Cross, militia, police, and other groups formed a United National Front. On August 21, two days after the Viet Minh takeover in Hanoi, these groups led a large demonstration in the streets of Saigon. Ngo Dinh Diem was one of the leaders of this front.

Two days later, Bao Dai abdicated and announced his support of the Viet Minh government in Hanoi, thereby defeating the hopes of monarchists. More to the point, Tran Van Giau persuaded some leaders of the United National Front that they would be handicapped when seeking international recognition because the Allies would view their organization as tainted by association with Japan. Consequently, many groups chose to join the public demonstration organized by the Viet Minh on August 25 at which Tran Van Giau announced a Southern Provisional Administrative Committee. However, when it became clear that communists dominated this committee the various groups began to go their separate ways.

In the spring of 1945, the Vichy sport and youth movement in Cochinchina had been reformed as a paramilitary organization under Japanese auspices. It was called Vanguard Youth and was led by Pham Ngoc Thao (1909–1968), a medical doctor trained in France who had become involved in politics during the Popular Front period. By September 1945, Pham Ngoc Thao was a secret member of the Indochinese Communist Party, and Vanguard Youth accordingly became the most important element in the southern Viet Minh. In the last days of August it was the Vanguard Youth that brought the revolution to the Cochinchinese countryside.

In western Cochinchina, however, the Hoa Hao resisted Viet Minh ascendancy, leading to episodes of violence, and Huynh Phu So publicly denounced Tran Van Giau. At Tay Ninh, the Cao Dai leadership split between those willing to cooperate with the Viet Minh and those who were not. Tran Van Giau eliminated many Trotskyists and other miscellaneous enemies of the party, but he could not form a government with broad popular support as the Viet Minh had done in Hanoi and in other cities further north. A Saigon rally that he organized on September 2 to coincide with the proclamation of independence in Hanoi turned into a bloody riot between Vietnamese and French residents of the city. He subsequently lost control of the Provisional Committee. His superiors in Hanoi later dismissed him from political work, considering his leadership in Saigon to have been heavy-handed and inept, but the situation in Cochinchina was beyond the grasp of any one man or party.

The 20th Indian Division, veterans of the Burma campaign, began to arrive in the second week of September. It was commanded by Douglas David Gracey (1894–1964), a career officer in the Indian army with a reputation for competence. The British recognized French sovereignty in Indochina. They were spread thin in Asia at that time, and Gracey limited his role to enforcing public order and facilitating the arrival of French forces. Under instructions to avoid getting involved in local politics and with inadequate numbers of troops, he occupied Saigon with caution.

The tension between the French and Vietnamese populations in the city was explosive. In late September, Gracey prematurely rearmed a French unit that had been interned by the Japanese. The French soldiers took possession of public buildings and expelled the Provisional Committee from the city. They went on to provoke a riot by assaulting Vietnamese civilians and taking many of them prisoner. Gracey sent the French back to their barracks, but within hours the Vietnamese underworld erupted against French civilians, killing around two hundred of them. To restore order, Gracey resorted to activating rearmed Japanese prisoners under his command. These events strengthened the determination of British authorities to turn the Indochina business over to the French as quickly as possible.

French post-war colonial policy vaguely envisioned a French Union in which a five-state Indochinese Federation existed under a French governor general. The states, corresponding to the five parts of French Indochina, would enjoy varying degrees of local autonomy while economic, military, and diplomatic powers remained with the French. Such was the plan announced by the government of Charles de Gaulle in early 1945. This plan may have been plausible if the end of the war had found the French still in power in Indochina, but the events of 1945 rendered this an antiquated dream. French aims required that the Vietnamese acquiesce to the return of French colonial rule. Although this was a vain hope, French policy remained stuck on this point, which meant that the first necessary step for the French was to reconquer the Vietnamese.

The men chosen by de Gaulle to do this were closely associated with him during the European war, men he trusted and who were devoted to him. General Philippe François Marie Leclerc de Hauteclocque (1902–1947) had a venerable aristocratic lineage. He commanded the first French units to reach Paris in 1944 and, as commander of French forces in Asia, represented France at the September 2 surrender ceremony in Tokyo Bay. He arrived in Saigon in early October with the first large infusion of French troops from Europe. Georges Louis Marie Thierry d'Argenlieu (1889–1964), with a mixed naval and monastic career, had risen to the rank of admiral in de Gaulle's navy. Appointed as high commissioner with supreme authority for implementing French policy in Indochina, he arrived in Saigon at the end of October. Leclerc and d'Argenlieu single-mindedly pursued a policy of reconquest.

By the end of the year, Leclerc had retaken most cities and towns in Cochinchina and southern Annam and the British were departing. By early 1946 Leclerc was making plans to attack Tonkin, but this would not be possible without some understanding with the Chinese. On February 28, 1946, French diplomats in Chongqing signed an agreement with Chiang Kai-shek by which France renounced the unequal treaties of the past and China recognized French sovereignty in Indochina. The next day, Leclerc departed Saigon with a large expeditionary force aboard a fleet of over thirty ships. Wanting to complete his Tonkin campaign before the monsoon rains began in May, he planned to arrive at Hai Phong on March 6 when a high tide would allow his heavy ships upriver to the docks. The next high tide would not occur until March 18, which in his calculations would be too late in the season.

The Chinese were unwilling to be caught in the middle of a war between the French and the Vietnamese and made it clear that they would not allow the French to land without Vietnamese approval. When French ships appeared at Hai Phong on the morning of March 6, Chinese forces fired on them and were prepared to contest their landing until word arrived that a Franco-Vietnamese agreement was being signed in Hanoi. This agreement postponed war in the north until after the Chinese departed six months later.

Finalized under the pressure of the high tide, the Franco-Vietnamese Agreement of March 6 contained provisions repugnant to both sides. Instead of obtaining French recognition of Vietnamese "independence," Ho Chi Minh agreed to his government being weakly identified as a "free state" (*état libre*) within the Indochinese Federation under the French Union. For their part, the French agreed to two provisions they had no intention of honoring. French troops north of the sixteenth parallel were limited to fifteen thousand men for a period of five years, and a referendum was to be held on the issue of unifying the Vietnamese regions. This agreement entangled the French and Vietnamese in joint military operations and fruitless negotiations for several months.

Outbreak of a new war

The central issue in subsequent Franco-Vietnamese negotiations was the status of Cochinchina. D'Argenlieu was determined to deny Ho Chi Minh's government any claim to the south. At a conference held during April and May in Dalat, a colonial resort in the Central Highlands, d'Argenlieu made it clear to the Vietnamese representatives from Hanoi that there would be no referendum. He was busy setting up a Republic of Cochinchina with Nguyen Van Thinh (1888–1946), a former Constitutionalist politician and a French citizen, as president. Many Vietnamese who had adapted to French colonialism and nurtured political ambitions gathered around Nguyen Van Thinh. In August, d'Argenlieu convened another conference at Dalat with pliant representatives from all five regions of Indochina. This conference denounced the Hanoi government and made plans for an Indochinese Federation. From d'Argenlieu's perspective, Ho Chi Minh's government was a temporary annoyance.

The scheme for a Republic of Cochinchina united virtually all of the southern groups, including the Cao Dai and the Hoa Hao, in opposition. The fighting between French and Vietnamese in Cochinchina that had begun the previous autumn intensified. Tran Van Giau was called back to the north and replaced by Nguyen Binh (1906–1951), a former Nationalist Party activist from near Hanoi who had meanwhile joined the communists. Nguyen Binh turned the Viet Minh into a military alliance against the threat of Cochinchinese separatism. He made extensive use of terror, including the detonation of bombs in public places, to discredit French authority. The fighting in Cochinchina continued through the summer and into the autumn of 1946.

Meanwhile, Ho Chi Minh and Pham Van Dong had traveled to France to negotiate directly with the government in Paris. This was a time of transition between the immediate post-war government of Charles de Gaulle, who had abruptly resigned in January 1946, and the constitution of the Fourth Republic, which would go into effect in January 1947. The dominant politician during this year was Georges Augustin Bidault (1899–1983), a former history teacher, pre-war Catholic anti-fascist youth leader, veteran of the wartime resistance, and Minister of Foreign Affairs since August 1944. He had supported de Gaulle but believed that de Gaulle's preference for a presidential, rather than a parliamentary, constitution was not plausible in the existing political situation. Bidault led one of the three main political parties at that time, the Mouvement Républicain Populaire (commonly referred to as the MRP), the other two being the Socialist Party and the Communist Party. The election of June 1946 resulted in Bidault forming a government that included socialists and communists. He served as both Prime Minister and Minister of Foreign Affairs in this government.

Ho Chi Minh was personally acquainted with some of the socialist and communist politicians because he had been a member of both parties during his residence in Paris a quarter-century before. Although he was welcomed warmly, there was no political will in France, even among socialists and communists, to support his negotiating agenda. In the uncertain political situation of 1946, no French politician was prepared to gainsay the Indochina policy established by de Gaulle and continued by Bidault, the main points of which were maintenance of the Tonkin–Annam–Cochinchina division and no recognition of the Democratic Republic of Vietnam as an "independent" state. Furthermore, with d'Argenlieu and Leclerc in Indochina actively implementing this policy, a more robust government than Bidault's ephemeral five-month coalition turned out to be would have been required to implement a change of course. Neverthe-less, d'Argenlieu was able to pursue this policy because French politicians over-whelming agreed with it, regardless of any supposed weakness of the Paris government.

In mid September, after two months of failed negotiations at the Paris suburb of Fontainebleau, the Vietnamese negotiator, Pham Van Dong, departed. At that moment, the last of the Chinese were leaving Tonkin. The Chinese had pro-longed their departure to enable thousands of troops from Yunnan and Guangxi to be shipped by rail to Hai Phong for embarkation to the civil war battlefields in northern China. Now, without their presence, the possibility of war breaking out between the Vietnamese and the French increased day by day. Even as the Chinese presence had produced the Franco-Vietnamese agreement of the previ-ous March, the Chinese absence led to another Franco-Vietnamese agreement designed to prolong the prospect of settling matters peacefully.

One day after Pham Van Dong's departure and three days before the last Chinese troops were scheduled to depart Hai Phong, Ho Chi Minh, who had been vainly trying to rally political support for his government among Paris politicians, signed a modus vivendi with the Minister for Overseas France, Marius Moutet (1876–1968). Moutet, a socialist, agreed in principle with the established Indochina policy, but, perhaps under the pressure of time, he was not alert to the practical effects of the modus vivendi. This agreement guaranteed the safety of French citizens and their property and established committees and commissions to address outstanding questions. The most important item in this modus vivendi, however, was the provision for a ceasefire in Cochinchina effective October 30. This ceasefire provision had far-reaching implications and results, for it diminished d'Argenlieu's scheme for a Republic of Cochinchina.

With this modus vivendi, the French government recognized the Vietnamese resistance in Cochinchina as a legitimate party to a ceasefire and not simply as terrorists beyond the law. The French government also acknowledged that Ho Chi Minh was competent to deal on behalf of the Cochinchina resistance. The modus vivendi undermined both d'Argenlieu's Republic of Cochinchina and the French doctrine of regional separation. Furthermore, when in fact Nguyen Binh and his Cochinchinese allies honored the ceasefire on October 30, it was obvious that Ho Chi Minh spoke for them. Nguyen Van Thinh, president of the Republic of Cochinchina, committed suicide ten days after the ceasefire went into effect.

Just as his Cochinchina policy suffered this setback, the November 10 election in France posed a further challenge to d'Argenlieu. Gains by the social-ists and communists brought the Bidault cabinet to an end. The new constitution of the Fourth Republic had been approved and would go into effect at the beginning of 1947. Meanwhile, socialists, some of whom had expressed criticism of d'Argenlieu, formed caretaker governments. D'Argenlieu departed for France three days after the election to ensure that political change in Paris did not disturb his Indochina policy. He left local matters in the hands of trusted subordinates, most important of whom was General Jean Etienne Valluy (1899–1970), who had replaced Leclerc the previous summer.

Since October, Valluy and d'Argenlieu had been making plans to initiate hostilities in the north in order to remove the Vietnamese government in Hanoi, thereby disposing of the main obstacle to the Indochinese Federation and invalidating the Cochinchinese implications of the modus vivendi ceasefire. Before departing for France, d'Argenlieu instructed Valluy to implement these plans. This was done without delay.

The situation in the north had greatly changed during the preceding months while Ho Chi Minh was in France. Most Chinese occupying forces had departed by June and with them went many of the anti-communist Vietnamese politicians who had sheltered under their protection, including Nguyen Hai Than, Nguyen Tuong Tam, and Vu Hong Khanh. The government consequently became more homogeneous and compliant with the communist leadership. Some groups, particularly members of the Nationalist Party, resisted the turn of events, but Vo Nguyen Giap attacked them, killing or arresting many hundreds. The French cooperated with this campaign because the Nationalist Party was more implacably anti-French than the Viet Minh. At the same time, a new front was assembled to bring several groups that had previously had a separate organizational existence into alliance with the Viet Minh, in particular unions and associations representing women, workers, and youth. This was known as the Lien Viet (Hoi Lien Hiep Quoc Dan Viet Nam, Vietnamese People's National United Association).

Meanwhile, Viet Minh agents were purchasing arms in various Asian countries, mainly China and Thailand, and stockpiling supplies in the mountains. Franco-Vietnamese tensions escalated in the seaport of Hai Phong, the main point of access for the Vietnamese to the outside world and for the French to Tonkin. Vietnamese and French military units coexisted in a volatile state of restrained antagonism with control of the docks being the focus of contention. After d'Argenlieu's departure for France in mid November, Valluy instructed his subordinates in Tonkin to escalate provocations. Open warfare eventually broke out on November 23 when the French seized Hai Phong after heavy fighting and a bombardment that killed thousands of civilians. At the same time, French forces seized Lang Son, where the railroad connected with Guangxi. The Vietnamese began to evacuate Hanoi, and, less than a month later, on December 19, fighting broke out there as the Vietnamese government and army shifted to the mountains.

In accepting this war, the French anticipated a short campaign that would be over long before 1950 when their calculations indicated that they would no longer be able to financially sustain a war in Indochina. Even French leaders who believed that French interests in Indochina could have been arranged without resorting to war were confident of a quick military solution. Leclerc, d'Argenlieu, and Valluy had implemented a policy that was widely supported by the French political establishment and the French people. That the war would last so long and that it would eventually become part of a global confrontation beyond the national interests of France were unforeseen.

A Franco-Vietnamese government

Although large numbers of Vietnamese rallied to the Viet Minh to defend national independence, there were also many Vietnamese who saw the underlying Viet Minh agenda of communist revolution as a threat to their vision of an independent Vietnam. They viewed a renewal of French colonialism as an unlikely long-term prospect in a decolonizing world, and they looked for ways to keep alive the possibility of an independent but non-communist Vietnam. These people needed some kind of plausible leader with a potentially broad national appeal, and some of them began to look in the direction of Bao Dai.

Bao Dai had earned a measure of good will among the Vietnamese by his abdication and willingness to be a "patriotic citizen" during the August Revolution. After a few months in Hanoi as "advisor" to the new government, he went to China and remained there, drawing the attention of both non-communist Vietnamese politicians and French administrators.

The new French constitution contained the legal basis for designing an Indochinese Federation within the French Union, which up until then had been simply a vague idea. In January 1947, the first government of the Fourth Republic was formed under the leadership of Paul Ramadier (1888–1961), a socialist. He envisioned an Indochinese Federation made up not of five or four parts as earlier concepts espoused by d'Argenlieu proposed, but rather three "associated states" for the Cambodians, the Laotians, and the Vietnamese. This willingness to speak of a united Vietnam, despite legal impediments entrenched in the special status of Cochinchina dating from the mid nineteenth century, became the basis for French discussions with Bao Dai. Another factor softening the French position was the Madagascar uprising, which prevented military reinforcements from reaching Indochina before the rains began. In early 1947, the French signed an accord with Cao Dai leaders and, after the communist murder of Huynh Phu So in April, also made an agreement with Hoa Hao leaders. Thereafter, the French subsidized and relied upon Cao Dai and Hoa Hao armies to fight the Viet Minh in rural Cochinchina. With the monsoon rains inhibiting military operations until autumn, the French seemed to be in a mood to talk, if not to negotiate.

In March 1947, Ramadier replaced d'Argenlieu with Émile Bollaert (1890–1978), a man with no experience outside of France. From a family of musicians, Bollaert earned a law degree; served with distinction in the army during the First World War; occupied a series of mid-level government posts, mostly provincial, in the inter-war period; served in the wartime resistance until captured; and ended the war in the Bergen-Belsen concentration camp. In the weeks before he was replaced, d'Argenlieu was beginning to promote the idea of using Bao Dai to rally Vietnamese behind French policy. Although not given the freedom of action that had been exercised by d'Argenlieu, Bollaert endeavored to open paths of consultation with Vietnamese who were willing to work with France in a process they were led to believe was aimed at dissolving the colonial relationship. Shortly after arriving in Indochina, Bollaert established contact with both Bao Dai and Ho Chi Minh.

At the time of Bollaert's initial contact with Ho Chi Minh in April 1947, Ho Chi Minh entertained the possibility that the French communists, who were then a significant part of Ramadier's government, could influence French policy in his favor. In the summer of 1947, he brought more non-communists into his government and attempted to project a demeanor of moderation, expressing a willingness to be in the French Union if Vietnam were independent and unified. The French were unwilling to go so far and, believing that military operations during the upcoming dry season would eliminate the Viet Minh, preferred to deal with Bao Dai, who was more malleable to their purposes.

In early 1947, leading figures in the Nationalist Party and the Revolutionary League who had taken refuge in China during 1946 gathered around Bao Dai. Subsequently, other prominent figures from inside Indochina also went to consult with Bao Dai, including Le Van Hoach (1896–1978), a member of the Cao Dai who had replaced Nguyen Van Thinh as president of the Republic of Cochinchina; the chief military leader of the Cao Dai; the ranking Vietnamese administrators of Tonkin and Annam; and Ngo Dinh Diem.

In September 1947, Bao Dai, in Hong Kong, issued a statement indicating his willingness to talk with the French on behalf of an independent and united Vietnam. Long-distance discussions between Bao Dai and Bollaert accelerated. In October, France signaled its abandonment of d'Argenlieu's Cochinchina separatism policy by changing the Republic of Cochinchina to the Provisional

Government of South Vietnam. At the same time, the French replaced Le Van Hoach, whom they did not trust, with Nguyen Van Xuan (1892–1989), a French citizen and a general in the French army who had collaborated with Nguyen Van Thinh and d'Argenlieu in forming the Republic of Cochinchina a year and a half before. Nguyen Van Xuan also supported an accommodation with Bao Dai.

Meanwhile, with the coming of the dry season, General Valluy made his move into the mountains to exterminate Ho Chi Minh's government. The operation was a dismal failure, and by the end of the year his men were forced to withdraw back to the lowlands. Thereafter, the war appeared to settle into a stalemate that worried the French because they understood that they could not sustain an interminable war. Furthermore, French policymakers were increasingly convinced that even battlefield success would lead nowhere without developing an alternative to the Viet Minh that was acceptable to a critical mass of influential Vietnamese. Despite the dramatic post-war growth of the French colon community, French authorities were dependent upon the service and cooperation of large numbers of Vietnamese civil servants, including police and soldiers. The politicians who represented these Vietnamese were using Bao Dai to press for change in the Franco-Vietnamese relationship.

In November 1947, Ramadier's government fell and was replaced by the more conservative government of Robert Schuman (1886–1963). Ramadier had been diffident about making an agreement with Bao Dai. That constraint was now removed. In early December, Bao Dai and Bollaert met and signed a statement that became the basis for further negotiations. In June 1948, Bollaert signed an agreement with Bao Dai that envisioned "independence" and "unity" for Vietnam. To facilitate this, a month earlier Nguyen Van Xuan's government in Saigon was renamed the Provisional Central Government of Vietnam. Now, for the first time, there were two Vietnamese governments claiming jurisdiction over all of Vietnam.

But Paris was preoccupied with the failure of three governments within two months, from July to September, and many Vietnamese politicians stepped away from Nguyen Van Xuan's government, which, despite the changed name, was primarily comprised of a residue of French and Vietnamese Cochinchina separatists. It took several weeks for French policy to regain momentum. In October, Bollaert was replaced with Léon Pignon (1908–1976). Pignon was a career colonial administrator who had been in Indochina since 1945. He had assisted in negotiating the Franco-Vietnamese agreement of March 6, 1946, and had been a principal advisor of d'Argenlieu. Bollaert did not trust Pignon because of his association with d'Argenlieu's policies, and Pignon was assigned to Cambodia during Bollaert's tenure.

Pignon was a strong advocate of setting up a Vietnamese government under Bao Dai to rally the non-communist Vietnamese. He believed that such a government could be given a countenance of sovereignty while France retained control of vital state functions. With his support, the Elysée Agreement was signed in March 1949, granting Vietnam independence and unity but reserving to France control of financial, economic, diplomatic, and military affairs and creating an autonomous territory for non-Vietnamese peoples in the Central Highlands. It took nearly a year before this agreement was fully ratified into law by the French National Assembly. Legal issues related to Cochinchina as a separate jurisdiction were finally resolved in June 1949, and at that time Bao Dai inaugurated his government in Saigon as the State of Vietnam. But not until February 1950 did the French National Assembly ratify the entire agreement. Outstanding issues were slated to be resolved in future negotiations.

Bao Dai's State of Vietnam rallied most of the heterogeneous groups in Cochinchina. While Cao Dai leaders were hostile to the French and wavered between support of Saigon governments and wartime neutrality, in 1949 they firmly supported Bao Dai. The Viet Minh murder of Huynh Phu So in 1947 had made the Viet Minh an enemy of the Hoa Hao. The French subsequently enlisted the Hoa Hao to maintain security in western Cochinchina. There was a pattern of dissention among Hoa Hao leaders, but most pledged their support to Bao Dai. An organization of river pirates in the Saigon–Cholon area had emerged in September 1945 as allies of the Viet Minh and thereafter became a local economic and political force called the Binh Xuyen. The Binh Xuyen pledged loyalty to Bao Dai and subsequently prospered under his patronage, eventually commanding both the criminal underworld and the police of the metropolitan area. Although Catholics in the north overwhelmingly supported the Viet Minh until 1950, Catholic militias had formed in the south for protection against Viet Minh attacks and gave their allegiance to Bao Dai.

Radicalization of the Viet Minh

Nguyen Binh, the Viet Minh leader in Cochinchina, continued a guerrilla war against the French and against the groups supporting Bao Dai until his death in 1951. He was able to establish bases in less-populated areas where the Hoa Hao or Cao Dai were not strong: in the Ca Mau region of the extreme south and in the swampy Dong Thap Muoi region west of Saigon along the Cambodian border.

The other main center of Viet Minh strength outside of northern Vietnam was in Quang Ngai, where the communist leadership had been relatively radical since

1945. In 1946 a Viet Minh military academy was established in Quang Ngai under the leadership of Nguyen Son (1908–1956) and several Japanese officers who chose to remain in Indochina to fight the French. Nguyen Son, originally from a Hanoi suburb, had joined the Chinese Communist Party in the 1920s and by the 1940s had risen to the top level of leadership among Chinese communists. He returned to Vietnam in 1945, bringing with him ideas about self-criticism and individual rectification for nurturing the new socialist personality. He was in Quang Ngai for only about a year, but his influence strengthened the Communist Party in Quang Ngai and made this province the revolutionary vanguard of the central coast.

In late 1947 and early 1948, a series of events led to the realignment of Vietnamese communist policies away from the national front concept and toward the international communist movement and revolutionary class struggle. At a plenum of the Vietnamese communist leadership in January 1948, three new aspects of thought and policy were addressed: the Zhdanov Doctrine, land reform, and party membership. In September 1947, one of Stalin's confidants, Andrei Zhdanov (1896–1948), founded what came to be called the Cominform (Information Bureau of the Communist and Workers' Parties) as a new Cold War version of the Comintern, which had been disbanded during the Second World War. Zhdanov announced what became known as the Zhdanov Doctrine asserting that the world was divided into two antagonistic camps: the imperialist forces led by the United States and the socialist democratic forces led by the Soviet Union. Although his ideas were formulated primarily in the realm of culture, their political implications were obvious: there could be no compromise with class enemies of the revolution. The Vietnamese plenum cited and acknowledged the Zhdanov Doctrine.

By the end of 1947, the Chinese communists were gaining victories in Manchuria and turning the civil war in their favor. At that time, the Chinese were implementing a radical program of homicidal land reform in parts of northern and northeastern China, and Mao Zedong made announcements emphasizing the importance of land reform in the struggle against anti-revolutionary enemies. Although the Vietnamese communists were not yet in a position to initiate such an ambitious land policy, their plenum in early 1948 nevertheless took an important step in that direction by calling for the confiscation of the land and property of "traitors." Although in Viet Minh terminology "traitors" were those who served the French, in communist terms they were class enemies of the revolution. In 1948 the two definitions of "traitors" began to be conflated by Vietnamese communist officials, hardening the boundary between the party and the front. Increasingly from this time, those who had joined the Viet Minh out of patriotism rather than commitment to communist revolution were marginalized.

This was a serious problem for the Vietnamese communists, because in
1945 and 1946 it had been necessary to allot several government ministries to
non-communists, in particular those dealing with education, trade, agriculture,
irrigation, and justice. After the Viet Minh government was driven into the
mountains in 1947, the usefulness of non-communist urban intellectuals and
French-trained professionals in these ministries declined. Yet, in the administration of justice, lawyers and judges continued to advocate an independent
judiciary to the chagrin of communist leaders, and the court system threatened
to thwart policies advocated by the party.

In the rush of patriotic enthusiasm that accompanied the August Revolution
and the outbreak of war, party ranks had more than tripled with thousands of
people whose commitment to communism was lukewarm or non-existent. After
the party had been ostensibly abolished in November 1945, it continued to exist
as a structure of command and status within the Viet Minh front. By late 1947,
when there was no longer any discernible benefit in displaying a moderate visage
to the French, the party began to change course.

The plenum of early 1948 decided to restrict new members to people from
correct class backgrounds, such as soldiers, workers, peasants, and ethnic minorities. Furthermore, new members would be required to undergo a period of
training and indoctrination. The idea was to build up a new core of obedient
and ideologically reliable party members who would eventually overwhelm those
who had rallied to the Viet Minh in 1945, 1946, and 1947 for mainly patriotic
reasons. This arousal of struggle within the party was gradual until 1950 when
the arrival of Chinese communists on the border enabled the Vietnamese communists to take a more peremptory attitude toward non-party colleagues in the
Viet Minh. Until then, the communists sought to retain the loyalty of people who
were susceptible to the Bao Dai appeal.

Beginning in 1948, Vietnamese communists aligned their party rhetoric with
the Cold War terminology of international communism, making social revolution the foundation of national liberation and espousing the Marxist-Leninist
"new democracy" being hailed in China and Eastern Europe. The decline of the
left in France dispelled the mirage of a potential ally there, and the Bao Dai
phenomenon sharpened the need to combat Vietnamese enemies as well as the
French. However, as long as the Vietnamese communists remained isolated from
potential allies, they could not afford to frighten away their non-communist
followers.

In February 1948, Viet Minh representatives attended two meetings in Calcutta: the Second Congress of the Communist Party of India, which announced a
new emphasis on class struggle, and the Conference of Youth and Students of
Southeast Asia Fighting for Freedom and Independence, which was organized by

groups associated with Soviet propaganda operations. Shortly after these meetings, there was an upsurge of communist activity in Burma, Malaya, and Indonesia. For the Vietnamese communists, the Calcutta meetings and their sequels added plausibility to the prospect of being part of an international movement. But it was the communist victory in the Chinese civil war that fundamentally altered the situation.

Chinese communist army units began to accumulate on the Sino-Vietnamese border in late 1949, and in December Ho Chi Minh set out for Beijing. In January both Mao Zedong's People's Republic of China and the Soviet Union announced diplomatic recognition of Ho Chi Minh's Democratic Republic of Vietnam. From Beijing, Ho Chi Minh continued on to Moscow to meet with Stalin. Stalin released some limited military equipment for transport to Vietnam, but the main burden for assisting the Vietnamese was assigned to the Chinese. By April 1950 a Chinese Military Advisory Group (CMAG) had been formed and Vietnamese military units were soon being trained in Yunnan and Guangxi as Chinese supplies and advisors began to arrive in Vietnam.

During the spring and summer of 1950, the Viet Minh proclaimed a general mobilization and conducted a series of activities to promote the recruitment of people into their ranks. By the end of the summer around twenty thousand troops had been trained and equipped in China. In September and October, a system of French forts and installations along the Sino-Vietnamese border were overrun, expelling the French from the uplands. This was followed by a series of major attacks into the Red River lowlands that continued for most of 1951. The military situation rapidly shifted against the French with the rise of the People's Republic of China.

The political situation also changed rapidly once the lifeline to foreign allies was established. In February and March 1951, the Second Congress of the Indochinese Communist Party was held in Tuyen Quang Province with around two hundred delegates (the first party congress had been held in 1935 in Macau). This congress created separate parties for Cambodia and Laos under the supervision of the Vietnamese party, which was renamed the Vietnamese Labor Party to indicate a new emphasis on class struggle in line with Chinese communist doctrine, which was strongly supported by Truong Chinh, the party secretary general. At the same time, the Viet Minh front had become so closely associated with its communist leadership that it no longer served as a "front organization," so it, along with the Vietnamese Labor Party, was merged into the Lien Viet front that had been organized in 1946 to bring various groups into alliance with the Viet Minh.

However, this effort to withdraw the Viet Minh behind an ostensibly more inclusive Lien Viet front did not have its desired effect. The movement of people from upland resistance bases to French-controlled areas, especially educated professionals and people from inconveniently non-revolutionary class backgrounds, previously a small but growing number, now became a significant shift of population. Most of these people dropped out of politics, being unwilling to follow either the communists or the French. They added to the ranks of those waiting for national independence without either communism or colonialism, those who were called *attentistes*, "those who wait," in French and *trum chan*, "those who cover their heads with a blanket," in Vietnamese.

The most respected leader of these people was Ngo Dinh Diem, an uncompromising nationalist and anti-communist. He had repeatedly warned Bao Dai against making a settlement with the French that compromised true independence. He believed that the Elysée Agreement was a sham and refused to be associated with it. In August 1950, when he heard rumors that the Viet Minh had issued instructions for his assassination, he left the country and by the end of the year was living in the United States.

The beginning of United States involvement

Until 1950, the United States was uninvolved in the Vietnamese conflict. While supportive of France as a Cold War ally in Europe, the Truman administration refrained from providing direct assistance to French operations in Indochina, not wanting to be associated with what it viewed as a colonial policy. In early 1949, with the ongoing Berlin Blockade, the United States was concerned to obtain full French participation in the North Atlantic Treaty Organization. American policymakers worried about the large representation of the French Communist Party in the French National Assembly and the instability of Fourth Republic governments. Although the American State Department considered the Elysée Agreement to be significantly less than the granting of independence and insufficient to rally Vietnamese nationalists, the United States kept these doubts to itself in view of the importance of France to American policy in Europe. But with the communist victory in the Chinese Civil War and the recognition of Ho Chi Minh's government by the Chinese and Soviet governments, the Cold War came to Asia, and the United States could no longer stand aloof. In February 1950, days after the French National Assembly ratified the Elysée Agreement, the United States and the United Kingdom announced diplomatic recognition of Bao Dai's State of Vietnam.

There was a contradiction at the center of American policy toward the Vietnamese situation, which was an extension of the contradiction at the center of French policy. Was France fighting to create a non-communist independent

Vietnam or to retain some form of neo-colonial control? Despite talk to the contrary, French behavior revealed that the answer to this question was the latter. For its part, the United States wanted France to grant Bao Dai's government the genuine independence required to compete with communists for the nationalist cause and to build a Vietnamese army able to take over the war, but it did not believe that it could force France to do this without erasing French incentive to continue the war and without risking a breakdown in the Cold War alliance. Beginning already in the late 1940s and continuing through 1950, various studies and memos produced in the American Departments of State and Defense debated the benefits and liabilities of getting involved in the Vietnamese war with cogent arguments on each side of the issue. However, the communist victory in China and concern about the extension of communist regimes elsewhere in Asia became the decisive consideration, overriding doubts raised by the afterlife of French colonialism.

Once the decision was made to grant diplomatic recognition to the Bao Dai government in February 1950, American involvement developed rapidly. In March, following a French request for help, President Truman released money previously allocated by Congress for "the non-communist areas of China," the first direct American funding for the French in Indochina. A mission sent to study French needs in Indochina reported that much greater assistance would be required. The outbreak of the Korean War in June appeared to American policy-makers as a second front in China's promotion of communist regimes in neighboring countries and accelerated plans to send assistance to Vietnam.

In July, the United States sent another mission to survey conditions in Vietnam. The report of this mission was pessimistic about the military situation, which it considered to be a stalemate in which the French were taking unsustainable casualties. It asserted that the war could not be won militarily and that the main problem required a political settlement that the French were unwilling to make. Because of the urgency of the situation, the report nevertheless recommended the formation of a Military Assistance Advisory Group (MAAG) to fill French military needs and to build a Vietnamese army. Despite French objections to the presence of an American MAAG, which they viewed as an unnecessary infringement upon their prerogatives, the United States established a MAAG in Saigon in the autumn of 1950 to deliver, account for, and evaluate the use of military material provided to the French.

American policy was aimed at providing what was necessary to keep the French military from defeat while maximizing the possibilities of building a Vietnamese army and government administration within the constraints imposed by the French. With this in view, in addition to the MAAG, the United States set up a Special Technical and Economic Mission (STEM) to work directly with the

Bao Dai government on civilian development projects. This irritated the French, who suspected that the Americans were seeking to displace them.

At the beginning of 1950, Bao Dai appointed Nguyen Phan Long, the veteran Constitutionalist politician of the 1920s and 1930s, as prime minister of the Saigon government. Nguyen Phan Long called for full independence, for American aid to be given directly to his government, and for rapidly building up a Vietnamese army. He had no personal political following, so it was easy for the French to obtain his replacement in April 1950 by the governor of Cochinchina, Tran Van Huu (1896–1984), a French citizen, wealthy landowner, and former partisan of the Cochinchina separatist movement. Despite his background, Tran Van Huu strained at the French leash to enlarge the Saigon government's authority. Notwithstanding the limitations of the Elysée Agreement, the French acquiesced to his opening diplomatic relations with the United States, the United Kingdom, Thailand, India, and other countries.

In June 1950, Tran Van Huu began what turned out to be five months of difficult negotiations at Pau in southwestern France with representatives of France and the other two associated states of Indochina, Cambodia and Laos. The agenda was to resolve issues remaining from the Elysée Agreement that were ostensibly to be handled at the federal level of the Indochinese Federation: communications, immigration, customs, foreign trade, and finance. Cambodia and Laos supported French involvement in these matters from fear of being dominated by their Vietnamese neighbor. Tran Van Huu vainly appealed to the Americans and British to pressure France to be more accommodating to the Vietnamese. The arrangements that were ultimately reached appeared to represent a compromise among all the concerned parties, but, when implemented, the French gave up very little of their control.

France's stubborn clinging to power frustrated both Tran Van Huu and the Americans and stymied any effort to raise the credibility of the State of Vietnam in what, beneath the surface of France's persistently colonial attitude and of the United States' Cold War agenda, was becoming more and more of a civil war among Vietnamese. During his two years as prime minister, Tran Van Huu became more nationalistic and revealed an increasing willingness to work directly with the United States, prompting French chagrin. In June 1952, the French obtained his replacement by Nguyen Van Tam (1893–1990), another French citizen and former Cochinchina separatist, who had made a reputation in military and security affairs. Nguyen Van Tam demonstrated subservience to French interests and to the commandeering style of Jean Letourneau (1907–1986), who combined the ministerial post in charge of the Indochinese associate states with the post of high commissioner for most of 1952 and 1953.

The military situation from 1950 to 1953, with the additional participation of China and the United States, attained a new level of stalemate. The French loss of their Sino-Vietnamese border forts in late 1950 prompted the appointment of a well-known and respected Second World War military leader to both command the armed forces and be high commissioner: Jean Joseph Marie Gabriel de Lattre de Tassigny (1889–1952). During 1951, Vo Nguyen Giap launched three major attacks from the mountains into the lowlands of the Red River, first from the north, then from the east, and finally from the southwest. De Lattre defeated all of these offensives with American logistical assistance. He built a string of forts along the edge of the deltaic plains to insulate the lowlands from the mountains. Known as the "de Lattre line," this defensive formation did not prevent routine communist infiltration of the plains, but de Lattre's strong personality and competent leadership briefly raised French morale.

De Lattre mixed talk of a truly independent Vietnam and measures to build up the State of Vietnam's army with acts that guarded French supremacy, such as vetoing a bilateral aid agreement between the Saigon government and the United States. Nevertheless, the United States was sufficiently impressed with his achievements to significantly accelerate the military supply line to Vietnam. After he died of cancer in January 1952, his successor was unable to sustain his moment of optimism, and French public opinion began to turn against the war. A series of military setbacks in 1952 spread gloom among French policymakers.

By January 1953, when René Mayer (1895–1972) became Prime Minister of France and Dwight David Eisenhower (1890–1969) became President of the United States, French war weariness and American skepticism of French policy had reached new levels of seriousness. In Vietnam, the French were mostly ascendant from Nha Trang south. Aside from that, they tenuously held a coastal strip from Da Nang to Dong Hoi, and in the Red River plain they held major cities and towns and were dominant in much of the countryside. French forces were for the most part tied down in static defensive positions and strongly invested in road-bound supply operations. They lacked sufficient manpower to undertake offensive operations and were slow to expand and train the Vietnamese army. When Mayer requested increased American funding for the war, the Eisenhower administration responded that before considering the request it would be necessary to see a French plan for defeating the enemy within two years.

Mayer and Letourneau visited Washington, DC, in March to make their request in person. Discovering that Eisenhower was serious about wanting to see a plan, Letourneau proposed a three-step scenario of building up the Vietnamese army to secure the south, of consolidating French forces in the north, and then of taking the offensive to finish the war in 1955. The Americans accepted this plan despite doubts and reservations.

In June, the newly appointed French commander, Henri Eugène Navarre (1898–1983), produced an accelerated version of the Letourneau plan that envisioned offensive operations as early as the autumn of 1953. The new French government of Joseph Laniel (1889–1975) publicly embraced this Navarre plan and indicated that substantial reinforcements would be sent from France. The Laniel government was a finely balanced coalition that included four former prime ministers, each with his own analysis of the Indochinese situation and his own circle of experts. French policy lost coherence as it entered a phase of keeping up wartime appearances while seeking a way to negotiate an end to the fighting. The idea of obtaining a favorable battlefield position from which to negotiate became the most plausible way to portray French policy under Laniel.

Reinforcements sent to Navarre were negligible, and he was left to his own devices. Although American officers assigned to the MAAG in Saigon reported that they could see no evidence of the Navarre plan being implemented, Navarre was determined to do what he could with available resources to demonstrate the aggressive intent of his plan. He was inhibited by elements in the Laniel government eager to negotiate an end to the conflict and that adjusted the administrative hierarchy in Indochina to increase civilian control over the military.

Paul Reynaud (1878–1966), a former prime minister prominent in the Laniel government, obtained the appointment of Maurice Dejean (1899–1982), then ambassador to Japan, to replace Letourneau. Reynaud had been Minister of Colonies in the early 1930s and had visited Indochina in the wake of the Nghe-Tinh soviet uprising. He was now in favor of negotiating an end to the war and estimated that Dejean, who had been a subordinate of his for a time in the late 1930s, would be an appropriate person to oversee matters in Indochina. Dejean, a career diplomat, would be disgraced in the 1960s after a scandal while serving as ambassador to the Soviet Union amid rumors that he had been recruited by Soviet intelligence during the Second World War or even earlier. There were stories of friction between him and Navarre because he was supposedly holding back the allocation of resources in accordance with a shadow policy of the Laniel government to minimize military operations while stalling for negotiations. Although both men publicly denied that this was the case, their sensing the need to do so revealed that French policy toward the war was shifting. In early July 1953, the Laniel government informed the associated states of Indochina that it was ready to discuss "the transfer of powers" and "the perfecting of independence and sovereignty." This, combined with the departure of Letourneau's heavy hand, brought Saigon politics to life with new energy.

The peace settlement

By 1953, the State of Vietnam had become an agglomeration of several elements. A cluster of politicians, most of whom had been part of the Cochinchina separatist scheme of d'Argenlieu, gathered in Saigon around Prime Minister Nguyen Van Tam. The Binh Xuyen was a crime syndicate in Saigon and Cholon in alliance with the Corsican mafia that handled the opium traffic. The Hoa Hao was ascendant in western Cochinchina. The main Cao Dai leadership at Tay Ninh was allied with Bao Dai, but splinter groups followed the Viet Minh or the maverick general Trinh Minh The (1922–1955), who opposed both the Viet Minh and the French. The Dai Viet Party was dominant in Tonkin except for the Catholic bishoprics of Phat Diem and Bui Chu near the coast south of Hanoi, which governed their own affairs. Bao Dai resided in Dalat surrounded by his favorites, one of whom one was General Nguyen Van Hinh (1915–2004), son of Nguyen Van Tam, a French citizen, and a former major in the French air force, now serving as commander of the Vietnamese army.

The remaining element was a disparate collection of people unwilling to participate in the false independence of the State of Vietnam and who were "waiting" for an opportunity to press for total independence. A leading figure among these was Ngo Dinh Nhu (1910–1963), a younger brother of Ngo Dinh Diem. Ngo Dinh Nhu had studied in France in the 1930s and, influenced by ideas of progressive French Catholic philosophers, endeavored to articulate an alternative to the extremes of communist collectivism and capitalist individualism.

Ngo Dinh Nhu rejected both the "masses" (*quan chung*) of communist ideology and the "individual" (*ca nhan*) of capitalism. He advocated instead the "person" (*nhan vi*) who both cooperated with others and retained an autonomous personal identity. His ideology, commonly translated as "personalism" and generally conflated with the "personalism" of Emmanuel Mounier (1905–1950), who influenced his thought, is probably more correctly translated as "personism" with its emphasis on the dignity of each person in the context of collective self-help. It was an adaptation of French "personalism" to an Asian society emerging from colonialism into the modern world.

Ngo Dinh Nhu aimed for a society based neither on submersion into the mass nor the isolation of individuality but rather on the integrity of persons who take responsibility for each other. He rejected the communist term for "labor" (*lao dong*) that was used in the communist party name, Vietnamese Labor Party (Dang Lao Dong Viet Nam), because it derives from a classical expression meaning to mobilize or to rouse to action, which implies labor under the pressure of an external authority. He preferred the term *can lao*, which derives from a classical expression meaning a willingness to work without coercion, which can be translated as "diligence." Ngo Dinh Diem easily understood these ideas, for he believed that neither the coercive collectivism of communism nor the alienating individualism of capitalism was a suitable model for his vision of a modern Vietnamese society.

After Ngo Dinh Diem went into exile in 1950, Ngo Dinh Nhu began to speak publicly about his ideas and to attract like-minded people. He lived for a time in Dalat where he established contact with Bao Dai. In 1953 he allied with a Saigon trade union leader and began to organize labor unions. He became a spokesman for those seeking total independence from the French. Before Bao Dai departed for France in August to follow up the Laniel government's July announcement, Ngo Dinh Nhu met with him to discuss the Vietnamese negotiating position.

Nguyen Van Tam was discredited, and under Dejean the French grip on Vietnamese political life had loosened. In early September, Ngo Dinh Nhu, along with the Cao Dai leader Pham Cong Tac (1890–1969), organized a congress in Cholon that included around fifty delegates from the Cao Dai, the Hoa Hao, the Binh Xuyen, the Vietnamese Nationalist Party, the Dai Viet Nationalist Party, and various Catholic groups. After lively debates, the delegates called for unconditional independence and a national assembly elected by universal suffrage. This congress brought to the surface widely shared opinions that had previously been pushed down by the French. Although it was an ad hoc event and lacked any official government standing, it opened political space and enabled Bao Dai to convene another congress in October. This congress, representing Bao Dai's government, called for total independence and sovereignty, rejected membership in the French Union in its current form, rejected any negotiated settlement made by an international conference that was not approved by the Saigon government, and designated Bao Dai to conduct negotiations with the French.

Nguyen Van Tam resigned in December and, in January 1954, Bao Dai appointed his cousin Buu Loc (1914–1990) to be prime minister. Meanwhile, the Laniel government was envisioning the prospect of negotiations with the Viet Minh as well, and the contradiction of simultaneously dealing with Bao Dai and Ho Chi Minh created difficulties for the French. The cases of Laos and Cambodia were simpler, and France concluded treaties granting independence to those countries by the end of 1953. When Buu Loc finally began negotiations with the French in early March of 1954, he discovered that the French were still not ready to take up his agenda. Within days, these negotiations were overshadowed by military events in Vietnam and by the impending international conference at Geneva, which had developed from the easing of Cold War tensions after Stalin's death.

Navarre, despite the lack of significant reinforcements from France and the lack of progress in expanding the Vietnamese army to the extent necessary for his plan, was under pressure from both the Americans and his own government to act, from the Americans to show evidence that his plan was still alive and from Paris to improve the French negotiating position. In November 1953 he began to garrison the valley of Dien Bien Phu, three hundred kilometers west of Hanoi near the Laotian border. There were five plausible reasons for this move, but they were unlikely to have been decisive without Navarre's need to demonstrate some kind of offensive operation as envisioned by his plan.

Dien Bien Phu was a major junction for routes between Vietnam, Laos, and China, and one reason for garrisoning this place was to inhibit the movement of enemy troops from Vietnam into Laos, as had occurred in the spring of 1953, which had distracted the French from Vietnamese battlefields to the defense of Laos. A second reason for going to Dien Bien Phu was to establish a base for offensive operations to bring the war into the enemy's territory. Related to this was a third consideration: to more effectively support and maximize the guerrilla operations of France's Tai allies in that region. A fourth idea was that a base at Dien Bien Phu would attract suicidal enemy attacks that could be destroyed by French firepower, as had happened the previous year at a mountain base named Na San. Finally, Dien Bien Phu was a major center of the opium trade, which was coveted by both the communists and the French. Controlling this place would deny a large source of income to the enemy and ensure that it came into French hands instead. But most important, the garrisoning of Dien Bien Phu was intended to restore a sense of mobility and an offensive spirit to an army that had become passive and road-bound.

The main problem with Dien Bien Phu was that it could be supplied only by air, and its distance from French airfields was near the limit of the amount of fuel a plane could carry for a return trip. This was not a serious problem so long as the Dien Bien Phu airfield was serviceable. More serious was that, by itself, without reinforcements or a major growth of the Vietnamese army, it took limited resources away from other priorities. This may not have been a factor if more men had been available and the move to Dien Bien Phu had promptly developed into a more general occupation of the surrounding area and pro- gressed to threaten communist supply lines from China. However, contrary to French expectations, Vo Nguyen Giap rather quickly surrounded Dien Bien Phu and installed heavy artillery in the mountains overlooking it. Once the battle began in mid March, the airfield was unusable and Dien Bien Phu became a trap for the French. The Eisenhower administration was uninterested in intervening militarily, and Dien Bien Phu fell to the communists one day before the Geneva conference took up the Vietnamese issue on May 8.

The fall of Dien Bien Phu, although not militarily decisive, broke the French will to continue the war. But even at this point, the issue of acknowledging Vietnamese independence remained unresolved. Under American pressure, a treaty granting independence to the State of Vietnam had been completed by late April, but the French delayed signing it. Negotiations were about to begin at Geneva, where Ho Chi Minh's government would also be represented, and, as long as the independence treaty with the State of Vietnam remained unsigned, the French could negotiate with the communists on behalf of the Saigon government without its approval.

However, Laniel's thinking about this changed somewhat in late May after Bao Dai summoned Ngo Dinh Diem from Belgium, where he was residing, and arranged for him to replace Buu Loc in June. Ngo Dinh Diem was famously anti-French and Laniel expected that dealing with him would be more difficult than with Buu Loc. At the same time, however, by late May it was clear to the French that a partition of Vietnam would be a fundamental part of the settlement. This was strongly opposed by Bao Dai, Ngo Dinh Diem, and other representatives of the State of Vietnam. Laniel accordingly wanted to get the independence issue out of the way without fanfare before the people around Bao Dai learned of the partition issue. Consequently, on June 4, Laniel and Buu Loc initialed the independence treaty, but it was not ratified with the signatures of Bao Dai and the French president. Nine days later, Laniel resigned and, four days after that, Pierre Mendès-France (1907–1982) became prime minister with the pledge to obtain a peace agreement within a month. Mendès-France had no intention of observing any assurances that had previously been made to the State of Vietnam about not negotiating a settlement without its approval.

France ostensibly released its colonial claim on Vietnam only at the last possible moment, after years of tortuous negotiations, in the calamity of repudiating a costly war, as a subsidiary aspect of larger diplomatic maneuvers, and with the anticipated embarrassment of breaking promises. And even then, it was not done, for the independence treaty would never be ratified. All the same, the State of Vietnam began to act as if it had been ratified and to establish relations directly with the United States, the only major power with a serious interest in its future. Ngo Dinh Diem had already left for Vietnam when Bao Dai proclaimed him as prime minister in mid June.

France, the People's Republic of China, the Soviet Union, and the United Kingdom were the major negotiating powers at Geneva. The Soviet Union and the United Kingdom were the co-conveners of the conference and drove the agenda. China posed as mentor and patron of its Vietnamese ally. Desperate for a settlement before his self-imposed deadline of thirty days, Mendès-France acted for France and left the newly independent Indochinese associated states to manage on their own. The interests of Cambodia and Laos, each of which had only one government, were generally observed by the major powers. The State of

Vietnam, however, was an orphan. The United States, while attending the conference, stood to one side, seeking to minimize being implicated in what it understood as a Cold War defeat. Its presence offstage, however, was an important influence on the outcome and confirmed the need to partition Vietnam between its two governments not just to end the current war but more importantly to prevent the outbreak of a new war.

It was obvious to nearly all the major powers that the only way to remove the likelihood of Vietnam again becoming a place of crisis in the Cold War was to separate the two Vietnamese governments, each in its own territory. However, Vietnamese of all political persuasions opposed a permanent partition of the country. Consequently, the expedient of a unification election in the future was contrived to conveniently dispose of the issue. Except for France, the major powers subsequently showed no further interest in the matter, understanding that Vietnam could not be united without war, and more war was what they hoped to preclude. Nothing of the Geneva settlement was signed except for ceasefire arrangements by mid-level representatives of the French and Democratic Republic of Vietnam's armies, thereby demonstrating the studied ambiguity of a document that affirmed the sovereign independence and unity of a country that it also partitioned between two rival armies and governments.

Mendès-France revealed the persistence of colonial habits by neglecting to ratify the independence treaty that had been initialed by Laniel and Buu Loc in early June, claiming that to do so would violate the Geneva provision for an election to unify the country and that, until the election was held, France was still responsible for southern Vietnam. At the same time he sent an envoy to Hanoi to sign a commercial treaty with the Democratic Republic of Vietnam that acknowledged French economic and cultural interests. He seemingly imagined that, by maintaining the upper hand in southern Vietnam until the elections, France could produce an electoral result that unified Vietnam under Hanoi while preserving French influence. Even after his resignation in February 1955, the momentum of French efforts to direct Saigon politics continued for another three months.

For his part, Ngo Dinh Diem regarded the State of Vietnam as fully independent and considered the Geneva agreement to be a vestige of French colonialism, having been negotiated without the participation or approval of his government. While he publicly accepted the line of partition, he would have nothing to do with unification elections, which he viewed as impossible in a northern Vietnam ruled by a communist regime and as an opportunity for France to continue its pretensions of sovereignty.

13 FROM TWO COUNTRIES TO ONE

Saigon

After Bao Dai went to France in late 1953 to pursue possibilities for negotiating full independence with the Laniel government, Ngo Dinh Diem departed the United States for Europe, sensing that he may find a role in the changing situation. Ngo Dinh Diem's youngest brother, Ngo Dinh Luyen (1914–1990), was a childhood friend of Bao Dai from their schoolboy days in France and served as a go-between. Although Bao Dai had never been comfortable with Ngo Dinh Diem's strong anti-French attitude, in May 1954 he turned to him because there was no other person of his stature and reputation as an uncompromising nationalist. Furthermore, Ngo Dinh Nhu's emergence as a political figure in Saigon the previous year suggested that Ngo Dinh Diem had a point of access into the political world of the State of Vietnam. Two other considerations were apparently on Bao Dai's mind. Ngo Dinh Diem's appointment would apply pressure on the French to sign the independence treaty, and no other Vietnamese politician was likely to elicit the American assistance that would be necessary for the future of his government. However, Bao Dai soon realized that with the appointment of Ngo Dinh Diem he had ended his role in the political life of his country, and he never returned to Vietnam.

In the summer of 1954, Ngo Dinh Diem was seemingly without any firm source of support. The United States was beginning to provide institutional assistance but was non-committal regarding Ngo Dinh Diem himself, being unsure of whether he would be able to surmount the daunting situation in Saigon. The French army had regrouped to southern Vietnam and was still the pre-eminent military force in the country. The French military commander and commissioner in Vietnam was General Paul Henri Romuald Ély (1897–1975), who made no secret of his opinion that Ngo Dinh Diem should be replaced. The French continued to insist that American military assistance to the Vietnamese army be channeled through them. General Nguyen Van Hinh, commander of the

Vietnamese army, publicly affirmed his intention to depose Ngo Dinh Diem until Bao Dai was persuaded to recall him to France in October. The various sect armies continued to receive subsidies from the French and showed little regard for Ngo Dinh Diem's authority. In May 1954, Bao Dai had sold control of the Saigon–Cholon police to the Binh Xuyen gangsters, and they, with the covert support of the French, were determined to resist Ngo Dinh Diem's authority.

Concerned about the direction of French activities in Saigon, the Eisenhower administration sent a senior French-speaking army general to Vietnam with ambassadorial rank, Joseph Lawton Collins (1896–1987), thereby providing an American peer of Ély. Collins and Ély worked well together and negotiated an arrangement for Americans to participate in training the Vietnamese army. Collins was susceptible to Ély's negative evaluation of Ngo Dinh Diem, however, and, in the spring of 1955, he began to report his opinion that Ngo Dinh Diem should be replaced.

This came during several weeks of crisis during which a coalition of sect armies led by the Binh Xuyen openly challenged Ngo Dinh Diem, seemingly with French encouragement. Against this threat, Ngo Dinh Diem rallied army units and sect leaders such as the Cao Dai maverick Trinh Minh The. The Binh Xuyen was destroyed and its allied sect armies were driven into the countryside. The United States promptly made a commitment to support Ngo Dinh Diem and, in May 1955, informed France that thereafter it would no longer consult about Vietnamese affairs. Within a year, all remaining French forces were evacuated and the French command in Vietnam was abolished, although French advisors to the navy and air force did not depart until 1957.

Ngo Dinh Diem stood for those who had had enough of French colonialism and its decaying residue, and he did not shrink from entering and mastering the ruthless world of Saigon politics. France never ratified the independence treaty initialed by Joseph Laniel and Buu Loc on June 4, 1954. Furthermore, Ngo Dinh Diem understood that his government would not be free of France until its link to Bao Dai was broken, for many aspiring Saigon politicians continued to shelter under Bao Dai's Francophile wings. Consequently, in October 1955 he staged a referendum to remove Bao Dai as head of state. The public campaign and voting procedure for this referendum was used to spread popular awareness of the new government and its break with the French past. With Bao Dai and his quasi-monarchical and colonial aura out of the way, Ngo Dinh Diem proclaimed the Republic of Vietnam. This was a declaration of independence from France.

In March 1956, elections were held for a constituent assembly, which drew up a constitution and then sat as a national assembly until legislative elections under the new constitution were held in 1959. Ngo Dinh Nhu had organized the quasi-clandestine Revolutionary Personalist Labor Party (Can Lao Nhan Vi Cach

Mang Dang), which did not directly participate in elections but selected and promoted candidates in allied parties, in particular the National Revolutionary Movement (Quoc Gia Cach Mang Phong Trao), which served as a front organization. Three major parties that supported Ngo Dinh Diem won two-thirds of the seats in the 1956 elections. As would be true in all the elections held under the 1956 constitution, opposition candidates fared best in Saigon where the urban and international environment was more congenial to constitutional freedoms than in the countryside where the level of education and understanding of democratic procedures was lower and where respect for those in power was more ingrained and more efficiently enforced.

The Geneva agreement provided for the redeployment not only of armies but also of civilians from one side of the armistice line to the other. Between eighty and ninety thousand people embarked for the north on Soviet Bloc ships from the two main areas ruled by communists: Ca Mau in the extreme south of the Mekong plain and the Quang Ngai and Binh Dinh region of the central coast. Many of these people were youths selected for education in the north. Around ten times this number of people shifted from the north to the south, one-third of them transported by the United States navy. Two-thirds of the immigrants into the south were Catholics, and Ngo Dinh Diem provided settlements for them in localities along the northern edge of the Mekong plain.

The arrival of large numbers of northern immigrants both strengthened the political base of Ngo Dinh Diem and introduced tension between northerners and southerners and between Catholics and non-Catholics, partly from resentment about resources devoted to the newcomers and partly from cultural differences between northerners and southerners. Southerners perceived northerners as "pushy" while northerners perceived southerners as "lazy." Furthermore, Catholics tended to live in close-knit communities under ecclesiastical leadership in a global hierarchy, which maximized their potential for economic success and a relatively high standard of living. This, along with lines of patronage via the Church to the Ngo Dinh family, inspired resentment among many non-Catholics.

The departure of people from Ca Mau and the central coast was accompanied by the extension of Saigon authority into those areas. During 1955 and 1956, the Republic of Vietnam launched a campaign to identify and eliminate communist leaders who had stayed behind. A few hundred people were imprisoned or killed in this "denounce the communist" (to cong) campaign. At the same time, Ngo Dinh Diem introduced a modest agrarian policy that limited land rent for tenants and the amount of land that any single person could own. According to redistribution legislation, about one-third of all tenanted land in the country was to be expropriated. Resistance from landowners and local officials inhibited

implementation, however, and only 40 percent of this land was actually transferred to farmers. Ngo Dinh Diem espoused the idea of "collective advance,"
which aimed to bring improvements to rural life without radical or violent
measures, such as were then being used in the north. Even so, many landowners
were embittered by their loss of land, including the father of Ngo Dinh Nhu's
wife, Tran Van Chuong (1898–1986), a career diplomat whom Ngo Dinh Diem
made ambassador to the United States. Although Ngo Dinh Diem tripled the
number of farmers owning land in the Mekong plain, the great disparity between
landowners and farmers that historically had characterized this region was not
significantly ameliorated.

One area that worried Ngo Dinh Diem was the Central Highlands, a vast
upland region sparsely inhabited by non-Vietnamese peoples along the Laotian
and Cambodian borders. He suspected that he had limited time to stabilize social
conditions and consolidate government authority in this remote region before the
communists became active there. The French had discouraged Vietnamese settlement in the Central Highlands and had tried to preserve it as an autonomous
non-Vietnamese region. In 1955, Ngo Dinh Diem initiated a program both to
settle Vietnamese in the highlands and to encourage peripatetic upland peoples to
make permanent settlements. In 1957, the United States took an interest in the
program and allocated money for it but withdrew after a year because of
disagreements about how it was being implemented. Ngo Dinh Diem believed
the matter was urgent and that it was more important to encourage a spirit of
self-reliance among the people than to wait for the American bureaucracy to
complete its studies and its paperwork before releasing allocated funds. Before
his death, he had settled a quarter of a million Vietnamese in the Central
Highlands.

On their side, American aid officials criticized the Central Highlands program
for being too hasty, too disorderly, and too undemocratic, an analysis that
became the standard institutional view of Ngo Dinh Diem's policies among the
American aid mission and embassy staff during the ambassadorship of Elbridge
Durbrow (1903–1997), who arrived in March of 1957. On the other hand,
General Samuel Tankersley Williams (1896–1984), commander of MAAG since
October 1955, saw Ngo Dinh Diem as doing the best possible in a difficult
situation. Williams had a colorful and valorous career as a combat officer in both
World Wars and Korea. He respected Ngo Dinh Diem as a strong leader who
understood the priorities of his situation. Durbrow, a career diplomat without
prior experience in Asia, began to advocate a policy of "linkage" between
American aid and Vietnamese government "reforms." Tension between
Durbrow and Williams over their divergent views was the beginning of a new
contradiction in American policy toward Vietnam that would eventually lead to

Ngo Dinh Diem's death in 1963. To some extent, this contradiction was an American version of the old French arguments about "assimilation," turning Vietnamese into French men and women or into Americans as the case may be, and "association," conceding space for the Vietnamese to develop their own way within the relationship of colonialism or Cold War alliance, as the case may be.

Military personnel attached to MAAG stabilized at around 650 men in early 1956, most being involved in training activities. The civilian aid establishment attached to the American embassy, with exceptions, became a critical mass of rotating people in culture shock, frustrated that Vietnamese did not act like Americans. This, combined with a sense of power and global responsibility, produced among many Americans a teachery attitude verging on the racist condescension typical of a colonial relationship. Furthermore, while claiming to be against colonialism, American policy appeared to dominate smaller countries through the flow of money and material goods, as demonstrated by the manner in which the United States provided monetary assistance to the Saigon government.

In 1955, the United States established the Commodity Import Program as the means for transferring funds to Ngo Dinh Diem's government. The United States provided dollars for purchase by Vietnamese importers. The dollars were spent in the United States for commodities, mainly consumer goods such as refrigerators, televisions, radios, stoves, air conditioners, and comestibles, which the importers then sold in Vietnam. Importers bought dollars with Vietnamese piastres at a fixed exchange rate that represented a subsidy for them. The piastres were placed in a "counterpart fund" for use by the Vietnamese government. Eighty percent of all American aid funds were provided through the Commodity Import Program. This scheme was intended to control inflation, prevent dollars from overwhelming the local economy, and keep taxes low. Negative effects included the retardation of local manufacturing; creating a Vietnamese government that was dependent on a foreign source of money rather than taxing its own citizens; corruption in the licensing of importers; non-market exchange rates; and the creation of an import-based urban consumer economy that artificially separated cities from the rest of the country.

The Commodity Import Program was controversial among Vietnamese. Phan Quang Dan (b. 1918), the main opposition politician in Saigon during the late 1950s, became well known for speaking out against the Commodity Import Program. Originally from Nghe An, he became politically active in 1945 and chose to follow Bao Dai to China. Disappointed with Bao Dai's lack of firmness in dealing with the French, he tried to form his own party before going to the United States, where he lived in exile until returning to Vietnam at the end of the war.

Ngo Dinh Diem was also critical of the Commodity Import Program and tried unsuccessfully to have aspects of it changed. The scheme created an institutional dependency that made Durbrow's "linkage" idea plausible as a way to force the Vietnamese government to follow American advice. The ultimate example of this occurred in October 1963 when the suspension of the Commodity Import Program was used as a signal to indicate American support for a conspiracy against Ngo Dinh Diem. The Commodity Import Program was in principle and in effect not very different from the manner in which Chinese and Soviet aid was provided to the government in Hanoi, except that with two rival patrons the northern government was in a better position to prevent either one from becoming dominant.

Hanoi

After shifting its headquarters from the mountains to Hanoi in late 1954, the Democratic Republic of Vietnam received large amounts of aid from China and the Soviet Union, including food, consumer goods, military and industrial equipment, and money. But the greatest foreign presence in North Vietnamese domestic affairs was Chinese supervision of the land reform program. Chinese involvement in Vietnamese land reform was not an exercise of unwanted influence but rather the provision of expertise eagerly sought and gladly accepted by the Vietnamese communist leadership. During the years of Chinese participation in the French war and the tenure of Luo Guibo (1908–1995) as Chinese ambassador from 1950 to 1954, a very close, albeit unequal, relationship was established between the two communist parties. Communist success in China was an object of admiration and emulation by the Vietnamese.

At the same time, there were reasons for land reform in Vietnam that had nothing directly to do with the Chinese model. Truong Chinh, the leader of the party since 1940, had co-authored with Vo Nguyen Giap a study of rural conditions, published in 1937–1938 during the Popular Front period, entitled *Van De Dan Cay*, "The Peasant Question." This work portrayed rural society with the five categories that became the basis for land reform in the 1950s. It described the system of landholding, taxation, and indebtedness that made peasant life difficult, but also described the peasant "mentality" as indoctrinated to accept exploitation through the influence of religious beliefs and an irrational respect for private property. While Mao Zedong's emphasis on the peasantry may be detected here, the work is more generally the application of Marxist analysis to the rural conditions in Vietnam, particularly northern Vietnam, where it was written and published.

The view of peasant life in *The Peasant Question* is very similar to what was portrayed in "realist" literature being published at that same time. For example, Nguyen Cong Hoan's *Buoc Duong Cung* (Impasse), published in 1938, depicts the tragedies of peasant oppression and attributes them to the stupidity of the peasants themselves, who are illiterate, do not understand why their lives are so bad, and have no idea about what to do. In 1937, the communist poet To Huu (1920–2002) published *Mo Coi* (Orphan), which expressed deep sympathy with the sufferings of the downtrodden. The Maoist idea of making revolution by mobilizing poor peasants to overthrow rural tyranny did not come as news to Vietnamese communists. Both China and Vietnam were overwhelmingly agrarian countries and aspiring revolutionaries could not avoid that fact.

In the late 1940s and early 1950s, Truong Chinh pushed for ever more radical rural policies as conditions permitted. Initially, during the first two years after the August Revolution of 1945, with the Chinese occupation and the outbreak of war with France, he was content to call for rent and debt controls. Beginning in 1948, he ordered census and land ownership surveys as an initial step in gathering information about rural conditions at the village level. This was primarily aimed at the provinces with relatively large peasant populations that were governed by the communists: Thai Nguyen, Thanh Hoa, Nghe An, and Ha Tinh. With the arrival of Chinese allies in early 1950, a flurry of decrees about land policy included conducting a census to sort the rural population into the five categories of landlord, rich peasant, middle peasant, poor peasant, and landless. This produced resistance from local officials who claimed that people had been incorrectly categorized, and a "rectification" was required later in the year. Local party leaders were not yet ideologically motivated to follow land reform instructions.

At the party congress in early 1951, land reform became a priority, and thereafter the Land Reform and Party Consolidation Section of the Chinese Political Advisory Group (CPAG) assisted in organizing a program of "purification" to prepare for land reform by re-educating party members through campaigns of criticism and self-criticism. As Chinese advisors became more involved in training and supervision, they began to influence the pace and details of implementing policy. In a document submitted to Vietnamese leaders entitled "Preliminary Comments on Mass Mobilization in 1953," dated September 3, 1952, Chinese ambassador Luo Guibo outlined a plan for land reform and asserted that it was time to begin. Shortly after this Ho Chi Minh went to Beijing, and by October was in Moscow with a land reform plan ostensibly written with the assistance of Liu Shaoqi (1898–1969), second after Mao Zedong in the Chinese party hierarchy. Ho Chi Minh presented the plan to Stalin and solicited his approval.

In early 1953, the Vietnamese communists held a conference on mobilizing the rural population. Truong Chinh personally chaired the committee assigned to implement land reform. At the same time, dozens of Chinese land reform experts were sent to join the Land Reform and Party Consolidation Section of CPAG in Vietnam. From April to August 1953, an experimental mass mobilization campaign was conducted in Thai Nguyen and Thanh Hoa. This was designed to provide training for land reform cadres and to evaluate the response of peasants. This was followed in September by codifying procedures for mobilizing villagers to overturn property relations and authority structures.

Cadres were to recruit the poorest villagers and train them to denounce and confiscate the property of people they identified as their oppressors. Land would then be redistributed, local government would be reorganized, and the culprits would be punished. Because of the implications of this for local party leadership, in November the party issued a directive for evaluating party cells and individual members based on class background, ideological correctness, competence, and willingness to follow instructions. In December, the first of several waves of land reform was begun in Thai Nguyen. The beginning of mass mobilization for land reform coincided with the mobilization of soldiers and supplies, including rice from Thanh Hoa, to the battlefield of Dien Bien Phu.

Thereafter, the land reform campaign was extended to all parts of the new Democratic Republic of Vietnam north of the post-Geneva line at the seventeenth parallel. However, reports of excessive violence accumulated, and by early 1956 war veterans were protesting. By late 1956, the party leadership acknowledged errors and in 1957 instituted a rectification campaign to correct injustices. But many thousands of people had been killed and local party members were in turmoil. The excessive violence was partly due to the application of a model designed for rural conditions in China, where class tensions were higher than in Vietnam. It also partly came from the enthusiasm of Vietnamese cadres in demonstrating revolutionary fervor to their superiors and fidelity to their Chinese mentors. Large numbers of them were from urban backgrounds, were unfamiliar with rural life, and relied on their theoretical training when intervening in village society. But more fundamentally the violence was an integral part of the plan for the party to gain firm control of the rural population, which included quotas for the number of people to be executed.

The negative reaction to land reform violence began to be a factor in party affairs in the wake of Nikita Khrushchev's famous speech at the Moscow party congress in February 1956 attacking Stalin's cruelty and personality cult. The Vietnamese delegates to this congress were Truong Chinh and Le Duc Tho (1911–1990). Le Duc Tho was from an upper-class family in the Nam Dinh area south of Hanoi. He had been an early member of the Indochinese

Communist Party and had spent much of the 1930s and early 1940s in prison. After regaining his freedom in 1944, he worked closely with Truong Chinh and was a leading figure at the Tan Trao conference in August 1945. He held responsibility for internal party operations. From 1949 to 1954 he was assigned to the south where in 1951 he helped to organize the party's Central Office for the Southern Region (Truong Uong Cuc Mien Nam; generally translated in English as Central Office for South Vietnam, COSVN). In 1954, he returned to Hanoi and was among the most powerful leaders in the party, nicknamed "the hammer" for his skill in enforcing discipline.

While he was in the south, Le Duc Tho became an associate of Le Duan (1907–1986). Le Duan was from a working-class background in Quang Tri Province. His party career was similar to Le Duc Tho's, being an early member and spending many years in prison. After emerging from prison in 1945, he obtained leadership of the party organization in the south, confining Nguyen Binh to military affairs until Nguyen Binh's death in 1951. While Le Duc Tho was educated and relatively cultured, Le Duan had a strong but rather uncouth personality. The two men nevertheless worked well together and established an enduring bond. When Le Duc Tho returned north in 1954, Le Duan remained as the senior party leader in the south. Dismayed by the effects of Ngo Dinh Diem's "denounce the communists" campaign, in early 1956 Le Duan sent a request to Hanoi to abandon the policy of non-violent struggle in the south and to make plans for armed resistance. This directly challenged the leadership of Truong Chinh, who favored Chinese advice to build socialism in the north and to postpone dealing with the southern question.

When Truong Chinh and Le Duc Tho returned from Moscow to Hanoi in early 1956, there were three vexing issues facing the party. In addition to land reform and the southern question was the question of how to respond to Khrushchev's speech with its critique of homicidal politics and the cult of personality. This speech could be locally interpreted as a critique of how the land reform was conducted and of Ho Chi Minh's cult of avuncular sainthood. Protocol required the Vietnamese to acknowledge the Moscow speech. This was done with a pro forma statement. But the speech simply punctuated a post-Stalin relaxation of discipline that was affecting many parts of the communist world.

In Poland, violent protests led to a change in government. In Hungary, replacement of the Stalinist party leader was followed within weeks by an uprising. In China, Mao Zedong proposed to allow public discussion to identify problems and strengthen the party, thereby initiating what became known as the "hundred flowers campaign." In Vietnam, young intellectuals, most of whom were party members and veterans of the war with France, wanted to express their own thoughts and feelings beyond wartime propaganda and political slogans, and they believed that doing this served both the party and national culture. A number of literary journals sprang up in 1956, the two most influential being *Nhan Van* (Humanity) and *Giai Pham* (Fine Arts). The editor of *Nhan Van*, and the doyen of what became known as the *Nhan Van Giai Pham* Affair, was Phan Khoi, the poet who a quarter-century before had started the New Poetry Movement.

The contributors to the new journals were emboldened by what seemed to be a relatively more open attitude toward diversity of thought throughout the communist world and by critical accounts of the land reform that began to surface in newspapers and party communications. They wrote against dogmatism, hero worship, and politicized art. They were for the most part not seeking to dissent from the revolution but rather to enrich it with the benefits of a more tolerant view of human creativity. The movement nevertheless tarnished Truong Chinh's leadership because he had taken the lead to mobilize intellectuals into the party during the 1940s and had posed as the party expert on cultural matters. Now, the two prime areas in which Truong Chinh had most distinctively exercised his leadership, land reform and culture, seemed to be slipping out of the party's control.

Within a year, important decisions were made about each of the three issues (land reform, intellectual ferment, and the southern question), but not before there was a change of leadership. In September 1956, Truong Chinh stepped down as leader of the party and was temporarily replaced by Ho Chi Minh. In early 1957, Le Duan returned to Hanoi to be leader of the party. He and his ally Le Duc Tho were thereafter the primary decision-makers in Hanoi. Le Duc Tho kept track of party personnel and ensured that Le Duan was obeyed. Ho Chi Minh, now most valuable to the party as a symbol of continuity and unity, was assigned to maintain fraternal relations with the Chinese and Soviet parties. Truong Chinh, Pham Van Dong, and Vo Nguyen Giap remained respected senior colleagues but had weak individual power bases. Leadership of the military shifted to Nguyen Chi Thanh (1914–1967), who came from a peasant background in the Hue area. Like Le Duan, he was not from the educated élite, as were most of the top party leaders, and he was from the central coast just south of the seventeenth parallel. He had joined the party in the mid 1930s, spent time in French prisons in the early 1940s, had attended the Tan Trao conference, and by the time of the second party congress in 1951 had risen to the rank of general and was in charge of political commissars in the army. In the late 1950s, he became an ally of Le Duan.

The party knew that it could not afford to either alienate or fail to control the peasantry. A rectification campaign to ostensibly redress the injustices committed during the land reform was begun, but not before the most famous episode of resistance to party authority occurred. This was in Quynh Luu district of Nghe An, one of the last places reached by the land reform. There, a large Catholic population had patriotically followed the Viet Minh during the French war but had been prevented from joining the Catholic exodus to the south in 1954. In the summer of 1956, land reform cadres arrived in Quynh Luu. Taking exception to both the religion and the relative wealth of the population, the cadres were especially brutal. When members of the International Control Commission, which had been set up to monitor compliance with the Geneva Accords comprised of representatives from Canada, India, and Poland, happened to drive through Quynh Luu district in November 1956, people gathered and appealed to them for assistance to go to the south. Local authorities were unable to disperse the demonstrators, and the army was deployed to restore order; there was loss of life.

Regardless of the "errors" that called for "rectification," most of which were beyond recall, the land reform program achieved what it set out to do. It eliminated anti-revolutionary class enemies in rural society, it instituted an ostensibly more equitable distribution of land usage, and it traumatized the rural population into obedience to the state. The latter achievement was particularly important for the larger agenda of the new Hanoi leadership. The land reform experience instilled an unquestioning compliance to authority that enabled the communist party to rely on the sacrifice and suffering of the people again and again during the next thirty years.

As for the intellectuals involved in the *Nhan Van Giai Pham* Affair, their journals were shut down, some of them were imprisoned, most of them were sent to work in factories or the countryside to be re-educated to think like proletarians. As part of the disciplining of the young intellectuals involved in this movement, the poets who had been at the forefront of the New Poetry Movement in the 1930s, and who had at that time gained fame for expressing their individualism, alienation, and romantic imagination, were now mobilized to criticize the younger generation for wanting to express their personal feelings. Ngo Xuan Dieu, Cu Huy Can, Luu Trong Lu, The Lu, and Che Lan Vien had all joined the revolution in the 1940s and wrote of their experience as a religious conversion, turning them away from the prison of their own feelings toward the common life of the people. They all wrote poems or essays to condemn the selfish, anti-social attitudes of the *Nhan Van Giai Pham* generation and to praise the infallible leadership of the party.

Cultural policy in the Democratic Republic of Vietnam aimed to replace prerevolutionary beliefs and practices with new cultic symbols of the state, such as Karl Marx, Vladimir Lenin, Joseph Stalin, Mao Zedong, and Ho Chi Minh. Village festivals were prohibited as superstitious and wasteful. Many temples and shrines were closed or turned into storehouses. Buddhist monks and Catholic priests were limited in number and carefully supervised. Traditional music, typically slow and melancholy, was speeded up to a cheerful marching beat. The singing of *ca tru* was suppressed as "feudal." The proscription of popular culture was part of the effort to nurture "the new socialist personality." In art and literature, heroic themes of peasants and soldiers advancing together into a bright future were celebrated.

Socialist realism as developed in the Soviet Union and China became the criteria for literary and artistic expression. A few pre-twentieth-century historical figures were portrayed as proletarian nationalists, especially the eighteenth-century Tay Son leader Nguyen Hue Quang Trung, who was celebrated for coming from an underclass, defeating the oppressive feudal regime, and leading armies against foreign invaders. But more effort was put into identifying and promoting the memory of exemplary cultic figures from more recent times, for example Mac Thi Buoi (1927–1951), a woman from the Hai Duong area with a reputation for bravery who was captured and killed by the French. In 1955, she was designated as a national hero and commemorated with a mausoleum, a statue, a shrine, and a postage stamp.

While religions such as Buddhism and Christianity were discouraged, Confucianism was both denounced as the ideology of the old feudal class and redefined as a source of redeemable tradition among the common people for whom it represented not only respect for authority but also a commitment to social justice and, in its Mencian form, a justification for revolution. Party cadres discovered that they could easily insert themselves into the space vacated by the old class of mandarins. The Democratic Republic of Vietnam became a local version of the type of modern totalitarian state that emerged in the twentieth century under the banners of fascism and communism.

Start of a new war

The ascendance of Le Duan brought the southern question into the center of party policy. His request to shift from political to military action in the south was rejected by the party's Central Committee when it met in April 1956. Instead this meeting subscribed to the "peaceful coexistence" line of Khrushchev's speech and focused on domestic economic problems such as food shortages and the lack of skilled labor. However, in December 1956, after Truong Chinh had stepped down as party leader, the Central Committee approved a clandestine policy of gradually rebuilding the party structure in the south and initiating selective terrorism to kill and kidnap southern government officials and community leaders. In fact, by this time, Le Duan had already begun to do this. Accordingly, during 1957, there was an upsurge of armed action against the Saigon government, a significant part of which was initially conducted by remnants of sect armies that had been defeated by Ngo Dinh Diem in 1955 and had subsequently allied with the communists.

Le Duan spent 1957 and 1958 consolidating his grip on party leadership. In 1957, the launching of a three-year economic plan absorbed the attention of the party. In November 1957, Le Duan went with Ho Chi Minh to a conference of communist parties in Moscow, gaining first-hand familiarity with the world of international communism that was vital to the survival of his government. This came after several uneasy months during which the Soviet Union had proposed United Nations membership for both the Saigon and Hanoi governments in a diplomatic gambit aimed at the German situation. During 1958, Le Duc Tho quietly reshuffled personnel in the party hierarchy to advance Le Duan's supporters.

Disturbing news from the south prompted Le Duan to make an inspection trip in December 1958. Upon his return in January 1959, he reported that the situation was dire. According to him, the Saigon government had successfully countered the communist policy approved two years before and was destroying the party's organizational infrastructure in the south; two thousand cadres had been killed during 1957–1958, and party membership had plummeted. Faced with what appeared to be an urgent situation, the Central Committee of the party approved what came to be known as Resolution Fifteen, which authorized a policy of war to unify the south with the north.

Although Ho Chi Minh immediately went to Beijing and Moscow for consultations and made two additional trips to those capitals during the course of 1959, there are no indications that either ally was enthusiastic about Hanoi's new policy toward Saigon. Mao Zedong was dealing with the disaster of his "great leap forward," and Khrushchev was planning a trip to the United States. Nevertheless, Le Duan's leadership would not have survived failure in the south. Furthermore, unification had been a cardinal tenet of communist policy since 1954. It could not be abandoned without serious damage to party discipline.

In May 1959, the Central Committee ratified Resolution Fifteen. Within months, communication and transportation routes into the south by land and sea were established and thousands of southerners who had regrouped to the north after Geneva and had since then received training were sent back south. Hanoi's war policy gained momentum in the south just as the Sino-Soviet dispute over leadership of the communist world was breaking into the open. Ho Chi Minh's main contribution to the new policy was to maximize its insulation from this dispute by maintaining good, if sometimes tense, relations with both powers.

The importance of Resolution Fifteen and its implications for the future of the country prompted the convening of the third national party congress in September 1960. The second congress had been held in 1951 to mobilize for war with France after the arrival of Chinese aid. The agenda of this third congress was related to economic and political aspects of the decision to authorize war in the south. A five-year industrialization plan was adopted to be the basis for a wartime economy. Le Duan, who since 1957 had been the "acting" leader, was officially ratified as the head of the party and his followers obtained key positions. Most immediately significant for policy in the south was adoption of a plan to create a front organization in the south to emphasize nationalism, democracy, and prosperity, but without any mention of communism.

The United States at this time appeared passive and vulnerable. After the death of John Foster Dulles in 1959, foreign policy drifted as Eisenhower was in poor health and the 1960 presidential election preoccupied the country. During the last months of 1960, a coup in Laos led to a government in Vientiane that was sustained by a Soviet airlift from Hanoi, prompting a Cold War crisis that led to another Geneva conference in 1961–1962. The Democratic Republic of Vietnam took a major role in the Laotian situation to protect its western border and to ensure that it had access to the western border of the Republic of Vietnam through southern Laos. An effort to open a supply route directly into the south through the mountains within Vietnamese borders at the seventeenth parallel had been defeated in 1959 by the southern army.

The 1959 legislative elections in the Republic of Vietnam encouraged public discussion of government policy in Saigon and relatively open dissent. The divergence of opinion among Americans in the military and civilian aid programs gave an impression of confusion and lack of commitment. By late 1960, trust between Ngo Dinh Diem and the American ambassador, Elbridge Durbrow, had been broken. It was a propitious moment for the communists to mobilize alienated southerners against the government.

In December 1960, the Communist Party's Central Office for the Southern Region (COSVN) established the People's Liberation Front for South Vietnam (Mat Tran Dan Toc Giai Phong Mien Nam Viet Nam). This front eventually included representatives of organizations that aimed to mobilize artists, Buddhists, Catholics, doctors, journalists, minorities, nurses, peasants, students, teachers, women, workers, writers, youth, and even Americans. It became widely known in English as the National Liberation Front (NLF). In early 1961, the Southern Region Liberation Army (Quan Giai Phong Mien Nam) was organized to create a command system for armed units in the south. In English this army became commonly known as the People's Liberation Armed Forces (PLAF) or as the Viet Cong, an abbreviation of Viet Nam and "communist" (cong san).

The Hanoi government developed its policy of war in the south at a time when the Eisenhower administration was losing focus and contradictions among American officials and between them and Ngo Dinh Diem were becoming serious. Ngo Dinh Diem endeavored to defeat the threat from the north while resisting American pressure to force him into a position of subordination that he believed would ruin his nationalist credentials. But the drumbeat of American criticism directed at Ngo Dinh Diem's government aroused expectations of opportunities among aspiring politicians in Saigon who were dissatisfied with how Ngo Dinh Nhu had controlled the National Assembly elections held in August 1959.

Ngo Dinh Diem between communists and Americans

The contradiction between French colonialism and American promotion of an independent, sovereign Vietnamese state had been a prominent aspect of US involvement in Vietnamese affairs in the late 1940s and early 1950s. In the late 1950s, although the French were no longer part of the situation, an analogous contradiction between controlling the policies of a client regime and respecting the sovereignty of an allied government became embedded in the US bureaucratic structure that grew up around the American commitment to defend a non-communist South Vietnam. This contradiction became increasingly volatile as the Hanoi decision to initiate war in the south gathered momentum and Saigon's dependence upon US assistance accordingly increased.

Ambassador Durbrow and others believed that the upsurge of insurrection produced by implementation of Hanoi's Resolution Fifteen in 1959 was primarily a political and not a military problem, and that the correct solution was for Ngo Dinh Diem to share power with his critics. This point of view began to appear in US press reports, which from a Vietnamese perspective were understood to represent official US policy. Durbrow's idea of "linking" US support for the Republic of Vietnam to liberalizing reforms became well known among Ngo Dinh Diem's Saigon critics and emboldened eighteen of them to sign a public manifesto in May 1960 that echoed American criticisms of Ngo Dinh Diem's government. This "Manifesto of the Eighteen" became popularly known as the Caravelle Manifesto after the name of the hotel in downtown Saigon where the group met.

The eighteen men who signed the Caravelle Manifesto included two who had served as provincial governors under the French, five who had served in pre-1954 Bao Dai cabinets, six who had briefly served in Ngo Dinh Diem's first cabinet in 1954, two professors, one elderly graduate of the 1903 doctoral examination, a Catholic priest, and a medical doctor (six of the others were also medical doctors). Their manifesto was addressed to Ngo Dinh Diem and reflected criticisms of his government that had begun to appear in both American and Vietnamese newspapers, such as charges of corruption, nepotism, and promotions in both the civil administration and the army that were based on personal loyalty rather than competence; the manifesto also asserted that the south could compete successfully with the north only by embracing liberal democracy and civil rights. The manifesto charged that the Ngo Dinh family had manipulated the legislative elections of the previous year to exclude those who were not members of its entourage and that the election was spoiled by censorship and politically motivated arrests. It lamented unemployment, poverty, and the lack of economic activity. It claimed that the elimination of sect armies simply left the countryside vulnerable to the communists and that the government's agrarian policy, which was then focused upon the building of rural towns called agrovilles, was provoking disaffection and giving ammunition to enemy propaganda.

There was substance to these complaints, particularly with how the agroville scheme had been implemented and how the legislative elections had been conducted during 1959. In both cases, the Ngo Dinh brothers had responded to the upsurge of communist-led insurgency by resorting to severe measures that alienated as well as mobilized. When they saw this, however, they endeavored to modify their policies. They abandoned the agroville plan in 1960 and subsequently loosened their control over electoral political activity. On the other hand, they sought to minimize American involvement in what they viewed as internal Vietnamese affairs. Meanwhile, their Vietnamese critics were beginning to think that they could legitimize a role for themselves in the Saigon government by championing American demands for political reform. The contradiction in US policy had expanded into Saigon's domestic politics.

The agroville concept had been hastily developed in early 1959 as part of a response to the rising communist challenge in the countryside. The idea was to concentrate the rural population into new towns where it could enjoy the benefits of urban life with schools, hospitals, stronger community organizations, and physical security. The people were expected to volunteer their labor to create the agrovilles and thereby gain a sense of self-sufficiency and develop a spirit of public service. American involvement was excluded to preclude the intrusion of foreign ideas and money that would simply induce an attitude of dependency upon the US. The Ngo Dinh brothers were influenced by their personalist ideology about modernizing through self-reliance and collective advance. They were also determined to keep American hands from reaching too deeply into Vietnamese society.

Within a year, however, the agroville experiment was discredited by the coercive practices of local officials seeking to meet unrealistic deadlines, the reluctance of rural people to relocate and to donate their labor for a project they did not understand, and by the success of communist agents in sabotaging and denouncing the policy. Around twenty agrovilles had been started when the scheme was discontinued in mid 1960. Not only had the agrovilles aroused internal opposition, but they also provided a new target for American criticism of Ngo Dinh Diem's government. By the autumn of 1960, Ambassador Durbrow's demands for reform were being expressed with greater urgency as warfare in the countryside intensified. At the same time, Ngo Dinh Diem lost his strongest ally among the Americans when General Lionel Charles McGarr (1904–1988) replaced Samuel Williams as the MAAG commander in the summer of 1960. McGarr's appointment was made in response to the upsurge of rural insurgency. He had been associated with studies of counterinsurgency, and he gave more attention to the details of small-unit action than Williams had been inclined to do.

Meanwhile, Durbrow's pressure for change increased. In October 1960, he conveyed to Ngo Dinh Diem a list of suggested reforms that included reorganization of the cabinet, restricting the Ngo Dinh patronage system, increasing the powers of the legislature, relaxing press censorship, raising the price of rice, and providing subsidies to people mobilized for community service. He also urged that Ngo Dinh Nhu be excluded from the government. Ngo Dinh Nhu was especially disliked by Ngo Dinh Diem's critics, both Vietnamese and American, because of his effectiveness in maintaining the security of the regime and his resistance to proffered American tutelage.

Durbrow's threat of "linkage" between Ngo Dinh Diem's compliance and continued US support was not a secret. The resonance of Durbrow's agenda with the Caravelle Manifesto of five months before was apparent to politically alert Vietnamese. Some disgruntled and adventurous Vietnamese imagined that the Americans were prepared to countenance a change of government, as had occurred in South Korea when Syngman Rhee was pushed out of power the previous spring. Criticism of the Saigon government in the American press and Durbrow's advocacy of political reform encouraged some of Ngo Dinh Diem's critics to imagine that the Americans would welcome his overthrow.

Three days after the election of a new American president in November 1960, some army units led by officers resentful about what they perceived as discrimination attempted a coup to unseat Ngo Dinh Diem. They were joined by some civilian political figures, including Phan Quang Dan, the most outspoken critic of Ngo Dinh Diem in the late 1950s, whose election to the legislature in 1959 had been annulled. Others who adhered to the coup were people associated with the Caravelle Manifesto and with political groups that had been sidelined by Ngo Dinh Diem, such as the Vietnamese Nationalist Party, the Dai Viet Party, the Hoa Hao, and the Cao Dai.

While the outcome of the coup hung in the balance, Durbrow struck a pose of neutrality and urged Ngo Dinh Diem to compromise with the coup leaders. This thoroughly alienated Ngo Dinh Diem from Durbrow and was the end of Durbrow's effectiveness as ambassador. It also aroused the specter of Syngman Rhee's overthrow, and Ngo Dinh Diem's sense of trust in the US was irreparably damaged.

The coup collapsed when army units loyal to Ngo Dinh Diem converged on Saigon. Military leaders of the coup escaped to Cambodia where they obtained asylum. Phan Quang Dan and several signers of the Caravelle Manifesto were arrested. This episode demonstrated the extent to which critics of the government were sensitive to indications of deteriorating American support for Ngo Dinh Diem, and its timing caught the attention of the newly elected American President.

The Kennedy escalation

At the end of 1960, American policy in Southeast Asia was in disarray with the Laotian situation threatening a Cold War confrontation and relations with Saigon in turmoil. During the next year, the administration of John Fitzgerald Kennedy developed new policies toward Laos and Vietnam that became the basis of subsequent US involvement in the region. An influential figure in formulating and implementing these policies was William Averell Harriman (1891–1986), a prominent businessman who had served as ambassador to London and to Moscow, as Secretary of Commerce in Harry Truman's cabinet, and as Governor of New York State. Kennedy successively appointed him Ambassador at Large (January 1961), Assistant Secretary of State for Far Eastern Affairs (November 1961), and Under Secretary of State for Political Affairs (April 1963).

As an elder statesman with extensive diplomatic experience and as a senior member of the President's political party, Harriman enjoyed Kennedy's confidence. Participation in wartime and post-war diplomacy during the Roosevelt and Truman administrations had inclined Harriman to believe that local conundrums could be sorted out by understandings reached among the major powers, who would in turn police their respective small-power clients. This perspective led to an international agreement to neutralize Laos and to the policy goal of unseating Ngo Dinh Diem for insufficient compliance with American instructions. Harriman strongly disliked Ngo Dinh Diem because of his resistance to

American supervision and his opposition to Harriman's effort to neutralize Laos. Ngo Dinh Diem saw that the Laos agreement in effect ceded to Hanoi control of South Vietnam's border with Laos, but Harriman trusted Moscow to keep Hanoi in line and viewed Ngo Dinh Diem as a recalcitrant beneficiary of American Cold War leadership. A group of men highly critical of Ngo Dinh Diem gathered around Harriman in the State Department.

At the same time, a different perspective developed in the Department of Defense under Secretary of Defense Robert Strange McNamara (1916–2009), a systems analyst with wartime experience in the 1940s as a logistics expert and with post-war experience in the automobile industry. He excelled at organizing available resources to attain assigned goals and was less concerned with formulating policy than with using quantitative methods of evaluation to guide policy implementation to get results. Another important figure in Kennedy's Department of Defense was General Maxwell Davenport Taylor (1901–1987), a man with a distinguished wartime record who, as Army Chief of Staff in the late 1950s, dissented from Eisenhower's defense policy of "massive retaliation," which threatened use of nuclear weapons and minimized the role of the army. Taylor resigned and, in 1960, published a book that argued the need for an army able to deal with situations short of nuclear war with a policy of "flexible response" to military threats. Kennedy was impressed with this book and made Taylor his military advisor. In October 1962, Kennedy appointed Taylor to be Chairman of the Joint Chiefs of Staff. McNamara and Taylor favored maximizing military assistance to Ngo Dinh Diem to deal with the security problem rather than encouraging his critics with demands for political reform.

Kennedy replaced Durbrow with Frederick Ernst Nolting (1911–1989), a former naval officer and career diplomat. Nolting arrived in spring 1961, just as Ngo Dinh Diem conducted a presidential election that he overwhelmingly won against two virtually unknown candidates. Nolting established a good relationship with the Ngo Dinh brothers, but they never fully trusted the US again. Nolting exercised his diplomatic skills in dealing both with the Ngo Dinh brothers and with his superiors in Washington, DC. He succeeded in minimizing US demands while eliciting small indications of Vietnamese cooperation, thereby restoring a façade of American respect for Vietnamese sovereignty and of Vietnamese compliance with American expectations.

However, during 1961, the Americans and the Vietnamese developed divergent policies toward the communist threat, not only with little prior consultation but also with the aim of avoiding the need for consultation altogether. By the end of the year, both Ngo Dinh Diem and Kennedy were pushing forward new counterinsurgency policies; but, while the Vietnamese sought to minimize dependence upon American assistance, the Americans sought to mask the scale of their escalating military presence in Vietnam from both the American public and the Vietnamese government.

Furthermore, the Ngo Dinh brothers understood that the communist supply lines through Laos into South Vietnam could not be stopped by an international agreement; they saw Kennedy's decision to support Harriman's policy on Laos as at best a miscalculation and at worst an indication that the US would eventually abandon them as it seemed to have abandoned the anti-communist Laotians. Nevertheless, while pursuing different paths, the Vietnamese and Americans implemented policies that by 1962 were showing signs of success against the Hanoi-supported insurgency.

After ending the failed agroville experiment in 1960, the Ngo Dinh brothers put their authority behind a new plan to build strategic hamlets. The strategic hamlet idea emerged by mid 1961 from local initiatives in Tay Ninh, Quang Ngai, and Vinh Long Provinces. It was elaborated by Ngo Dinh Nhu's personalist philosophy of modernizing rural communities by fostering collective effort and self-reliance. It aimed to bring revolutionary change to the countryside by fostering an attitude of "struggle" for a better life with a new generation of leaders unspoiled by the corruption and passivity associated with habits remaining from the French colonial experience. The idea of strategic hamlets was to minimize relocating people as much as possible and to reorganize communities for self-defense, self-government, a more egalitarian society, and a more dynamic economy.

The personalism of the Ngo Dinh brothers was a relatively abstract and idealized formulation, but no more vague and incomprehensible to Vietnamese peasants than was Marxism-Leninism. The critical factors in comparing the two Vietnams at this time are that the Ngo Dinh regime, unlike the rulers in Hanoi, did not have the benefit of a disciplined one-party totalitarian state to enforce its version of modernism and that it was challenged at every turn by an active and externally directed enemy. In the Vietnams of that time, both north and south, the effective exercise of power was the first step to obtain popular obedience or, at least, compliance. In the north, this was achieved with the land reform and the disciplining of intellectuals during the 1950s. In the south, Ngo Dinh Diem strove to modernize rural society while at the same time protecting it from an externally directed and supplied enemy. The strategic hamlet program was his final experiment for achieving this goal.

An important role in implementing strategic hamlets was assigned to the Republican Youth Movement, which had been organized in 1960 to mobilize young people to be activists in moving the country out of the colonial mentality that remained strong among the older generation. Within two years, over a million and a half young people were trained and assigned to participate in the strategic hamlet program. Their task was to revolutionize rural communities by propagating an attitude of self-reliance and by helping to prepare and organize elections for local leaders, thereby releasing latent talent and energy inhibited by the existing structure of authority. In the larger scheme of Ngo Dinh Nhu's thought, this would ideally be the beginning of a self-generating form of Vietnamese democracy that, spreading from the countryside, would eventually overcome the poisonous residue of French colonialism that was still strong among urban intellectuals.

Strategic hamlets were designed not only as a response to the communist insurgency but also as a response to the threat of American interference in Vietnamese domestic affairs, for the Ngo Dinh brothers feared that American largess and instruction would destroy the self-reliance and national pride that they understood to be the key to building up a social and administrative structure that could withstand the challenge from the north. As the Americans gradually became aware of the program and saw the merit of it, they instinctively wanted to support it with their resources and expertise, and to the extent that this was done without compromising Vietnamese aims and authority it was welcomed. But Americans quickly developed ideas about how the program should be conceptualized and implemented as an extension of their aid and advisory mission, and these ideas diverged from the aims of the Vietnamese government.

The Ngo Dinh brothers pressed for urgent speed in implementing the program, seeing it as a way to foster local initiative, on which they wished to rely rather than waiting for American money and supervision. There were around five hundred strategic hamlets by the end of 1961. By the end of 1962, the number was up to four thousand. Americans got involved by providing material resources and advisory assistance in certain areas, but they were dismayed by what they saw as undue haste and lack of systematic planning. While the Ngo Dinh brothers were counting on a release of energy among the people to gain sufficient momentum to overcome obstacles, American critics could not see beyond the apparent confusion and friction produced by this effort to revolutionize rural society. Americans viewed the pace of implementation as unrealistic and argued that the program should be slowed down to consolidate success in one place before extending the process to adjacent localities. On the other hand, the Ngo Dinh brothers believed that a rapid pace of implementation was necessary to preclude being overwhelmed by the insurgency.

A more serious aspect of the pace of implementation is that, in their haste to meet assigned deadlines, provincial authorities sometimes resorted to coercion and intimidation. This compromised the revolutionary goal of nurturing a Vietnamese version of grass-roots democracy espoused by the Republican Youth Movement. It also provided fuel for communist propaganda, which denounced the program as a form of exploitation and oppression. The great outcry of communist propaganda, however, came not simply from whatever popular resentment the program produced in some places. It was more directly an indication that the program, however poorly implemented, created serious problems for the insurgency by disrupting its links to the rural population. In 1962, the insurgency suffered serious setbacks and appeared to lose the initiative that it seemed to have had in 1961. South Vietnamese and American authorities were tempted to think that the strategic hamlet program might be the answer to turn back communist influence in the countryside.

While the strategic hamlet program was the central focus of the Ngo Dinh brothers, it was but a minor aspect of what the Americans were doing in 1962. In late 1961, Kennedy decided to increase by many thousands the number of US military advisors, to send bombers and helicopters, and to delegate direct supervision of this escalating American presence in Vietnam to Robert McNamara. Kennedy temporarily shelved criticism of Ngo Dinh Diem in favor of a major escalation in training, advising, and providing support to the Vietnamese army. In early 1962, a new command system was established for the US army in Vietnam. The MAAG was absorbed into the Military Assistance Command, Vietnam (MACV) under General Paul Donald Harkins (1904–1984). During the next two and a half years, Harkins presided over a steady increase of US military personnel from less than one thousand to over sixteen thousand.

Characteristically, this new American policy was decided with a minimum of consultation with the Vietnamese government. Within months, the thousands of Americans entering the country "without passports" were a source of dismay to Ngo Dinh Diem, who began to worry that the sovereignty of his country was being compromised. While grateful for American assistance, he did not trust American advisors to resist the temptation to take command of military and civil operations, thereby pushing aside his government. While the combination of the strategic hamlet program and the American military escalation dealt the communist insurgents major setbacks, it also exacerbated the tensions between the US and the Republic of Vietnam.

With the dramatic increase of American advisors came greater scrutiny from the American press. The official position of the Kennedy administration was that Americans were advising the Vietnamese army but were not directly involved in combat. American news reporters soon learned otherwise, and a pattern of dissimulation by Harkins and of skepticism by American reporters created sharp tension in MACV news briefings. Even more ominous for the US–Vietnamese relationship was the clash of cultural values produced by many thousands of American advisors with limited or no Vietnamese language ability attempting to work with their Vietnamese counterparts. The result was a critical mass of frustrated American advisors who did not understand Vietnamese culture and were alienated by what they imagined that they had learned about it. A "frustrated advisor" syndrome was combined with a "critical reporter" syndrome, and the two groups of young Americans, soldiers and reporters, shared information and opinions that were reflected in the American press as charges of corruption and incompetence against Ngo Dinh Diem's government. American reporters were given freedom to gather information and to file reports without any limitations, which soon became a factor in internal Vietnamese politics as their reports critical of the Vietnamese government were recycled back into the Vietnamese press and widely understood as representative of official US government views. In fact, Kennedy was particularly solicitous of the press, and press reports came to play a prominent role in how he understood events in Vietnam and in how he responded to those events.

Seeing this, Ngo Dinh Diem felt increasingly cornered and diminished by an overwhelming American presence that threatened to deprive him of legitimacy among Vietnamese nationalists. He was also concerned that the host of American advisors was instilling a colonial mentality in the new generation of Vietnamese officers. But, as long as the counterinsurgency efforts appeared to bear fruit, he chose to trust Nolting's assurances that the situation was temporary and that the number of American advisors would be reduced as soon as possible. He was also comforted by the hope that success of the strategic hamlet program would eventually make such intensive American involvement in his country unnecessary.

The Kennedy escalation produced a dramatic growth in the American military and civilian bureaucracy in Vietnam. This upsurge of activity was initially funded by purchase of local currency with dollars, but after a year these funds were expended, and the US wanted the Vietnamese government to contribute directly to a "counterinsurgency fund" that was under American control. Ngo Dinh Diem resisted this as a loss of authority over his national budget and a diminution of Vietnamese sovereignty. In the spring of 1963, after weeks of negotiations, Nolting eventually arranged a compromise acceptable to both sides.

Assassination of Ngo Dinh Diem

The Vietnamese–American relationship unraveled in 1963 as a result of several factors. The flawed Laotian agreement of 1962 facilitated North Vietnamese use of southern Laos to supply communist forces in South Vietnam. This assisted Hanoi's response to the challenge of strategic hamlets and of escalating American advisory, logistical, and air support activities. Harriman, the chief architect of the

Laos agreement, bitterly resented Ngo Dinh Diem's criticism of it. Harriman was the most influential among a group of officials in the State Department and the National Security Council that pressed for Ngo Dinh Diem's removal from power. These officials were emboldened when he began to appear increasingly vulnerable during the course of 1963. This vulnerability developed from at least five sources: French foreign policy, which aimed to extend to South Vietnam the neutralization scheme that had been imposed on Laos; disenchanted erstwhile American supporters; the response of American public opinion to critical news reports from Saigon; a movement to overthrow him led by Buddhist monks; and military officers susceptible to signs of American encouragement for them to organize a coup.

President de Gaulle imagined a role for France in Southeast Asia as the patron of neutral countries who desired to avoid the bipolar Cold War alternatives. Norodom Sihanouk (1922–2012), the leader of Cambodia, was an enthusiastic supporter of this, and the Laotian agreement of 1962 appeared to offer an example of power sharing between communists and non-communists. The Hanoi government professed to see benefit in this French initiative. In the south, some Vietnamese saw it as a way to avoid war and to reverse the tide of American advisors. Officially, the Saigon government and the US considered neutralism as simply a step toward surrender. However, as the Ngo Dinh brothers became increasingly alienated from the Americans during 1963, this path out of the American shadow acquired some plausibility, and rumors of contact between the two Vietnamese governments added to the rising tension between Saigon and Washington, DC.

In 1961, some American academics who had participated in an aid and advisory program in Vietnam sponsored by Michigan State University published articles denouncing Ngo Dinh Diem as a dictator. With the dramatic escalation of American assistance to Saigon during 1962, a dissenting view that American aid was being wasted on behalf of an unworthy tyrant gained traction among some American intellectuals. The most influential of these critics was Michael Joseph Mansfield (1903–2001), a former Professor of Latin American and Far Eastern History who in 1961 became the majority leader of the US Senate. Mansfield was a senior member of Kennedy's political party who, like Kennedy, had voiced strong support for Ngo Dinh Diem in the 1950s. However, after a visit to Saigon in late 1962, he advised Kennedy that Ngo Dinh Diem was unworthy of continued American assistance. Mansfield was widely respected for his expertise on Asia and for his thoughtful, considered manner. The official report of his trip to Vietnam was published in February 1963. It asserted that continued support of the Saigon government was a waste, and it recommended that the US should withdraw from the Vietnamese situation. The Mansfield report raised doubts about Vietnamese policy in the minds of some American politicians and officials, and it damaged Ngo Dinh Diem's confidence in the future of Vietnamese–American relations.

Meanwhile, a group of young American reporters had become advocates of overthrowing the Ngo Dinh brothers. In January 1963, a small battle in which communist forces inflicted disproportionate damage on South Vietnamese forces was reported from the vantage of an American advisor who had participated in the battle and who blamed its outcome on the corruption and incompetence of the Vietnamese government. This battle, which the Americans called the Battle of Ap Bac, was not representative of military activity in the country at that time, but it was reported in American newspapers as a major defeat for Saigon, a turning point in favor of the communists, and an indictment of Vietnamese leadership. Reports of this event in the US cast doubt on the efficacy of American efforts in Vietnam so long as the Ngo Dinh brothers remained in power.

Despite the negativity generated against the Ngo Dinh brothers in the American press and among American officials, Kennedy remained confident in McNamara's positive evaluation of progress on the battlefield and in the importance of Ngo Dinh Diem for maintaining political stability in Saigon. This changed with the eruption of the Buddhist movement in the summer of 1963. Although the Ngo Dinh brothers had successfully asserted their ascendancy over the religious sects in the Mekong River plain and over rival urban-based political parties such as the Nationalists and the Dai Viet, and although they had shown an ability to compete with communists for control of the rural population, they were relatively oblivious to the vulnerability created by their adherence to Roman Catholicism, and particularly to how this vulnerability was exacerbated by Ngo Dinh Thuc (1897–1984), the eldest living brother who, after serving more than twenty years as a bishop at Vinh Long in the Mekong plain, had been appointed Archbishop of Hue in late 1960.

The great infusion of Catholic refugees from northern Vietnam in 1954, added to southern Catholics, was a ready source of support for the Ngo Dinh brothers, who tended to rely upon Catholics not only because of their relatively high level of education, economic prowess, and community discipline, but also because of the role of the Church in recommending and guaranteeing the behavior of loyal people. Catholic refugees contributed to the larger tension between northerners and southerners, between immigrants benefiting from government assistance and local inhabitants struggling for a livelihood. But beyond this, many southerners converted to Catholicism as a step closer to the center of power, and advantages gained thereby were resented and viewed as discriminatory by those who chose not to take that path.

Ngo Dinh Diem had no discernible intention to discriminate against non-Catholics, and he labored to establish good relations with the Buddhist monkhood. He subsidized the building and repair of Buddhist temples and guaranteed freedom of religion. Yet, the undercurrent of incipient favoritism toward Catholics remained. This may never have broken into the open as it did in 1963 without the destabilizing activities of Ngo Dinh Thuc as Archbishop of Hue, for Hue also happened to be the center of a Buddhist leadership disposed to challenge Ngo Dinh Diem on both religious and political grounds.

Ever since the "Buddhist revival" led by Vien Chieu in the 1920s and 1930s, there was a strong tendency toward radical political activism among some Buddhist monks with nationalist inclinations. By the 1940s, Vien Chieu and others had gone so far as to leave the monkhood and to join the Indochinese Communist Party. In the early 1950s, many young Vietnamese circulated between the monkhood and the Viet Minh struggle against French colonialism. After 1954, some monks continued to maintain contact with one another across the demilitarized zone. In the early 1960s, many monks supported the idea of neutralism as a way to avoid civil war. In their opinion, the Ngo Dinh regime discriminated against Buddhists in favor of Catholics and had furthermore opened the country to American domination and civil war. The Kennedy administration's military escalation produced a sense of urgency among monks to stop the slide into a war.

Young Vietnamese monks were encouraged to take an active part in public affairs by the larger movement of Asian Buddhists that had arisen in the 1950s from nationalist struggles against colonialism and in reaction to the Cold War clash of non-Asian ideologies. This was in contrast to older, more conservative, monks who tended to be based in rural areas and who preferred to avoid the vicissitudes of politics. Hue was a former royal capital and colonial cultural center. Monks there tended to be politically alert with a sense of responsibility for the country.

Until the appointment of Ngo Dinh Thuc as Archbishop of Hue, Ngo Dinh Can (1911–1964), a younger Ngo Dinh brother, had effectively governed the northern part of South Vietnam and maintained good relations with the local Buddhist monks, including Thich Tri Quang (b. 1924), a leader among the younger, more politically inclined monks based at Hue. However, Ngo Dinh Thuc overshadowed his younger brother and destabilized the situation by mixing his efforts to promote Catholicism with his influence over government administration. He demonstrated a high-profile arrogance and insensitivity toward non-Catholics that alienated many Buddhists from the Saigon government. Buddhist leaders accused him of aggressive proselytizing with the weight of the government behind him. Ngo Dinh Diem could not bring himself to acknowledge that his elder brother, to whom he had given respect and deference throughout his life, was creating a problem.

In early May 1963, uproar broke out in Hue over the discriminatory enforcement of regulations about the flying of religious flags. The twenty-fifth anniversary observance of Ngo Dinh Thuc's ordination as a bishop had flourished Catholic flags, but shortly after this some local officials tried to prevent the flying of Buddhist flags during the observance of Vesakha, commonly referred to in English as Vesak or "the Buddha's birthday." Vesak was a relatively new Buddhist holiday that had been established in 1950 at the inaugural conference of the World Fellowship of Buddhists in Colombo, Sri Lanka, which thereafter encouraged the promotion of Buddhism in national cultures.

Thich Tri Quang had studied in Sri Lanka and became active in the Vietnam General Buddhist Association that was founded in 1951 by monks who were inspired by the Colombo meeting. After 1954, this organization was abolished in North Vietnam when the communist authorities implemented a policy to control and discourage religion, but it continued to exist in South Vietnam, based at Hue, where by 1963 Thich Tri Quang had become one of its leaders. A French colonial law that permitted the term "church" to be used only by Catholics had produced the term "association" in the organization's name. That this law had never been revoked is an indication of Ngo Dinh Diem's lack of awareness or concern about the resentment it produced and about the danger of allowing his elder brother to flaunt Catholicism in the region most committed to a Buddhist version of nationalism.

Thich Tri Quang was prominent in organizing the 1963 Vesak observance as a response to Ngo Dinh Thuc's activities. He was determined to use the occasion to rally public resentment against the archbishop and against the official policy of discrimination that the archbishop seemed to promote. Although government officials quickly disowned and reversed the effort to prevent display of Buddhist flags, Thich Tri Quang and his followers aroused a campaign of protest against religious discrimination of which the flag controversy was symbolic. Thich Tri Quang led a demonstration to the Hue radio station with the intention of broadcasting his complaints against the government. After soldiers arrived on the scene, explosions killed several demonstrators.

According to various theories, the soldiers, or the communists, or even the Americans had set off the explosions, but evidence for assigning culpability remains inconclusive and controversial. Nevertheless, Thich Tri Quang took the most plausible and expedient line of blaming the government, which was widely believed. He presented the government with five demands: freedom to fly Buddhist flags, revocation of the law forbidding Buddhist organizations the legal status of a "church," indemnification for the families of those who died at the radio station, punishment of those responsible for the deaths, and the end of all discrimination against Buddhists.

Ngo Dinh Diem was slow to respond to these demands. He was reluctant to acknowledge any official policy of religious discrimination, and he blamed the radio station deaths on the communists. He preferred to deal with older, less radical monks, but did not arrive at an agreement with them until mid June, by which time Thich Tri Quang and his activist followers had expanded their anti-government activities to Saigon and staged the public immolation of a monk to protest what was reported in the American press as "religious persecution." This event provoked widespread outrage against Ngo Dinh Diem's government in the US and turned the Kennedy administration against him.

Kennedy replaced Nolting with Henry Cabot Lodge, Jr. (1902–1985), a former senator, ambassador to the UN, and candidate for vice president who came from a social background similar to Kennedy and Harriman and who shared Harriman's disdain for uncooperative leaders of client states. By the time Lodge arrived in Saigon in August, the Vietnamese government had ended a summer of Buddhist street demonstrations by declaring martial law, seizing temples, and removing activist monks to prison or to the custody of senior monks in rural areas. Thich Tri Quang took refuge in the US embassy where Lodge treated him as an honored guest and where he acknowledged that his aim was to bring down the government.

Buddhists and foreign newsmen charged that the suppression of the Buddhist movement during the raids on temples had been excessively violent and that many people had been killed. Ngo Dinh Diem subsequently requested and obtained a UN "fact-finding team" that arrived in October and was permitted to investigate without restrictions. The UN report, made public after Ngo Dinh Diem's downfall, claimed that there had been no deaths and that those imprisoned had all been released.

Meanwhile, Ngo Dinh Diem held elections for the National Assembly that had been scheduled at the end of August but were postponed due to the imposition of martial law. Martial law was lifted in mid September and the election was held at the end of the month. This was the most open and least manipulated national election held under Ngo Dinh Diem. The number of elected members affiliated with the National Revolutionary Movement that served as the front organization for the Ngo Dinh brothers fell from seventy-six to fifty-five while those unaffili-ated with the regime increased from thirty-six to sixty-six. Ngo Dinh Diem accepted the election results and opened the new, albeit relatively powerless, legislature shortly before his death. By this time, US policymakers were no longer interested in electoral reform, having already decided the fate of Ngo Dinh Diem's regime.

In late August, Lodge endeavored to promote a military coup against Ngo Dinh Diem in response to instructions from the State Department drafted by

Harriman and his collaborators, which Kennedy subsequently approved. The senior generals on whom the Americans began to place their hopes had begun their careers with the French army; some had been French citizens. The leading figure among them was Duong Van Minh (1916–2001), the son of a wealthy Cochinchina landowner whom Ngo Dinh Diem had retired from active service. The catalyst for the flurry of plotting in late August was the arrival of Lodge and his clandestine contacts with disgruntled officers. On the other hand, Harkins made no secret of his lack of enthusiasm for a coup, which, along with a lack of mutual trust among the generals, initially stymied efforts to organize a conspiracy.

In July, at the peak of the Buddhist demonstrations, Ngo Dinh Diem staged trials of civilians who had been arrested in connection with the coup attempt of November 1960, and other former political figures were summoned for questioning as well. This was a warning to aspiring politicians tempted to support Thich Tri Quang's call for a change of government. Ngo Dinh Diem had excluded from his government people associated with the Nationalist and Dai Viet Parties, ostensibly because of their past status as clients of China and Japan and their participation in Bao Dai's governments in the early 1950s. They also represented rival networks of men with political and administrative experience. In February 1962, two air force pilots had bombed the presidential mansion; one of them was the son of a Nationalist Party leader who had been briefly jailed in 1960. The plotting military officers had no ability to govern, but there were many doctors, lawyers, former administrators, and other professional people who were alienated from the Ngo Dinh regime and were ready to serve if given an opportunity.

During September and October 1963, Kennedy leaned toward the State Department view of Ngo Dinh Diem and waited on Lodge's efforts to encourage the generals to seize the government. The plotters asked that the Commodity Import Program be suspended as a signal that the US government fully supported them; this was done in mid October. After a final face-to-face meeting between Lodge and one of the generals to convey assurance that the US approved the conspiracy, Ngo Dinh Diem and Ngo Dinh Nhu were seized and killed at the beginning of November. Ngo Dinh Thuc was out of the country at the time and never returned. Ngo Dinh Can was killed six months later. The overthrow of Ngo Dinh Diem was Kennedy's most fateful achievement in Vietnam. It fundamentally changed the Vietnamese–American relationship and set US involvement in Vietnam in a new direction.

Ngo Dinh Diem had stabilized a government in South Vietnam that resisted Hanoi's efforts to destroy it by means of political agitation, terrorism, and insurgency. His strength lay in the desire of various groups to maintain a non-communist option for the future of the country, in his reputation as a nationalist, and in his ability to elicit American aid. However, when Hanoi resorted to military means to overthrow his government in 1959, each of these strengths became a weakness. His strict attitude toward national sovereignty, a vestige of his disgust with French colonialism, also extended toward critics and potential allies, and he withdrew into the inner circle of his family and personal entourage. The widespread desire for an effective anti-communist leader had benefited him in the mid 1950s, but he alienated many public-spirited people who were disappointed at being denied an opportunity to contribute to national affairs. His blindness to the seriousness of his elder brother stirring up religious resentment in the northern part of the country made him vulnerable to both his Vietnamese and his American critics. Increasingly concerned about the double threat of communist insurgency and American intrusion, he allowed the monk-led demonstrations against his government to continue for nearly four months, undermining his control of the military and his relationship with the United States. American support became the poison he feared; it overwhelmed and finally discarded him. Without American encouragement, the army generals would never have moved against him. The generals were united not so much against Ngo Dinh Diem as by the opportunity offered by the Americans.

Political turmoil in Saigon

Despite filling the role of "first among equals" during the planning and execution of the coup, Duong Van Minh was indolent and without ideas aside from removing Ngo Dinh Diem's officials and abandoning his policies. In a matter of days, the structure of authority created by the Ngo Dinh brothers was dismantled and the strategic hamlet program came to a halt. During the three months of Duong Van Minh's regime, most government activity had to do with sorting out a shifting pecking order among military officers and allotting the spoils of power. Duong Van Minh was susceptible to the views of the Buddhist activists, and to the extent that a general policy for his government could be discerned, his rivals and the increasingly appalled Americans accused him of favoring the neutralism touted by the French and by Sihanouk. Sihanouk ended his relationship with American foreign aid after Ngo Dinh Diem's death, fearing that it could have a similar effect in Cambodia, and he called for a neutralization of Indochina. Duong Van Minh resisted extension of the US advisory program and appeared to encourage the activist monks to believe that their anti-war and anti-American views were important for national policy.

Duong Van Minh failed to establish successful working relations with civilian politicians, with his fellow generals, and with the Americans. The cabinet appointed by the generals to administer the country excluded some groups, such as the Dai Viet and the Hoa Hao, who instinctively began to work to bring down the government. There was also a falling out into factions among the generals themselves. General Tran Thien Khiem (b. 1925), a Catholic and godson of Ngo Dinh Diem, had joined the coup plot but resented Duong Van Minh's decision to kill the Ngo Dinh brothers. He and other military officers were dissatisfied with how authority was apportioned after the coup. The Americans soon decided that the results of the coup were a step backwards in terms of government stability and battlefield performance. The military situation had begun to shift in late summer when the attention of the commanding generals was diverted from fighting to plotting. In the wake of the coup, many experienced and competent officers and officials were discarded, the battlefield situation became grim, and Duong Van Minh had no plans.

Under the new American President, Lyndon Baines Johnson (1908–1973), initiative for policy shifted from the embassy of Ambassador Lodge to the MACV command of General Harkins. Harkins had never agreed with the scheme for removing Ngo Dinh Diem, and he had little esteem for the group of opportunistic generals gathered around Duong Van Minh. He identified General Nguyen Khanh (b. 1927) as someone more likely to share the American concern to fight communists and encouraged him to take power. Nguyen Khanh, like Duong Van Minh, was the son of a wealthy Cochinchina landlord. He had received military training in France in the late 1940s and in the US in the late 1950s. He had helped to foil the 1960 coup plot. In 1963, with a command just north of Saigon, he had remained aloof from the plotters until joining the coup as it occurred. Duong Van Minh then reassigned him to command the northern part of the country, which made him very dissatisfied. His new second-in-command was Nguyen Chanh Thi (1923–2007), who had been a prominent member of the 1960 coup attempt against Ngo Dinh Diem and had gone into Cambodian exile until rehabilitated in November 1963. Nguyen Khanh, along with Nguyen Chanh Thi, Tran Thien Khiem, and other officers who were alienated by Duong Van Minh's lack of initiative, his vulnerability to the Buddhist activists, and his inability to maximize benefits from the American relationship staged a mostly bloodless coup at the end of January 1964 with the active encouragement and support of the Americans.

Nguyen Khanh was the pre-eminent figure in the Saigon government for the next year. He was opportunistic and he lacked political ability, but he was indebted to the fact that American policy was in an era of passivity as Johnson waited for the election of 1964 to give him the political clout to respond to what under Khanh's wavering leadership became an increasingly chaotic situation. Nguyen Khanh initially turned to the Dai Viet politicians who had been excluded from power by both Ngo Dinh Diem and Duong Van Minh. But political parties in Vietnam had arisen during French colonial rule and consequently were oppositional, conspiratorial, and unwilling to take responsibility for governing. Furthermore, the Dai Viet politicians did not form a coherent party organization but rather had become groups vaguely allied as opponents of Ngo Dinh Diem.

There were at least four groups of Dai Viet politicians, three of them aligned in factions associated with the three parts of Vietnam – north, center, and south. The most prominent Dai Viet figure was Phan Huy Quat (1908–1979), whom Nguyen Khanh made his Foreign Minister. Phan Huy Quat, a medical doctor, was from the northern Dai Viet faction. He had served as Minister of Education under Bao Dai in 1949 and as Minster of Defense during the brief Nguyen Phan Long government of 1950, and again in the Nguyen Van Tam government of 1953–1954. He briefly served as acting Prime Minister in 1954 between Buu Loc and Ngo Dinh Diem and was touted by some as an alternative to Ngo Dinh Diem in 1954. He was a signer of the Caravelle Manifesto in 1960. In February 1964, he refused to join some Dai Viet figures who were plotting to seize control of Nguyen Khanh's government. This plot disabused Nguyen Khanh of relying on civilian politicians associated with "parties."

Because he had overthrown those who had eliminated Ngo Dinh Diem, Nguyen Khanh was vulnerable to accusations of wanting to re-establish the Catholic regime of the Ngo Dinh family. His support of the Dai Viet politicians was intended to negate this accusation because the Dai Viet politicians had the reputation of being opponents of Ngo Dinh Diem. However, when he realized that the non-sectarian political parties, including the Dai Viet, were incoherent and untrustworthy because of their lack of organization and their conspiratorial culture of opposition, he began to look elsewhere for a political base. During the spring and summer of 1964, he attempted to cultivate the support of the Buddhist monks and of the younger generation of military officers.

After the overthrow of Ngo Dinh Diem, activist Buddhist leaders reorganized themselves into the Vietnamese Buddhist United Church, which included around three thousand monks and six hundred nuns and claimed three million lay adherents. They became experts at pressuring Saigon governments with street demonstrations. Student groups, particularly in Saigon, being inspired and influenced by the Buddhists, had developed their own style of street politics beginning in the late summer of 1963, and they continued their efforts to affect national policy during 1964. In May 1964, the Buddhists and students successfully demanded that Nguyen Khanh kill Ngo Dinh Can to prove that he had repudiated Ngo Dinh Diem's political heritage. From this, they understood that Nguyen Khanh was a weak leader who could be pressured from the streets.

More important than the civilian politicians or the Buddhists and students were the junior colleagues of Nguyen Khanh in the military. He was a relatively lonely generational figure between the Francophile senior generals who had gathered around Duong Van Minh and junior officers who represented a more pro-American and anti-communist perspective. During the first half of 1964, Nguyen Khanh made sure to recognize the loyalty of his junior colleagues with promotions. Aside from Nguyen Chanh Thi, two other prominent figures in this group of so-called "Young Turks" were Nguyen Van Thieu (1923–2001) and Nguyen Cao Ky (1930–2011). Nguyen Van Thieu, from a coastal region not far north of Saigon, had converted to Catholicism during Ngo Dinh Diem's rule. In 1963, he was the commander of a key unit near Saigon and had joined the coup against Ngo Dinh Diem when it became clear that it was going to succeed. He subsequently joined the plot led by Nguyen Khanh. He was a cautious man, determined to be on the winning side of military politics and convinced that the exercise of power depended upon American support. Nguyen Cao Ky, a pilot who had become the commander of the air force, was also alert to the winds of change. However, unlike Nguyen Van Thieu, who was introverted and secretive, Nguyen Cao Ky was open, outspoken, transparent, and with no hint of corruption.

As Nguyen Khanh endeavored to keep his position atop the shifting sands of Saigon politics, American policy prepared for greater intervention as it became clear that the battlefield situation had turned dramatically against Saigon after the death of Ngo Dinh Diem. No major initiative was politically possible until after the presidential election of November 1964. Until then, US policy in Vietnam was subordinated to electoral politics. Nevertheless, early in his presidency, Johnson had authorized sabotage and intelligence gathering operations by Taiwanese and Vietnamese commandos along the coast of North Vietnam in the Gulf of Tonkin. In August 1964, this resulted in an attack by North Vietnamese patrol boats upon a US destroyer, just at a time when Johnson needed to demonstrate his anti-communist resolve to silence criticisms from his presidential opponent. He ordered a retaliatory air strike against North Vietnam and obtained congressional approval of the so-called "Gulf of Tonkin Resolution" that authorized him to wage war in Southeast Asia. This helped Johnson to silence his militant critics, but it also had an effect upon Saigon politics.

During the summer of 1964, Buddhist militants organized the National Salvation Council with provincial committees to stage demonstrations against what they continued to view as the danger of a return to power of Ngo Dinh Diem's people. Many public confrontations with Catholics turned violent, and Catholics began to denounce what they viewed as religious persecution. Activists on both sides influenced student groups, who began to stage demonstrations in Saigon not directly related to religion. In late July, students led a large demonstration in Saigon denouncing what they saw as French interference in Vietnamese affairs. Nguyen Khanh appeared irresolute amidst the clamor of street politics.

The Gulf of Tonkin episode with retaliatory US air strikes on North Vietnam and a warlike congressional resolution inspired Nguyen Khanh to try some similarly dramatic initiative to overcome his reputation for vacillation. He declared a national emergency, imposed press censorship, and persuaded his military colleagues to issue the Vung Tau Charter, giving him near-dictatorial powers. After ten days of public demonstrations in which Buddhists denounced these moves and mobs of Buddhist and Catholic youth brawled in the streets, Nguyen Khanh backed down and rescinded the Vung Tau Charter.

Nguyen Khanh's military colleagues were losing confidence in him, yet no one else was in a position to push him aside. Maxwell Taylor had just replaced Lodge as US ambassador and, at the same time, General William Childs Westmoreland (1914–2005) replaced Harkins as MACV commander. Taylor and Westmoreland wanted to avoid any dramatic political change while rebuilding a civilian government.

By the end of August, Nguyen Khanh entered a kind of triumvirate with Duong Van Minh and Tran Thien Khiem. In mid September, Tran Thien Khiem was implicated in a coup attempt plotted by two other Catholic generals and, consequently, sent out of the country to be ambassador to the US. The Young Turks thwarted the coup and their influence accordingly grew. In November, Duong Van Minh was eased out and sent abroad as a "roving ambassador." Meanwhile, in early September the High National Council was formed of sixteen civilians with responsibility to write a constitution, to function as a temporary national assembly, and to restore a civilian administration.

Phan Khac Suu (1893–1970) was chosen as Chairman of the High National Council. He was an agricultural engineer and a member of the Cao Dai who had served in Bao Dai's cabinets. He had signed the Caravelle Manifesto in 1960 and was subsequently jailed by Ngo Dinh Diem. Under his leadership, at the end of October, the High National Council promulgated a "provisional charter" to serve as a temporary constitution. He was elevated to serve as Chief of State, and he chose Tran Van Huong (1902–1982) to be the prime minister. Tran Van Huong had a reputation for honesty and competence. A secondary school teacher, he spent most of the French war working for the Vietnamese Red Cross in southern Vietnam. Under Ngo Dinh Diem, he was the mayor of Saigon for several months and then became Secretary General of the Vietnamese Red Cross Society, a position he held when he signed the Caravelle Manifesto in 1960. Duong Van Minh made him a member of his powerless Council of Notables after the coup against Ngo Dinh Diem. He was once again the mayor of Saigon when Phan Khac Suu called on him to be Prime Minister.

Tran Van Huong stood for establishing public order against the street politics of the student and Buddhist activists. He sponsored a Buddhist church organization of monks opposed to the militancy of Thich Tri Quang and insisted that politics and religion should not be mixed. Although his ability to exercise strong leadership was hindered by controversy over his selection of cabinet ministers in the High National Council, now functioning as a legislative body, he forcefully responded to Saigon street disturbances in late November by declaring a state of emergency, closing schools, banning public meetings, and authorizing the local military commander, General Pham Van Dong (1919–2008), to search and arrest without warrant. These measures were popular in Saigon where street politics had been disrupting life for months, but Nguyen Khanh and the Young Turks viewed Pham Van Dong as a potential rival.

Pham Van Dong had a long record of service in the French and Vietnamese armies. Americans praised his competence on the battlefield, and he had a reputation for being politically astute and personally honest. He kept a small private army of men from a northern upland ethnic minority, into which he had married, and accordingly enjoyed a measure of independence in relation to other military officers. Tran Van Huong's reliance upon him to restore a semblance of public order raised the profiles of both men as effective leaders. However, the Buddhist activists, whose influence on government depended upon their skill in street politics, were unhappy. Nguyen Khanh, who remained susceptible to the idea of increasing his authority in alliance with the militant Buddhists, was also unhappy. Neither were the Young Turks happy with the ascendancy of Pham Van Dong, which threatened to intercept their path to power.

Nguyen Chanh Thi, a prominent Young Turk, was closely associated with both Nguyen Khanh and the militant monks based at Hue. When the High National Council resisted pressure to expand its membership to include supporters of Thich Tri Quang, the young generals demanded that it pass a law to retire military officers after twenty-five years of service. This measure was aimed at Pham Van Dong, who had enlisted in 1939, a year earlier than Duong Van Minh. When this demand was refused, Nguyen Khanh and his young colleagues dissolved the High National Council and arrested some of its members along with other political figures. They nevertheless continued to express support for the Tran Van Huong government and pretended that the powers of the High National Council had passed to Phan Khac Suu. This action weakened Tran Van Huong while strengthening Nguyen Khanh and the Buddhist activists.

Taylor reacted angrily to the apparent reassertion of Nguyen Khanh's authority and to the setback in building a civilian government. The two men fell out,

596 / A history of the Vietnamese

each demanding that the other leave the country. Tran Van Huong managed to defuse the situation and by mid January 1965 had restored a measure of calm to Vietnamese–American relations. Taylor's reaction was to some extent aggravated by American plans to escalate involvement in Vietnam, which after the US presidential election were now rising in priority. The Americans wanted a stable civilian Vietnamese government to facilitate and legitimize an increase in US involvement. Nevertheless, political turmoil in Saigon continued during the next two months as dry-season battlefield activity intensified and American military intervention began to materialize.

In late January, Tran Van Huong aimed to strengthen his government by proposing a new cabinet that included four generals. This prompted Buddhist militants led by Thich Tri Quang to call for Tran Van Houng's resignation and to mobilize violent anti-American demonstrations in Saigon and in Hue. Responding to this, Nguyen Khanh solicited Buddhist support by persuading the generals to remove Tran Van Huong from office.

By mid February, Nguyen Khanh had named Phan Huy Quat to be prime minister. Phan Huy Quat, a Dai Viet leader who had been in Nguyen Khanh's first cabinet, was a Buddhist from the north widely considered to be a political enemy of those who had supported Ngo Dinh Diem. Most of the men he appointed to his cabinet were from the north or center of the country. He was acceptable to the Buddhist militants, but Catholics and southerners distrusted him.

In late February, southern Catholic officers attempted to stage a coup that was suppressed by Nguyen Chanh Thi and other generals who took the occasion to send Nguyen Khanh into exile. Thereafter, as American bombing of North Vietnam started and American troops began to arrive, Nguyen Chanh Thi established himself in the Hue/Da Nang region of the central coast with strong Buddhist support. Meanwhile, the Phan Huy Quat government limped along in Saigon, handicapped by its unpopularity among Catholics and southerners, which prompted another unsuccessful coup attempt in late May.

By early June, the government was paralyzed by a dispute between Phan Huy Quat and Chief of State Phan Khac Suu over the composition of the cabinet. The National Legislative Council, which had been formed in February to replace the High National Council, was too weak to solve the problem. Consequently, Phan Huy Quat resigned and handed the government back to the generals, who decided on Nguyen Van Thieu as Chief of State and Nguyen Cao Ky as Prime Minister. These two generals, along with Nguyen Chanh Thi, had emerged as the most influential among the military officers after Nguyen Khanh's departure. Nguyen Chanh Thi preferred to establish his personal bailiwick in the northern part of the country rather than to enter the politics of the Saigon-based generals. In mid June, Nguyen Cao Ky formed a war cabinet as American intervention accelerated.

Formation of the Second Republic of Vietnam

Lyndon Johnson accepted the American commitment to defeat the communist attempt to take over South Vietnam, but he subordinated the implementation of this commitment to the presidential election of 1964 and to his ambitious domestic legislative agenda, which occupied him during the first half of 1965. Consequently, when, in March 1965, he opened direct American participation in the war, he endeavored to minimize drawing attention to it. The Hanoi government had been rapidly increasing its military involvement in the south ever since the death of Ngo Dinh Diem, hoping to gain victory before the US could react. By early 1965, the military position of the Saigon government was deteriorating so quickly that direct American intervention was needed to avoid a debacle. Phan Huy Quat was not enthusiastic about American intervention but had no way of resisting it. The generals understood that American intervention ensured the survival of their armed forces and would fundamentally change the context of Vietnamese politics in their favor.

After four months of a US bombing campaign against North Vietnam and of piecemeal deployments of thousands of American ground troops to South Vietnam, in July of 1965 Johnson finally announced his policy toward Vietnam. He proposed an open-ended increase in US troops, the amount to be determined by the number necessary to obtain his aim, which was to persuade Hanoi to abandon its policy of seizing the south. His approach followed a "limited war" theory that had been developed by some academics, which proposed that one could persuade an enemy to renounce its goal through a limited application of military action; it was not necessary to actually force defeat upon an enemy in order to obtain one's own goal but merely to convince an opponent that it was in its best interest to stop fighting. This theory was combined with the "flexible response" idea that Kennedy had ostensibly embraced to produce the concept of "graduated pressure," according to which the US would apply increasing levels of military action in Vietnam until Hanoi decided to give up.

Ambassador Taylor had argued against the deployment of ground troops, fearing that it would destroy the nationalist credentials of the anti-communist Vietnamese. Johnson replaced him with Lodge, who for the next two years watched from the embassy as more and more American troops arrived. Without a clear strategy for defeating the enemy and gaining victory, American forces concentrated upon logistics, at which they excelled, moving men and material halfway around the world to Vietnam. Westmoreland was tasked with using his increasing resources to cause maximum battlefield damage to the enemy. Handicapped by being unable to control the movement of men and materials through Laos and Cambodia into Vietnam, Westmoreland resorted to a policy of "search and destroy" in which American forces endeavored to locate and apply their superior firepower to communist forces. The result was that communist forces learned how to be "found" in ways that maximized their advantages and consequently they were able to initiate around 80 percent of all combat encounters. It began to look like a war of attrition by 1966 and 1967.

The momentum of American escalation pushed aside the South Vietnamese army and it was relegated to so-called "pacification duties," dealing with local insurgents and the chaos in civilian life caused by the increase in warfare. Meanwhile, American forces attempted to engage the units of the North Vietnamese army that increasingly appeared from across the Laotian and Cambodian borders. In addition to the land route from North Vietnam through southern Laos, supplies also reached communist forces by ship to the Cambodian port of Sihanoukville. Sihanouk allowed the movement of military supplies through Cambodia to the Vietnamese border in exchange for a percentage of the shipments.

The first major battle between American and North Vietnamese army units occurred in autumn 1965 at what became known as the Battle of Ia Drang, in the Central Highlands near the Cambodian border, in which US airmobile units, recently arrived from the US, endeavored to destroy a large concentration of North Vietnamese soldiers. The North Vietnamese considered the battle a victory because, after inflicting significant casualties upon the Americans, they were able to withdraw in good order across the Cambodian border where they enjoyed immunity from American attack. Although Americans officially claimed the battle as a victory because their casualties were fewer than those of the North Vietnamese, McNamara's analysis of the battle was the beginning of his doubts about the war. He concluded that the bombing campaign could not sufficiently diminish the movement of men and materials into the south nor could US search and destroy operations disable North Vietnamese units fast enough for any discernible scenario leading to success. Although McNamara persuaded Johnson to order a brief bombing halt in early 1966 to explore the possibility of negotiations, the basic war policy remained unchanged with continued bombing and ever-increasing numbers of US troops being sent to South Vietnam.

By early 1966, the activist monks based in Hue were pressing for the election of a constituent assembly to write a constitution and to re-establish a civilian government. The Americans also endorsed this agenda. Ambassador Lodge, who in 1963 had established a good relationship with Thich Tri Quang, endeavored to keep the Buddhists calm while nudging the Nguyen Cao Ky government in this direction. Complicating this issue was the personal falling out between Nguyen Chanh Thi, who was closely associated with Thich Tri Quang, and the Saigon generals, which exacerbated the alienation of the Buddhist population in the northern part of the country from the government in Saigon.

After Nguyen Cao Ky was publicly insulted during a visit to Hue and Da Nang in early March, the Saigon generals decided to relieve Nguyen Chanh Thi of his command. In response to this, Thich Tri Quang began to broadcast anti-government messages from the Hue radio station and a resistance movement led by monks and students spread to major cities along the central coast and in the Central Highlands, and also to Saigon. In addition to calling for an end to the military government, the demonstrators also aired anti-American slogans. They expressed a Buddhist fear that the military government was bringing back officials who had worked for the Ngo Dinh brothers as well as a more general dismay at the increasing numbers of US combat troops in the country and the expansion of warfare.

During the following three months, two important developments simultaneously occurred. Soldiers, teachers, students, and others in the Hue–Da Nang region joined Buddhist activists in resistance against the Saigon government. This was eventually suppressed by force, and many of the most militantly anti-government people fled to join the communists in the mountains. At the same time, and to some extent as a political response to the revolt, a committee was formed to draft laws for electing and administering a constituent assembly that would write a constitution. The work of this committee was completed and approved in June 1966, just as the revolt was coming to an end.

The election for the constituent assembly was held in September 1966 with 401 candidates standing for 117 seats and around 80 percent of the electorate participating. The election revealed strong regional and sectarian differences. Initially, the largest bloc was mainly comprised of people from north and central Vietnam and included Dai Viet politicians, some Catholics and a few people associated with the military. This bloc was eventually equaled in size by the combination of a Catholic group and a group of southerners led by Hoa Hao leaders that attracted some independents and formed a bloc that supported Nguyen Cao Ky's efforts to mediate between the assembly and the generals. There was a smaller bloc of militant southern regionalists, an echo of the old Cochinchinese separatist movement of the late 1940s. The Buddhist activists had been discredited by the revolt and consequently there was no significant bloc of people representing their agenda.

In October, as the constituent assembly was organizing itself, a crisis erupted when southerners in Nguyen Cao Ky's cabinet threatened to resign over what they viewed as discriminatory treatment of southerners in favor of northerners. This crisis resonated with the formation of regional blocks in the constituent assembly. Nguyen Cao Ky, a northerner, succeeded in calming the matter and maintaining the unity of his cabinet. He thereafter gave much attention to negotiating compromises between the constituent assembly and the generals. The constitution that was finally completed and approved in March 1967 was the result of significant concessions from both groups. It provided for a strong presidency, a bicameral legislature, and an independent judiciary.

After a complex series of procedures and maneuvers in the summer of 1967, eleven men were officially approved to run for president. Although Nguyen Cao Ky was keen to run for president, his military colleagues forced him to run for vice president under Nguyen Van Thieu, who was his senior in rank; the generals feared that without a united military ticket they could lose the election. Of the ten civilian candidates, Phan Khac Suu and Tran Van Huong were the most prominent. Thich Tri Quang called on his followers to boycott the election.

The election was held under the gaze of dozens of American and other international observers. Despite many problems, it was generally evaluated as an accomplishment on the road toward building a democratic political system in wartime. Despite the advantage of holding power, the military ticket received only around 35 percent of the votes. Phan Khac Suu and Tran Van Huong polled well in the cities with each receiving around 10 percent of the votes. Two other candidates received between 5 and 10 percent, and five candidates received less than 5 percent. The surprise of the election was that a man named Truong Dinh Dzu came in second with around 17 percent of the votes.

Truong Dinh Dzu (1917–1980s), originally from Binh Dinh Province, studied law in Hanoi and from 1945 practiced law in Saigon. He was rumored to have communist acquaintances, but he also had business relations with people related to Ngo Dinh Diem. He was an active member of the Rotary Club, becoming the head of the Rotary Club organization in Southeast Asia. He had been investigated for bribery, illegally transferring funds abroad, and tax irregularities, but nevertheless managed to gain approval to run for president. He was an effective speaker and attracted attention with his platform of peace and of negotiation with the communists. He ran well in contested rural areas that were susceptible to communist influence. After the election he was jailed on a currency transaction charge.

The Second Republic of Vietnam was inaugurated at the end of October 1967 after completion of National Assembly elections. The government was a civilian–military hybrid, a structure inhabited by military authority with built-in democratic tendencies that required ongoing negotiation and compromise with civilian constituents. During the year and a half of preparing and bringing into operation the new constitution, American intervention rose to half a million troops in the country. This dominating American presence had a stabilizing influence on the country's politics. In 1967, Ellsworth Bunker (1894–1984) was named US ambassador. He was an experienced, competent, and effective career diplomat who, during his six years in Saigon, preserved a predominantly cooperative relationship between the US government and Nguyen Van Thieu. Nguyen Van Thieu's lack of ability as a political leader was to some extent offset by his caution, his consistency, his mastery of military politics, and his ability to work with Americans.

During the four years between the end of the Ngo Dinh regime and the beginning of the Second Republic, the politics of South Vietnam developed amidst an externally supported insurgency and a massive American intervention. A large theme was competition for ascendancy between the two groups that had brought down Ngo Dinh Diem: the Buddhist activists and the military officers. Eventually, the Buddhists were forced to yield. Within the military, a junior cohort relatively susceptible to American influence came to the fore. A large and varied population of civilian politicians, often with strong sectarian and regional affiliations, actively participated in the many experiments in government. After a year of negotiation and compromise, a constitutional structure was adopted that provided a legal framework for politics and administration until dismantled by the communists seven and a half years later.

The communist offensive of 1968

Between the 1959 decision to force a military solution upon the southern question and the death of Ngo Dinh Diem in 1963, Le Duan and his associates in Hanoi were constrained by party members who believed that economic development was a higher priority than military confrontation with the south and that, in fact, developing a strong economy was an essential first step toward overcoming the south. The Le Duan leadership group tightened its control over the party, the army, and intellectuals during the third party congress in late 1960, but internal resistance and the indifference of China and the Soviet Union continued to inhibit policy toward Saigon. By late 1962, after the strategic hamlet program was launched and Kennedy escalated American military involvement, there was much uncertainty and vacillation in the party. After the agreement to neutralize Laos was completed in the summer of 1962, the Soviet Union lost interest in Southeast Asia. China continued to support the Laotian and Vietnamese communists but was distracted by mass starvation and by border tensions with India, Taiwan, and the Soviet Union. Party leadership in Hanoi was divided over the relative importance of the Soviet model of a centralized bureaucratic state and the Chinese model of mass mobilization and permanent revolution.

The November 1963 coup in Saigon awakened the Hanoi leadership from the conundrums of socialist internationalism and its manifestations within the Vietnamese party. The sudden, dramatic dismantling of the Ngo Dinh Diem regime opened the prospect of victory in the south much sooner than it had been thought possible. Within weeks of Ngo Dinh Diem's death, the central committee of the party resolved upon an aggressive policy of "general offensive and general uprising" to take over the south. Dissenting party members were demoted, marginalized, put under house arrest, or imprisoned. Students in the Soviet Bloc countries were recalled for re-education. A campaign to enforce intellectual conformity among writers and artists was launched. North Vietnamese army units began to move into South Vietnam through Laos and Cambodia.

By the time of the 1965 Johnson escalation, Khrushchev had been deposed, and the new Soviet leadership challenged the expansion of American military action in Vietnam by giving strong support to Hanoi. China followed suit and within two years stationed nearly two hundred thousand troops between the Chinese border and Hanoi. The Chinese troops handled air defense, logistics, and construction. Their presence enabled the Vietnamese to allocate more manpower to the south.

Nguyen Chi Thanh, the commander of communist forces in South Vietnam, believed that the Vietnamese disadvantage in battlefield technology could be overcome by high morale. He aimed to break the will of Americans to fight in Vietnam by seeking direct engagement with American units to inflict maximum casualties. The high cost of this strategy provoked dissent within the North Vietnamese army. In 1966 and the first half of 1967, Vo Nguyen Giap spoke out against what he considered to be the wasting of the army in high casualty engagements. He advocated an emphasis on guerrilla operations and protracted warfare to minimize the damage suffered from superior US firepower. In reply, Nguyen Chi Thanh argued that the US strategy of limited war and attrition could be overcome by an aggressive strategy that prevented Americans from becoming comfortable in Vietnam and that a shift to guerrilla warfare would damage the morale of the communist soldiers.

Voices of moderation within the party began to rise as the human and material cost of the war became increasingly apparent. US bombing disrupted and degraded the country's industrial and transportation infrastructure and forced major relocations of population. Many party members were dismayed to see plans for economic development sacrificed to a war they considered unnecessary. They called for peace talks to end the war, believing that a better way to unify the country was through economic development, confident that a vibrant socialist economy would eventually overwhelm southern resistance. These people were encouraged by the growing involvement of the Soviet Union in the war effort. They admired the Soviet model of state building, being repelled by the chaos of China's Cultural Revolution, and they supported the Soviet Union's call for a negotiated settlement.

By 1967, the rising involvement of both the Soviet Union and China in the war brought the Sino-Soviet conflict into the center of party politics. The Soviet Union provided military material for conventional war but advocated negotiations with the Americans. China advocated a protracted guerrilla war and opposed negotiations. In mid 1967, disagreements within the army about battlefield strategy and pressures from rival allies about diplomatic strategy became entangled with the problem of party leadership. The death of Nguyen Chi Thanh and the declining health of Ho Chi Minh raised the profile of Vo Nguyen Giap and the prospect of a challenge to Le Duan's position at the head of the party. Le Duan felt the need to reassert his authority by distancing himself from his foreign allies and silencing his domestic critics.

Prior to his death in July 1967, Nguyen Chi Thanh proposed a major offensive in 1968 to break the seeming stalemate on the battlefield, to rally the southern population behind the party, and to turn back the tide of American intervention. The virtue of this proposal was that it asserted a Vietnamese strategy for victory that rebuffed both the Chinese advocacy of protracted guerrilla warfare and the Soviet advocacy for a negotiated peace settlement. This would enable Le Duan to separate himself from both allies, thereby avoiding the morass of their rivalry.

The debate about battlefield strategy ended with Nguyen Chi Thanh's death. Without him, Le Duan's control of the army was threatened. Le Duan countered opposition to Nguyen Chi Thanh's plans by purging party members inclined toward a guerrilla strategy and peace talks; these people viewed Vo Nguyen Giap, now the dominant military figure, as their leading spokesman. During the last half of 1967 as plans for the 1968 offensive were completed and negotiating possibilities were rejected, several hundred people were disciplined or arrested, including members of Vo Nguyen Giap's personal staff; this series of purges was called the "revisionist anti-party affair." Plans for the offensive of 1968 were closely related to Le Duan countering threats to his authority both from his foreign allies and from within the ruling party. Beginning in the late 1950s, Le Duan and Le Duc Tho repeatedly renewed their ascendancy in the party by enforcing their policy of war to conquer the south. The purges of late 1967 brought an end to debates that had begun with the decision to accelerate this policy that had been prompted by Ngo Dinh Diem's death.

At the end of January 1968, Hanoi initiated the first phase of its offensive. Six cities, thirty-six provincial capitals, and sixty-four district capitals were attacked, primarily by the People's Liberation Armed Forces, commonly called the Viet Cong, the military arm of the communist movement in the south. The attacks were rapidly defeated everywhere except in Hue. The communists held Hue for about a month, during which time people from Hue who had joined the communists after the revolt in spring 1966 returned and attempted to establish a revolutionary regime. The communists arrested around three thousand people in Hue; most of these were later found massacred in shallow graves outside the city. A second wave of attacks in May and a third wave in August were on a much-reduced scale and were no more successful.

One result of the offensive was that the southern communists were virtually wiped out as a military force and thereafter the North Vietnamese army was forced to assume a defensive pose; the communists lost control of much of the territory that they had previously taken. On the other side, the new government of the Second Republic in Saigon benefited from a rise of popular support as people rallied against the attackers with a new sense of appreciation for what was at stake. For many people in relatively protected urban areas, what had been a war in the countryside was suddenly in their streets and homes. The fighting of 1968 strengthened the Saigon government and stimulated a surge of volunteers into its armed forces.

What anti-communist Vietnamese experienced as a victory, American reporters, opinion makers, and politicians perceived as a defeat. The reason for this was that Johnson's limited war strategy did not account for the vital connection between Le Duan's leadership and Hanoi's uncompromising pursuit of victory in the south. There was no way to persuade Le Duan to renounce his war policy in the south because his authority depended upon it. Yielding to American pressure would have meant the downfall of Le Duan and his associates, which they were determined to prevent. American public opinion turned away from the war when the 1968 offensive revealed that the enemy was far from giving up. Johnson saw that he was politically vulnerable and decided against running for re-election. At the same time, at the end of March 1968, he responded to criticism of his policy in Vietnam by unilaterally restricting US bombing of North Vietnam to an area on its southern border and by calling for negotiations to end the war.

Seeing the effect of the offensive on American politics and sensing that the American will to continue the war had been broken, Hanoi agreed to peace talks, which opened in Paris at the beginning of May 1968. From the beginning, the peace talks served the non-negotiable American desire to disengage from the war and the non-negotiable Hanoi determination to gain control of South Vietnam.

On the other hand, the survival of an independent non-communist South Vietnam was negotiable. In June, the National Assembly in Saigon protested the US negotiating matters related to South Vietnamese sovereignty without its participation, but Ambassador Bunker failed to obtain assurances from the State Department that the Saigon government would be fully informed and consulted.

From the beginning, Hanoi demanded that the US cease all bombing of North Vietnam as a precondition for continuing the talks. Johnson acceded to this demand just before the presidential election in November 1968. In late 1968, the US forced Nguyen Van Thieu to accept a negotiating formula of "two sides, four parties" that compromised his government's claim of sovereignty over South Vietnam. The US and the Republic of Vietnam formed one side while North Vietnam and the National Liberation Front were the other side. This acknowledgment of equal status between the Republic of Vietnam and the National Liberation Front as two governments each claiming to rule all of South Vietnam became even more explicit a year later when the National Liberation Front was redesigned as the Provisional Revolutionary Government of South Vietnam. Despite the battlefield victories of 1968, American eagerness to negotiate an exit from the war forced the Republic of Vietnam into a negotiating stance that threatened its continued existence.

US redeployment out of Vietnam

When the two-sided four-party Paris peace talks began in early 1969, it was quickly apparent that they were little more than a propaganda platform. Hanoi was occupied with rebuilding its military capability in the south without the large southern component that had been sacrificed in 1968 and was content to delay serious negotiations until it had gained a stronger position on the battlefield. Under strong political pressure to end American involvement in the war and with the Paris negotiations at an impasse, the new administration of Richard Milhous Nixon (1913–1994) shifted to a strategy of removing American forces from Vietnam and giving responsibility for the anti-communist struggle back to the South Vietnamese. This was possible because the Second Republic government in Saigon was stable and enjoyed a relatively high measure of popular support, and also because the communist defeats in 1968 had temporarily, but significantly, reduced the battlefield threat.

Secretary of Defense Melvin Robert Laird (b. 1922) made plans to redeploy nearly all American military forces out of Vietnam by the end of 1972. The first redeployment was announced in the summer of 1969 and the drawdown continued thereafter on schedule. General Creighton Williams Abrams, Jr.

(1914–1974), who replaced Westmoreland in 1968, espoused a new strategy of "one war," which aimed to integrate the operations of the Vietnamese and American armies and also to integrate civilian and military operations.

Under Westmoreland's command, the Vietnamese army was for the most part pushed aside from battlefield responsibilities as American forces conducted search and destroy operations. Furthermore, the equipment provided by the Americans to the Vietnamese was generally inferior to that available to communist forces, particularly in the quality of small arms and individual weapons. Under Abrams, the South Vietnamese army was equipped with up-to-date weapons that were equivalent to the quality of arms used by its enemy. Abrams organized joint Vietnamese–American operations that were to some extent designed as training exercises. As American redeployment progressed, the Vietnamese increasingly assumed responsibility for defending the country. At the same time, American programs for assisting civilians in battle zones that from 1967 had begun to be integrated into American military operations were turned over to the Vietnamese. These policies, commonly referred to as "Vietnamization," needed time for implementation, and major campaigns in Cambodia and Laos during 1970 and 1971 aimed to gain time by keeping communist forces off balance and away from South Vietnamese cities.

In early 1970, the Cambodian army commander, Lon Nol, who opposed the arrangements that had allowed the Vietnamese communists to use Cambodian territory, deposed Sihanouk. Sihanouk then joined a Chinese-sponsored alliance between the Vietnamese and Cambodian communists as Lon Nol appealed to the US for assistance. South Vietnamese and American forces advanced into Cambodia, forcing the Vietnamese communists to evacuate their headquarters and supply bases. These events were accompanied by widespread massacres of Vietnamese residing in Cambodia, victims of Cambodian resentment against the dominance of Vietnamese communists that Sihanouk had allowed in the eastern part of the country. Americans and South Vietnamese believed that this operation, which continued into the summer of 1970, helped to keep Vietnamese battlefields relatively quiet for a year, enabling the Vietnamization process to gain momentum. Opposition to this operation in the US Congress, however, resulted in a law prohibiting American ground troops from thereafter entering Cambodia or Laos.

War continued between Lon Nol and the Cambodian and Vietnamese communist forces, but the port of Sihanoukville was thereafter closed to the communists, and North Vietnam became more dependent upon its supply lines through southern Laos. In early 1971, South Vietnamese forces entered southern Laos in an operation designed to sever the communist supply lines during the winter dry season. In a series of battles, North and South Vietnamese forces both suffered heavy casualties. Although the initial aim of the operation was not fully reached, North Vietnamese plans were sufficiently disrupted to give the Vietnamization policy another year of relative calm. By early 1972, the number of US ground troops in Vietnam was insignificant and the American presence had become more like the Kennedy phase of advising with logistical and air support.

At the international level, Nixon endeavored to exploit the deepening Sino-Soviet dispute by diplomatically engaging each of these major communist powers and persuading them that they had more to gain from strengthening relations with the US than from supporting the North Vietnamese. Nixon understood that the Cold War was shifting from a bipolar confrontation toward a three-corner game with possibilities for prying one or both of the communist powers away from Hanoi. China had begun to withdraw its troops from North Vietnam after the end of American bombing and the beginning of American redeployment, and it began to be apparent that the Chinese were not in favor of Hanoi gaining control of South Vietnam. While China had supported Hanoi so long as the American presence in South Vietnam was on a threatening scale, it was not keen to have a united Vietnam on its southern border. On the other hand, the Soviet Union was ready to provide Hanoi with all that it needed to conquer the south and thereby gain a potential ally in the increasingly rancorous confrontations that were characterizing Sino-Soviet relations.

The troubled state of Sino-Soviet relations made both powers want to strengthen ties with the US in order to isolate the other. Nixon enjoyed the benefit of China and of the Soviet Union competing to build strategic relation-ships with the US. There were plans for Nixon to visit both countries during the first half of 1972. Le Duan understood that the international situation was changing in a direction that threatened to downgrade the importance of North Vietnam to its allies and decided to try for a quick military victory.

The Second Republic

North Vietnamese leaders worried not only about the diminishing importance of their struggle in the context of world politics but also about the success of the Second Republic in stabilizing South Vietnam. Nguyen Van Thieu was not a very inspiring leader, but neither was he known for either excessive corruption or egregious abuse of power. He was a relatively competent administrator, and he was inclined to avoid violating constitutional formalities. He countenanced opposition in the legislature, a judiciary to some extent beyond his control, and relative freedom of the press without prior censorship. To an extent, his behavior was influenced by American expectations as Ambassador Bunker endeavored to gently coach him about American norms of constitutional practice.

Elections for the National Assembly under the Second Republic elicited participation by a wide range of groups. The first Senate election was held at the same time as the presidential election in early September 1967. The sixty-member Senate was elected with a system of ten-member slates; the six slates that received the most votes were elected. Of sixty-four aspiring slates, forty-eight were approved to stand for election. Two slates associated with Thich Tri Quang's militant Buddhists were among those not approved. A moderate Buddhist slate was approved, but did not win election. Slates associated with the Hoa Hao, with Nguyen Cao Ky, and with Truong Dinh Dzu were approved but were also unsuccessful in the election. The successful slates included people who had both supported and opposed Ngo Dinh Diem but they were generally favorable toward Nguyen Van Thieu. Around 40 percent of those elected were Catholics. Although Catholics amounted to not much more than 10 percent of the population, they were more organized than others, and they strongly supported the Second Republic.

Three years later, half of the senators, who had drawn three-year terms, as opposed to the regular six-year senatorial term, either stood for re-election or stood down from the Senate. In the 1970 senatorial election, sixteen of eighteen aspiring ten-member slates were approved, and a slate supported by the militant Buddhists led by Thich Tri Quang was one of the three slates elected. Among the new senators seated in this election were members of the Hoa Hao and the Cao Dai, a Khmer Theravada Buddhist, and a Cham Muslim. The results of this election significantly increased the number of senators who opposed or were critical of the government.

The last senatorial election was held in August 1973, when the Second Republic was in the early stage of abandonment by the US and beginning to suffer economic problems. Election rules were changed to make it more difficult for oppositional politicians to be elected. Four fifteen-member slates were allowed to campaign and two were elected. During the Second Republic, the Senate was under strong presidential influence but not control; many senators were critical of the government and forced it to publicly defend its policies. Even more lively debate and opposition to the government was characteristic of the House of Representatives.

In the first House election, held in October 1967, more than 1,150 candidates competed for fewer than 150 seats. About one-third of those elected were Buddhists, including several militant followers of Thich Tri Quang. Other major religious groups represented were Catholics, who made up 25 percent, and Hoa Hao, 10 percent. Among those elected was Ho Huu Tuong, the Trotskyist activist in the 1930s who spent several years in French prisons. In the late 1940s he turned away from communism and worked as a journalist in Saigon. In 1955, he was imprisoned when he supported the sects against Ngo Dinh Diem. After his release from prison in 1964, he returned to journalism. When his slate for the Senate election was disallowed, he ran for the House instead and served there to the end of the Second Republic as a respected critic of the government.

The second and last election for the House, in which members held four-year terms, was in August 1971. Of members seeking re-election, only 40 of 119 were successful; of these 40 about half supported the government and about half were oppositional. The largest single bloc of winners were supporters of Thich Tri Quang's militant Buddhists, constituting 15 percent of the House, of whom over half were under the age of 40. The new House in comparison with the outgoing House was better educated, less corrupt, and included more independent and oppositional members.

In these elections, voter turnout varied from around 65 percent to 85 percent of registered voters. The relatively high percentage of voters may to some extent be attributed to the importance of demonstrating one's loyalty to the government in wartime by being able to produce a voter card proving that one had voted. But beyond this, considering the press coverage of the elections and the eagerness of people to run for office, the Second Republic demonstrated a certain plausible success as a government based on relatively free elections. There were many charges of fraud in these elections, but there were procedures for investigating them that came to depend upon an increasingly independent judiciary. Many fraud charges were simply part of the political process as it was understood and practiced at that time; losers charged fraud because they had asserted before the election that they could lose only if there was fraud.

The Supreme Court was established in 1968 with justices chosen by the National Assembly. It was generally comprised of highly qualified people and included some who were openly critical of Nguyen Van Thieu's administration. In dealing with electoral fraud charges, it demonstrated that it had achieved credibility as a relatively neutral interpreter of the law. During the course of its existence, it established the procedure of judicial review and was not shy about declaring legislation and administrative acts to be unconstitutional.

The most controversial election in the history of the Second Republic was the October 1971 presidential election. During the preceding summer, Duong Van Minh, who was living in retirement, and Vice President Nguyen Cao Ky were poised to run against the incumbent. As a man out of power, Duong Van Minh was perceived as an opposition candidate. He believed that he had a chance of winning if Nguyen Cao Ky and Nguyen Van Thieu split the pro-government vote. Conversely, Nguyen Van Thieu believed he could defeat Duong Van Minh if Nguyen Cao Ky was out of the race. In June 1971, after rancorous debate, the National Assembly passed a new law requiring candidates to obtain a certain number of endorsements from elected officials. Nguyen Van Thieu proceeded to gather all available pro-government endorsements, shutting out Nguyen Cao Ky. Duong Van Minh received the necessary endorsements, but when he saw that Nguyen Cao Ky was disqualified he dropped out of the race. Shortly after this, the Supreme Court ruled that it was illegal for Nguyen Van Thieu to accumulate excessive endorsements. Although Nguyen Cao Ky was then approved to run, he nevertheless quit the race, the result being that Nguyen Van Thieu ran for re-election unopposed with Tran Van Huong as his vice presidential candidate. The election further marginalized Nguyen Cao Ky and his followers while consolidating Nguyen Van Thieu's position, but the election also demonstrated that legislative and judicial acts were accepted as matters of law and were not under executive control.

While constitutional development enabled participation in national politics by a relatively diverse range of constituencies, dramatic developments in rural areas were at least as important to the stability of the Second Republic. Southern communists suffered a sharp decline in numbers and influence after the 1968 fighting. Defections to the Second Republic reached an all-time high in 1969. Local government in rural areas experienced a minor revolution with elections for village and hamlet officials. Furthermore, in a move resisted by the army but popular among rural people and strongly pushed by Nguyen Van Thieu, weapons were provided to local self-defense units that were under the control of village officials. The Ngo Dinh dream of strategic hamlets was to some extent realized under the Second Republic.

The most important aspect of rural policy was land reform legislation, which built on prior redistribution laws that had never been fully implemented due to wartime conditions and government weakness. In 1969 and 1970, rural areas became more secure and the legal structure of the Second Republic was able to effectively address agrarian issues. Within three years, redistributed land amounted to two and a half times what had been transferred during the previous decade and a half. The maximum amount of land anyone could own was reduced by 85 percent. While owners were compensated, tenants received land free of charge, as did landless farmers, war veterans, families of war dead, and others. Farmers were allowed to keep land that had been redistributed by communist authorities, and all new owners received permanent deeds, which they were forbidden to sell during fifteen years. In some areas that had been controlled by communists, by 1968 the taxes collected by communist authorities from those to whom they had given land exceeded the rent of tenants in adjacent government-controlled areas. Rural taxation under the Second Republic was comparatively light.

Cultural and intellectual life under the Second Republic was to some extent an echo of the lively debates and diversity of views that had characterized Saigon in the 1920s and 1930s. The experience of the heavy American military presence during the late 1960s stimulated extensive discussion about negative American influences and the importance of a Vietnamese cultural identity. As the American presence rapidly declined in the early 1970s, a southern Vietnamese perspective on national culture focused on issues larger than the war. This was different from North Vietnam, where thought and culture were entirely subordinated to the war and to politics. Southerners enjoyed the freedom to speak and to write about matters not directly related to the war or to politics. Journalism, literary works, magazines, and academic journals reflected a wide range of interests, ideologies, and opinions about culture, politics, religion, science, youth, gender, family relations, international trends, and personal life. Compared with cultural life in North Vietnam, this sometimes appeared chaotic and disconnected from the wartime situation, but it was a typical expression of southern openness to new ideas and to the outside world. Furthermore, it demonstrated why the war was being fought.

The victory of Hanoi

When Ho Chi Minh died in mid 1969, Le Duan decided to enshrine public memory of him with the goal of conquering the south, thereby adding an aura of saintliness to the party's policies and authority. The tightening of domestic social control became increasingly important not only to mitigate war weariness but also to maintain discipline as it became increasingly difficult to dismiss doubts about the Sino-Vietnamese alliance, which had been the cornerstone of victory in the French war. China was uninterested in having a united Vietnam on its southern border and was eager to establish a relationship with the US to give it leverage in relations with the Soviet Union. Although China continued to voice support for Hanoi, it slowly backed away from the war in South Vietnam and instead strengthened its relations with the Cambodian communists who were seeking to overthrow Lon Nol. While the Soviet Union moderated its public support of Hanoi to facilitate relations with the US, it was willing to supply Hanoi with whatever it needed to win the war, gambling on the chance for an alliance with a united Vietnam on the southern border of its Chinese antagonist.

With Nixon's diplomatic game gathering momentum, Le Duan and Le Duc Tho worried that the time available to achieve their goal in the south was ebbing away. By 1972, there were very few American ground troops in Vietnam, but the Second Republic was looking increasingly formidable. The Paris peace talks were at an impasse. Nixon had conceded the right of the North Vietnamese army to remain in South Vietnam after an agreement, but he rejected Hanoi's precondition of dismantling the Second Republic. However, 1972 was an American presidential election year, and public opinion in the US and internationally was opposed to continued American involvement in Vietnam. This raised communist hopes that Nixon would be as vulnerable to a major offensive as Johnson had been in 1968 and that he would acquiesce in a Hanoi victory.

In the spring of 1972, North Vietnam mobilized virtually its entire military potential, including strategic reserves, to launch a three-prong invasion of South Vietnam with the goal of winning the war immediately. The South Vietnamese army defeated this invasion with American logistical and air support. Furthermore, Nixon mined North Vietnamese harbors and initiated a new bombing campaign against North Vietnam. His escalation of American involvement did not damage American relations with either China or the Soviet Union. Hanoi's gamble had failed, and, when it became apparent that Nixon would be re-elected, Le Duc Tho signaled to his American negotiating partner, Heinz Alfred (Henry) Kissinger (b. 1923), Nixon's National Security Advisor, that he no longer demanded the dismantling of the Second Republic before an agreement could be reached.

Le Duc Tho and Kissinger had been conducting secret negotiations separate from the official four-party peace talks, which had never developed beyond issuing propaganda. After the defeat of Hanoi's spring offensive of 1972, Le Duc Tho was keen for an agreement that would eliminate the US from the war and compromise the Second Republic. The push for an agreement from the American side came from Kissinger's personal investment in it and from the election of an anti-war congress in the autumn of 1972 that threatened to legislate an end to American involvement in Vietnam when it convened in January 1973.

The agreement drafted by Kissinger and Le Duc Tho provided for the release of American prisoners of war and the end of American military intervention. It allowed the North Vietnamese army to remain in South Vietnam and provided for a political process to supersede the Second Republic with a coalition government that would include communists and neutralists. It abandoned the aim of preserving a non-communist South Vietnam and discarded the sovereignty of the Second Republic, which was accorded a status equal with the communist Provisional Revolutionary Government of South Vietnam.

There were strong public expressions of opposition to this agreement in South Vietnam. The House of Representatives of the National Assembly rejected the political provisions that nullified the Second Republic's sovereignty. Nguyen Van Thieu announced that he could not accept the agreement without changes. He wanted to initiate direct Hanoi–Saigon negotiations, but the US, just as France had claimed to negotiate for Saigon in 1954, was determined to avoid direct contact between the Vietnamese sides. Nguyen Van Thieu understood that he was powerless to influence the peace talks and trusted Nixon's assurance that adjustments would be made and that the US would continue to support the Second Republic regardless of any agreement made.

However, when the US proposed changes, Le Duc Tho withdrew a concession previously made that was particularly important to the Americans: separation of the release of American prisoners of war from the issue of releasing political prisoners held by the Second Republic. Nixon needed this concession, for without it American prisoners would remain hostage to the disposition of Vietnamese prisoners, which was a difficult and unpredictable issue. With a newly elected Congress that was determined to legislate the end of American involvement in Vietnam scheduled to convene in a matter of weeks, Nixon resorted to a bombing campaign that in a few days destroyed North Vietnam's air defense capability and persuaded Hanoi to restore the prisoner of war concession, which led to the signing of an agreement in late January 1973 by which the US military presence in Vietnam was terminated within two months.

The political provisions of the Paris Agreement were never implemented, and the war continued in South Vietnam without American participation. After the North Vietnamese defeats in 1972, the Soviet Union provided all that was necessary to rebuild and supply communist forces in South Vietnam. An all-weather road and a pipeline were constructed from North Vietnam through the uplands to a point not far from Saigon, and plans were made for offensive operations to destroy the Second Republic.

Within a year of the agreement, South Vietnam began to experience severe economic and military problems as a result of the 1973 oil embargo crisis and the progressive reduction of US aid. The communist military build-up coincided with American disengagement as Nixon's political problems and eventual resignation ended the prospect of any further US interest in Vietnamese affairs. The military balance shifted in favor of North Vietnam as South Vietnamese forces suffered shortages of petrol, spare parts, and ammunition. Widespread economic distress led to Saigon street demonstrations in the autumn of 1974. Nguyen Van Thieu's political career had been based on a trust in the American alliance. As it became apparent that this alliance no longer existed, he was unable to think beyond it and was paralyzed by the looming communist threat, vainly hoping that the US would come to the rescue.

In early 1975, North Vietnamese leaders determined that the US would not return and initiated a campaign that within two months obtained total victory. Days later, fighting broke out between the Vietnamese and the Cambodian communists, who had just gained control of Cambodia with Chinese support. These hostilities were quickly halted, but they foreshadowed another war and demonstrated that American withdrawal had enabled the Sino-Soviet confrontation to come alive in the region.

The Sino-Khmer War and renovation

Hanoi moved rapidly to unify the country. The Provisional Revolutionary Government of South Vietnam was pushed aside and administrators were sent from the north to establish the new regime in the south. Many Second Republic officials were killed and hundreds of thousands of people were sent to concentration camps, ostensibly to re-educate them to live in a socialist society. A system of registering the population was instituted to ensure that those whose families had supported the Second Republic were penalized by denial of employment, education, and food rations. An ambitious plan for economic development was initiated, but within three years the country was facing political, economic, and diplomatic failures. These failures became parts of a crisis that led to a new war.

The harsh official attitude toward the defeated population squandered a potential reservoir of good will among many southerners who were ready to turn their backs on the past and to contribute to building a new united country. The Hanoi government even marginalized southern communists. Many people from urban areas were relocated with a minimum of preparation in relatively remote "new economic zones" in rural areas. Large numbers of these people surreptitiously returned to the cities. Efforts to collectivize southern agriculture were stymied by the resistance of the rural population. In the shadow of a new war, the Hanoi leaders rushed to gain control of the south and to integrate its resources into its militarized economy.

The strategic situation after the withdrawal of American power shifted rapidly as China and the Soviet Union competed for influence in Southeast Asia. The pressure point of this confrontation was the Cambodian–Vietnamese border, a border that, while drawn by French colonial administrators in the 1930s, was very close to the border that existed prior to the French arrival in the nineteenth century. This border was based on the Vietnamese acquisition of formerly Cambodian territories in the seventeenth and eighteenth centuries. While it was considered to be a satisfactory border by Vietnamese authorities, Cambodian nationalists were unreconciled to the loss of the lower Mekong plain, and this was particularly true of the Cambodian communists who gained control of Phnom Penh in 1975 under the leadership of Saloth Sar (1925–1998), also known as Pol Pot.

Added to the sense of a historical grievance was the strong resistance of Pol Pot to what he understood as the threat of Vietnam dominating Cambodia in the same way that it dominated Laos. Some Cambodian communists, particularly those in the eastern provinces along the Vietnamese border, were willing to collaborate with the Vietnamese and even to defer to Vietnamese leadership. Pol Pot, full of nationalist fervor and feeling surrounded by enemies, was eager to eliminate what he viewed as colonial residue, whether French, Vietnamese, or Cambodian. He initiated a homicidal policy against urbanites, people with education, and the people of the eastern provinces.

By 1977, Pol Pot, with the benefit of Chinese economic and military assistance, initiated attacks across the Vietnamese border to eliminate the Vietnamese population in areas that Phnom Penh claimed as Cambodian. In response, Vietnam briefly campaigned into Cambodia in late 1977. Between two and three hundred thousand Cambodians fled their country and followed the Vietnamese withdrawal back into Vietnam where they constituted a large refugee population. Hanoi's efforts to negotiate a settlement of the border issue were rejected by Phnom Penh, and it became apparent that Cambodian intransigence on the border issue was tacitly supported by China.

The next phase of sliding into war focused on the ethnic Chinese population in Vietnam. This population had developed differently in northern and southern Vietnam. Southern Chinese had been forced to take Vietnamese citizenship in the late 1950s. In the north, however, the relatively smaller Chinese population had been accorded a special status: it was allowed to retain Chinese citizenship with its privilege of travel to China and was exempted from Vietnamese military conscription and from certain tax liabilities. Chinese in the north were experts in the unofficial Sino-Vietnamese cross-border trade and in the south had accumulated wealth from their business skills and international contacts. By early 1978, Vietnamese authorities perceived the Chinese communities as not only threats to their plans for a socialist economy but also a fifth column allied with China in the armed confrontation that was rapidly materializing. When the Vietnamese acted to confiscate the property of Chinese in the south and to force the southern Chinese population into the socialist economy, thousands of southern Chinese fled from the country by sea. At the same time, Hanoi endeavored to restrict the Chinese population in the north, fearing their vulnerability to being manipulated by China. When China announced that Vietnam was persecuting the Chinese and that it was sending ships to rescue them, there was a stampede of northern Chinese to the Sino-Vietnamese border.

By the summer of 1978, the prospect of a Sino-Vietnamese war loomed over the region as China continued to build up the Cambodian army and concentrated troops along the Sino-Vietnamese border. The Vietnamese economy was in shambles with confiscation of private property and the penalization of people with wealth in the south, with the ruin of southern agriculture by the failed collectivization effort, and with plans for industrial development in the north stillborn by lack of investment and the return of wartime priorities.

Added to the turmoil in domestic affairs and in relations with China and Cambodia, Vietnam fell afoul of the Cold War shift from China and the Soviet Union against the US to China and the US against the Soviet Union. Failing in negotiations to normalize relations with the US, Vietnam signed a strategic treaty with the Soviet Union and made plans to strike Cambodia before China could act, thereby initiating a war that for the next ten years kept Vietnam encircled by enemies with a thin lifeline to the Soviet Bloc countries.

After organizing the semblance of an allied Cambodian government from among the Khmer refugees, Vietnam invaded Cambodia at the end of 1978 and within days had defeated the Cambodian army and sent Pol Pot and his associates fleeing to the Thai border. China, having just normalized relations with the US and eager to demonstrate its strategic value as an anti-Soviet ally, briefly invaded Vietnamese border provinces in early 1979 and then withdrew after destroying the economic and administrative infrastructure there. Thereafter, Sino-Vietnamese hostilities continued with cross-border shelling and raids while the main arena of the war was in Cambodia, where Vietnam supervised the establishment of a Cambodian army and government.

Contesting Vietnamese ascendancy in Cambodia were three Cambodian groups operating from bases along the Thai border with the logistical support of the Thai army. China provided supplies primarily to Pol Pot. The neighboring countries that had allied with the US in the 1960s, which included Thailand, Singapore, Malaysia, Indonesia, and the Philippines (the five ASEAN countries), mainly supported a royalist group led by Sihanouk. The US gave support to a third group espousing parliamentary democracy led by Son Sann (1911–2000), a veteran politician who had been active in politics since the 1940s. Supervised by China, the US, and the ASEAN countries, the three groups were diplomatically organized, presented, and acknowledged in the United Nations as the legitimate coalition government of Cambodia, thereby preventing the government formed in Phnom Penh, supported by Vietnam and the Soviet Bloc countries, from receiving UN recognition.

The three anti-Vietnamese Cambodian groups established bases just inside the Cambodian border from where they launched guerrilla operations. During the 1984–1985 dry season, Vietnamese forces attacked and destroyed all of these bases. Thereafter, Vietnam began to withdraw its army back to Vietnam, handing responsibility for defending the country to its client government in Cambodia, which from 1985 was led by Hun Sen (b. 1952), a former follower of Pol Pot who had defected to Vietnam in 1977.

The collapse of the Soviet Union removed the rationale of the war. Vietnam accordingly completed its withdrawal from Cambodia in 1989. In the early 1990s, the UN sponsored a ceasefire and elections in Cambodia, which led to a brief coalition between the royalists and Hun Sen, yet Hun Sen and his followers continued to dominate Cambodian politics well into the twenty-first century. This superficially appeared to vindicate Vietnam's war aims. However, regional politics shifted sharply in the 1990s with Vietnam joining ASEAN and making peace with China. Furthermore, the price paid by Vietnam for this war was very high, bringing unprecedented economic distress. It also contributed to an exodus of people fleeing the country by sea, sojourning in regional refugee camps, and emigrating to foreign lands.

In the early years of the Sino-Khmer War, deepening poverty forced Hanoi to acquiesce in a new system of agriculture that restored some incentive for private initiative with contracts for farmers to supply the state with specified amounts of produce and allowing anything beyond that to be freely marketed for private profit. This somewhat alleviated the food supply and led to relative well being in the countryside. During the 1980s, villagers in northern Vietnam began to invest their private earnings in building brick homes to replace their thatched wooden dwellings. Urban populations, however, suffered from a lack of income, a deteriorating infrastructure, a scarcity of consumer goods, and hunger.

The death of Le Duan in the spring of 1986 made possible a shift in domestic policy. Truong Chinh presided over the party for six months during which Nguyen Van Linh (1915–1998) rode the pressures for reform to replace him. Nguyen Van Linh was originally from Hanoi, had joined the party in the 1930s, and spent several years in French prisons. In 1975, he became the leader of the party in the south where he had been assigned since the early 1960s. By the mid 1980s, he was known to be at odds with Le Duan over economic and cultural policy. He favored a loosening of state control over markets, religious and cultural activities, and journalism. During his years as head of the party, from late 1986 to mid 1991, he nurtured a younger generation of party leaders and initiated what became known as the *doi moi* policy, literally "to change to the new," commonly rendered in English as "renovation." As the Sino-Khmer War ended and the Soviet Bloc disappeared, he restored trade with China and encouraged foreign investment from Japan, South Korea, Taiwan, Singapore, and other countries. He invited journalists to report on corruption and abuse, allowed publication of literary works critical of party policies, and encouraged the restoration of temples and local festivals.

One aspect of the renovation policy was an effort to create a sense of continuity with pre-revolutionary culture by cultivating new versions of traditional art, music, theater, village festivals, and religious pilgrimage sites. The rebuilding and repair of temples became possible with contributions from a rising class of businesswomen who worked in the urban markets. Many temples in northern Vietnam had been neglected and not a few were even plundered and destroyed by greedy or fanatical officials. Perhaps the most notorious example is the many lavishly furnished temples on Mount Yen Tu, around 125 kilometers east of Hanoi, which dated to the Tran dynasty and were a major pilgrimage destination for centuries. By the time of the renovation policy, they had all been stripped of valuables and burned down under the supervision of local officials. In the early 1990s, a monk returned to the mountain and, with government approbation, began to rebuild one of the temples with contributions of pilgrims. Within a few years, the government had built a new road to the foot of the mountain and a welcoming center for the growing number of pilgrims.

At the party congress in 1991, Nguyen Van Linh stepped down, ostensibly because of poor health, and was replaced by Do Muoi (b. 1917). Do Muoi was born near Hanoi, had joined the party in his youth, and had made his career in the state bureaucracy. During his six years at the head of the party, the *doi moi* policy was basically preserved. At the same time, there was a stronger emphasis upon internal security measures to affirm the party's control over public opinion and political activity. In 1997, Do Muoi was succeeded by his protégé Le Kha Phieu (b. 1931). Le Kha Phieu had made his career in the military and was critical of corruption and factionalism in the party. However, his anti-corruption campaigns united virtually all the party factions against him, and, in 2001, he was forced to retire. Nong Duc Manh (b. 1940), a forestry expert from the mountains north of Hanoi rumored to be a son of Ho Chi Minh, replaced him and remained head of the party for ten years with a policy of economic development and strong party control modeled on the example of China.

One of Le Kha Phieu's unpopular acts was completing a treaty with China that demarcated the land border and the Gulf of Tonkin sea border. Many Vietnamese considered that this treaty conceded too much to China and represented a proffering of homage to the big northern neighbor. However, with communist parties losing power in many countries during the 1990s, the Chinese and Vietnamese parties gradually built a new version of the close relationship that had existed between the two countries for centuries. But new conditions in the twenty-first century placed limits on this relationship and created a contradiction for party leaders.

On the one hand, by the first decade of the twenty-first century, the Vietnamese ruling party's ability to maintain power depended upon the continued success of the Chinese ruling party to control China. Any political change in China that displaced the Chinese party would have made it very difficult for the Vietnamese party to avoid political change as well. A close and mutually supportive relationship between the two parties helped to sustain the regime in Vietnam.

On the other hand, the rise of popular nationalism in both countries exacerbated the underlying tension in the relationship between a China seeking regional dominance and a Vietnam determined to resist subordination. This tension was concretely expressed in the growing dispute over the islands in the South China Sea. The Hoang Sa (Paracel) archipelago had been inherited from France and occupied by South Vietnam until it was seized by China in 1974. The Truong Sa (Spratley) archipelago was claimed and partly occupied by China but parts of it were also claimed and occupied by Vietnam, the Philippines, and other countries. Hanoi appeared to acknowledge Chinese sovereignty over the islands in the late 1950s when it was dependent upon China for its policy of taking over the south, but from 1975 the Vietnamese government forcefully announced its claim to the islands.

After the Sino-Khmer War, Vietnamese foreign policy experts debated whether to follow China and to prosper as a junior regional partner in what was imagined as an inevitable Chinese hegemony over eastern and southeastern Asia, or whether to follow a multi-directional policy aimed to maximize anti-Chinese leverage in cooperation with the ASEAN countries, Japan, and the US. This debate continued into the twenty-first century, fueled by the island dispute and the fear that China would eventually enforce its claims unless the US remained a balancing presence in the region. At the beginning of the twenty-first century, having weathered the storms of French colonialism, the Japanese Empire, and both phases of the Cold War, the Vietnamese faced the prospect of returning to a Sinic world order, unsure about how feasible for the long term a multi-lateral foreign policy option might be. In general, northerners view such a prospect with less dismay than do southerners.

RETROSPECTIVE

Considering the events discussed in this book, no conclusion can be drawn in the sense of discovering some deep logic governing a presumed destiny of the Vietnamese people. Knowledge of the Vietnamese past in the English language accumulated in the late twentieth century in the shadow of war; academics, journalists, and politicians accorded the chief privilege of shaping that accumulation to the group of Vietnamese fortunate enough to have allies that remained relatively steadfast until the last battle. What accumulated came from wartime propaganda based on a stridently nationalistic version of Vietnamese history that featured, first, an affirmation of Vietnamese identity pre-dating contact with the ancient Chinese and, second, dominant themes of rebellion against colonial oppression and resistance to foreign aggression; neither of these ideas can be sustained by a study of existing evidence about the past.

More appropriate than a conclusion is a retrospective in the sense of a reappraisal that keeps close to surviving materials from the past and that aims to see the Vietnamese and their ancestors through their own eyes in various times and places. To some extent, what we see is "just one random thing after another"; but this in itself is important because it alerts us to the fallacy of putting faith in a rigid overarching narrative of "the Vietnamese people" or "the Vietnamese nation." There is no discernible pattern to explain how times of prosperity and well being alternated with times of misery and violence. As this book demonstrates, the Vietnamese past is, among other things, a great swath of failed experiments in social organization and governance.

It is instructive to realize that an event trumpeted by Vietnamese historians as a great moment of glory – defeat of the Mongol invasions in the thirteenth century – was followed by nearly a decade of famine and starvation leading to the enslavement of a large part of the rural population by the warriors who had fought off the Mongols. Similarly, victory over the French at Dien Bien Phu was followed by a homicidal cauterization of the northern rural population into the discipline of obedience to state authority. On the other hand, the French conquest of northern Vietnam ended decades of lawlessness during which the Vietnamese government was powerless to stop women and children from being routinely kidnapped for sale as slaves in China. A serious consideration of what happened in the past makes it difficult to sustain the visions of heroes and villains favored by those who write about the past in service to state authority.

The retrospective that emerges from the narrative constructed in this book shows three main reconsiderations. These reconsiderations are about the Vietnamese relationship with China, about the relationship between northern and southern Vietnamese, and about the relationship of the Vietnamese with the non-Chinese world.

It is clear that who and what we call Vietnamese did not exist prior to the centuries during which Vietnamese ancestors lived as inhabitants of Chinese dynastic empires. Every aspect of Vietnamese culture appeared as a result of being in that empire and from the existence of a large Chinese-speaking population that developed over several generations and that eventually melted into the local population when the imperial connection was severed. Vietnamese language, literature, education, religion, historiography, philosophy, family system, social and political organization, cuisine, medicine, music, and art: all are deeply imprinted with the marks of what is commonly called East Asian or Sinitic civilization. This occurred differently from the other peripheral members of this civilization: the Japanese and the Koreans.

Relative isolation on islands off the continent enabled a process of picking and choosing that allowed Japanese rulers to keep China at arm's-length. On the other hand, Koreans absorbed Sinitic influence in a particularly thorough, albeit idiosyncratic way that achieved a countenance of cultural and political legitimacy enabling survival on a peninsula of pressure between Chinese, Japanese, and various powers inhabiting Manchuria. Vietnamese grew from within the Sinitic imperial world, as the ancient Koreans also initially did; but while Korean kingdoms began an autonomous existence after the fall of the Han dynasty, a similar Vietnamese event did not occur until after the fall of the Tang dynasty.

The Vietnamese did not live on islands or on a peninsula where the power of Chinese dynasties could be either ignored or balanced with other Sinicizing powers. They came from a place where Chinese speakers, during the course of a millennium, were constantly reinforced by immigration from the northern empire; these people were eventually cut off from the north and gradually faded into the local population through a process of mutual absorption that produced what we call Vietnamese. For centuries, this was a strategically and economically important jurisdiction of successive Chinese empires; for centuries thereafter, local rulers posed as vassals of Chinese dynasties. No powers or civilizations other than China have seriously competed for the attention of people living here with the brief exceptions of France, Japan, the USSR, and the US in modern times.

After the tumults of the nineteenth and twentieth centuries, a fundamental long-term pattern in Vietnamese historical experience of being ineluctably connected to the Chinese political world has re-emerged. For example, it is difficult to imagine any significant political change in Vietnam without a prior change in China. For one thing, the Vietnamese cannot avoid living as a neighbor of China, and they understand that they must show to China a visage that does not contradict Chinese interests and that is congruent with Chinese political practice. Any effort to change the Vietnamese political system without Chinese precedent would be likely to create opportunities for Chinese involvement in domestic affairs that could compromise the measure of independence currently exercised. Vietnamese autonomy with regard to China, now as in the past, remains dependent upon a successful practice of mimicry.

At the same time, the temptation to pull away from the Chinese model remains alive among the Vietnamese, particularly southerners. However, potential balancing options involving non-Chinese Asian neighbors and possibly the US are fraught with uncertainty and doubt. It is easier for most Vietnamese leaders to trust the Chinese than to trust non-Chinese neighbors and allies because they know and understand the Chinese to a much greater degree than they know and understand any other people. Although they have no doubt that a strong China will never lose a chance to squeeze them, they also know that for many generations with few exceptions Vietnamese leaders have successfully maintained acceptable relationships with Chinese governments. Vietnamese are culturally familiar, even intimate, with the Chinese. The historic relationship, involving mixtures of subservience and non-compliance, has existed through the vicissitudes of centuries of experience.

The nationalistic conceit of being in a constant state of aggravation with the Chinese has no basis in fact. For centuries, during the first millennium of the Common Era, ancestors of the Vietnamese lived in relative peace and security as residents of the Sinitic empire. Subsequently, Chinese military operations were launched against Vietnamese rulers only five times, and each of these times resulted from unusual circumstances. In the 930s, the Southern Han campaigned in northern Vietnam amidst the post-Tang competition among regional powers. In 980, the rising Northern Song dynasty followed the pattern of previous dynasties in viewing northern Vietnam as an integral part of the empire, albeit after this pattern was no longer feasible; in 1075, border problems became entangled in Song bureaucratic factionalism, emboldening a Vietnamese attack into southern China that provoked a counterattack; in 1407, the ascendant Ming dynasty endeavored to take advantage of dynastic change among the Vietnamese to restore the Han-Tang imperial borders but soon discovered that this was not a realistic policy; in 1979, China attacked Vietnam to prevent Soviet influence from stabilizing in Vietnam and Cambodia after American withdrawal from the region. In each case, Chinese interest in attacking Vietnam arose from specific and contingent circumstances, and it quickly evaporated once those circumstances had changed.

On the other hand, refugee Song Chinese armies were allied with the Vietnamese during the Mongol Wars of the thirteenth century. In the eighteenth century, Qing China sent an expedition to support its vassal, the Le dynasty king, against rebels, but had no ambition to take over the country. In the 1880s, China, at great cost and with little prospect of success, honored its obligations to the Vietnamese court by attempting to prevent the French conquest of northern Vietnam. In the early 1950s, China served as the ally of an aspiring Vietnamese protégé. With few and very episodic exceptions, Vietnamese and Chinese have lived in peace and amity.

The controversy over the islands in the South China Sea is more of a regional than a purely Sino-Vietnamese issue. It arises because the future direction of international relations in the region remains in question and the islands have become symbolic of that uncertainty. Should a relatively stable and widely shared understanding of regional security be achieved, there is unlikely to be any insurmountable impediment to working out acceptable accommodations among the disputants and other interested powers. An obstacle to Chinese and Vietnamese governments making such accommodations is the nationalistic enthusiasms with which they have educated their peoples.

The second reconsideration warns against the conceit of a unified Vietnamese people. Any effort to describe the Vietnamese must be alert to the many regional differences among them. For example, even among northerners, people from Thanh Hoa, Nghe An, and Ha Tinh sometimes express disdain toward those who live in the Red River plain, considering them as passive and susceptible to Chinese blandishments. On the other hand, people of the Red River plain resent what they view as the arrogance and pushiness of people from the three coastal provinces immediately to their south, the birthplaces of Le kings, Trinh lords, and of many cadres of the communist party who flooded into Hanoi to occupy positions of authority after 1954. This is a difficult inter-regional relationship that goes back to the wars between the Mac and Le dynasties in the sixteenth century and to the generations of Trinh misgovernment in the seventeenth and eighteenth centuries.

Elsewhere, one cannot ignore Hue's proud heritage of presiding over the centuries-long process of Vietnamese becoming southerners as well as bringing into existence the country of Vietnam as it now exists with its modern borders.

This pride is susceptible to a desire to speak on behalf of the entire country with an air of moral authority, a tendency that remains strong among Buddhist leaders based in Hue. In contrast, the people of the Da Nang region, with a mixed Cham–Viet heritage, a milder climate, and a good harbor, are less interested in virtue from the past and more interested in wealth from maritime trade. Further south, the regions between Da Nang and Saigon where the bitter battles of the 1790s and the early 1800s were fought retain distinctive provincial outlooks that in various ways seek to minimize connections with the larger Vietnamese realm, echoes of Nguyen Nhac's Tay Son perspective.

Above all these differences is the contrast between north and south epitomized by the cities of Hanoi and Saigon. The large stereotypes of northern and southern Vietnamese mask many regional differences, but nevertheless reflect a fundamental divergence among Vietnamese. Northerners are more disciplined to accept and to exercise government authority, they are proud of inhabiting what they view as the center of Vietnamese culture, they tend to be cautious about contact with the overseas world, and they are inclined to view what is happening in China as a model. Southerners are more individualistic, egalitarian, entrepreneurial, interested in wealth more than in authority, proud of carrying within themselves their own sense of culture, open to the outside world, and wary of how things are done in China. Northerners, more than southerners, see virtue in poverty, a legacy from three centuries of misgovernment under Vietnamese regimes from the seventeenth to the nineteenth centuries. Southerners, more than northerners, see virtue in having options and possibilities to explore, a legacy from the frontier experience and the relatively light touch of Nguyen government. The generally ineffective Nguyen government in the mid nineteenth century posed few problems for southerners, many of whom by the 1860s were being governed by the French; but for northerners, after having been inured to the discipline of Confucian administrators and to the authoritarianism of the Trinh regime in Hanoi, the lack of a functioning government produced political, social, and economic chaos that was finally brought to an end by the French. Any discussion of the Vietnamese cannot avoid the ambiguities created by northern and southern viewpoints. These ambiguities can be viewed either as a problem or as an asset, as creating tensions that lead to frustration or to opportunities for mutual benefit.

The emergence of a southern Vietnamese perspective was much more complex than the cliché of "southern advance" (*nam tien*) implies. There was no single historical process impelling Vietnamese southward. The movement of Vietnamese into the south was fundamentally episodic, reflecting a variety of different causes and motivations depending upon time and place, over a period of several centuries and from region to region over great distances. Furthermore, this was not a purely Vietnamese phenomenon. Chams, Chinese, Khmers, as well as upland peoples of the Central Highlands all participated significantly in this long historical process, often contributing a willingness to accept the ascendancy of Hue in exchange for peace and security. Many of the actual battles were between Chams serving the Vietnamese and Chams resisting the Vietnamese, or between Chinese and Khmers, or between Khmers allied with the Vietnamese and Khmers allied with the Siamese. Southerners entered multi-ethnic, multi-cultural, multi-lingual realms open to the outside world as was not possible in the north. This was reinforced by two and a half centuries of political separation and military confrontation between two rival versions of being Vietnamese, and the legacy of this is still alive.

Finally, the idea that the Vietnamese have preserved an ancient, or at least a pre-modern, identity through the vicissitudes of the modern age must be reconsidered. During the last century and a half, the Vietnamese have experienced an intense engagement with Europe, not only France, but also, from the 1920s through the 1980s, with the Soviet Union and other Soviet Bloc countries, not to mention the brief American involvement in the south during the 1950s, 1960s, and early 1970s. At the same time, the cultural connection with China based on an educational system in Literary Chinese came to an end. Ideas about society, politics, government, education, scholarship, literature, art, and music have all been transformed by ideologies and practices coming from Europe, whether the capitalist and democratic "west" or the communist and totalitarian "east." In the 1950s and 1960s, the Maoist version of the East European form of modernization was added to the mix of revolutionary thought and action. In the 1990s and 2000s, the Deng Xiaoping version of market economics inspired efforts to renovate the relationship between government and the production of wealth. The idea of attributing economic success to a Confucian past gained some attention in the late 1980s and early 1990s but quickly faded away.

The search for the "real" Vietnam or for the "cultural core" of being Vietnamese is bound to fail. There is an accumulation of different religious, ideological, and cultural orientations among people who speak Vietnamese. Any effort to privilege one over the others simply produces arguments without resolution. Being Vietnamese has many forms. The only unifying characteristic is a use of the Vietnamese language and a connection to a particular place on the planet. What makes this place distinctive is its location between what we commonly categorize as East Asia and Southeast Asia: on the one hand, the Sinitic world of Confucianism, Mahayana Buddhism, popular Daoist spirit cults, and imperial administrative procedures of which Vietnamese are unambiguous members; and, on the other hand, the realms of entourage politics, Cham Hinduism, Indo-Malay Islam, Theravada Buddhism, overseas Chinese and South

Asian communities, and Catholic Philippines, with which Vietnamese, especially southerners, have some degree of familiarity and a sense of neighborhood. Christianity, the new religions of Cao Dai and Hoa Hao, Marxism-Leninism, and Maoism must also be included in any effort to describe the Vietnamese. Being Vietnamese offers many options.

An enduring feature of Vietnamese experience is the fundamentally compliant relationship with China enforced by governments modeled on what exists in China. An aspect of this is that government tends to be didactic with weak connections to popular aspirations. Since the fifteenth century, and continuing to the present time, governments in Hanoi have endeavored to promote particular ideals and practices by enforcing habits of obedience, whether to be good Confucians, vanguard socialists, or patriotic producers of wealth for the state. Despite lofty intentions, the undercurrent of corruption, injustice, and oppression remains. Nevertheless, there are countercurrents of thought that flow elsewhere than to China or to the past and that continue to be refreshed by the Vietnamese diaspora. Although subordinated and harnessed by an authoritarian regime, and although wounded by a faithless ally in 1975, these countercurrents nevertheless remain alive in dreams of Vietnamese futures.

BIBLIOGRAPHIC ESSAY

Materials in Asian languages

Much of this book is based upon materials written in Literary Chinese (Han) and, to a
lesser extent, in Literary Vietnamese (Nom). For readers who wish to consult these
materials, I can do no better than to refer them to Tran Van Giap, *Tim Hieu Kho Sach
Han Nom* (Investigation into the Storehouse of Han and Nom Books), 2 vols. (Hanoi:
Van Hoa, 1984–1990). That bibliography is built upon the earlier work of Émile
Gaspardone, "Bibliographie Annamite," *Bulletin de l'École Française d'Extrême-Orient*
34 (1934), which had been preceded by the pioneering work of Léopold Michel Cadière
and Paul Pelliot, "Première Étude sur les Sources Annamites de l'Histoire d'Annam,"
Bulletin de l'École Française d'Extrême-Orient 4 (1904). A good reference for materials
held at the Institute of Han-Nom Studies in Hanoi and in various collections in Paris is
Tran Nghia and François Gros, *Di San Han Nom Viet Nam Thu Muc De Yeu (Catalogue
des Livres en Han Nom)*, 3 vols. (Hanoi: Nha Xuat Ban Khoa Hoc Xa Hoi, 1993). For
the pre-tenth-century period, see Tran Nghia, *Suu Tam Va Khao Luan Tac Pham Chu
Han Cua Nguoi Viet Nam Truoc The Ky X* (Search and Analysis of Works in Han
Written by Vietnamese Before the Tenth Century) (Hanoi: Nha Xuat Ban The Gioi,
2000). For inscriptions, see Nguyen Quang Hong, ed.-in-chief, *Van Khac Han Nom Viet
Nam* (Han and Nom Inscriptions in Vietnam) (Hanoi: Nha Xuat Ban Khoa Hoc Xa Hoi,
1992). A good reference for examination graduates through the centuries is Ngo Duc
Tho, ed., *Cac Nha Khoa Bang Viet Nam 1075–1919* (Vietnamese Examination
Graduates 1075–1919) (Hanoi: Nha Xuat Ban Van Hoc, 1993).

Textual information for events before the tenth century is virtually all found in the
dynastic histories and related writings from China; for these works, see Keith Weller
Taylor, *The Birth of Vietnam* (Berkeley: University of California Press, 1983). Works
with information about the era of historiographic transition from texts based on Chinese
materials to texts based on Vietnamese materials are discussed in K. W. Taylor, "The
'Twelve Lords' in Tenth-Century Vietnam," *Journal of Southeast Asian Studies* 14, 1
(March 1983):46–62. For studies of Chinese texts related to events in Vietnam since the
tenth century, see Yamamoto Tatsuro, ed., *Betonamu Chugoku Kankeishi* (History of
Sino-Vietnamese Relations) (Tokyo: Yamakawa Shupansha, 1975). A good study of the
Mongol Wars in the thirteenth century based on Chinese and Vietnamese texts is Ha Van
Tan and Pham Thi Tam, *Cuoc Khang Chien Xam Luoc Nguyen Mong The Ky XIII*
(Resistance to the Yuan–Mongol Invasions in the Thirteenth Century) (Hanoi: Khoa Hoc
Xa Hoi, 1968).

Han and Nom texts written by Vietnamese with information about people and events in the past form a large archive that also includes much about literature, religion, government, geography, economics, law, philosophy, military affairs, medicine, and education. The best catalogue of this archive is Tran Nghia and François Gros, *Di San Han Nom Viet Nam Thu Muc De Yeu*, cited above. Here I will briefly mention the main sources that I have consulted for this book. All of these works were written in Literary Chinese (Han) unless otherwise noted; most are available today in Vietnamese translations or, in the case of Nom texts, alphabetic transcriptions.

One of the earliest surviving annals is the *Viet Su Luoc* (Historical Annals of Viet), which covers the Ly dynasty (eleventh and twelfth centuries) with some materials mostly taken from Chinese sources for earlier times, written without attribution in the thirteenth or the fourteenth century. The *An Nam Chi Luoc* (Annals of Annam) was written in the fourteenth century by a Vietnamese exile in China and is largely based on Chinese sources. In the fifteenth century, a collation of historical materials resulted in the *Dai Viet Su Ky Toan Thu* (Complete Book of the Historical Records of Great Viet). This annal begins in ancient times and ends with the founding of the Le dynasty in 1427. It became the basis of later historical studies that continued the annal to 1675, which was xylographically printed in 1697; this printing is the Chinh Hoa edition of the work that has survived to the present time and which preserves a Hanoi perspective. By this time northern and southern historians were separately compiling the histories of their respective realms, and existing historical materials for the eighteenth century mostly reflect the work of Nguyen dynasty scholars in the nineteenth century.

An exception to this is what has been assembled by French and Vietnamese scholars and recently translated from Han into Vietnamese with the title of *Dai Viet Su Ky Tuc Bien – 1676–1789)* (Continued Compilation of the Historical Records of Great Viet – 1676–1789), being the combination of two texts held by the Institute of Han-Nom Studies in Hanoi: *Ban Ky Tuc Bien* (Continued Compilation of the Basic Records), which was produced by Trinh historians in Hanoi in the 1740s covering the years 1676–1740, and *Hau Le Thi Su Ky Luoc* (Record of Events of the Later Le Dynasty), apparently produced by historians in Hanoi in the 1790s during Tay Son rule, which covered the final years of the Le dynasty from 1741 to 1789. For this, see Ngo The Long and Nguyen Kim Hung, trans., *Dai Viet Su Ky Tuc Bien – 1676–1789* (Hanoi: Nha Xuat Ban Van Hoa – Thong Tin, 2011); first edition was published in 1991.

In the nineteenth century, three principal works of history were produced at the Vietnamese court. The *Dai Nam Thuc Luc* (True Records of the Great South) begins in 1558 when the Nguyen family established a separate base of power in the southern Vietnamese territories and ends in 1888 amidst the French conquest. It was compiled over a period of decades and achieved its final form in 1909. The *Dai Nam Liet Truyen* (Biographies of the Great South), compiled along with the *Dai Nam Thuc Luc*, contains biographies of kings, princes, princesses, prominent officials, rebels, and other personalities. The *Kham Dinh Viet Su Thong Giam Cuong Muc* (Imperially Ordered Completely Researched General Survey of Viet History) begins in earliest antiquity and stops with 1789 when the Le dynasty ended. It was compiled over a thirty-year period and completed in 1881 and is an erudite collation of all available information from Chinese and Vietnamese texts.

There are some texts that provide additional information about particular times and places. For example, *Lam Son Thuc Luc* (True Records of Lam Son), completed in 1431, is a detailed account of Le Loi's career fighting with Ming armies and establishing the Le dynasty. In the early eighteenth century, Nguyen Khoa Chiem wrote what is now known as *Viet Nam Khai Quoc Chi Truyen* (Stories about the Founding of the Country of Viet Nam), an anecdotal history of southern affairs from the mid sixteenth century to the early eighteenth century.

Two texts are often categorized together as containing folklore or popular tales, though they are very different. *Viet Dien U Linh Tap* (Departed Spirits of the Vietnamese Realm) was compiled in the early fourteenth century and contains information about deified beings from twenty-seven cults, mostly dating from the Ly dynasty, that were recognized by the Tran dynasty as "kingdom protecting spirits." These include spirits of historical figures, earth spirits, mountain spirits, and water spirits. *Linh Nam Chich Quai* (Strange Tales Collected South of the Mountains) is an accumulation of tales said to have been collected from villagers that assumed its present form in the late fifteenth century under the sanitizing and editorializing brushes of Confucianist scholars; many of its stories were added to historical annals to give substance to ancient times for which information did not exist. Each of these works, in its own way, provides information about religion and politics during the Ly, Tran, and early Le dynasties.

In the sixteenth century, Nguyen Du's *Truyen Ky Man Luc* (Record of Strange Tales) appeared, influenced by a trend in Ming China toward writing stories in which ghosts, demons, and deities establish contact with human beings. Doan Thi Diem, a woman famed as both a poet and a writer of prose, wrote a work in this genre called *Truyen Ky Tan Pha* (New Collection of Marvelous Stories). These works reveal educated people's reaction to popular forms of religious practice. Both of these authors were from the region surrounding Hanoi.

In the eighteenth and early nineteenth centuries, three collections of stories and anecdotes appeared that include much information about academic examinations, life in officialdom, the culture of educated people, sightseeing, curious legends, temples and shrines. *Cong Du Tiep Ky* (Writings at Leisure) by Vu Phuong De (b. 1698, active from 1730s) is full of lore current among the Vu family who came from near modern Hai Duong and were prominent in government. Pham Dinh Ho, from near Hanoi, wrote *Vu Trung Tuy But* (Going with the Writing Brush through the Rain) and, with Nguyen An, his literary accomplice, *Tang Thuong Ngau Luc* (Records of Chance Vicissitudes).

A source for how Zen masters in the Tran dynasty constructed a spiritual genealogy to connect themselves with what they believed to be the true source for the transmission of enlightenment is the *Thien Uyen Tap Anh* (Compiled Extracts About Zen Worthies), compiled in the Tran dynasty. The *Co Chau Phap Van Phat Bon Hanh Ngu Luc* (Record of What has been Said about the Origin and Deeds of the Cloud Dharma Buddha at Co Chau), written in both Han and Nom, is an accumulation of accounts about the female Buddha worshiped at Chua Dau (Mulberry Temple) east of Hanoi, considered to be the first Buddha to appear among the Vietnamese, in the early third century; it was published in its present form in the mid eighteenth century.

There are many collections of poetry in both Han and Nom from the fifteenth to twentieth centuries, but works to be performed on stage are rare. The most interesting exception is the *Sai Vai* (Monk and Nun), written in Nom by Nguyen Cu Trinh, a southerner with a distinguished career as both an administrator and a literary figure. For general introductions to works of literature, see Maurice M. Durand and Nguyen Tran Huan, *An Introduction to Vietnamese Literature* (New York: Columbia University Press, 1985) and Maurice Durand, *L'Univers des Truyen Nom* (Hanoi: Nha Xuat Ban Van

Hoa, 1998); Huynh Sanh Thong, trans., *An Anthology of Vietnamese Poems: From the Eleventh through the Twentieth Centuries* (New Haven: Yale University Press, 2001).

Suggested readings in English and French organized by chapters

Introduction

On the geological formation of the Vietnamese region, see Robert Hall and Derek J. Blundell, eds., *Tectonic Evolution of Southeast Asia*, Geological Society Special Publication No. 106 (London: Geological Society, 1996). On the Red River Fault Zone, see Philippe Hervé Leloup et al., "The Ailao-Shan–Red River Shear Zone, Tertiary Transform Boundary of Indochina," *Tectonophysics* 251 (1995):3–84; Erchie Wang et al., *Late Cenozoic Xianshuihe-Xiaojiang, Red River, and Dali Fault Systems of Southwestern Sichuan and Central Yunnan, China*, The Geological Society of America Special Paper 327 (Boulder, CO: Geological Society of America, 1998); Lindsay M. Schoenbohm et al., "Miocene to Present Activity along the Red River Fault, China, in the Context of Continental Extrusion, Upper-crustal Rotation, and Lower-crustal Flow," *Geological Society of America Bulletin* 118, 5/6 (May/June 2006):672–688.

On changing sea levels and their relation to early archaeological evidence, see Neil Jamieson, "A Perspective on Vietnamese Prehistory Based upon the Relationship between Geological and Archaeological Data: Summary of an Earlier Article by Nguyen Duc Tam," *Asian Perspectives* 24, 2 (1981):187–192.

On the physical environment of Vietnam, including flora and fauna, see Eleanor Jane Sterling et al., *Vietnam: A Natural History* (New Haven: Yale University Press, 2006).

On Sino-Vietnamese-Muong historical linguistics, see the following works by John D. Phan, "Re-imagining 'Annam': A New Analysis of Sino-Viet-Muong Linguistic Contact," *Chinese Southern Diaspora Studies* 4 (2010):3–25; "Muong is not a Subgroup: Phonological Evidence for a Paraphyletic Taxon in the Viet-Muong Sub-family," *Mon-Khmer Studies* 40 (2012): 1–18; and "Lacquered Words: The Evolution of Vietnamese under Sinitic Influences from the 1st Century BCE through the 17th Century CE," Doctoral Dissertation (Cornell University, 2012).

An available reference work is Bruce Lockhart and William J. Duiker, *Historical Dictionary of Vietnam*, 3rd edn (Lanham, MD: Scarecrow Press, 2006).

Chapter 1 (to the 10th century CE)

On archaeology, see Olov R. T. Janse, *Archaeological Research in Indo-China*, 3 vols. (Cambridge, MA: Harvard University Press, 1947 and 1951; Bruges: St. Catherine Press, 1958); Louis Bezacier, *Le Viet-Nam de la Préhistoire à la Fin de l'Occupation Chinoise* (Paris: A. et J. Picard, 1972); Nguyen Phuc Long, "Les Nouvelles Recherches Archéologiques au Vietnam," *Arts Asiatiques*, Special Number, 31 (1975); Jeremy H. C. S. Davidson, "Archaeology in Northern Viet-Nam since 1954," in R. B. Smith and W. Watson, *Early South East Asia: Essays in*

Archaeology, History and Historical Geography (Oxford: Oxford University Press, 1979), pp. 98–124; Charles Higham, *The Archaeology of Mainland Southeast Asia* (Cambridge: Cambridge University Press, 1989); Charles Higham, *The Bronze Age of Southeast Asia* (Cambridge: Cambridge University Press, 1996); Marilynn Larew, "Thuc Phan, Cao Tong, and the Transfer of Military Technology in Third Century BC Viet Nam," *East Asian Science, Technology, and Medicine* 21 (2003):12–47; Nam C. Kim, Lai Van Toi, and Trinh Hoang Hiep, "Co Loa: An Investigation of Vietnam's Ancient Capital," *Antiquity* 84 (2010):1011–1027; Anne-Valerie Schweyer, *Ancient Vietnam: History, Art and Archaeology* (Bangkok: River Books, 2011); Ambra Calo, *The Distribution of Bronze Drums in Early Southeast Asia: Trade Routes and Cultural Spheres*, BAR International Series No. 1913 (Oxford: Archaeopress, 2009); Andrew Hardy, Mauro Cucarzi, and Patrizia Zolese, eds., *Champa and the Archaeology of My Son (Vietnam)* (Singapore: NUS Press, 2009); James C. M. Khoo, ed., *Art and Archaeology of Fu Nan: Pre-Khmer Kingdom of the Lower Mekong Valley* (Bangkok: Orchid Press, 2003); and an exhibition publication: Nancy Tingley, *Arts of Ancient Viet Nam: From River Plain to Open Sea* (Houston: The Museum of Fine Arts, 2009).

Studies of archaeology and textual sources with a focus on southern China having significance for understanding early Vietnam can be found in Shing Muller, Thomas O. Hollmann, and Putao Gui, eds., *Guangdong: Archaeology and Early Texts (Zhou-Tang)* (Wiesbaden: Harrassowitz Verlag, 2004) – useful chapters in this book are: Francis Allard, "Lingnan and Chu during the First Millennium B.C.: A Reassessment of the Core–Periphery Model," pp. 1–21; Geoff Wade, "Lady Sinn and the Southward Expansion of China in the Sixth Century," pp. 125–150; Claudine Salmon, "Tang-Viet Society as Reflected in a Buddhist Bell Inscription from the Protectorate of Annam (798)," pp. 195–216; James K. Chin, "Ports, Merchants, Chieftains and Eunuchs: Reading Maritime Commerce of Early Guangdong," pp. 217–239.

For general surveys of pre-modern Vietnamese history, somewhat dated, see the two books by Le Thanh Khoi: *Le Viet-Nam: Histoire et Civilisation* (Paris: Editions de Minuit, 1955) and *Histoire du Vietnam des Origines à 1858* (Paris: Sudestasie, 1981).

For a survey of Vietnamese history to the tenth century, see K. W. Taylor, *The Birth of Vietnam* (Berkeley: University of California Press, 1983). Also see Nguyen Phuong, unpublished manuscript available in some university libraries, entitled "The Ancient History of Viet-Nam: A New Study" (1976), being based to some extent upon his *Viet Nam Thoi Khai Sinh* (Vietnam at the Time of its Birth) (Hue: Sao Mai, 1965). For an analysis of evidence about perceptions of ethnicity, see Erica Brindley, "Barbarians or Not? Ethnicity and Changing Conceptions of the Ancient Yue (Viet) Peoples, ca. 400–50 B.C.," *Asia Major*, 3rd series, 16, 1 (2003):1–32. For a study of settlement patterns, see Nishimura Masanari, "Settlement Patterns on the Red River Plain from the Late Prehistoric Period to the Tenth Century AD," *Indo-Pacific Prehistory Association Bulletin* 25, Taipei Papers, Vol. 3 (1999):99–107. On the problem of terms used to identify ancient peoples, see Michael Churchman, "Before Chinese and Vietnamese in the Red River Plain: The Han-Tang Period," *Chinese Southern Diaspora Studies* 4 (2010):25–37.

For the early historical period from Qin/Han to the sixth century, see Matsumoto
   Nobuhiro, "Religious Thoughts of the Bronze Age Peoples of Indochina," in
   N. Matsumoto and T. Mabuchi, eds., *Folk Religion and the Worldview in the
   Southwestern Pacific* (Tokyo: Kokusai, 1968); Yamamoto Tatsuro, "Myths
   Explaining the Vicissitudes of Political Power in Ancient Vietnam," *Acta Asiatica*
   18 (1970):70–94; Émile Gaspardone, "Champs Lo et Champs Hiong," *Journal
   Asiatique* 243 (1955):461–477; Paul Wheatley, *Nagara and Commandery: Origins
   of the Southeast Asian Urban Tradition* (Chicago: University of Chicago Press,
   1983), pp. 365–397; Bui Quang Tung, "Le Soulèvement des Sœurs Trung,"
   Bulletin de la Société des Études Indochinoises 36 (1961):78–85; Stephen
   O'Harrow, "From Co-loa to the Trung Sisters' Revolt: Viet-Nam as the Chinese
   Found it," *Asian Perspectives* 22, 2 (1979):140–164; Jennifer Holmgren, *Chinese
   Colonisation of Northern Vietnam: Administrative Geography and Political
   Development in the Tongking Delta, First to Sixth Centuries* A.D. (Canberra:
   Australian National University Press, 1980); Henri Maspero, "Études d'histoire
   d'Annam," *Bulletin de l'École Française d'Extrême-Orient* 16 (1916):1–55 and 18
   (1918):1–36; K. W. Taylor, "Perceptions of Encounter in *Shui Ching Chu* 37," *Asia
   Journal* 2, 1 (1995):29–54.
On Shi Xie, see Stephen O'Harrow, "Men of Hu, Men of Han, Men of the Hundred
   Man," *Bulletin de l'École Française d'Extrême-Orient* 75 (1986):249–266.
On the Han prefecture of Nhat Nam and the rise of Lin Yi, see Rolf A. Stein, "Le Lin-Yi,"
   Han-Hiue II, Fasc. 1–3 (Peking: Université de Paris, Centre d'Études Sinologiques
   de Pekin, 1947).
A good study of the history of Hanoi from the seventh century to the present is Philippe
   Papin, *Histoire de Hanoi* (Paris: Fayard, 2001); another good study of ancient
   Vietnam by the same author is "Géographie et Politique dans le Viet-Nam Ancien,"
   Bulletin de l'École Française d'Extrême-Orient 87 (2000):609–628.
For the Tang period, see Henri Maspero, "Le Protectorat Général d'Annam sous les
   T'ang," *Bulletin de l'École Française d'Extrême-Orient* 10 (1910):539–682;
   Edward H. Schafer, *The Vermilion Bird* (Berkeley: University of California Press,
   1967); K. W. Taylor, "Phung Hung: Mencian King or Austric Paramount?" *The
   Vietnam Forum* 8 (summer–fall 1986):26–59.
On the tenth century, see Ken Gardiner, "Vietnam and Southern Han," *Papers on Far
   Eastern History* 23 (March 1981):64–110; K. W. Taylor, "The 'Twelve Lords' in
   Tenth-Century Vietnam," *Journal of Southeast Asian Studies* 14, 1 (March
   1983):46–62.

Chapter 2 (10th–12th centuries)

On the Hoa Lu kings and the founding of the Ly dynasty, see K. W. Taylor, "The Rise of
   Dai Viet and the Establishment of Thang Long," in K. R. Hall and J. K. Whitmore,
   eds., *Explorations in Early Southeast Asian History: The Origins of Southeast
   Asian Statecraft*, Michigan Papers on South and Southeast Asia, No. 11 (Ann
   Arbor: University of Michigan Center for South and Southeast Asian Studies,
   1976), pp. 25–60. On the religious policy of the Ly dynasty in the eleventh century,
   see K. W. Taylor, "Authority and Legitimacy in Eleventh-Century Vietnam," in
   D. B. Marr and A. C. Milner, eds., *Southeast Asia in the 9th to 14th Centuries*

(Singapore: Institute of Southeast Asian Studies, 1986), pp. 139–176. For a comparison of annalistic accounts of two eleventh-century kings, see K. W. Taylor, "Looking Behind the Vietnamese Annals: Ly Phat Ma (1028–54) and Ly Nhat Ton (1054–72) in the *Viet Su Luoc* and the *Toan Thu*," *The Vietnam Forum* 7 (winter–spring, 1986):47–68. On the Nung Tri Cao uprising, see James Anderson, *The Rebel Den of Nung Tri Cao: Loyalty and Identity Along the Sino-Vietnamese Frontier* (Seattle: University of Washington Press, 2007). On a late eleventh-century poet, see K. W. Taylor, "The Poems of Doan Van Kham," *Crossroads* 7, 2 (1992):39–53.

On the historiography of an early twelfth-century reign, see Oliver William Wolters, "Le Van Huu's Treatment of Ly Than Ton's Reign (1127–1137)," in C. D. Cowan and O. W. Wolters, eds., *Southeast Asian History and Historiography* (Ithaca: Cornell University Press, 1976), pp. 203–226. On the Ly court in the mid twelfth century, see K. W. Taylor, "Voices Within and Without: Tales from Stone and Paper about Do Anh Vu," in K. W. Taylor and J. K. Whitmore, eds., *Essays into Vietnamese Pasts* (Ithaca: Cornell Southeast Asia Publications, 1995), pp. 59–80. On late twelfth-century and early thirteenth-century Chinese accounts of Vietnam, see John Kremers Whitmore, "Elephants can Actually Swim," in D. G. Marr and A. C. Milner, eds., *Southeast Asia in the 9th to 14th Centuries* (Singapore: Institute of Southeast Asian Studies, 1986), pp. 117–133. On the port of Van Don, see Tatsuro Yamamoto, "Van-don: A Trade Port in Vietnam," *The Memoirs of the Toyo Bunko* 39 (1981):1–28.

Chapter 3 (13th–14th centuries)

O. W. Wolters has written extensively on the historiography, poetry, and intellectual history of the Tran dynasty: "Narrating the Fall of the Ly and the Rise of the Tran Dynasties," *Asian Studies Association of Australia Review* 10, 2 (November 1986):24–32; "On Telling a Story of Vietnam in the Thirteenth and Fourteenth Centuries," *Journal of Southeast Asian Studies* 26, 1 (March 1995):63–74; "Historians and Emperors in Vietnam and China: Comments Arising out of Le Van Huu's History, Presented to the Tran Court in 1272," in A. Reid and D. M. Marr, eds., *Perceptions of the Past in Southeast Asia* (Singapore: Heineman Educational Books, 1979), pp. 69–89; "Possibilities for a Reading of the 1293–1357 Period in the Vietnamese Annals," in D. M. Marr and A. C. Milner, eds., *Southeast Asia in the 9th to 14th Centuries* (Singapore: Institute of Southeast Asian Studies, 1986), pp. 369–410; "Min-Ton's Poetry of Sight, Light, and Country," in O. W. Wolters, *Two Essays on Dai Viet in the Fourteenth Century*, Lac-Viet Series No. 9 (New Haven: Yale Council on Southeast Asia Studies, 1988), pp. 54–165; "Assertions of Cultural Well-Being in Fourteenth-Century Vietnam," first published in *Journal of Southeast Asian Studies* 10, 2 (September 1979):435–450 and 11, 1 (March 1980):74–90, reprinted in *Two Essays on Dai Viet in the Fourteenth Century*, Lac-Viet Series No. 9 (New Haven: Yale Council on Southeast Asia Studies, 1988), pp. 3–53; "Pham Su Manh's Poems Written While Patrolling the Vietnamese Northern Border in the Middle of the Fourteenth Century," *Journal of Southeast Asian Studies* 13, 1 (March 1982):107–119; *Monologue, Dialogue, and Tran Vietnam* (published online at http://ecommons.library.cornell.edu/handle/1813/13117);

"Chu Van An: An Exemplary Retirement," *The Vietnam Review* 1 (autumn–winter 1996):62–96. On Chu Van An, also see J. K. Whitmore, "Chu Van An and the Rise of 'Antiquity' in 14th century Dai Viet," *Vietnam Review* 1 (1996):50–61.

On poetry, see Jason Hoai Tran, "Aesthetics and Self-Image in Dai Viet Buddhist Poetry during the Ly and Tran Dynasties," M.A. Thesis (Cornell University, 2006).

For an essay on the historiography of the Tran period, see Shawn Frederick McHale, " 'Texts and Bodies': Refashioning the Disturbing Past of Tran Vietnam (1225–1400)," *Journal of the Economic and Social History of the Orient* 42, 4 (1999):494–518.

On Vietnamese Buddhism prior to and during the Tran period, see Cuong Tu Nguyen, *Zen in Medieval Vietnam: A Study and Translation of the* Thien Uyen Tap Anh (Honolulu: University of Hawai'i Press, 1997). Philippe Langlet, *La Sagesse bouddhiste aux débuts du Viêt Nam* (Paris: Les Indes Savants, 2012).

On trade, culture, and ethnicity along the coast of northern Vietnam during this time, see Li Tana, "A View from the Sea: Perspectives on the Northern and Central Vietnamese Coast," *Journal of Southeast Asian Studies* 37, 1 (February 2006):83–102; J. K. Whitmore, "The Rise of the Coast: Trade, State and Culture in Early Dai Viet," *Journal of Southeast Asian Studies* 37, 1 (February 2006):103–122; J. K. Whitmore, "Brush and Ship: The Southern Chinese Diaspora and Literati in Dai Viet during the Twelfth and Thirteenth Centuries," *Chinese Southern Diaspora Studies* 4 (2010):38–41; and Nola Cooke, Li Tana, and James A. Anderson, eds., *The Tongking Gulf Through History* (Philadelphia: University of Pennsylvania Press, 2011).

Chapters 4 and 5 (15th–16th centuries)

On Ho Quy Ly, see Émile Gaspardone, "Le Qui-ly," in L. C. Goodrich, ed., *Dictionary of Ming Biography* (New York: Columbia University Press, 1976), pp. 797–801; J. K. Whitmore, *Vietnam, Ho Quy Ly, and the Ming (1371–1421)*, The Lac Viet Series No. 2 (New Haven: Yale Council on Southeast Asia Studies, 1985); O. W. Wolters, "Celebrating the Educated Official: A Reading of Some of Nguyen Phi Khanh's Poems," *The Vietnam Forum* 2 (summer–fall 1983):79–101.

On Ming Giao Chi, see O. W. Wolters, "A Stranger in His Own Land: Nguyen Trai's Sino-Vietnamese Poems Written During the Ming Occupation," *The Vietnam Forum* 8 (summer–fall 1986):60–89; Alexander Barton Woodside, "Early Ming Expansionism (1406–1427): China's Abortive Conquest of Vietnam," *Papers on China* 17 (Cambridge, MA: Harvard University East Asia Research Center, December 1963):1–37.

On Le Loi, see Émile Gaspardone, "Le Loi," in L. C. Goodrich, ed., *Dictionary of Ming Biography* (New York: Columbia University Press, 1976), pp. 793–797; Stephen O'Harrow, "Nguyen Trai's *Binh Ngo Dai Cao* of 1428: The Development of a Vietnamese National Identity," *Journal of Southeast Asian Studies* 10, 1 (March 1979):159–174.

On the development of the Le dynastic regime, see J. K. Whitmore, "The Development of Le Government in Fifteenth Century Vietnam," Ph.D. Dissertation (Cornell University, 1968); Esta Serne Ungar, "Vietnamese Leadership and Order: Dai Viet under the Le Dynasty (1428–1459)," Ph.D. Dissertation (Cornell University, 1983). Concerning Le dynasty historiography, see Liam C. Kelley, "The Biography of the Hông Bang Clan as a Medieval Vietnamese Invented Tradition," *Journal of Vietnamese Studies* 7, 2 (Summer 2012):87–130.

On the reign of Le Tu Thanh, see O. W. Wolters, "What Else May Ngo Si Lien Mean? A Matter of Distinctions in the Fifteenth Century," in A. Reid, ed., *Sojourners and Settlers: Histories of Southeast Asia and the Chinese* (Sydney: Allen & Unwin for the Asian Studies Association of Australia, 1995), pp. 94–114; J. K. Whitmore, "The *Tao-Dan* Group: Poetry, Cosmology, and the State in the *Hong-duc* Period (1470–1497)," *Crossroads* 7, 2 (1992):55–70; J. K. Whitmore, "Two Great Campaigns of the Hong Duc Era (1470–1497) in Dai Viet," *Southeast Asia Research* 12 (2004):119–136.

On Confucianism, see A. B. Woodside, "Classical Primordialism and the Historical Agendas of Vietnamese Confucianism," in B. A. Elman, J. B. Duncan, and H. Ooms, eds., *Rethinking Confucianism: Past and Present in China, Japan, Korea, and Vietnam* (Los Angeles: UCLA Asian Pacific Monograph Series, 2002), pp. 116–143. Also see Vo Van Thang, "Ancestor Worship in Vietnam: A Study of Books and Rituals and Practices in a Village," M.A. Thesis (Cornell University, 1997).

On military technology, see Sun Laichen, "Military Technology Transfers from Ming China and the Emergence of Northern Mainland Southeast Asia (c. 1390–1527)," *Journal of Southeast Asian Studies* 34, 3 (October 2003):495–517.

On the Mac dynasty, see J. K. Whitmore, "Mac Dang-dung," in L. C. Goodrich, ed., *Dictionary of Ming Biography* (New York: Columbia University Press, 1976), pp. 1029–1035; J. K. Whitmore, "*Chung-hsing* and *Cheng-t'ung* in Texts of and on Sixteenth-Century Viet Nam," in K. W. Taylor and J. K. Whitmore, eds., *Essays into Vietnamese Pasts* (Ithaca: Cornell Southeast Asia Publications, 1995), pp. 116–136; Olga Dror, *Cult, Culture, and Authority: Princess Lieu Hanh in Vietnamese History* (Honolulu: University of Hawai'i Press, 2007).

On Buddhist temples and *dinh*, see Ha Van Tan and Nguyen Van Ku, *Buddhist Temples in Vietnam* (Hanoi: Social Sciences Publishing House, 1993); Ha Van Tan and Nguyen Van Ku, *Community Halls in Vietnam* (Ho Chi Minh City: Ho Chi Minh City Publishing House, 1998).

On literature, see Minyan Peng, "For Qing or for Didacticism? A Comparative Study of the Love Tales in *Jiandeng Xinhua* and *Truyen Ky Man Luc*," M.A. Thesis (Cornell University, 2002).

Chapters 6, 7, and 8 (17th–18th centuries)

For studies that present comparative perspectives on northern and southern Vietnamese government and society, see: Nguyen Thanh-Nha, *Tableau Économique du Viet Nam aux XVII et XVIII siècles* (Paris: Éditions Cujas, 1970); and Dang Phuong-Nghi, *Les Institutions Publiques du Viet-Nam au XVIII siècle* (Paris: École Française d'Extrême-Orient, 1969). For European accounts of the north and the south in the seventeenth century, see Olga Dror and K. W. Taylor, *Views of Seventeenth-Century Vietnam: Christoforo Borri on Cochinchina and Samuel Baron on Tonkin* (Ithaca: Cornell Southeast Asia Program, 2006). On the Trinh–Nguyen wars, see M. Léopold Michel Cadière, "Le Mur de Dong-Hoi: Étude sur l'Établissement des Nguyen en Cochinchine," *Bulletin de l'École Française d'Extrême-Orient* 6

(1906):87–254; Charles B. Maybon, *Histoire Moderne du Pays d'Annam (1592–1820)* (Paris: Librairie Plon, 1919); K. W. Taylor, "Surface Orientations in Vietnam: Beyond Histories of Nation and Region," *The Journal of Asian Studies* 57, 4 (November 1998):949–978.

For studies that focus on the north, see: Philippe Langlet, *La Tradition Vietnamienne: Un État National au Sein de la Civilisation Chinoise* (Saigon: B.S.E.I., New Series, Vol. XLV, 2–3, 1970); Nguyen Ngoc Huy and Ta Van Tai, *The Lê Code: Law in Traditional Vietnam*, 3 vols. (Athens, OH: Ohio University Press, 1987); Insun Yu, *Law and Society in Seventeenth and Eighteenth Century Vietnam* (Seoul: Asiatic Research Center, 1990); Alexandre de Rhodes, *Histoire du Royaume du Tonkin* (Paris: Éditions Kimé, 1999); K. W. Taylor, "The Literati Revival in Seventeenth-Century Vietnam," *Journal of Southeast Asian Studies*, 18, 1 (March 1987):1–23; A. B. Woodside, "Central Viet Nam's Trading World in the Eighteenth Century as Seen in Le Quy Don's 'Frontier Chronicles'," in K. W. Taylor and J. K. Whitmore, eds., *Essays into Vietnamese Pasts* (Ithaca: Cornell Southeast Asia Publications, 1995), pp. 157–172; A. B. Woodside, "Conceptions of Change and of Human Responsibility for Change in Late Traditional Vietnam," in D. K. Wyatt and A. B. Woodside, eds., *Moral Order and the Question of Change: Essays on Southeast Asian Thought*, Monograph No. 24 (New Haven: Yale University Southeast Asia Studies, 1982), pp. 104–150; K. W. Taylor, "Literacy in Early Seventeenth-Century Northern Vietnam," in M. A. Aung-Thwin and K. R. Hall, eds., *New Perspectives on the History and Historiography of Southeast Asia: Continuing Explorations* (London: Routledge, 2011), pp. 138–200.

For studies that focus on the south, see: Yang Baoyun, *Contribution à l'Histoire de la Principauté des Nguyên au Vietnam Méridional, 1600–1775* (Geneva: Olizane/ Études Orientales, 1992); K. W. Taylor, "Nguyen Hoang and the Beginning of Viet Nam's Southward Expansion," in A. Reid, ed., *Southeast Asia in the Early Modern Era* (Ithaca: Cornell University Press, 1993), pp. 42–65; Li Tana and A. Reid, eds., *Southern Vietnam under the Nguyen: Documents on the Economic History of Cochinchina (Dang Trong), 1602–1777* (Singapore: Institute of Southeast Asian Studies, 1993); and Li Tana, *Nguyen Cochinchina: Southern Vietnam in the Seventeenth and Eighteenth Centuries* (Ithaca: Cornell Southeast Asia Program, 1998); Claudine Ang Tsu Lynn, "Statecraft on the Margins: Drama, Poetry, and the Civilizing Mission in Eighteenth-century Southern Vietnam," Doctoral Dissertation (Cornell University, 2012). On trade and shipbuilding in the eighteenth century, see Nola Cooke and Li Tana, eds., *Water Frontier: Commerce and the Chinese in the Lower Mekong Region, 1750–1880* (Lanham, MD: Rowman & Littlefield, 2004). On Chinese immigrants in the south, see Nguyen Hoi Chan, "Some Aspects of the Chinese Community in Vietnam, 1650–1850," *Papers on China* 24 (1971):104–124; Émile Gaspardone, "Bonzes des Ming réfugiés en Annam," *Sinologica* 2 (1950):12–30; and Charles Wheeler, "Buddhism in the Re-ordering of an Early Modern World: Chinese Missions to Cochinchina in the Seventeenth Century," *Journal of Global History* 2 (2002):303–324.

For the wars of the late eighteenth century, see George Dutton, *The Tay Son Uprising: Society and Rebellion in Eighteenth-century Vietnam* (Honolulu: University of Hawai'i Press, 2001); Dian H. Murray, *Pirates of the South China Coast, 1790–1810* (Stanford, CA: Stanford University Press, 1987); and Truong Buu Lam, "Intervention versus Tribute in Sino-Vietnamese Relations, 1788–1790," in J. King

Fairbank, ed., *The Chinese World Order* (Cambridge, MA: Harvard University Press, 1968), pp. 165–179.

On Vietnamese envoys to the Qing court, see Liam C. Kelly, *Beyond the Bronze Pillars: Envoy Poetry and the Sino-Vietnamese Relationship* (Honolulu: University of Hawai'i Press, 2005).

On Cambodia, see Mak Phœun, *Histoire du Cambodge de la Fin du XVI siècle au Début du XVIII* (Paris: École Française d'Extrême-Orient, 1995); Khin Sok, *Le Cambodge entre le Siam et le Vietnam de 1775 à 1860* (Paris: École Française d'Extrême-Orient, 1991); and Alfons Van Der Kraan, *Murder and Mayhem in Seventeenth-century Cambodia* (Bangkok: Silkworm Books, 2009).

On international trade, see Pierre-Yves Manguin, *Les Portugais sur les Côtes du Viet-Nam et du Campa* (Paris: École Française d'Extrême-Orient, 1972); Pierre-Yves Manguin, *Les Nguyen, Macau et le Portugal* (Paris: École Française d'Extrême-Orient, 1984); Hoang Anh Tuan, *Silk for Silver: Dutch–Vietnamese Relations, 1637–1700* (Leiden: Brill, 2007); Robert LeRoy Innes, "The Door Ajar: Japan's Foreign Trade in the Seventeenth Century," Ph.D. Dissertation (The University of Michigan, 1980); Danny Wong Tze-Ken, "The Nguyen Lords and the English Factory on Pulo Condore at the Beginning of the 18th Century," in F. Mantienne and K. W. Taylor, eds., *Monde du Viêt Nam–Vietnam World: Hommage à Nguyên Thê Anh* (Paris: Les Indes Savantes, 2008), pp. 371–384.

On European missionaries, see: André Marillier, *Nos Pères dans la Foi: Notes sur le Clergé Catholique du Tonkin de 1666 à 1765* (Paris: Églises D'Asie, 1995); Alain Forest, *Les Missionnaires Français au Tonkin et au Siam, XVII–XVIII siècles*, 3 vols. (Paris: L'Harmattan, 1998); Alexandre de Rhodes, *Histoire du Royaume du Tonkin* (Paris: Éditions Kimé, 1999); Olga Dror, *Adriano di St. Thecla's "A Small Treatise on the Sects among the Chinese and Tonkinese": A Study of Religion in China and North Vietnam in the Eighteenth Century* (Ithaca: Cornell Southeast Asia Program, 2002); Peter C. Phan, *Mission and Catechesis: Alexandre de Rhodes and Inculturation in Seventeenth-century Vietnam* (Maryknoll, NY: Orbis Books, 1998); Brian Eugene Ostrowski, "The Nom Works of Geronimo Maiorica, S. J. (1589–1656) and their Christology," Ph.D. Dissertation (Cornell University, January 2006); Nola Cooke, "Strange Brew: Global, Regional and Local Factors behind the 1690 Prohibition of Christian Practice in Nguyen Cochinchina," *Journal of Southeast Asian Studies* 39, 3 (October 2008):383–409; Frédéric Mantienne, *MGR Pierre Pigneau, Évêque d'Adran, Dignitaire de Cochinchine*, Archives des Missions Étrangères, Études et Documents 8 (Paris: Églises d'Asie, Série Histoire, 1999); Georges Taboulet, *La Geste Française en Indochine*, Vol. I (Paris: Adrien-Maisonneuve, 1955); Micheline Lessard, "Curious Relations: Jesuit Perceptions of the Vietnamese," in K. W. Taylor and J. K. Whitmore, eds., *Essays into Vietnamese Pasts* (Ithaca: Cornell Southeast Asia Publications, 1995), pp. 137–156; Nicole-Dominique Le, *Les Missions-Étrangères et la Pénétration Française au Viet-Nam* (Paris: Mouton, 1975).

Chapter 9 (early 19th century)

On the political and cultural history of the Nguyen dynasty, see Philippe Langlet, *L'Ancienne Historiographie d'État au Vietnam*, 2 vols. (Paris: École Française d'Extrême-Orient, 1985–1990); A. B. Woodside, *Vietnam and the Chinese Model:*

A Comparative Study of Vietnamese and Chinese Government in the First Half of the Nineteenth Century (Cambridge: Harvard University Press, 1971); Maurice Durand, *L'Oeuvre de la Poétess Vietnamienne Hô Xuân Huong*, Collections de Textes et Documents sur l'Indochine IX, Textes Nôm No. 2 (Paris: École Française d'Extrême-Orient, 1968); *Spring Essence: The Poetry of Hô Xuân Huong*, translated by John Balaban (Port Townsend, WA: Copper Canyon Press, 2000); *The Kim Vân Kiều of Nguyen Du*, translated by Vladislav Zhukov with introduction by K. W. Taylor (Ithaca: Cornell University Southeast Asia Program Publications, 2013). On the reign of Minh Mang, see Choi Byung Wook, *Southern Vietnam under the Reign of Minh Mang (1820–1841)* (Ithaca: Cornell Southeast Asia Program Publications, 2004). On examination graduates, see Nola Cooke, "Nineteenth-Century Vietnamese Confucianization in Historical Perspective: Evidence from the Palace Examinations (1463–1883)," *Journal of Southeast Asian Studies*, 25, 2 (September 1994):270–312. On trade and Chinese immigrants in the Mekong delta, see Nola Cooke and Li Tana, *Water Frontier: Commerce and the Chinese in the Lower Mekong Region, 1750–1880* (Singapore: Rowman & Littlefield, 2004). For Cambodian–Vietnamese relations, see Khin Sok, *Le Cambodge entre le Siam et le Vietnam (de 1775 à 1860)* (Paris: École Française d'Extrême-Orient, 1991).

On Siam–Vietnamese relations, see Mayoury Ngaosyvathn and Pheuiphanh Ngaosyvathn, *Paths to Conflagration: Fifty Years of Diplomacy and Warfare in Laos, Thailand, and Vietnam, 1778–1828* (Ithaca: Cornell Southeast Asia Program Publications, 1998); J. K. Whitmore, "The Thai–Vietnamese Struggle for Laos in the Nineteenth Century," in N. S. Adams and A. W. McCoy, eds., *Laos: War and Revolution* (New York: Harper & Row, 1971), pp. 53–66.

On contacts with Europeans, see Alastair Lamb, *The Mandarin Road to Old Hue: Narratives of Anglo-Vietnamese Diplomacy from the 17th Century to the Eve of the French Conquest* (Edinburgh: Archon Books, 1970); Georges Taboulet, *La Geste Française en Indochine*, Vol. II (Paris: Adrien-Maisonneuve, 1955); Frédéric Mantienne, "The Transfer of Western Military Technology to Vietnam in the Late Eighteenth and Early Nineteenth Centuries: The Case of the Nguyen," *Journal of Southeast Asian Studies* 34, 3 (October 2003):519–534.

Chapter 10 (late 19th century)

On the French conquest and rule, see John F. Cady, *The Roots of French Imperialism in Eastern Asia* (Ithaca: Cornell University Press, 1954); John Laffey, "Les racines de l'imperialisme française en Extrême-Orient: A propos des thèses de J.-F. Cady," in J. Bouvier and R. Girault, eds., *L'Imperialisme Française d'avant 1914* (Paris: Mouton, 1976); Milton E. Osborne, *The French Presence in Cochinchina and Cambodia: Rule and Response (1859–1905)* (Ithaca: Cornell University Press, 1969); Charles B. Maybon, *Lectures sur L'Histoire Moderne et Contemporaine du Pays d'Annam de 1428 à 1926* (Hanoi: Imprimerie D'Extrême-Orient, 1927); Jean Chesneaux, *Contribution à l'Histoire de la Nation Vietnamienne* (Paris: Éditions Sociales, 1955); Philippe Devillers, *Français et Annamites: Partenaires ou Ennemis? 1856–1902* (Paris: Éditions Denoël, 1998); Charles Gosselin, *L'Empire d'Annam* (Paris: Perrin, 1904); Henry McAleavy, *Black Flags in Vietnam: The Story of a*

Chinese Intervention (New York: Macmillan, 1968); Amaury Lorin, *Paul Doumer, Gouverneur Général de l'Indochine (1897–1902)* (Paris: L'Harmattan, 2004); John DeFrancis, *Colonialism and Language Policy in Vietnam* (The Hague: Mouton, 1977).

On the Vietnamese experience, see Yoshiharu Tsuboi, *L'Empire Vietnamien face à la France et à la Chine, 1847–1885* (Paris: Éditions L'Harmattan, 1987); Truong Buu Lam, *Patterns of Vietnamese Response to Foreign Intervention: 1858–1900*, Monograph No. 11 (New Haven: Yale University Southeast Asia Studies, 1967); Truong Buu Lam, *New Lamps for Old: The Transformation of the Vietnamese Administrative Elite* (Singapore: Maruzen Asia, 1982); Truong Buu Lam, *Resistance, Rebellion, Revolution: Popular Movements in Vietnamese History* (Singapore: Institute of Southeast Asian Studies, 1984); Tran My-Van, *A Vietnamese Scholar in Anguish: Nguyen Khuyen and the Decline of the Confucian Order, 1884–1909*, Journal of Southeast Asian Studies Special Publications Series No. 2 (Singapore: National University Singapore, 1992); Le Van Phuc, "La Vie et la Mort du Maréchal Nguyen Van Thieng," *Bulletin de la Société des Études Indochinoises*, 1, 33 (1941); Mark W. McLeod, *The Vietnamese Response to French Intervention, 1862–1874* (New York: Praeger, 1991); Charles Fourniau, *Annam-Tonkin 1885–1896: Lettrés et Paysans Vietnamiens face à la Conquête Coloniale* (Paris: L'Harmattan, 1989); Hue-Tam Ho Tai, *Millenarianism and Peasant Politics in Vietnam* (Cambridge: Harvard University Press, 1983); David G. Marr, *Vietnamese Anticolonialism: 1885–1925* (Berkeley: University of California Press, 1971); and K. W. Taylor, "A Southern Remembrance of Cao Bien," in P. Papin and J. Kleinen, eds., *Liber Amicorum: Mélanges offerts au Professeur Phan Huy Lé* (Hanoi: École Française d'Extrême-Orient, 1999), pp. 241–258.

On the geography, economy, and administration of the Mekong delta, see Philippe Langlet and Quach Thanh Tâm, *Atlas Historique des Six Provinces du Sud du Vietnam du Milieu du XIXe au Début du XXe siècle* (Paris: Les Indes Savantes, 2001); Pierre Brocheux, *The Mekong Delta: Ecology, Economy, and Revolution, 1860–1960* (Madison: University of Wisconsin, 1995). On the Central Highlands, see Oscar Salamink, *The Ethnography of Vietnam's Central Highlanders: A Historical Contextualization, 1850–1990* (Honolulu: University of Hawai'i Press, 2003).

Chapters 11 and 12 (early 20th century)

For a good general survey of the French colonial regime, see Pierre Brocheux and Daniel Hémery, *Indochina: An Ambiguous Colonization, 1858–1954* (Berkeley: University of California Press, 2009). On French colonial prisons, see Peter Zinoman, *The Colonial Bastille: A History of Imprisonment in Vietnam 1862–1940* (Berkeley: University of California Press, 2001). On French policy toward ethnic minorities, see K. W. Taylor, "On Being Muonged," *Asian Ethnicity* 2, 1 (March 2001):25–34. Two overviews of the Franco-Vietnamese colonial relationship are Ralph Bernard Smith, *Viet-Nam and the West* (Ithaca: Cornell University Press, 1968); and A. B. Woodside, *Community and Revolution in Modern Vietnam* (Boston: Houghton Mifflin, 1976). On education, see: Gail

P. Kelly, *Franco-Vietnamese Schools, 1918–1938: Regional Development and Implications for National Integration*, Paper No. 6 (Madison: University of Wisconsin Center for Southeast Asian Studies, 1982); and Gail P. Kelly, *French Colonial Education: Essays on Vietnam and West Africa* (New York: AMS Press, 2000).

On the monarchy, see Nguyen The Anh, *Monarchie et Fait Colonial au Viet-Nam (1875–1925): Le Crépuscule d'un Ordre Traditionnel* (Paris: Éditions l'Harmattan, 1992); and Bruce McFarland Lockhart, *The End of the Vietnamese Monarchy* (New Haven: Yale University Council on Southeast Asia Studies, 1993).

On early Vietnamese responses to French colonialism, see Phan Boi Chau, *Overturned Chariot: The Autobiography of Phan Boi Chau* (Honolulu: University of Hawai'i Press, 1999); Phan Chu Trinh, *A Complete Account of the Peasants' Uprising in the Central Region*, University of Wisconsin Center for Southeast Asian Studies Monograph 1 (Madison: University of Wisconsin, 1983); Phan Chau Trinh (Vinh Sinh, ed. and trans.), *Phan Chau Trinh and his Political Writings* (Ithaca: Cornell Southeast Asia Program Publications, 2009); Tran My-Van, *A Vietnamese Royal Exile in Japan: Prince Cuong De (1882–1951)* (New York: Routledge, 2005); Vu Duc Bang, "The Dong Kinh Free School Movement," in W. F. Vella, ed., *Aspects of Vietnamese History*, Asian Studies at Hawaii, No. 8 (Honolulu: The University Press of Hawai'i, 1973), pp. 30–95; Truong Buu Lam, *Colonialism Experienced: Vietnamese Writings on Colonialism, 1900–1931* (Ann Arbor: The University of Michigan Press, 2000); Kimloan Vu-Hill, *Coolies into Rebels: Impact of World War I on French Indochina* (Paris: Les Indes Savantes, 2011); Tran Tu Binh, *The Red Earth: A Vietnamese Memoir of Life on a Colonial Rubber Plantation* (Athens: Ohio University Press, 1985); Jayne Susan Werner, *Peasant Politics and Religious Sectarianism: Peasant and Priest in the Cao Dai in Viet Nam* (New Haven: Yale University Southeast Asian Studies, 1981).

On Franco-Vietnamese collaboration, see Milton Osborne, "The Faithful Few: The Politics of Collaboration in Cochinchina in the 1920s," in W. F. Vella, ed., *Aspects of Vietnamese History*, Asian Studies at Hawaii, No. 8 (Honolulu: The University Press of Hawai'i, 1973), pp. 160–190; R. B. Smith, "Bui Quang Chieu and the Constitutionalist Party in French Cochinchina, 1917–30," *Modern Asian Studies* 3, 2 (1969):131–150; Megan Cook, *The Constitutionalist Party in Cochinchina: The Years of Decline, 1930–1942* (Clayton: Monash University Centre of Southeast Asian Studies, 1977); and William H. Frederick, "Alexandre Varenne and Politics in Indochina, 1925–1926," in W. F. Vella, ed., *Aspects of Vietnamese History*, Asian Studies at Hawaii, No. 8 (Honolulu: The University Press of Hawai'i, 1973), pp. 96–159.

On the response of Vietnamese to French colonialism during the later period, see David G. Marr, *Vietnamese Tradition on Trial 1920–1945* (Berkeley: University of California Press, 1981); Charles Keith, "Annam Uplifted: The First Vietnamese Catholic Bishops and the Birth of a National Church, 1919–1945," *Journal of Vietnamese Studies* 3, 2 (summer 2008):128–171; Charles Keith, *Catholic Vietnam: A Church from Empire to Nation* (Berkeley: University of California Press, 2012); Hue-Tam Ho Tai, *Radicalism and the Origins of the Vietnamese Revolution* (Cambridge, MA: Harvard University Press, 1992); Hue-Tam Ho Tai, *Passion, Betrayal, and Revolution in Colonial Saigon: The Memoirs of Bao Luong* (Berkeley: University of California Press, 2010); George Dutton, "Ly Toet in the

City: Coming to Terms with the Modern in 1930s Vietnam," *Journal of Vietnamese Studies* 2, 1 (winter 2007):80–108; Shawn Frederick McHale, "Mapping a Vietnamese Confucian Past and its Transition to Modernity," in B. A. Elman, J. B. Duncan, and H. Ooms, eds., *Rethinking Confucianism: Past and Present in China, Japan, Korea, and Vietnam* (Los Angeles: UCLA Asian Pacific Monograph Series, 2002), pp. 397–430; Shawn Frederick McHale, *Print and Power: Confucianism, Communism, and Buddhism in the Making of Modern Vietnam* (Honolulu: University of Hawai'i Press, 2004); K. W. Taylor, "Vietnamese Confucian Narratives," in B. A. Elman, J. B. Duncan, and H. Ooms, eds., *Rethinking Confucianism: Past and Present in China, Japan, Korea, and Vietnam* (Los Angeles: UCLA Asian Pacific Monograph Series, 2002), pp. 337–369; Christoph Giebel, *Imagined Ancestries of Vietnamese Communism: Ton Duc Thang and the Politics of History and Memory* (Seattle: University of Washington Press, 2004); Christopher E. Goscha, "Widening the Colonial Encounter: Asian Connections Inside French Indochina During the Interwar Period," *Modern Asian Studies* 43, 5 (2009):1189–1228; Huynh Kim Khanh, *Vietnamese Communism 1925–1945* (Ithaca: Cornell University Press, 1982); Sophie Quinn-Judge, *Ho Chi Minh: The Missing Years* (Berkeley: University of California Press, 2002); Céline Marangé, *Le Communism Vietnamien* (Paris: Sciences Po, 2012); Peter Zinoman and Nguyen Nguyet Cam, *Dumb Luck: A Novel by Vu Trong Phung* (Ann Arbor: The University of Michigan Press, 2002); Vu Trong Phung, *The Industry of Marrying Europeans*, translated by Thuy Tranviet (Ithaca: Cornell University Southeast Asia Program Publications, 2005); Vu Trong Phung, *Luc Xi: Prostitution and Venereal Disease in Colonial Hanoi*, translated by Shaun Kingsley Malarney (Honolulu: University of Hawai'i Press, 2011); Sébastien Verney, *L'Indochine sous Vichy entre Révolution Nationale, Collaboration et Identities Nationales, 1940–1945* (Paris: Riveneuve Éditions, 2012).

Chapter 13 (late 20th century)

For a relatively detailed survey of the three Indochinese countries during this period, see Arthur J. Dommen, *The Indochinese Experience of the French and the Americans* (Bloomington: Indiana University Press, 2001). A good reference work is Christopher E. Goscha, *Historical Dictionary of the Indochina War (1945–1954): An International and Interdisciplinary Approach* (Honolulu: University of Hawai'i Press, 2011).

On the events of 1945–1946, see David G. Marr, *Vietnam 1945: The Quest for Power* (Berkeley: University of California Press, 1995); Stein Tonnesson, *Vietnam 1946: How the War Began* (Berkeley: University of California Press, 2010); Vu Ngu Chieu, "The Other Side of the 1945 Vietnamese Revolution: The Empire of Viet-Nam (March–August 1945)," *The Journal of Asian Studies* 45, 2 (February 1986):293–328.

On the Franco-Vietnamese War, see Philippe Devillers, *Histoire du Viet-Nam de 1940 à 1952* (Paris: Éditions du Seuil, 1952); Ellen J. Hammer, *The Struggle for Indochina* (Stanford: Stanford University Press, 1954); Christopher E. Goscha and Benoît de Trégladé, eds., *Naissance d'un État-parti: Le Vietnam depuis 1945* (Paris: Les Indes Savantes, 2004); Christopher E. Goscha, "Building Force: Asian Origins of

Twentieth-century Military Science in Vietnam (1905–54)," *Journal of Southeast Asian Studies* 34, 3 (October 2003):535–560; Christopher E. Goscha, *Thailand and the Southeast Asian Networks of the Vietnamese Revolution, 1885–1954* (Richmond: Curzon Press, 1999); Bao Dai, *Le Dragon d'Annam* (Paris: Plon, 1980); William J. Duiker, *Ho Chi Minh* (New York: Hyperion, 2000); Tuong Vu, "'It's Time for the Indochinese Revolution to show its True Colours': The Radical Turn of Vietnamese Politics in 1948," *Journal of Southeast Asian Studies* 40, 1 (October 2009):519–542; Qiang Zhai, *China and the Vietnam Wars, 1950–1975* (Chapel Hill: The University of North Carolina Press, 2000); Alex-Thai Dinh Vo, "Agrarian Policies in Northern Vietnam During the Resistance War, 1945–1953," M.A. Thesis (Cornell University, 2010); Thomas Engelbert, "Vietnamese–Chinese Relations in Southern Vietnam during the First Indochina Conflict," *Journal of Vietnamese Studies* 3, 3 (fall 2008):191–230; and Christopher E. Goscha and Christian F. Ostermann, eds., *Connecting Histories: Decolonization and the Cold War in Southeast Asia, 1945–1962* (Stanford: Stanford University Press, 2009); Fredrik Logevall, *Embers of War: The Fall of an Empire and the Making of America's Vietnam* (New York: Random House, 2012).

On non-communist nationalists, see François Guillemot, "Vietnamese Nationalist Revolutionaries and the Japanese Occupation: The Case of the Dai Viet Parties (1936–1946)," in Li Narangoa and R. Cribb, eds., *Imperial Japan and National Identities in Asia, 1895–1945* (London and New York: Routledge Curzon, 2003), pp. 221–248; Hoang Van Dao, *Viet Nam Quoc Dan Dang: A Contemporary History of a National Struggle 1927–1954* (Pittsburgh: Rose Dog Books, 2008); François Guillemot, *Dai Viêt, Indépendence et Révolution au Viêt-Nam: l'Échec de la Troisième Voie (1938–1955)* (Paris: Les Indes Savantes, 2012); Edward Miller, "Vision, Power, and Agency: The Ascent of Ngo Dinh Diem, 1945–54," *Journal of Southeast Asian Studies* 35, 3 (October 2004):433–458; Edward Miller, *Misalliance: Ngo Dinh Diem, the United States, and the Fate of South Vietnam* (Cambridge: Harvard University Press, 2013).

Edward Miller and Tuong Vu, "The Vietnam War as a Vietnamese War: Agency and Society in the Study of the Second Indochina War," *Journal of Vietnamese Studies* 4, 3 (fall 2009):1–16, introduces a journal issue with several fine studies of the period 1954–1975. For a study of how various groups created allegories about modern Vietnamese history, see Wynn Wilcox, *Allegories of the Vietnamese Past: Unification and the Production of a Modern Historical Identity*, Monograph 61 (New Haven: Yale Southeast Asia Studies, 2011).

On North Vietnam, see Peter Zinoman et al., "Forum: Memories of Land Reform," *Journal of Vietnamese Studies* 2, 2 (summer 2007):231–297; Peter Zinoman, "Nhan Van-Giai Pham and Vietnamese 'Reform Communism' in the 1950s," *Journal of Cold War Studies* 13, 1 (winter 2011):60–100; Ken Maclean, "Manifest Socialism: The Labor of Representation in the Democratic Republic of Vietnam (1956–1959)," *Journal of Vietnamese Studies* 2, 1 (2007):27–79; Lien-Hang T. Nguyen, "Between the Storms: North Vietnam's Strategy during the Second Indochina War (1955–73)," Ph.D. Dissertation (Yale University, 2008); Lien-Hang T. Nguyen, "The War Politburo: North Vietnam's Diplomatic and Political Road to the Tet Offensive," *Journal of Vietnamese Studies* 1, 1–2 (February/August 2006):4–58; Merle L. Pribenow II, "General Vo Nguyen Giap and the Mysterious Evolution of the Plan for the 1968 Tet Offensive," *Journal of Vietnamese Studies* 3, 2 (Summer 2008):1–33; Patricia M. Pelley, *Postcolonial Vietnam: New Histories of*

the National Past (Durham, NC: Duke University Press, 2002); Kim N. B. Ninh,
*A World Transformed: The Politics of Culture in Revolutionary Vietnam, 1945–
1965* (Ann Arbor: The University of Michigan Press, 2002); Lien Hang T. Nguyen,
Hanoi's War: An International History of the War for Peace in Vietnam (Chapel
Hill: The University of North Carolina Press, 2012).

On South Vietnam, see Peter Hansen, "Bac Di Cu: Catholic Refugees from the North of
   Vietnam, and their Role in the Southern Republic, 1954–1959," *Journal of
   Vietnamese Studies* 4, 3 (fall 2009):173–211; Jessica W. Chapman, "The Sect Crisis
   of 1955 and the American Commitment to Ngo Dinh Diem," *Journal of
   Vietnamese Studies* 5, 1 (winter 2010):17–85; Edward Miller, "Grand Designs:
   Vision, Power and Nation Building in America's Alliance with Ngo Dinh Diem,
   1954–1960," Ph.D. Dissertation (Harvard University, 2004); Edward Miller, "The
   Origins of the Buddhist Movement of 1963 in South Vietnam," (unpublished
   paper); Ronald H. Spector, *Advice and Support: The Early Years of the U.S. Army
   in Vietnam 1941–1960* (New York: The Free Press, 1985); Philip E. Catton, *Diem's
   Final Failure: Prelude to America's War in Vietnam* (Lawrence: University Press of
   Kansas, 2002); Anne Blair, *Lodge in Vietnam: A Patriot Abroad* (New Haven: Yale
   University Press, 1995); Ellen J. Hammer, *A Death in November* (New York:
   E. P. Dutton, 1987); Francis X. Winters, *The Year of the Hare* (Athens: University
   of Georgia Press, 1997); Hoang Ngoc Thanh and Than Thi Nhan Duc, *Why the
   Vietnam War? President Ngo Dinh Diem and the US: His Overthrow and
   Assassination* (San Jose, CA: Tuan-Yen and Quan-Viet Mai-Nam Publishers,
   2001); Vinh-The Lam, *Republic of Vietnam, 1963–1967: Years of Political Chaos*
   (Hamilton, Ontario: Hoai Viet, 2010); Martin Loicano, "Military and Political
   Roles of Weapons Systems in the Republic of Viet Nam Armed Forces," Ph.D.
   Dissertation (Cornell University, 2008); Nguyen Cong Luan, *Nationalist in the Viet
   Nam Wars* (Bloomington: Indiana University Press, 2012); Howard R. Penniman,
   Elections in South Vietnam (Stanford: Hoover Institution, 1972); Nguyen The Anh,
   "L'Engagement Politique du Bouddhisme au Sud Viet-Nam dans les Années
   1960s," in A. Forest et al., eds., *Bouddhismes et Sociétés Asiatiques: Clergés,
   sociétés, et pouvoirs* (Paris: L'Harmattan, 1990), pp. 111–124; Tran Ky Phuong
   and Bruce M. Lockhart, eds., *The Cham of Vietnam: History, Society and
   Art* (Singapore: NUS Press, 2011).

On the Sino-Khmer War, see Nayan Chanda, *Brother Enemy: The War After the War*
   (New York: Harcourt, 1986); Jap van Ginneken, *The Third Indochina War and
   Conflicts between China, Vietnam and Cambodia* (Amsterdam: University of
   Leiden, 1983); David W. P. Elliott, ed., *The Third Indochina Conflict* (Boulder:
   Westview Press, 1981); Steven L. Rundle, "The Vietnamese Army in Cambodia
   1978–1990," M.A. Thesis (Cornell University, 1992); Thomas Englebert and
   Christopher E. Goscha, *Falling out of Touch: A Study on Vietnamese Communist
   Policy Towards an Emerging Cambodian Communist Movement, 1930–1975*
   (Clayton: Monash University Centre of Southeast Asian Studies, 1995).

On cultural trends in contemporary Vietnam, see Miranda Arana, *Neotraditional Music
   in Vietnam* (Kent, OH: Nhac Viet Publications, 1999); Nora A. Taylor, *Painters in
   Hanoi: An Ethnography of Vietnamese Art* (Honolulu: University of Hawai'i Press,
   2009); Heonik Kwon, *Ghosts of War* (New York: Cambridge University Press,
   2008); K. W. Taylor, "Locating and Translating Boundaries in Nguyen Huy
   Thiep's Short Stories," *The Vietnam Review* 1 (autumn–winter, 1996):439–465.

FIGURES

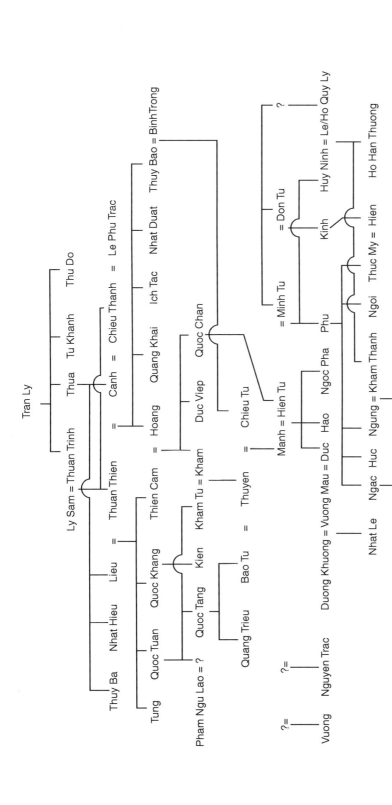

Figure 1. Tran dynasty genealogy

646

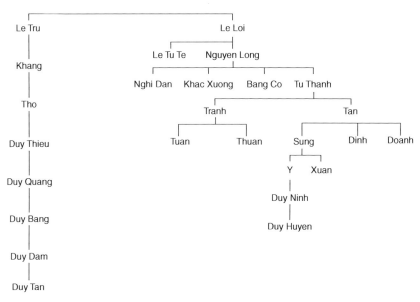

Figure 2. Le dynasty genealogy (15th & 16th c.)

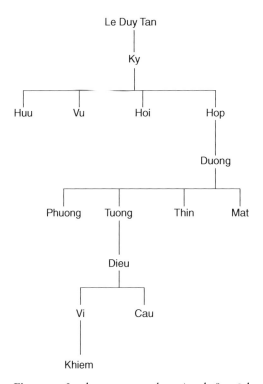

Figure 3. Le dynasty genealogy (17th & 18th c.)

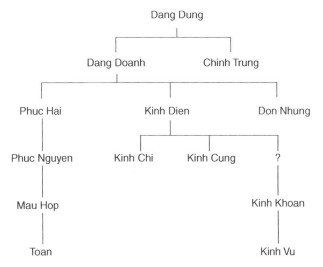

Figure 4. Mac dynasty genealogy

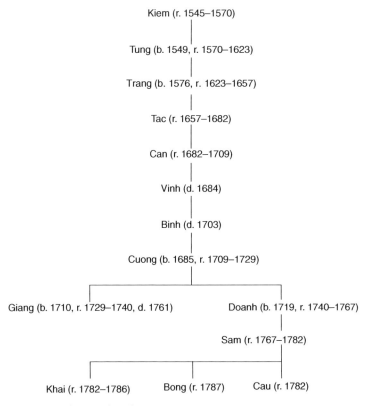

Figure 5. The Trinh rulers

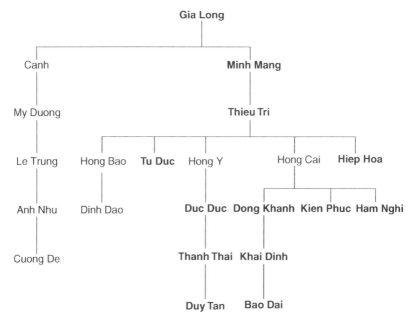

Figure 6. Nguyen dynasty genealogy

TABLES

Table 1. *Hoa Lu king list*

Name	Posthumous title	Born	Reigned
Dinh Bo Linh	Dinh Tien Hoang	924	965–979
Le Hoan	Le Dai Hanh	941	980–1005
Le Viet	Le Trung Tong	983	1005
Le Dinh	Le Ngoa Trieu	986	1005–1009

Table 2. *Ly dynasty king list*

Name	Posthumous title	Born	Reigned
Ly Cong Uan	Ly Thai To	974	1009–1028
Ly Phat Ma	Ly Thai Tong	1000	1028–1054
Ly Nhat Ton	Ly Thanh Tong	1023	1054–1072
Ly Can Duc	Ly Nhan Tong	1066	1072–1127
Ly Duong Hoan	Ly Than Tong	1116	1127–1138
Ly Thien To	Ly Anh Tong	1136	1138–1175
Ly Long Trat	Ly Cao Tong	1173	1175–1210
Ly Sam	Ly Hue Tong	1194	1210–1224
Ly Chieu Thanh	Ly Chieu Hoang	1218	1224–1225

Table 3. *Tran dynasty king list*

Name	Posthumous title	Born	Reigned
Tran Thua	Tran Thai To	1183	1225–1234
Tran Canh	Tran Thai Tong	1218	1225–1277
Tran Hoang	Tran Thanh Tong	1240	1258–1290
Tran Kham	Tran Nhan Tong	1258	1279–1310
Tran Thuyen	Tran Anh Tong	1276	1293–1320
Tran Manh	Tran Minh Tong	1300	1314–1357
Tran Vuong	Tran Hien Tong	1319	1329–1341
Tran Hao	Tran Du Tong	1336	1341–1369
Tran Phu	Tran Nghe Tong	1321	1370–1394
Tran Kinh	Tran Due Tong	1337	1373–1377
Tran Hien	Tran Phe De	1361	1377–1388
Tran Ngung	Tran Thuan Tong	1378	1389–1399
Tran An	Tran Thien De	1396	1399–1400
Tran Ngoi	Tran Gian Dinh De		1407–1409
Tran Quy Khoang	Tran Trung Quang De		1409–1413

Table 4. *Le dynasty king list (15th & 16th c.)*

Name	Posthumous title	Born	Reigned
Le Loi	Le Thai To	1385	1428–1433
Le Nguyen Long	Le Thai Tong	1423	1433–1442
Le Bang Co	Le Nhan Tong	1441	1442–1459
Le Nghi Dan		1439	1459–1460
Le Tu Thanh	Le Thanh Tong	1442	1460–1497
Le Tranh	Le Hien Tong	1461	1497–1504
Le Thuan	Le Tuc Tong	1488	1504
Le Tuan	Le Uy Muc	1488	1505–1510
Le Dinh	Le Tuong Duc	1495	1510–1516
Le Quang Tri		1508	1516
Le Y	Le Chieu Tong	1500	1516–1525
Le Xuan	Le Cung Hoang	1506	1523–1527
Le Duy Ninh	Le Trang Tong	1515	1533–1548
Le Duy Huyen	Le Trung Tong	1534	1548–1556
Le Duy Bang	Le Anh Tong	1531	1556–1573
Le Duy Dam	Le The Tong	1566	1573–1599

Table 5. *Le dynasty king list (17th & 18th c.)*

Name	Posthumous title	Born	Reigned
Le Duy Tan	Le Kinh Tong	1588	1600–1619
Le Duy Ky	Le Than Tong	1606	1619–43, 1649–62
Le Duy Huu	Le Chan Tong	1629	1643–1649
Le Duy Vu	Le Huyen Tong	1653	1662–1671
Le Duy Hoi	Le Gia Tong	1660	1671–1675
Le Duy Cap	Le Hy Tong	1663	1675–1705
Le Duy Duong	Le Du Tong	1679	1705–1729
Le Duy Phuong	Le De Duy Phuong		1729–1732
Le Duy Tuong	Le Thuan Tong	1698	1732–1735
Le Duy Thin	Le Y Tong	1718	1735–1740
Le Duy Dieu	Le Hien Tong	1716	1740–1786
Le Duy Khiem	Le Man De	1765	1786–1788

Table 6. *Mac dynasty king list*

Name	Posthumous title	Born	Reigned
Mac Dang Dung	Mac Thai To	1483	1527–1541
Mac Dang Doanh	Mac Thai Tong		1530–1540
Mac Phuc Hai	Mac Hien Tong		1541–1546
Mac Phuc Nguyen	Mac Tuyen Tong		1546–1561
Mac Mau Hop			1562–1592
Mac Toan			1592
Mac Kinh Chi			1592–1593
Mac Kinh Cung			1593–1625
Mac Kinh Khoan			1625–1638
Mac Kinh Vu			1638–1677

Table 7. *List of Nguyen Phuc rulers*

Lord = Chua (C.); Duke = Quan Cong (Q.C.); King = Vuong. Prince Duong was called Dong Cung, "Eastern Palace," meaning Crown Prince, for crown princes had resided in the Eastern Palace since the early eleventh century. When Nguyen Phuc Anh proclaimed the Gia Long reign period in 1802, he was announcing himself as "high king" or "emperor."

Name	Born	Ruled	Lord	Duke	King
Hoang	1525	1558–1613	C. Tien	Doan Q.C.	
Nguyen	1563	1613–1635	C. Sai	Thuy Q.C.	
Lan	1600	1635–1648	C. Thuong	Nhan Q.C.	
Tan	1620	1648–1687	C. Hien	Dung Q.C.	
Tran	1648	1687–1691	C. Nghia	Hoang Q.C.	
Chu	1675	1691–1725	Quoc C.	To Q.C.	
Tru	1695	1725–1738		Dinh Q.C.	
Khoat	1713	1738–1765			Vo Vuong
Thuan	1754	1765–1777			Dinh Vuong
Duong		1776–1777			"Dong Cung"
Anh	1761	1780–1802			Nguyen Vuong
		1802–1820			Gia Long

Table 8. *Descendents of Nguyen Phuc Khoat who were crown princes or kings*

First son (2nd crown prince): Nguyen Phuc Chuong (1730–1763)
Second son (3rd crown prince): Nguyen Phuc Con (1731–1765)
   His son (king 1780–1820): Nguyen Phuc Anh (1761–1820)
Ninth son (1st crown prince): Nguyen Phuc Hieu (1738–1760)
   His son (crown prince 1774–76; king 1776–77): Nguyen Phuc Duong (d. 1777)
Sixteenth son (king 1765–1777): Nguyen Phuc Thuan (1754–1777)

Table 9. *Nguyen dynasty king list*

Reign name	Date of birth	Reign	Date of death
Gia Long	1762	1802–1820	1820
Minh Mang	1791	1820–1840	1840
Thieu Tri	1807	1840–1847	1847
Tu Duc	1829	1847–1883	1883
Duc Duc	1852	1883	1883
Hiep Hoa	1847	1883	1883
Kien Phuc	1869	1883–1884	1884
Ham Nghi	1872	1884–1885	1943
Dong Khanh	1864	1885–1889	1889
Thanh Thai	1879	1889–1907	1954
Duy Tan	1899	1907–1916	1945
Khai Dinh	1885	1916–1925	1925
Bao Dai	1913	1925–1945	1997

MAPS

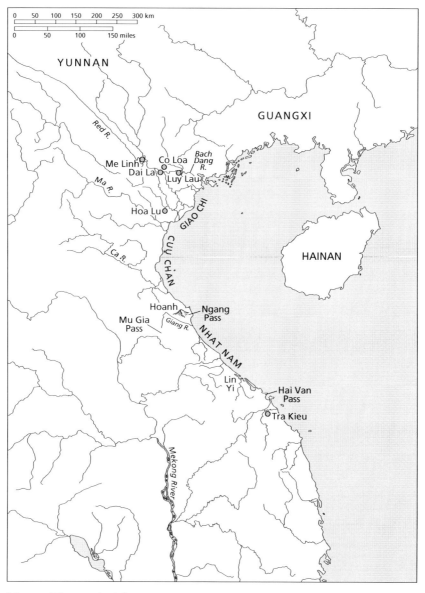

Map 1. The provincial era

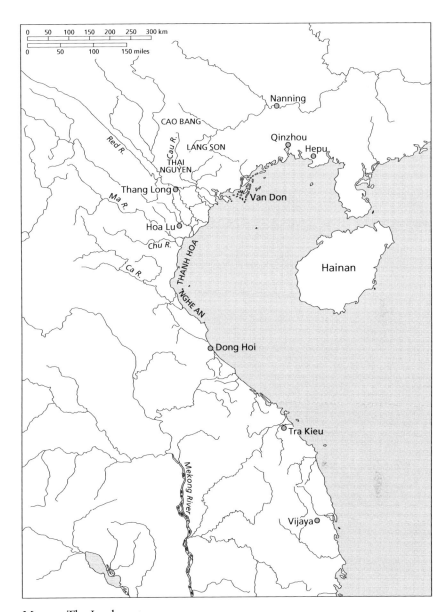

Map 2. The Ly dynasty – map 1

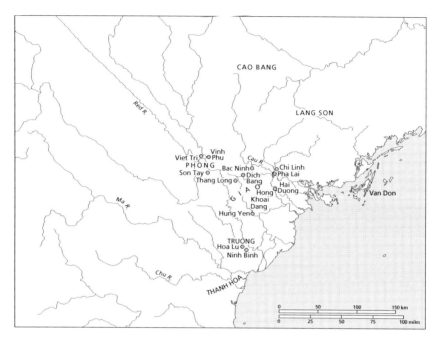

Map 3. The Ly dynasty – map 2

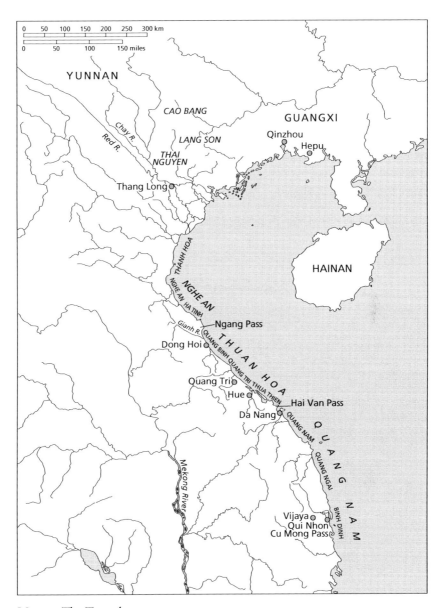

Map 4. The Tran dynasty – map 1

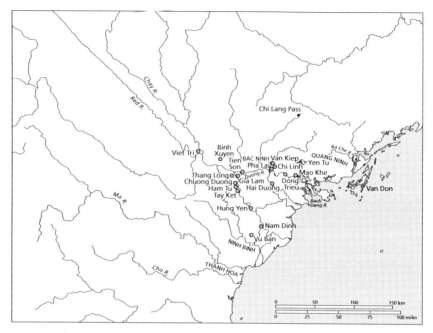

Map 5. The Tran dynasty – map 2

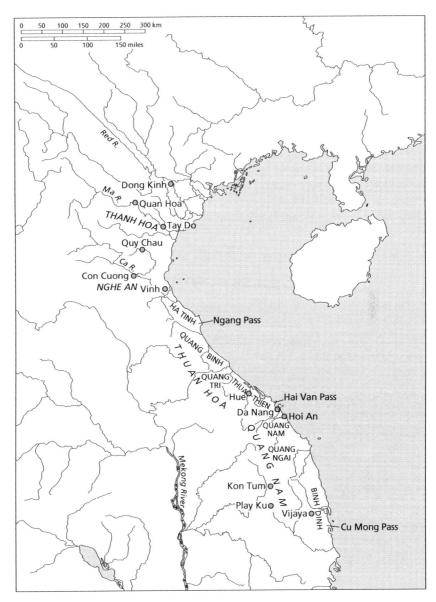

Map 6. The Le dynasty – map 1

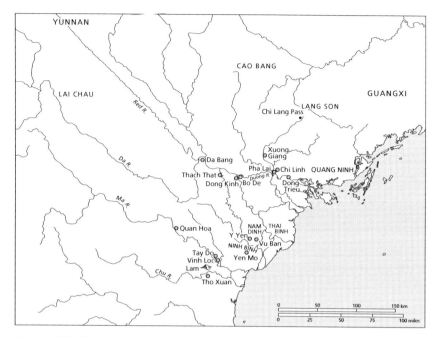

Map 7. The Le dynasty – map 2

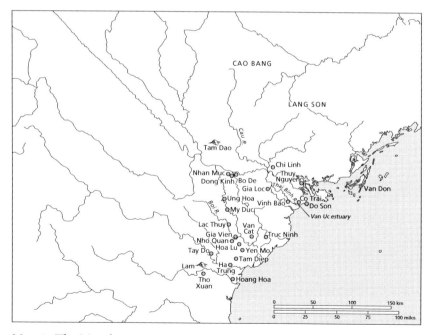

Map 8. The Mac dynasty

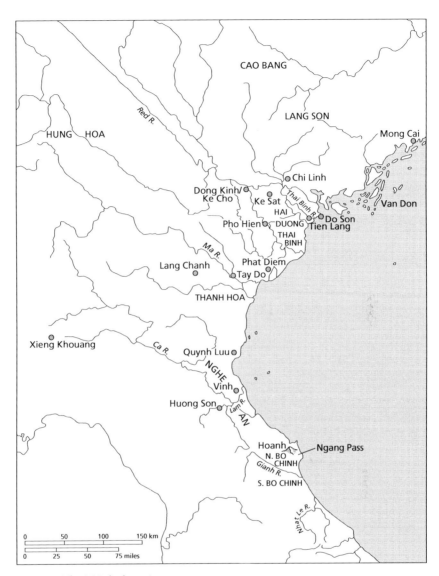

Map 9. The Trinh domain

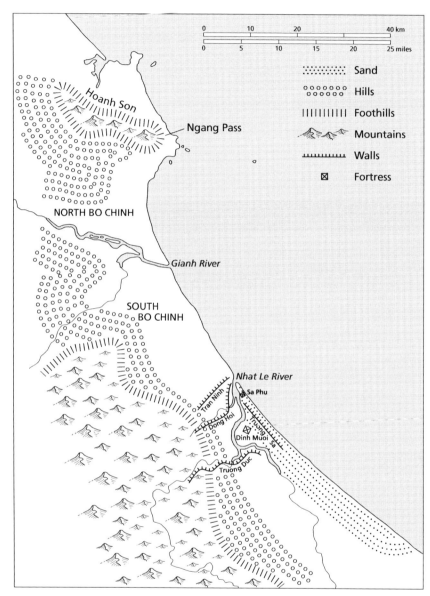

Map 10. The Trinh–Nguyen border

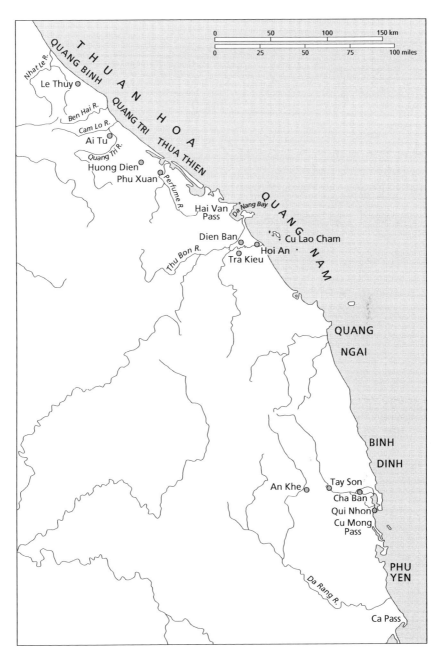

Map 11. The northern Nguyen Phuc domain

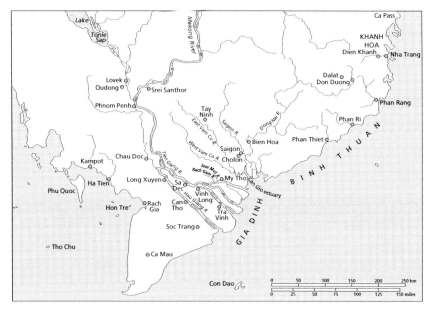

Map 12. The southern Nguyen Phuc domain

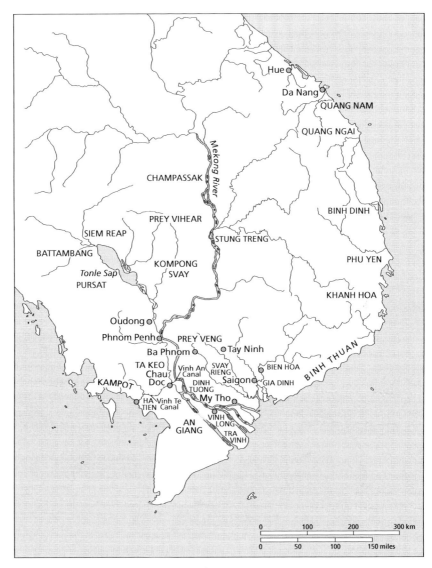

Map 13. The Nguyen dynasty: south

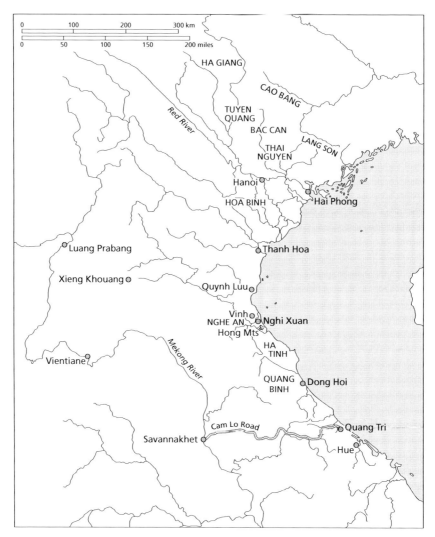

Map 14. The Nguyen dynasty: north

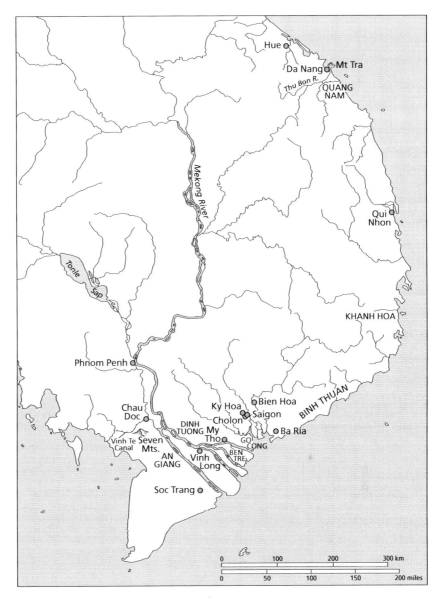

Map 15. The French conquest: south

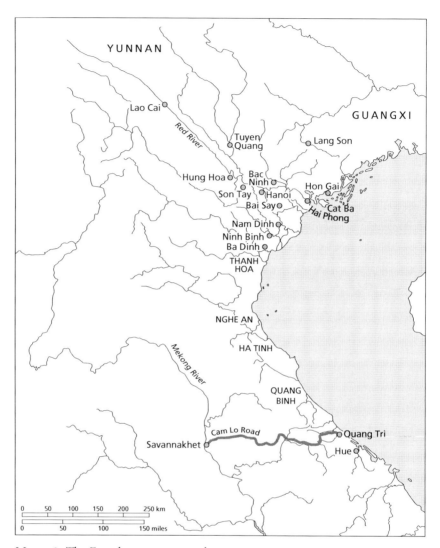

Map 16. The French conquest: north

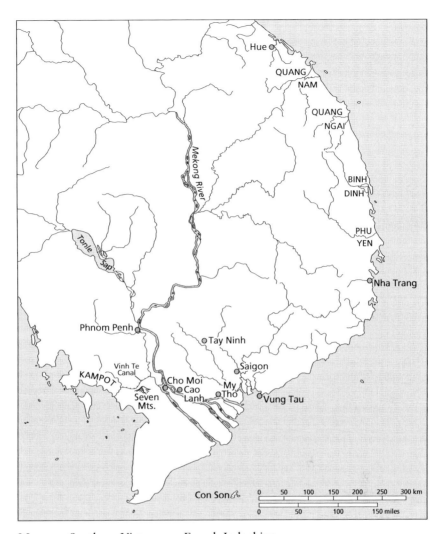

Map 17. Southern Vietnamese French Indochina

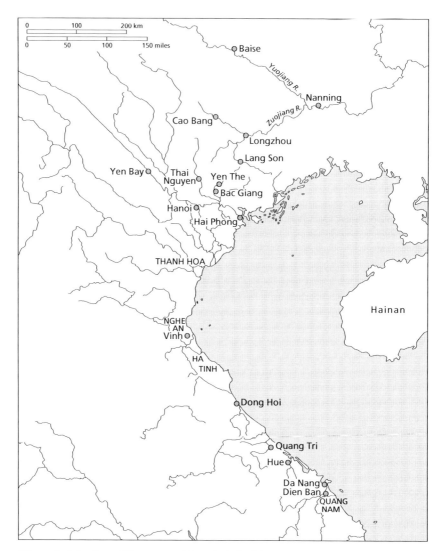

Map 18. Northern Vietnamese French Indochina

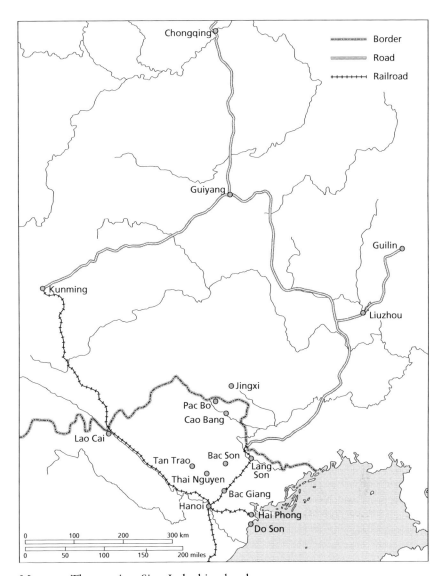

Map 19. The wartime Sino-Indochina border, 1940s

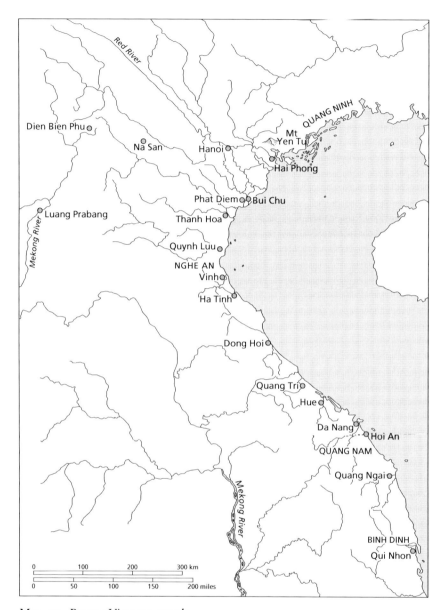

Map 20. Recent Vietnam: north

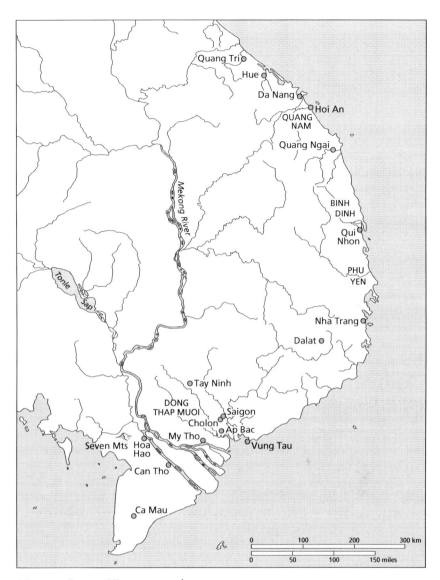

Map 21. Recent Vietnam: south

INDEX